UCLA Basketball Encyclopedia: The First 100 Years

SPENCER STUEVE

FOREWORD BY MARQUES JOHNSON

SPORTS PUBLISHING

Sports Publishing books may be purchased in bulk at special discounts for sales promotion, corporate gifts, fund-raising, or educational purposes. Special editions can also be created to specifications. For details, contact the Special Sales Department, Sports Publishing, 307 West 36th Street, 11th Floor, New York, NY 10018 or sportspubbooks@skyhorsepublishing.com.

Sports Publishing® is a registered trademark of Skyhorse Publishing, Inc.®, a Delaware corporation.

Visit our website at www.sportspubbooks.com.

10 9 8 7 6 5 4 3 2 1

Library of Congress Cataloging-in-Publication Data is available on file.

Cover design by Tom Lau
Cover photo credit Getty Images

ISBN: 978-1-68358-319-6
Ebook ISBN: 978-1-68358-320-2

Printed in the United States of America

Contents

Foreword

I was named after the famous Harlem Globetrotter Marques Haynes, whom my dad, Jeff, saw play in Shreveport, Louisiana, on several occasions in the early 1950s. My dad thought Haynes was the best basketball player he had ever seen, and if he had a son, his name would be Marques.

My father was a highly successful high school basketball coach at Central High School in Natchitoches, Louisiana. I still run into former players of his, sixty years after the fact, who tell me he was way ahead of his time. His motion offense and arduous conditioning drills were straight out of Kentucky coaching legend Adolph Rupp's book *Championship Basketball*, written in 1948.

When I was three years old, I sat next to my dad during games while he was coaching. During timeouts and halftime, I would speed dribble, or "dibble" as I pronounced it, up and down the court. The crowd would go crazy; the more they cheered, the faster I would dibble. My father—my first coach—taught me all the fundamentals of the game until I became adept at executing them.

We moved to Los Angeles, California, when I was five years old. One reason was to escape the racial prejudice in the South. Another reason was that since both my parents were educators, they dreamed that each of their four kids at the time would attend UCLA. I have a baby picture of myself sitting in a metal chair in our backyard in Natchitoches. The inscription written at the bottom says UCLA Bound.

The *Pittsburgh Courier* and *Chicago Defender* were two of the most prominent black newspapers of the time. Blacks in the South subscribed to both newspapers to keep up with the national news as it pertained to African Americans. My parents would read about the athletic exploits of the great Jackie Robinson, or the high-level Nobel Prize diplomacy of Dr. Ralph Bunche. They knew both these gentlemen attended UCLA. The school became a symbol of hope and upward mobility, and Los Angeles represented the opportunity for social and economic advancement blacks rarely found in the South.

I started playing organized basketball at Sportsman Park in 1964. Of course, my dad was the coach of our team, The Raiders, in the Tiny Division. We went undefeated that season, and I was awarded the Most Valuable Player trophy at season's end. One of my teammates and childhood friends was NFL Hall of Fame wide receiver James Lofton. James tells the story of how during one game, my dad and I didn't arrive until halftime. Our Raiders squad was down, 20–1. After I got there, we wound up winning, 25–24, with me scoring every point in the second half. I won the MVP trophy every year for the next five seasons.

I attended Audubon Junior (Middle) School from the seventh through ninth grades. The school produced some terrific athletes who made it all the way to the professional ranks. UCLA great Wendell Tyler won a Super Bowl with the San Francisco 49ers. Michael "Butch" Johnson had one of the greatest catches in Super Bowl history for the Dallas Cowboys. My fondest memory happened in what was called the Bird Bowl. The lower half of the seventh grade played against the slightly older upper half. It was a lunchtime battle that we wound up losing, but I had a great game, scoring over 30 points in a forty-minute game. My dad had taught me this up-and-under move off a shot fake. I used it over and over again to score. When I got to my fifth-period class late after a change of clothes, the students gave me a standing ovation. The teacher was unaware and had to be told what all the commotion was about.

Ricky "Tex" Walker stood six feet, four inches tall in the ninth grade and was the best player in school, destined for greatness. We both attended Dorsey High School as sophomores. He made the varsity, and because I was only fourteen at the time, I had to play junior varsity. We found out that other high school players convened at UCLA to play on Sunday mornings at ten. I had been aware of UCLA basketball since the days of Walt Hazzard and Gail Goodrich. I had followed them even more closely after the phenom from New York, Lew Alcindor, led his freshman team to a victory over the number one ranked varsity.

I still remember the disappointment when the Bruins lost to the Big E, Elvin Hayes, and the Houston Cougars. I watched as a record fifty thousand fans showed up to see these two titans battle. Lew (Kareem) had a scratched cornea and was not at full strength. When the two teams met in the Final Four semifinals, it was a different story.

Tex was older and had a car and a license, and he would pick me up in his mother's gray Ford Galaxie. Those Sunday morning games were great. Just walking onto the hallowed floor of Pauley Pavilion was a special honor for me. The nets were so taut that some of my shots would go more than halfway down and then spin completely back out. Future Bruins Roy Hamilton and Brad Holland were there most Sundays, as were guys like John Davis, Lew, Malek Mansour, and American triple jump record-holder Milan Tiff. We had hoped to play against my idols, Sidney Wicks and Curtis Rowe, but never got the chance then.

After I transferred to Crenshaw High School, my basketball career really took off. Playing for the great Willie West was a key to my further development. My dad had made sure I was fundamentally as sound as could be. Coach West and my Crenshaw teammates gave me that inner toughness and spirit to have the confidence that no one could beat us. We practiced three-and-a-half and sometimes four hours every day, with conditioning taking up a large part of those practices. The other time was spent honing our offensive and defensive execution with a precision rarely seen in high school basketball in any era.

During this time, UCLA had begun to express some interest in me. My parents had a coworker named Bruce Tenen, who worked as a scorekeeper for Bruins games and alerted the coaching staff that there was a player at Crenshaw they should keep an eye on. Tex Walker, still at Dorsey, was playing great our junior year also. UCLA showed interest in other players in the area: Jackie Robinson was a muscular, high-jumping forward who played for Jim Harrick at Morningside High. Lewis Brown was an enigmatic 6-foot-9 center at powerhouse Verbum Dei High School. Steve Cantor was at Fairfax; he and I played together for a year at the Westside Jewish Community Center. Gavin Smith was a super-athletic forward from Van Nuys High in the San Fernando Valley.

The summer after an undefeated junior season, we played in the annual Watts Summer Games basketball tournament final. We were matched up against Morningside High, the number one ranked team in the nation. We were missing two key rotation players and still almost won the game. UCLA assistant coach Frank Arnold watched the game at Cal State Los Angeles, perched over a railing on the second level. I had my summer look going—huge afro parted down the middle, cutoff navy blue sweat pants, black high-top Chuck Taylor Converse sneakers, floppy heavy tan work socks, and my rawhide knotted necklace I had fashioned around my neck. I played great, finishing with 36 points and close to 20 rebounds. One sequence in particular, Coach Arnold told me later, sealed the deal in my favor. Late in the game, Jackie Robinson got the ball close to the basket. You couldn't dunk in those days, which made shot blocking a little more predictable. I had gotten the best of Jackie all game, so to vent his frustration he attempted to dunk on me. I blocked it cleanly, and he got the ball right back. He drop-stepped, rose high in the air, and once again tried to dunk. I blocked the second attempt also.

Coach Wooden finally saw me play in person during the city playoffs my senior year. The games were played right at Pauley Pavilion, and I remember Coach sitting by himself off in a corner, watching intently. I played two great games, and Crenshaw won the city championship, undefeated once again. I was voted the Most Outstanding Player, Best Offensive Player, and Best Defensive Player. Afterward, my parents and I dined with Coach Wooden and Frank Arnold at Chasen's Restaurant in Beverly Hills. It was a magical evening, and my mind was pretty much made up about where I would attend college.

I started a handful of games my freshman year. The most notable was the rematch game against Notre Dame—they had ended our 88-win streak the week before. We avenged that loss with a double-digit beatdown. I had 17 points and seven rebounds, most coming when we opened up the lead in the second half.

That season I thought we were pretty much guaranteed a national championship. David Thompson and North Carolina State had other ideas, defeating us in double overtime in the semis.

I worked harder than ever that summer going into my sophomore season. I ran hills, the deep sand at the beach, and stadium steps at Drake Stadium. I worked on my vertical leap and my body obsessively. Bucks exec Wayne Embry watched me play against some pros in town for the LA Summer League in Pauley one afternoon. After seeing me dismantle older, more experienced players, he publicly stated that I was the "best forward in America, college or pro."

Unfortunately, I contracted a serious bout of hepatitis two days before fall practice was to begin in October. I lost 20 pounds in a week and was hospitalized for a few days. I never regained full strength that season, or the remainder of my career. The good news is that UCLA basketball team was able to give John Wooden his 10th and final championship. Even though I struggled mightily with my conditioning, I was still a major contributor to our success.

Coach Wooden retired, and I played for Gene Bartow my final two years. We reached the Final Four my junior year and won the conference both my junior and senior seasons. After giving some thought to turning professional after my junior year, I decided at the eleventh hour to return for my final year as a college student at UCLA. I majored in Television and Film Production in the Theater Arts Department, making documentary films that caught the attention of fellow students like future filmmaker Jamaa Fanaka. I hosted my own campus television show, *Searching*, that featured a variety of non-sports-related topics. I starred in a play written by Jim Birge about an athlete struggling to find himself. It was the best time of my life, capped off with me winning the first-ever John Wooden Award for the best player in college basketball.

I have had two sons play for UCLA, Kris and Josiah. Kris was a member of the 1995 national championship team, led by the great Ed O'Bannon. I was working games for UCLA radio at the time and watched firsthand the grit and determination that team showed under the leadership of coach Jim Harrick (from Morningside High). That title made my son Kris and me the only father-and-son tandem to win a championship at the same school. Kris finished in the top 25 of all-time Bruins in points scored.

My son Josiah excelled academically at UCLA and used his experience as the basis for an animated series he helped create, still shown on Comedy Central, *Legends of Chamberlain Heights*.

I still maintain my connection with the school and team, hosting or attending various events. I ushered my Bruins teammate Richard Washington into the school's Hall of Fame by serving a second stint on the selection committee.

UCLA will forever hold a special place in my heart. Through all the ups and downs, the victories and defeats, my time there was by far the best experience of my life. And for that, I will be eternally grateful.

—Marques Johnson

CHAPTER 1
Fred Cozens (1919–1921)

Before John Wooden, before Larry Brown, before Jim Harrick, there was Fred Cozens. Before Red Sanders, before Terry Donahue, before Jim Mora, there was Fred Cozens. Before John Savage, there was Fred Cozens. Before he went on to a long, distinguished career as UCLA's athletic director, Fred Cozens was the first basketball, football, and baseball coach in UCLA history.

Fred Cozens was a first-generation American, born in Portland, Oregon, to Frederick and Carrie Cozens on November 19, 1890. Little is known about his childhood. However, when Fred reached college, he knew his calling. He was an intellectual who enjoyed studying and learning about physics, history, and biology. He received a bachelor's degree from the University of California Berkeley; later, in 1918, he received a master's degree from Cal, as well. A decade later, his educational pursuit continued, and in 1928, he was awarded a PhD from the University of Oregon.

After coaching freshman baseball at Cal his junior and senior seasons, Cozens moved south to a new school, still in the making, the Southern Branch of the University of California (soon to be renamed the University of California Los Angeles). Along with coaching basketball, football, and baseball, Cozens followed his first love, academics. Fred was an associate of Physical Education from 1912 to 1942. In the United States census of 1920, and again in 1930, Fred listed his occupation as an educator. Fred married Helen Kerron in 1916 and had two boys, Frederick Jr. and James.

Fred Cozens, 1919 (Southern Campus Collection).

Despite a promising future as an educator and a growing family, Cozens had other thoughts on his mind upon graduation in 1918. Cozens would continue to educate not only in the classroom but also as a coach. The popularity of basketball and football in 1919 were growing. In basketball, backboards were implemented in 1909, and open nylon nets were approved in 1912. The game was still in infancy, ever evolving and growing. Fred Cozens was a successful basketball coach, though he was certainly not a strategic expert. In his two years as the Southern Branch basketball coach, Cozens compiled a 20–4 record and won the Southern California Intercollegiate Athletic Conference in 1921. Cozens's favorite sport, however, was baseball. Much like the rest of the country at the time, Cozens believed that baseball was the true American pastime, a perfect contrast to America's other athletic love, boxing. Cozens coached baseball at UCLA for five years and improved his record every year, twice winning the conference. College football took center stage on fall Saturdays. Yale and Princeton dominated the late nineteenth century, but Knute Rockne and the Notre Dame Fighting Irish, along with Fielding Yost at Michigan and Charlie Daly at West Point, ushered in a new era. Fred Cozens, far from the glamour of Notre Dame or the ascent of Michigan into a football powerhouse, ushered in a new era as well. He only coached football at SBUC for one year before focusing on his other pursuits. The 1919–20 athletic/academic year was a year to set the bar, and each coach since has been tasked with raising that bar. Coach Cozens was the man who got it all started.

1919–20

The University of California Southern Branch officially opened September 15, 1919, and eighteen short days later, the history of UCLA basketball and football began. On October 3, the Southern Branch basketball team had its first intrasquad scrimmage, and the football team played its first official game.

After the Southern Branch Cubs football team lost its first game in school history, and then went on to finish the inaugural season with a 2–6 record, Coach Fred Cozens had to switch his focus from football to basketball. December 12 marked the first basketball game. Unlike the football program, the basketball program started with victory. The men on the gridiron fell by the score of 74–0 to Manual Arts High School in its opening game more than two months earlier. Coach Cozens had a young hoops squad, with the school only having a freshman class, and several of the players were playing organized basketball for the first time in their lives. Still, the team was good. The Cubs whipped the Manual Arts boys by the score of 46–38. The Cubs played three more games against high school opponents and won all three. It was time to take on conference opponents. The Southern Branch was a member of the Southern California Intercollegiate Athletic Conference (though unofficially until 1920–21), consisting of six teams, divided into two divisions. The first conference foe, the University of Redlands, playing in its home gym, handily beat Coach Cozens's Cubs, 34–21. Though the final outcome of the game provided little drama, the Cubs showed promise: they were quick and well coached. They simply struggled to score the ball.

Following the first loss in school history, the Cubs regrouped and found its rhythm. The first captain in program history was Si Gibbs, and in the game against Occidental College, he played his finest game of the season. He hit a variety of shots, from both near and far, from straight on to the corners. Coach Cozens stressed during practices that the ball must move, but ultimately it was to land in the hands of the most capable of scorers, and Gibbs proved that his coach was right. In the ensuing games, the team continued to win. Pomona College, Whittier College, and Caltech—none stood a chance.

1920 Southern Branch team photo (Southern Campus Collection).

Much like the Pac-10 Conference would do many years later, prior to the expansion to the Pac-12, the Southern California Intercollegiate Athletic Conference (SCIAC) played a double round-robin schedule. All teams that SBUC had played already in conference would get another shot. The Bruins were 4–1 in conference play and hoped to avenge their lone loss to Redlands. First, they had to beat the other teams in the way. The Cubs easily dismantled Occidental, before taking on the Pomona Sagehens for the second time. This time around the game was much closer, but the Cubs again came out on top. Eddie Rossell was on the mark from deep, and "Bugs" Woodard constantly found himself shooting foul shots, which he made at a high mark. The final score was 33–30. The Cubs would run its winning streak to six after beating Whittier, 33–21, again behind Woodard's stellar shooting and smothering defense. The Cubs then slipped up, however; in the second matchup against the men from Caltech, the Cubs winning streak came to a close. The offense performed at a similar pace, but on defense the Cubs could not do enough. The final score was 41–30.

SBUC was 11–2, and though the team would not win the conference, Coach Cozens and his squad of nine desperately wanted to win the rematch against the University of Redlands. The game was played on a Thursday evening, February 19, 1920, in front of a large crowd of 400 fans. The game was hard fought. Both teams played stifling defense, and neither was able to score much. The players needed a team effort to stay in the game, as Redlands was a budding powerhouse program. The five starters played the entirety of the game, with Raymond McBurney and Rossell starring on defense, and Gibbs, Woodard, and Sterling Tipton scoring whenever they could. After the rough, physical game finally ended, the Cubs had done it. They had avenged their loss from earlier in the year, 23–17. It was the first loss for the University of Redlands in its two years of playing intercollegiate basketball.

While the 1919–20 SBUC basketball team is not one of the most memorable in school history, it is historically significant. Coach Cozens and his men forged a path for future success, the likes of which have not been matched anywhere. To Woodard, Tipton, Rossell, McBurney, and the rest of the team, a thank-you is owed. The Cubs finished with a 12–2 record and were optimistic about their future. The 1920–21 season would be one for the record books.

New York University and the University of Pennsylvania claim national champion status for 1920.

1920–21

Coming into season number two, there were considerable expectations. Coach Fred Cozens, no longer the football coach, was able to spend more time focusing on basketball. The entire team from the year prior returned, and the Cubs were looking to improve on the already impressive 12–2 inaugural season. They would prove to be a fine team once again and contend for the conference crown.

The Cubs opened its season with a slew of high school opponents. The games were not official, only scrimmages, but they gave Coach Cozens, as well as fans and students, a taste of what was to come. The Southern Branch team was good, easily dismantling the younger competition. The first official game, however, would not be like the scrimmages. SBUC took on its older brother, the University of California Berkeley. As with the football team in the Southern Branch's earliest days, the basketball program was not at the level of Cal's. The team was, however, more than simply competitive. It was impressive even in defeat. The game was played in Berkeley, and the home crowd expected an easy victory. The game was dubbed a race. Both teams played at a frantic, up-and-down pace, and while neither team shot particularly well, the level of play was still high. The fast pace of the game helped the Cubs players, who were much smaller but also quicker. Eventually the Bears wore down the Cubs, both with size and depth. When the final seconds ticked off, the score read Bears 36, Cubs 28.

The hard-fought game against the men from Berkeley helped the young Cubs. When they took on the Redlands Bulldogs in the first conference game, they were ready. Redlands was the heavy favorite, having returned the majority of its roster from the 1920 conference champion team. The game would be low scoring with neither team being able to break away from the other, and the score remained close throughout. Finally, however, the Cubs did enough to take the lead and hold it in the final minute, finishing at 29–26. The games would not get easier for the majority of the season. The Cubs played many close games, including the third game of the season, a three-point victory over Pomona. Sitting at 2–1 and 2–0 in conference play, the Cubs were in a fine early-season position. The team was sure not to slip up against Caltech, remembering the heartbreaking loss of one year prior. It easily dismantled them by 14 points. Despite Caltech's fine passing and player movement, the Cubs were better, with more men capable of scoring.

Perhaps the finest moment of the season for Coach Cozens and the Cubs came in the rematch against the Redlands Bulldogs, though it didn't seem to be early on. At halftime, the Cubs trailed 13–3. Coach Cozens, however, was not worried about making strategic adjustments. He felt his team was doing a fine job of getting shots in positions they could score. The shots were simply not falling. He was tasked with keeping his players optimistic about making a second-half comeback. When the two teams returned after intermission, they seemingly switched jerseys. Suddenly, the Cubs were the better team and shot lights out from the floor. The defense was stingy, as it had been all season. The final score was 26–22, with the Cubs on top.

Due to a series of postponements earlier in the season after experiencing travel issues, the Cubs had several games to make up on the back half of the schedule against conference foes they had yet to play. The Cubs were nothing other than solid on offense all season, but the defense was very strong. Against Occidental College, the team was again able to keep its opponent from scoring in bunches and won by the score of 36–26. The following week, the Cubs beat the Whittier Poets twice, 18–16 and 26–24.

With two conference games to play and an undefeated conference record, the Cubs were in position to bring home the first conference championship in school history. The rematch against Pomona was much like the first matchup earlier in the season. The Cubs easily won by a dozen points. In the final game of the season, the Cubs were playing for their goal. After defeating Caltech by 15 points, the Cubs won the 1920–21 Southern California Intercollegiate Athletic Conference championship, the first of many championships to come in program history.

The Cubs were 9–1 and riding a nine-game winning streak when it again took on the California Golden Bears. While the game was meaningless in the grand scheme of things, it was important to the players, as they hoped to improve on their season-opening performance. The seven varsity letter winners made the trip to Berkeley to take on the deep squad of ten opposing them. Cubs Captain Raymond McBurney, the vocal leader, as well as an excellent defender and rebounder, was tasked with leading the team over the top. It wasn't to be, however, and the Bears beat the Cubs, 46–29.

In two years, Coach Cozens compiled a 21–4 record as the Southern Branch basketball coach and was responsible for the first conference championship in school history. After the 1921 season, however, he would step aside and focus on baseball for the next four seasons and teaching for the rest of his working career. The new coach that took over the varsity program was a familiar face. Pierce "Caddy" Works was the freshman coach before his promotion, and he continued the growing basketball legacy at the new school in Los Angeles. He coached at SBUC/UCLA for 18 seasons and took the team to new heights.

No team claims national champion status for 1921.

CHAPTER 2
Pierce "Caddy" Works (1921–1939)

Whereas the Southern Branch's first coach, Fred Cozens, was slightly out of his comfort zone when coaching football and basketball, SBUC's next coach was not considered a typical coach of any sport now or even then. Pierce Works, nicknamed "Caddy," was not even a coach, or an athlete, for most of his life. He was a lawyer.

Born on January 2, 1896, Caddy, like many young boys at the time, experienced sports on the periphery when he was a child. He enjoyed watching early twentieth-century baseball, and boxing was, of course, something he often heard about. Basketball was a growing sport, but for many, it would be years before they even heard of the game. Caddy liked basketball from a young age, but his goal was never to play it at the highest level. He wanted to become a lawyer. But he had other goals in mind; he was talented. He played baseball and basketball at the University of California Berkeley and enjoyed a short stint in minor-league baseball with the Wichita Falls (Texas) Spudders, an affiliate of the Pittsburgh Pirates.

Caddy would, in time, reach his larger goal. He became a full-time lawyer at the firm of O'Melveny, Tuller & Myers. The firm dealt primarily with tax litigation, which suited Works's mind just fine. He was a numbers-driven man, and he was considered a very good, prominent Los Angeles lawyer.

Coach Caddy Works, 1924 (Southern Branch Collection)

Works always enjoyed basketball, however, though he was never a strategic expert. In 1920–21, the Southern Branch of the University of California had its first sophomore class, and thus a freshman team was born. While Coach Cozens taught the men on the varsity, Caddy Works coached the freshmen—his first coaching job. For Works, however, basketball was merely a hobby. He remained a full-time lawyer and would go from his day job to the Vermont Avenue campus to coach the team at night.

When Fred Cozens stepped away from basketball following the 1921 season, Coach Works was the logical choice to take over the varsity job, though he still had no plans for dedicating himself to basketball full time. For a substantial period, Works was able to balance both his day job and coaching a rising basketball program just fine, but eventually the demands of the job became too much, and the program began to suffer.

Still, Works was a winner, and he did most of his winning in his earliest years. While Cozens's two teams played very good defense and were selective on offense, Coach Works taught a different style of play. SBUC played fast. The players took lots of shots and pressed full court on defense. It was often said that Coach Works's teams played out of control, but the frantic pace was exactly what he wanted. In Works's first six seasons, the Cubs, who would later become the Grizzlies and then the Bruins, won five conference titles, all of which came in the Southern California Intercollegiate Athletic Conference. His success, however, did not last, at least when it came to conference crowns. As basketball evolved and UCLA played a tougher schedule, eventually moving to the Pacific Coast Conference, balancing basketball and his work as an attorney became increasingly difficult. In basketball, UCLA took a backseat to the college's crosstown rival, the USC Trojans, led by Coach Sam Barry. Over time, Coach Works was forced to change his style. While the early teams played fast and seemingly carefree, eventually they played methodically, dragging out the games and hoping to have a chance at the end. Coach Works would never win another conference crown, but he would provide stability, even if fans hoped for more dedication. When Coach Works finally ended his coaching career, he had accumulated 173 wins and 159 losses. He coached for 18 seasons and was UCLA's all-time leader in wins until John Wooden passed him in 1954. Coach Works is, to this day, number four all-time in wins in UCLA history.

Coach Caddy Works would continue to work as a lawyer for several more years and eventually retire to his Beverly Hills home. In July of 1982, he passed away at age 86.

1921–22

With a new coach in charge, there were, of course, questions and concerns coming into the 1921–22 season. The Southern Branch program was still in its infancy, but the college had two successful seasons on the hardwood and were hoping to have a third, even better season. Every major contributor from the previous two seasons returned, and the program continued to add depth with each ensuing year. A key issue was whether Coach Caddy Works could balance his work as an attorney and as the head coach of the SBUC basketball program.

Prior to the official beginning of the basketball season, the Cubs played a series of exhibition games. Although the score was not kept in each game, and they were nothing other than glorified practices, the games meant a lot to the athletic administration. They were an opportunity to see where the Cubs stacked up against foes. The games were close, but the Cubs were the inferior team in each matchup. Los Angeles Athletic Club, Santa Clara, and Cal Berkeley each bested the Bruins, but all three games were highly competitive. In the lone exhibition game that the Cubs clearly won (though the score was not kept), Coach Works and his boys defeated the California freshmen team.

The official season opener pitted the SBUC Cubs against the Caltech Engineers. Though the game was not pretty, it showed Coach Works's change in style. The Cubs played much faster than they had in the past, and though the team shot the ball poorly, they beat the Engineers by the score of 30–12. Starting forwards Cy Eaton and "Bugs" Woodard led the way in the first Cubs victory of the season.

The Cubs looked to continue its winning ways, but another conference crown would not be easy. In the second game of the season, much like the first, the Cubs shot the ball poorly. The team played fast, which pleased Coach Works. But again players failed to score consistently. Still, the Cubs led, 24–20, with time winding down in the second half. The University of Redlands, though trailing, was not out of the game. With time ticking down, the Bulldogs made three consecutive baskets and stole victory in the very last minute, 26–24. The loss hurt, but it was not soul-crushing. With eight games to play, the Cubs just needed to improve and win the remaining games, and the team would again be at the top of the Southern California Intercollegiate Athletic Conference.

Winning games was not much of an issue for the Cubs in 1922. A large crowd saw the Cubs take care of a weak Occidental squad. Prior to the next game, rumors circulated that the Whittier Poets had a strong team, but Coach Works and the Bruin five proved they were even better. The Poets stood no chance, losing 29–9, with nine points the least amount SBUC had given up in its brief hoops history at the time. The winning streak would run to four with a comfortable win over the Pomona College Sagehens. Halfway through the season, the Cubs stood at 4–1, with the second half of the round-robin schedule set to begin. Conference superiority was still clearly attainable; the Cubs just had to keep winning.

In the second matchup with Caltech, the game was sloppy, much like the first matchup, but it was thrilling nonetheless. The game was the fastest paced one of the year, but it also was one of the lowest scoring. At halftime, the score was 7–6 in favor of the Cubs, and with time ticking down in the second half, the score was tied, 17–17. SBUC had the ball; in the waning seconds, the players did what they seldom had done all season: they held the ball and played slowly. With no shot clock, the only way for the Engineers to get the ball back was to play tight defense and force the action, but they were content with playing slow as well. As time ticked off the clock, the ball found its way into the hands of SBUC's most reliable player, its captain, Si Gibbs. From the center of the court, near the free-throw line, Gibbs released a shot that found its way through the basket with no time remaining. The Cubs won, 19–17. It was time for the rematch against Redlands.

The rematch was no contest. The Southern Branch played its best game of the season and thoroughly defeated their conference rival. SBUC had its highest scoring game of the season thus far and played strong defense, resulting in the final score of SBUC 41, Redlands 19. The rest of the year went much the same. The Cubs were the best team in the SCIAC and proved it each time they played. They beat Occidental by 20 and then beat Whittier College in front of a large crowd to clinch the conference crown for the second year in a row. With one final game remaining, the Cubs continued to play well. Pomona College played many of their backups against SBUC, and it paid the price, losing 46–18. Coach Works's style of play was jelling, and opponents struggled to keep up. The solid play of Captain Si Gibbs all season; the shooting of "Bugs" Woodard, the best shooter in the conference; and the contributions of Tim Scott, Lamar Butler, Cy Eaton, and rest of the squad was a winning combination. The year 1922 was another good season for the young squad, which hoped to continue its success in 1923.

Wabash College and the University of Kansas claimed national champion status for 1922.

1922–23

After three consecutive successful seasons on the hardwood, two of which culminated in conference championships, the Southern Branch was buzzing. While the men on the football field were still trying to find their footing, the players in the gymnasium had no such problem. Over 100 men tried out for the team in the fall of 1922, and because of Coach Works's fast-paced system, the majority of those who tried out were forwards, the men who Coach Works insisted take the vast majority of shots. When the season finally came around, Coach Works had found his combination of men. The team goal was simple: to again win the Southern California Intercollegiate Athletic Conference. It would not be easy.

The season-opening game, played in front of a capacity crowd at the Pasadena YMCA, pitted the Caltech Engineers against the Southern Branch Cubs. The game marked a new wrinkle in Coach Works's preferred style of play. Whereas Works had only experimented before with a four-man defense, with the fifth cherry-picking for the majority of possessions, he stepped up the use of this strategy during the 1922–23 season. Against the Engineers, it worked. Buck Beeson, Horace Bresee, Bill Goertz, Cy Eaton, and Si Gibbs all played well, and the Cubs cruised to a 40–15 victory.

Throughout the early part of the season, it appeared no team stood a chance against the Cubs. UCLA's four-man defense and fast-paced offense was too much for Redlands. The Cubs won by a comfortable 13-point margin. The

1922 Southern Branch Cheer Squad (Southern Branch Collection).

matchup with Occidental was not much of a basketball game, but more of a brawl. SBUC, the more skilled team, eventually prevailed, beating Oxy by 22 points. Whittier went down, as well, as did Pomona College. Against the Sagehens, Captain Si Gibbs recorded a game-high 17 points and 12 rebounds. After beating Caltech by 29 points during the rematch on February 14, the Cubs' record was a perfect 6–0.

The game against Redlands was a crucial game in the conference race, and though the Cubs had defeated the Bulldogs soundly earlier in the season, Coach Works knew that his opponent was strong. The game would go back and forth for the majority of the two halves. Gibbs once again performed admirably, leading the Cubs with 10 points. In the final seconds, the score was tied at 24 and Redlands had possession. The final basket would come with just seconds left, and it was not a Cub who shot the ball, but a Bulldog. Redlands made a long jump shot to win the game and end the Cubs' perfect season.

SBUC bounced back from the loss, taking out all their frustration on their next opponent, Occidental. The Cubs won by nearly 50 points, 61–12. Every player on the roster got into the game, with the backups playing significant minutes and scoring seemingly at the same pace as the starters. The Cubs would continue to beat their opponents in convincing fashion, but the schedule was back-loaded with tough opponents. After beating Pomona and Whittier by double digits, the Cubs felt for the first time what it was like to be on the wrong side of a one-sided game. The California Golden Bears beat the Cubs by the score of 47–15, the largest loss in the young program's history.

One of the best rivalries in college basketball began in 1923. SBUC and the University of Arizona Wildcats played four games against each other, and, as would be the case in the decades to come, the two teams were closely matched. While Arizona and SBUC each won twice, none of the four games were particularly close. In the first matchup, the Cubs won, 43–30. Arizona would then beat SBUC by 11 in the second matchup in Los Angeles. Following the two games played in California, two games were played in Tucson, Arizona. The Cubs won the first game, 43–30, and the Wildcats won the next, 32–22.

Despite losing twice to the University of Arizona and also losing to the California Golden Bears, the Cubs were again the SCIAC champion, losing only one conference game. In four seasons, the Cubs had won three conference titles. However, in 1923–24, there would be change. The first graduating class in school history included some of the key contributors of the successful, early teams. Captain Si Gibbs was gone, and replacing him would be a challenge for Coach Works. In 1923, there would be other changes as well at the Southern Branch.

The University of Kansas claims national champion status for 1923.

1923–24

At the Southern Branch, basketball was becoming the athletic calling card. The team was good; the program was strong. Under Fred Cozens and Caddy Works, the Cubs had won three consecutive conference championships and were looking for more. In sunny Southern California, Coach Jimmie Cline entered his second year as the head coach of the Southern Branch football program, but unlike on the hardwood, it would take much longer for SBUC to find success on the gridiron.

For the basketball team, Coach Works was just trying to keep the train on the tracks following the loss of key players to graduation. Off-the-court changes were in store, as well. Though certainly not the consensus, many students on campus started calling their university the "University of California at Los Angeles." They believed "Southern Branch" did not give due respect to the university. The name would eventually stick, but in '23 and '24, the name was still the University of California Southern Branch.

With Si Gibbs moving on following graduation, the new team captain was Bill Goertz. Though he had already played significant time prior to the new season, in 1923–24, he assumed the role as SBUC's key player. He was the leading scorer for the Cubs and the leading scorer in the Southern California Intercollegiate Athletic Conference. After the season, he would be named to the mythical All-Southern California Conference team, made up of all schools in the Southern California region.

Although the games against Redlands had been the key matchups in the conference race in previous years, the main challenge for the Cubs would come

1924 Southern Branch captain Bill Goertz (Southern Branch Collection)

not against the Bulldogs of Redlands, but against the Whittier Poets. Despite some close games with other teams, it was clear early in the season that the race was a two-team battle. The Cubs were scheduled for 10 games, and the eight played against other conference foes would all go the Cubs' way. In the two games against Caltech, the Cubs dominated. Goertz scored 22 points in the first matchup, as the Cubs won by over 30 points. In the return matchup, played in Pasadena, the game was a bit closer, but still noncompetitive. Goertz, Horace Bresee, and Wilbur Johns all played well, and the Cubs won handily.

Unlike the two matchups against the Caltech Engineers, the games against Redlands were close, but in both games, the Cubs came out on top. In the first game against Occidental, the Cubs led, 28–1, at halftime and finished with a 41–9 advantage. The second game would be much closer, but the Cubs again won, this time by six. Like the games against Caltech, Redlands, and Occidental, the two games against Pomona College would be all Cubs. SBUC won both. The two games that ultimately decided the SCIAC crown came against Whittier.

The first matchup, in the Whittier College home gym, was competitive, a back and forth affair. At halftime, the Cubs led, 12–10, but in the second half, the Poets played much better. Still, the game was close and could have gone either way. In the final minutes, the Poets outplayed the Cubs and came away with a two-point victory, 22–20. Though the loss was disappointing, it was not debilitating. The Poets would lose one conference game itself before the two teams met up in the conference-deciding game on March 5, 1924, at the USC Pavilion. The game went much the way of the first matchup. It was close throughout, with no team ever leading by more than three points. At halftime, the Cubs led, 11–8. If the team could hold its advantage throughout the second half, it would win the SCIAC once again. In the second half, both teams seemingly found their way on offense, at least in terms of taking better shots. Still, neither team shot particularly well. In the final seconds, the score was tied at 21. Whittier had the ball, and, with time ticking down, the ball was heaved from just inside halfcourt. As the ball came down, it went right through the hoop and the Poets were the SCIAC champions, breaking the three-year Southern Branch stranglehold.

While the ending to the 1924 season was undoubtedly disappointing, and the first taste of defeat on a conference level for many of the players involved, it was not altogether surprising. The varsity team had replaced many of its key players from the previous four seasons, and the team outperformed the expectations of most. The freshmen squad in '24 was the best in school history to that point, so the future for hoops at the Southern Branch looked bright.

The University of North Carolina and Butler University claim national-champion status for 1924.

1924–25

In 1924, Soviet dictator Vladimir Lenin died. The Ottoman Empire was toppled. The British Mount Everest expedition ended in tragedy when George Mallory and Andrew Irvine disappeared trying to be the first people to reach the summit. In Los Angeles at Southern Branch, there was one notable change. While "Southern Branch" would remain, "Cubs" was no more. Students wanted a more ferocious name, and administrators wanted to stick to the University of California theme. In 1924, the Southern Branch athletic teams became known as the "Grizzlies."

Entering his fourth season, even the most pessimistic of people were inclined to say Coach Caddy Works was doing a fine job, though he was still a full-time attorney and coached the basketball team at nights, after work. He had won the Southern California Intercollegiate Athletic Conference twice in his first three years, and in his fourth season, the team would again be good. The Grizzlies would play all its home games at Manual Arts High School, and many of the games became must-watch action. The team was exciting, played at a fast pace, and was to play its toughest schedule of any season to date. SBUC's leading scorer for the season was Wilbur Johns, a third-year player and the captain of the varsity team. While Johns got the most attention, junior Horace Bresee was the unsung hero and the vocal leader on the team. He was quiet off the court, but he was a motivational teammate on it, and his toughness was never questioned.

Another man, just a sophomore and new to the varsity squad, was Ralph Bunche. Though in '25 he was known simply for his aggressive play and underhand shooting, he would soon be known for much more. Bunche was black, the first minority player in Southern Branch/UCLA basketball history. Simply playing for the team is an achievement to be recognized, but it seems now like just a minor accomplishment on his impressive life resumé. As a boy, he was primarily raised by his grandmother after both of his parents died at a young age. When Ralph was ten, he began working, selling newspapers, working for a carpet-laying company, and even appearing as an extra in movies. He found his most success, however, in the classroom. In elementary school, he won awards for his work studying both history and English. Bunche was the valedictorian of his high school. When he arrived at the Southern Branch on a full basketball scholarship, he set his goals not only for the hardwood but also for academic success. While also spending time working as a janitor, Bunche thrived in every aspect of his studies. He graduated in 1927 *summa cum laude* and again was named valedictorian. Bunche went on to Harvard University and received a master's degree in just one year and spent the majority of his career working in research and history. He studied social studies, world economics, political science, and philosophy. Bunche was one of the original founders of the United Nations and earned a Nobel Prize for his studies of the Arab-Israeli conflict in Palestine. He was later awarded a Medal of Freedom and was one of the preeminent twentieth-century Civil Rights leaders. Today, Bunche is honored on the UCLA campus with a building named after him, Bunche Hall, featuring his bust at the entrance.

With Johns, Bresee, Bunche, and the rest of the Grizzlies squad ready to play, the season began against the University of La Verne. The nonconference schedule was difficult for the Grizzlies, and the team stumbled through the difficult stretch. But during the earliest games, the Grizzlies were dynamic and played well. In the first game, SBUC won by a staggering margin, beating ULV, 54–11. Though San Diego College did better, the Grizzlies again dominated in the second game of the season, winning by 20 points. Overall, the Grizzlies played seven total nonconference games, but it won just those two. The team lost close games to both Oregon and Stanford early in the season. Over Christmas break, Coach Works took ten of his players to the Bay Area to play a series of games. The team lost to Stanford again, to California Berkeley, and to the local Olympic Club team.

In conference play, the Grizzlies performed much better than they did in nonconference games. After smashing the University of Redlands, 48–5, in the conference opener, the Grizzlies took on the Whittier Poets, the favorite to win the SCIAC. At halftime, the Grizzlies led, 12–6. The players were not shooting to Coach Works's liking, but they played smothering defense. In the second half, the shooting picked up, and the defense remained strong. The Grizzlies won by the score of 32–11.

For much of the season, it appeared no team in the SCIAC stood a chance against the Grizzlies. The team pummeled Pomona in consecutive games, beat Redlands again, and then crushed Occidental College by 16 points. The rematch against Occidental was surprising, however. Playing one night after the initial matchup, the Oxy Tigers and the Southern Branch Grizzlies appeared to have switched uniforms. Bunche would start at guard for the first time in his career, and Edward Prigge would start at center, replacing Bill Goertz, who was out with an injury. The game went to overtime, and when the time expired after the extra five minutes, the Grizzlies were on the wrong side of the 24–23 score.

The final game had conference implications. With a win, SBUC would again win the conference crown, its fourth in five years. With a Whittier win, there would be a three-way tie between the Grizzlies, Whittier Poets, and Occidental Tigers. The first half was a seesaw contest. Both teams played well on defense and alternated the lead for much of the half. At the break, SBUC led, 12–10. The beginning of the second half was the same, and the game seemingly would come down to the final minutes. Midway through the half, however, the Grizzlies made a run and took control of the game. The final score was 22–15, with SBUC on top. Again, SBUC won the conference title. The 1925 team was tested outside the conference, and although the players knew they had a long way to go, the program was successful.

Washburn University and Princeton University claimed national champion status for 1925.

1925–26

Entering the 1925–26 season, the Grizzlies were expected to win. The team had won four conference titles in five years since officially joining the SCIAC, including three conference crowns in four years under Coach Works. The Grizzlies played a difficult schedule, its toughest yet, but the team was supremely talented. Horace Bresee was a senior and team captain; he was to have his best season yet. When the '26 season ended, all close observers considered Bresee to be the best player yet in the young history of the university. He was a solid scorer, a smart offensive player, and a good rebounder for a guard. His prowess, however, came on the defensive end. He was feisty and aggressive and had a knack for the ball unmatched in the SCIAC.

While Bresee was the Grizzlies' best defensive player, Ed Prigge, the captain-elect, was the main threat on the offensive end. He was tall, lanky, and an excellent offensive center. The season opened on December 12 against the Hollywood Athletic Club on Hollywood Court, and though the game was surprisingly close, due to the sloppy play of the Grizzlies, Coach Works and his men prevailed by the score of 27–25. Though not impressive, the win satisfied Coach Works. The Grizzlies ran its record to 3–0 by beating the Los Angeles Athletic Club by five points and trouncing San Diego State Teachers College by 15. Over Christmas break, several more nonconference games were played, and SBUC came out victorious in each. Montana State College and Oregon Agricultural College each lost by double figures, before the Grizzlies took on Stanford in Palo Alto. Though the Grizzlies were considered underdogs, they proved to be the superior team, trouncing the Stanford varsity, 28–15. It was the first victory for SBUC over Stanford in school history.

On January 9, the quest for another conference crown began. SBUC was without its top player, Horace Bresee, due to illness, and on the court it showed. The Grizzlies were not sharp offensively, but the opponent, the Redlands Bulldogs, proved to be no match. Redlands hoped to make the game a physical battle that the Bulldogs preferred. Although the game was rugged and SBUC guard Jimmy Armstrong fouled out, the final score showed the difference between the two teams. After leading, 14–1, at halftime, the Grizzlies cruised to a 32–8 victory. The win over Redlands would be a sign of things to come. SBUC beat Occidental, 38–11, and though it barely snuck by the Tigers in a rematch just days later, winning 15–11, sportswriters started to believe the Grizzlies were the best team on the West Coast. In the following game, Ed Prigge led the team with 15 points, and the Grizzlies' unbeaten season remained intact.

On Friday, February 5, SBUC took on the Stanford team in a rematch, this time in Los Angeles. SBUC was 10–0, and Stanford's lone loss came six weeks earlier at the hands of the Grizzlies. Over five thousand fans showed up and saw a thriller. Though both teams would start slow on the offensive end, soon they were able to find the basket. Throughout the first half, the lead repeatedly changed hands. At the break, SBUC led, 16–13, and the game was tough throughout. SBUC consistently got shots closer to the basket, but the Stanford players made tough shots to

1926 Southern Branch team photo (Southern Branch Collection).

remain close. The early portion of the second half was a disaster for the Grizzlies. After SBUC quickly scored two baskets to extend the lead to seven, Stanford Coach Andy Kerr had seen enough. He removed all five of his starters and brought in a new wave. Suddenly the fresh Stanford squad looked to be the better team. Stanford went on a 15–2 run, and for the first time all season, SBUC trailed late in a game. SBUC cut the Stanford lead to three with two minutes to play. In the final minutes, the Grizzlies hit a basket and a free throw, but so did Stanford. When the final seconds ticked off, the score read Stanford 32, SBUC 29. The perfect season was over. While the Southern Branch varsity was certainly talented, they lacked the depth of the Stanford squad, and ultimately it cost them the game. In the following game, the California Golden Bears proved that Stanford and SBUC were not the only two teams on the West Coast that knew how to play ball. The Bears thrashed the Grizzlies, winning 22–8.

While the Grizzlies' depth was a problem against Stanford, it would not be when the team returned to conference play. Coach Works wanted to rest his usual starters when playing the Caltech Beavers. None of his usual five played in the first half. At the break, SBUC led just 9–7, but in the second half, with the help of the regulars, SBUC held on to win another conference game, 27–21. With three games to play, the Grizzlies were in a position to win the conference title with one victory. Coach Works still was unsure of the best lineup to start. Three players who were usually reserves—Scribner Birlenbach, Arthur Williams, and Franklin Pierce—started. The plan backfired, however, and soon the Grizzlies were down by five. Coach Works played his usual starters for the rest of the game, and the team easily came out on top. SBUC beat Whittier again the next day; then in the final game, it destroyed the Redlands Bulldogs, 46–17. The Southern Branch Grizzlies finished the season with a 14–2 record, and a perfect 10–0 conference record. SBUC again was the conference champion, and despite the hectic work schedule of Coach Works, he appeared to master his craft. The results of the '26 season, beyond the conference title, served as a measuring stick for the young athletic program. With Coach William Spaulding leading the football program to the first winning season in '25, and Coach Works leading the basketball program to consistent success in the SCIAC, the Southern Branch was on the rise. The team saw that it could beat Stanford on the hardwood, and though they lost to California, the team believed they were in the same class and could beat California in '27. A new team that SBUC had never played was suddenly in the discussion, as well. Coach Works and his young squad wanted to play USC.

Syracuse University claimed national champion status for 1926.

1926–27

Prior to the 1926–27 season, change at the university hadn't quite arrived; the period was more a time of reflection. The late '20s would see many changes that shaped the future of athletics at the still new university. Until then, some changes had begun. In '26, a new nickname was born, though it would not be official for another year. Many students who found the name "Southern Branch" insulting started calling the school "University of California at Los Angeles." They believed doing so would force the change amongst administrators. Eventually they were proved right, but most in the media and all administrators still stuck with the old name. Though nothing abnormal would change with the basketball program prior to the season, obviously the Grizzlies would not be long for the Southern California Intercollegiate Athletic Conference. Football was improving under Coach William Spaulding each year, the basketball program was the strongest program on campus, and the other sports were also doing quite well. The '26–'27 season would be the last for the basketball program in the SCIAC. In the six years the Cubs/Grizzlies competed in the SCIAC, they had finished at the top five times. In Coach Caddy Works's five seasons, the varsity squad had a record of 54–13. In the final season in the SCIAC, Coach Works hoped to do what he had done so many times already—win.

Despite the loss of much of the conference championship roster of the season prior, the Grizzlies entered the season again as favorites and would again have a strong team. The new team captain was Jimmy Armstrong, a fast yet composed guard. He had the capability to play at a speed few could match, and his style worked well in Coach Works's frantic offense. He was able to set his feet before shooting better than most players with his speed, and his two-hand jump shot was accurate. He was a vocal leader, as well, and the best perimeter defender on the squad.

Throughout the season, the Grizzlies would play six nonconference games, and as had been the case in recent years, the opponents in those games challenged the Grizzlies the most. In the first nonconference game, played over Christmas break, the Grizzlies won, 32–22 over the Oregon Agricultural College Aggies. Along with Armstrong, the other four starters—Milo Young, Jack Ketchum, Ralph Bunche, and Sam Balter—played well.

SBUC, hoping for an undefeated season, would not be so lucky. Though they beat Stanford twice in close games, they lost handily to the University of Idaho, Hollywood Athletic Club, and Pacific Coast Club.

Despite just a 3–3 nonconference record, which failed to include a game against USC despite the urging of many Southern Branch fans, Coach Works and players knew that the conference games were of much greater significance. On January 7, the SCIAC season opened with a tilt between the Grizzlies and the Occidental College Tigers. The game went through two distinct phases. Early on, Occidental played a stalling game, taking only wide-open shots, holding the ball for minutes at a time. Nevertheless, the Tigers trailed. When the Grizzlies had the ball, the players pushed the pace and scored quickly. Midway through the first half, the Occidental strategy changed, and with it, so did its hopes. Their players attempted to match SBUC's speed, but to no avail. The Grizzlies won, 32–17, and were 1–0 in conference. As was the case for the majority of conference foes, there would be two meetings. In the second meeting with the Oxy Tigers, SBUC again won, this time by 28–14. SBUC beat San Diego State College twice, by a margin of more than 15 points per contest. The team beat Caltech in the lone encounter; Pomona twice, with Ketchum starring in both contests; and Redlands by 18 points.

While the Grizzlies were easily dismantling all their conference foes, so were the Whittier Poets. Although the matchups on the football field between SBUC and Whittier are more memorable, it was on the hardwood where conference crowns were decided. In the first matchup between the two teams, Whittier was superior from start to finish. The Poets held a lead for much of the game of around three to five points, but with a few timely baskets toward the end, the game was put away. The final score read Whittier 31, Southern Branch 22. The final matchup between the Grizzlies and Poets also concluded the conference season. Whittier held a 9–0 record, and SBUC came in at 8–1. With a win, Whittier would be the SCIAC champion. With a Southern Branch win, there would be a tie. Before the game, conference officials discussed the feasibility of a playoff tiebreaker, but they decided that an SBUC win would result in two cochampions.

The second matchup was one of the best games in school history at the time. The Poets jumped out to a quick lead. The two teams were getting quality looks at the basket, but only one team consistently scored. Unfortunately for Coach Works, the men able to find the hoop were wearing Poet uniforms. At the break, the score was 16–7. It appeared unlikely that SBUC would make a charge to win the conference crown alone again. However, the style of play in the second half again differed greatly from that of the first. In the opening half, the teams had constant motion, and though only Whittier shot the ball well, free-flowing offense was on both sides. In the second half, both teams played very physical defense, with many fouls called. With eight minutes left, the Grizzlies still seemed unlikely to win—the score stood at 20–12. SBUC's inability to score was letting them down. Coach Works would make a key change, however, and suddenly the tide began to shift. Bill Woodruff, an oft-used backup center, was inserted into the game and instantly made an impact. Taking the ball back to nearly half court to get separation from the stingy defense, Woodruff fired a long shot, and to the amazement of all in the arena, it fell through the net. The Grizzlies' scoring barrage was just beginning. Armstrong and Balter each hit short shots in succession to bring the score to 20–18. Whittier responded with a quick basket to grow the lead to four, but Balter and Ketchum again scored for the Grizzlies and suddenly the game was tied for the first time since the early minutes. After forcing a stop, super sub Woodruff scored again, and then put the game away with another late basket, bringing the score to 26–22. In the final desperate minutes, Whittier threw up several long shots, but its lone point came on a free throw. The Grizzlies played error-free in the final minutes and won, 29–23. The 17–3 scoring run following the insertion of Woodruff into the game helped the Grizzlies win the third consecutive SCIAC title, and the graduating seniors would finish their careers having never lost the SCIAC crown as members of the varsity squad.

Soon, the competition would get much more difficult. While Coach Works was able to balance his work as an attorney during the day and his coaching at night with stunning success in his first six seasons, he thereafter found success much harder to obtain.

The University of Notre Dame claimed national champion status for 1927.

1927–28

The year 1927 brought more change. The nickname that was born in 1926 became reality in 1927. No longer was there a University of California Southern Branch. The new name was the University of California at Los Angeles ("at" was removed in 1958). Although the football program remained in the Southern California Intercollegiate Athletic Conference for one more year, the basketball team, along with several other teams in other sports on campus, joined the preeminent college athletic conference on the West Coast, the Pacific Coast Conference. In basketball, there would be two divisions, the North and the South. The North Division had six teams: Washington, Washington State, Oregon, Oregon State, Idaho, and Montana. The South Division had just four teams: UCLA, USC, Cal, and Stanford. The winner of the conference was not decided by a conference championship game at the end, but simply by conference record. Although the PCC crown was the goal for each team, the reality of the scheduling dictated that the more immediate goal was to win the division. The northern teams played their northern rivals twice each, and southern teams played their southern rivals three times each. There would be no crossover between divisions.

While the 1927–28 Grizzlies were solid, the switch to the PCC, as well as the acceleration of basketball competition on the West Coast, made Coach Caddy Works's job even more difficult. Whereas conference and division rivals each had full-time coaches, Coach Works's first obligation was to his legal practice and would remain so for the entirety of his career. In the first year for the Grizzlies in the PCC, the situation did not pose much of a problem, but soon the program fell behind.

UCLA began the season with six nonconference games before the start of PCC play. With an added interest in basketball on campus amongst students, the Grizzlies set out to prove itself. In the six preliminary games, the Grizzlies went 5–1. The nonconference games are memorable for two reasons. Most important to the long-standing record, they were a success on the scoreboard. Though the squad lost a close game to the Los Angeles Athletic Club, it also trounced several opponents, including a 53–32 win over Pomona and a 70–10 win over Caltech, in which every Grizzly player appeared in the game. However, not all was great for Coach Works in the early-season slate. The Grizzlies outscored the six opponents by 229–156, but the man most responsible for the scoring would not play again for quite a while. Guard Bob Baker started the season excellently, but he was injured in the final tune-up before PCC play. Suddenly Coach Works had to replace a key player.

UCLA opened PCC play with a three-game series against new rival Stanford. Though the two teams had played in recent years, the games took on more importance with UCLA's arrival to the PCC. Coach Works always measured his success against his rivals from Palo Alto. When the UCLA team took off on the trip to Palo Alto for the first two games, a crowd of more than two thousand fans wished them well. The rally at the Glendale Station for the departing men turned into an impromptu party, and though the players would have loved to stay with their beloved classmates, they knew they had a job to do. Playing in Stanford's gymnasium was a challenge. Practically no fans ever attended, and while Stanford was a good team, the games therefore always felt substandard. Early in the game, Stanford struggled to keep up with the fast pace of play by the Grizzlies. Though the game remained frustratingly close for Coach Works, when the final seconds ticked off the clock, UCLA was victorious, 29–22. Jack Ketchum led the way with 13 points for the Grizzlies.

One day later, the two teams played again, and though the score was almost identical, the game was much different. UCLA's speed was vanquished. Stanford played better transition defense and forced the Grizzlies to score in the half-court offense. The Grizzlies were the more disciplined team, however, which showed most prominently in the second half. UCLA continued to pass the ball for an open shot, even if doing so took minutes off the clock. Stanford was more rushed and took many long shots. All but 10 attempts for Stanford were from long distance, and even down low their players struggled, finishing just 2-for-10 on layup attempts. William Woodroff was the leading man for the Grizzlies, finishing with 12 points. The final score was 28–22, making the Grizzlies 2–0.

The third game in the Stanford series disappointed Coach Works in many ways. At 2–0, UCLA was tied with USC at the top of the division standings, and a sweep over a strong Stanford team would go a long way toward helping reach the end goal. In front of a large crowd back home at Olympic Auditorium, the Grizzlies stormed out to what seemed like an insurmountable 24–13 halftime lead. In the second half, however, things changed dramatically. The Stanford men found their rhythm on offense, and the Grizzlies played sloppily, not showing the patience they exhibited one week earlier. Stanford outscored UCLA, 19–3, to win by a five-point margin.

If the loss to Stanford frustrated all UCLA rooters, the first game of the series against California was heartbreaking. With the score tied at 34 with five seconds left, a foul was called on UCLA. Vern Corbin of California would make one free throw, and the Golden Bears came away with the one-point win. In the second game, the Grizzlies changed strategy. Despite being much smaller and faster, Coach Works wanted to muck the game up. UCLA played a physical brand of basketball, knowing it would force the Bears to match their physicality. The plan worked, as the second half ended up being essentially a free-throw contest in between periods of wrestling. The Grizzlies were the better shooting team and came away with a 12-point victory. The plan gave the Bears an idea of what would happen again in the rematch one day later. Instead of trying to avoid the physical strategy, Cal doubled down and played an even more physical game. This time, however, the team also shot the ball well. In the rubber match between the two UC rivals, the men from Berkeley won, 33–26.

UCLA and USC met at Olympic Auditorium in 1928 for the first matchup between the two schools in a major sport in history. Coach Works and many of his players had hoped to play the Trojans in nonconference games for years; now, they needed to beat the men they had asked for. The games against USC meant more to the players than those against early rivals Stanford and California. USC entered the first matchup with a 22–2 overall record and a 5–1 conference record. The Grizzlies came in at 8–4, with a 3–3 conference record. On paper the Trojans seemed superior, so Coach Works needed to convince his players that they could beat USC. As was to be the case so often in many sports, the games were close, and drama was always one possession away. In the first matchup, the sportswriters appeared to be right. Though the game was tied at 32 deep into the second half, the Trojans rallied and won, 45–35. UCLA would get revenge, however, and win the second game of the series. UCLA's starting five, Ketchum, Woodruff, Larry Wilds, Sam Balter, and Bob Baker each played well. Baker, who was injured in the final nonconference tune-up, returned for the USC series, and was a key player in the Grizzlies' victory.

The final game of the season brought with it the largest crowd to date at Olympic Auditorium. Fans stood outside, just trying to glimpse the action. The first half was a battle, as both teams were sharp. They played strong, tight defense, but they were equally impressive on the other end. With the score tied at 20, USC scored just before half to take a two-point lead into the break. In the second half, the Grizzlies played the finest basketball of the year. Players smothered the Trojans on defense and executed flawlessly on offense. An 11–0 UCLA run to start the half proved to be the difference. Though USC would make a run of its own, the surge was not enough. UCLA finished with a flurry and won, 47–37.

The 1928 Grizzlies did not win the PCC, instead finishing just third in the South Division. But the team was undoubtedly impressive in its initial PCC season. With a 10–5 overall record and a 5–4 mark in conference play, the squad exceeded all outside expectations. Going forward, however, the team was about to enter into the darkest period in UCLA basketball history.

The University of Pittsburgh claimed national champion status for 1928.

1928–29

Prior to the start of the 10th season in UCLA basketball history, more change occurred. Unlike with the basketball side, the football PCC conference was not split into divisions; teams could play any team in the conference. The University of Montana Grizzlies was a member institution, and the PCC would not allow two teams to have the same nickname. Gone were the days of the UCLA Grizzlies. In 1928, every athletic team on campus was called the UCLA Bruins.

Caddy Works's eighth season was unlike every other season in his career to that point. For the first time, UCLA struggled. Although the team was relatively experienced, the returning players did not play as successfully as in previous seasons, nor did any newcomers pick up the slack. Coach Works constantly fiddled with his lineup trying to find the right combination, but nothing seemed to work. Twelve players earned a varsity letter during the season, but none stood out as true stars. Larry Wilde, Dick Linthicum, Milo Young, Bill Woodroff, Sam Balter, Bob Baker, and Al Sunseri each started at different points during the season. Key scorers Balter, Baker, and Sunseri were all of similar size and skill, and all graduated at the end of the season. The Bruins big men, on the other hand, were younger but struggled mightily for the majority of the season.

When looking at just the results of the early contests, one would be shocked to find out how poorly the season turned out. The Bruins, as was expected, started the season with a flurry of wins. On December 14, the ball was in the air for the first time during the new season. The game was played at Pomona College and the Sagehens were no match. UCLA won, 43–22. One day later, the Bruins took on La Verne College and again won decisively, this time by the score of 46–24. The Bruins cruised through the next two opponents, beating Hollywood Athletic Club by 17 and Los Angeles Club by 18. Sam Balter was the Bruins' best early-season scoring threat and led on the defensive end as well. UCLA finished the nonconference slate by beating the University of Utah in the first ever meeting between the two schools, in Salt Lake City. The thrill of victory did not last long, as Utah won the rematch one day later. Finally, the nonconference slate finished with another Bruins victory on January 4, this time over the University of North Dakota.

With a 6–1 record, Coach Works, as well as players and fans, was confident that 1929 could be a championship season. The offense was strong in early-season play and the defense was much improved over the prior season. But their early hopes and dreams were not based in reality. In the first conference game of the season, the Bruins defense played well, but the offense suddenly went cold. When UCLA headed to Berkeley to take on the Bears, they went to win the series and return home to study for final exams the following week. In the first half, the Bruins outplayed the Bears but struggled to score when they had open looks at the hoop. The two teams exchanged the lead several times, but the half-time score was just 10–7 in favor of the Bruins. In the second half, scoring picked up, but only slightly. The score was tied at 19 with under eight minutes to play. In the final minutes, however, only the team from Berkeley rose to the occasion, outscoring the Bruins, 7–2, and winning the game, 26–21.

The second game against the Bears was not much like the first, but the end result was nevertheless frustrating. UCLA led 15–14 at half, but the Bears stormed out of the break and rallied to take a 35-24 lead. Though UCLA would score the final seven points, it wasn't enough. The Bruins had chances, but the game was lost at the free-throw line. Three Bruins fouled out (four fouls was the maximum at the time) in the physical game. Cal shot 14 free throws, making 12. UCLA shot 17, only making nine. Though the final game of the three-game series would be played weeks later at Olympic Auditorium in Los Angeles, it mattered little. The Bears crushed the Bruins and swept the three-game series.

Though Stanford was not the team that Cal was, and two of the three games would be played in Los Angeles, the result was the same in the second series of the season. Stanford was big and strong, whereas UCLA was fast and shifty. In the end, size won decisively. Stanford won by double digits in the first game. In the second game, Coach Works's frustration began to show. He started three players who were normally substitutes: Al Sunseri, Erwin Piper, and Carl Knowles. It didn't work, and the Bruins fell to 0–5 in conference play. The five-game losing streak would reach six, then seven, and then eight. The latter two losses would come against the University of Southern California.

With an abysmal 0–8 conference record, Coach Works struggled to find the words to motivate his men to finish the season strongly. Many of his players were multisport athletes who started to focus on their next season. Still, some were seniors thinking about life after school.

USC, however, also stuggled. Its only two wins in conference play had come against the Bruins, and the Bruins hoped to return the favor in one final showdown. Sophomore Dick Linthicum, who played only the first half, was expected to be the star in the coming years, and against USC, he had his finest half of the season. He scored 12 points before watching the second half from the bench. Seniors Sammy Balter and Bob Baker got their last wish, winning in the final game of their careers. The score was 44–33, bringing some comfort to a disappointing season. UCLA finished with a 1–8 conference record and just a 7–9 overall mark. The season was the first losing one in school history, and the eight-game losing streak was the longest in history. The Bruins finished in last place in the four-team South Division and had the worst record of any school in the ten-team Pacific Coast Conference.

Montana State University and Butler University claimed national champion status for 1929.

1929–30

The 1929–30 season was in a way one of redemption, but it was also one of disappointment. The Bruins, under Coach Caddy Works, improved greatly from the prior season, but still the squad failed to reach the success of just a few years earlier. Though Coach Works implemented a fast-paced offense like that of his first year at UCLA, his defense began to stand out. For years, he was flexible with his chosen defenses, implementing strategies still common today. Whereas almost every team played exclusively man-to-man defense, Coach Works and the Bruins implemented zone defense, as well as tactics that became known later as "box and one" and "triangle and two" coverages. By the 1930 season, however, UCLA did not mix defenses much. They played almost exclusively zone.

Leading the way for the Bruins on the court was Captain Larry Wilds. As a three-year varsity letter winner, Wilds was the most consistent Bruin on the court, and the coaching staff claimed he was the most mature, the man they could always trust to make the correct play. Though the 1929 season was the worst thus far in UCLA history, word had spread that Coach Works had built a strong program, and the student body caught basketball fever. The 1930 Bruins had 18 varsity players, more than any thus far in school history. Along with Wilds, Richard von Hagen, Carl Knowles, Frank Lubin, and Carl Shy were the usual starters. Coach Works was well aware that the 1930 season would need to be a strong one. The team was experienced, senior-laden, and coming off of a disappointing prior season. Though the freshmen of 1930 were splendid players, the best thus far in school history, Coach Works knew that 1930 brought a unique opportunity to win, and early in the season, the Bruins did just that.

The Bruins played eight nonconference games against teams they were expected to handle easily to open the season, and they won them all. Carl Knowles led the Bruins in scoring in the first game of the season, thrashing the much larger Elks Club, 51–34. As it turned out, nearly every team was much bigger than the Bruins. Yet the team possessed excellent ball-handling skills and accurate shooting and was able to wear down many of their opponents with sheer pace. This was displayed in the second game of the season against the University of La Verne, which was able to keep up with the Bruins through the first half before tiring in the second, losing by 15 points. The Bruins played fine basketball in the remaining early nonconference games. The team's largest victory came by 29 points over Pomona. It also beat Occidental by 25 and thrashed Caltech again by 29 in the final tune-up game. The closest affair came against Los Angeles Athletic Club in a low-scoring game, just 23–17.

Coach Works and the Bruins believed the following series against nonconference Brigham Young University was vitally important to their success, more so than the previous eight games. BYU was a strong team. In the first game of the series, the tables were turned on UCLA: BYU played a similar style, but the men from Provo played it better. The players excelled on timing, with excellent passing and constant movement. To the surprise of everyone in attendance, UCLA was tired. Its speed and conditioning advantage was nonexistent here. BYU played an excellent game, but still the Bruins were close. In the end, the difference was just seven points: BYU 47, UCLA 40. The second game was much like the first, though the outcome was different. Rather than trying to change the way the Bruins played, Coach Works drilled in his players the importance of teamwork. He wanted them not to try to beat BYU by themselves, but rather to note how their opponent beat them the day before—with teamwork and excellent passing. This was the UCLA way, and it would be the strategy going forward. Despite playing much better, the Bruins still trailed by two points at halftime. The second half would be a back-and-forth battle, with each team exchanging the lead several times. In the end, the victor earned the victory at the free-throw line. UCLA was the better foul-shooting team and came away with a 47–43 victory. The Bruins were 9–1.

Next on the schedule was the University of Utah. The series would be one of highs and lows for fans of the Bruins. In the first game, UCLA easily dismantled the men from Salt Lake City. In the second game, however, a flaw in the Bruins surfaced. After jumping out to a fast start and building a 14-point lead, Coach Works pulled his starters and inserted backups. He hoped they would gain valuable experience, play well, and give the starters rest. With four minutes remaining, however, the contest was knotted. Coach Works put all five starters back in the game. UCLA went on a run to close the game and finished with an 11-point victory. With two wins over Utah already in the books, Coach Works chose to play his backups for the majority of game three. Though the normal starters would eventually reenter, it was too late. After falling behind by 14 points, the Bruins lost, 52–44.

The rest of the season would consist of three three-game series in conference play. There were several thrilling moments for Bruins fans, but none would top the first matchup with Stanford. Though heavy underdogs, the Bruins played its finest basketball. The game was at Olympic Stadium, and the Bruins faithful showed in full force. Both teams started slowly, and several minutes in, the score was just 2–1. The game seemed like it would be a low-scoring, slug-it-out affair, but soon things changed. The Bruins would find their shot over and over again. The Stanford players and coaches were stunned. UCLA could seemingly do no wrong. Knowles led the Bruins with 20 points, and Wilds finished with 19. When the final seconds ticked off the clock, the final score was UCLA 63, Stanford 30. The 63 points scored was the most in the history of the Pacific Coast Conference to that point.

As would be an issue throughout all conference play, the Bruins were inconsistent in the second matchup with Stanford. The game was played in Palo Alto three weeks after the first game, and it appeared early to be much like the game in Los Angeles. The Bruins built a 13-point lead at halftime, but it did not last. Stanford charged back to take a lead. Trailing by two points with less than 30 seconds to play, Wilds hit a shot for the Bruins to send the game to overtime, but the Bruins lost in the extra period.

Unlike the previous two matchups, the third meeting was low scoring. The final score was just 20–15, and though the game was not aesthetically pleasing, and resembled a football game more than a basketball game, the Bruins won the slugfest to take two out of three.

UCLA was still an underdog against the California Golden Bears in the next game, and in the first half, one could see why. UCLA was unable to do anything well on offense, and on defense, it couldn't stop Kent Pursel, who accounted for 13 points in the first half. The Bruins trailed, 22–11, at the break. In the second half, the Bruins picked up their offense a bit, but their defense brought them back. California hurt itself as well in the half. It finished just 1–6 from the free-throw line, and remarkably, the one point was the only one it scored all half. UCLA tallied 15 second-half points and won, 26–23. The breaks evened out in the second game, however, and though UCLA outplayed Cal for much of the game, the Bears finished with three more points, winning, 32–29. The final game against Cal was one that players and coaches would have to think about for the entirety of the offseason. UCLA led, 30–28, with time ticking down in the final minute. UCLA would have won if they were simply able to get a stop and then stall to run out the clock. Joel Cottfield was able to hit an incredible long-range shot for the Bears, however, and suddenly the game was tied. UCLA failed on the offensive end, and Cal's best player, Kent Pursel, then hit the game-winning shot to break the Bruins' hearts. The chance at a conference crown was over.

The final games against the University of Southern California were anticlimactic. The Bruins could not win the conference title, and the team was without one of its better players for the first two games. Carl Shy was sick, and Dave Williams, a strong defensive player but not the offensive scorer Shy was, didn't make up the difference. USC beat UCLA in all three contests, winning 33–16, 42–30, and finally, 33–28. Shy played in the final game; by scoring 15 points, he secured the title of leading scorer in the South Division of the Pacific Coast Conference. UCLA finished with a 14–8 record, but just 3–6 in conference play.

The University of Pittsburgh claimed national champion status for 1930.

1930–31

By the fall of 1930, the United States was in a period of prolonged struggle. The collapse of the stock market in '29 triggered uncertainty. The economy collapsed, and a brief upswing was a mirage. Lives were destroyed, professions ceased to exist, and many were left to start over. For UCLA basketball, the 1930–31 season was much like the early years of the Great Depression. In the 1920s, both the US economy and the UCLA basketball program were strong. As the Roaring Twenties ended, so did the success of UCLA basketball, a growing regional power. In the first dozen years that SBUC/UCLA played basketball, the varsity team finished with a winning record eleven times and six times officially won the conference title. In 1930, the Bruins won 14 games but had an overall losing record in Pacific Coast Conference play. In 1931, the Bruins would accomplish the same feat again. They were good enough to finish with more wins than losses, but not good enough to compete for a conference crown. Things looked bleak, with the Bruins disappointing for the second year in a row, but times would only get worse. The Bruins wouldn't have an overall winning record for twelve more years, and the team was never again competitive under Coach Caddy Works. Fifteen more years elapsed until UCLA had a winning record in conference play. While many understand today that UCLA basketball has a rich tradition of winning, these years were truly dark for the program. Crosstown rivals USC would start beating UCLA repeatedly, with the UCLA coach a laughingstock in his own town. Coach Caddy Works was no longer the right man for the job, but still he remained, and still the Bruins continued to lose.

The 1931 Bruins were the last of Coach Works's teams with promise. To be certain, the squad was quite talented. Leading the Bruins was senior Carl Knowles, the elected team captain. Knowles, a product of local Fairfax High School, was not always a sure thing. In high school, he was not even a starter on the varsity team, and he rarely got any playing time even with the second string. He had more value on the practice court than during games. Still, he continually worked hard and steadily improved.

He enrolled at UCLA following his graduation from Fairfax in 1927. Much like his time with the Fairfax basketball squad, his experience on the freshmen team at UCLA was rather forgettable. He was awkward without much talent. As a sophomore on the Bruins varsity squad, Knowles showed vast improvement, and though he was not a regular contributor, for the first time he showed potential. As a junior in '29–'30, he was a valuable member of the team and the best all-around player. By '30–'31, he had progressed from below average high school player to the best player on the Bruins squad. He was not the best shooter, though his one-hand shot had become a strong weapon. He was not the best passer, though he was mostly reliable in making the correct pass. His athleticism was still a question mark, and he was still a bit awkward at times. But he was smart, and he was the man that all could trust.

Joining Knowles on the varsity were six other players. The senior class of '31 was strong. Two other senior starters played key roles for the starting five, including Dick von Hagen, who led the conference in scoring, and Frank Lubin, the most intense player on the squad. Though three seniors led the team, the most talented player was Dick Linthicum, and Dudley Tower was a reliable fifth starter. Coming off the bench for the majority of the season was Ted Lemcke, who improved greatly as the season went on, and backup center Carson Binkley.

Strategically, the team was much like previous years. It still relied heavily on outpacing the other teams and playing zone defense, but as PCC opponents became familiar with the Bruins' tactics, the tactics were less successful. Coach Works had begun to use stalling tactics sporadically the previous few years, and he would continue to do so in '31. The Bruins would play a condensed schedule compared to the year prior. Six nonconference games began the season; like they had done one year earlier, the players got off to an excellent start.

The season opened against former rival Whittier College. Once a leading contender, along with the Bruins, in the old Southern California Intercollegiate Athletic Conference, Whittier was a shell of itself. UCLA had outgrown Whittier, and easily handed the Poets a defeat, 57–23. The Bruins led wire-to-wire, and Linthicum led the team with 20 points. All Bruins fans, players, and coaches expected to come away victorious in the opening game, but they knew the schedule would eventually get tougher. The margin of victory, however, surprised even the most optimistic of Bruins. In the following game, Pomona was no match for UCLA. Coach Works mixed some normal starters with several backups, and UCLA cruised to a 28-point win. UCLA would continue to win games throughout the nonconference season, but one defeat is most memorable. The underdog Los Angeles Athletic Club trounced the Bruins, 41–24, and soon the once promising season took a turn for the worse.

Captain Carl Knowles, the most important player on the team, and Coach Works's most trusted confidant, was sick. He was unable to play more than a few minutes against the Montana Grizzlies, and his illness would be a large part of the poor close to the season. Without Knowles, UCLA squeaked by Montana, 29–28, in a closer than expected game. UCLA played much better in the second matchup, winning by over 20 points. The Bruins had a strong record, but entering the three series that always defined the PCC season, the team would need their leader at full strength.

When UCLA took on Stanford, California, and USC, they were in for a challenge every year. In '31, all had strong teams, and the South Division of the PCC was wide open to any of the four. Coach Works believed the "Red Men" from Stanford were the conference favorites. All week he drilled into his players that they needed to be their best to win. So when UCLA went north to Palo Alto, players brought with them an intensity they had not yet shown all season and a skill Stanford did not expect. In the first game, UCLA stunned Stanford with its teamwork. The Bruins passed the ball well, were in sync on defense, and shot well enough to build a lead. Though Stanford would close the gap, the Red Men never seriously threatened, and UCLA won, 32–23. The second matchup against Stanford was much like the first. UCLA built a 10-point lead, and Stanford then made a run. Though the Stanford Indians would inch closer in the second affair, UCLA held on to win again, this time by 28–26. Going for the season sweep would not be easy, however, and the third game was a back-and-forth matchup. With under a minute on the clock, UCLA led, 28–27, but the game-winning shot was hit by Stanford, and the Bruins lost by one.

The series with the California Golden Bears was

a microcosm of the season. UCLA was a good team, but far too often it came up short. In a home matchup against the Bears at Olympic Auditorium, the Bruins lost by two points, 24–22. It was the second consecutive game that the opponent scored right at the end to beat the Bruins. The Bruins would have no better luck in the next matchup, losing, 43–39, and in the final game of the three, the team again lost a close one, this time by 30–28, with Cal again scoring in the final seconds to beat the Bruins.

While the three close losses to California doomed the Bruins' hopes for a conference title, there was hope heading in to the series with USC. After battling illness for much of the season, Knowles felt much better, and he would play against the Trojans. In the first matchup, the Bruins won a dull game by 25–16. UCLA built a comfortable lead early, and neither team made another noteworthy run for the rest of the game. Unlike the first matchup, the second game between the two rivals offered much to talk about. UCLA seemingly was the better team, but the referees were whistle-happy, and UCLA was unable to keep USC from the free-throw line. Despite just one first-half field goal for the Trojans, USC led by a point at the half. In the second half, UCLA continued to foul, and USC finally started making outside shots, dooming the Bruins. In the final game, UCLA led, 19–9, at half. In the second half, USC slowly closed the game, inching closer to the Bruins. It looked to many like UCLA would lose again at the end, a theme for the '31 season. UCLA went on a run in the final few minutes, however, playing its best basketball of the entire season. After a 21–2 run, the game was essentially put away, and the Bruins cruised to a dominant win. Although the Bruins finished the season with a 9–6 record, the 4–5 conference mark clearly disappointed. With a talented senior class moving on, the season was Coach Works's last chance at a conference title. The series with the Golden Bears and inability to win close games ruined UCLA's season. The '31 squad was one of UCLA's best early teams, but those that can't win at the end can't be champions.

Northwestern University claimed national champion status for 1931.

1931–32

The 1931–32 Bruins players were an interesting bunch. The starting five was young but talented. Coach Caddy Works was still seen in a positive light, but his best days were behind him, and his darkest days lay ahead. Joining the returning players on the varsity team were two sophomores who were key contributors. Don Piper started, and though he was not a star by any means in his first year, he was a steady performer and became one of the most trusted Bruins in 1931–32. The second sophomore, Lou "Bud" Rose, also started, and though he was more inconsistent than Bruins rooters had hoped, he was immensely talented, as well. Ted Lemcke was the captain-elect, and his backcourt defense was superb. "Jimmy the Windmill" Soest started alongside Lemcke in the backcourt, but he was known more for his success in another sport. Soest was one of the top amateur boxers in the United States and hoped to one day make it big as a fighter, not a baller. Rounding out the starting five was captain Dick Linthicum, best known today as the first All-American in not only UCLA basketball history but also all of UCLA athletics. He was truly the glue that held the Bruins together. Joining Linthicum on the All-America team was a man unknown to almost all in Southern California, a man who would eventually become synonymous with UCLA basketball and American athletics in general. In 1932, Purdue guard John Wooden's name was right beside Dick Linthicum on the All-America list.

The Bruins opened the season, as always, with a stretch of nonconference games against seemingly inferior teams. The first game of the season pitted UCLA against the Hollywood Athletic Club. The Bruins had no problem dispatching its opponent, winning by 35–20. Linthicum led the way with 12 points. UCLA won its next two games by an average of 16 points, both coming against the Whittier Poets.

In the early-to-mid-twentieth century, scheduling was much different than it is today. During World War II, military teams, filled with many current college-age men and even players who had already used their collegiate eligibility, were formed. They played games that counted on the official record even though they were seemingly at an advantage. The practice happened before the war as well, though many sports historians don't recognize that. Those teams were usually part of a club rather than the military, however. UCLA's fourth game of the season came against one of these teams: the Pasadena Majors consisted of many UCLA basketball alumni, as well as several former USC players. The Bruins were no match for the older, better players and lost, 34–24.

UCLA was 3–1 in nonconference play and few were discouraged by the loss to the Pasadena Majors. The following three-game series with Utah State, however, humbled the Bruins. The team was thoroughly dismantled twice, losing by double digits in both affairs. Though they beat USU in the third game and then Los Angeles Athletic Club to close out nonconference play, its 5–3 record was disappointing.

In the early years of UCLA basketball, success was most clearly defined by the games against Stanford, Cal, and USC. They were the Pacific Coast Conference South Division competitors. The Bruins opened conference play against Stanford, and the worries that Coach Works had following the nonconference slate proved to be legitimate. The first game was mostly a back-and-forth affair. The game was tied at 22 with one minute to play, but the Indians scored the final basket and added a free throw to win, 25–22. One night later, the teams played again, and though the game was much different than the first, the result was the same. UCLA started slowly, made a major run, and then faltered at the end: Stanford 31, UCLA 26. The Bruins were 0–2 in the conference. Things changed, however, when the Indians came south to take on the Bruins at the Olympic Auditorium. With six minutes to go, the game was tied. Unlike in Palo Alto, however, the Bruins would not falter down the stretch. Bud Rose played a brilliant final five minutes, and the Bruins won, 35–31. The second game back in Los Angeles was different than the previous three games played thus far. It was a blowout. UCLA led, 19–5, at halftime, and the final outcome was never in doubt. Linthicum led all scorers with 10 points.

Although splitting four games with the Indians was not ideal, the result was also not crushing. Stanford was a strong team in '32, but the tougher test was the California Golden Bears. Any hope of winning the conference crown would soon be dashed. The two teams played four games, two in Berkeley and two in Los Angeles. Cal won all four contests, and the Bruins were eliminated from conference contention. After losing by double digits in the first matchup, the second game was a nail-biter. Cal's Ted Ohashi scored in the final seconds of regulation to send the game to overtime, and in the extra period, Cal snuck by, 26–25. In Los Angeles, much was the same. Cal won by six and then won again in overtime in the final game. Losing four in a row to Cal crushed the Bruins' season.

Though the 1932 team was not remembered for success on the hardwood, pride was still on the line when it took on the USC Trojans. The teams played three times, and the Bruins won twice. There was also a fight in the final game, and the Bruins won that too. USC's coach, Sam Barry, was, in a way, innovative. Stalling tactics were nothing new in college basketball, but Coach Barry took stalling to a new level. In '31–'32, the pace of play for the Trojans suddenly came to a crawl. Barry knew that his tactic was successful, but he was often influenced by public pressure. His plan was to hold the ball as long as possible, even minutes at a time, without even looking to score. UCLA played almost primarily zone defense, and he wanted the Bruins to overextend pressure so his team could pick apart the zone. In the first half of the first game, neither side caved. Coach Works demanded that his players stay back in their zone, and Coach Barry demanded that his men wait it out. The first half was a total bore. Fans booed, yelled, and even threw things on the court. After a while, players noticed not angry fans, but distracted ones. Many took to reading the newspaper during play, knowing they weren't missing any action. In the second half, the public pressure got to Coach Barry and he called off his "stationary offense." It was time to play. UCLA, though, was the better team. The game was close, but UCLA prevailed, winning by 19–17 on a half-court shot by Bud Rose.

The second game was different than the first, but the scoring hardly indicated so. Despite abandoning slow tactics for the majority of the game, UCLA and USC still hardly scored. With time ticking down, the score was 24–22, USC. The magic of one night prior was still with the Bruins, however. Rose again proved he was clutch and tied the game at 24, and then captain Dick Linthicum won it with a last-second shot. The season had been a disappointment, but beating the Trojans in the final series of the season was sweet. With one final game to play, the Bruins hoped to go out with a third victory over USC. It wasn't to be, however, as USC won the final game, 35–31. The game is most notable not for the final score but for the big fight. After a hard foul, in which James Soest was sandwiched between two Trojans defenders, fists flew. Little did USC know that Soest was an elite amateur boxer. He didn't need any help, and he resolved the situation in the way he knew best. He knocked two Trojans to the floor with his thundering right hand. Others tried to get in on the action, but it was soon broken up. The Bruins had fight in them the entire season, but for Coach Works, a man who had far exceeded expectations in his early years, it was another disappointing season. The Bruins finished the year with a 9–10 overall record and were 4–7 in conference play. For Dick Linthicum, the season was unquestionably a success. Though his name has long been lost to history for many UCLA fans, he should always be remembered as the first All-American for the Bruins. The man who joined him on that list will never be forgotten. John Wooden was a senior in '32. His college playing career was over. It was time to start the next phase of his life.

Purdue University claimed national champion status for 1932.

1932–33

While athletic greatness was seen throughout Los Angeles during the Summer Olympic Games in 1932, the UCLA basketball team was far from great. Coach Caddy Works was still supported by the vast majority of the UCLA faithful, but doubters believed that coaching the Bruins basketball team on a part-time basis was becoming too difficult. The UCLA yearbook of '31 called Coach Works a "genius." The yearbook of '32 called him "brilliant." Opposing teams were not intimidated, however. The Bruins had become a pushover in recent years, and the '32–'33 season was another in the long streak of losing seasons.

Dick Linthicum, the All-American of one year prior, was gone; replacing him was a monumental task. He was the best player yet in UCLA history. Ted Lemcke was in his third season on the varsity squad and was elected captain by the coaching staff, but his play was slowed for much of the season by a bum ankle. Fellow captain Don Piper, chosen by the players, was the best all-around scorer on the team, and one of the best in the conference. He finished the season second in the Pacific Coast Conference South Division in scoring and earned the nickname "Dynamite Don." Carson Binkley, Cordner Gibson, Bill Maxwell, George Brotemarkle, Shelby Johns, and a plethora of players off the bench received significant playing time. Though many played well at moments, none were consistent performers.

The Caddy Works brand of basketball had usually been fast. He wanted his team to run the floor, fast-break at every opportunity, and beat the other team with conditioning. Over the previous several years, however, Coach Works began to doubt his own ability, and the ability of his team to play with pace. He mixed in periods of stalling, with usually poor results. In the '32–'33 season, he was committed to playing his way. He wanted no longer to shorten the game by holding the ball. The squad would play fast, and if it didn't work, Coach Works was determined to abandon it all together. The season would be a test. If 1933 didn't produce a winner with speed, 1934 would bring an entirely new style.

UCLA's season was a tale of two parts. The season began in incredible fashion. During nonconference play, the Bruins put on a show, playing with speed and grace. The team shot the ball especially well. In ten nonconference games, the Bruins won nine, including wins over Nevada, Utah, and Santa Clara. Then came conference play. The team that dominated early in the season was steamrolled the rest of the way. Many of UCLA's losses were close affairs, and some on campus believed the Bruins were jinxed. UCLA started the conference season against California in Berkeley. In the first game, the Bruins laid an egg. At halftime, the Bears led comfortably,

UCLA vs. Santa Clara, 1933 (Southern Branch Collection).

and though UCLA played a strong second half, the Bears won, 40–37. The two teams played again one night later, and the game unfolded much the same way. Hal Eifert, Cal's top scorer, finished with 19 points. Ted Lemcke was the high man for the Bruins, but the home team again came away victorious. The final score was 33–29 in favor of the Bears.

Following the two losses to Cal, UCLA returned to Los Angeles to take on USC. The games against the Trojans in '33 did not have the drama of the big fight or the boredom of stalling in '32. In the first matchup in '33, USC coach Sam Barry did not need to stall. His team got out of the gate fast and never looked back. USC cruised to a 22-point victory.

The Bruins were 0–3 in conference play after the game against the Trojans, and in the blink of an eye, their 0–3 mark turned to 0–5. They traveled north to Palo Alto for the second road trip of the conference season and came home with two more losses. Much like early in the conference season, the Bruins returned to Los Angeles following their two losses up north with hopes of beating their crosstown rival. Just like earlier, however, the Trojans weren't keen to let the Bruins have their way. In the second matchup between the two, USC won again, this time 39–33.

UCLA's strong season had quickly turned into a porous one during conference play. The Bruins and their fans once believed the team had a chance to win the PCC, but after starting 0–6 in conference play, the goal shifted to simply winning a game. With consecutive games against Cal at Olympic Coliseum in Los Angeles, the Bruins seemed to have a chance to come out on top. In the first game, however, UCLA fell once again. With Piper being the only effective offensive player for the Bruins, UCLA was easily dismantled. The second game, however, was competitive the entire way. At halftime, the score was tied at 18. UCLA held a small lead for much of the second half. With under two minutes to play, Cal finally overtook the Bruins and held on to win, 37–36. The Bruins were still winless in PCC play. The team was finally able to win a game at the end of the conference season over Stanford but lost two more to finish with a 1–10 conference record after starting the season 9–1 in nonconference play. For the first time, UCLA had two consecutive losing seasons.

No school claimed national champion status for 1933.

1933–34

The 1933–34 UCLA basketball season turned out to be the worst thus far in school history. The team was loaded with inexperienced sophomores who had yet to see varsity action. Many of the upperclassmen had spent the previous years playing in limited roles, and now they were tasked with carrying the load for the Bruins. One of the few experienced players on the team was captain Don Piper, who was the only consistent performer for the Bruins and one of the top scorers in all of Pacific Coast Conference play.

Like so many seasons before this one the nonconference slate for the Bruins was not particularly difficult. Though the season turned out to be subpar for the Bruins, it was impossible to tell by judging the early season games. UCLA tipped off its season against Long Beach Junior College and easily won, 50–29. The Bruins had a balanced attack and shot the ball well. UCLA continued its hot start by beating Whittier by 10, La Verne by 24, and Los Angeles Junior College by 19. Along with Piper, Clem Melancon and Don Ashen were the two performers who caught the attention of Bruins rooters early in the season.

After starting the season undefeated in their first four contests, the Bruins went north. On back-to-back nights, the Bruins took on Chico State and came away with two wins. The team then beat St. Mary's by double digits and beat Athens Club Aggregation, 33–26. The Bruins were 8–0 with three nonconference games to play before it was time for the PCC. The first loss of the season came at the hands of the Olympic Club Cagers, who beat the Bruins, 35–30. UCLA then lost twice more to Santa Clara, stumbling into conference play with a three-game losing streak.

The conference season would, as always, consist of matchups with three South Division rivals. The Bruins didn't know what to expect. On paper, Stanford, Cal, and USC were all expected to be better than the Bruins, but college athletics are always hard to predict. The Bruins had new players that their conference mates had yet to see, and Coach Works instilled a new brand of basketball. Though the Bruins would still fast-break during nonconference games against inferior opponents, the game plan in conference games emphasized slowing the pace. Coach Works was determined to run a stalling offense, just as Coach Sam Barry had so successfully implemented at USC. The results were disastrous.

In the four games against Stanford, three were fairly close, but the Indians proved to be superior to the Bruins in totality. The first game, the only non-competitive game of the three, finished with a score of 45–26, with the Bruins on the losing side. UCLA fans at Olympic Auditorium were predictably upset, but one night later, they saw a reversal. The Bruins trailed for much of the night, but in the final minutes, Bill Athey, Ralph McFadden, and Shelby Johns each hit clutch shots, and the home team stole a victory: UCLA 32, Stanford 31. When the series resumed in Palo Alto, the Bruins had no such fortune. Stanford won both games.

The series against the California Golden Bears was much like the series against Stanford. The Bears won three of the four games and were clearly the better of the two teams. In Berkeley, neither game was particularly close. Despite the slow play, UCLA's defense struggled for much of the year. Against Cal, the Bruins gave up an average of 40 points per game in the first two contests. When the Bears made their way to Los Angeles to take on UCLA in back-to-back nights at Olympic, the games were a bit different. Though UCLA lost again in the first game, they played better offensively and kept the game close. In the final game against Cal, the Bruins finally broke through. Piper hit a late shot to send the game into overtime, and McFadden hit two free throws in the extra period to secure the victory.

UCLA basketball uniform, 1934 (Southern Branch Collection).

USC was the class of the South Division of the PCC, and beating the Trojans seemed much harder than beating Stanford or California. Though Coach Works tried his best to motivate his men, USC was much too talented, and UCLA was much too weak. The Trojans were bigger, had more offensive skill, and were coached better. The four games were each blowouts. USC won the first game, 39–26. They followed that up with a 39–22 win. The third game was even worse for the Bruins: USC won 46–21. In the final clash, the Bruins put up a bit more of a fight but still succumbed to the Trojans by 32–23. Despite an 8–0 start, the season was miserable for the Bruins.

The University of Wyoming claimed national champion status for 1934.

1934–35

By the time the 1934–35 season tipped off, Coach Pierce "Caddy" Works was in his fourteenth year as the UCLA basketball head coach. Since leaving the Southern California Intercollegiate Athletic Conference following the 1927 season, UCLA had failed to capture a single Pacific Coast Conference title. Despite accumulating winning records in three of the first four seasons in the PCC, the previous three seasons all resulted in losing records, even with an increase in nonconference games against subpar opponents.

In 1935, UCLA improved, but only slightly. The team still played slowly, and scores were often very low. But the Bruins were a good offensive team, though they failed to show it in the early games of the season. The team was loaded with good scorers but didn't have enough talent to win consistently in a strong conference. The squad struggled on defense, and despite shortening games by stalling, many times UCLA was unable to maintain defensive effort and focus for the entirety of the game. One player who was able to lead by example was captain Cordner Gibson. Along with Gibson, Bill Maxwell and John Wells, both seniors, started the majority of the games. Joining the senior trio were John Ball and Don Ashen, who each earned All-PCC recognition. Several others contributed as well, as Coach Works continually looked for the right combination of players.

In the first game of the season, the Bruins traveled to Whittier to take on the old foe, the Whittier Poets. The Bruins played well, though the Poets were a notch below the level of the Bruins. UCLA was expected to win comfortably, and it did, 47–30. The 1–0 Bruins record soon became 2–0 after UCLA doubled up Los Angeles Junior College, 30–15, in what many saw as an unimpressive performance. In the third game of the season, UCLA suffered one of its most embarrassing losses thus far in school history, to a private club team put together by Universal Pictures. The Universal Pictures team only had five players, but they were good enough to drop the Bruins from the ranks of the unbeaten. More embarrassing than the loss, however, was the dismal offensive showing. The final score was just 20–11. UCLA was a good offensive team in '35, but when players struggled to shoot the ball well, there was no alternative to their slow play. They continued to play slowly even when all in attendance knew it was time to pick up the pace.

Next, the Bruins set out on its annual barnstorming tour in Northern California. The results were mixed. The team beat Fresno State and Chico State in close games. It also lost close games to St. Mary's and Santa Clara and then finished the five-game trip with a 10-point win over San Jose State before returning to Los Angeles. After a few practices back at Olympic Stadium, the Bruins went south to take on San Diego State. UCLA won both affairs in the final nonconference tune-up games.

The conference schedule was, like always, a California affair. The South Division of the PCC consisted of UCLA, USC, Stanford, and California. Though the Northern California schools were once UCLA's greatest competition, Sam Barry had built a winner at USC, and that team was the prohibitive favorite going into every game. As was expected, the games against Stanford and California were very competitive. The games against the Trojans were much tougher.

In the first conference game of the year, sophomore center John Ball was the star for the Bruins. He racked up 19 points and was also key in the Bruins' zone defense that held Cal to just 25 points. The final score was 36–25, and the Bruins began conference play with a much-needed confidence boost. In the second game in Los Angeles against the Golden Bears, the script was flipped. Cal easily won, racking up a double-digit victory, 38–26. Cal and UCLA were evenly matched, and it showed in Berkeley as much as it did in Los Angeles. In the return trip, the Bruins won the first game due to the clutch shooting of Bill Reitz, and the Bears won the second game. The two teams split their four contests on the year.

UCLA vs. Cal, 1935 (Southern Branch Collection).

The four games against Stanford were much like the games against Cal. UCLA won the first game at home by the score of 34–27. Despite an excruciatingly slow first half, in which the score was just 10–9, the second half was action-packed, and the Bruins pulled away for the victory. UCLA then won again the next night and was 2–0 against the Indians. Several weeks later, the Bruins went north to Palo Alto and looked like a different team. Stanford won both games. Ultimately, the two teams tied for third place in the South Division of the PCC.

While UCLA, Stanford, and Cal were all competitive, USC was the dominant team of the year. The Bruins played its best game of the series in the first matchup. UCLA led for much of the first half but ultimately fell, 39–34, as USC played a much better second half. In the following two games, USC played focused basketball the entire way, and its superior talent and coaching was more evident than ever. USC won the second matchup, 52–22, and the third, 55–22. The losses were embarrassing, and though UCLA played better in the fourth and final game, losing, 43–33, it showed itself a second-rate team in Los Angeles. The season was another disastrous one, with a final record of 11–12. Though the 11 wins for UCLA was the most since 1930, the Bruins finished with just a 4–8 conference record. All luster from UCLA's early basketball success was gone. The Bruins' basketball program was a train wreck.

Louisiana State University claimed national champion status for 1935.

1935–36

The 1935–36 UCLA basketball team consisted of a fine mix of seniors, juniors, and sophomores. There were five seniors, including both backcourt starters, Don Ashen and Ralph McFadden. There were five juniors, as well, with John Ball starting at center and Orv Appleby starting at forward. Chet Freeze showed the most potential early among the six sophomores on the roster, starting the majority of games at the other forward spot. Sophomore George Robinson was valuable when he was inserted into the starting lineup midway through the year at the news that Don Ashen had eligibility issues. Freeze shifted from the backcourt to the frontcourt to make way for Robinson at the other forward position. Though UCLA had a solid starting five, one man was the clear star of the team. John Ball was UCLA's best player and a unanimous choice for Pacific Coast Conference honors.

UCLA began its season as they had so many seasons in recent memory, with a handful of home games before going on a Northern California barnstorming tour. As had been the case in recent years, UCLA won the majority of its preseason games. The first game of the year pitted the Bruins against the Baxter Club of Glendale, a private club team consisting of mostly former players from the Rocky Mountain region. The Bruins trailed for much of the game but eventually pulled ahead to win, 36–28. The following weekend, UCLA took on a pair of local junior colleges, beating Los Angeles Junior College and then crushing Glendale Junior College. The Bruins were 3–0 with one game to go before the early-season road trip. In the fourth game of the season, UCLA took on the Universal Studios club they had lost to one year prior. Universal Studios had improved their roster and were led by three former Bruins—Frank Lubin, Carl Shy, and Carl Knowles. Despite being considerable underdogs, UCLA looked the better team much of the day. When the game ended, the Bruins were atop on the scoreboard. UCLA was 4–0.

UCLA's Northern California road trip consisted of four games, and the Bruins were expected to sweep the competition and remain undefeated. In the first game, the Bruins took on College of the Pacific and were stunned, losing, 31–28. Two nights later, UCLA captured a win against San Jose State, though with an underwhelming performance. With the exception of John Ball and Alex Widlicska, who was the first man off the bench for Coach Works, the Bruins struggled mightily to score. The backcourt was anemic offensively to start the season. After two subpar performances, UCLA looked strong against Santa Clara, playing its best game of the year thus far. Orv Appleby and Chet Freeze played much better, and Ball continued to lead the way for the Bruins. The final game of the trip was played against Utah State, which traveled to Northern California to meet the Bruins at a neutral site. UCLA was unable to come away with a victory this time, and its trip ended with a 2–2 record. After returning to Los Angeles, the Bruins practiced for a full week before resuming the nonconference slate. UCLA took on the Joe E. Brown All-Stars, a club team that handily defeated the defending PCC champion USC Trojans already. UCLA played its A game, however, and pulled off the shocking upset, 36–26. Keeping with the theme of inconsistent play to start the season, UCLA lost the final nonconference game one week later to Utah State and finished the early-season slate with an 8–3 record.

While the aggregate result of the nonconference slate was disappointing (some observers expected the school to finish the nonconference portion undefeated), it actually represented the high point of the season. The Bruins at least accomplished the most basic of goal in sports: it won at a fairly high clip. Conference play was much more difficult. The Bruins began on the road with two games against conference favorite Stanford. Hank Luisetti was Stanford's star player, but in the games between the two teams, John Ball won the statistical battle over Luisetti. Ball dominated the two games up north, finishing with 15 points and then 21 points the next night, leading all scorers in both games. UCLA lost the first game, but upset the Indians, 44–37, in the second. It was the only game Stanford lost all season on their home court, as it indeed won the PCC as most predicted. In the return trip to Los Angeles, some things stayed the same and some changed. Ball was again the best player on either team. He finished the two games with 21 and 26 points. He outscored Luisetti in all four games. But Stanford was the better team, winning both games at Olympic Stadium.

The four games played against the California Golden Bears were all extremely close games. The 1936 UCLA yearbook would say of the matchups, "This year's basketball series with the University of California at Berkeley was probably the closest and most exciting series of games ever played in the history of the two schools." The games were no doubt exciting, but frustrating, like much of the last half decade for the Bruins. The Bruins lost by two, and then four, and then two again. The Bruins were at a major disadvantage, however. Orv Appleby didn't play because of a minor operation. John Ball, too, was out for much of the series. After suffering a sprained ankle, he was limited to only a few ineffective minutes. Despite the personnel issues, UCLA won the third game, 32–28.

Bruins fans, players, and coaches would like to forget the games against USC. The Trojans came away victorious in each of the four. Two of the games were close, but two were blowouts. UCLA finished the conference season with a 2–10 record and had an overall record of 10–13, its fifth straight losing season. The Bruins hadn't beaten USC since 1932. Things would get worse.

University of Notre Dame claimed national champion status for 1936.

1936–37

In 1936, UCLA football was led by veteran head coach William Spaulding and coming off the two best seasons in school history. The Westwood campus was buzzing with sports fever, but the UCLA basketball team was just an afterthought. They had played well in previous years in late fall and early winter, only to fall apart when conference season came around in the New Year. Unfortunately, the theme continued in the new season, and UCLA was again poor.

The Bruins basketball squad of '36–'37 faced a new challenge. Though it would again go on an early-season barnstorming tour, they faced a much tougher schedule. Wins would be hard to come by, and the usual pushover games that appeared on the schedule in previous years were now gone. The Bruins replaced the second-tier programs with West Coast powerhouses and mixed in nonconference games with Midwest teams, as well. The Bruins started the season with two consecutive wins against junior college programs. But in early-season play, UCLA finished with just four wins, to go along with five losses. UCLA lost to Oregon, Washington State, Idaho, Washington, and Ohio State. Its only semi-impressive early-season performance came against Oregon State, in which the Bruins came away on top.

The Bruins opened the 1937 Pacific Coast Conference season against the USC Trojans. UCLA outplayed USC for much of the game and held a three-point halftime lead, but the Trojans stormed back in the final 10 minutes and defeated UCLA, 41–31. Orv Appleby, the captain of the 1937 squad, was the high scorer for UCLA with 13 points. The game story was a pattern for the Bruins against the Trojans. In the second matchup two weeks later, the Bruins again led at halftime and fell. The third game was much the same. John Ball of UCLA and

1936 UCLA team photo (Southern Branch Collection).

Eddie Oram of USC each had 16 points, but Ball was without help for much of the game. Oram, on the other hand, had his USC teammate Gail Goodrich (father of the more famous UCLA and NBA player by the same name) by his side. Goodrich added 13 points, and the Trojans won. After three heartbreaking losses to USC, the fourth matchup late in the season was not competitive. The Trojans cruised to another season sweep over the Bruins. Coach Caddy Works could not crack the Trojan code.

Things weren't any better for the Bruins against the Stanford Indians. In four games, the Bruins finished 0–4. One year prior, John Ball vs. Hank Luisetti went the way of Ball, at least in individual success. The script was flipped in '37 and Luisetti outscored Ball in three of the four games. In the one game in which Ball topped Luisetti, the Bruins kept the game close before losing, 42–40. In the other three games, the Indians easily topped the Bruins.

Although games against USC and Stanford clearly showed that the Bruins were a long way from the top of their division, the games against Cal were more competitive. In the second week of conference play, Coach Works and the Bruins traveled to Berkeley. As was the trend throughout the season, the Bruins led at halftime, but fell apart in the second half and lost. The second matchup was different. There were no long runs for either team, and the game was close throughout. When the final seconds ticked off the clock in the second half, the teams were tied. The game went to overtime; in the extra session, Bill Robinson scored three of his game-high 13 points, and the Bruins won, 46–44. Along with Robinson and Ball, Crossan Hays and Paul Slaughter played extraordinarily well. The two teams would not meet again until late in the season in Los Angeles. The Bruins beat the Bears once again in the first game of the two-game series. Ball scored 16 points and Jack Cooper added 10. The next night, the shots were no longer dropping, and UCLA lost, 43–31. When the season came to a close, the games against Cal were the only ones the players, coaches, and fans thought

Bill Reitz, 1937 (Southern Branch Collection).

Kenny Lueke drives to the basket against Cal, 1937 (Southern Branch Collection).

were even worth remembering. The season had been a disaster, but it is hard to say whether it was a disappointment. The Bruins had become accustomed to losing, and no change appeared in sight.

Stanford University claimed national champion status for 1937.

1937–38

After the 6–14 season of 1936–37, few felt the lack of experience on the '37–'38 team was something to worry about. Sure, the Bruins were young, but the experienced team of one year prior finished with the worst record in school history. The situation would only get worse. The 1937–38 UCLA Bruins basketball team is the worst in school history to this day. The six leading scorers of the year prior were gone, and their replacements were incapable of winning games at a high or even average clip. Coach Works was in his seventeenth season. Long gone were the days of fast-paced hoops and top conference finishes. Winning any game was a struggle, as was drawing enough interest from fans who clamored for a more exciting brand. The Bruins played at a snail's pace, and it didn't work.

The first game of the season was slated for December 1 against a poor Los Angeles Junior College team. Neither team played particularly well, but the Bruins did just enough in the second half to secure victory. The University of La Verne outplayed the Bruins for much of the second matchup, but the Bruins finished with the top hand on the scoreboard. So too did Chico State outplay the Bruins. For the vast majority of the game, the Bruins trailed, but in the final few minutes Bob Calkins found his shot, and the Bruins escaped with a win. UCLA was 3–0, but the season would not be defined by the pre–New Year's Day games.

UCLA's annual barnstorming tour in the Northwest was a disaster. Six games were played on six consecutive days, and the Bruins finished with six losses. Oregon State won by 14. Oregon won by 21. Washington State won by 23 and then again by nine. UCLA failed to even keep any of the games close, as they lost the last two to Idaho by 14 and then nine. The Bruins, who went north with a 3–0 record, returned with a 3–6 record and shattered confidence.

There were few high points during the '38 season, but the game against the Loyola Marymount University Lions was one of them. The prior year, the Lions wanted to play UCLA because the team believed it could stack up well against a program in a top conference and UCLA was the best matchup. UCLA refused to play, saying its schedule was full. This year, the Lions got the matchup. The game went back and forth, but in the end the Bruins were the top team. The final score was 29–26, and the six-game losing streak was over. When one losing streak ended, however, another soon began. Purdue and Indiana traveled to Los Angeles to take on UCLA and USC. The first game for the Bruins was against the Hoosiers, and UCLA played respectably, considering they were a major underdog. The final score was 42–33. The next night UCLA took on Purdue, and the result was much different, but not in a way Coach Works had hoped. The game was an embarrassment, the worst loss in UCLA's young history, 69–33 in Purdue's favor. Fans in attendance and local reporters admitted that Purdue toyed with the Bruins. It could have been worse.

Following the disastrous nonconference season, UCLA began conference play against the USC Trojans, who had won 20 consecutive games over the Bruins in the previous five seasons. The game was no match, as proved to be the case for most conference games. USC easily beat UCLA. The Bruins then took on California at home, and the results were no better, at least in terms of wins and losses. In both games, the Bears finished with more points than the Bruins, though the games were fairly competitive. UCLA was unable to break the losing streak in the next game, either, and USC once again beat UCLA.

Sitting at 0–4 in the conference, the next task seemed monumental. The Bruins took on Stanford University, the defending national champions and one of the best teams in the nation, led by Hank Luisetti, one of the best players in college basketball history. In the four games played during the conference season, UCLA won none. Expectations had so been lowered that the UCLA Yearbook believed the trip was a success simply because UCLA kept Luisetti from scoring a record amount of points in a single game in any of the four meetings. UCLA was slaughtered in each, however, and Stanford's second string, nicknamed the "Laughing Boys," played huge chunks of time in each of the games.

1939 UCLA team photo (Southern Branch Collection).

UCLA went to Berkeley and the losing streak continued. In two games, in which both teams played incredibly slowly, the Bruins were on the losing side. The Bruins sat at 0–10 in conference play with two games left. In the first game of the final weekend against USC, Will Munkers and Paul Slaughter each played well, but it was not enough to topple Hal Dornsife and the Trojans. Following the final game, a season celebration was scheduled at Coach Works's home, and the Bruins planned to go out with one final win. It wasn't even close. USC crushed UCLA again. The Bruins ended their season on a 14-game losing streak, and the losing streak against the Trojans stretched to 24 games.

Temple University claimed national champion status for 1938.

1938–39

Coach Caddy Works in the 1938–39 season once again decided to change his offense. In his earliest days at UCLA, his teams played fast, but over time they increasingly employed the stalling tactic. In recent years before this season, the complete offensive strategy was to play slow, extremely picky offense. In what would be Coach Works's last season at UCLA, he decided to revert back to what worked in his early days. Assistant Coach Dick Linthicum, former All-American under Works, was in charge of installing and teaching the new fast-paced offense. In part because of the new strategy, and in part because the team was more talented than the previous year and the schedule was easier, the Bruins appeared to be an improved team.

The Bruins began the season in Northern California, playing three games in Berkeley—one each against Ohio State, Nebraska, and Cal. Though Cal was in the Pacific Coast Conference, the game would not count as a conference affair. Bob "Ace" Calkins proved during the early games that he was the best offensive weapon on the team, and he was able to continue his fine play for the entirety of the season. The team had a number of other key contributors, but none played with the consistency of Calkins. The Bruins began the season with a 1–1 record after losing to a strong Ohio State team and then beating Nebraska the next night. In the third game up north, Cal and UCLA played a close game, but the Bears finished on top. The Bruins played twelve more nonconference games before the start of the conference season, their largest nonconference slate to date. UCLA finished with seven wins before starting PCC competition.

Though UCLA was 7–8 going in to conference play, there was a sense that UCLA was an improving team. Its style was more attractive to fans, and they had already nearly doubled the win total from the previous year. Early conference play, however, showed UCLA clearly was still not what any fans had hoped. For the second season in a row, UCLA went winless in PCC play. The Bruins and the Stanford Indians played a competitive four games, but the men from Palo Alto came out on top in each matchup. The games against Cal and USC were much more decisive. Cal was led by Bill Ogilvie, a 6'6", 222-pound big man, and the Bruins were powerless to stop him. The final two games were played at the San Francisco Fair, and everyone in attendance saw a show. Cal won by an average of 21 points. Against USC, the Bruins again stood no chance. USC forward Ralph Vaughn was too much to handle. In one game, he scored 36 points, breaking the PCC single-game scoring record. UCLA finished with a 0–12 conference record.

After the season, Coach Works resigned as the UCLA head basketball coach to devote more time to his law practice. The writing was on the wall. He wasn't getting the job done, and though he still had support from the UCLA athletic administration, confidence was quickly dissipating. Though the resignation was notable in Westwood, something more notable occurred in college basketball: in 1939, a new way to determine the national champion was introduced.

In 1939, a postseason basketball tournament was organized by the NCAA for the first time. Though the NIT (National Invitation Tournament) was still seen as the decider of the national champion, time has since added relevance to the first NCAA Tournament, and most now see the winner of the 1939 NCAA Tournament as the true national champion. In the first ever tournament, only eight teams were invited. It was a single-elimination tournament and the winners of the first round all made it to the semifinals, which was then dubbed the "Final Four." The eight teams to compete in the first ever NCAA Tournament were Oregon, Texas, Oklahoma, Utah State, Villanova, Brown, Wake Forest, and Ohio State, with Oregon, Oklahoma, Villanova, and Ohio State advancing to the Final Four. On March 27, 1939, the first national championship game was played in Philadelphia between Oregon and Ohio State.

For UCLA's best player, Robert "Ace" Calkins, 1939 would be his last season at UCLA because he graduated. Soon he would was in a place he never would have expected to be. When the United States was attacked in 1941 and entered World War II, Calkins quickly joined the fighting force. He served in the European theater, but his story in the military is one of tragedy. On May 16, 1943, Calkins, of the 341st Bomb Squadron, died as a POW in a military hospital in Lucca, Italy.

The University of Oregon won the NCAA basketball national championship in 1939.

CHAPTER 3
Wilbur Johns (1939–1948)

Wilbur Johns's job was not easy. He inherited an abysmal program. But the UCLA alumnus and former basketball player understood winning. In 1922, Johns starred on the UCLA freshman team. From 1923 to 1925, he was one of the better players on the varsity team. As a senior, he was team captain. In his three seasons on the varsity, his teams accumulated a 31–12 overall record and twice won the Southern California Intercollegiate Athletic Conference.

Though inheriting a poor program fifteen years after his last season as a player was not what Johns hoped to do, he helped turn around the team. Before his arrival, UCLA finished with a losing record in eight straight seasons and it was still trending down, finishing with the worst three seasons in school history just prior to his arrival. In Johns's first three seasons, he asserted his authority as the head coach with mixed results. The team showed some signs of improvement, and Johns was respected by all, as he was fully committed to turning around the program. But the Bruins still lost more than they won. In 1943, however, UCLA finally turned the corner and finished with a winning season for the first time in twelve years. For the majority of his tenure, UCLA was around a .500 program, but in 1945, the Bruins won the team's first Pacific Coast Conference championship, and two years later, the team was even better.

UCLA Head Coach Wilbur Johns, 1941 (Southern Branch Collection).

Coach Johns coached the UCLA basketball program for nine years and was an athletic administrator for over a decade before taking the job. But his time as the UCLA athletic director is most memorable. In 1947, Wilbur Johns was hired as the AD at UCLA. He finished his coaching career with one final season and then searched nationally for his own replacement. The UCLA head coach position was not considered an elite job, but he was able to proudly say the program was in a better place than when he inherited it. The man Johns ultimately chose turned out to be the best coach in organized sports history. Wilbur Johns hired John Wooden, and the results were astonishing. While his hire of Wooden would eventually grab the headlines, he did so much more. He appealed to Coach Wooden's sense of duty and honor to convince Wooden to stay when the early years were the toughest. Johns was a key figure in the construction of Pauley Pavilion, and he helped UCLA build itself into a college athletic powerhouse. He pulled Red Sanders from the South to come west and coach the Bruins football team, and he was the AD when UCLA brought home its lone football national championship. Wilbur Johns retired as the UCLA athletic director on July 1, 1963, and less than one year later, the Bruins' basketball program won its first national championship. Upon his retirement, Johns said, "Over the past thirty-eight years, I have seen the athletic program at UCLA grow to full maturity, and it has been my privilege to have been a part of this."

Johns stayed active in athletics for the rest of his life. He advised members of the Pacific Coast Conference on a number of issues and was a voice within the administration of the NCAA offices, as well. He served on the NCAA Bowl and Executive Committees, as well as the NCAA Olympic Committee. With the split of the Pacific Coast Conference, Johns was integral in the formation of the Athletic Association of Western Universities. Johns was named the UCLA Alumnus of the Year in 1955, but his greatest honor, the one that would have made him the most proud, happened after his death. Johns died of cancer in 1967, and eighteen years later, the man who dedicated his life to UCLA athletics was honored for his work. He is a member of the second UCLA Athletics Hall of Fame class, joining Red Sanders and John Wooden, who were inducted the year prior.

1939–40

In 1939, the UCLA football team was brilliant. Led by the masterful Kenny Washington and coached by first-year man Edwin Horrell, the Bruins finished with six wins, zero losses, and four ties. (The four ties is still the NCAA record for most ties in a season.) Joining Washington in the backfield was another man who would make history one day. In 1938, Jackie Robinson joined the UCLA football team. He played three years of football for the Bruins, one year of track and field, and one year of baseball. He also played two years of basketball for the Bruins, leading the South Division of the Pacific Coast Conference in scoring each season. Although Robinson would go on to fame playing baseball, he did little to help the Bruins win on the diamond, struggling for the entirety of his one season. He starred in his three other sports. He was one of the best punt returners and big-play offensive weapons in college football, won the NCAA broad jump championship in track and field, and was the best player on the Bruins' basketball team in each of his two years in Westwood. Washington and Robinson would each go on to be civil rights icons, with Washington integrating the National Football League in 1946, and Robinson integrating Major League Baseball in 1947. When UCLA's football season ended and Robinson joined his basketball teammates on the hardwood, Coach Wilbur Johns hoped some of the magic of the fall football season would rub off on the Bruins ballers.

The Bruins basketball team improved in Coach Johns's first year, but only slightly. Coach Johns was committed to changing the Bruins' style of play, but it would take time for him to fully implement his style and find the right mix of players. Johns wanted his team to run. He believed it necessary to have multiple players who could handle the ball and move up court at the same time, and he wanted everyone to be in premiere shape to fast-break the entire game. Coach Johns experimented with different lineups throughout the season in search of the perfect combination. Along with a new coach and a new strategy,

Jackie Robinson, 1940 (Southern Branch Collection).

the Bruins had a new style in 1939–40—flashy blue and silver uniforms. Players hoped to play as well as they looked.

The Bruins' early-season nonconference slate was a mixed bag. UCLA lost the first game of the season to a strong San Diego State team on the road, but the next day, they beat the same foe. UCLA split a doubleheader with San Jose State but beat the California Aggies and St. Mary's Gaels. The Bruins also played a handful of games against private club teams, including a win over Bank of America, 39–38, and losses to North American Aviation and Fox Studios.

When it came time for conference play, the Bruins had a record of five wins and eight losses. As usual the Bruins played 12 conference games, four each against Cal, Stanford, and USC. Conference play was still a struggle under Coach Johns, though the team appeared markedly better than the previous few years. The Bruins would have the most success against the California Golden Bears. Though the team lost the first game in Berkeley, 39–36, it came back the next night to win its first conference game in two-and-a-half years. In the return trip to Los Angeles later in the year, the script was nearly identical. The Bruins lost the first game but won the second. Robinson scored the game-winning basket with just seconds remaining on the clock.

Against Stanford, things didn't go quite as well, but the Bruins broke the long losing streak against the men from Palo Alto. The Bruins went 1–3 in the four contests, but there were several bright spots. Robinson was the best player on either team, and in the first matchup he scored 23 points, the most by any player in the PCC in 1940. In the final game between the two, played back home at Westwood Gym, UCLA won in overtime and ended the four-year losing streak to the Indians. The losing streak would not end against USC, however. The Bruins hadn't beaten the Trojans in eight years, and the streak would continue into year nine. The Bruins finished the season with an overall 8–17 record in Coach Johns's first year.

Indiana University won the NCAA basketball national championship in 1940.

1940–41

The Bruins played a full 26-game schedule in 1940–41. After showing slight improvement one year prior, Bruins rooters hoped that Coach Wilbur Johns could continue the momentum in season two. Jackie Robinson, the leading scorer in the PCC in 1940, returned and was again one of the top players on the West Coast, again leading the PCC in scoring. Along with Robinson, Ernie Handelsman and Lloyd Anderson were the primary weapons in UCLA's fast-break offense. The Bruins began the season at home with two matchups against San Diego State and one against the 20th Century Fox club team. Fans saw these early games as an indicator of how the rest of the season would go. The Bruins once again let down their most ardent supporters. The team lost all three, including two heartbreakers to SDSU.

The 1941 Bruins were not the best team in UCLA history, nor were they the best for Coach Johns, nor the best in the pre-Wooden days, but the team held one distinction. It was the most widely traveled. After starting the season 0–3 at home, the team went to Michigan for a Midwest barnstorming tour, the first in UCLA history. Most in the UCLA athletic administration felt the UCLA team was better for taking

1941 UCLA team photo (Southern Branch Collection).

the trip, but the results suggested otherwise. UCLA lost all four games, to DePaul, Western State, Bradley Tech, and Illinois Normal. When the Bruins returned home, the team was 0–7, and the losing continued. Indiana crushed UCLA before the Bruins finally eked by Loyola for a one-point victory, the first of the season. UCLA won two of the next three before conference play and entered the PCC season with just a 3–9 record.

Right out of the gate, UCLA had a chance to do something they had failed to do over the previous nine seasons—beat USC. Yes, it would be an immense challenge, as USC was a far superior program, but Coach Johns dreamed of nothing more than topping the men from Troy to start the season. The game turned out to be a wake-up call. Some still believed that UCLA was on the right track, and that its lack of success in nonconference play was because players sleepwalked through the games they deemed unimportant. When USC thrashed UCLA, 56–35, even the most optimistic UCLA supporters knew the reality that faced them. UCLA was not very good and had not been good for a very long time.

The games against Cal in 1941 are the ones most memorable now. When UCLA went to Berkeley following the loss to USC to start conference play, they went with shattered confidence, and the result of the first game did nothing to help the Bruins' psyche. Players were heckled by the fans in Berkeley like never before, and they played an undisciplined, angry brand of basketball. The crowd got to the Bruins and helped its team win. The first game ended with the hometown Golden Bears starters on the bench, relishing the easy victory: Cal 42, UCLA 32. One night later, things changed. The Bruins played the best game of the season thus far as a balanced team, with Robinson, Handelsman, and Anderson receiving plenty of support from teammates "Long John" Fryer, Bob Alshuler, and Bob Null. After losing by 10 the night before, the Bruins beat Cal by two to grab their first PCC win of the year.

The season had its highs and lows. Following the win over Cal, UCLA lost to the Bank of America club team, and then were beaten by the Indians of Stanford. The Bruins did to Stanford what the team had done to Cal—in the next game, the squad beat the rival from Palo Alto by one point. It was the best win of the season, as Stanford was the class of the PCC. The Bruins lost the final two games to both Cal and Stanford later in the season and tacked on one win in a nonconference game against St. Mary's late in the season. UCLA fans wanted to finally beat USC. After losing to the Trojans once again in the middle of the season, the team had two final chances in the last two games of the year. In the second-to-last game, UCLA outplayed USC for much of the contest, but USC made a late run to take control of the game. USC won again, this time by the score of 53–47. Lastly, USC ended the careers of Robinson, Null, Anderson, and Clark George with another defeat. The 6–20 record marked another disastrous campaign in Westwood. The seniors were off to another chapter in their lives, one that for Jackie Robinson would be much more important than his days on the hardwood.

University of Wisconsin won the NCAA basketball national championship in 1941.

1941–42

Coach Wilbur Johns's third season as the UCLA basketball coach was one of distraction, by no fault of his own. The world was a mess, and soon things would become much worse. When the season kicked off, Coach Johns had several things to worry about. Soon, all of UCLA basketball and the world had something else to think about. The United States was about to enter World War II.

The loss of Jackie Robinson hurt; he was one of UCLA's finest players in its early history, the best scorer the Bruins had in recent years, and the best scorer in the Pacific Coast Conference. Replacing him would be Coach Johns's toughest task. The two captains of the '41–'42 squad were nicknamed "Big Guns," and they had big responsibilities. Ernie Handelsman and Bob Alshuler were expected not just to be leaders on the team and top performers in games but also to essentially be co-coaches. Johns trusted his two captains to call timeouts during the games, speak with referees, call offensive plays, He also wanted them to make sure everyone was attending classes, getting good grades, and going to bed on time. Coach Johns was committed to winning, and even though the turnaround would be slow, he was adamant the losing would eventually stop.

UCLA's preseason slate of games featured nine games before PCC play began. Though the Bruins

Roger Terry flying high against Stanford, 1942 (Southern Branch Collection).

beat Loyola, Nebraska, and Santa Clara and lost the other six, the story of the early season, of late 1941, was not basketball. The United States was at war.

For Coach Johns, like Coach Horrell of the football team, suddenly everything changed. He was a wartime coach, so his job description had now changed. He was tasked with leading men in a confusing time, knowing the same young men he bonded with on and off the court could one day find themselves in battle in either the Pacific or in Europe.

The UCLA basketball season as a whole was no better than the previous two. The Bruins finished with just a 5–18 record, 2–10 in conference play. The team beat Stanford by double digits one time, but lost the other three matchups by an average of 13 points. Similarly, the Bruins beat Cal once and lost the other three. Again, UCLA failed to beat USC, and the losing streak against the Trojans reached an unbelievable 39 games, the longest losing streak to one opponent in NCAA history to that point.

Over the course of the offseason, the United States war effort would become the focus of Americans in every corner of the country, in every industry. For Coach Johns, he needed to balance his roles as mentor and coach and prepare his best for his upcoming fourth season in Westwood. His first three weren't good enough.

Stanford University won the NCAA basketball national championship in 1942.

1942–43

The 1942–43 UCLA basketball team was one of the most interesting teams in the pre–John Wooden days at UCLA. With the United States war effort picking up by fall of '42, for many, sports became an afterthought. But for some, it became an outlet. The war affected each roster at every school differently. For the UCLA football team, not until 1943 did the team suffer attrition caused by the war. In fact, the '42 Bruins football team won the Pacific Coast Conference and went to the first Rose Bowl in school history. For the basketball team, several notable personnel moves were directly influenced by the war. At the beginning of the season, the Bruins' starting five consisted of Dick West and Mickey Panovich at the forward positions, John Fryer and Jack Baddeley at guards, and Marvin Lee at center. Fryer, the team captain, and key reserve Bill O'Brien both left during the season to serve overseas. With the Bruins short on players, Coach Johns got creative. He planned on recruiting the junior college circuit hard in the offseason, but he decided to move up his timeline. He convinced Marin Junior College hoopster Don Barksdale to transfer to UCLA midyear and join the team. Barksdale became one of the best players in UCLA history.

The 1942–43 season was a breakthrough. For the previous 11 seasons, UCLA had failed to finish with more wins than losses, including each of Coach Wilbur Johns's first three seasons. Due to the war, the conference schedule was reduced. In '43, there was only eight conference games instead of the usual 12. In '44, there was just six, and in '45 only four. In the early days of the Pacific Coast Conference, the Bruins played well in nonconference games before faltering against the tougher opponents in the PCC. Later, the Bruins won neither in conference nor out of conference, at least not at a high enough clip to please the fans. In '43, things changed in nonconference play. The Bruins would play 13 nonconference games, 12 of which came before PCC play. The Bruins finished at 11–2. UCLA was able to beat Vega Aircraft, a military team, as well as Loyola and San Francisco State, all by one point. It fell to Whittier, 44–42, but beat the Fox Studio Club team two out of the three meetings. In nonconference play alone, the Bruins clinched a winning season, the first since 1931, before Hitler was even a citizen of Germany.

In the conference opener, Dick West stole the show. A transfer from Long Beach City College, West played with an energy and pace that set him apart from most in the PCC. He poured in 18 points, good for team best, and the Bruins beat the Bears, 49–40. Following the victory over Cal, the Bruins played two games against the men from Palo Alto. The games were polar opposites. In the first game, the Bruins' high-scoring offense was too much for the Indians five. Though the game ended with a relatively close 60–57 score, the Bruins were in control for the majority of the game. The key to the Bruins' win was Coach Wilbur Johns's decision to move Dick Perry from forward to guard. Though the forwards would take the majority of shots in Coach Johns's offense, Perry had a scoring mind-set and continued shooting the ball often despite the position change. The second matchup would not go as well. Nothing worked for the Bruins, and the Indians easily came away with a 61–41 win. Following the Stanford game, the Bruins again took on the California Golden Bears, and though the team was sluggish for much of the game, it finally surged ahead and won, 42–40.

The games against Cal and Stanford were important in the conference race, but the games against USC were important for morale going forward. The losing streak was tiresome and embarrassing. The streak would continue, however, when the two teams met the first time: USC 60, UCLA 49. In the second meeting, the scores were lower for each team, but the Bruins were unable to claw any closer: USC 51, UCLA 39. In the third game, Bruins fans saw something they had yet to see in over a decade. Perry and Ainslie Bell guarded their Trojan counterparts closely, Panovich shot through passing lanes and disrupted the USC offense the entire game, and Don Barksdale was a wizard in the offensive post, totaling 18 points. When the clock ticked down to zero, the scoreboard read UCLA 42, USC 37. The 41-game losing streak was over. Though the Trojans would beat the Bruins in the fourth and final contest between the two, the season was unquestionably a success. The Bruins finished with a 14–7 overall record, the best winning percentage since 1928, including a 4–4 conference record, the best too since 1928. UCLA beat USC for the first time in 11 years, and most important, there was hope was again for Bruins basketball.

University of Wyoming won the NCAA basketball national championship in 1943.

1943–44

After the team logged a 14–7 record in 1942–43, fans approached the '43–'44 season with cautious optimism. Was the prior season a fluke? Or were the Bruins back? Seventeen years had elapsed since the Bruins' last conference title in basketball, and that was as a member of the Southern California Intercollegiate Athletic Conference. Since joining the PCC, the Bruins had only finished in the top two of the South Division just once, the year prior.

The season would again result in a second-place finish for the Bruins in the South Division, but the conference results or even the overall record was not most meaningful in '44. The games against USC were. With only six conference games, one might think that the Bruins would play the Trojans, Bears, and Indians twice each, but that was not the case. UCLA would play Cal twice, USC four times, and Stanford not at all. One year prior, UCLA ended the historic losing streak to USC, and the Trojans were eager to make it known that the team was still the best in Southern California. UCLA was determined to win more than one in '44.

The nonconference season started in strange fashion. In the first nine games, UCLA won five games and lost four. Eight of the nine games were not competitive. In UCLA's four losses, the team went down by an average of nearly double digits, which in the day was a blowout margin. In UCLA's five wins, the team won by an average of over 14 points. The Bruins played five more out-of-conference games throughout the year, mixed in with the conference slate, and they were polar opposites of the early-season games. UCLA beat Occidental and Pepperdine by two points each, and lost to Caltech and March Field, a military team, by two points each. The only comfortable game was played against the San Diego Navy, and the comfortable team was not the Bruins, but the boys in the service. The Bruins fell, 43–36.

The Bruins had bigger challenges than the nonconference games. Cal was the conference favorite, and the Bruins lost both matchups. UCLA had taken

Don Borden shoots against Cal, 1944 (Southern Branch Collection).

a step back in results on the court from the prior year, but if it could play well against the Trojans, there would be positives to extract from an otherwise underwhelming season.

The Bruins were led by "Tricky" Dick West, one of the best players on the West Coast. He was a consummate floor general who handled the ball well and set up his teammates in advantageous spots. He was the best perimeter defender on the roster and was the man trusted most by Coach Johns. West would split time between the frontcourt and the backcourt, and his versatility was his greatest asset. As the season went on, however, he became even more than just a passer and defender. He started shooting the ball more, especially as he saw more time at forward; when the season came to a close, he was the top scorer in the PCC. Joining West in the starting lineup was Bill Rankin, a sophomore guard, who led the conference in scoring for much of the season until West surpassed him late in the year. Jack Heald, a transfer from Stanford, held down the center position for much of the year, though an injury late in the year shortened his season. Rounding out the starting five were Bill Putnam and Dave Brown. Brown was a busy man. He also played on the Bruins football team under Babe Horrell. He, like Heald, was a transfer from Stanford, and Coach Johns was happy to have them both.

In the first game against the Trojans, 2,600 fans showed up at Westwood Gym to see the two teams face off. The squad of '44 was not the greatest offensively during Coach Johns's tenure, but the team was certainly one of the best defensively. In the first half, the Bruins held the Trojans to just seven points and led by eight going in to the break. In the second half, Coach Johns rotated his players to keep them fresh, and with every move he saw results. Bill Rankin scored 15 points, and the Bruins won, 33–19. The second game was frustrating. UCLA got off to a strong start, leading 5–0, before the Trojans went on a scoring binge. The Bruins kept chugging along, however, and finally clawed back into the game. With the score tied at 29 in the second half, the Bruins had foul problems. In a matter of minutes, West, Rankin, and Brown all fouled out, and the Bruins lost by seven points.

In big games, teams often lean on star players. In the third matchup, the Bruins relied on the captain and best player, Dick West. With the score tied and 10 seconds to play, West hit a high arcing jump shot to win the game. It was the finest moment of his career. Despite trailing at halftime in the fourth and final game, the Bruins played a strong second half to beat the Trojans for the third time that season. It was the first time UCLA took a season series against USC since 1932. The Bruins finished with an overall 10–10 record, going 3–3 in conference play.

The University of Utah won the NCAA basketball national championship in 1944.

1944–45

The Bruins of 1944–45 had an incredible season, in both a good and bad sense. After beating Los Angeles Community College, the Bruins lost seven consecutive games. Of the seven teams to down the Bruins, four were military teams loaded with former college athletes. The Bruins would later in the year play a military team called Camp Ross, whose best player was the brilliant former and future Bruin Don Barksdale. The Bruins finally ended the streak by beating Caltech, but then the team lost three more. UCLA and USC played each other four times during the season, but only two counted in the conference standings. In the first matchup, the Trojans easily won, outscoring the Bruins, 53–25. Unfortunately for the Bruins, this one counted in the conference standings. Though the Bruins were just 2–10, the team turned the season around, beginning with the matchup against the California Golden Bears.

Grant Clothier grabs a rebound against Cal, 1945 (Southern Branch Collection).

The Bruins were led all season by the strongest starting five in recent Bruins history. Bill Rankin was named to the All-PCC South Division First Team for the second season in a row, and Bill Putnam and Bob Arnold joined him on it. The other two starters were no slouches, as both Hal Michaels and Dick Hough were named to the Second Team. When the Bruins went north to take on the Bears in Berkeley, Coach Johns was unsure what his team was capable of. He came back pleasantly surprised. The game was never in doubt. Six minutes in, the Bruins led, 12–3, and at halftime, UCLA led, 21–12. In the second half, the Bruins played steady, unspectacular offense, and tight defense. The final score was 37–26. Cal's best player, Gus Mota, was defended almost entirely by Putnam, who held him to just nine points.

With the Bruins at 1–1 in conference play, a long stretch of nonconference games began. Unlike the early-season struggles, the Bruins played much better this time around. USC was one of the games that didn't count on the conference slate, but it felt great for the Bruins to knock the Trojans off, 41–36.

When conference play started again, the Bruins once more took on Cal, this time in Westwood. Though UCLA would fall behind, 17–10, early, the team rallied to take a three-point lead into halftime. Rankin was dealing with the flu and would not play for the Bruins in the second half, but the team did enough to win, this time by the score of 50–44.

The PCC season of '45 was a strange one when looking back on it now. The war decimated many programs, and schedules were condensed greatly. The Bruins only played four conference games, and the fourth one, against USC, was the deciding game in the South Division. The Bruins jumped out to a large lead early, leading, 14–3, midway through the half. A Trojans run, however, closed the gap before halftime, and the UCLA lead was just six points. Though USC would tie the game at 25, the Bruins were the better team and showed it in the final minutes. Rankin played his best game of the year, scoring 14 points to lead the way. With the victory, UCLA won the South Division of the Pacific Coast Conference for the first time since joining the conference sixteen years earlier. There would be no PCC championship series against the North Division champion, and the Bruins were named PCC Champions. The Bruins and Trojans would play one more time in a nonconference affair to close the season, and the Bruins fell, 37–20.

The Bruins finished the season with just an 11–12 overall record but won the PCC. Soon, the war would end, bringing some change to college campuses.

Oklahoma A&M College (now Oklahoma State University) won the NCAA basketball national championship in 1945.

1945–46

By late fall 1945 when basketballs were bouncing and coaches everywhere were teaching chest passes and defensive slides, the war that forever changed the world was over. Men who left college to serve came home, and the college athletic scene was changing. Though the '45–'46 season had players older than the typical college athletes, teams in the '46–'47 and '47–'48 seasons typically saw a spike in former military men rejoining college programs. For Coach Johns, the '45–'46 season was one of excitement. For the first time in many years, the Bruins actually had high expectations going into the season, including the possibility of reaching the NCAA Tournament for the first time. The past three seasons were the best since their days in the old Southern California Intercollegiate Athletic Conference, and the team had an abundance of talent from the previous year. But the Bruins would instead close out a terribly disappointing season.

The year before, UCLA struggled mightily to begin the season but eventually avenged the early-season losses by playing strongly in conference play. After the war ended, the conference schedule went back to a more normal form—meaning 12 games in PCC play. Before the conference slate, however, the Bruins took on a number of nonconference foes, including AAU teams, military teams, and other local colleges and universities. The previous year, the Bruins lost frequently out of the gate. Coach Johns hoped to avoid the slow start, but it happened again nonetheless. UCLA lost seven of the first eight, including another against Camp Doss, still led by former and future Bruin great Don Barksdale. The Bruins then defeated Caltech by a dominant 33–9 score, but the Bruins finished nonconference action with just a 3–9 record.

The Bruins began conference play by trekking north to take on the Cal Bears, led by Coach Nibs Price and the high-scoring duo of Andy Wolfe and Bob Hogeboom. The first half was a tight game with plenty of action on both sides. With under a minute to go in the half, the game was tied at 16. The Bears made one last shot before the break to take an 18–16 lead. The team never looked back, running away with the game in the second half. The final score was Cal 45, UCLA 33. The second game was much like the first half of the first game. It was back and forth for its entirety, and finally came down to a last-second shot. With the score tied at 35, Cal reserve forward Bob Anderson saw a crease and drove hard to the basket. No Bruin was quick enough to stop him and he laid the ball off the backboard and through the hoop. Chuck Stewart got one last shot up for the Bruins from near halfcourt, and it nearly went in. After rolling around on the rim, it fell off, and the Bruins lost.

The games played next against the Trojans were not quite as competitive. USC, under Sam Barry, had taken a step back in recent years, and the Bruins took full advantage then, turning the rivalry to the Bruins' favor. The script would be flipped again in '46, when the Trojans were the better team. In the first matchup, UCLA lost by 10, despite the strong performance from freshman Chuck Clustka. The next game was close for most of the way, but the Bruins collapsed in the final minutes. With the score tied at 38, USC scored seven straight. Bob Arnold knocked down a long shot from 25 feet away in the closing seconds for the Bruins, but they fell by a score of 45–40.

UCLA was 0–4 in conference play, but it would soon start winning. When the Bruins took on the Stanford Indians, the team showed they were better than the current record. The players dominated the game, leading between eight and 18 points the entire way. When the game ended, the Indians had only tallied 18 points, and though UCLA's offense wasn't particularly strong in this game, its 35 points were more than enough. One night later, the result was the same. Though Stanford actually led at half, Clustka and George Englund dominated the second half, and UCLA came away with a convincing win.

UCLA's winning streak would be short, however. When Cal came south to meet the Bruins in Westwood, it won both meetings. The Bruins got back on track by beating Stanford two more times before taking on USC in the final two games of the season. Thus far, UCLA had gone 0–4 against Cal, 4–0 against Stanford, and 0–2 against the Trojans. In the third game against the Trojans, Clustka, fast becoming a star, scored 16 points, and Hal Michaels added 12 for the Bruins. UCLA beat USC by double digits. There was no conference championship in '46, nor was there a division championship or a tournament appearance. In the final game, however, the Bruins were hoping to split the season series against the Trojans and finish .500 in conference play. But Clustka struggled in the second game, and no one picked up the scoring slack. USC played fine offense, UCLA's defense struggled, and the game was a rout. USC won, 60–43, and the season was over. The Bruins finished with a disatrous 8–16 record.

Oklahoma A&M College (now Oklahoma State University) won the NCAA basketball national championship in 1946.

1946–47

For the past two seasons, UCLA had played against a military team called Camp Doss. Though the Camp Doss team was littered with many older players, one man, Don Barksdale, who still retained eligibility amazed Coach Johns. He was tall and lean—6'6", 200 pounds. Unlike most centers of the day, he was mobile. He could run, jump, shoot, score, and defend the post. Coach Johns had recruited Barksdale before. He badly wanted him on the'43–'44 team, but because of war attrition, he convinced him to enroll early and finish the '42–'43 season with the Bruins. Barksdale would not be long for Westwood, however. He was soon off to war, and for three seasons, Coach Johns wondered if Barksdale would ever wear "UCLA" across his chest again. When he returned from the service, the answer was easy. He finished his playing career at UCLA, and Bruins everywhere are thankful that he did.

Along with Barksdale, the Bruins had plenty of talent on the team. Dick West, Bob Arnold, and Chuck Clustka were fantastic players in their own right, and teamed with Johnny Stanich, Davage Minor, Marv Lee, Dick Perry, Bill Rankin, and the rest, the Bruins had the potential to be a very good team. UCLA began the season with wins in four of their first five nonconference games, a welcome change from years past. For Christmas 1946, the Bruins were not home, but on the East Coast. UCLA beat Wyoming by 13 points in Brooklyn, and then won in a thriller against a strong Saint Joseph's team by two points in Philadelphia. Next, the Bruins played in one of the first truly grand-scale games in school history, against New York University. The game was played in the venue that would one day become known as the Mecca of hoops. Despite 23 points from Barksdale, NYU beat UCLA, 66–49, in Madison Square Garden.

Conference play started at the beginning of 1947, when the Bruins were back home in California. Playing Stanford on back-to-back nights, the Bruins split the series with the Indians. UCLA would remain in Los Angeles the next week, but not at home. Playing USC at Shrine Auditorium, the Bruins beat USC, and then one night later back in Westwood, UCLA beat them again. UCLA traveled outside Los Angeles for the first time in PCC play the next week and split the two games with Cal, the early South Division favorite. Though most expected Cal to eventually break loose from the Bruins and surge ahead in the conference standings, that never happened. The Bruins kept winning, and the most trouble came not from Cal, but Stanford. The Bruins took two out of the four against the Indians, compared to the three they won against the Bears. Most notable in the games played against those rivals from the North, however, was the third game against the Bears. UCLA scored 85 points, holding Cal to just 52. The Bruins were led by Barksdale, Minor, and Stanich, who each put the ball through the hoop with record-setting accuracy. The 85 points scored by the Bruins was the most ever in a PCC game to that point.

With two conference games to play, the Bruins were in the driver's seat in the South Division. If UCLA beat USC in both games, it would win the division and head to the championship series against the North Division winner. Though the first game was close, the Bruins won by five, 71–66. The next night, the Bruins clinched the division title by winning, 66–54. Bring on Oregon State.

If the Bruins could beat Oregon State College in the three-game championship series, the team might head to the NCAA Basketball Tournament and compete for a national championship. With a loss, however, the season would end. The championship format was easy. The games would be played in

Corvallis, Oregon, and the first team to two victories was the champion. Though it would be great for Coach Johns to say he had climbed the mountaintop of West Coast hoops, it would have to wait. Oregon State was a much better team. Red Rocha defended Barksdale better than any opponent had all season, and the Beavers won in convincing fashion both nights.

College of the Holy Cross won the NCAA basketball national championship in 1947.

Don Barksdale

Donald Argee "Don" Barksdale was born on March 31, 1923, in Oakland, California. Of the 10 players to have their jersey number officially retired by UCLA, only Don Barksdale played in the pre–Wooden era. He is one of only two that didn't win a National Championship and one of two who was never a consensus First Team All-American. He is one of just three who was never named National Player of the Year. Still, Don Barksdale is every bit as deserving as the rest. While John Wooden may be the father of UCLA basketball, Don Barksdale is the grandfather. His legacy is more far-reaching and long-lasting than the earliest coaches or players in UCLA history. His impact on the United States is undoubtedly significant, and his impact on UCLA athletics is worth remembering.

Don Barksdale's development as a basketball player was unlike nearly all athletes who eventually reach fame in their sport. He did not play in high school. Barksdale went to Berkeley High School, and because of the color of his skin, he never saw action with the team. The head coach at Berkeley had a "black quota." He only permitted one black player to play on his team each season, and though Barksdale would try out for the team three times, he was never the one chosen. Instead, he perfected his craft on the Northern California playgrounds. Though the game was much different in the late '30s and early '40s than what it is today, Barksdale was different than most. His style was modern. He was fast and athletic. He played above the rim. He was said to "jump out of the gym" and he had a fancy flair to his game. His style can be attributed at least in part to his games on the playgrounds, where the style was just plain different no matter where you went. Though many consider New York, Los Angeles, and Chicago to be the Meccas of playground hoops, playing in Northern California provided Barksdale with a similar experience. Fouls were rarely called, fights were frequent, and toughness was valued.

Despite not playing in high school, Barksdale's career would soon take off. He played at Marin Junior College for two years, winning the California Junior College championship in 1942 and 1943, before earning a scholarship to UCLA under Wilbur Johns. After enrolling midyear in 1943, Barksdale was one of the most valuable pieces to the Bruins puzzle that ended USC's 41-game winning streak over the Bruins. His time in Westwood would be brief, however. Like so many young men of the time, Barksdale left to fight in World War II. Barksdale served in the United States Army, and though his military service delayed his basketball career, the more successful part of his career was still left. In 1946, he returned to UCLA; this time, he was there for the full season, better than ever. During the '46–'47 season, Barksdale was a sight to behold. One of Barksdale's best friends, Arthur Lewis, a teammate of his on the track team, said of his friend, "He was a superior athlete, definitely. He had very good running abilities, and in basketball, he could get up and down the court like Wilt Chamberlain, for example. He was probably the best basketball player that UCLA ever had up to that point." Barksdale could do it all. He was 6'6" with incredible leaping ability, and though most centers of the day played a different style, Barksdale was unique. He was too quick for bigger defenders and jumped too high for smaller ones. He would be named an All-American, and then he was gone. Barksdale only played one season at UCLA before graduating in 1948, but like fellow Bruins Jackie Robinson and Kenny Washington, he would make history.

In 1948, Barksdale became the first black player to ever play for the United States Basketball team. Prior to the Olympics, the US team played an exhibition game against the University of Kentucky, and Barksdale was the first black player to ever play against the Wildcats. Though he was often forced to stay at different hotels than his teammates, and he received death threats often, he did not let that deter him. In the Olympics, the US team was perfect. They went undefeated in tournament play and came home with a gold medal.

Though Barksdale had proven to be one of the best young players in the country, he was left without a spot in the NBA. Washington had integrated the NFL, and Robinson integrated MLB, but the NBA (then known as the Basketball Association of America) was still a white man's league. Barksdale would instead work a series of odd jobs in the Bay Area. He was a radio disc jockey, the first black DJ in San Francisco. He owned a beer distribution company and worked on television, while playing AAU basketball on the side. Still, Barksdale longed for greater competition and hoped for a chance to play basketball at the highest level.

Despite wanting to play pro basketball, there was another problem. When the NBA finally integrated black players into the league in 1950, the pay was not satisfactory incentive to leave behind his current work. NBA teams repeatedly called Barksdale to gauge his interest, but he continually turned them down. In 1951, Barksdale finally accepted an offer. He signed a contract with the Baltimore Bullets and became one of the highest paid players in the NBA.

As a 28-year-old rookie, Barksdale was a hit. In his second season, he was named to the All-Star team, the first black man to ever make the team. He was traded in the offseason to the Boston Celtics and play two more years., When healthy, he was effective, but ankle injuries derailed his career. After just four seasons, Barksdale retired.

Following his brief but meaningful career, Barksdale had a successful career in radio, and he also opened his own nightclub and founded a record company. In 1983, he launched Save High School Sports Foundation, which helped fund local sports in his hometown of Oakland. Though Barksdale averaged just 11 points and eight rebounds per game during his NBA career, he received the ultimate honor for a basketball player in 2012. Nearly 60 years after his retirement, he was posthumously inducted the Naismith Memorial Basketball Hall of Fame. He is a member of the Pac-12 Conference Hall of Fame and the UCLA Athletics Hall of Fame. His number 11 jersey is retired by UCLA. Barksdale died in 1993, but every time UCLA fans look to the rafters and see his jersey hanging in Pauley Pavilion, they are reminded of the man who was there before Wooden. They are reminded of a pioneer and a great Bruins legend.

1947–48

The 1947–48 season would be the last for Coach Wilbur Johns as the head coach of the UCLA basketball program, although he continued his duties as the athletic director. He soon hired a new man to take over the basketball program.

Coach Johns had the goal of leaving UCLA on the upward swing. Over the previous five seasons, UCLA accumulated an overall 61–52 record, two South Division titles, and one PCC championship. The success was modest, but the Bruins were headed in the right direction.

More than 50 students showed up to the annual basketball tryouts in the fall of 1947. The men who made the team were the best of the bunch, and Coach Johns made them earn their spot on the roster. Forwards John Stanich, Chuck Clustka, Dick West, and guard Davage Minor were the most effective players on the team. Filling out the roster were quality players Bill Rankin, Don Seidel, Ron Pearson, Wayne Boulding, Guy Buccola, Eldon Bennett, Jim Baker, Ernie Johnson, George Stanich, Gene Williams, Alan Sawyer, and Ray Alba. The roster was deep with talent, the deepest in Coach Johns's nine seasons as the UCLA head basketball coach.

The Bruins began with their usual nonconference slate of solid opponents mixed with subpar teams. The Bruins did well for the most part, finishing with a 9–3 nonconference record. The season began with consecutive games against the Loyola Lions, both of which were won by the Bruins in dominant fashion. UCLA hoped for the same outcome against the Santa Clara Broncos, but was unable to complete the sweep. UCLA won the first matchup by five and then lost the next night by the same amount. At 3–1, the Bruins traveled north. The Bruins had no problem playing Nevada Reno in San Francisco, beating the team by 13 points. One night later, the Bruins faced a tougher task and saw a familiar face. Like he had done while playing on military teams during World War II, Don Barksdale now faced his alma mater, the UCLA Bruins. Barksdale was the star player of the AAU squad Oakland Bittners. Though the Bruins were considered heavy underdogs, the game was close, and with time ticking down, UCLA led by two. Like they had seen so many times before, the Bruins saw up close the brilliance of Barksdale. With under five seconds to play, he

Gene Williams shoots a hook shot against Cal, 1948 (Southern Branch Collection).

hit a running shot to tie the game at 60 and send the game to overtime. The Bittners then scored seven points in the extra period, and the Bruins scored just three. UCLA then returned home for two games, losing to Baylor and then beating College of the Pacific before heading east.

The most memorable moments of the '48 season came on the three-game trip to the East Coast. In the opener, the Bruins beat St. Joseph's, 64–54, as West, Minor, and John Stanich all played well. The next night, the Bruins took on Long Island University at Madison Square Garden, with 18,478 fans to watch a thrilling game. Though UCLA led most of the way, LIU scored in the final 10 seconds to send the game to overtime. In the OT period, Dick West grabbed the victory for the men from Westwood. With 50 seconds left, he hit a running shot to give UCLA a 66–64 lead and the Bruins finished with a win. One overtime was not enough for the game against Cornell, however. For the first time in school history, the Bruins played a double-overtime game, winning, 50–47.

UCLA was a different team in PCC play. After three weeks off, they played Cal in the conference opener and showed that the players were not in the same class as the men from Berkeley. On the year, UCLA played the Bears four times and lost each game, with the closest game being a 41–37 loss in the final matchup. The Bruins fared better against Stanford, though it were only able to split the four games played. Against USC, the Bruins won just one of four. The lone UCLA win was close. With UCLA down one and shooting a free throw for the tie, John Stanich grabbed the miss and laid it in with 15 seconds to play to give the Bruins a 51–50 win.

When the season came to a close, the Bruins had a disappointing 12–13 record and finished third in the South Division of the PCC. Johnny Stanich earned a place on the All-Southern Division team, joining Davage Minor. Dick West and Bill Rankin ended their very strong careers as seniors and were on to the next phase of their lives. Although the graduating senior class would be missed, the hiring of John Wooden for the next season was to eventually far overshadow the loss.

University of Kentucky won the NCAA basketball national championship in 1948.

CHAPTER 4
John Wooden (1948–1975)

The story of John Wooden's life could fill a book itself. In fact, as of this writing, over one hundred books have been written about him. For UCLA basketball, he was a godsend. But he was so much more than just a basketball coach. John Wooden became, in time, a national icon, respected as much for his dignity, humanity, and grace as he was for his legendary coaching career. When Wooden passed away at ninety-nine years old, he had lived a full life. He had affected the lives of more people than anyone could ever estimate. He had lived a life in the public eye, but wherever he went and whatever he did, scandal stayed away. He was untouchable, beloved, and brilliant. He is the man in which every coach looks to for guidance. Men who never met him idolize him. While Coach Wooden would study Abraham Lincoln and find guidance in one of America's greatest leaders, others would study him and find guidance in America's greatest coach. When searching for Coach Wooden's influence today in athletic circles, one must look no further than the writings of others. No matter the sport, no matter the age of the coach, no matter his success or failure, when you read a book about a coach, you are sure to see Coach Wooden's influence. You will read about his humanity, his morals, his guidance, his love. While Coach Wooden's success is well publicized, his life was so much more than the moments on the sideline coaching the UCLA Bruins. Though Coach is now gone, his legacy lives. It began in a small town in Indiana.

On October 14, 1910, John Robert Wooden was born in Hall, Indiana. The middle child of five to Hugh Joshua Wooden and Roxie Wooden, John's life as a young boy was not easy. His family was poor, his father working as a tenant farmer. He would eventually find a new job, however, but the family financial situation didn't improve much at all. Wooden's father, who would go by his middle name Joshua, became a mail carrier, while also working part time on a small farm. Though John's early childhood could be seen as rough by today's standards, young John never thought of his time in Hall as difficult. He found joy in ways that young children are often able when they are too young to know the worries of their parents. John loved his father's horses and loved joining his father on his buggy while delivering the mail. John's first goal in life was not to become a basketball player or a coach. He simply wanted to own a buggy of his own, one with red wheels, pulled by a black mare.

In 1918, just before John's eighth birthday, the family inherited a 60-acre farm near Centerton, Indiana. The family moved to the much more rural town. There was no electricity or plumbing, and the family got water from a well. The Wooden farm grew corn, wheat, alfalfa, watermelons, and tomatoes. Working the farm was the job not just of Joshua Wooden but also of the whole family. While working the farm one day, John's brother Cat playfully flipped a chunk of manure off of a pitchfork onto John's face. John was angry and charged his brother, calling him a "son of a bitch." Joshua was close by, and he would not take well to the language of his son. Both Cat and John faced the wrath of their angry father, but in his father's eyes John's language was worse than Cat's error in judgment. Joshua made sure to get his point across that losing control of emotions and swearing were unacceptable at the Wooden household. John took the lesson to heart. Years later, both Coach Wooden and his former players would often tell others that Coach Wooden's worst language would usually be "Goodness gracious, sakes alive!"

John's father was a man of high moral standards, as was his son. John idolized his father, and after graduating from county day school, John was given a gift more valuable than any toy. His father gave him a piece of paper with a handwritten creed:

1. Be true to yourself.
2. Make each day your masterpiece.
3. Help others.
4. Drink deeply from good books, especially the Bible.
5. Make friendship a fine art.
6. Build a shelter against a rainy day.
7. Pray for guidance, count and give thanks for your blessings every day.

We can see now the influence Joshua had on his son, as this creed resembles what most think about Coach Wooden today. John carried the paper in his wallet for many years, until the paper was worn out. He then had copies made and carried a copy with him for the entirety of his life.

Along with the creed, Joshua provided John with something that became his passion. When John was in third or fourth grade, his father built an iron basketball ring and fixed it to the side of a barn as close to regulation height as he could. Hay blocked the hoop, but the faster the Wooden boys would remove and distribute the hay for the animals, the sooner they had access to the hoop. Basketball was not the only sport for John, though, nor was it his favorite. His father leveled a field and made a baseball diamond on the family land, and John fell in love with America's pastime. As a thirteen and fourteen year old, he played on a local club team with boys as old as their early twenties. He dreamed of one day playing in the major leagues.

Joshua was good with land and animals, but many things were beyond his control. When all his hogs died of cholera in 1924, following a bad vaccination, suddenly the family was in a bad way financially. The family could no longer pay the mortgage and lost the farm. John was just fourteen years old, but most boys his age were no longer enrolled in school, instead opting to work. John, too, expected his academic pursuits to end when the family was forced to move to Martinsville. His parents were adamant, however, that he remain in school. They would find a way to survive, and he would have a better life for himself than they had. Joshua took a job at a sanitarium, and worked there until he died in 1950. While a freshman at Martinsville High School, John met his future wife, Nellie Riley. The two eventually married, and their love story is that of fairytales.

Prior to John's first game on the varsity team as a sophomore in 1926, a tradition was born. John looked over to Nellie and winked at her; she then put her index finger to her thumb, making an *O* and signaling good luck. The two would do this every game, though eventually the wink became a wave of John's signature rolled-up game program.

As a sophomore, John was a very good basketball player. Playing for Glenn "The 'ol Fox" Curtis, the Martinsville Artesians lost in the Indiana state championship game. Curtis would be one of Wooden's earliest mentors, but things didn't begin well for the two. Early in John's sophomore season, he was told he would come off the bench instead of start. He passionately disagreed with his coach, so he quit. For two weeks, he vowed he would never play for Coach Curtis. Like many impressionable and emotional young men, Wooden let his feelings get the best of him. He entered the season with the belief that Coach Curtis played favorites, as his brother Cat told him from his experience. But after getting to understand the reasoning behind Coach Curtis's decision, John relented and rejoined the team. He ended up starting the majority of the season.

In 1927 as a junior at Martinsville, John got his first, but certainly not his last, taste of winning. His team won the state championship, and he was the best player. As a senior, the repeat hopes came down to the final seconds. After Wooden missed a shot that would have given the Artesians a three-point lead, Charie Secrist of Muncie High School scored the game-winning basket to win the state title. More than seven decades after the disappointing loss, Coach Wooden said, "To this day, it is the highest arched shot I have ever seen. It seemed to go up through the rafters and come straight down through the hoop.

Losing that game was the most disappointing thing that ever happened to me as a player."

Following the 1928 basketball season and graduation from Martinsville, John enrolled at Purdue University and played under Coach Ward "Piggy" Lambert, another man who would have an enormous impact on him. Wooden said years later, "Piggy Lambert was the greatest influence on me from both the standpoint of playing and coaching. Coach Lambert had a fetish for details." John Wooden's playing career at Purdue was legendary. He was a good scorer, good defender, and an instinctive player. He was hardnosed and extremely aggressive. He would earn the nickname "Indiana Rubber Man" because he was always diving on the floor and bouncing back up. He was three times named to the All–Big Ten Team and three times a consensus All-American, the first three-time AA in college basketball history. Twice Purdue won the Big Ten, and twice Wooden was named team captain. The Boilermakers won the 1932 college basketball national championship, and Wooden was named the 1932 College Basketball Player of the Year. Wooden earned the prestigious Big Ten Medal for Scholarship and Prowess and later was inducted into the Basketball Hall of Fame as a player. Wooden graduated in 1932, married Nellie in August, and then began his long coaching career one month later.

Coach Wooden always fancied himself a teacher. In his first job out of college, he taught not only on the hardwood but also in the classroom. John Wooden coached the Green Devils of Dayton High School in Dayton, Kentucky, for two years. Along with coaching the basketball team, he also served as the athletic director and English teacher. The '32 Green Devils team was the worst team Coach Wooden ever coached, finishing with a 6–11 record, the only losing season Wooden ever experienced as a player or coach. Following his departure from Dayton, John and Nellie move to South Bend, Indiana, where John coached the basketball and baseball teams at South Bend Central High School, as well as teach English and work part-time at a local book publishing company. For eleven years, at both Dayton and South Bend Central, Coach Wooden learned on the job. He strategized and adjusted, built his philosophy, and gained experience that shaped him as a man and a coach. But now he was off to war.

In 1942, Coach Wooden became Lieutenant Wooden in the United States Navy. Ultimately, fate intervened to save the life of the man who would become an American icon. Lieutenant Wooden was assigned to the USS *Franklin*, but a ruptured appendix changed everything. He had emergency surgery, and though he survived, his replacement was not so lucky. A kamikaze pilot struck the Franklin, and the man who took his place died. Upon his release from the Navy four years later, Wooden briefly returned to South Bend Central. He soon moved on to Indiana State Teachers College (now Indiana State University), replacing his old high school coach, Glenn Curtis. In his first year, 1946–47, Indiana State finished with a 17–8 record but declined to play in the prestigious National Association of Intercollegiate Basketball tournament because the tournament would not allow one his players, Clarence Walker, a black man, to play. Wooden remained at Indiana State for one more year, in which the team had a 27–7 record, winning the Indiana Intercollegiate Conference for the second year in a row. This time the team accepted an invitation to play in the NAIB tournament. Walker was allowed to play this time, and in doing so, he became the first black player to ever play in an NCAA postseason tournament. Indiana State lost to Louisville, the only time Wooden would ever lose a championship game as a coach. Soon, Coach Wooden, the Midwestern boy, was in an entirely new element—he would soon be in Westwood.

Coach Wooden's plan was going exactly how he hoped two years earlier. He wanted to coach at a school with less pressure, playing in a small conference, before joining a big-time college basketball league. He hoped to coach in the Big Ten and felt if he was successful, he would get that chance. Though he turned down a chance to be an assistant coach and coach-in-waiting at Purdue one year prior, he knew he was ready to be the man in charge of a major program. Following the '48 season, two schools were interested in Coach Wooden, UCLA and Minnesota. The Golden Gophers were Coach Wooden's first choice, but he decided to do his due diligence. He visited both places, and promised the athletic directors at both schools he would give them his answer on an agreed-upon date. Minnesota was to call at 6:00 p.m. and UCLA was to call at 7:00 p.m. When 6:00 rolled around, Coach's phone remained quiet. Still no call came in at 6:15,

6:30, 6:45. At 7:00, the phone rang. It was Wilbur Johns, and Coach Wooden agreed to accept the UCLA job. The news of Coach Wooden's acceptance went straight to the press in Los Angeles. One hour later, Frank McCormick of Minnesota called and expected to confirm he had a new coach. Coach Wooden told McCormick, "It's too late. I have already accepted the job at UCLA." Coach Wooden badly wanted to go to Minnesota, and McCormick badly wanted him. He pleaded with Wooden to call Johns back and tell him he would instead go to Minnesota. Wooden refused, despite finally hearing that the reason McCormick was unable to call at 6:00 was because he was stuck in a major snowstorm. Wooden felt bad for Minnesota, and McCormick specifically, but he had given his word to Johns, and he would not back out. It was the greatest snowstorm in UCLA history.

Though Johns and the Bruins got the man they wanted, much work was still to do, and much doubt remained for all Bruins. Coach Wooden had only coached for two years at the collegiate level and was yet to ever coach in a major conference. He believed the facilities at UCLA were not only subpar but also atrocious. When he first conducted practice with the Bruins in spring, he thought the team was very bad, and that Indiana State would handle the team easily.

First year UCLA head coach John Wooden, 1949 (Southern Branch Collection).

In 27 seasons as the UCLA basketball head coach, John Wooden won the conference title 19 times, including his last nine seasons. The Bruins won the national championship 10 seasons. He was named the NCAA Basketball Coach of the Year seven times. He was inducted into the Basketball Hall of Fame as a coach in 1973, becoming the first inductee as a player and a coach. In 2006, he was a founding member of the College Basketball Hall of Fame. In 2009, he was inducted into the Missouri Valley Conference Athletics Hall of Fame. While his multiple inductions into different halls of fame are noteworthy, many more honors have been bestowed on Coach Wooden that are too numerous to count. He was named *Sports Illustrated*'s Sportsman of the Year and the *Sporting News*'s Greatest Coach of All Time. There is John Wooden High School, John Wooden Post Office, John Wooden Drive, John Wooden Center, and, on Pauley Pavilion, Nell and John Wooden Court, known by many as "The House that Wooden Built." In 2003, he was awarded the Presidential Medal of Freedom, and in 2012 a bronze statue of Wooden was erected in front of the newly renovated Pauley Pavilion.

When Coach Wooden retired following another national championship in 1975, he was far from finished living a miraculous life. Coach Wooden wrote books, spoke to huge crowds, and ran basketball camps for kids. He attended UCLA games, sitting in the same seats, which to this day are reserved for the Wooden family. He welcomed visitors and was graceful even as he aged. John Wooden's former players are his biggest fans, and his greatest spokesmen. You can hardly think of Kareem Abdul-Jabbar, Bill Walton, Jamaal Wilkes, or any other Bruin without also thinking of Coach Wooden, and that's how the players like it. They loved him, and fans loved him just as much. On the UCLA campus today, you find symbols of Coach Wooden all over the place. His Pyramid of Success is everywhere. Industriousness, friendship, loyalty, cooperation, and enthusiasm are the foundation upon which all success is built. Then comes self-control, alertness, initiative, and intentness. The heart of the pyramid is condition, skill, and team spirit. Poise and confidence are connecting blocks, and nothing is complete without the apex,

Coach John Wooden, 1975 (Southern Branch Collection).

competitive greatness. The Pyramid took Coach Wooden fourteen years to complete, and through countless hours of refinement, it is perfect.

Coach Wooden has been called many things. He has been called the greatest of all time. He has been called a teacher, a moral compass, and a legend. He is the Wizard of Westwood, an icon, a larger than life figure, and a brilliant man. He is a lot of things to a lot of people, but at UCLA, he is, to this day, called one thing—Coach. While it is impossible to detail Coach's brilliant life in full, his legacy lives on through the impact he had on others, and we see Coach Wooden at UCLA every day. We see him in his predecessors. We see him in each other. Coach Wooden died on June 4, 2010, and to all who remember it, it is the saddest day in UCLA history. It has now been more

John Wooden looks on from his seat at a UCLA basketball game in 2009 (Erkki Corpuz Collection).

than seventy years since John Wooden came west and stepped foot on the ground in Westwood and built UCLA into the greatest college basketball program of all-time. UCLA fans will forever be thankful.

John Wooden Quotes

"Talent is God given. Be humble. Fame is man-given. Be grateful. Conceit is self-given. Be careful."

"If you're not making mistakes, then you're not doing anything. I'm positive that a doer makes mistakes."

"Things turn out best for the people who make the best of the way things turn out."

"If you don't have time to do it right, when will you have time to do it over?"

"Success comes from knowing that you did your best to become the best that you are capable of becoming."

"Success is never final, failure is never fatal. It's courage that counts."

"Success is peace of mind, which is a direct result of self-satisfaction in knowing you made the effort to become the best of which you are capable."

"Just try to be the best you can be; never cease trying to be the best you can be. That's in your power."

"A coach is someone who can give correction without causing resentment."

"The most important thing in the world is family and love."

"Failure is not fatal, but failure to change might be."

"Do not let what you cannot do interfere with what you can do."

"Be more concerned with your character than your reputation, because your character is what you really are, while your reputation is merely what others think you are."

"Never mistake activity for achievement."

"It's what you learn after you know it all that counts."

"Don't measure yourself by what you have accomplished, but by what you should have accomplished with your ability."

"Winning takes talent, to repeat takes character."

"Don't give up on your dreams, or your dreams will give up on you."

"Discipline yourself, and others won't need to."

"The main ingredient of stardom is the rest of the team."

"Somebody asked me, 'You know, how come it took you so long to win a national championship?' And I said, 'I'm a slow learner; but you notice when I learn something, I have it down pretty good.'"

"You can't live a perfect day without doing something for someone who will never be able to repay you."

"If I am through learning, I am through."

"Be quick, but don't hurry."

"The best thing a father can do for his children is to love their mother."

"Never make excuses. Your friends don't need them, and your foes won't believe them."

"Seek opportunities to show you care. The smallest gestures often make the biggest difference."

"It is amazing how much can be accomplished if no one cares who gets the credit."

"Failing to prepare is preparing to fail."

"Happiness begins where selfishness ends."

"Although there is no progress without change, not all change is progress."

1948–49

John Wooden would not take long to show he was unlike any other coach in UCLA history. He would win early and often. His tenure began not with optimism, however, but with worry.

In 1948, basketball programs commonly conducted spring practice, much like is now standard for football. During spring, Coach Wooden was amazed by the team he had chosen to coach. He believed there was a lack of talent, athleticism, and teamwork. He vowed to help them become better, and he would do so by conditioning them. If UCLA was to have a successful season in '48–'49, players had to be in better shape than their opponents. Coach Wooden's practices seemed endless. They were organized down to the minute, and they were efficient. UCLA's earliest practices were all about conditioning, fundamentals, basic basketball drills, and understanding Coach Wooden's early basketball philosophy. He believed in running, a full-court pressing defense, constant movement, and unselfishness on both ends of the floor. By the end of spring practice, he believed his team had improved greatly.

Along with Eddie Sheldrake, Ronnie Pearson, and Chuck Clustka, Coach Wooden found new players in the fall that he believed would help the team win. Alan Sawyer, who did not participate in spring, was a player Wooden came to trust. Coach Wooden, unfamiliar with junior college basketball when he accepted the job, quickly learned the ins and outs of recruiting JC players. He believed first in acquiring talent from high schools, but he also learned that acquiring talent from JCs to fill the gaps was necessary at times. In his first year, he quickly filled spots with transfers Carl Kraushaar and Paul Saunders. There were other players, as well, and by the time the season began, Coach Wooden had quality depth. Ray Alba, Art Alper, Wayne Boulding, and Guy Buccola would all contribute in their own way, either in games or on the practice court.

Coach Wooden's first season would be one of great triumph. UCLA won Coach Wooden's first game in Westwood by the score of 43–37 over Santa Barbara College. The game was not always pretty, as UCLA missed more shots than Coach would have liked, but the win got UCLA off in the right direction. It turned out to be one of many. UCLA finished the nonconference slate with 12 wins and three losses. The first team to beat UCLA was Wisconsin, and the most meaningful was a loss to Oregon State, a game that counted as a nonconference affair, though both were members of the PCC. The two would meet again.

UCLA was picked to finish last in the South Division of the PCC, but the preseason prognosticators knew little about UCLA's new phenom coach. They couldn't have been more wrong. Though UCLA lost to Stanford in the conference opener, it would lose just one more in the conference. The Bruins took three out of four against the Indians of Stanford, three out of four against the Trojans of USC, and all four against the Golden Bears of California. After finishing with a losing record just one year prior, UCLA won the South Division and took on the Oregon State Beavers in the PCC Championship series.

The series was to be a best out of three, and the winner would head to the NCAA Tournament. OSU won the first game, 53–41, but the Bruins bounced

1949 UCLA team photo (Southern Branch Collection).

back to take the second game, 46–39. In the third and final game, UCLA's offense struggled, and though its defense performed well, 35 points weren't enough, as the Beavers scored 41 to win. OSU would head to the tournament and advance to the semifinals, now called the Final Four, before losing. Coach Wooden and the Bruins won 22 games, the most ever for a UCLA team, topping the previous best of 18 wins two years prior. The Bruins were good in '49. They would be even better one year later.

University of Kentucky won the NCAA basketball national championship in 1949.

1949–50

In Wooden's second year, the Bruins did not have star power, but the team had strength in numbers. Coach Wooden was often said to have used his bench very little. While this was true when he had elite starters, in 1950 he did not, so he used all the weapons he had. UCLA's leading scorer was Alan Sawyer, a 6'5" forward who averaged 12.6 points per game. Eddie Sheldrake, a guard, would average 9.1, and Carl Kraushaar, George Stanich, Ralph Joeckel, and Jerry Norman were also key contributors.

The Bruins began the season against Bruins alumni ballers. Though the game was seen as serious, it did not count on the official all-time game record, and it really was no contest. The current Bruins cruised past the alumni Bruins, 81–44. It was surely a sign of things to come. UCLA won many games by large margins. They started 5–0, with crushing defeats of Arizona State, San Diego State, Pepperdine, and Santa Clara. Though the team lost to the University of San Francisco in the sixth game of the year, Coach Wooden learned from the early blowouts and settled in to a tighter rotation. The following games were more difficult, but UCLA was better for it. The squad beat Illinois and La Salle in close games before taking on City College of New York, a brilliant New York City–based team. After UCLA shocked the home team, winning, 60–53, at Madison Square Garden, the Bruins received a level of notoriety never been seen in school history. UCLA shot all the way up to No. 9 in the Associated Press rankings. The Bruins slowed down after the big win, but still had a solid 14–5 record in nonconference play.

Against the California Golden Bears, the first conference opponent, UCLA players showed that they simply had too much speed for their older brothers from the North. In the first half, however, UCLA appeared to be going through the motions. Coach Wooden would send a message, however, and in the second half, the Bruins woke up from their hibernation and came away victorious. In 1950, students gave Westwood Gym had a new nickname, and it was perfectly fitting for the team: the "racetrack." Against Stanford in the second conference game of the year, the Bruins were too fast, agile, and good. UCLA ran away with a big win to improve its PCC record to 2–0.

Though the Bruins were a well-balanced team, they were beaten almost singlehandedly by USC. Bill Sharman scored 32 for the Trojans, and UCLA lost for the first time in conference play. Though the Bruins were no longer perfect, the team was contending once again in the South Division of the PCC. One night after losing to the Trojans by 13, UCLA beat USC by 21. The Bruins cruised through the rest of conference play, sweeping both Stanford and California on the season, winning twice at home and twice in the Bay Area against each. The most exciting game came in the final affair against Cal. With the score tied at 44, Sawyer scored the game-winning basket with under 10 seconds to play to seal the victory for the Bruins. Just as UCLA was jubilant after defeating Cal, the school was on the other end of a similar game. In the second to last conference game of the year, UCLA lost to USC by two points. The next night, however, the Bruins handily beat the Trojans, despite 24 points from Sharman, and won the South Division of the Pacific Coast Conference.

George Stanich, 1950 (Southern Branch Collection).

For the second consecutive year, the Bruins played a three-game series to decide the conference championship. This year, the opponent was the Washington State Cougars, led on the sideline by Coach Jack Friel, and led on the court by senior Ed Gayda and the very tall sophomore Gene Conley. The game would be one to remember. UCLA led for much of the game but in the waning minutes seemed to lose composure. Bruins forward Ralph Joeckel took ill-advised shots and continued to miss. As the Bruins bricks were building, the Washington State comeback was, as well. In the final seconds with the score tied, Washington State finally missed, and the Bruins had a chance to win at the end. Though Joeckel had struggled for much of the late going, he was the hero of the final seconds of game one. Jumping off of one foot, he leaped from just beyond halfcourt and released a shot high into the rafters. When the ball came down, it hit the backboard and went straight through the net with no time on the clock. The Bruins won, 60–58, and the crowd went wild. Fans stormed the court, filling every inch of the hardwood. Joeckel was carried off by the fans and taken to the locker room to continue the celebration. Though the Bruins won the game, there was a lesson to be learned. In the locker room, Joeckel would say to Coach Wooden, "I sure tried to throw the ball game away, didn't I, Coach?" Coach Wooden replied, "You sure did" and preached to his team the importance of taking smart shots. One night later, there would be less drama. Bruins players took Coach Wooden's advice and played a clean, smart game, winning, 52–49. The win gave the Bruins its first Pacific Coast Conference crown and first conference title since the final year in the Southern California Intercollegiate Athletic Conference 23 years before. More important, however, the season was not over. UCLA earned a berth in the NCAA Tournament for the first time.

Coach Wooden believed UCLA had a fine chance to take home the NCAA championship in 1950, but it wouldn't be easy. UCLA had made too many errors in the PCC Tournament. With only eight teams in the NCAA Tournament at the time, the Bruins would face the Bradley Braves in the first round. It was no match. UCLA played sloppy basketball from the tip, and though the team scored 59 points, it was not enough. UCLA turned the ball over far too many times, took too many bad shots, and made too many defensive errors. The Braves scored 73 and advanced to the semifinals. UCLA played for the third-place prize in the West Region but again struggled. BYU beat UCLA, 83–62. George Stanich was named to the All-Region team at the end of the tournament. UCLA's season ended in disappointment. In the school's first trip to the NCAA Tournament, the team lost in embarrassing fashion. The losses of 1950 would eventually be forgotten. UCLA's long relationship with the NCAA basketball tournament was just beginning. The Bruins finished the season ranked No. 5 in the country, the highest ranking in school history to that point.

City College of New York won the NCAA basketball national championship in 1950.

1950–51

UCLA's biggest challenge prior to the 1950–51 basketball season was not figuring out a way to improve upon the prior seasons results. It was not about going further in the tournament or winning more games. The first, and what proved to be the most important, challenge was to make the coach happy. John Wooden had been at UCLA for two years, and he was already the most successful coach in UCLA history. The Bruins had won a school record 22 games in 1949 and then won 24 in 1950. Other schools took notice. Wooden's alma mater, Purdue, wanted its favorite son to come home. The Boilermakers offered him substantially better contract to than the Bruins could afford to pay. Though Coach Wooden had signed a three-year contract, he was ready to leave one year early if he could gracefully get out of the final year of his deal. When approached by Coach Wooden, Athletic Director Wilbur Johns and Graduate Manager Bill Ackerman of the Associated Student organization reminded Coach Wooden he had one final year on his contract. Johns and Ackerman were sure Wooden would leave when his contract expired so they chose to increase his salary for the final year. This time, Coach Wooden reminded them of his commitment. He turned down the salary increase and coached the final season under the terms he had

Coach John Wooden, 1951 (Southern Branch Collection).

originally agreed to. Though there was uncertainty about Coach Wooden's future in Westwood, his family had grown to love California. At the end of the season, he decided he was there to stay. Bruins fans are forever thankful.

The success of the 1951 team was something almost unimaginable at UCLA just three years earlier, but now with raised expectations under Coach Wooden, it appeared to some as a step back. The Bruins were again quite good, finishing with the third most wins in a single season in UCLA history, only behind Coach Wooden's first two seasons. UCLA finished with an overall record of 19–10 and a 9–4 record in PCC play. The Bruins began the season by beating the Bruin Alumni squad by nearly 30 points and then beating nonconference foe Arizona State by exactly 30 in the next game. UCLA was inconsistent, however, for much of the early-season action. They beat Oregon by 22, but then lost by 18 to the same Webfoots team in the next game. They beat Santa Clara and San Jose State but then lost to a strong Bradley team and got blown out by Long Island and Iowa. There were few close games on the weird nonconference schedule in '50–'51. The Bruins were on the winning side and losing side of many blowouts.

Conference games finally were tight, however. The Bruins beat the California Golden Bears three out of four times, losing only in the first matchup, 62–60. UCLA took care of Stanford in each of the four

Eddie Sheldrake attempts a hook shot vs. Stanford, 1951 (Southern Branch Collection).

games, averaging 75 points per game. The Bruins and the Trojans played five times in 1951, more than the customary four matchups. While the Bruins offense clicked against Stanford all year, the games against USC were typically defensive battles. The first game was a wake-up call. The Trojans defense was smothering, and the Bruins only scored 34 points. USC beat UCLA by 19 points. The rest of the games would all be much closer. UCLA won two of the next three, and the final matchup was the deciding game of the PCC season. The Bruins beat USC, 49–41, and win the South Division of the PCC for the third year in a row.

UCLA's chances in the 1951 Pacific Coast Conference championship series were derailed by the flu. UCLA went north to take on the Washington Huskies, but leader Eddie Sheldrake and Art Alper were unable to play, and UCLA lost to the Huskies twice. The season was over. UCLA did not build on the success of the 1950 season in a definitive way on the court, but the season was still quite good. UCLA had won the South Division of the PCC for the third year in a row and won 19-plus games in each season.

University of Kentucky won the NCAA basketball national championship in 1951.

1951–52

In his fourth season, Coach Wooden hoped for a return trip to the NCAA Tournament. In three seasons, Coach Wooden's Bruins had won the South Division of the Pacific Coast Conference each season and would again be a very good team in '52. Every season has challenges, however, and nothing is easy. This was never more clear than in 1952.

For different periods in the history of UCLA basketball, freshmen were allowed to play on the varsity squad. In UCLA's first season in 1920, back when the university was still known as the Southern Branch, there were no students other than freshmen. During parts of World War II and during the Korean War, the NCAA allowed freshmen to compete on varsity. Coaches treated the authorization differently. Some chose not to play freshmen, knowing the rule was only temporary. Others played their best players, regardless of age. In 1951–52, UCLA leaned on freshmen like never before. Don Bragg, a freshman forward from San Francisco, and Johnny Moore, a center from Indiana, each started for much of the season and were key members of a very good squad.

No player was more of a challenge than Jerry Norman. Norman was a senior cocaptain, one of the best players in the Pacific Coast Conference, and he was what Coach Wooden called a "rebel." For four years, Norman and Coach Wooden were in a constant battle. Personally, Wooden liked Norman, but coaching him was often impossible. Coach Wooden described him as "very head-strong, set in his ways, and profane." Norman was dismissed from practice regularly for cursing, he would throw crosscourt passes that Coach Wooden warned him about, and he used the wrong hand on layup attempts, something that frustrated Wooden constantly. He was suspended multiple times during the season for failing to fix his cursing habit, but he was always a good teammate. He was unselfish, trusted others around him, and played hard. In 1952, the situation came together well for Norman. The good and the bad were always apparent, but with the help of his friend and teammate Eddie Sheldrake, the good finally outweighed the bad.

Don Johnson and Ron Livingston started in the backcourt, joined on the starting five with Bragg, Moore, and Norman. Johnson was a big, strong guard, while Livingston was smaller and faster. Both were ideal in Coach Wooden's mind, as they had versatility to direct the offense from either guard position.

The Bruins played a full 19-game nonconference schedule in 1952. In the opening game, the Bruins took on the UCLA Alumni squad and, once again, won handily. UCLA then crushed Arizona State by 29 points before taking on the two PCC foes from the state of Washington. Though the games against the University of Washington and Washington State University counted as nonconference affairs, the games had a psychological effect on the Bruins. After losing to both the Huskies and the Cougars, the Bruins could see that they were not the class of the PCC, at least not yet. UCLA would win 11 nonconference games, including wins over strong Saint Mary's and San Francisco teams. It would also lose to Illinois and Santa Clara and get crushed by the defending national champion Kentucky Wildcats.

UCLA began conference play with two games against the media favorite to win the South Division. In the opener, the Bruins crushed the Stanford Indians 81–63, but one night later, Stanford got its revenge and won a close game, 73–71. The Bruins of '52 were not dominant in conference play, but neither were the Indians, Bears, or Trojans. The key to the season would be peaking at the right time, and the Bruins did that. After splitting the opening two games, UCLA took both games against USC, but then lost two in a row to Cal. With a 3–3 conference record, the Bruins were seemingly treading water. In the next two games against Stanford, the teams again split the pair. With four games to go, the Bruins likely needed to win out to go to another conference championship series. The Bruins beat Cal, 67–54, then 68–52. In the final two games of conference play, UCLA beat USC by 15 points and then snuck by in a nerve-wracking six-point game against the Trojans. UCLA did indeed win those final four games and made the conference championship tournament for the fourth year in a row.

When UCLA went north to take on the Washington Huskies in the Pacific Coast Conference championship series, the players remembered the early-season loss to the Huskies. The Bruins had no problem with the Huskies in the first game, winning, 65–53, but the next night was much more difficult. The game was close, as UCLA's offense struggled for much of the night. When the clock hit :00, UCLA was on the wrong end of a 53–50 score. The Bruins would prove the next night, however, that the team

Jerry Norman goes up for a layup vs. Cal, 1952 (Southern Branch Collection).

was superior. In a game more like the first matchup than the second, the Bruins won, 60–50, and were off to the NCAA Tournament.

The second representation in the tournament in school history was unfortunately the same as the first. Prior to the first game, Don Bragg stumbled while getting out of the shower and broke his toe. He would be unavailable during the NCAA Tournament. It was a big blow for the Bruins, as the freshman Bragg was UCLA's top rebounder and second leading scorer. Santa Clara knocked off the Bruins, 68–59, and Oklahoma City beat the Bruins in a consolation game. The season was over, and though the end was disappointing, Coach Wooden had done a miraculous job. His team was young. He had to deal with a talented player who was often tough to coach. The team had to overcome injuries in the face of raised expectations. While many other successful seasons ultimately were remembered by Bruins for decades, the 1952 season was one of Coach Wooden's finest coaching jobs. He hoped to build off the success and carry the Bruins into a successful offseason.

University of Kansas won the NCAA basketball national championship in 1952.

1952–53

In Coach John Wooden's 27 seasons at UCLA, the 1953 team was perhaps his worst. Only once did the Bruins win as few as the 16 games won that season and never did a Wooden team have a conference record as poor as the 6–6 recorded in '53. The Bruins were the four-time defending South Division champions of the Pacific Coast Conference and twice had won the conference championship, but in Coach Wooden's fifth season, nothing worked. The team had poor on-court chemistry, and the expected improvements from the returning players from the '52 squad were unrealized. The team certainly was not bad, but Coach Wooden had achieved so much in his short tenure that Bruins fans expected more. While the UCLA football team was in the midst of its greatest period of glory, the Bruins ballers took a step back.

Looking back, one can see that the '53 season was not exactly normal. Oddly enough, the Bruins started the season in a fashion never before seen at UCLA: the team rattled off 10 consecutive wins to begin the season. They beat strong teams from out of conference and teams from the North Division of the PCC in games that didn't count toward the conference record. Four times UCLA beat Oregon State. The team also split a pair of games against the University of Washington and beat Bradley, Michigan State, and others. The only two losses in nonconference games came in the final two nonconference games, to Washington and Notre Dame.

The UCLA basketball program had a number of firsts when conference play began. After losing to Cal, 72–68, and then losing again to the Bears, 69–66, and dropping a game to the USC Trojans, 65–54, the Bruins had lost five games in a row, marking the first time a John Wooden team had lost five straight games. It was the first time, too, that the Bruins had lost three straight home games, as all three conference games were played at the Men's Gym, nicknamed the "BO Barn." It also was the beginning of the end of UCLA's four-season streak of winning the South Division of the PCC.

The Bruins would indeed fail to win the division crown, but the team didn't give up its title easily. After starting 0–3 in PCC play, the Bruins won the next four games. UCLA was not as strong as they had been, but during the winning streak, players made the right plays down the stretch and won close games. After beating USC by double digits, they beat Stanford by just one and then again by three and then beat Cal by four. The winning streak would end when the Bruins took on Cal for the fourth and final time, losing, 70–62, but UCLA then blew out Stanford two times before the final series of conference play. In that final series, UCLA lost twice to USC on the road and the season was over. The Bruins had lost three of four to Cal on the year, lost three of four to USC, and beat Stanford all four meetings. The season was not one that Coach Wooden and the Bruins would celebrate, but there was reason to be optimistic. The Bruins of '53 were young. They started the conference season slowly, but improved as the year went on to finish with an overall 16–8 record, not bad for Coach Wooden's worst season ever. The freshmen team had also been inconsistent during its season, but Coach Wooden was looking forward to several of the players joining varsity next year.

Indiana University won the NCAA basketball national championship in 1953.

1953–54

Coming off the disappointing season of 1953, Coach John Wooden entered his sixth season with something to prove. His success in Westwood was undeniable, but oftentimes coaches succeed early but are unable to continue winning. Coach Caddy Works won five conference titles in his first six years in the SCIAC. With the move to the Pacific Coast Conference, Works's winning days were gone. Wilbur Johns won the PCC once but finished with an overall record 27 games under .500. Wooden was not Works, however, nor was he Johns. The Bruins would not regain the form of 1950 or 1952 immediately, but the team was greatly improved from the prior year, even if the record showed only modest improvement.

Captain Ron "Doctor" Livingston led the team in '54. Although he had been a constant contributor in his first two seasons with the Bruins varsity, in '54 he took his game to new heights. At the conclusion of the season, he was UCLA's all-time leading scorer. Don Bragg also had a strong year. Though Livingston and Bragg led the Bruins most consistently, the '54 team was incredibly deep, and many players were the star of the day. Livingston's defense and clutch scoring against California and Bragg's 10-for-10 performance from the field against Oregon were memorable. So, too, was Willie Naulls's 16-point first half against USC. Hank Steinman led a second-half rally to beat Duke. Denny Miller scored 13 points against Stanford. Ed White shot 90 percent from the free-throw line for the year. John Moore scored 23 against Cal, 21 of which came in the second half. Ron Bane, Mark Costello, Morris Taft, Dick Ridgway, and Mike Hibler all performed well throughout the year.

UCLA head coach John Wooden and assistant coach Doug Sale, 1954 (Southern Branch Collection).

After finishing 10–2 in nonconference play one year earlier, the Bruins went 11–2 in 1954. The season, like all early years, would be about conference play. After finishing just 6–6 in the conference the year prior, the Bruins looked for a bounce-back season, but things didn't start well. UCLA lost both of its opening matchups with the California Golden Bears and then lost to USC at Loyola Gym. In the second game against USC, the Bruins looked to be on the way to 0–4 in the conference, but Naulls's big game sparked a Bruins win. After defeating USC, 81–63, the Bruins found their rhythm, especially on offense. UCLA played fast, outscoring every opponent. The team scored 92 against Stanford and then 77 the next night, winning both. The Bruins beat Cal twice in the rematch series, scoring 82 and then 71. When UCLA took on Stanford for the second series of the year, it again beat the opponent twice, putting up big numbers (averaging 90 per game). With two games left against USC, the Bruins had to win just one to clinch the division title. In the first game, however, USC smashed UCLA by double digits. The next night, the game was much closer, but Roy Irwin and the Trojans outlasted Livingston and the Bruins, 69–67. UCLA lost the division race by one game, and the season was over. It was a heartbreaking way to end the year.

La Salle University won the NCAA basketball national championship in 1954.

1954–55

While the Bruins basketball players prepared for what would turn out to be a strong basketball season, Bruins fans had their eyes on their other favorite Westwood team. The 1954 UCLA football team was the greatest in school history. Led by the great Red Sanders, the Bruins had the number-one offense and number-one defense in the country. UCLA finished

Johnny Moore vs. Cal, 1954 (Southern Branch Collection).

the football season undefeated and was named national champion by the United Press International poll. In the Associated Press poll, UCLA finished No. 2 despite its perfect record. The poll ranked Ohio State, which also finished undefeated, No. 1. At the time, the UPI and the AP polls were the two significant ones, and both teams would forever be considered 1954 national champion. In a later time, a situation such as this would have been settled on the field. The polls chose the national champion before the bowl games were played, and one of the greatest potential games of all time was thwarted by another rule. The no-repeat rule barred teams from participating in the Rose Bowl in back-to-back years, so UCLA was ineligible to play in the game. UCLA and Ohio State had two opponents that appeared on each of their schedules, Cal and USC, and UCLA beat both by a wider margin than the Buckeyes.

Despite the euphoria over the football team, fans would continue to feel joy about basketball if UCLA could once again dominate opponents. Coach Wooden's accomplishments were remarkable considering the state of UCLA basketball before his arrival. Fans trusted Wooden and hoped that the '55 season, his seventh, would be one of the best yet in school history.

The UCLA team had a wealth of talent, and it showed. Don Bragg finished the season as UCLA's second all-time leading scorer, with over 1,000 points scored. John Moore, from Gary, Indiana, was the leading scorer for the season, averaging 13.6 points per game. Junior Willie Naulls set a PCC record with 163 total rebounds on the season. Morris Taft, Ronnie Bane, Mark Costello, and a handful of younger players all were great contributors at times for the '55 Bruins.

The Bruins began the season with an impressive nonconference showing, routing Kansas State by 29 points in the season opener. The team then crushed Santa Clara by 35 and beat the University of San Francisco, 47–40, in New York City. The great center Bill Russell led the Dons. With the guidance of head coach Phil Woolpert and the All-America play of Russell, the Dons did not lose another game all season; at the end of the year, that team won the national championship.

UCLA ran through much of its schedule with relative ease. When nonconference play ended, the Bruins were clearly better than the team had been the previous two years. In conference play, that belief was solidified. After losing to Stanford in the first game by five points, UCLA beat Stanford the next night by 16. They beat USC twice in a row and then beat Cal twice, 83–64 and 84–63. Then they beat Stanford 85–63 and again 72–59. UCLA then blew out Cal two more times and beat USC twice more to run its winning streak to 11 straight games. For the fifth time in the last seven years, UCLA won the South Division of the PCC and headed to the championship series. Despite the brilliant season thus far, the Bruins' luck would not continue in the postseason. Oregon State, led by "Big Swede" Halbrook, swept UCLA, winning by seven and then 19. UCLA's season was over. Through seven years, John Wooden's record at UCLA was now 139–56. UCLA's best season yet was one year away.

University of San Francisco won the NCAA basketball national championship in 1955.

1955–56

Coming off a South Division title in 1955, during no other season in UCLA history to that point were fans more optimistic about the prospects of their basketball season. Coach Wooden had proven his worth, and the team was certainly on an upward swing. UCLA athletics were in a time of glory, as the football team was in the midst of the finest three-year stretch in school history and the '56 Bruin basketball team had its finest year to that point.

The offseason was actually one of considerable intrigue. Those on the outside believed the team would be quite good, but the loss of key players from the year before led to many questions, and players were tasked with greatly improving their own individual skills in the offseason. The feelings of fans were based not primarily on remaining personnel but on trust in Coach Wooden, which solidified in the 1955 season. Many new names joined the roster. Carroll Adams, Jack Arnold, Dick Banton, Conrad Burke, Bill Eblen, Jim Halsten, Allen Herring, Art Hutchins, Willie Naulls, Ben Rogers, and Morris Taft were roster mainstays. Bruins fans may have forgotten many of the players, with the exception of Naulls, but the team was the greatest in UCLA history to that point.

The PCC schedule reflected an important change for the '56 season. Since joining the PCC 28 years before, UCLA played primarily against just three schools—USC, California, and Stanford. In '56, the PCC still had North and South Divisions, but teams in both would play all teams in the conference during the regular season.

In nonconference play, the Bruins struggled early. In the season-opening two-game series against BYU, the Bruins were twice defeated, losing by 17 and then by two. UCLA then won two in a row over Denver and Purdue but lose twice more after that. The Bruins defeated St. John's and Duquesne but then lost to defending national champion University of San Francisco in the final nonconference game. The two would meet again.

UCLA took on a North Division foe in the first game of conference play in '56. After crushing Idaho in both meetings, the Bruins had a winning streak, and it wouldn't end any time soon. UCLA was the cream of the crop in the PCC, and few were even able to keep close with the Bruins. The team crushed Washington State twice and beat Washington, Stanford, Oregon State, Oregon, Cal, and USC twice. Only three times were opponents able to stay within 10 points of the Bruins, with the closest game being a 61–60 victory over the University of Washington. Willie Naulls kept the Bruins' perfect conference record alive with a tip in at the buzzer for the win. In UCLA's 16–0 conference season, the Bruins won by an average of 14 points and scored an average of 89 points. The team was truly a juggernaut.

At the conclusion of the perfect conference season, the team advanced to the NCAA Tournament for the third time in Coach Wooden's eight seasons. What UCLA had done under Wooden was remarkable. It

Morris Taft vs. Idaho, 1956 (Southern Branch Collection).

Teammates celebrate with Willie Naulls after he made the game-winning basket at the buzzer against Washington, 1956 (Southern Branch Collection).

had won the South Division of the PCC six times and won the PCC three times. The team still had goals to reach, however, that had never been done before at UCLA. After losing to Bill Russell and the USF Dons over two months earlier, UCLA was to play the University of San Francisco again.

After losing only one game, at the hands of the Bruins, en route to a national championship the year prior, the Dons were perfect in '56. While Russell would be forever remembered in USF lore, he was not alone. Complimenting Russell was K. C. Jones and a very balanced team. Though USF had crushed the Bruins by 17 in the earlier meeting, the Bruins were understandably confident, riding a 16-game winning streak. The game ended up being a dud. USF jumped out to an early lead, and though the Bruins remained in striking distance, UCLA was never able to close the gap completely. When the final seconds ticked off, the Bruins' chances at a championship were over. Though the team played a regional third-place game against Seattle University and won, the tournament was a disappointment. With the expansion of the tournament to 25 teams, there was added interest in postseason college basketball, but the Bruins were unable to take advantage of the new system. The '56 team was one to remember at UCLA, but the squad ran into a buzzsaw and fell to a much better team.

University of San Francisco won the NCAA basketball national championship in 1956.

1956–57

Coming off a season in which the Bruins finished with a perfect 16–0 conference record and won more than 20 games for just the fourth time in school history, the glass-half-empty fans had to remind the glass-half-full fans that it was just one year. Yes, under Coach John Wooden, the Bruins had reached levels of success they had only dreamed of before his arrival, but they still had yet to win an opening-round NCAA Tournament game. A national championship still seemed distant. Coach Wooden and the Bruins would have to prove themselves every single year.

The '57 Bruins had a solid mix of players. At guard, Dick Banton led the way. Banton averaged 14.1 points per game, good for tops on the team, and 7.0 rebounds per game, second behind his backcourt mate, Walt Torrence, who averaged 7.1. Along with his strong rebounding, Torrence averaged 12.3 points per game, as well. Jim Halsten and Ben Rogers were the other two players who averaged double-digit scoring, averaging 10.8 points per game each. UCLA was loaded with depth. Coach Wooden would have a larger rotation than in many years, and 10 Bruins saw significant time during the season.

After a 9–0 nonconference season, the Bruins began Pacific Coast Conference action against the Idaho Vandals. With roughly 3,500 fans in attendance for each game, the Bruins and Vandals played two thrillers in back-to-back nights. In game one, UCLA fell behind early and played from behind for much of the game. With less than nine minutes to play, the Bruins ramped up their already aggressive full-court defense and started to cut into the Vandal lead. Due to the rampant pace of play and the turnovers UCLA forced, the Bruins climbed back from a 14-point deficit. Art Hutchins and Dick Banton were the main cogs in the comeback. With just 40 seconds left, Banton tied the game at 59. In overtime, Walt Torrence was the key. Though it would take a second overtime, Banton, Hutchins, Torrence, and the Bruins came out on top: UCLA 64, Idaho 63. As frustrating as the end result was for the Vandals in game one, so too it was for the Bruins in game two. This time the game was close throughout, but the Vandals made the big shots down the stretch, beating the Bruins by one point, 69–68. Luckily for the Bruins, only the first game counted against the conference record, as the second matchup was scheduled as a nonconference game ahead of time.

When UCLA took on Washington State in the second series of the season, there was much less

Coach John Wooden, 1957 (Southern Branch Collection).

drama. In both games, the Bruins jumped out to big leads and played many backups in the second half. The same could be said about the games against Oregon State. Though they were lower scoring, the results were the same. UCLA beat OSU, 59–37, and then 64–53. The 37 points scored by OSU in game one was the least scored by any Bruin opponent in eight years. Next, the Bruins went to Seattle to take on a strong Huskies team in an intimidating environment. Edmondson Pavilion was large, and the fans were always rowdy. Over ten thousand fans showed up for each game, and they were a difference maker. In the first game, however, the Bruins dealt with the elements and came out on top. Nolan Johnson played his best game of the season, leading the Bruins' second-half surge. UCLA won, 68–64, and with the win, ran its PCC winning streak to 23 games, the longest in conference history. The streak bested the one put together by the Washington Huskies from 1943 to 1944. The Bruins' streak would not be extended, however. The next night, the Huskies shot extraordinarily well from the field and crushed the Bruins, 90–74.

Though UCLA would continue to play well throughout the rest of conference play, there was no room for error, as the conference was extremely strong. UCLA beat Stanford in both their meetings, despite 50 fouls called in the first game. They beat Oregon twice on famed McArthur Court. With four games to play, the Bruins likely needed to go 4–0 to win the PCC again, but they were playing two very good teams. In the opening matchup with USC, the Bruins' defense again failed. Despite scoring 80 points, they gave up 84 and lost. Banton, the Bruins' senior leader, played his best game of the season the next night as UCLA avenged the defeat, and then they would split the two matchups with California, but that was not enough. The Bruins finished the season with an overall record of 22–4 and a conference record of 13–3, for the third consecutive season winning 20-plus total games and 10-plus conference games. In 1958, the Bruins would have many questions to answer and many holes to fill.

University of North Carolina won the NCAA basketball national championship in 1957.

1957–58

The 1958 UCLA yearbook described the basketball season best: "The 1958 basketball season was a slightly disappointing one as gauged by past Bruin cage marks, but the team hustled all the way and did end up with a 16–10 record to keep Coach John Wooden's string of winning seasons intact. His clubs

UCLA Spirit Squad, 1958 (Southern Branch Collection).

have never had a losing year in his ten seasons at Westwood." The season was a disappointment, but Coach Wooden and the Bruins were still steady, solid, and in the race for the PCC crown for the entirety of the season.

Whereas the '57 team was deep, the talented '58 team lacked depth. Only six players saw significant playing time. At 6'6", Ben Rogers was the tallest man on the team. He started at center and led the team in scoring. Walt Torrence was back, and he had another strong season. Jim Halsten contributed double-digit scoring for the season, and Roland Underhill, Conrad Burke, and Denny Crum each played significant minutes. Denny Miller and Rafer Johnson did not see much time throughout the year, but in the final games and throughout the practice season, they showed great potential. Miller was back at UCLA after two years in the military and Johnson would try his hand at basketball while juggling his other athletic exploits. The Bruins would only average 65.2 points per game, and the offense was not of typical Wooden fashion. Still, the team won its share of games and could have won even more.

The Bruins played only 10 nonconference games all season, and in the first two weeks, things appeared to be going well. UCLA started 4–0, but then lost four straight. The Bruins would win their final two nonconference games to finish with a 6–4 record. When conference play began, the Bruins played well enough to remain in the hunt.

UCLA began conference play in Eugene, Oregon, against the Oregon Webfoots on Friday, January 3. Despite falling behind early and trailing at halftime, the Bruins came back to beat the home team, 64–58. One week later, when Oregon traveled to Los Angeles for the second game, the result was the same. Despite the hot shooting from Oregon, UCLA held on and swept the season series. UCLA then took on Idaho and again came out on top. The Bruins at times appeared ready to dominate the PCC again, but particular losses made fans think the team wasn't ready. The Bruins beat USC twice, including a 52–51 win in which Torrence stole the ball and scored in the final seconds to win. The Bruins beat Washington State and Washington twice each and also beat a very strong California team by two points. But UCLA lost to Cal and Stanford and twice was beaten by Oregon State. Idaho beat UCLA behind 37 points from sharpshooter Gary Simmons. Ultimately, the season ended with immense frustration, and for the first time, and arguably the only time, a John Wooden-coached team seemingly could have been better. The Bruins finished with a 16–10 overall record and a 10–6 conference mark.

University of Kentucky won the NCAA basketball national championship in 1958.

1958–59

Prior to the 1958–59 UCLA basketball season, tragedy struck the UCLA athletic department. Despite Wooden's success, the most popular coach in Westwood in 1958 was Red Sanders. Coach Sanders was actually the original "Wizard of Westwood," earning the nickname because of the brilliant success of the Bruins football program in the 1950s. In August 1958, Red and the Bruins were preparing for the start of a new season. The team had finished the previous season with an 8–2 record and was gearing up for another shot at the PCC crown and the national title. At 4:30 p.m. on August 14, 1958, shocking news hit radio and television sets everywhere: Red Sanders was dead. Complaining of the heat and humidity in his hotel room on Beverly Boulevard, Red had asked a friend of his, W. T. Grimes, to grab him a refreshment. When Grimes returned, he found a nonresponsive, shirtless Sanders lying on the floor motionless. When Grimes had walked out, Sanders grasped for air and clutched his chest, succumbing to a massive heart attack. Though unknown at the time, Red had an enlarged heart, nearly twice the size of what is considered normal. Scar tissue also indicated long-standing heart disease. His heart was a ticking time bomb, and when his time ran out, UCLA and the college football community lost one of the greatest coaches of all time at only 53 years old. Replacing him was an impossible task. Following the death of Sanders, George Dickerson was named the next Bruins head coach, but his time would be short. In August, he was hospitalized for nervous exhaustion. He would return to work, but three weeks into the football season, he could handle no more, and Bill Barnes, a man who would become a friend to Coach Wooden, was named the new head coach. The glory days of UCLA football were over.

Coming off a 16–10 season, few knew what to expect in '58–'59. The Bruins could bounce back to top form, or this could be the new norm—solid, yet unspectacular. The team turned out to be remarkably similar to the team of one year prior. The Bruins finished 6–4 in nonconference play in '58, and in '59, they finished 6–3. For the second season in a row, the Bruins finished with a 10–6 conference record in third place in the PCC. A number of moments are worth recognizing, however.

The Bruins beat the Oregon Webfoots in both matchups, once in Eugene and once in Los Angeles at the Pan Pacific Auditorium. Walt Torrence was the star against the Webfoots, scoring 26 in the first matchup. Oregonians said of the two games against the Bruins, "There was just too much Torrence." For many of the PCC members, there was too much Torrence. In his senior season, Torrence went out in brilliant fashion. He led the Pacific Coast Conference in scoring, racking up a total of 537 points (21.5 points per game), third most in a single season in UCLA history to that point and leading the PCC in '59. His marvelous senior season earned him unanimous All-PCC recognition at the end of the year.

Against Idaho, the Bruins won the early-season matchup, but fell late in the year. The loss to the Vandals in Los Angeles came in the midst of the worst stretch of the season for UCLA, in which they lost four consecutive games. Although the losing streak ultimately doomed UCLA's chances at the PCC crown, the five-game winning streak later in the season salvaged what had been a disappointing year. Included in the winning streak were wins over Colorado, Oregon State, and USC, each swept by the Bruins. While UCLA finished with a mediocre 16–9 record, it proved it could play with nearly every team on the schedule; UCLA just lacked consistency. Saint Mary's, which beat UCLA in the season opener; Santa

UCLA forward Rafer Johnson scores against the Idaho Vandals, 1959 (Southern Branch Collection).

UCLA forward Rafer Johnson soars to the basket against Washington, 1959 (Southern Branch Collection).

Clara, which bested the Bruins early in the season; and the brilliant California Golden Bears were the only teams on UCLA's schedule that UCLA failed to beat at least once.

The 1950s was the greatest decade in UCLA football and UCLA basketball history to that point. On the gridiron, the football team won more games than any previous decade and also won its lone national championship. In the 1950s, John Wooden had brought success to Westwood that was never before seen in basketball. Though the end of the decade closed with a bit of a lull, the 1960s would bring success that is still almost unimaginable to this day.

University of California won the NCAA basketball national championship in 1959.

1959–60

For the entirety of the history of the UCLA basketball program, the Bruins never had a gym to call their own. They played at high schools and public gyms, at the Westwood Gym and Pan Pacific. In 1959–60, the Bruins again had a new place to play their home games, and it was right in enemy territory. When Coach Wooden chose to come to UCLA over a decade earlier, he was told that UCLA would upgrade its facilities. The process became very frustrating. Instead of opening a new gym on campus, the Bruins now played their home games in the new gym on USC's campus. The Los Angeles Sports Arena was brand new, and UCLA and USC shared the arena, much to Coach Wooden's dismay. Though the Sports Arena has come to be the butt of jokes about poor facilities, it was once a splendid basketball facility, surely an upgrade over what UCLA had played in every season for the previous four decades.

Changing the Bruins' home gym was not the only major change in 1959–60. The Pacific Coast Conference was no more. A pay-for-play scandal in football, involving UCLA, USC, Stanford, California, and others had been exposed. The process after the scandal, not the punishment itself, ultimately led to the demise of the PCC. Both the Bruins and the Trojans had dominated the football scene on the West Coast throughout the 1950s, and when news of the scandal continually seeped to the public, most all in Southern California had the same view of the scandal: it was a witch hunt. The Bruins and the Trojans were guilty of relatively minor infractions, no more than any other member of the conference was, but they were punished severely, while the others weren't. Finally, they had enough. Along with Cal, the Bruins and the Trojans led the push to create a new conference. In fall of 1959, the Athletic Association of Western Universities was officially formed. Only five teams—UCLA, USC, Cal, Stanford, and Washington—made up the conference. Three years later, Washington State joined, and two years after that Oregon and Oregon State joined. In 1968, the conference changed its name to the Pacific-8 conference. Eventually the scandal was forgotten, and the current Pac-12 Conference has absorbed the defunct PCC into its record books.

The drama off the court was much more interesting than the Bruins product on the court. The Bruins finished with less wins than in any other season in Coach Wooden's tenure at UCLA. They would tie the 1952 Bruins for most losses by a Wooden-coached team. They never could quite get on track, as they were an extremely young team, the most inexperienced team of Wooden's tenure so far. The only senior, "Clever" Cliff Brandon, averaged just 4.4 points per game, though he was an excellent defensive guard. Guard John Green led the team in scoring at just 10.2 PPG. The Bruins rotation was ever-changing, as Coach Wooden tried to find the right combination to win more games. The Bruins played a plethora of sophomores and was inconsistent for the entirety of the season.

After beating USC in the season opener to officially open the Sports Arena, the Bruins faced a Kentucky Wildcats team that had come west, and head coach Baron Adolph Rupp was the coach everyone thought to be the best in college basketball. Coach Wooden's team would play well, however, and the game would come down to the wire. At halftime, the Bruins led, 34–28, and held the lead until, with 5:59 remaining in the game, Don Mills knocked down a shot to put Kentucky ahead. The game would continue to go back and forth, and with under a minute to play, the score was tied at 66. Sid Cohen, a Brooklyn boy playing for the Wildcats, hit the go-ahead shot, and the Wildcats held on to win by a bucket. Bill Ellis was the top performer for the Bruins, scoring 20 points, while Kent Miller grabbed 15 rebounds. The Bruins were 1–1 on the season.

Many nail-biters like the Kentucky game happened during the season; more so than in years past, the Bruins were unable to pull out a victory. In non-conference play, the Bruins finished with just seven wins in 14 games. UCLA, USC, Cal, Stanford, West Virginia, Illinois, Northwestern, and Michigan all played in a December tournament held at the Sports Arena. In the L.A. Classic Tournament, the Bruins were up and down. After winning two opening-round games, the Bruins lost to West Virginia, led by Jerry West, and Cal. In the third-place game, USC beat UCLA, and the tournament was a disappointment for the cohost Bruins.

In conference action, the Bruins took on Washington in the first two games of the season, and both came down to the final minute. On January 2, the Bruins beat the Huskies, 57–55. Sophomore John Green led the way with 15 points. Two days later, the two-point margin was cut to one. The Bruins won, 55–54, overcoming a double-digit deficit in the final nine minutes. Kent Miller scored the game-winning basket for the Bruins and then blocked the last-ditch

UCLA vs. USC, 1960 (Southern Branch Collection).

shot for the Huskies at the buzzer. The Bruins were 2–0 in the conference. UCLA then lost to Cal but bounced back to beat USC and then beat Stanford twice to start 5–1 in conference play. But soon the bottom fell out. Coach Wooden relied on young players who seemingly hit a wall. The Bruins lost four out of their next five, with the only win coming in blowout fashion, 48–19 over the Stanford Indians. Though UCLA won the last game over USC, it was not enough. The Bruins finished in second place in the AAWU with a 7–5 conference record. They finished just 14–12 overall. Beginning in 1961, UCLA would ride an escalator to the top of the college basketball world. It has since only won 14 games or fewer three times, the next not coming for another 42 years.

Ohio State University won the NCAA basketball national championship in 1960.

1960–61

The Bruins had a lot to prove in '61, and so did their coach. After winning just 14 games the year prior, would UCLA continue the downward trend? Could the team find its winning ways again? Coach Wooden dug deep to answer these questions himself. He looked at what had gone wrong the previous season and wrestled with ideas of how to correct what held UCLA back in the past. He reconfigured the UCLA conditioning program, as he felt many of his recent teams faded as the season went on. He looked at substitution patterns as well. Though he always played his starters the vast majority of minutes, he knew that injuries, foul difficulties, and unexpected poor results would force his hand at times. One example of a way that Coach Wooden changed the practice norms was in five-on-five scrimmaging. In prior years, Coach Wooden always split the first team against the second team. In 1960–61, he began splitting them up by mixing starters with nonstarters. With 15 members on the team, five on the side shot free throws while the other 10 scrimmaged. Rather than simply shooting on their own, however, Coach Wooden changed the way they practiced, as well. One player shot free throws at a time; when he made a predetermined number of them, he moved near Coach Wooden. At the next stoppage of play, he would rotate in. Thus UCLA players became accustomed to playing with every teammate, and the practice also helped UCLA at the free-throw line and in the midrange game, as there was more incentive for them to get a high number of shots up in practice.

Coach Wooden analyzed every aspect of his prior teams and reset the program. While many of his new drills and philosophies helped improve the team, a great amount of talent was on the team. Gary Cunningham, the junior forward, was named to the All-AAWU team, and earned honorable mention All-America honors. John Berberich joined Cunningham on the All-AAWU team and was the Bruins' leading rebounder. Ron Lawson, just a sophomore, led the Bruins in scoring, averaging nearly 14 points per game. John Green averaged 12.5 PPG, and senior Bill Ellis contributed solidly on both ends of the floor.

For the second season in a row, UCLA and USC hosted an early-season basketball tournament. From December 28 through December 30, the Los Angeles Basketball Classic pitted the two Los Angeles schools, as well as Cal, Indiana, Iowa, Michigan State, Minnesota, and Stanford, against one another. Indiana, led by All-American Walt Bellamy, was the favorite in the single-elimination tournament, but when they faced the Bruins in the semifinal, it proved no competition. Berberich outplayed Bellamy, and the Bruins outplayed the Hoosiers: UCLA 94, Indiana 72. While the Bruins represented Los Angeles well, USC didn't do the same in its semifinal. After losing to Iowa, the Trojans beat Indiana in the third-place game, and the Bruins took on the Hawkeyes in the championship. While offense wasn't an issue against Indiana, nor was it against Iowa in the first half, it was a problem in the second half for the Bruins. UCLA went cold, and Don Nelson and Iowa did enough to overcome a halftime deficit. The final score was 71–65, Iowa.

Throughout the nonconference season, the Bruins were generally strong, but they were not perfect. The team finished with 11 wins and three losses before beginning AAWU play. In the conference opener, UCLA traveled to Seattle to take on the University of Washington Huskies. The two teams played on back-to-back nights; UW won the opener, and UCLA won the next night. Late in the season, the two met again, and though the game was close early, Cunningham and Ellis took over late, and the Bruins won by a comfortable margin. The Bruins beat a poor California team twice at the Sports Arena, but a late-season loss to the Bears in Berkeley was a heartbreaker. The game itself was disappointing, as Cal won, 66–65, despite a brilliant performance by Cunningham. The loss made it almost impossible for UCLA to win the conference, and ultimately it fell just short. The Bruins took two out of three against Stanford. Had the Bruins not lost to California in upset fashion in their final meeting, UCLA would have only needed to beat USC once in the final three games to win the conference. Instead, it needed two, and USC was a very good team. The two teams split the first two games, and the final game went down to the wire. After the end of regulation, the score was tied, and in overtime, USC came out on top, winning by just one point and winning the AAWU crown. UCLA's season was over, and though it ended in great disappointment and the team missed the NCAA Tournament for the fifth consecutive season, the season was a major improvement from the prior year. The Bruins finished with an 18–8 record, the most wins since 1957.

University of Cincinnati won the NCAA basketball national championship in 1961.

1961–1962

In 1961–62, Walt Hazzard joined the UCLA basketball program, marking the beginning of what was one of the greatest stretches in the history of college athletics. For the previous five seasons, the Bruins failed to win a single conference title and were left out of the NCAA Tournament in each year. Coach Wooden had been at UCLA for 13 years and six times won a conference title. With the addition of Hazzard, the Bruins expected to win titles once again. Though only a sophomore, the 6'2" guard contributed immediately, scoring 13.2 points per game and grabbing nearly six rebounds per game. All-American John Green was Hazzard's backcourt mate, and he led the Bruins in scoring, averaging 19.3 PPG. Gary Cunningham and Pete Blackman held down the two forward spots, with each averaging in double figures. Starting at center was Fred Slaughter, who averaged a tick under 10 rebounds per game.

Coming into the season, preseason prognosticators believed the Bruins were the fourth-best team in the five-team Athletic Association of Western Universities Conference. Early on, Bruins doubters seemed right. UCLA started extremely slowly. In the season opener on December 1, the Bruins took on BYU in Smith Fieldhouse in Provo and lost by two points, 68–66. One night later, the team lost again to BYU in another close game: BYU 86, UCLA 83. Though UCLA beat Kansas and DePauw University at the Sports Arena, it dropped a game to Colorado State and then dropped two in a row on the road to Creighton and Houston. When the Bruins returned to Los Angeles for the holidays, they beat Texas A&M to run their record to 3–5 before the start of the third annual Los Angeles Classic.

In the L.A. Classic, the Bruins opened with Army. The cadets from West Point couldn't keep up, and the Bruins began with a win. Cunningham scored 21 for the Bruins and Dave Waxman added 15. The next game was not as easy, however. On December 28, the Bruins took on the No. 1-ranked team in the country, the Ohio State Buckeyes. Though UCLA played well on offense, its defense struggled. UCLA shot 49 percent from the field,

UCLA vs. BYU, 1962 (Southern Branch Collection).

aided by 23 points from Blackman and 22 from Cunningham. The biggest star on this day was not a Bruin, however. It was a Buckeye. All-American Jerry Lucas scored 30 points and grabbed 30 rebounds. The final score was Ohio State 105, UCLA 84. One day later, in the third-place game, the script was nearly identical. All-American Billy McGill scored 29 points and had 24 rebounds for Utah, and the Bruins fell again. UCLA was just 4–7 and the season looked anything but special.

Following a short holiday break, the Bruins returned to the hardwood on January 5 for conference play. UCLA took on the University of Washington at the Sports Arena and twice won in comfortable fashion. In the first game of the conference season, Cunningham led all scorers with 21 points. One night later, Green scored 29, and the Bruins swept the first AAWU matchup. While December was frustrating, January was exhilarating. The Bruins played their finest basketball in years, and the results showed in the standings. The Bruins followed up their two wins over UW with a win over Cal, and two wins in nonconference play over Texas Tech at Santa Monica City College gym. UCLA finished the month of January with a 5–0 record, winning by an average of 19 points per game. February was not as easy, however, as the schedule was much more difficult.

On February 2, UCLA took on the No. 5 University of Southern California Trojans. The game was a mismatch. UCLA blew out USC, winning by 14 points to remain perfect in conference play. UCLA then trounced the Stanford Indians by 18 points before setting the stage for a rematch with the Trojans. Against USC, the script was flipped from just two weeks earlier—the Trojans beat the Bruins handily. One night later, the two crosstown rivals met again, in the third and decisive meeting in the season series. UCLA got off to a horrendous start and trailed by double digits early. The Bruins kept plugging along, however, and by halftime, they had clawed back in the game. In the second half, UCLA took the lead, but it would not hold for the rest of the way. The lead changed hands multiple times, but with 2:40 left to play, John Green's layup put the Bruins ahead for good, and they went on to win, 69–62. Every UCLA starter scored double digits.

Coach John Wooden, 1962 (Southern Branch Collection).

Following the win over USC, clinching the AAWU title was a mere matter of time. UCLA won four of its final five games, dropping only a game on the road at Stanford Pavilion. After starting the season with just a 4–7 record, the Bruins finished with a 16–9 regular season mark, 10–2 in conference play, and won the AAWU Conference.

UCLA accepted an invitation to the NCAA Tournament, one of 25 teams to participate. UCLA was slotted in the West region, and after Utah State beat Arizona State in the regional quarterfinals, the Bruins, after a first-round bye, took on Utah State in the semifinals. Against USU, the UCLA was the clearly superior team, but it almost blew a chance to advance. After leading by 16, the Bruins let their guard down, and soon the entire lead evaporated. Jarred, UCLA put its foot back on the gas and cruised to an 11-point win. In the regional finals against Oregon State, UCLA got off to a similar strong start but never let up. Their fast-break offense was too much for the Beavers, and UCLA won 88–69.

With the two tournament wins, the Bruins were in a place they had not been before: the Final Four. The national semifinal pitted the Bruins against the defending national champion University of Cincinnati. The game was played at Freedom Hall in Louisville, Kentucky, and 18,274 fans saw one of the best games of the year. Like they had done against USC earlier in the year, the Bruins got off to an inexplicably slow start, trailing 18–4 early. The Bruins climbed back methodically, however. After fully erasing the deficit, Coach Wooden and the Bruins needed to finish the job. The game was close coming down to the wire. Green scored 27 for the Bruins, Cunningham scored 19, and Hazzard added 12 points. Paul Hogue, who scored 36 points and pulled down 19 rebounds for the Bearcats, was the best man on the court. With the score tied at 70 with 10 seconds to play, Cincinnati had the ball, and Hogue was the obvious go-to man. It would not be easy to get him the ball, however, as UCLA knew that Hogue was the likely target. *Sports Illustrated*'s Ray Cave described the final sequence: "Cincinnati couldn't manage [getting the ball to Hogue], however, so it tried the first option off the play. [Tom] Thacker drove to the right side, jumped and sank a 25-footer with three seconds left. Thacker is not a good outside shot. He had missed all six shots he had taken up to that point. Yet he made the one that mattered—which is what Cincinnati has done all year." It was an unlikely end result to a fantastic game, and for UCLA, it was unfortunate. There would be no national championship in 1962. That would have to wait. One night later, UCLA lost the third-place game to Wake Forest, and the season was over.

University of Cincinnati was the winner of the NCAA basketball national championship in 1962.

1962–63

The 1962–63 season was much like the season before. A new player would come along: guard Gail Goodrich. Although he wasn't the Bruins star in his first season on varsity, he left a lasting legacy with the Bruins recognized by generations of fans. Like the prior season, the Bruins of '62–'63 would not be dominant, but they would be highly successful. After finishing fourth in the country in '62, many questions had to be answered in '63. All-American John Green was gone, as was Gary Cunningham. Stepping up would be junior Walt Hazzard, who led the team with 16.3 points per game. Fred Slaughter, Jack Hirsch, and Gail Goodrich each averaged between 10.4 and 10.9 PPG, as well. The Bruins were not as deep as the year before, but Coach Wooden worked with the team he had. The season began on November 30, and it would again be a memorable one for the fans in Westwood.

The 1963 season would be one of the most improbable seasons in UCLA history. The Bruins began their season by whipping the University of Denver Pioneers by nearly 30 points at the Los Angeles Sports Arena. They then beat Santa Clara by 25 before taking to the road for the first trip of the season. Unfortunately, UCLA did not have the same success on the road. They lost a pair of games in the state of Colorado, one to the Buffaloes in Boulder and then to the Rams in Fort Collins. After the disappointment, UCLA returned home to play its finest ball of the season. The Bruins crushed Oklahoma, 101–64, at the Santa Monica City College gym and then beat Missouri in convincing fashion one night later. The Bruins then continued their fine play when they went on their second road trip of the season, this time in the Midwest. UCLA beat Butler by 18 in Indianapolis, Northwestern by seven in Evanston, and Wisconsin by 14 in Madison.

With a five-game winning streak, the Bruins once again took part in the Los Angeles Classic. On December 26, the Bruins faced off against Utah State at the Sports Arena. The first ten minutes were close, as the teams appeared evenly matched, but UCLA made a run before half and jumped out to a 16-point lead at the break. In the second half, the Aggies made a run of its own, and the Bruins lead was cut to five. Following a timeout by Coach Wooden, UCLA scored four straight baskets, one each by Jim Milhorn and Slaughter, and two by Hazzard. The Bruins cruised the rest of the way to win by 14. UCLA had no trouble in the second game of the tournament. St. Louis University played a physical brand of basketball, but despite the rough tactics used against them, the Bruins' superior skill was the deciding factor. Milhorn once again played well for UCLA, as did Hazzard and Jack Hirsch. UCLA won, 85–66, and advanced to the championship game of the tournament, a rematch against the Colorado State Rams, which just three weeks earlier beat UCLA on the road by a single point. UCLA had a balanced scoring attack, as Hazzard led the team with just 10 points. Bill Green was the leading scorer for CSU, netting 17, but UCLA came out on top, 68–64.

The Bruins' record stood at 10–2 when 1962 turned to 1963 and nonconference play turned to conference action. Following the win in the L.A. Classic, the Associated Press ranked UCLA No. 9. The Bruins would not stay ranked long, however. On New Year's Day, the Bruins took on the University of Washington in Seattle. UCLA only connected on 25 percent of its field-goal attempts in the AAWU opener but hung around for much of the game. When the final seconds ticked off the clock, UW had defeated UCLA by one point, 62–61. Four days later, the teams met again, and the result was nearly identical. UCLA shot poorly, just 34 perfect from the field, and UW won another close game, this time by the score of 67–63.

In the third conference game one week later, the Bruins again looked out of sync for much of the way. They struggled in the first half, but in the second half, things started to come together. Walt Hazzard led the way, and UCLA beat Cal in another close game. After 13 days off, UCLA traveled to Lubbock, Texas, for two nonconference games against Texas Tech, each of which the Bruins won handily, by 20 and then 23. Back in California after the trip, the Bruins continued their winning ways, beating USC twice, with Hazzard scoring 27 in each game to lead all scorers.

After starting 0–2 in conference play, UCLA had seemingly turned around its season and were expected to run away with the conference, as they had done so often. On February 9, UCLA traveled to Palo Alto to take on No. 9 Stanford. The games led to ultimate disappointment for the Bruins. The Indians won both games, and UCLA's chances at the AAWU crown and another trip to the tournament seemed all but dead. The Bruins won their next game over Cal, but then dropped a close game to USC. With three games left to play, Stanford led UCLA by three

Walt Hazzard finds Fred Slaughter for an easy basket against Cal, 1963 (Southern Branch Collection).

games in the standings. On March 2, UCLA beat Washington, 80–52, at the Santa Monica gym, and USC beat Stanford 60–58 at the Sports Arena. Six days later, the Indians had another chance to clinch the AAWU, but they would have to beat the Bruins to do it. UCLA again stayed alive, beating Stanford by 10. Though the Bruins had closed the gap, Stanford still controlled its AAWU destiny. On March 9, UCLA defeated Cal in the last regular-season game, and USC again defeated Stanford. There was a tie in the AAWU.

On March 12, UCLA and Stanford played a one-game playoff to determine the AAWU champion, with a bid to the NCAA Tournament. The game was low scoring. The Bruins scored only 51 points, their lowest total the entire season. Stanford would score only 45, however, the second-lowest total it scored all season and the lowest for a Bruins opponent since the first two games of the season. The game was certainly not pretty, but the result was just right for the Bruins. The Stanford collapse was complete, and Coach Wooden and his men were champions once again.

On March 15, UCLA took on the No. 4 Arizona State Sun Devils in the NCAA Regional semifinal played in Provo, Utah. The Bruins were considerable underdogs, but they also finished the regular season hot and hoped to carry it into the NCAA Tournament. The Bruins success would continue no further, however, as ASU essentially ended the game by halftime. The Sun Devils hit 19 of their first 21 shots and scored 62 points in the first half alone. UCLA played valiantly in the second half but fell by the score of 93–79. The Bruins would lose once more, this time to USF in the regional third-place game one day later. The 76–75 loss was the sixth loss of the season by five points or less and third by a single point. The Bruins finished with an overall record of 20–9. The Bruins had just completed their second straight season of great success, and they were just getting started. Henceforth, only national championships were deemed successful in Westwood. The 1963 team was good; the 1964 squad was a team of destiny.

Loyola University (Chicago) won the NCAA basketball national championship in 1963.

1963–64

The 1963–64 UCLA basketball season was different. Coming off a 20-win season and back-to-back

AAWU Conference titles, the Bruins were on an upward swing. Just four years earlier, the Bruins reached the low point of the John Wooden era, a 14–12 season and a frustrated fan base. Coach Wooden had raised expectations in Westwood, and when the team started to slide in the wrong direction, fans were upset. With the minor tweaks implemented by Coach Wooden since the disappointing 1960 season, the Bruins found more success. After winning just 14 games, the team won 18 games two years in a row, and then 20. In 1964, the team again increased its win total and cemented its legacy as one of the greatest teams of all time. Coach Wooden had begun using a full-court 2-2-1 zone press in recent years, but in '63–'64, the zone press became the most lethal defensive and offensive weapon in college basketball. The Bruins defense was smothering, the fast-break offense was breathtaking, and the winning was constant.

The Bruins of '63–'64 had a marvelous mix of talent, teamwork, and commitment to the sole task of improving each day, whether in practice or in games. Gail Goodrich and Walt Hazzard, the great guard tandem, led the team. Goodrich excelled in the scoring department, averaging 21.5 points per game for the season. Hazzard was right behind him, averaging 18.6 PPG. Jack Hirsch and Keith Erickson each averaged double digits in scoring, and Fred Slaughter anchored the Bruins defense from the center position. Kenny Washington, a 6'3" forward, was not a high scorer for the Bruins, but he was a steady performer off the bench, the best sixth man of Coach Wooden's tenure so far.

When the Bruins met the Brigham Young University Cougars in the first game of the season, the visiting team had no chance. UCLA opened the season December 6 with a dominant 113–71 thrashing of the Cougars, and it was just getting started. UCLA beat Butler by 15 points the next night and then wiped out Kansas and Kansas State the following week. In the third week of the season, the Bruins continued to shine. Now ranked as the sixth-best team in the country by the Associated Press, the Bruins beat Baylor, 112–61, and then Creighton, 95–79. The Bruins were 6–0, but the competition got more difficult.

By the start of the L.A. Classic, the Bruins had risen to No. 4 in the rankings, and one team ranked ahead of them stood in their way. After dispatching Yale behind Goodrich's early scoring barrage, the Bruins took on the Michigan Wolverines. Michigan, coached by Dave Strack, came into the game ranked No. 3 in the country. It would be the first big test for the Bruins all season. From the opening tip to the end of the game, the Bruins' press defense was relentless. Just 19 seconds into the game, the Bruins had scored, gotten a steal, and scored again. Michigan's Cazzie Russell was thoroughly

UCLA Cheerleaders, 1964 (Southern Branch Collection).

frustrated by the Bruins. Goodrich scored 30 points for UCLA, and against the best team they faced all season, the Bruins made a statement: UCLA 98, Michigan 80.

In the L.A. Classic final, the Bruins understandably looked sluggish. It was the third game in three days, and there was an emotional letdown following the win over Michigan. The Bruins staved off the Illinois Fighting Illini, however, and remained unbeaten on the season. As the final seconds ticked off the clock, Bruin fans in the crowd loudly chanted, "We're number one! We're number one!"

The Bruins' time at the top would have to wait, though once they finally reached the top, they never looked back. The Bruins began the New Year ranked No. 2 in the country, just before AAWU play. In the first game of the conference season, UCLA again came out sluggish. They beat Washington State, 88–83, but it took 28 points from Goodrich and 23 from Hirsch to get the job done. One night later, UCLA had no such problem. On January 4, 1964, UCLA put on a performance that has seldom been matched or exceeded in school history. Playing in the second game of a back-to-back series, UCLA demolished Washington State in Pullman. All five Bruins starters scored in double figures. The press defense was a sight to see, and despite Coach Wooden substituting frequently in the second half, the Bruins kept pouring it on. When the final seconds ticked off the clock, the score read UCLA 121, Washington State 77. The 121 points was the most scored in a game in UCLA history to that point, and those who still believed that any team in the country was better than UCLA were wrong. In the next AP rankings, the voters got it right—UCLA was the No. 1 team in the nation.

Simply holding the No. 1 ranking at any given time during the season is not an accomplishment in itself, and the Bruins knew it. The conference season was still just getting started, and sloppy play could derail the Bruins' hopes at any time. Coach Wooden wouldn't let that happen, however. Against USC, Hazzard scored 21 in the opener and the Bruins won two consecutive games over their crosstown rival. The Bruins then smashed Stanford twice, easily took care of UC Santa Barbara on back-to-back nights, and then beat California by 20 in Berkeley. On the second night in Berkeley, however, the Bruins played their worst game of the season. UCLA's defense was solid, but the team wasn't able to force the as many turnovers as usual, and players were unable to ignite their fast-break offense. Cal played slowly and was in the game the entire way. With under a minute to play, the Bruins led by just one, but clutch free-throw shooting by Hazzard helped UCLA escape with a 58–56 win. No other team would stay within single digits the rest of the conference season. Against Washington, Walt Hazzard scored 15 points, giving

1964 UCLA team photo (Southern Branch Collection).

him 1,226 for his career and making him UCLA's all-time leading scorer. UCLA beat Washington three times down the stretch by an average of almost 16 points per game. UCLA beat Stanford once more, this time by 12 points. It crushed Washington State by 37, beat Cal by 30, and then finished the regular season with a perfect 26–0 record by beating USC. The Bruins of 1964 had already proven to be the best UCLA team in history. The NCAA Tournament gave the team the chance to cement their legacy as one of the greatest teams in NCAA history.

Every game in the 1964 NCAA Tournament, still comprised of 25 teams, was difficult, and one bad game would end an otherwise brilliant season with disappointment. UCLA took on Seattle in Corvallis in the first game. The Bruins were able to jump out to a nine-point lead at halftime, but Seattle kept hanging around, frustrating the Bruins. Though the score was closer than expected, UCLA won, 95–90. The West Region would be settled the following night, as UCLA took on the University of San Francisco. At one point, the Bruins' season seemed like it would end in unimaginable disappointment. As the Bruins had done several times earlier in the season, they started slowly. USF built a 13-point lead in the first half, and though UCLA cut into the lead before halftime, still it trailed by eight at the break. In the second half, the Bruins outscored USF, 48–36, and climbed all the way back. The final score was 76–72. The Bruins advanced to the Final Four.

The 1964 Final Four was played in Kansas City in Municipal Auditorium, and here the legend of John Wooden was born. Though Coach Wooden had achieved miraculous success thus far in his Bruins coaching career, for many he would be defined by championships. In two close games, first against Kansas State and then against Duke, the Bruins showed their incredible depth and teamwork. Against KSU, the Bruins trailed by five with 7:20 to play but marched all the way back and won by the score of 90–84. Hazzard and Goodrich received the most acclaim throughout the season, but Keith Erickson had a career night, scoring 28 points, and that made the difference against KSU. The Bruins headed to the national championship, and again a man few talked about was the greatest difference maker. On March 21, 1964, Kenny Washington scored 26 points, and the UCLA Bruins defeated the Duke Blue Devils, 98–83, to win the first national championship in school history.

Teammates Gail Goodrich and Fred Slaughter celebrate as UCLA wins their first National Championship in school history, 1964 (Southern Branch Collection).

The '64 Bruins were a truly remarkable team, perhaps the greatest press defensive team ever coached by John Wooden. Gail Goodrich, Walt Hazzard, and the twelve other Bruins each played an important role in creating an unstoppable team. The Bruins finished with a perfect 30–0 record. They had climbed the mountain top.

1964–65

Getting to the top is difficult, but staying there is even harder, as the old sports adage goes. The Bruins were the defending champions, and the 1965 team exemplified the greatness of college sports. Unlike professional athletics, college athletics has a constant influx of new players, as well as the departure of those moving on with their lives. One of UCLA's all-time greatest players, Walt Hazzard, was gone to the NBA. While replacing others was also difficult, Hazzard was different. He was already a UCLA legend, and his nearly 19 points per game was almost impossible to replace.

UCLA did indeed take a step back offensively. After averaging 88.2 points per game in '64, the Bruins averaged 85.4 in '85. Their defense was also slightly worse statistically, giving up one more point

Edgar Lacey, 1965 (Southern Branch Collection).

per game. The Bruins' press defense in '64 was the greatest asset, offensively or defensively, UCLA had ever known, and it would again be essential to the Bruins' success of '65. Gail Goodrich returned to have the single greatest individual season for any Bruin ever to that point, in his senior season. He averaged 24.8 PPG and added over five rebounds per game. Olympic volleyball player Keith Erickson, Freddie Goss, and Edgar Lacey all averaged double digits points, as well, with Lacey also pulling down 10.2 rebounds per game. Kenny Washington was again a key contributor; Mike Lynn and Doug McIntosh contributed as well.

The season started not with a continuation of the previous season but with a shocking blowout loss. The Bruins began play on December 4, 1964, against the University of Illinois at Assembly Hall. The hometown Fighting Illini, which averaged 91.7 PPG for the season, crushed the Bruins. UCLA's defense was nonexistent, as Illinois continually broke the full-court pressure and scored layup after layup. UCLA did well enough offensively, scoring 83 points, but shockingly gave up 110 on the other end.

One night after the opening-game debacle, the Bruins were back in action again, and they looked more like the team Bruins fans had become accustomed to seeing. This time, they were the ones to put up huge offensive numbers, scoring 112 points and beating Indiana State by 36 points. When the Bruins came home, they picked up where they left off. Though the team had fallen from No. 2 in the rankings to No. 7, the season was still obviously young, and it would improve from game one to the end of the season more than any team in Coach Wooden's tenure. UCLA knocked off Arizona State, again breaking the 100-point barrier, beating the Sun Devils, 107–76, at the Sports Arena. They beat Oklahoma State by 16 the next night and then beat Marquette and Boston College in back-to-back nights one week later in the Milwaukee Classic. Against BC, the Bruins scored 115 points.

After climbing up to No. 4 in the rankings, the Bruins competed again in the Los Angeles Classic, and again, they won the tournament. By the start of the New Year, the Bruins were back where they felt they belonged. They had won nine consecutive games since the loss to Illinois and were now the No. 1-ranked team in the nation. UCLA would have very few close games in the months of January and February. Only three of the next 14 were decided by less than 10 points. The Bruins beat both the Oregon schools on the road by an average of 17.5 points per game. They beat Cal and Stanford at the Sports Arena by an average of 13 points per game.

With UCLA's winning streak up to 13 games, the Bruins took on the Iowa Hawkeyes on January 29, 1965, at Chicago Stadium. The game was much like the season opener for the Bruins, though the game was closer. UCLA's offense was good, scoring 82 points, but the defense struggled. When the Bruins' press defense wasn't working, opponents were able to score at a high clip for much of the season. Though the Hawkeyes were just 7–4 at the time and were just 1–3 against ranked opponents, they were able to do what seemed impossible: beat the Bruins. The final score was Iowa 87, UCLA 82. The game was a wake-up call for the Bruins. When they lost the season opener, it proved they were not invincible. When they lost to Iowa, it proved that regaining their championship form was difficult, and they would have to continue to improve to again raise the trophy in March.

Despite the two losses, UCLA was still a championship contender, and was on a collision course

The 1965 UCLA basketball team after winning their second consecutive national championship (Southern Branch Collection).

with another team with championship aspirations. The Michigan Wolverines were ranked No. 1 for the majority of the season; UCLA lost to Iowa, the Bruins came in at No. 2. Though both teams stumbled at times throughout the season, they were the two best and proved it. UCLA beat Loyola by 13 and each Washington school twice, including a 52-point win over the Cougars. They beat both schools from Oregon, and both from Northern California. In the final AAWU series of the season, they beat USC twice and finished with a perfect 14–0 conference record. The Bruins were again the AAWU champs, but it was not a conference title they dreamed of. It was time to play for another national title.

The 1965 NCAA Tournament featured 23 teams, and most fans believed UCLA and Michigan had a chance to bring home the title. Coach Wooden did not allow his team to overlook any other team, however, as his team showed they were beatable. UCLA's offense was clicking at the right time, however, and in the opening game, the Bruins looked like a juggernaut. At Smith Fieldhouse in Provo, Utah, the Bruins took down BYU, 100–76 in the Regional Semifinals. One day later, they again topped the century mark, beating the University of San Francisco, 101–93. The Bruins were again in the Final Four and off to Portland, Oregon, and Veterans Memorial Coliseum. Wichita State waited for them there.

In the NCAA semifinals, the Bruins did what they had done in the previous two games. Their offense was so fast and their press defense so lethal that they shocked their opponent. UCLA beat Wichita State, 108–89, and for the second year in a row, the Bruins would play for the national title. On March 20, 1965, the top-seeded Michigan Wolverines, as expected, took on the No. 2 seed UCLA Bruins for the national championship.

The Michigan Wolverines were talented and well coached. Cazzie Russell, Oliver Darden, and Bill Buntin played well offensively against the Bruins. UCLA, however, had one man that Michigan did not—Gail Goodrich. Though Kenny Washington had one of his best games all season, Goodrich stole the show. He finished with 42 points, the most points ever scored in a game by a UCLA Bruin, the most ever scored in an NCAA championship final at the time, and still the second-highest total ever scored in the NCAA championship. Many experts saw the game as a battle between Michigan's superior size, in both height and weight, and the UCLA's superior speed, agility, and skill. At halftime, the score was 47–34, Bruins, as the Wolverines size advantage had become a size and mobility disadvantage against the ever-attacking Bruins. UCLA won the game, 91–80, to take its second national championship in a row. Goodrich's performance, his last at UCLA, cemented his already incredible legacy with the Bruins. He was named a First Team All-American and is considered one of the finest college basketball players of all time.

Goodrich had a successful NBA career after leaving, and as one star left, another arrived. Ferdinand Lewis Alcindor, a young man from New York City with incredible size, agility, skill, and grace, joined the Bruins basketball dynasty. UCLA would open a new gym prior to the start of the 1965–66 season, a college basketball cathedral located in the heart of campus. The Bruins had won two national championships and established themselves as one of the premier contenders for the foreseeable future with the signing of one of the most elite high school prospects of all time. Going forward, every season was championship or bust.

UCLA legends John Wooden and Gail Goodrich at the 1965 national championship rally (Southern Branch Collection).

Gail Goodrich

In the grand history of UCLA basketball, few players were more prominent and successful than Gail Goodrich. Yet despite his storied career both with UCLA and in the NBA, he is often overlooked. Kareem Abdul-Jabbar, Bill Walton, Reggie Miller, and others are seen as the faces of UCLA basketball, along with Coach Wooden, of course. Gail Goodrich, however, is the man that got it all started. Other players, like Don Barksdale and Walt Hazzard, came before Goodrich and created an incredible legacy all their own. When looking at the success of UCLA basketball during Coach Wooden's tenure, we look not at single moments of brilliance but at sustained excellence over time. Goodrich's career at every level was about excellence. He won at UCLA, in a number of ways. While Coach Wooden and the Bruins community were blessed to see Goodrich play in Westwood and spark the true Bruin basketball revolution, it almost wasn't to be. He grew up in a Trojans family, and dreamed of donning the cardinal and gold USC uniform.

Gail Goodrich Jr. was born on April 23, 1943, in Los Angeles, California. Unlike many of the stars still to come after Goodrich, he was not easily identifiable as a basketball player. He was never particularly tall, as he stood at less than six feet tall while in high school. He would eventually grow to 6'1", still below average for a college or pro player, though not necessarily too short for a shooting guard at the time. Coaches worried about his height while in John H. Francis Poly High School, but he was one of the top high school players in the country. In his final game, Goodrich was at his best, though he was injured. Goodrich was the leading scorer in the L.A. City Championship, scoring 29, despite breaking his ankle during the game.

His father had starred on the USC basketball team decades earlier, and Jr. wanted to be just like Sr. and play for the Trojans. Coach Wooden would be less concerned than Coach Forrest Twogood at USC. Wooden and UCLA recruited Goodrich harder than the crosstown Trojans, and in 1961, Goodrich enrolled at UCLA, not his childhood-favorite USC.

Goodrich would recover in time to build a legacy at UCLA that was unmatched by any Bruin to that point. After one season on the freshmen squad, Goodrich joined the varsity and made an incredible impact. In 1963, as just a sophomore, Goodrich averaged double-digit scoring and laid the groundwork for what was to come. UCLA had experimented with its soon-to-be legendary press defense in the past, but with Goodrich, the team took it to the next level, as Coach Wooden fully believed in his new weapon. In 1964, the UCLA basketball team was one the greatest teams of all time. The Bruins offense was breathtaking, and Goodrich was one of the main reasons why. He averaged 21.5 points per game during the year the Bruins stayed perfect and won the first national championship. Along with the incredible offense was the lethal press defense. In 1965, the defense wasn't quite as strong as the year before, forcing less turnovers and giving up more points. The UCLA offense took a slight step back, as well, not scoring as many points in transition. Goodrich, on the other hand, improved his game, and as the season wore on, the Bruins improved as a team. Goodrich averaged 24.8 points per game, and the Bruins again won the national championship. He scored 1,691 points in his three-year varsity career, making him the highest scorer in UCLA history to that point. He is currently the fifteenth-highest scorer in UCLA history in total points, despite the increase in number of games and current eligibility for freshmen.

During much of his NBA career, Goodrich's teams fell just short. In 1965, he was drafted by the Los Angeles Lakers, and the same perceived problems that he had dealt with his entire life were brought up once again. He was said to be too small, he wouldn't be able to get his shot off against bigger defenders, and he was not athletic enough to make a real impact. He was nicknamed "Stumpy" by teammate Elgin Baylor, and for much of his rookie season, the doubts that many had proved to be accurate. He struggled as a rookie, scoring only 7.8 points per game and shooting poorly from the field. As a second-year player, his opportunity increased, as he split time with former UCLA teammate Walt Hazzard, starting alongside Jerry West. He bumped his scoring average to 12.4 PPG, but his season was inconsistent. In 1967, as a third-year player, Goodrich came into his own, steadily improving, though many in the Lakers organization still doubted his ability and his minutes were still limited. He bumped his scoring to 13.8 PPG, a very respectable number, but his time in Los Angeles was running out.

Gail Goodrich vs. USC, 1965 (Southern Branch Collection).

In 1968, the Lakers lost Goodrich to the Phoenix Suns in the expansion draft, and though he would be away from his hometown team, he would finally have a chance to prove his value. He became a full-time starter, and an immediate star. In his first season in Phoenix, he averaged nearly 24 points, as well as six assists and five rebounds, and was named an All-Star for the first time. He had another good season in 1970 but was then traded back to the Lakers, where he would continue to play his finest basketball. Under Coach Bill Sharman, West shot the ball less, passing more, and being more of a playmaker. On the other end of many of West's passes was Goodrich, and in his second year back with the team, he was a key piece in one of the greatest teams of all time. The 1972 Lakers were special, and no man put the ball through the hoop like Goodrich. Though West and Wilt Chamberlain were certainly the two biggest names, the top scorer was Goodrich, who averaged a career best 25.9 points, and the Lakers won the championship. The '72 season also began a stretch for Goodrich of four consecutive All-Star nods, all coming with the Lakers. The year 1976 would be Goodrich's final season in Los Angeles, as his scoring had dipped in his eleventh season in the league. He spent his final three years with the New Orleans Jazz, where he averaged 14.2 points.

In 14 seasons, Goodrich averaged 18.6 points, was a five-time All-Star, won a championship with his hometown team, and did it all despite the doubts of many outsiders. He was not too small or too slow. His skill was incredible. He was a crafty left-hander, who got to his spots, made and took his shots, and was fundamentally well schooled, just as Coach Wooden had taught him. He eventually put his principles to paper, writing a book called *Winning Basketball*, in which he covered the proper drills to hone the fundamentals that led to his success. He talks about the usage of both hands, proper shooting form, pivoting, passing, individual and team defense, and every other simple part of the game that led him to a brilliant career.

Following his playing career, Goodrich worked for a number of golf companies, living in multiple states. He has also analyzed basketball on television and for a brief time was a hot name in coaching circles. Even after his playing career ended, the honors kept coming. In 1996, he was elected to the Naismith Memorial Basketball Hall of Fame, and the Lakers retired his number 25 jersey. In 2003, his high school number was retired, and one year later, his number 25 was retired by UCLA. In 2006, he was inducted into the College Basketball Hall of Fame, joining Coach Wooden, who thankfully didn't believe Goodrich was too short.

1965–66

In 1965, Pauley Pavilion opened, and UCLA finally had a home to call its own. When Coach Wooden accepted the job at UCLA nearly two decades prior, he was told that UCLA would stop traveling to home games soon, with a new gym built on campus. Not until November 27, 1965, did the promise come to fruition.

UCLA was the top-ranked team in the nation and two-time defending national champions, but they were blown out by a team of the future. The final score was 75–60, but the game did not count. UCLA's opponent was UCLA, the varsity going down to the freshmen. Leading the way for the youngsters was Lewis Alcindor, who would become the greatest player in college basketball history and was already better than anyone on the Bruins varsity roster. A crowd of 12,051 showed up at Pauley Pavilion to see the exhibition game; though the hype surrounding Alcindor's arrival in Westwood was hard to ignore, all those sitting in the stands would be lying if they said they weren't stunned. Alcindor could do everything—run, jump, score, rebound, defend, and pass. He was even the key difference maker for the freshmen in breaking the varsity press defense. Alcindor would stand near midcourt, and within one or two passes, he would receive the ball, holding it up higher than the defense could reach, and find streaking guards going the other way. The Bruins freshmen, led by Coach Gary Cunningham, put on a clinic. Alcindor scored 31 points, grabbed 21 rebounds, and was the talk of the town already. When the game ended, the freshmen ran off the court chanting, "We're number one! We're number one!" For one day at least, they were right. They knocked off the best team in America, and it didn't even count. While fans may have been surprised, Coach Wooden was not, and neither was Alcindor. Coach Wooden said when asked if he thought the game was a true stunner, "Not at all." Alcindor said later, "That game was easy for us." The freshmen team won all 21 of its games in '65–'66, including a 103-point victory over Mira Costa College.

Even though the future was bright for the UCLA basketball program, the 1966 season would be a tremendous challenge for Coach Wooden. While many in the media were already imagining three consecutive titles for the varsity with Lew Alcindor, and six consecutive overall, the Bruins had something else to worry about. Alcindor and the rest of the talented

1966 UCLA freshmen team photo (Southern Branch Collection).

freshmen team were still one year away from varsity eligibility, and the current varsity team had holes to fill. They overcame the loss of Walt Hazzard to the NBA one year earlier, but replacing Gail Goodrich was more difficult. No star players returned, and on top of the challenges of replacing a legend, UCLA was hit with the injury bug in 1966. Mike Lynn led the Bruins in scoring and rebounding but missed time with the flu. Kenny Washington had his finest season in Westwood but suffered a midseason muscle pull. Freddie Goss, who averaged more than 13 points per game, missed time with a stomach ailment. Edgar Lacey suffered a fracture of his knee cap. Doug McIntosh bruised his back. The Bruins played 26 games in 1966; when fully healthy, they only lost once in league play, but they were rarely healthy. Mike Warren had a strong season, and he was the only regular rotation player to stay healthy for the entire year., But he was just a sophomore, and at times he seemed to carry the Bruins on his back. It was not a recipe for success, but Coach Wooden did not let his team be controlled by luck, or lack thereof. He prepared his players for every game, and the results would speak for themselves.

The opening night of the season was on December 5, when the Bruins took on the Ohio State Buckeyes at Pauley Pavilion. The game went as expected, with the Bruins winning, 92–66. The next night, they ran their record to 2–0 by beating Illinois, 97–79. The season became more difficult, however.

John Wooden, 1966 (Southern Branch Collection).

In one week, the Bruins were set to head to Durham, North Carolina to take on the Duke Blue Devils. Duke was one of the best teams in the nation, and for the first time for all the Bruins basketball players, they took the court against a team better than them. The Blue Devils had no problem with the Bruins' press defense and beat UCLA, 82–66, and 94–75 in back-to-back nights. The losses to Duke were disappointing, but UCLA was still strong and plenty of season remained. When UCLA returned to Pauley Pavilion, they had fallen to the No. 8 spot in the country. The team took on the fourth-ranked Kansas Jayhawks. Mike Lynn scored 26 points for UCLA, and the Bruins upset the eventual Big Eight champs. One night later, things took a turn. An inferior Cincinnati squad upset UCLA. At 3–3, UCLA looked anything but special. It started the year in mediocre fashion, and unless something changed, the freshmen would remain the main attraction on campus.

The Bruins were able to get on track. UCLA raced past USC at the Sports Arena and then won three games in a four-night span to win the Los Angeles Classic for the fourth consecutive year, beating USC again in the championship game. When league play began, the Bruins were ranked No. 10 in the country, and they appeared well on their way to another AAWU crown the first weekend. UCLA dismantled Oregon State, which tried to play a slow, stalling game. The Beavers were unable to score themselves, however, and eventually the floodgates opened for the Bruins offense. The final score was UCLA 79, Oregon State 35. UCLA then crushed the Oregon Ducks and next beat Cal six days later.

Despite the upswing, the 1966 season would not be magical for the Bruins. After starting 3–0 in conference play, UCLA lost three of the next four, including a game in which it gave up 106 points to a strong Loyola-Chicago team. UCLA beat Arizona but lost to Washington State when Doug Cloke made two free throws for the Cougars with five seconds left to put WSU up for good. UCLA still won seven more games, dropping only two, but the losses were critical to the Bruins finishing in second place in the conference. After beating Oregon State by 44 points in January, the Bruins lost to the Beavers by 13 in February. When UCLA lost to the Oregon Ducks the next night, the conference race was all but over. UCLA finished with an 18–8 overall record and 10–4 in AAWU play. Oregon State finished with a 12–2 record and would receive the lone tournament bid for the AAWU.

UCLA's season ended in disappointment, and its run of consecutive championships was over. No matter what team, and no matter what sport, no championship is ever a sure thing, and there were never any guarantees that UCLA would win again. Even with Lew Alcindor, the best player to ever play, waiting in the wings, the sting felt by the players when they were knocked off their mantle was significant.

The 1966 season was thought at the time to be one of the most forgettable seasons of the Wooden era. Instead it turned out to be one of the most memorable, as remembering the years UCLA did not win the national championship was easier than the years it did.

Texas Western College (now the University of Texas-El Paso) won the NCAA basketball national championship in 1966.

1966–67

With the addition of Lew Alcindor to the varsity squad in 1966–67, Coach Wooden had a weapon unlike any he had ever had before. Coach Wooden's teams were often built on speed, not on size. Things would be different for the Bruins going forward, at least when they were in the half-court offense. Coach Wooden anticipated having to find ways to utilize Alcindor's tremendous ability, spending a tremendous amount of time over more than a year running through scenarios in his mind, imagining what he would do when he was able to use his 7'2", graceful, skilled big man. In *They Call Me Coach*, he described the year leading up to Alcindor's varsity debut: "I had spent literally hundreds of hours from the time Lewis entered as a freshman and the beginning of his sophomore year in 1967 talking to coaches whom I respected about the low post offense, diagramming plays and analyzing the consequences and trying to determine just how this seven foot plus youngster would fit in with others." Ultimately, Coach Wooden implemented a single low post offense. He wanted Alcindor "no more than eight feet away," and the other four would play off the big man, roaming the perimeter and finding slashing lanes, but not bogging down Alcindor or limiting his space to operate.

Coach Wooden's time and effort, as well as Alcindor's transcendent ability, ultimately paid major dividends. Though expectations for the Bruins were almost impossibly high, with many in the media predicting a perfect season, the Bruins did not disappoint. The team was made up of more than Alcindor, however. At the beginning of the season, the Bruins started four sophomores, with Lynn Shackelford, Kenny Heitz, and Lucius Allen joining Alcindor. The only starter with any varsity experience was Mike Warren, a solid fit at guard.

UCLA began the season on December 3, and the world got a glimpse of Alcindor for the first time. The Bruins took on crosstown USC at Pauley Pavilion, and for one of the few times in Alcindor's career, he faced a strictly man-to-man defense. Teams would quickly learn that you couldn't simply play Alcindor straight up. He was a nightmare for the Trojans. In UCLA's 105-90 win, Alcindor hit 23 of 32 shots from the field and 10 of 14 from the free-throw line. In his first varsity game, Alcindor scored 56 points, an all-time UCLA record.

John Wooden, 1967 (Southern Branch Collection).

UCLA students mocking USC's stalling offense, 1967 (Southern Branch Collection).

The Duke Blue Devils, third-place finisher in the 1966 NCAA Tournament, made the return trip to Westwood. One year earlier, Duke embarrassed UCLA in Durham, North Carolina; things would be different this time around. The Blue Devils were ranked number seven in the country, but they were a junior varsity team in comparison to the mighty Bruins. Duke put two or three guys on Alcindor all game, holding him to just 19 points. He didn't even take a shot for almost eight minutes, but the Bruins easily dispatched the Blue Devils, as others found openings and converted over and over. Lucius Allen scored 19 for the Bruins, and Shackelford put in 13. The next night, the two played again, and this time it was the Alcindor show. With 38 points and 22 rebounds, he proved just how difficult playing UCLA would be. Teams had to make choices on how they would defend the Bruins, and no choice was a good one. UCLA won, 107–87, in game two.

In reality, opposing coaches had only one option. They were forced to play an old-fashioned stalling game, the likes of which hadn't been seen often in college basketball in over a generation. When teams played a normal brand of basketball, they were shredded by the Bruins offense. Notre Dame lost by 29 points, unable to contain Alcindor. UCLA demolished Wisconsin, Georgia Tech, and USC in the L.A. Classic, losing by 44, 19, and 24, respectively. The Bruins were 8–0 when conference play began, and AAWU opponents fared no better than the nonconference teams did. On January 7, Washington State became the first team to stay within single digits of the Bruins, losing by only nine. Most teams weren't so fortunate. UCLA beat Stanford, 116–78; Portland, 112–57; and UC Santa Barbara, 119–75. Then the team went to Chicago to beat the University of Illinois, 120–82, at Chicago Stadium, with Alcindor scoring 45. The Bruins appeared on track for a perfect season, but every game is different, and being perfect is never easy.

By the time February rolled around, UCLA was 16–0. They had been ranked No. 1 from the beginning of the season and seemed to have a firm grasp on the position. When it took on USC on February 4 at the Sports Arena, however, UCLA had its toughest test of the year. The Trojans did not play the Bruins in a normal manner. They waited and waited. Players would have an open shot but continue passing the ball until someone had an ever more open shot. The plan worked, to an extent. The Bruins averaged nearly 90 points per game on the season, but against the stalling Trojans, they scored only 40. With USC leading, 31–27, with four minutes to play, Warren hit a jumper, and two minutes later, Allen knocked down two free throws to tie the game. The game went to overtime, an accomplishment in itself for the inferior Trojans. In the OT period, the Bruins pulled ahead behind Warren's clutch play. The final score was just 40–35, but the game was another win for UCLA over USC, their thirteenth in a row.

No team the rest of the way would have a chance against the Bruins. UCLA beat Oregon and Oregon State twice each, even though the second matchup with the Ducks saw the same strategy implemented that the Trojans tried. UCLA beat Washington to run its record to 22–0, and one night later, on February 25, the Bruins had a chance to clinch the AAWU crown against the Washington State Cougars at Pauley Pavilion. In what ended up being the conference-clinching game for the Bruins, Alcindor poured in 61 points, hitting 26 of 35 shots and nine of 18 free throws, and he pulled down 24

The 1967 Bruins after winning the national championship (Southern Branch Collection).

rebounds. The Bruins won the AAWU for the fifth time in the previous six seasons, but they strived to achieve more.

After finishing the regular season with a perfect 26–0 record, including another win over USC that pushed the streak to 14 straight over the Trojans, UCLA began the NCAA Tournament in a familiar fashion: it crushed the opponent. In the opening-game regional semifinals in Corvallis, Oregon, the Bruins cruised to a 49-point win over Wyoming. They beat Pacific the next night by 16 to advance to the Final Four, played at Freedom Hall in Louisville, Kentucky. The venue may have changed, and the opponents may have been tougher on paper, but the results were the same. When No. 7 University of Houston and star center Elvin Hayes faced off against UCLA, the Cougars' strategy was clear. The team was going to be extremely physical with Alcindor, hoping to get the Bruin star in foul trouble. Hayes was an aggressive player and tried to play mind games with his opponents. Alcindor was calm, trusted his ability, and trusted his teammates. The strategy didn't work for Houston, and though Hayes played well, his team fell. The final score was UCLA 73, Houston 58.

Though the final game was a serious affair for Coach Wooden, the Bruins, and the Dayton Flyers, it also seemed like just the final game in a season that was destined to go the Bruins' way. UCLA was the best team from start to finish; it won, 79–64. Alcindor scored 20 points and hauled down 18 rebounds. Allen scored 19, Warren 17, and Shackelford 10. For the third time in four years, the UCLA Bruins were the national champions. Alcindor was named National Player of the Year by every recognized poll and was named Player of the Tournament, as well. Coach Wooden was named National Coach of the Year, a well-deserved honor after he made wholesale changes for the betterment of the team. Alcindor had 29.0 points and 15.5 rebounds per game for the season. Allen had 15.5 PPG and 5.8 RPG, as well. The Bruins were perfect, four of their five starters were just sophomores, and all five starters would be back the following year. It was hard to imagine any team ever topping the 1967 Bruins, but Coach Wooden helmed plenty more teams that would earn their way into the conversation of greatest team ever. Just three years prior, the '64 Bruins made their case for greatest team of all time, and now in the minds of most they had been clearly surpassed.

1967–68

After the Bruins' dominant season in 1967, something had to change—at least in the minds of the people atop the NCAA rules committee. As a sophomore, Lew Alcindor was the best player in America, almost completely in three ways. He dunked, finger-rolled, and shot short jumpers from the right block. Beginning in the 1967–68 season, one of Alcindor's three weapons would be gone, but ultimately his greatest weapon would develop. Prior to the season, the NCAA banned dunking during games. Reasons cited went beyond just slowing down Alcindor. Practically speaking, dunking was bad for the game because modern rims and backboards could not support dunking like they do now. Games were suspended or cancelled because of broken backboards at an increasing rate. With every broken backboard came broken glass, spewed all over the court and on top of the dunker. Dunking was a safety issue, and outlawing the dunk eliminated the problem. Then there was the hard to ignore Alcindor factor. Banning the dunk might open up the competition in '68, allowing other teams to compete with the Bruins.

Coach John Wooden supported the dunking rule (others called it the "Lew Alcindor Rule"), believing it was good for the game as a whole and for individual players. It certainly proved to be good for Alcindor. Though he had used a hook shot in the past, learning it when he was very young, the hook shot now became his go-to move. The hook shot was not simply about putting the ball in the air in a sweeping motion toward the basket; it required grace, fluidity, footwork, and touch. Alcindor was able to perfect the age-old move, holding the ball high up in his right hand, jumping off his left foot, following through, and splashing the ball through the basket. He went to the middle of the paint from the left block or to the baseline from the right. Eventually, he polished his game even more, using his left hand from close distance and stepping further away from the basket and using his right hand as his game continued to develop. Alcindor's shot would become known as the "skyhook," and it became the most lethal offensive weapon in basketball history. No one has since repeated the skyhook with the effectiveness or consistency of Alcindor. In 1968, however, Coach Wooden, Alcindor, and the Bruins were simply adjusting.

The 1968 season was ultimately remembered for two games, though the many more played included a

Lew Alcindor, 1968 (Southern Branch Collection).

thrilling season opener. The 1967 UCLA Bruins were rarely challenged, so when the first game of the '68 season was a nail-biter, it was shocking. Playing in Purdue Arena in West Lafayette, Indiana, the Bruins took on the Purdue Boilermakers, coach Wooden's alma mater. With fourteen thousand in attendance, the game was tied at 71 with seven seconds to play. Boilermaker All-American Rick Mount was at the free-throw line shooting two with a chance to upset the top-ranked Bruins in the season-opening game. Mount missed the first attempt. On the second shot, the ball hung on the rim, and then fell just off. Alcindor grabbed the rebound and fired an outlet pass to Mike Warren. With four seconds left, Warren turned, dribbled once, and passed to Bill Sweek, who let go a shot from 30 feet away with two seconds on the clock. The ball came down through the net, and the Bruins won, 73–71, at the buzzer! Sweek averaged just 3.6 points per game on the year, but no shot was bigger than this one.

The Bruins crushed every opponent on the rest of the schedule before conference play. Six days after the close call against Purdue, the Bruins began a stretch of five consecutive games scoring at least 109 points. They would score no less than 93 for the next 10 games and scored 120 and 121 in consecutive games against Wichita State and Iowa State. UCLA seemed unstoppable. On January 12, the Bruins wrapped up another dominant victory, beating the Cal Golden Bears, 94–64, in Berkeley. The 30-point win moved the Bruins' record to 11–0 overall, and 3–0 in conference play. During the game, however, Alcindor's eye was badly injured. He was sent to the hospital and treated for a scratched cornea. For much of the following week, Alcindor was isolated from his team, spending most of his time in a dark room in the Jules Stein Eye Center on the UCLA campus. When he left the Center, he had to wear a thick patch on his eye. Alcindor would not play against Stanford, nor would he play against Portland five days later.

UCLA won both games without Alcindor, but on January 20, 1968, they had a new test that would be much more difficult. The game was played in the Houston Astrodome, with 52,693 fans, the most for a basketball game, watching the two top-ranked teams in the nation play. The attraction was not just UCLA vs. Houston, it was Alcindor vs. Hayes, or at least UCLA hoped it would be. All week, no one was sure when Alcindor would return. He made the trip with the team, however, and he played. The game would go down as the most important in the history of college basketball, though the quality of play was actually very poor. Neither team shot well, and both teams complained of the arena lighting. The game was said to be the brightest ever played indoors, with the stadium lights distracting players as they went for rebounds. The court, which was shipped from Los Angeles (the same court used at the L.A. Sports Arena), was placed where second base would be on the baseball field at the Astrodome, and the fans were farther from the court than ever before at a basketball game. Alcindor, in his return, struggled like never before. He made just four of his 18 field-goal attempts, the only game thus far in his career in which he shot under 50 percent from the field. He never again shot under 50 percent for the rest of his college career. One man, however, did play well: Elvin Hayes. In the first half alone, Hayes scored 29 points, and in the closing seconds of the game, his total was up to 37. The score was tied late, but Hayes was not done. He scored his 38th and 39th points in the final minute from the free-throw line to lift the No. 2 Cougars over the top-ranked Bruins. UCLA's 47-game winning streak was over. Fans at the Astrodome stormed the court in celebration. Houston had topped college basketball's biggest giant and, more important, did it on the biggest stage.

The game was quickly dubbed the "Game of the Century," and the name has stuck for over 50 years. It was not the prettiest game, nor was it the greatest upset ever, but it set in motion changes that would ultimately make college basketball one of America's most popular sports. The game was nationally televised, drawing the largest audience to ever watch a college basketball game at the time. Sports fans would never again consider college basketball to be a minor sport. It had reached the status of big-time entertainment.

As Houston players ran off the court, they yelled, "The King is dead!" They soon learned they were wrong. Alcindor bounced back, as did the Bruins. Revenge was just two short months away.

The Bruins plowed through most of the rest of the opponents that stood in their way, though the occasional close game occurred. Boston College

UCLA vs. Houston, the "Game of the Century," 1968 (Southern Branch Collection).

kept the game within single digits at Madison Square Garden, and Oregon State stayed close to UCLA at Gill Coliseum in Corvallis, losing by only three points. The Trojans only lost by eight in the final conference game of the season, but this followed a 34-point drubbing in the previous meeting. The rest stood no chance whatsoever. In the other nine games following the loss to Houston, UCLA outscored its opponents by almost 32 points per game. The Bruins again finished perfect in AAWU play with a 14–0 record.

Other games in the NCAA Tournament were worthy of recognition, but everyone had their eyes on the looming rematch. Coach Wooden kept his team focused on the simple task of beating the team at hand, and two teams took on the Bruins before the Cougars. UCLA beat New Mexico State and Santa Clara in Albuquerque to reach the NCAA Final Four. The team waiting for them was the undefeated No. 1 in the country, the Houston Cougars. The rematch was even more anticipated than the original.

On March 22, 1968, UCLA demolished the Houston Cougars in the Final Four. Alcindor was healthy, and the Bruins were determined to exact revenge. "It was the greatest exhibition of basketball I have ever seen," said Houston Coach Guy Lewis. Following the incredible performance by Hayes at the Astrodome, Coach Wooden pondered what he would do if he faced him again later. UCLA could implement a box-and-one, in which UCLA would play a 2-2 zone defense, with one defender shadowing Hayes wherever he went. It could play man defense again or go strictly to a conventional zone. Wooden found the perfect fit, but it would not come in a conventional way. UCLA played a diamond and one. The Bruins went to a diamond zone defense as the base, with Lynn Shackelford following Hayes everywhere he went and Alcindor staying just behind, ready to help from the middle of the paint. It worked spectacularly, holding Houston to just 28 percent from the field and Hayes to just 10 points and five rebounds. On the other side, UCLA's offense was brilliant, and it wasn't just Alcindor. The Bruins center scored 19 points and pulled down 18 rebounds. Lucius Allen and Mike Lynn each scored 19, as well, Shackelford added 17, and Mike Warren scored 14. The final score was 101–69. UCLA advanced to the national championship game again, while Houston was left with just a memory of the game in the Astrodome.

The national championship game of 1968 was not remembered like the two games against Houston. The Bruins had taken on their toughest foe, and it wasn't the North Carolina Tar Heels. UCLA beat UNC in the national title game, 78–55, to win its second consecutive national championship and fourth in the last five years. With the dominant NCAA Tournament performance of 1968, UCLA proved they were still the king of college basketball. Meanwhile, the UCLA freshmen team finished with a perfect 19–0 record and would be joining the varsity the following year.

1968–69

The 1968–69 season was more of the same for UCLA basketball, but for the country, it was a trying time. Before the basketball season began, Martin Luther King Jr. was assassinated, as was Robert F. Kennedy. The Vietnam War raged on, and protests at college campuses increased. The 1968 Summer Olympics were held in Mexico City. Lew Alcindor turned down a spot on the US basketball team, believing that his participation would be an endorsement of the treatment of blacks in America. Tommie Smith and John Carlos would not boycott the Olympics, but they would steal the show. After winning gold and bronze in the 200-meter dash, they held up their gloved fists during the playing of the national anthem, signifying the Black Power movement. They were then thrown off the Olympic team, seen by some as heroes and others as villains.

For the UCLA basketball team, it was a simpler time. They were again ranked No. 1 to begin the season and again expected to win the national championship. Some players, Alcindor included, were already looking forward to leaving UCLA and starting the next phase of their lives. Though the roster was stacked with seniors who had already dominated college basketball for two years, Coach Wooden allowed no letdown. As long as his players wore the four letters across their chest, they would play the Wooden way.

Despite any depth and experience on the roster, nothing in college athletics is certain. Prior to the season, Lucius Allen was suspended for the entire year for his second marijuana citation. Without Allen or the graduated Mike Warren, the Bruins backcourt was a major question mark. To begin the season, seniors Bill Sweek and Don Saffer were named starters, but Saffer eventually quit the team, and Sweek alternated as a starter with John Vallely and converted forward Kenny Heitz. But the frontcourt was tremendous. Along with Alcindor at center, forwards Curtis Rowe, Sidney Wicks, and Lynn Shackelford were intimidating all season.

John Vallely drives to the hoop, 1969 (Southern Branch Collection).

UCLA began its season by taking on three straight ranked opponents, and though all three games were closer than fans had expected, the Bruins won them all. In the season opener at Pauley, they beat 10th-ranked Purdue 94–82 and then knocked off 13th-ranked Ohio State and fifth-ranked Notre Dame in back-to-back games on the road. The Bruins got back to their dominant ways, not merely happy finishing with more points than the opponent but striving to be the best, which almost always meant crushing teams by extraordinary margins. UCLA did just that in beating Minnesota by 39 points and then West Virginia by 39 again the next night. The Bruins continued to cruise when they went east to play in the ECAC Holiday Tournament at Madison Square Garden. They dispatched Providence, Princeton, and

Saint John's to win the trophy, and then went home to destroy Tulane in the final nonconference game before the start of the conference season.

Prior to the start of the 1968–69 basketball season, the Athletic Association of Western Universities was no more. The name changed to the Pacific-8 Conference. No matter what the conference was called, everyone knew what team owned the conference on the hardwood. UCLA was gunning for its seventh conference title in the last eight years. During the conference season, no one could compete with UCLA. The Bruins swept the opening road series against the schools from Oregon, winning by an average of 24 points per game. They crushed three more nonconference teams and then did the same to the Pac-8 schools from Northern California, beating Cal by 35 and Stanford by 37. Washington played a slow brand of basketball but fell twice at the hands of the Bruins. Washington State, which played at a normal pace, still lost both games by an average of 26 points. Even in the worst game of the year to date, UCLA still survived, beating Cal in an overtime game on March 1, thanks to the clutch play of Curtis Rowe. UCLA was 24–0, perfect in Pac-8 play, and well on its way to another perfect season—that is, until it took on the USC Trojans.

The Trojans used the same tactics that other teams had tried for years—play slowly, drag the game out, and hope the Bruins would make mistakes at the end that they could capitalize on. The game, on March 7 at the Sports Arena, would be close throughout, as the Trojans' patience was keeping them in the game. At the end of regulation, the score was tied, and for the second game in a row, UCLA went to overtime. The game was still tied with 10 seconds remaining in overtime when USC sank a short jumper for a two-point lead. Coach Wooden called a timeout to set up the offense, and when the Bruins came back out onto the court, they executed perfectly. Shackelford knocked down a high-arching 30-foot jump shot at the buzzer, sending the game to a second overtime period. From there, the Bruins rose to the challenge and finally accomplished what many thought was a foregone conclusion before the game started. UCLA won, 61–55, to stay perfect on the season.

One night later, on March 8, the two teams played again, this time at Pauley Pavilion. UCLA had already clinched the Pac-8 crown. This time, however, the clutch play of the Trojans was the deciding factor. With the score tied at 44, Ernie Powell knocked down a long jump shot and beat the Bruins in dramatic, shocking fashion. The loss ended the Bruins' 41-game winning streak and was the first loss since losing to Houston at the Astrodome the prior year. It was also the first home loss for UCLA since December 1965.

UCLA cheerleaders, 1969 (Southern Branch Collection).

Despite the loss, UCLA was still the number-one team entering the 1969 NCAA Tournament, and they played the first two games at Pauley Pavilion. No. 12 seed New Mexico State did not hide what its strategy would be going into the game. Coaches openly talked about employing the stall, believing that UCLA was too undisciplined to play focused basketball against the strategy. Despite the loose lips and brash confidence, the players stood no chance. The game was over by halftime, and UCLA won, 53–38. The next game was the last at Pauley Pavilion for Lew Alcindor, arguably the greatest college player of all time. He certainly would not go out with a loss, and the Bruins crushed Santa Clara to advance to another Final Four.

On March 20, the Bruins took on the Drake University Bulldogs at Freedom Hall in Louisville, Kentucky. A crowd of 18,435 saw the game, and it was one to remember. Though the game was close, UCLA again won, this time by the score of 85–82, again advancing to play for a national championship. Most sportswriters believed UCLA would play North Carolina in the national championship game, but Rick Mount and the Purdue Boilermakers had other ideas. Mount was the hottest man in the tournament, and stopping him would be the toughest test for the Bruins. With UCLA's close call in the semifinals, many started to believe the Bruins could actually lose, something that was unthinkable just a few short weeks earlier. When the game got under way, however, it didn't take long to see which team was better. Kenny Heitz guarded Mount for most of the game, and he did so in splendid fashion. It was the greatest defensive performance of the year by any guard in the country, as he completely frustrated one of the top players in America. Mount had the worst game of his career, and though he scored 28 points, he shot just 12-for-36 from the floor, grabbed only one rebound, and had zero assists. UCLA's star would not have the same problems. Alcindor finished his brilliant career with another classic performance, pouring in 37 points on 15-for-20 shooting and grabbing 20 rebounds. Purdue never had a chance. It trailed, 42–31, at halftime and lost, 92–72. UCLA became the first team to win three consecutive national championships.

Lew Alcindor following his final collegiate game and third consecutive national championship, 1969 (Southern Branch Collection).

The game marked the end of Lew Alcindor's magnificent college career. His arrival at UCLA sparked expectations never before placed on a college player, and he matched or exceeded them in every way. He averaged 26.4 points per game for his three-year career, which has never been matched at UCLA in one season since. UCLA had to fill a massive void left by Alcindor's graduation, but Coach Wooden had certainly proven to be the right man for the job. The end of the 1960s marked a decade of dominance—UCLA won five national titles. Despite the loss of Alcindor, UCLA aimed to dominate the '70s too.

Kareem Abdul-Jabbar

Kareem Abdul-Jabbar, born Lewis Ferdinand Alcindor, is a complex man. The man who became one of the most accomplished basketball players to ever live was born on April 16, 1947, in Harlem. Alcindor's spent most of his early childhood in Manhattan, where he was raised in the Inwood section housing projects. For Alcindor, it was an exciting place to grow up. As a young boy, he was interested more in learning than in athletics, and Inwood exposed him to a wide variety of different cultures. In *Becoming Kareem*, he spoke of his early childhood surrounded by a "mini United Nations" in Manhattan.

He did not realize until third grade that he was different than most of his classmates. When one of Lewis's classmates, a boy named Michael, brought a Polaroid camera to school and the class decided to take a class photo, Alcindor suddenly noticed what wasn't so clear before. The photo would be passed around to the students, each taking a look at the group of classmates together; when Alcindor got his hands on the picture, he noticed not the group as a whole, but himself as an individual—a black boy towering awkwardly over all of his classmates. He was not the only black child in his class; he was one of three. But he saw the three as distinctly different from the others. For the rest of his life, race would be at the center of the way Alcindor thought about life, society, and America.

Alcindor's parents had not planned on athletics for him. He was raised in a strict household; his parents viewed his education as the primary (and secondary) pathway to future success. Though he would have spats with his parents, as all children do, this was not a problem for Lewis. He was always curious, loved reading, and had a passion for learning. While Lewis's mother pushed him to succeed academically, Lewis's father was the emotionally distant figure that provided the example. He was a police officer, a music aficionado, an avid reader, and someone Lewis was never quite able to figure out. He was a strict father who tried to keep Lewis on the right path, yet it was hard for Lewis to get to know his father. Still, they had commonalities, none more so than their love of music. Educated at the Julliard School of Music, his father played the trombone, sang in the Hall Johnson Choir, and loved jazz. Alcindor would say of his father, "When he was either playing or dancing, he was smiling and happy. When he wasn't, it was as if someone had opened his valve and let all the air out." Alcindor would share his father's interest in music, playing the sax, idolizing John Coltrane, and studying music history in his free time.

When Lewis was eight years old, he first took part in organized athletics, playing Little League baseball. Alcindor played for four years, calling the sport his first love. His first taste of basketball was not what one may imagine. His dad tried to teach him qualities that would make a good player, but instead he physically dominated him, and their first time playing together would be their last. Instead, Alcindor stuck to baseball and his other interests, including Western movies, civil rights, and the space race.

Though Lewis was an ideal student at St. Jude, a strict Catholic School, his parents decided to send him to a boarding school for the fourth grade. Holy Providence was not what Lewis envisioned. He believed he was sent there for educational opportunities, but he quickly learned that it was a reform school, meant to "transform tough kids into model students." Behavioral issues were not a concern for Lewis in the past, and they would not be a problem for him at Holy Providence. The greatest problem was race. He was said to act too white for the black kids, and he was too black for the white kids. The other black children, led by a boy named Sylvester, bullied Lewis. It was the toughest year of his early life. He felt abandoned by his parents and felt he didn't fit in with any particular group of peers at Holy Providence. He did, however, find something glorious during such difficult times. Because of his height, he was chosen to be on the school basketball team, through no decision of his own.

Lewis was clumsy, didn't run fast, could not jump high, and didn't have a good shot at the basket. He was shy, lacked confidence on the court, and was far from one of the better players on the team. During one game, however, he received the ball down low, and though he looked to pass back out to his teammates, no one was open. He began to panic, and in a hurried attempt to get the ball out of his hands as quickly as possible, he swung his arm toward the basket, letting go of the ball. It was the first time Alcindor ever attempted a hook shot. He missed the shot badly, but the feel of the move excited Alcindor, and he tried it again the very next time down the court. He missed again. Lewis's hook shot improved throughout high school and college and became the greatest offensive weapon in basketball history while in the NBA. It all started on the blacktop courts at Holy Providence, a place where Alcindor felt so alone.

Lewis spent just one year at the boarding school, but it changed who he was. The tough year had turned him from an optimistic, interested boy to a quiet, lonesome child who rarely smiled and rarely talked unless necessary. Back in New York, he viewed himself more every day as someone who would be defined by his race and height and who needed to safeguard himself from others. He became more aware of issues involving race relations nationwide, and that changed him. While other things occupied his mind off the court, Alcindor continued playing basketball. Though he still struggled to find positive results, he found a believer. Coach Farrell Hopkins believed Alcindor had talent; it just needed to be refined. He connected Lewis with a local college player, George Hejduk, who helped him develop skills. Lewis continued to improve. By seventh grade, he was a good player, the best on the team, and he was no longer unenthusiastic about the game. It had become a passion. By eighth grade, Lewis stood at 6'8", towering over all the other players, and he was already easily able to dunk a basketball.

Catholic high schools across the northeast wanted Alcindor to play for their program, to help them become the best high school team in the nation. Alcindor decided to stay home and attend Power Memorial Academy in downtown Manhattan. He played for Coach Jack Donahue, whom Alcindor greatly admired and then later despised, only to make up with decades later.

When Lewis began high school, he was 6'10", mature, smart, focused, and expected to be one of the best players on the team right away. Alcindor got good grades throughout high school, something his parents still valued more than his basketball skills. While at Power Memorial, Lewis continued his interest in race relations and pay close attention to the growing civil rights movement across America. He developed his own beliefs, followed his own new idols, and pictured how he could one day influence the world like the men he followed closely. He questioned his religious beliefs, his formal education, and what his greater purpose in life was. What he saw mostly angered him, and he wished he could do more to make the difference he believed was necessary in the country. But he was only 14, just a freshman. He needed an outlet, and it was basketball.

Though Alcindor practiced with the junior varsity during the preseason, he would make the varsity team as a freshman, going from sparse playing time to playing a key role as the season progressed. He was certainly not the elite player he would later become, but he was competing with the older, more polished, more confident, stronger players, and it served him well. Playing for Coach Donahue inspired Lewis. He had never played for such a strong-willed coach, someone who would be blunt and honest with him, and someone who so clearly believed in him and wanted him to succeed. Power Memorial lost six games Lewis's freshman year. Colleges were already recruiting him, and things would only continue to improve for him on the court.

While the spectacular indoor, hardwood gym facility at Power Memorial was a refuge for Lewis, it was not the only court that helped change his life. Outside was the world-famous blacktop Rucker Park, and the annual summer Rucker Tournament. Prior to his sophomore year, Lewis was at the tournament when he met another basketball great who would influence his life. Wilt Chamberlain was already the greatest player in basketball, a larger-than-life figure everywhere he went. Alcindor was introduced to Chamberlain, and though their first interaction was brief, it started a friendship that would eventually turn into a professional rivalry. Chamberlain was honest with Alcindor. He gave him tips on basketball and life and gave him a glimpse of what was possible if he reached the top of the game. Chamberlain's off-the-court exploits are nearly as famous as what he did on the court, and Lewis saw in Chamberlain what was possible if he continued to get better.

Power Memorial finished the season undefeated with Alcindor as a sophomore. The next year, it won the high school national championship, and in Alcindor's senior year, it was the runner-up. All three years, the school was the New York City Catholic champion. Alcindor finished his high school career with more than 2,000 career points, a New York City record at the time. Though high school basketball brought great success, it also brought a moment of betrayal, one that would be more memorable for Alcindor than any success on the court. In Alcindor's junior season, in a game against St. Helena's High School, Power Memorial and Alcindor had a sluggish first half. Though the team led at halftime, the margin was much closer than Coach Donahue thought it should have been. As the players filed into the locker room, Coach Donahue followed behind his team, closed the door, and ripped into them. He was an emotional coach, a screamer, and such a tantrum was not new. After throwing verbal daggers at the team, Coach Donahue turned to his star player. "And you, Lew. You go out there and don't hustle. You don't move. You don't do any of the things you're supposed to do. You're acting just like a nigger!"

Lewis didn't say anything; he couldn't. He was crushed. Alcindor looked up to Coach Donahue, and the coach just broke his heart. Power Memorial won the game, but the words of his coach stuck with Lewis. In the locker room afterward, Coach Donahue called Lewis into his office. "See! It worked! My strategy worked. I knew that if I used that word, it'd shock you into a good second half, and it did! I know it seemed harsh at the time, but it got you going." For Lewis, he used his coaching hat to conceal his racism, all for the good of the team. He wanted to transfer immediately, believing he could no longer play for the man he used to admire. Lewis's parents understood why he wanted to leave, but also knew how impractical it was. Instead, he would remain at Power, winning games for a coach he no longer could trust. Coach Donahue and Lewis had a strained relationship for decades, but in 1998, the broken pieces were put back together. While visiting Coach Wooden in his home, Wooden brought up the incident, explaining to then Kareem Abdul-Jabbar that everyone makes mistakes and if it is warranted, Coach Donahue is worthy of forgiveness. Minutes later, the phone rang, and it was Coach Donahue. Coach Wooden handed the phone over to Kareem; the two finally spoke again, beginning to fix a decades-long broken relationship.

As a senior, Lewis had an important decision to make; which college he would attend. For years, he had been receiving scholarship offers, but Coach Donahue always hid correspondence from Lewis, telling him that it would all work itself out. He was told he could attend any school in the country, and this was a fact. He was one of the most recruited athletes in prep sports history. Lewis had three specific criteria in choosing where he wanted to attend:

Alcindor blocks a shot, 1968 (Southern Branch Collection).

- He had to be a primary focus of the offense and had to be on a team that won at a very high level.
- He needed a great education, because he knew that basketball could be taken away at any time, and injuries must not prevent him from becoming a successful person.
- He had to leave New York to get away from home.

The four schools Lewis finally narrowed his choices to were the University of Michigan, Columbia University, St. John's University, and UCLA. After weighing the pros and cons of each school, seeing which matched the criteria he valued, and dreaming of the place where he would next live and play, he decided to visit UCLA; if his visit went well, that's where he would attend. On his visit to UCLA, he met with Coach John Wooden in his office. He expected to hear a typical sales job from a coach. After an awkward silence, Coach Wooden finally said, "I'm impressed with your grades, Lewis." The visit solidified in Lewis's mind that he wanted to attend UCLA, but one more step was needed. Coach Wooden went east to visit the Alcindor home. There, after exchanging pleasantries and talking briefly, Lewis's mom asked Lewis to wait in his room while they talked. For one hour, the Alcindor parents and Coach Wooden spoke, with Lewis desperately trying to hear through the sound of the walls in his room. Finally, he was called back out, just in time to say goodbye. Coach Wooden had already won over Lewis; this time he won over his parents. Lewis's mom would call Coach Wooden "a gentlemen, not the kind of man who will take advantage of you." His father called him "dignified." With that meeting, it became a certainty. Coach Wooden had just found his next star. Lewis Alcindor would go west.

Alcindor became a star on the UCLA court (as discussed earlier) and a changing man off of it. Like most college students, Alcindor's four years at UCLA were a time of great personal evolution. He had been politically and socially conscious for years, but while in college, he became more active. He took deep interest in the civil rights movement, the

Black Power movement, African history, and politics. He got to know Muhammad Ali, studied Malcolm X, and participated in the Cleveland Summit with Jim Brown, Bill Russell, and others. He boycotted the 1968 Olympics, studied under Bruce Lee, and developed his love of writing. While in college, he also studied religion. For years, he had quietly questioned his Christian faith, and in college he finally found answers. He read about Buddhism, Taoism, Hinduism, and other religions, but none made sense to him except Islam. Fans would question why he would choose a religion seen as so foreign to American culture, and Alcindor took no offense to the questioning. He had his reasons, backed up by his beliefs, formed through his studies, and it was finally his decision.

After converting to Islam prior to his senior season at UCLA, Alcindor believed something more had to change. He saw that many of his idols who were also Muslim had changed their names, believing that their birth names were merely reflections of their prior life. Lewis was given the name Kareem ("generous") Abdul ("servant of Allah"). The name would be kept quiet, however. Lewis believed he needed to further his education and harden his positions before publicly pronouncing his new name and officially changing it. After the season, however, he again had a new name. His teacher Hamaas Abdul-Khaalis believed his name lacked spirit. He would add Jabbar, meaning "powerful." He was now Kareem Abdul-Jabbar, at least in his inner circle.

In 1969, Alcindor was drafted by the Milwaukee Bucks with the first overall pick in the NBA draft and first overall in the ABA draft by the New York Nets. It was a dream scenario. He wanted to play for the Nets of the ABA, but he could also use the NBA as leverage in contract negotiations. Alcindor and his advisor told both teams to submit one offer only, hoping that they would silently seek to outbid each other by raising the value of the contract. He would simply choose the highest bidder.

When the two offers came in, Alcindor was shocked. The Bucks offered a generous contract, and Alcindor expected the Nets to offer significantly more. Instead, it was less. He had wanted to join the Nets, but he also had researched enough on Wisconsin to convince himself that it would be a great place to start his career. He informed the Bucks he would sign with them, but it was not without drama. Before making the deal official, he heard again from the Nets with a new offer. They would give Alcindor three times the money the Bucks offered. It was a dream come true. He would get to go home, and for more money. But he had given his word to the Bucks and would not change plans. He would take less money to play in a city he viewed as a second choice.

As a rookie with the Bucks, Alcindor averaged 28.9 points and 14.5 rebounds per game. He played in every game and was instantly one of the best players in the entire league. One year later, the Bucks acquired All-Star guard Oscar Robertson and won the NBA title. Alcindor was named MVP of the league in just his second year, averaging 31.7 PPG in the process. On May 1, 1971, the day after winning the NBA title, Lewis Ferdinand Alcindor officially became Kareem Abdul-Jabbar. Nationally, the change seemed radical, but it was who he had been for years. Kareem continued his magical career with the Bucks, winning two more MVP's in the next four years. In six seasons with the Bucks, Kareem won three MVP's and one championship, he and averaged 30.4 points per game. His time in Milwaukee is just a footnote in his legendary career.

In 1975, Kareem was traded from Milwaukee to the Los Angeles Lakers. For 14 seasons, he was the man in the middle for the purple and gold, nicknamed the "Captain," and winning at an incredible rate. He would eventually be teamed up with Magic Johnson and later Jamaal Wilkes, Norm Nixon, James Worthy, and the rest of the "Showtime" Lakers, forming one of the greatest dynasties in sports history.

During his magnificent NBA career, Kareem won six NBA championships, six MVPs, 19 All-Star selections, 15 All-NBA selections, 11 All-NBA Defensive selections, a Rookie of the Year award, and numerous other honors. He compiled 38,387 career points, most in NBA history. He grabbed 17,440 rebounds, fourth most all-time. His 3,189 blocks rank third all time. His number 33 jersey is retired by the Milwaukee Bucks and the Los Angeles Lakers. He is a member of the Basketball and the College Basketball Halls of Fame.

On February 3, 1990, his number 33 jersey was retired by the UCLA basketball program, never to be worn again by a UCLA Bruin. The list of accomplishments on Kareem's incomparable resume is long, but it does not include basketball only. He is the author of over a dozen books, ranging from politics to history to basketball and has appeared in multiple movies and television shows. He is a documentary filmmaker and a political activist. He has served as a Cultural Ambassador for the United States and as a member of the President's Council of Fitness, Sports, and Nutrition. He is a cancer survivor, a philanthropist, and a father. In 2016, President Obama awarded him the Presidential Medal of Freedom, the highest civilian honor in the United States.

1969–70

When most college basketball fans think of the UCLA success under Coach Wooden, they think of the '64 team, the three straight championships with Lew Alcindor leading the way, the 88-game winning streak, or the years with the Big Redhead, Bill Walton. UCLA's success under Coach Wooden certainly provided great memories for Bruins fans everywhere, but some teams mostly forgotten are equally important to the mystique of the Bruins dynasty. The 1970 team is one of those. Few historians throw the 1970 team into the all-time great discussion, and they were certainly not the greatest UCLA team of all time. It was, however, incredibly successful. With the loss of Alcindor to the NBA, many other coaches around the country believed they had a chance, that the Bruins would fall back. With Alcindor gone, no clear dominant force could almost single-handedly guarantee another national championship. But UCLA had teamwork. Steve Patterson at center averaged a double-double. Junior Curtis Rowe averaged more than 15 points per game as a hybrid guard-forward. Sophomore guard Henry Bibby put in 15.6 PPG, and senior captain John Vallely added another 16.3 to give the Bruins one of the best backcourts in America. The biggest star for UCLA on the court in 1970 was Sidney Wicks. After playing a complimentary role the prior season, Wicks became one of the best players in America in 1970, earning All-America status and National Player of the Year recognition. The 6'8" 225-pound Wicks averaged 18.6 points and 11.8 rebounds per game on the season.

The Bruins began the season not in their familiar spot at the top of the college basketball ranking, but actually at No. 4 in the AP poll. The ranking was not entirely surprising, given the hole to fill. UCLA began the season by winning and then winning more and more. The season began on December 1, and the Bruins crushed the University of Arizona, 90–65 at Pauley Pavilion. Not all the games would be that easy. Five days later, the Bruins traveled to Minneapolis to take on the University of Minnesota at Williams Arena. The Bruins escaped with a win but were far from dominant, beating the unranked Golden Gophers by a single point.

Following the close call, the Bruins got back on track, beating Miami by 58 points, LSU by 49, Texas by 45, and Georgia Tech by 31 in consecutive games. In the game against LSU, the Bruins scored 133 points, a single-game school record. Pistol Pete Maravich scored 38 points, but shot just 14-for-42 from the field and committed 18 turnovers. Despite winning the previous four by more than 45 points, UCLA inexplicably struggled at home against Princeton, led by Geoff Petrie and John Hummer, both NBA first-round picks, in the Bruin Classic. UCLA again snuck by, winning, 76–75, and remained unbeaten on the season. UCLA was 7–0, though they had yet to play any ranked teams. In their next game, it got the first chance at another AP top team, the 13th-ranked Notre Dame Fighting Irish. The Bruins returned to top form, winning by 31 points and proving to the nation that they were still the team to beat in the country.

Beating UCLA would not be easy, even if every opponent was gunning for them, hoping to knock off the top team in the land. When conference play began on January 9, the Bruins were back in the top spot in the AP rankings, and Pac-8 opponents were back to wondering what they could possibly do to stop the juggernaut in Westwood. The answer was not much. UCLA beat both Oregon schools, though the game against OSU was another one-point affair, then took on four straight nonconference foes, easily dispatching them as well. When conference play resumed, the Bruins continued their winning ways, beating both Washington schools twice and again beating Oregon State, this time by 15 on the road.

UCLA was 21–0 and seemed indestructible. Another perfect 30–0 season was what most expected by now, but what they got in Eugene was surprising to

Curtis Rowe, 1970 (Southern Branch Collection).

everyone. UCLA not only lost, but got crushed. The final score was 78–65, in favor of Oregon. Knowing that students would rush the court at the end of the game, Coach Wooden walked over to Oregon head coach Steve Belko and shook his hand before the final seconds ticked off. When the clock hit :00, fans stormed the court, and the winning streak was over. With the loss came the destruction of UCLA's invincibility. The team could be beat, and a national championship was not a sure thing. The loss on February 21 would not be just a bad game, or bad luck. It was the first of two losses for the Bruins heading into the NCAA Tournament. After beating Stanford and Cal by an average margin of 22 points, the Bruins took on USC on March 6 at Pauley Pavilion and lost again. It was just the second loss ever for the Bruins at Pauley Pavilion, and though they would rebound the next night to beat USC at the Sports Arena, 91–78, the loss at home cost the Bruins the top overall seed in the NCAA Tournament. UCLA had won the Pac-8 conference again, but because of the tremendous success during the previous years, the standard for the Bruins was national championship or bust. They would enter the tournament as the No. 2 overall seed, behind the Kentucky Wildcats.

The games of the West Region of the 1970 NCAA Tournament were held in Seattle, and the Bruins took on Long Beach State, coached by Jerry Tarkanian, on March 12. The 49ers entered the game with an impressive 19-game winning streak, but left the arena with a one-game losing streak. Bibby and Wicks each scored 20 for the Bruins, Rowe added 15, Vallely 14, and Patterson scored 13. The performance was typical for the 1970 Bruins, and in the eyes of Bruins fans, it was perfect. They simply needed to do it again three more times. Two days later, UCLA took on a strong Utah State team in the regional final. Wicks and Rowe each scored 26 to lead the way, and four of the five starters scored in double figures. UCLA trounced USU, 101–79, and advanced to another Final Four.

The Final Four was held at Cole Field House, the

home gym of the University of Maryland. The semifinal game against New Mexico State was another perfect Bruins recipe, a game with great balance and incredible teamwork. In the opening game of the tournament for UCLA, Bibby and Wicks shared game-high scoring honors. The next game, Wicks and Rowe shared the honors. In the semifinal against New Mexico State, Vallely, who scored 23 points, led the scoring. Wicks added 22 points and 16 rebounds, and Rowe added 15 points and 15 rebounds. The final score was UCLA 93, NMSU 77. The Bruins once again advanced to the national championship game.

The matchup contrasted two styles: UCLA, a speedy, pressing team, which thrived in the open court, versus Jacksonville University, a huge team that already knocked off top-seeded Kentucky earlier in the tournament. The Dolphins were led by 7'2" center Artis Gilmore and 7'0" forward Pembrook Burrows III. The Dolphins jumped out to a quick nine-point lead, leading 16–7 early, but UCLA's balance, teamwork, and incredible speed and agility eventually wore down the bigger Dolphins. Wicks played perhaps the finest defensive game of his career, blocking five of Gilmore's shots and holding him to 19 points on just nine of 29 from the field. Wicks also added 17 points of his own, grabbed 18 rebounds, and was just one of the main ingredients for the Bruins. Rowe scored 19 points, Patterson scored 17, and Vallely added 15 points. The Bruins beat the Dolphins, 80–69. The victory was their 24th consecutive in the NCAA Tournament, and the title was the fourth consecutive and sixth in the past seven years. Rowe and Vallely were named to the NCAA Final Four All-Tournament Team, and head coach John Wooden was named National Coach of the Year by nearly every media outlet.

The 1970 Bruins proved they could win without Lew Alcindor. The question going forward—how long could they keep doing it? The two thousand UCLA fans who met the Bruins at Gate 36 at Los Angeles International Airport would think about that later. It was time to party.

1970–71

When UCLA won the national championship in 1970, many college basketball fans were surprised. Like the 1965 team, the 1970 Bruins were not expected to be as good as the season before. Still, the team persevered. Going forward, no one would underestimate Coach Wooden. He had won with Hazzard and Goodrich and Alcindor. He could and would keep winning. No longer was Sidney Wicks underrated. He stepped out of the giant shadow left by Alcindor, and after a brilliant season in 1970, he was to be even better in '71. He finished with a 21.8 points per game average and hauled in nearly 13 rebounds per game. Curtis Rowe continued his incredible career, finishing second on the Bruins in scoring and rebounding, averaging 17.5 points and 10 rebounds per game Steve Patterson and Henry Bibby were excellent players, as well, and a strong bench supported the four main weapons. The 1971 Bruins were in the middle of an incredible stretch of success, and they forged their own legacy, won their own way, and lived on in college basketball lore.

UCLA began the season again ranked No. 1 in the country and proceeded to win its first 14 games. UCLA averaged nearly 92 points per game during that stretch and gave up a tad under 70 points per game. They were blowing opponents out, and many in the media were already calling Wicks, Rowe, and Patterson the greatest frontcourt in college basketball history. The three were dominating opponents not with sheer size, but with athleticism, timing, leaping ability, coordination, skill, energy, and an incredible press defense that led to fast-break offense.

Though the Bruins were 14–0, they had yet to play a ranked team heading into the matchup against the ninth-ranked Notre Dame Fighting Irish on January 23, 1971, at the Athletic and Convocation Center in South Bend, Indiana. The Bruins, and especially Wicks, started slowly. For the first eight minutes of the game, Wicks was unable to make a shot, UCLA's guards were unable to take care of the ball, and the entire team was unable to stop Notre Dame star Austin Carr. UCLA was down by 13 points, trailing, 37–24, but it soon righted the shipped—or so it seemed. By halftime, UCLA had cut the lead to five, trailing just 43–38.

In the second half, Wicks picked up his game, and so did the Bruins offense, but stopping Carr was an entirely more difficult task. UCLA tied it up at 47 just three minutes into the second half but would trail for much of the way, as Notre Dame bounced right back to regain control. UCLA trailed, 82–78, with three minutes to play. In order to complete the comeback, the team would have to get stops, but Carr could not be stopped on this day. He scored six more points to finish it out for the Fighting Irish. Wicks finished the game with 23 points, leading the Bruins, but the story was Carr: he finished with 46 points. The final score was Notre Dame 89, UCLA 82. Coach Wooden gave Carr the credit he deserved after the game, saying, "Austin Carr is tremendous, and today we met a team that played better than we did." The loss was the first for UCLA against a nonconference foe in 48 games. One streak came to a close. Another was set to begin.

UCLA fell to No. 3 in the nation following the loss to Notre Dame, and it would not get any easier going forward. After beating UC Santa Barbara, the Bruins took on the No. 2 USC Trojans on February 6 at the Sports Arena. The '71 Trojans were possibly the greatest team in USC basketball history, led by Dennis Layton and Paul Westphal, both guards, and both incredible scorers. They were undefeated going into the game, with a 16–0 record and wins over three ranked teams already. The game was not pretty. Scores in the 60s were not ideal for UCLA, a team with an incredible offense and pressing defense. The team wanted to run, to play a free brand of basketball with scores in the 90s or 100s. Against USC, the game was much slower. The final score was 64–60, and again the team that owned Los Angeles in college basketball was the team to finish on top.

Following the game against USC, the Bruins kept winning. They would win their next eight games, though they were not dominating teams. They beat Oregon by just one point, and then Oregon State by two the next night. They beat Oregon by just seven in the return trip to Los Angeles, and later beat Washington State by just four and Washington by two.

Going into the final game of the season, the Bruins were coming off their best two games in over a month. After struggling for much of February, they beat Cal, 103–69, and Stanford, 107–72, in early March. The Pacific-8 Conference title would come down to one final game. Since losing to UCLA, USC had not lost again. They had a record of 24–1 and was now ranked No. 3 in the country. Its season would be for naught, however, if it did not beat UCLA. The NCAA Tournament allowed only one team per conference to participate up until 1975, so USC was playing for its season. A win over UCLA would result in a one-game playoff for the Pac-8 title and a trip to the NCAA Tournament, where the participant would be the betting favorite to take home the crown. The game was a tale of two different Bruins teams. In the first half, UCLA's offense smacked USC in the mouth. It raced out to a 19-point lead. In the second half, UCLA's offense slowed, but its defense was smothering. It was the best game UCLA played all season, as it cruised to a 73–62 win. USC finished No. 5 in the country but would not make the tournament. Westphal later explained what he believed the conference championship would have meant for USC: "It would have been just another championship at UCLA. If we win here, it will be unique. It's more of an achievement to beat Coach Wooden than to win for him." Westphal would never beat Wooden again.

Like much of the season, the NCAA Tournament was difficult. The Bruins didn't crush opponents every step of the way, with the exception of BYU in the first round. The games were close, especially the Regional Final game against Long Beach State. Jerry Tarkanian's 49ers scared the Bruins like no team in the tournament had during their championship era. The 49ers implemented a 2-3 zone, completely shutting down Bibby, Booker, and Patterson in the first half. They shot 0-for-17 combined, and the Bruins were in trouble. Wicks was in foul trouble most of the way, and Tarkanian's 49ers implemented a stall tactic to shorten the game. The Bruins clawed back, however, and though the game was close, with the final score just 57–55, Bruins, the streak continued. UCLA was still alive.

The Final Four was played in the Astrodome, a familiar venue for Coach Wooden. Against Kansas, a team effort led to another UCLA victory. Wicks scored 21, Bibby put in 18, and Rowe scored 16, and UCLA advanced to the national championship game once again. This time the Bruins would take on the Villanova Wildcats, the 19 seed in the tournament, and a decided underdog. Whereas Wicks and Rowe grabbed the headlines most of the year, Patterson starred for the Bruins on March 27, 1971. He played the game of his life, scoring 29 points, 20 of which came in the first half. Rowe took only three shots, scoring eight points. Wicks scored just seven. A

The 1971 Bruins after winning their fifth consecutive national championship (Southern Branch Collection).

crowd of 31,765 was in attendance, and though most expected UCLA to win, it was the way they won that surprised most there. Whoever was needed for the Bruins in '71 performed up to the task, and Patterson was the man to do it in the national championship game. Wicks was the big star for the Bruins, winning National Player of the Year honors, but the team was the star for Coach Wooden.

A new unique player and personality joined the varsity in '72. The big redhead, Bill Walton, was set to take center stage.

Sidney Wicks

Rarely can any honest UCLA basketball fan describe the beloved program as underrated. The success of UCLA basketball, and its individual players and individual Bruins teams, is well documented. Sidney Wicks is different—he is underrated. ESPN ranked Wicks as the 37 greatest college basketball player ever. *Bleacher Report* ranked him as the fifth greatest Bruin. These are both fine accomplishments. But Wicks was much more than just fine, however. He was brilliant.

Sidney Wicks was born on September 9, 1949, in Los Angeles, California. As an L.A. kid, growing up during the '50s and early '60s, Wicks naturally rooted for UCLA. Under Coach Wooden, the Bruins became the premier hardwood attraction in Los Angeles, and at the same time, the Bruins were in their greatest decade of football prosperity in history. UCLA and the newly arrived Los Angeles Dodgers were the talk of the sports town in Southern California. As a high school player at Alexander Hamilton High School, Wicks was certainly qualified to attend UCLA and play for Coach Wooden, but he struggled academically. Instead of choosing to go elsewhere, Wicks chose to follow his dreams. He briefly considered playing at California or Utah State, but he wanted to play at UCLA, and in order to do so, he needed to first attend Santa Monica College for a year and receive qualifying grades. For Wicks, the decision to attend SMC and then transfer to UCLA was easy. He said of the opportunity to be a Bruin, "At that time, there was no question UCLA had a fantastic tradition. They had the best coach in college basketball; they had the best team in college basketball. I said to myself, 'Why would I go anywhere else if these guys want me?'" When asked why UCLA stood out from other schools who recruited him, Wicks said, "It was so cool to see that type of basketball being played. The way the guys played, it was the way you wanted to play. They didn't make any mistakes. Everybody did the right thing, everybody said the right thing. They moved the right way, they looked the right way. It was so cool. Why would anybody want to go somewhere else?" Wicks's mind was made up. He wanted to be a Bruin. After one year at Santa Monica, his grades came in, and he qualified. He transferred to UCLA in the fall of 1968.

For one season, 1968–69, Wicks played with Lew Alcindor, the greatest college player of all time. The Bruins were the two-time defending national champions, and Wicks was a sophomore joining a loaded senior-laden roster. His role was minimal his first varsity season. He played in each game, averaging 7.5 points and 5.1 rebounds per game. He was an important contributor to be sure. For the rest of his career, he would be a star.

As a junior, the expectations for the UCLA team were much lower than they had been in recent years. Alcindor was gone, and so were much of the key pieces around him. Wicks picked up the slack, however, and begin to show the world that he was one of the greatest power forwards in college basketball history. As a junior, he averaged 18.6 PPG and pulled down 11.9 RPG. He was named First Team All-Pac-8 Conference. The Helms Foundation named him National Player of the Year. He was a consensus Second Team All-American. The Bruins again won the national championship, and he was named the tournament's Most Outstanding Player.

As a senior, he was even better. After averaging 21.3 points and 12.3 rebounds per game, he was again named National Player of the Year by the Helms Foundation. He also earned that honor from the United States Basketball Writers Association and *The Sporting News*. Wicks was a consensus First Team All-American and First Team All-Pac-8, and he again won the national championship at UCLA, his third title. After finishing his college career in 1971, he was drafted by the Portland Trail Blazers with the No. 2 overall pick in the NBA draft. He was in instant sensation, but it would not last.

Sidney Wicks, 1971 (Southern Branch Collection).

In Sidney Wicks's 10-year NBA career, his scoring average decreased in each year, but that isn't to say he wasn't a very good professional player. He just set the bar extraordinarily high as a rookie. After being drafted by the Trail Blazers, Wicks won Rookie of the Year Honors in 1972, and earned a spot on the All-Rookie team. He was an NBA All-Star his first year, averaging 24.5 points and 11.5 rebounds per game. It was an incredible first season for Wicks. Though year two would see a drop in scoring, as his averaged dipped to 23.8, Wicks would again earn a spot on the All-Star team in his second season, as he did in his third and fourth seasons as well. Though he was an accomplished player already through four seasons, his career, from a simple productivity standpoint, was trending in the wrong direction, or so the Blazers thought. Though his scoring was down, he still averaged 21.7 PPG in his fourth year and hauled in 10.7 RPG. Paradoxically, while his scoring numbers slowly dipped, his field-goal percentage steadily rose. Still, he only played one in more season in Portland.

In October of 1976, Wicks's contract was sold to the Boston Celtics, where he would again prove to be a valuable player, but his numbers continued to trend the wrong way. In his first year in Boston, he averaged a double-double (15.1 PPG, 10.0 RPG). He would play just one more season in Boston, however, before he was traded to the San Diego Clippers for Tiny Archibald, Marvin Barnes, Billy Knight, and two draft picks. He played three seasons with the Clippers before retiring from the NBA, and he finished his career in Italy. In 1982, he played for the Reyer Venezia Mestre club team in Venice. Though Wicks's NBA career is seen by many as a disappointment, his career numbers prove he was a very good player. In 10 seasons, he averaged 16.8 points and 8.7 rebounds per game. He finished with a scoring average of at least 20.0 PPG four times, averaged double-digit rebounds four times, and was a four-time All-Star. Since earning All-Star status as a rookie in '72, only 19 other rookies have been named to the All-Star team.

While Wicks's career as a player saw him in the spotlight for a decade and a half, his life post-basketball has been one of quiet comfort. As a retiree, he has remained behind the scenes. Wicks's only association with basketball after his playing days came back at UCLA. While Walt Hazzard coached the Bruins from 1985 to 1988, Wicks was beside him on the bench, serving as an assistant coach. Since his last days as an assistant, however, Wicks has nearly vanished from public eye.

Following his stint with the Bruins, Wicks searched for what to do next in his life. For a brief time, he owned and operated six dry-cleaning agencies in San Diego. He later moved on to the real estate industry and has lived in California, Georgia, North Carolina, and Florida. He is a private person who enjoys spending time with his daughter and working out. Wicks rarely speaks with the media, though he is cordial whenever approached. Wicks has become a model citizen and a loving father. Nearly 30 years ago, however, he nearly lost it all. On December 5, 1989, Wicks was in a serious car accident in San Diego. Driving a 1974 Cadillac, Wicks and the passenger riding in his car were struck by a loaded cement truck that ran a red light. Wicks suffered a ruptured spleen and several facial injuries. The passenger in his car suffered minor injuries. His fitness was said to have helped aid in his recovery.

Today, Wicks is 70 years old, and while many Bruins fans still have fond memories of watching his incredible athletic feats on the hardwood at Pauley Pavilion, they must know they are not alone. Wicks still cherishes his time as a Bruin and actively roots for his alma mater every year. He said of his experience at UCLA, "It was the best college experience a kid could have. Athletically, it was the best. Personally and academically, it was the best situation you could have at any college. The curriculum, the campus life, the way of life there was unbelievable." Wicks's number 35 jersey was retired at UCLA on February 1, 1996. When fans look to the rafters and see the name "Wicks," they are seeing the jersey of one of the greatest power forwards in college basketball history, and more important, a proud Bruin.

1971–72

Coach John Wooden had made it a habit to write and distribute an annual letter to his players in the summer before basketball season started. In the summer of 1971, Coach Wooden knew his team would be young. Wicks, Rowe, and Patterson were all gone, and Henry Bibby was the only returning starter. Still, Coach Wooden was excited for the upcoming season. In the first sentence of his letter, he wrote, "It has been a long time since I have looked forward so eagerly to a coming basketball season, and I hope that you share this enthusiasm." He continued, "The 1971–72 Bruins will be short on experience in comparison with most of our recent teams, but it will not be short on talent, and I would much rather have talent without experience than experience without talent."

Along with Bibby, there was a plethora of talent, including sophomore guards Greg Lee and Tommy Curtis, junior forwards Larry Hollyfield and Larry Farmer, and quality backups Gary Franklin, Vince Carson, and Swen Nater. Two men, however, would stand out above the rest. Keith Wilkes, a 6'6" sophomore from Santa Barbara with a funky shot coming from behind his right ear before being released high above his head, turned into a star. His mid-range jump shot would be his signature, and he was a perfect match with his other star teammate,

Bill Walton. At 6'11", Walton was the second elite big man that Coach Wooden had ever coached. Walton would have difficulty matching the play of Alcindor, the greatest college basketball player ever, but he didn't have to. Though he was not quite the dominant offensive scorer as Alcindor, he was a better defender, and a slightly better rebounder. He was a brilliant passer in the half-court offense. He was capable of playing backline defense and then quickly taking the ball off the board, turning and firing an outlet pass better than any Bruin in history, and possibly better than any player in college basketball history. As a sophomore, Walton averaged 21.1 points and 15.5 rebounds per game. Bibby was second on the team in scoring, putting in 15.7 PPG, and Wilkes averaged 13.5.

As had become an annual late fall tradition, the Bruins began the season ranked No. 1 in the country, and unlike in the previous two seasons, close games were few in 1971–72. The Bruins destroyed their opponents. On December 3, 1971, the careers of the brilliant sophomore class began, and the Bruins easily beat The Citadel. Walton finished with 19 points and 14 rebounds in his first career game, and his roommate, Keith Wilkes, scored 14. Bibby, however, was the star, leading all scorers with 26. Nater scored 16 off the bench. The Bruins were 1–0, winning, 105–49, and running their winning streak to 16 games.

One night later, Bibby scored 32, Farmer had 21, and the Bruins beat Iowa by 44 points. The early season would continue in the same fashion. High-scoring performances were registered by a number of Bruins, including 31 for Walton, 21 for Hollyfield, 22 for Wilkes, and multiple 20-plus point performances by Bibby, all in the month of December. The biggest win came against UCLA's upcoming rival. On December 22 at Pauley Pavilion, UCLA dominated Notre Dame in a way almost unseen in college basketball history. The Bruins jumped out to a 17–0 lead.

Henry Bibby, 1972 (Southern Branch Collection).

They led 53–16 at halftime, and went on to win by 58 points, more than doubling up their opponent, 114–56. Bibby led the way with 28 points. Walton finished with 20 points and 19 rebounds. Notre Dame head coach Digger Phelps would say of the Bruins, "This is the greatest team John Wooden has ever had. That Walton is the best big guy in the country. They don't have any weaknesses." The Bruins just kept rolling through the closing days of 1971. After scoring at least 100 points in each of the first seven games, UCLA was held to just 79 in the final game of the Bruin Basketball Classic against Ohio State. The Buckeyes played a slow style, led by 7'0" center Luke Witte. UCLA was fine playing any style, however, and sixth-ranked Ohio State stood no chance. Despite foul trouble for Walton, UCLA won, 79–53.

The New Year brought no hope for opponents. UCLA was king. The conference opener was the toughest game of the regular season for UCLA, mostly because they played far below its usual standard. Against Oregon State on January 7, UCLA committed 30 turnovers and let the Beavers' best player, Freddie Boyd, shred the defense for 37 points. Walton had strep throat, and the entire Bruins team seemed a step slow. The final score was 78–72, and though the game was ugly for UCLA, it again finished on top, running their record to 9–0 and their winning streak to 24.

The Bruins wouldn't have the same problems they had against the Beavers again for a long time. One night later, Walton scored 30 and the Bruins won with Nater brilliant off the bench. Walton kept playing well as the Bruins regained their form after the temporary slip in performance. Against Stanford, he scored 32. Against Cal, he blocked or deflected 14 shots or passes, and the Bruins held the Bears to under 25 percent shooting for the night. On January 21, the Bruins held Santa Clara to a Pauley Pavilion–record low scoring first half, with the Broncos scoring only 13. One night later, against the University of Denver Pioneers, Walton scored just eight points but did everything right for UCLA. His passing was brilliant, as he would pass up open shots to find his teammates for even better looks. Coach Wooden called it one of Walton's "finest games."

On January 29, UCLA retuned to South Bend, Indiana, to take on the porous Notre Dame squad they had crushed earlier in the season. It was the site of their last loss, and though Coach Phelps hoped to knock off the Bruins again, it wouldn't happen this night. The Irish played slowly, as Phelps knew he had no chance if they decided to run with the Bruins. The final score was 57–32. The Bruins left with another blowout win. UCLA beat USC twice by an average of 19 points and Washington State twice by an average of 30.5 points. They beat Washington twice by an average of 33. The Bruins smashed the two Oregon schools in the return trip to Pauley Pavilion, beating Oregon by 22 and Oregon State by 19. Neither Cal nor Stanford stood a chance either; both were destroyed at home. UCLA finished the regular season with a 26–0 record, 14–0 in Pac-8 play.

On March 16, 1972, UCLA began its quest for another title as it took on the Weber State Wildcats in Provo, Utah. The tournament would not begin well for Walton. He scored a season-low four points, dealing with foul trouble nearly the entire game. Nater filled in more than admirably, however, and the Bruins easily won and advanced. Two nights later, UCLA smashed Long Beach State and Coach Jerry Tarkanian. Bibby scored 23, Walton scored 19, and the Bruins won, 73–57, over the No. 5 overall seed in the tournament. Tarkanian and several of his players loudly complained that the Bruins received unfair positive treatment from the officials, making it impossible to stop the already superior Bruins. The 49ers would have plenty of time to think about the perceived injustices. Their season was over.

In the Final Four, everything was familiar for UCLA. The Bruins took on four-seed Louisville, coached by former Bruins player and assistant coach Denny Crum. The game was played at the Sports Arena, and it would not be easy for the Bruins. Louisville played excellent defense, forcing the Bruins into 21 turnovers. When UCLA took care of the ball, however, and was able to feed Walton in the post, Louisville could do nothing to stop him. Walton finished with 33 points on just 13 field goal attempts and hauled in another 21 rebounds. The Bruins played better as the game progressed and finally broke free and cruised to a 96–77 victory.

In the championship game on March 25, all the pressure was on the Bruins. They were 16-point favorites, an enormous margin for a championship game, and no one expected Florida State to keep the game close. UCLA got off to a terrible start, however. The Bruins trailed, 21–14, before they were able to finally turn the game in their favor. With 11 minutes to play, UCLA led comfortably by 13 when Walton picked up his fourth foul and would have to go to the bench. Florida State would make a run and keep the game interesting, but the cushion was too large for the Bruins and UCLA was too deep. Nater again played well, and the Bruins stars all had fine performances. Walton finished with 24 points and 20 rebounds. Wilkes scored 23 and Bibby finished with 18. The 1972 UCLA Bruins had done it again. They were the national champions, and one of the best teams to ever lace them up on a college hardwood. UCLA finished with a 30–0 record, the third time the Bruins had finished with a perfect record under Coach Wooden. It was their eighth championship in the last nine years. UCLA was criticized at times throughout the year, and again after the championship game, for not appreciating what victory meant. Whether true or not, it meant nothing to the story that history tells. The '72 Bruins were perfect.

1972–73

On August 1, 1972, Coach John Wooden once again penned a letter to his team. In writing it, he outlined the new challenge. Though UCLA had won the previous six national championships, their 1972–73 squad would be a unique team. Not since Lew Alcindor's junior and senior seasons had there been such overwhelming belief in the final outcome of the season before it even started.

Coach Wooden wrote, "It is my sincere hope that the 1972–73 UCLA varsity basketball team will be made up of players who love a challenge . . . I must caution that you cannot live in the past. The 1971–72 season is now history and we must look to the future."

While Coach Wooden and the '73 Bruins could not look to the past to guarantee success for the present, it was a fine time for fans to reflect on what had been accomplished under Coach Wooden's tenure. Through the 24 seasons of Wooden's tenure, the Bruins had gone from doormat to the greatest program of all time. The '64 team, along with the '67 and '72 teams, all finished with perfect 30–0 records. The Bruins had won with the greatest players in college basketball history, and at times when most thought they would fall back to the pack. The '73

Coach John Wooden, 1973 (Southern Branch Collection).

team was special as well. Walton and Wilkes carried the load again, with Walton averaged 20.4 points and 16.9 rebounds per game. Wilkes poured in nearly 15 PPG himself, and Larry Farmer and Larry Hollyfield each scored in double digits as the next two options.

At the start of the season, UCLA had already racked up 45 consecutive wins, just 15 short of the all-time NCAA record. The early games of the season were like so many of the recent past. The unanimous preseason No. 1 Bruins easily dispatched every opponent in their way. The first game of the season pitted the Bruins against the Wisconsin Badgers at Pauley Pavilion. Walton scored 26 points, grabbed 20 rebounds, blocked eight shots, and dished out seven assists. His first game of the year would be a masterpiece. His last would be legendary.

UCLA kept on winning, though opponents routinely tried the old stall tactic. Against Bradley, UCLA scored only 28 points in the first half, but still led by 18 at the break. It easily cruised to a 35-point win. In game three, Wilkes led the way with 18 points. The matchup was Coach Wooden's 1,000th career game as a coach, including his time coaching high school and his two years at Indiana State. The Bruins were 3–0, and with two weeks before their next game, Coach Wooden planned to practice his Bruins hard, sharpening them up before they took on the University of California-Santa Barbara. Plans changed. On December 11, Coach John Wooden suffered a heart attack. It was the middle of the night, and when he felt the agonizing pain in his chest, Coach thought he could just tough it out. It persisted, however, and at 1:45 a.m., he woke Nellie, and they drove to St. John's Hospital in Santa Monica, where Coach remained for eight days. One of the great memories Coach Wooden would have of an otherwise frightening event was the support he received from UCLA fans, administrators, and his players. After returning home, but still on a strict activity restriction, Coach Wooden heard the doorbell ring. Nellie had gone to the store, so Coach answered, and on the other side was Bill Walton. He had ridden his bike more than ten miles to see his coach, and it brightened the spirits of Wooden and made him proud.

Against UCSB, Gary Cunningham filled in for Wooden. For the first time in his entire coaching career, and for the first time at UCLA since 1948, Coach Wooden wasn't there. UCLA played for its coach, and the team did just fine: UCLA 98, UCSB 67. Walton scored 30 and grabbed 22 rebounds.

Larry Farmer, 1973 (Southern Branch Collection)

Six days later, UCLA played again, and this time, Coach was there. At halftime, he received the *Sports Illustrated* Sportsman of the Year award. UCLA beat Pitt, 89–73, for its 50th consecutive win.

UCLA just kept winning. On December 30, it closed out the Sugar Bowl Classic tournament with a seven-point win over Illinois. Walton said after the game, "That's our first championship this year." He certainly planned for another. As December turned to January, and 1972 turned to 1973, the Bruins crushed Pac-8 opponents, beating their first four conference mates by an average margin of 24 points. UCLA had run their winning streak to 57 when it took on the No. 10 University of San Francisco Dons. USF was the current record holder for longest winning streak in men's basketball history at the collegiate level, winning 60 straight in the mid-1950s under the leadership of Bill Russell and K. C. Jones. The current USF squad was very good, but Russell and Jones were gone, and no one could contain Walton. He finished with 22 points and 22 rebounds, with seven assists.

One night after knocking off the No. 10 team in America by 18 points, UCLA thrashed the No. 9 Providence Friars by 24. With the streak at 59 games, the Bruins had a chance to make history. On January 25, 1973, UCLA took on the Loyola University Ramblers in Chicago. Walton scored 32 points and hauled in a career-high 27 rebounds. UCLA won, 87–73. They had tied the record! Two nights later, UCLA took the court again, in a fitting place against a familiar opponent. On January 27, 1973, the UCLA Bruins beat the Notre Dame Fighting Irish, 82–63, in South Bend. They had done it. They had won 61 consecutive games. Wilkes led the way with 21 points. For Hollyfield and Farmer, this game was especially meaningful. They were the only remaining Bruins to have lost a game in college, against Notre Dame more than two years earlier.

The record was great, but UCLA still had more goals left to accomplish. Ten games were left on the schedule, and the Bruins were playing incredible basketball. They won all 10. Oregon State and Washington were the only opponents to stay within single digits of the Bruins. They beat USC twice by an average of 22 points and Washington State twice by an average of 35 points. There was no one, or no team, that could slow down UCLA. It finished

Bill Walton vs. Notre Dame, 1973. The win over the Fighting Irish was UCLA's 61st consecutive win, a new NCAA record. (Southern Branch Collection).

the regular season with a 26–0 record and would, of course, be the No. 1 seed again in the NCAA Tournament. The quest for another title would begin at Pauley Pavilion.

For the first two games, UCLA played in Los Angeles in front of enthusiastic crowds. Against Arizona State, Walton led the way with 28 points, Hollyfield scored 20, and the Bruins won by 17 points. The following game was not as easy. In the Regional Final, the Bruins took on the red-hot USF Dons. Though they had beaten them handily earlier in the year, USF played much better in the tournament. At halftime, UCLA led by only one point. In the second half, however, Curtis and forward Dave Meyers led the way. UCLA won, 54–39, in an agonizingly slow game and advanced to the Final Four once again.

On March 24, UCLA took on the No. 6 Indiana Hoosiers, coached by a young Bobby Knight in his second year. Knight was brash, hostile, loud, and arrogant. He led by fear and was a completely different man than Coach Wooden. Still, his teams won. The semifinal game was again tough for UCLA, at least by its lofty standards. The game was close throughout, with UCLA leading by just two points with a touch under six minutes to play. UCLA went on a 10–0 run, however, to seal the win. For the second game in a row, Tommy Curtis was a star for UCLA, finishing with 22 points to lead the way. Walton was one assist short of a triple-double.

On March 26, 1973, one of the all-time greatest individual performances in college athletics took place at St. Louis Arena. It was the NCAA basketball championship game, with UCLA going for its seventh consecutive title. Bill Walton had been a star for UCLA since the day he first stepped foot on the hardwood in UCLA practice attire. Against Memphis State, Walton could not be guarded. In the first half, the game was close, and at halftime, the score was tied at 39. Walton had a field day with any defender Memphis State Coach Gene Bartow threw his way. The Tigers tried everything they could to slow down Walton, but nothing worked. They guarded him straight up, fronted him, double-teamed him, triple-teamed him, and picked him up full-court. It didn't matter, and he didn't slow down in the second half. Greg Lee kept feeding the ball into Walton, and he finished by putting the ball in the hoop over and over. He scored in a variety of ways, hitting short bank shots, jump hooks, layups as he cut to the basket, and rebound put backs. He finished with an incredible 21 made field goals in 22 attempts. His only struggle was at the free-throw line, where he made only two of his five attempts. He was dominant from start to finish, and even had four dunks that were waved off due to the no-dunking rule. Even Walton's lone miss

The 1973 Bruins pose after winning their seventh consecutive national championship (Southern Branch Collection).

turned into two points, as he gathered his own miss and laid it back in. Though Walton has come to be known for his outrageous personality and seemingly endless chattering, he rarely talks about his incredible performance. He has never watched the game film and claims that he was just a product of a great system and great teammates feeding him the ball in the right spots. His 44 points in the championship game is still the most by any player ever, breaking the old record set by former Bruin Gail Goodrich in 1965. UCLA won the game, 87–66. Following the game, there was speculation that Walton would leave early for the NBA. He had proven all that many felt he needed to prove in college, and one more season would just be a waste. He didn't believe them. He loved UCLA, and he would be back.

1973–74

In 1974, a new market developed in Westwood—student ticket scalpers. In previous years, student tickets at Pauley Pavilion would be given on a first-come-first-served basis. Prior to the season, a new plan was made. There would be a lottery system, and those lucky enough to get tickets to see the Bruins play the entire season now had a valuable product. Students who chose to scalp their tickets were known as "student parasites." Though scalping was not permitted at UCLA, students did it anyway, but unfortunately for them, the market in '74 was not what they had hoped. As had been the case in 1969, when Lew Alcindor was a senior, in '74, there was less basketball buzz on campus. General seating in Pauley Pavilion would be filled for nearly every game, but student attendance lagged behind. Many believed winning an eighth consecutive championship was a foregone conclusion.

The 1974 season was a challenge, however, and it was a lifelong disappointment for many of the Bruins players. After winning back-to-back championships at the varsity level as sophomores and juniors, the brilliant senior class was tasked with repeating again. The Bruins frontcourt was stellar all season, as many had predicted. Walton had another brilliant individual season, averaging 19.3 points, 14.7 rebounds, 5.5 assists and being a steady anchor on the defensive end. Keith Wilkes was again a perfect match to play alongside Walton. He poured in nearly 17 PPG Dave Meyers also played well at the other forward position. Guard play would not be up to the Bruins standard for much of the year, however. Tommy Curtis and Greg Lee were inconsistent. Pete Trgovich and Andre McCarter also struggled in their limited playing time. UCLA had one more player who was a constant contributor in 1974, a forward by the name of Marques Johnson. Though the NCAA had allowed freshmen to play varsity basketball beginning in 1972, it was not until 1974 that a freshman became a key contributor for the Bruins. Johnson was the first, averaging 7.2 PPG and shooting 63.4 percent from the field.

UCLA entered the season with a 75-game winning streak and easily extended the streak to 76 by trouncing Arkansas 101–79 in the season opener. Walton scored 23 points and pulled down 17 boards. Wilkes started his senior season with a 16-point performance. The 1974 season was different than any in recent history for UCLA, as there were far more letdowns than most fans were used to. In game two at the Pauley Pavilion, the Bruins struggled mightily, and the streak appeared to be in great jeopardy. A matchup of Walton vs. Len Elmore, the star for the fourth-ranked Maryland Terrapins, the game came down to the final seconds. With the Bruins on top, 65–64, seldom-used freshman Richard Washington, who was in for the Bruins after Wilkes fouled out, stood at the free-throw line. Washington missed the front end of the one-and-one, and Maryland grabbed the rebound. John Lucas handled the ball for the Terps, and as he drove toward the basket, Dave Meyers knocked the ball away. Curtis grabbed it and ran the clock out. The Bruins survived by a single point. Walton scored 18 points and grabbed 27 rebounds. Elmore scored 19 and had 14 boards.

After the close call, the Bruins hit their stride. Walton notched a triple-double against SMU, the Bruins blasted No. 2 NC State by 18 points in St. Louis behind 27 points from Wilkes, and they beat Ohio State by 47 points and then St. Bonaventure by 53. The streak was up to 81 at the beginning of the Bruin Classic. In the two games played at Pauley Pavilion, UCLA won by an average of 24 points, easily dispatching Wyoming and Michigan. When Pac-8 play began, it was much of the same. The Bruins ran their record to 9–0 by beating the University of Washington, 100–48, in Seattle. The 52-point loss is the worst in UW history. Two nights later, the Bruins won again, but their short-term future took a hit and Walton's long-term future was quickly brought to reality. With the Bruins leading Washington State comfortably with ten minutes to play, Walton fell hard on his back. He would miss the next three games. In his place, Ralph Drollinger started, but Wilkes carried the load. UCLA beat Cal, Stanford, and Iowa to remain perfect. Coach Wooden said after beating Iowa, "I think Bill will play [against Notre Dame in two days]; the streak is important to him."

On January 19, 1973, UCLA faced Notre Dame once again, this time at the Athletic and Convocation Center in South Bend. With 3:30 to play, it appeared the Bruins were cruising to victory once again. Curtis had just knocked down a mid-range jump shot after driving to the right and leaping high over the defender to get the shot off. Curtis's jumper gave UCLA a 70–59 lead. After calling timeout, Notre Dame head coach Digger Phelps put in his best press defensive lineup. Facing a press was usually no worry for the Bruins. Walton indeed played, and he was the ultimate press-breaker. So many times the Bruins were able to push the ball upcourt and find Walton, and he would make the smart play with numbers to their advantage. Notre Dame quickly scored out of the timeout, set up the press, got a steal, and scored again. The Bruins' 11–point lead was cut to seven. After the Bruins started to stall a bit on offense, the aggressive Notre Dame defense finally stole the ball and scored again.

With the lead cut to five, the Bruins seemed nervous. Dick Enberg said of the crowd, "Pandemonium now!" Notre Dame set up the press again, and this time the Bruins broke free. Curtis released deep and caught a long pass over his shoulder from Wilkes. He had a clear lane to the basket, but the referee nearest the play called traveling. The television broadcast showed that no such traveling occurred. The Irish cut into the lead once more, this time on a mid-range jump shot from Gary Brokaw. With 1:49 remaining, UCLA's lead was cut to three. After Meyers missed a short jumper for the Bruins, Brokaw knocked down another short shot to cut the lead to just one. With 49 seconds on the clock, the ball was thrown into Wilkes on the right block. He turned and drove past the Irish defender and had a clear path to the basket. As he loaded up to jump, the whistle blew. The referee called an offensive foul as Wilkes's elbow hooked around the body of the defender. With 45 seconds to play and trailing by one, the Irish had the ball and a chance to take the lead. Notre Dame worked the ball around the perimeter. The Bruins knew the Irish were trying to find Brokaw. The defense was all over him, however, but that left Dwight Clay open along the right baseline. The ball was thrown to Clay, and, fading toward the end line, he threw up a high-arching shot that rattled in to give Notre Dame the one-point lead.

Wooden was never one to overuse his timeouts, and he would likely let his players determine the outcome for themselves, but Walton quickly went to the referee and called timeout himself. The final possession was one of the most embarrassing offensive sets for the Bruins in years. After nearly turning the ball over trying to feed Walton, UCLA panicked. Curtis flung up a long shot, well beyond what is now an NBA-distance three pointer. He missed, but the Irish lost the ball out of bounds with six seconds remaining. UCLA was able to get the ball inbounds cleanly this time, finding Walton on the right block about eight feet from the basket. After catching the pass, Walton quickly turned clockwise and without squaring his feet to the hoop, flung up a shot off the board. He, too, missed. A scramble for the offensive rebound ensued, and Meyers finally missed a short tap-in. The clock ran out and the game was over. UCLA's 88-game winning streak was over. As fans stormed the court from every direction, the Bruins were left with a feeling that was completely foreign to all of them. They had never lost in college before, and they shouldn't have lost this game. They led by 11 before allowing the Irish to score the final 12 points. Notre Dame head coach Digger Phelps would not let the win go to waste. To this day, he regularly talks about the victory over UCLA on January 19, 1974.

As it turned out, the loss to Notre Dame was not the only disappointment in '74, and the team did not make up for the shocker in South Bend with later success. Though Bruins fans felt great pride when UCLA dominated the rematch in Pauley Pavilion one week later, winning by 19 points, the Bruins were unable to regain their dominant form for long. Though UCLA was ranked No. 1 again after just one week in the No. 2 position, they found more trouble in a few short weeks. Against Oregon State and Oregon, the unthinkable happened. The Bruins lost both. Each game was close, with the Bruins losing by four to

OSU and then by five to UO. Suddenly, the Bruins were in a position of urgency. They would have to finish strong to win the Pac-8 conference and have a chance to defend their previous seven national titles in the NCAA Tournament. UCLA did, in fact, play well enough down the stretch to win the conference, winning its final five games, though two were by single digits.

In the opening game of the NCAA Tournament, the Bruins took on the Dayton Flyers at McKale Center in Tucson, Arizona. UCLA was the No. 2 seed, and Dayton was the No. 20 seed in the 25-team tournament. You wouldn't know if you watched it. UCLA struggled to ever pull away, as Dayton played tough the entire way. Though UCLA led by 12 at half, they were never able to push the lead enough to feel comfortable. In the second half, Dayton came all the way back. At the end of regulation, the score was tied, 80–80. The game would go to overtime, and then double overtime, and then triple overtime. It was a classic. Finally in the third extra session, the Bruins wore Dayton down and pulled away, winning, 111–100. Meyers led the way with 28 points and 14 rebounds. Walton scored 27 and grabbed 19 rebounds. It wasn't pretty for UCLA, but it was a win. Two days later, the Bruins returned to their old form. They crushed USF and advanced to another Final Four.

On March 23, 1974, UCLA took on the North Carolina State Wolfpack, which they had crushed by 18 points more than three months earlier. For the second time in three games, the Bruins played more than just regulation basketball. In double overtime, the Bruins led, 75–74, with Meyers at the line shooting one-and-one. He missed the front end and NC State grabbed the rebound. With 50 seconds left, Wolfpacks star David Thompson hit a running jump shot off the board to give NCSU the lead. The Bruins weren't able to respond. After a missed shot by Lee and loose-ball foul on Wilkes, Thompson went to the line for the Wolfpack and knocked down two free throws to essentially seal the game for NCSU. UCLA lost, 80–77, and the streak was over. UCLA had won the previous seven national championships, but a new champion was to reign in '74. The Bruins beat Kansas in the consolation game, but it was not the final game they wanted to play. Over the years, many people have blamed Walton and Wilkes for the 1974 season not ending in a title, saying they lost focus, had other interests, or weren't good enough team players. These are all weightless excuses, as Walton and Wilkes carried the team, with Walton again earning National Player of the Year honors. It wasn't to be for the '74 squad, but '75 presented an all-new, exciting challenge, with new players and new stars, but the same coach on the sidelines. Coach Wooden was now tasked with doing what he had done following the departure of Lew Alcindor five years earlier. He would save his best coaching job for last.

North Carolina State University won the NCAA basketball national championship in 1974.

Jamaal Wilkes

On May 2, 1953, Jackson Keith Wilkes was born in Berkeley, California. He would go by his middle name, Keith. The son of Leander Wilkes, a Baptist minister, and Thelma Wilkes, who raised Keith along with his four other brothers and sisters, he went his own way and find direction in life. From a young age, Keith was in love with the game of basketball. In his autobiography, *Jamaal Wilkes: Memoirs of the Original Smooth as Silk*, Wilkes wrote about his interest in practice growing up. He said, "During practices, I really paid great attention to detail with a sense of urgency." His hard work and focus paid off. Though he had spent most of his young life in Santa Barbara after moving from Berkeley, he finished high school in Ventura. After his father accepted a job as the pastor of the Second Baptist Church in Santa Barbara, the All-CIF player and student-body president was on the move. At Santa Barbara High School, Wilkes won CIF Player of the Year and was part of one of the best teams in the state. He was just getting started. In high school, he was called the "Spider," a nickname he didn't enjoy. Soon he upgraded his nickname and upgraded his stardom. He was off to UCLA, and the legend of "Silk" was born.

In 1971, Wilkes began his career at UCLA on the freshman team, and while the varsity won the national championship again, Wilkes and his roommate Bill Walton were just beginning their legendary careers in Westwood. When Wilkes was a sophomore in 1972, the Bruins were perfect. Averaging 13.5 points and 8.2 rebounds per game was nice as a sophomore, but he continued to improve. He increased his scoring in each of his final two seasons in Westwood, averaging

16.7 points per game as a senior, playing alongside one of the greatest players in college basketball history. The Bruins won two national championships in Wilkes's three seasons on the varsity team, and Wilkes earned consensus First Team All-America recognition as both a junior and a senior. He also earned Academic All-America honors in each of his three seasons. Like many great players before and after him at UCLA, he was interested in much more than basketball. As he left UCLA in 1974 after being drafted by the Golden State Warriors, he took the lessons he learned from his time in Westwood, both on and off the court, and applied them to his life. He continued to be one of the great basketball players in the world, as well as a kind, humble man, and someone who was always searching for ways to better himself.

Just as was the case with Kareem Abdul-Jabbar, he changed his life through religion. In 1975, Wilkes announced he had converted to Islam and legally changed his name to Jamaal Abdul-Lateef, though he would continue to use his surname for public recognition. Jamaal also tried his hand at acting. In 1975, he starred in the movie *Cornbread, Earl and Me*, in which he played a lead role as the character Cornbread. He continued to expand his general knowledge of world affairs, always looking to be comfortable as a conversationalist, someone willing to listen and talk to others as a way of improving himself.

As a rookie with the Golden State Warriors, Wilkes was an instant success. He won the Rookie of the Year Award, averaging 14.2 points and 8.2 rebounds per game while winning the championship with the Warriors. He upped his scoring to nearly 18 PPG over the next two years with Golden State, quickly becoming a fan favorite. Just as he had done at UCLA, his smooth, graceful style, combined with his unorthodox, yet lethal short-to-mid-range jump shot made him a joy to watch. He seemed to always be in the right spot at the right time, had tremendous hands, was a good outlet passer, ran the floor well, and played tremendous defense. He was an all-around player, and in his second season, he earned his first All-Star trip. In both his second and third seasons, he was named to the All-NBA Defensive Second Team. His time in Northern California would be short-lived, however. His career mirrored that of his early childhood: He was going south. He was coming home.

Prior to the 1978–79 NBA season, Wilkes joined the Los Angeles Lakers as a free agent, teaming up with Kareem Abdul-Jabbar and later Magic Johnson on some of the greatest teams in NBA history. Over the next eight seasons with the Lakers, Wilkes won three more NBA championships and was named an All-Star two more times, all the while being the third or usually fourth option on the team. From 1980 to 1982, he averaged at least 20 PPG in each season and was again a fan favorite. His greatest individual moment, like much of his career, is one in which he was overshadowed. In 1980, with Abdul-Jabbar out with an injury, rookie Magic Johnson laid one of the cornerstones of his own legacy, starting at center and leading the Lakers to the championship-clinching game over the Philadelphia 76ers. Wilkes, meanwhile, had a game to remember of his own, scoring a career-high 37 points and knocking in seemingly every mid-range shot that legendary Lakers broadcaster Chick Hearn called a "20-foot layup."

Like so many other great players, Wilkes did not end his career with the team he is most remembered for playing with. In 1986, he joined the Los Angeles Clippers, where he played in just 13 games before retiring. Though gone from basketball, Wilkes did not just disappear. His legacy would live on.

Wilkes has remained active in many ways, and he is often still seen at games cheering on his beloved Bruins and Lakers. Following his playing days, he was a coveted motivational speaker, as his soft tone and knowledgeable, conversational style captivated listeners. He briefly worked for the Los Angeles Stars of the American Basketball Association and wrote his autobiography. He has earned many honors since retiring, having his number retired by both high schools he attended. In March 2007, he was inducted into the Pac-10 Basketball Hall of Honor. In 2016, he was named to the National College Basketball Hall of Fame class, as well, 32 years after being named to the UCLA Athletics Hall of Fame. He was named to the Naismith Memorial Basketball Hall of Fame in 2012, and shortly after receiving the honor his number 52 was retired by both the Los Angeles Lakers and the UCLA Bruins.

Despite all the accolades, no greater honor comes for a UCLA Bruin than the approval of Coach Wooden. When asked by the *New York Post* in 1985 to describe the perfect basketball player, Coach

Wooden replied, "I would have the player be a good student, polite, courteous, a good team player, a good defensive player and rebounder, a good inside player and outside shooter. Why not just take Jamaal Wilkes and let it go at that?" That's legendary.

Bill Walton

When people think of UCLA basketball, three names usually come to mind first: John Wooden, of course—inarguably the greatest college basketball coach of all time; Kareem Abdul-Jabbar, formerly Lew Alcindor, and the clear top player in college basketball history; and then Bill Walton. Coach Wooden carefully chose his words, defined and refined his philosophy on not just basketball but life over and over, and was seen as a professional in every aspect of his life. Abdul-Jabbar is shy, often awkward, and just as careful with his words as Coach. He is mindful of the opinions of others and guards his reputation by putting up a personal shield. Walton is different. He is one of the most outspoken public figures in America, energetic and carefree. He is intelligent and frustrating. He is quick to tell a story about world events in the fifteenth century and even quicker to talk about American politics today. He was once one of the best athletes in the world and now has metal plates, rods, and screws throughout his body. He is nice, but combative. He is lighthearted, but confident. Some find him hysterical; others find him annoying. Walton is a simple yet complicated man. He is a hippie who grew up, but never lost his love for the 1970s teenage lifestyle that shaped him. He is a competitor, a winner, a Bruin, a Trail Blazer, a Clipper, a Celtic, a writer, a survivor, and so much more. Bill Walton is unique, a man you may love on a Thursday night when you listen to him on Pac-12 Network and a man you may despise two nights later when you hear him on ESPN. Walton is now in his mid-60s, and though he lives with joy, it wasn't always like that for the big redhead. His life has had many ups and downs, many bumps and breaks. He has raised trophies overhead and has fallen flat on his back, unsure if he'd ever recover.

Bill Walton was born on November 5, 1952. He spent his childhood in San Diego, a place that he called paradise. His childhood was perfect. He had friends, family, and an adventurous spirit. He loved school, received good grades, and had an early interest in history, writing, and especially music. Though he had a severe stuttering problem, Walton found joy with his small group of friends, and when he wasn't with them, he enjoyed life in his own world by himself. He also had another love that would take him places in real life that his imagination had already taken him. When Walton was eight years old, he started playing basketball. Along with Walton's first coach, a local fireman named Rocky, the sound of Chick Hearn on the radio brought basketball to life. Although Walton wasn't yet able to do on the court what Hearn described on the radio, the image was planted in his mind. Walton's philosophy on basketball is pure: throw the ball out there, and let's play. Run the court, get layups, play hard, don't call very many fouls, substitute infrequently, and have fun. Basketball for Walton is the most beautiful game—ten players on two teams playing in unison, competing with each other, all while helping each other achieve greatness. For many young boys, sports is an outlet. For Walton, basketball is more. It is freedom.

Unfortunately, the freedom of basketball was not always there for Walton. He was burdened with injuries nearly his entire life. By sheer numbers, he is the most injury-riddled athlete in American professional sports history, though he admits that many of his injuries as a player were not of the severity that have ruined the careers of football players, hockey players, and others. His first encounter with the knife came when he was just 14 years old. In the summer of 1967, Lew Alcindor was prepping for his first year on the UCLA varsity team, and Bill Walton was a 6'1", 110-pound kid kicking everyone's ass in the Helix High School gymnasium. While '67 was a great year for Alcindor and the UCLA basketball team, it was the beginning of a trend for the future Bruins star from San Diego. While playing pickup ball against much older men, Walton was taken out. He was high-lowed by two frustrated guys, tired of seeing the young, skinny kid scoring at will. Walton's knee was shot. Though he tried to rehab the knee for several months, he ultimately was forced to undergo major knee surgery. After the operation, the doctor told Walton, "We don't know how this is going to play out, Billy. Just go home and lie down for a few months and we'll hope and pray for the best." Walton would recover, though he never again felt completely healthy. In his time off from the game, something else happened that changed Walton's life—he grew. By the time he was ready to join the varsity team as a junior, he was 6'9". He would reach 6'11" by graduation.

At Helix High School, Walton won championships. As a junior, his team won the final 16 games of the season. As a senior, the team went undefeated. After enrolling at UCLA, the freshmen team was perfect, as was the team in 1972 and 1973, when Walton was a sophomore and junior. Finally in 1974, UCLA lost, ending its 88-game winning streak, a record that still stands today. Walton went nearly five-and-a-half years without losing a single basketball game.

Whereas Walton received some local attention for his exploits as a player at Helix, he became a national name while at UCLA. His choice to play for the Bruins was easy. Walton later called himself Coach Wooden's easiest recruit. The Bruins style of play fit Walton perfectly, and though Wooden and Walton were two very different men and never quite saw eye to eye when Walton was a player in Westwood, Walton's immense respect and love for Wooden as a teacher and a man was exactly what he needed. Wooden was a father figure for Walton, and like all father-son relationships, there is never unanimous agreement on all things. Coach Wooden brought out the best in Walton, however, and the Bruins saw incredible success. Walton saw incredible individual success, as well. He was National Player of the Year all three of his varsity seasons. He was an academic All-American, won two national championships, and was the No. 1 overall pick in the 1974 NBA Draft.

Bill Walton in the 1973 national championship game (Southern Branch Collection).

In the NBA, Walton was not the scoring machine that Lew Alcindor was, and he did not become the iconic player that many expected, but he was a fabulous player with an incredible skill set nonetheless. Walton played in the NBA for 13 years, but injuries took an incredible toll not only on his body, but on his time on the court. When added all together, Walton missed the equivalent of nine-and-a-half seasons of play, mostly because of reoccurring foot and ankle problems.

After graduating from UCLA, Walton, like Alcindor, had a choice. He could join the NBA or the ABA, or he could accept the prestigious Rhodes scholarship and continue his education, putting basketball on hold, and live in Oxford, England. When faced with the decision, Walton did what felt right. After four years at UCLA, he didn't want to be told what to do. He wanted to grow his hair long, stop shaving, and live life how he felt he should. He felt living in Portland and playing for the Trail Blazers was the place for him. He was right. Walton only played four seasons in Portland, but they are the ones he is most remembered for in the NBA.

When joining the Blazers, Walton learned an important lesson. The things that were common at UCLA were not common with his teammates or many of the other players in the NBA. Simple fundamentals that were drilled repeatedly at UCLA were not practiced by his teammates. Dribbling without looking at the ball, shooting with the off hand, and proper footwork in the post were all skills that UCLA players had that many pro players lacked. It was sure to be a process in Portland.

As a rookie, Walton had difficulty adjusting to the differences between the college and NBA games, as well. For Walton and teammate Sidney Wicks, the NBA game was so different from what they were used to at UCLA. The ball constantly moved for the Bruins, but for the Blazers, it constantly bounced. Players played off their own dribble, not off the motion of the offense and the passing from their teammates. After a stretch of healthy play for the Bruins, the injury bug again bit Walton as a rookie. He underwent a second knee operation, and for the first time in his life felt the pain of an injured foot. Without knowing the exact time the injury occurred, Walton one day felt a sharp, burning pain in his foot. He couldn't run; he could barely walk. His foot injury went undiagnosed for a long time, with some believing his problem was mental. Others blamed his diet, claiming that he wasn't eating enough red meat. His first season as a pro was limited to just 35 games. He showed incredible potential, however. He scored 12.8 points per game, grabbed 12.6 rebounds per game, dished out almost five assists per game, played strong defense, and was an all-around team player. He was incredible at taking the ball off the defensive backboard, keeping it high, and firing an outlet pass to a streaking guard. While two fellow NBA big men, Wes Unseld and Kevin Love, are also known for their outlet passes, the three had different passing styles. Unseld and Love threw long, length-of-the-court passes for quick scores. Walton was an expert at getting the ball and quickly throwing intermediate-distance passes to ignite the fast-break.

As a second-year player in 1975-76, even more was expected of Walton. He was the highest paid player already in NBA history and was supposed to be as good as Kareem Abdul-Jabbar. He was miserable. It would get worse. The 1976 team was improved on paper, but preseason predictions never account for injuries. Walton missed several games early in the year with a sprained ankle. He came back and broke his nose. Later in the year, he broke his wrist. Playing with a large cast, Walton tried to fight through the injury. The very next game after the wrist injury, Walton fractured and dislocated two fingers on his good hand. Late in the year, it went from bad to worse. He suffered a major break in his leg, and his season was over.

Although the injuries seemed like flukes, they proved to be all too common for the rest of his career. At times, however, Walton stayed on the court long enough to enjoy incredible success. In 1977, the Blazers were a new team. Dr. Jack Ramsay was now the coach, and Walton was joined by others in an upgraded roster. Walton's season was not totally injury-free. He missed 17 games with foot, ankle, and Achilles injuries. Still, the Blazers had the best record in the league, and Walton finished second behind Abdul-Jabbar in MVP voting. The playoffs weren't easy, but the Blazers were the best team and proved it. In the NBA Finals, they beat the Philadelphia 76ers in six games. Walton was named Finals MVP. After the clock ticked down to :00 in the deciding game, Walton ripped off his jersey and threw it into the crowd. The Blazers were the champions, the youngest team in NBA history to win the title.

Things seemed to be coming together for Walton. In '78, he was having another brilliant season, but then he got hurt—again. The injury was the worst one yet. In a late February game against the 76ers, in what was dubbed a "We Owe You One" contest, Walton felt a sharp, burning sensation in his foot once again. Again, team doctors couldn't figure out the problem. Walton's toughness was questioned. He felt alone. Team doctors took him to a hypnotist, who swung a watch in front of his face and chanted "Your feet are feeling better!" He saw faith healers. Nothing worked. Despite missing the final 22 games of the season, Walton was named league MVP, but the great honor didn't help heal his foot. Walton tried to return for the playoffs, but things only got worse. He was ineffective in Game One of the first round. Before game two against Seattle, team doctors had a plan. They injected a dosage of xylocaine just above Walton's ankle. At first, it seemed like a breakthrough. He felt no pain for the first time in months. He played, but when the medicine wore off, he had a big problem: his foot was worse. After the game, Walton was sent to the hospital to receive X-rays. The navicular bone in his foot had split in half. He was done for the rest of the playoffs. He never put on a Blazers uniform again.

Walton wanted to return home and play for the San Diego Clippers. Because of NBA free agency rules at the time, it took a while for the Blazers and the Clippers to work out an agreement that allowed Walton to play for San Diego, but it was eventually approved by the league. Walton's ties to the Portland team doctors were severed for good, and he began a new working relationship with Dr. Tony Daly. Though there was never any easy fix for Walton's foot problems, he found a doctor who truly cared about him and wanted what was best for him. Daly performed more than 20 foot and ankle surgeries on Walton over the years, including an operation to trim excess bone from both ankles prior to his first season with the Clippers.

After missing an entire season, Walton returned to the court, but it didn't go how he or his new doctor hoped. In a preseason game, he broke his foot again. Most thought his season was over before it even began, and others thought he was done for good. Doctors, engineers, chemists, and everyone else who knew about Walton's problems seemed to have ideas on what to do with him, but nothing ever worked. He was able to get back on the court, however, and he played 14 games in 1979–80 for the Clippers. Just as he was starting to play well, he broke his foot again. Now, almost everyone thought he was done. It was time for the big redhead to hang it up.

In the spring of 1981, well into the NBA season that Walton was unable to play in, a doctor from Whittier, California, named Bill Wagner, presented his idea on what to do about Walton's foot. He explained a complicated surgery to a room of so-called experts who were dumbfounded by Walton's feet. Most said his surgery had no chance. It had only been performed ten times before, and in none of those cases were the patients able to fully recover. Wagner was honest with Walton: "I'm not doing this so you can go out and try to play basketball again. I'm trying to give you some kind of life here, and to hopefully save you from having the whole thing cut off."

Wagner wasn't thinking about basketball for Walton, and Walton had begun to think about life without basketball. He had a growing family and many interests, including educational goals. Walton enrolled at Stanford Law School and began preparing for life without hoops. The Walton family moved to Northern California, buying a house and settling in while Bill was in school. Over time, his feet and ankles started to feel a little better. He increased his physical activity. One day while playing football in the yard with his young boys, he suddenly ran after the kids. Everyone was stunned. They couldn't remember the last time he ran. His climb back to the top of the athletic world started not with basketball, but with football and softball.

Toward the end of Walton's first year in Palo Alto, he was asked to join the Law School's intramural softball team and play first base. He was told not to worry about his lack of mobility. He would just have to stand there most of the time. When he was at the plate, special rules allowed Walton to hit and a designated runner to take off on contact. Eventually, however, Walton's natural athletic ability started to show. As he continued to get healthier, his range in the field increased, and he started running for himself. In the summer, he even played basketball, joining Henry Bibby, Walt Hazzard, and others in a UCLA vs. UNLV alumni tournament. After missing two full NBA seasons, Walton finally returned to the NBA, at first playing just weekends while still attending law school, but eventually making a full return as a serious player. For the next five years, Walton continued playing in the NBA, though he never had a single season in which he was fully healthy. He had ankle and foot surgeries in every season and averaged an estimated three to five surgeries every single year.

After three seasons with the Clippers, Walton was ready to move on. He wanted to play for the Lakers, but Dr. Jerry Buss wasn't interested. He then called Red Auerbach in Boston. At the time of the call, Auerbach was in his office with Larry Bird. When Walton asked if the Celtics were interested, he paused for a moment, asked Bird what he thought, and then replied to Walton, "Okay, we'll do it." Walton's first year with the Celtics proved to be one of the best of his career. He played in 80 games, more than in any season in his entire career. The Celtics won the championship, and Walton was named NBA Sixth Man of the Year.

In the summer following the 1986 championship season with the Celtics, Walton was a happy man. He was healthy, and the joy he felt just from being able to play the game he loved was uncontrollable. It was a joy he hadn't felt in years, and he was a new man. Early in the 1987 season, Walton broke his finger in a pickup game. He was relegated to weight training and the stationary bike in his short recovery. While riding the bike one day, a familiar pain returned. He again felt a sharp pain in his "good" foot. It was broken. He never played basketball again. Walton retired from basketball averaging 13.3 PPG for his career. He hauled in 10.5 rebounds, blocked 2.2 per game and averaged over three assists per game. Still, his NBA career is most remembered for what it could have been. He was one of the most talented players of his generation, but he was robbed of a potential legendary career by structurally unsound feet. He remained in the limelight, doing something that most thought impossible years earlier—talking for a living.

Though Walton's ankles are now fused, he is not confined to a stationary life. Since retiring in 1987, Walton has continued to do many of the things he loves, and he has found new passions. He rides his bike, plays with his dogs, lifts weights, and spends time with his wife and kids. He has attended over one thousand Grateful Dead concerts. He also happens to be an announcer.

Walton, the one-time stutterer, owes much of his career in announcing to two men—Marty Glickman and Ralph Lawler. Glickman, a legendary sports broadcaster, became Walton's speech coach, transforming him from a man who could not speak in public at all and struggled even in private conversation to one who dominates the microphone (much to the chagrin of David Pasch) during basketball games. Though Walton had an idea that he wanted to become an announcer, and friends pushed him in that direction, finding a job wasn't easy. Everyone knew of his speaking problems, and few were willing to believe they wouldn't sprout up again while on television. One team, however, was willing to give him a chance, and one man was willing to be his partner. Ralph Lawler gave Walton the opportunity to be his color commentator for Los Angeles Clippers games for 13 seasons. He also took gigs with network television, calling NBA games on NBC beginning in 1990 and later working for ESPN and ABC. Walton's broadcast style was always interesting. He was more outgoing than most, though his early years were nothing compared to his current style. His catchphrase was "Throw it down, big man." He was entertaining and popular. Then he was gone.

In November 2009, Walton left ESPN as a result of debilitating back pain, the extent of which nobody outside his inner circle knew for years. Walton had lived with excruciating back pain for over a year and a half, and it was getting worse. In his book *Back From the Dead*, Walton explained what his life had become: "I was on the ground, incapable of anything. I went through all the stages: I'm going to die. I want to die; and the worst stage of all—oh my gosh, I'm going to live and this is what I'm stuck with-forever."

This was Walton's life for three years. He was depressed and suicidal and felt he was a burden. He dreamed big but was confined to the area his body covered on the carpet at his home. Then one day, he made a choice. He felt he should just wait the pain out. It will go away. Maybe he could just work it out or ignore it. It was no use. The pain was getting worse. Finally, he did the last thing he wanted to do—see Dr. Steven Garfin and schedule spinal reconstruction surgery.

During Walton's initial preoperative exam, he crumbled to the floor during the 50-foot walk from the parking lot to the office. He needed help. Surgery lasted eight-and-a-half hours, and the recovery was slow. Bill's wife, Lori, was by his side every step of the way. He couldn't ride in a car for three months. He couldn't walk. The pain remained excruciating. But he slowly recovered. With each new accomplishment, Lori left a note to encourage him, such as the following:

- Today, you turned over in bed by yourself.
- Today, you were able to sit on the edge of your bed.
- Today, you were able to feed yourself—a little bit.
- Today, you went from your wheelchair to your walker.
- Today, you went from your walker to your cane.
- Today, you could pet the dog.

Eventually, Lori didn't need to write notes any longer. He recovered. He walks and lives more normally. He loves life, especially since it was once nearly taken from him, lying on the floor, unable to move.

Walton brings a special chair with him wherever he goes. He walks upright and slower than before. His back, ankles, and feet have been operated on more times than he probably cares to recall, but he persevered. His body failed him many times, but he kept chugging along.

Walton completed his comeback in July 2012 when he was hired by Pac-12 Network and ESPN as a full-time college basketball analyst. His style is even more outgoing and outrageous than before. Some fans love him; some can't stand him. Many more are completely unsure what to think of him. He wears tie-dye sitting in a row full of suits and ties. His hyperbole is over the top. His passion for the Conference of Champions is oftentimes overwhelming. His love for UCLA, sometimes shown in extreme bias and other times in extreme criticism, is off-putting for some. He is, however, himself.

Bill Walton's list of accomplishments is extremely long. He is a two-time college national champion and two-time NBA champion. He was named National Player of the Year three times in college and won one NBA MVP. He is in the Oregon Sports Hall of Fame, the UCLA Athletics Hall of Fame, the Basketball Hall of Fame, and the College Basketball Hall of Fame. His number 32 is retired by the Portland Trail Blazers and the UCLA basketball program. For those that know his story, they likely draw inspiration not from his time as a player or announcer and not even for his many comeback attempts from various ankle and foot injuries. They are inspired by his time lying down, unable to move, thinking about death but just wanting to live. It has been almost 50 years since he called Westwood home, and many UCLA fans never got the chance to actually see him play. His post-UCLA career saw several mountaintops, but it spent far too much time exploring the low valleys. Walton is healthy now, as healthy as his body will likely ever allow, and that is truly a blessing. Coach Wooden's easiest recruit ever has become one of UCLA's proudest alumni, and for Walton, that is one of many reasons to be happy to be alive.

1974–75

The 1975 Bruins basketball team was far from the most talented. No Alcindor-like figure was on offense, nor was there a dominant all-around star like Walton or incredible athletic wonder like Wicks. Someone like Goodrich or Hazzard didn't exist. Yet, the team was not without star power. Many think of Marques Johnson when they think of the '75 team because of the career he had, but the team of '75 was led not by Johnson, but by Dave Meyers. For two years prior, Meyers was a key contributor for the Bruins but was seldom talked about in the media or by the fans. He was overshadowed by Walton and Wilkes, and his legacy has been buried behind the stars that came before and after him. Yet in '75, the Bruins followed him. He took a backseat to no one. Meyers, a 6'8" forward who played a key role on the previous two teams, became an All-American. He earned consensus All-American status in '75, leading the Bruins in scoring (18.3 PPG) and rebounding (7.9 RPG). He earned NCAA Tournament All-Region and All-Tournament recognition at the end of the year, as well. The 1975 team was one of Coach Wooden's favorite teams.

Dave Meyers, 1975 (Southern Branch Collection).

Pete Trgovich and Andre McCarter in the back-court joined Meyers in the starting lineup. Trgovich would have his finest season in Westwood as a senior in '75, and McCarter was a defensive menace the entire season. Three players battled for minutes at the other two spots. Johnson, a 6'7" sophomore, and fellow classmate Richard Washington, another sophomore who stood at 6'11", each played a major role. Washington averaged nearly 16 PPG for the season, while Johnson added almost 12. Rotating with the two was Ralph Drollinger, who stood at 7'2" and was, along with Alcindor, the tallest player to ever play at UCLA to that point.

On November 29, 1974, the season began with the Bruins ranked No. 2 in the country. UCLA started the season with four consecutive wins, beating Wichita State, DePaul, Loyola-Chicago, and Oklahoma State by an average margin of 18 points. Still, the Bruins dropped in the rankings, falling to No. 3. UCLA just kept winning, however, running off eight more wins in a row, including a 113–94 win over 11th-ranked Memphis State, an 85–72 victory over No. 12 Notre Dame the next night, and 47-point win over Oklahoma.

The Bruins were back in the No. 2 spot in the AP rankings by the time the New Year rolled around and Pac-8 Conference play began. After sweeping the Washington schools at home, the Bruins' record now sat at 12–0 when they took on Stanford on the road. It was Friday night, January 17, and the game would be one of the most memorable in Stanford basketball history. The game was played in small Maples Pavilion, and the capacity crowd of 7,803 was into every play. Special sections were opened up just for this game. Behind the energetic crowd, Stanford got off to a quick start, jumping out to a shocking 37–24 lead at the break. The lead would grow to 15 in the second half, and when Drollinger picked up his fourth foul just minutes into the half, everything was seemingly going wrong for the Bruins.

Richard Washington would lead the comeback. After trailing by 15, UCLA reeled off 11 straight points to cut the lead to four. Stanford could do nothing to stop Washington. They would steady their play, however, and play the Bruins even the rest of the way. It was a frustrating game for the Bruins, as they had their chances in the final minutes, but Stanford was the better team on this day. The loss, now known as the Miracle at Maples, snapped a 17-game winning streak for the Bruins over their conference rivals from Palo Alto and was just the sixth loss for the Bruins in the last six seasons. It wouldn't be the last.

The '75 Bruins were not the dominant force that many of the previous great Bruin teams were, but they were still a great team. They had moments of classic Wooden dominance, like beating Cal by 30 one night after losing to Stanford, but they also had more close calls and losses than most teams of the '60s and early '70s, including losses to Notre Dame and a blowout loss to Washington. The Bruins did, however, have a nice list of wins on their resume. They beat highly ranked USC twice and ranked squads from Oregon and Oregon State twice each. The Bruins finished the regular season with another Pac-8 title and a 23–3 overall record.

They were the No. 2 seed heading into the NCAA Tournament, which had expanded in '75 from 25 teams to 32. Because tournament byes were eliminated, UCLA would have to win five games to bring home another title. (The year also marked the first time the tournament allowed more than one team from a single conference to participate.) It wouldn't be easy, but Coach Wooden liked the Bruins' chances.

On March 15, UCLA took on the University of Michigan in Beasley Coliseum in Pullman, Washington. The game was a battle throughout. In the first half, UCLA appeared lost in trying to stop the Wolverines. At the break, Michigan led, 50–46. In the second half, UCLA's defense recovered, slowing down Michigan, while also scoring enough to stay in the game. They weren't able to come all the way back and win in regulation, however. The game would go to overtime. After being tied 87-all through 40 minutes, the Bruins dominated the extra five, outscoring UM, 16–4, and winning, 103–91. Meyers scored 26, and Johnson and Washington each added 22.

In the second round, the Montana Grizzlies stuck with UCLA the entire way, with the final score being just 67–64 in UCLA's favor. Eric Hayes scored half of the Montana points, lighting up the Bruins for 32. UCLA played its finest game of the tournament against Arizona State in the regional final, and Marques Johnson played the greatest game of his career so far. Despite dealing with hepatitis during the season that restricted his playing time, he felt better by March, and it showed against ASU. He scored a game-high 35 points and pulled down 12 rebounds, and the score was UCLA 89, ASU 75.

The Bruins were off to the Final Four once again, this time played at the San Diego Sports Arena. The game would be a unique challenge for both coaches, as they were well accustomed to the styles of one another. The Bruins took on Louisville, coached by former Bruins player and assistant coach Denny Crum. The two teams played a nearly identical brand of basketball, and the game was a thrill to watch. Coach Wooden called the game one of the most beautifully played games he could remember. Fittingly, the game was close, as the two teams were tied at the end of regulation and would play an overtime period. With Louisville ahead, 74–73, with

50 seconds to play, Coach Wooden subbed in sophomore Jimmy Spillane, a fast, aggressive defensive player. Despite defensive pressure, UCLA was unable to create a turnover, and with 20 seconds to play, Spillane fouled Terry Howard, sending him to the line for a one-and-one. Howard missed, Washington grabbed the rebound, and the Bruins brought the ball up court. Coach Wooden called a timeout with five seconds remaining to set up a shot. The Bruins set up a play for a short baseline shot for Washington. It was executed perfectly. The shot went in with two seconds left. Crum called a timeout, but Louisville could get nothing going on its end and heaved up a wild, desperation shot. UCLA won, 75–74, a heartbreaker for Louisville but an incredible moment for the Bruins.

After the game was over, Coach Wooden felt something he had never yet felt during his coaching career—fatigue. Fans had stormed the court, Coach slithered his way through the crowd to shake Coach Crum's hand, waved to adoring spectators on the way to the locker room, and wondered if he could still do this much longer. He would say to himself, "Gee, if I'm feeling like this after such a beautiful game, maybe it's time to get out." When Coach reached the locker room, he told his team that the championship game on Monday would be his last as the UCLA coach. He had thought about retirement before, but his final decision was made in that moment as he left the court after beating Louisville. Although he had worried before about the state of the team going into '76 and beyond, the returning talent was enough going forward that he felt comfortable walking away. Still, he had one more game to coach, and it was for another national title.

On March 31, 1975, UCLA took on the University of Kentucky Wildcats in the national championship game and won by the score of 92–85. Though the game was close, with UCLA leading by just three at half and winning by just seven, the game could not have ended any other way. It was Coach Wooden's final game, and he and the Bruins did what they did best—raised the trophy overhead, champions of the college basketball world. Washington led the way for the Bruins with 28 points and 12 rebounds. He was named the tournament's Most Outstanding Player. Meyers and Drollinger each played well also. With the win, Coach Wooden was now 10–0 in national championship games. He had long ago proven to be the greatest college basketball coach of all-time, and the 1975 season may have been his best coaching job yet.

Wooden's shoes were impossible to fill, and no one has since been able to step out of the incredible shadow of the Wizard of Westwood. The Bruins continued to be a top basketball program going forward, and the UCLA brand is still amongst the elite in sports. With the retirement of Coach Wooden, however, the Bruins lost more than just a great coach. They lost a sense of invincibility. He would still be around campus for a long time, taking in games and rooting for the Bruins from his seat at Pauley Pavilion. Gene Bartow stepped forward to claim his role in the history of UCLA basketball. His task wouldn't be easy.

Coach John Wooden, 1975 (Southern Branch Collection).

CHAPTER 5
Gene Bartow (1975–1977)

No job in college sports history has been as difficult as the job Gene Bartow was asked to do when he was hired in 1975 to replace Coach John Wooden. Though an accomplished coach before his arrival in Westwood, he had big shoes to fill. Sure, the Bruins continued to win at a high clip, but the bar had been raised to a level no coach, besides Wooden, could ever reach. Bruins fans craved not only national championships but also dominant teams. They wanted what Coach Wooden brought them. Coach Bartow was a fine coach, but he wasn't the Wizard of Westwood.

Born in Browning, Missouri, on August 18, 1930, Gene Bartow was a product of the Great Depression. By the time he reached high school, the country was in the midst of World War II. His early life was challenging, but by the time he was off to college, things seemed to be turning around. The Depression was over; so was the war. Following high school, Bartow enrolled at Northeast Missouri State University, now known as Truman State University, in 1948, choosing to play basketball but knowing that his future would come on the sidelines. During his three years of varsity play, his time on the court was limited, but the team saw tremendous success, losing only one game. As a senior, while playing for his college team, he also coached high school. At nearby Greentop High School, Bartow got his first shot at coaching, and his team did fairly well, finishing with a 16–6 record.

After graduating from Northeast Missouri State, Bartow joined the United States Army, serving for two years at Fort Bliss in Texas and playing on the Army basketball team. Upon returning to civilian life, Bartow picked up where he left off, coaching prep basketball in Missouri for six years. In his first year after his return, he coached South Shelby High School in Shelbina, Missouri, winning 30 games, losing just six, and reaching the state tournament. He left South Shelby, however, to take the open job at St. Charles High School, where he found even more success. Over four years, he finished with a 145–49 record and won the 1957 Missouri state championship.

Though Bartow had a long and distinguished coaching career at multiple stops at the collegiate level, his time at UCLA is most memorable. To get to UCLA, however, he had to work his way up. Following two years as an assistant coach at the University of California-Santa Barbara, Bartow accepted his first head-coaching job at Central Missouri State, where he would coach for three seasons, finishing with a 47–21 record. In 1965, he moved on to Valparaiso. In six years, he took the Crusaders to the NCAA Tournament twice before moving on again. Bartow's greatest success came as the coach of Memphis State. For four seasons, he coached the Tigers, twice winning the Missouri Valley Conference. His greatest season came in 1973. The Tigers finished with a 24–6 record, reaching the national championship game. There, Bartow had an up-close view of Bill Walton's 44-point masterpiece. Despite success in Memphis, Bartow was never apt to stay at one place for long early in his career. In 1974–75, he coached at the University of Illinois, finishing with just an 8–18 record. A long rebuild lay ahead for Bartow in Champaign, and he was up for the challenge. Soon, UCLA called, and he could not turn that school down.

Taking over the UCLA job was uniquely challenging for Bartow, and the role of head basketball coach at UCLA has been an incredibly difficult job, filled with immense pressure, ever since. Shortly after taking the job, Bartow told *Sports Illustrated*, "I figure this nostalgia for Coach Wooden will pass in about a year, as long as UCLA keeps winning." Bartow won at UCLA, and his numbers in his brief stint in Westwood would have been viewed as a success at any other place. In two years, UCLA finished with a 52–9 overall record, won the Pacific-8 Conference both years, and made two tournament appearances. It reached the Final Four and the Sweet 16. UCLA still had the premier basketball program on the West Coast, but it wasn't good enough. UCLA didn't win it all.

Personally, the fans liked Bartow. He was a good man—caring, generous, available to the public. He embraced the UCLA way of doing things. *Sports Illustrated* said of him, "He doesn't smoke, doesn't swear, leaves the vodka out of his screwdrivers, goes home to his wife and three kids at night, goes to church every Sunday, gets his hair cut regularly, shaves every morning, and insists that his players put their dirty towels in the laundry bin to make the manager's job easier." In many ways, he was like Coach Wooden, but in one way he was different. He didn't raise the trophy overhead or cut down the nets in March.

Following the 1977 season, Bartow jumped at the chance to escape the pressure of Westwood. He decided to take over the University of Alabama Birmingham athletic program. The school was new to athletics, and he would be the first athletic director and first basketball coach in school history. Eight years later, he considered leaving for Kentucky but ultimately chose to stay. In 2009, when reflecting on that decision, Bartow said, "Probably the smartest thing I ever did. Or the second smartest. The first may have been getting out of UCLA alive."

Bartow had time to build something all his own and escape from the giant shadow of Coach Wooden that is still present in Westwood. In 21 seasons in Birmingham, Bartow compiled a 366–203 overall record. Following the 1996 season, Bartow retired

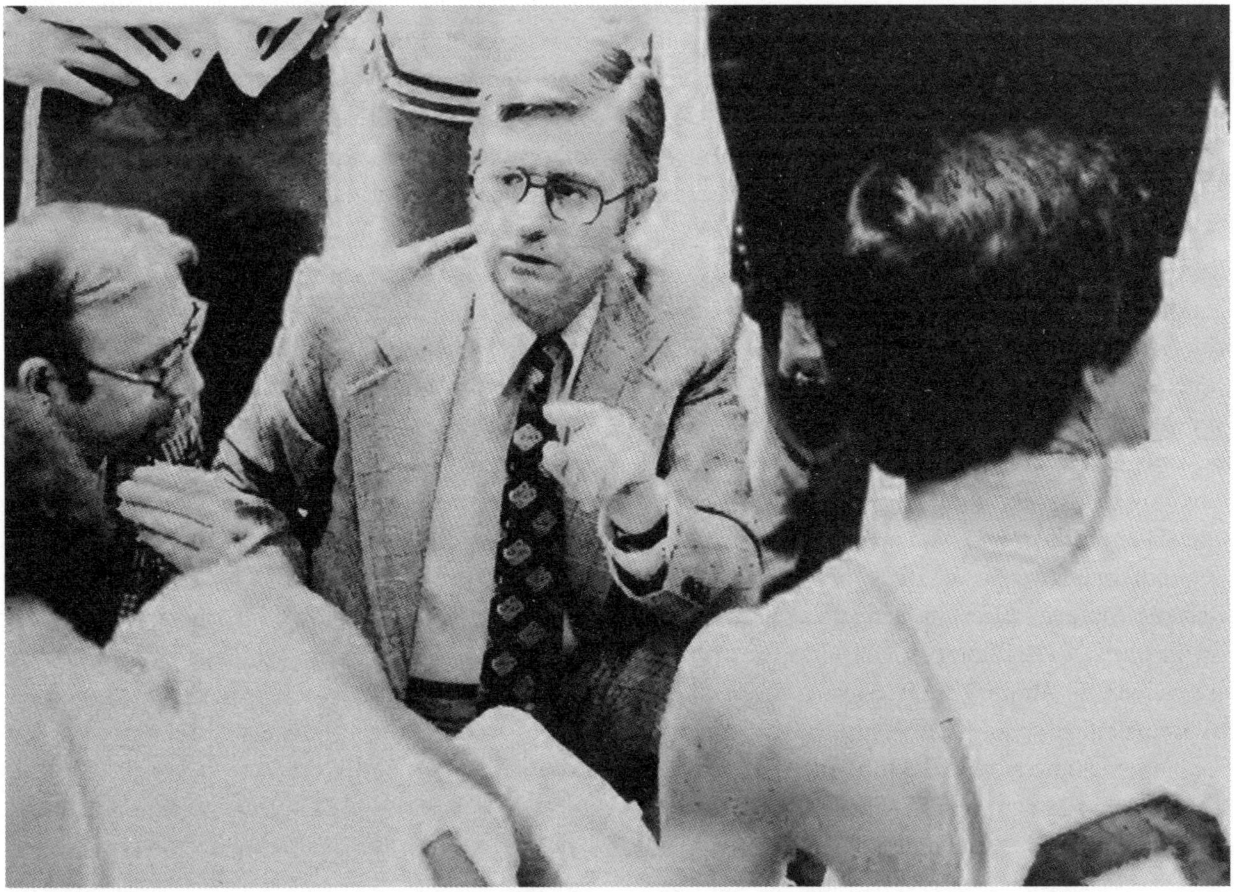

Head coach Gene Bartow, 1976 (Southern Branch Collection).

from coaching and named his son Murry the new head coach. Because he is considered the "Father of UAB Athletics," the gymnasium is fittingly named in his honor as Bartow Arena. He remained athletic director at UAB until 2000. In 2001, he was named special advisor to the newly-relocated Memphis Grizzlies.

Throughout Bartow's life, he has received many great honors. He is a member of 10 different halls of fame, including the National College Basketball Hall of Fame. He is not a member of the UCLA Athletics Hall of Fame, even though he had recognizable success. At the time of his hiring in 1975, he said, "I think they'll be patient with me. If not, well I used to teach driver's ed and badminton in high school. I've always got those skills to fall back on." Thankfully for Coach Bartow, he didn't need to. He was a basketball man who enjoyed a tremendous career, even if he wasn't fully appreciated at UCLA.

On January 3, 2012, Gene Bartow died of stomach cancer. Forty-three years after Bartow was named the head coach at UCLA, his son Murry was named an assistant coach for the Bruins, and he soon became UCLA's interim head coach. The Bartow basketball family legacy continues.

1975–76

When John Wooden was hired as the UCLA basketball coach prior to the start of the 1948–49 season, many things were different than when Coach Gene Bartow took the reins. UCLA basketball was just another program, a West Coast team at the tail end of a decade and a half of misery on the court. Fast forward to Coach Bartow's first season, when the coach was seemingly in an entirely different world. UCLA basketball was no longer a program in shambles. They were now the greatest program in America, and Coach Bartow had a seemingly impossible job.

In Coach Bartow's opening game, all eyes on his team not only because he was new but also because of the team UCLA faced. No. 2 UCLA took on No. 1, coached by Bobby Knight, at St. Louis Arena in Missouri. A crowd of 19,115 was in attendance, and the game was all but over just a few minutes in. IU hit 10 of its first 14 shots, while holding UCLA to 3 of 13 from the field and forcing five turnovers. UCLA settled down, however, and at halftime the score was just 36–28 in favor of IU. Richard Washington and Marques Johnson each played well for UCLA, scoring 28 and 20 points, respectively, but that wasn't enough. IU was the better team and began its legendary season with a convincing win over Coach Bartow and the Bruins. The final score was IU 84, UCLA 66.

Despite the opening-game loss, the Bruins were clearly one of the top teams in America. Following the game against IU, the Bruins got on track. They won their next 15 games, including two in the Bruin Classic in December and one over No. 5 Notre Dame at Pauley Pavilion. UCLA was ranked No. 6 in the country when it traveled to South Bend, Indiana, for a rematch. Adrian Dantley was the star of the game, pouring in 30 points for the Irish and handing UCLA its second loss of the season. The Bruins lost to the Irish in South Bend for the third consecutive season.

Despite the slight drop in quality of play, the Bruins won the Pac-8 Conference for the 10th consecutive year in '76. The margin of victory for the Bruins in many of the conference matchups was less than in the past, but they were winning nonetheless. The only conference loss came at the hands of the unranked Oregon Ducks on February 21. UCLA came into the game ranked No. 5 in the country, but Oregon played extremely tough in the prior matchup in Eugene, falling by only one point. In the return trip to Pauley, Oregon smoked UCLA, beating the team by 20 points and holding it to just 45 total.

The defeat was embarrassing, but the season wasn't over. After winning its final three games, UCLA entered the NCAA Tournament as the No. 6 team and the second seed in the West Region. The Bruins made quick work of their first three teams, beating San Diego State by 10, Pepperdine by nine, and Arizona by 16. The Bruins reached another Final Four, and though the team they faced was one of the best in college basketball history, the buzz was all about the Bruins. Could UCLA, winners of 10 of the previous 12 national championships, knock off the undefeated, top-ranked Indiana Hoosiers?

Despite the postseason experience edge going to the Bruins, the Hoosiers had something the Bruins didn't—one of the best defenses in college basketball history. The Final Four game was much like the season-opening game in November. The Hoosiers got off to a quick start, held a comfortable lead, and prevented UCLA from making any serious runs. Like the November matchup, UCLA was led by Washington and Johnson but got little help from the other key players. When the final seconds ticked off, the Bruins had just their second tournament loss in the last 14 years.

The Bruins finished by beating Rutgers in the third-place game, but it was still a disappointing season in the minds of most fans. As was the case in the two games with Indiana, the '76 Bruins were led by two men who had great seasons, but they were oftentimes forced to do too much. Washington led the way for UCLA in the scoring department, averaging 20.1 points per game. Johnson scored 17.3 PPG and led the team in rebounding, hauling in 9.4 rebounds per game. The Bruins as a team averaged 82.7 points per game, good for 38th in the country, but it was a two-point drop-off from the season prior and a large decrease from Coach Wooden's finest teams. Coach Bartow had done a fine job in guiding the Bruins to the Pac-8 title in '76, but conference crowns were hardly recognized in Westwood. Coach Bartow returned in '77, but he wasn't long for Westwood.

Indiana University won the NCAA basketball national championship in 1976.

1976–77

No one expected Coach Gene Bartow to be John Wooden, and certainly the results of his first year were neither Woodenesque nor poor. Going 28–4, winning the conference crown, and finishing the season ranked No. 4 in the country is a fine season at most places. Fans, students, players, coaches, and media understood that the era of domination would come to an end at some point and the glory days would become a memory. Coach Bartow in his second year and the Bruins hoped they could push back the inevitable. UCLA could return to the top of the college basketball world now and fall back later, so they thought. The goal in '77 remained the goal in every season for the prior decade and a half, which that remains today: win it all.

The Bruins were led by a pair of forwards in '77. Marques Johnson was now a senior and saved his best season for his last. After averaging 21.4 points and 11.1 rebounds per game, Johnson was named First Team All-Pac-8, earned consensus All-America honors, and was named the winner of the inaugural John R. Wooden Award, presented to the best player in America. Playing at the opposite forward position was David Greenwood, a 6'9" sophomore from Lynwood, California who poured in 16.7 points and 9.7 rebounds per game for the season. The other three starters were solid as well. Roy Hamilton and Jim Spillane were the two primary guards, and Brett Vroman was the top center on the team.

Coach Bartow and the Bruins began the season ranked No. 4 in the country and played their first 13 games at Pauley Pavilion. After defeating San Diego State on November 26, UCLA ran its record to 2–0 with a win over No. 18 DePaul, 76–69. Yes, the early win was over a ranked team, but the close score was worrisome. All in Westwood were still adjusting to the new reality that large blowouts over ranked teams were no longer the norm.

Part of the new reality unfortunately included losing more games. On December 11, No. 3 UCLA took on No. 7 Notre Dame. Once again, the Irish had the Bruins' number, knocking them off, 66–63. After dropping to No. 9 in the rankings following the loss, UCLA seemingly started to improve as it continued nonconference play at home. The Bruins won seven games in a row, including a 47-point win over Rice.

On January 7, 1977, UCLA began Pac-8 Conference action against the Oregon Ducks at Pauley Pavilion. The men from Eugene prevailed, winning a squeaker, 61–60. The story was what happened when the next rankings were released. UCLA dropped to No. 12 in the rankings, the first time UCLA was out of the Top 10 since 1966. The Bruins bounced back, however, making a run that put them once again in contention for the title in March. They won their next nine games, including a five-point win in a rematch against Notre Dame, a 14-point win over No. 7 Tennessee, and dominant performances against many of their Pac-8 mates. The Bruins climbed all the way back up to No. 2 in the rankings with six games to go in the season. Though the Bruins lost two of the final six conference games, including the rematch against Oregon, they again claimed the conference title, their 11th straight.

UCLA entered the 1977 NCAA Tournament as the No. 2 overall seed in the 32-team bracket. On March 12, it began the quest for championship number 11 against the Louisville Cardinals in front of 10,897 fans in Pocatello, Idaho. The game was close throughout, too close for comfort. At halftime,

Marques Johnson vs. USC, 1977 (Southern Branch Collection).

UCLA led by just three. In the second half, the two teams were still close, but UCLA did just enough to win the game. UCLA's offense scored 48 points in the second half to win by a final score of 87–79. Johnson led the Bruins with 17 points and 14 rebounds. Spillane added 16 points and led the way with six assists. It wasn't an easy win to start the tournament, but UCLA would take it nonetheless. The second round looked to be easier, but nothing is ever a given in the NCAA Tournament. When the Bruins took on the Idaho State Bengals on March 17, 1977, with a large TV audience watching on NBC, one of the most memorable games of the 1970s took place. The Bruins were on the wrong side of the thriller.

The Bruins had been to 10 straight Final Fours, and though reaching an 11th straight would take two more wins, things seemed to once again line up for the Bruins to make a deep run in March. Most pundits and fans thought Idaho State was nothing special, a team UCLA would stomp on their way to another championship run. The Bengals thought differently. The team was tremendous offensively, and its outside shooting was better than any opponent UCLA saw all season. But the Bengals were not just perimeter shooters; the team had a balanced offense. Steve Hayes, a 7-foot center, made the offense go. He was multitalented and, most importantly, smart. He had a left-handed Kareem Abdul-Jabbar–style skyhook that nobody could block. When defended one-on-one with space to work, he was a terror to defend in the post. His passing, however, was just as valuable as his scoring. He repeatedly kicked the ball out to his teammates on the perimeter or cutting across the lane.

Hayes said of the team he faced, "For all of us growing up, all we had ever seen was UCLA win every year." Hayes and his teammates wrote a new script, and this time the Bruins weren't the champions in the end. In one of the most stunning upsets in college basketball history, ISU beat UCLA, 76–75. Johnson and Greenwood were the stars for the Bruins, scoring 21 and 20 points each, but the best player on the court that day was Hayes. His 27 points and 12 rebounds led the way in the upset.

With the loss to Idaho State, many believed the dynasty was now truly over for UCLA.

Marquette University won the NCAA basketball national championship in 1977.

Marques Johnson

Marques Johnson is considered by many UCLA fans to be the last great player of the John Wooden era. Though he would not become the breakout star in Westwood until after Wooden's departure, Johnson was a key member of the last Wooden-led championship team in Westwood and one of the best players to ever don the four letters across his chest.

Born on February 8, 1956, in Natchitoches,

Louisiana, Johnson and his family moved to Los Angeles when he was a young boy. He was raised in the city and developed his game at Crenshaw High School. Just like his basketball idol Julius Erving, Johnson had great flair. As a high school senior in 1973, Johnson won the City Section Player of the Year award. It was just one of many accolades he would earn in his playing career. Following graduation, he was off to UCLA.

When Johnson arrived in Westwood, things were much different than in high school. The Bruins were the best team in America, and competition was fierce. No longer could he just step on the court and dominate. No longer was he the best player everywhere he went. He was a freshman in 1974, and the Bruins were riding a seven-year national championship streak. Freshmen were still new to varsity basketball, and though Johnson would indeed be one of the first freshman contributors in UCLA basketball history, his first season was difficult. The Bruins, presumed by nearly all to win the championship again in '74, didn't win, and Johnson was not the immediate star that many of the other all-time great Bruin players were before him. He had a solid freshman campaign, averaging 7.2 points and just over three rebounds per game.

In '75, things began to change in Westwood. The Bruins were no longer quite as dominant as they had been in recent years, and for the first time in over a decade the Bruins weren't considered a sure thing to win in March. UCLA was a young team, and though the team struggled at times, Coach Wooden and the Bruins peaked when it mattered most. In Coach Wooden's final season at UCLA, Johnson and the Bruins brought home the 10th national championship in the last twelve years. In the championship campaign of '75, he averaged 11.6 PPG and 7.1 RPG. He would be even better in his final two seasons.

Though Coach Wooden would never again roam the sidelines for the Bruins basketball team, UCLA kept chugging along in Johnson's final two seasons. Both years UCLA was good, but both years they lost in the NCAA Tournament. Johnson transitioned from a good player to one of the best in America. He bumped his scoring up to 17.3 PPG as a junior and up again to 21.4 as a senior. His rebounding continued to improve, as well, and in his senior year he averaged over 11 boards per game. He was named First Team All-Pac-8 both seasons, was a Second Team All-American in '76, and was a consensus First Team All-American in '77. He was named National Player of the Year by multiple outlets his senior season, and was the winner of the first ever John R. Wooden Award, presented to the top player in America. For his incredible college career, Johnson later earned two more prestigious honors. In 1996, his number 54 jersey was retired by UCLA basketball. In 2008, he was named to the Pac-10 Hall of Honor.

On June 10, 1977, the Milwaukee Bucks selected Johnson with the third overall pick of the NBA draft. He did not disappoint. As a rookie, he averaged 19.5 PPG, along with 10.6 RPG and was named to the NBA All-Rookie team. His second year was even better, arguably the best of his entire career. In 1979, Johnson finished third in the NBA in scoring, pouring in 25.6 PPG for the season and earning First Team All-NBA recognition. Over the following two years, Johnson continued his fine play, earning Second Team All-NBA in each season and beginning a stretch in which the Bucks were a consistent contender in the postseason. For five straight seasons, Johnson led the Bucks to the playoffs, winning the division title each season.

Despite the success of the team and the success of Johnson, Milwaukee dealt him to the Los Angeles Clippers following the '84 season. In seven seasons with the Bucks, Johnson was a four-time All Star and averaged 21.0 PPG. He would play for three more years with the Clippers, still scoring at a high clip, and earning another All-Star berth. But in '86, just 10 games into the season, Johnson ruptured a disc in his neck in a collision with teammate Benoit Benjamin. His season was over, and so was his career, basically. Johnson missed two full years following the injury, and though he made a brief comeback in 1989, playing 10 games for the Golden State Warriors, he was done. On December 27, 1989, he officially retired from basketball.

Johnson finished his career as a five-time All-Star and is frequently mentioned as one of the top players not in the Basketball Hall of Fame. Though he is now likely to remain just outside the doors of the Hall, his career should not be diminished. He was one of the best players of the late '70s and '80s. He was a player with incredible skill in the post and a lethal midrange jump shot. In 2019, his jersey number 8 was retired by the Milwaukee Bucks. He was once the top player in college basketball and a champion. Though his playing career was cut short, his life continued. There is more to Marques Johnson than just basketball, and he was just getting started.

Since retiring from basketball 30 years ago, Johnson has earned 26 acting credits, including roles in *White Men Can't Jump* and *Blue Chips*. He has worked as a color commentator for the Seattle SuperSonics, Milwaukee Bucks, Los Angeles Clippers, and Fox Sports as a Pac-10/12 analyst. Johnson has seven children—five sons, including two that played basketball at UCLA, and two daughters. His children have followed in their father's footsteps, excelling in athletics and entertainment.

Johnson's time in the NBA and his post-playing career are notable in many ways, but it was his four years as a UCLA Bruins basketball player that he is most remembered for. From time to time, Johnson sits at Pauley Pavilion, watching his Bruins play. For those who saw him play, the sight must bring back memories of a young man with a large Afro and a larger skill set. He was a player of incredible talent who left an impression on all those who saw him play. He was a Bruin, and a champion, and though his career was cut short by injury, his memory lives on today.

CHAPTER 6
Gary Cunningham (1977–1979)

Finding a replacement for Coach John Wooden that could both win at a high clip and handle the pressure of the toughest job in America has been a challenge for UCLA. After two years with Gene Bartow leading the Bruins, the search for his replacement began again. The task of taking UCLA back to the top was then passed to Gary Cunningham, and like the man before him and his three immediate successors, Cunningham would not be long for the job. Twenty-plus wins in a season weren't considered successful.

Gary Cunningham's UCLA story began not as a coach, but as a player. After enrolling in the fall of 1958, Cunningham played on the UCLA freshmen team in '59 and then was a solid contributor to the varsity squad under Coach John Wooden. As a sophomore, the 6'6" forward averaged nearly eight points and four rebounds per game. He upped his production the following year, scoring 12.9 points per game, and then as a senior, he had his finest season. Along with averaging 13.4 points and 6.9 rebounds per game, the Bruins won the AAWU Conference title and reached the first Final Four in school history.

Following his playing career at UCLA, the Cincinnati Royals chose Cunningham with the 58th pick of the NBA draft, but he never played. Instead, Cunningham began the next phase of his life. While he continued his studies at UCLA, eventually earning a master's degree in Physical Education and doctorate in Education, he saw a future in basketball as a coach. In 1965–66, Cunningham coached for the freshmen team, led by Lew Alcindor, that beat the two-time defending national champion varsity squad in the first-ever game at Pauley Pavilion. For 10 seasons, Coach Cunningham coached hoops at UCLA, including the majority of his time with the varsity team, becoming Coach Wooden's right-hand man and earning his trust, along with eight national championships.

Though he was considered for the opening following Coach Wooden's retirement in 1975, Cunningham was passed on for Gene Bartow. Cunningham was out of basketball for two years, serving as the executive director of the UCLA Alumni Association, but when Bartow moved on, Cunningham was suddenly under consideration as head basketball coach. Cunningham was hired as the sixth head coach in UCLA basketball history and coached the Bruins for two seasons. During

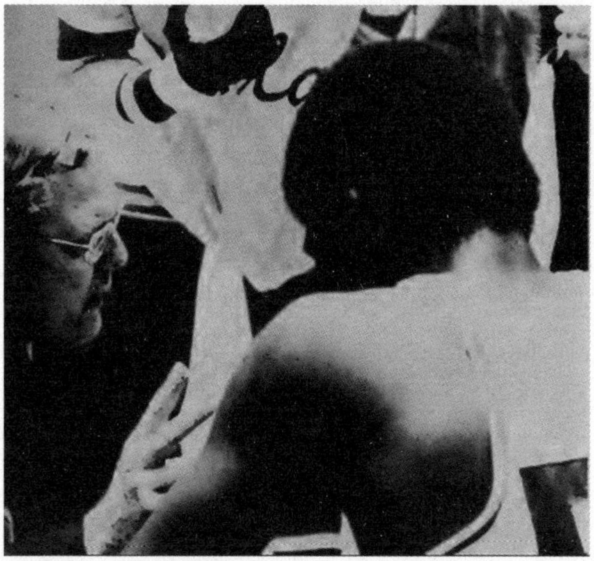

Coach Gary Cunningham speaking to his team, 1979 (Southern Branch Collection).

his tenure, he achieved what other programs would consider great success.

After the 1979 season, it was time for Cunningham to move on. He had proven himself as a good player and later a good coach, but his interest was no longer in coaching basketball, especially under the incredible pressure of the UCLA fan base.

While the pressure to perform at UCLA drove Coach Bartow away, for Coach Cunningham, the pressure was not the main factor in his departure. He never thought anyone was gunning for his job, and he felt supported by the vast majority of fans. His passion was no longer to roam the sidelines but to work behind a desk. Cunningham stepped away from coaching to pursue a career in athletic administration, and though the glory of his chosen profession rarely put him in the national limelight like that of top college coaches, he would have it no other way.

In 1979, Cunningham was named the athletic director and associate professor at tiny Western Oregon State College. He was out of the big city lights and was now working in relative obscurity in the overall college landscape. He said, "Nobody would ever understand it but Gary Cunningham."

After two years, Cunningham moved on to the University of Wyoming and then later worked at Fresno State for nine years and the University of California-Santa Barbara for thirteen. At each stop, Cunningham left the athletic department in a better place than it was when he had entered. His work was not just done at the university level but also at the conference and the national level. Along with serving on several conference committees at multiple stops, Cunningham was a member of the NCAA Division I ADA Executive Committee, the NCAA Men's Basketball Committee, the Basketball Issues Committee, the NCAA Committee on Women's Athletics, the NACDA Finance and Management Committee, and even the NCAA Committee on Committees. Cunningham served as president of the National Association of Collegiate Directors of Athletics, and, in 1999, he was named NCAA Division I-AA National Athletic Director of the Year.

Of course, Cunningham is still most often remembered for his time in Westwood. Along with his quality playing career, he twice won the conference championship as a head coach, eight times won the national championship as an assistant, and was named the 1978 Pac-8 Coach of the Year. His .862 winning percentage is still the highest in UCLA history. In 2001, Cunningham was named a member of the UCLA Athletics Hall of Fame.

1977–78

The 1977–78 season was again one of change for the Bruins. Seniors played for their third coaching staff in four years. Former three-time national champion Larry Farmer and rising coaching star Jim Harrick were the top two assistants for Coach Cunningham

UCLA was deep in '78, and scoring the ball at a high clip was never a problem. Junior forward David Greenwood, who scored 17.5 points per game and hauled down 11.4 rebounds per game, led the Bruins. Guard Roy Hamilton was right behind Greenwood in the scoring department, averaging 17.2 PPG and leading the Bruins with 6.0 assists per game. Senior Guard Raymond Townsend was a strong scorer, as well, averaging 14.7 PPG Kiki Vandeweghe was a solid contributor, and James Wilkes was the top Bruin defender. The Bruins, as they had done so often over the previous two decades, were one of the finest teams in America. They averaged 85.2 PPG as a team and held opponents to just 67.4. They were again the class of the Pac-8 Conference and a national contender. The Bruins had one problem, however. No team fared better against the Bruins in the 1970s than the Notre Dame Fighting Irish. UCLA played that team twice, and the two games were classics.

The Bruins began the season ranked No. 6 in the country by the Associated Press, and though they would play several quality opponents early, the first 10 games for the Bruins were all at Pauley Pavilion, which offered an advantage. After escaping with a narrow two-point win over BYU in the season opener, the Bruins knocked off Seattle, Colorado, and Santa Clara before they met the Fighting Irish for the first time. On December 10, No. 5 UCLA took on No. 3 Notre Dame in front of 12,829 fans at Pauley Pavilion. Though the game received significant hype, it wasn't pretty. Since the retirement of Coach Wooden, the Bruins and the Irish had split the four meetings between them, and in the fifth game, Notre Dame prevailed, 69–66. UCLA looked to be a very good team, but the Irish looked even better.

UCLA won the next four games before the start of conference play.

UCLA began their quest for another conference crown at home against Arizona on December 29, but many looked forward to the rematch against Notre Dame looming ahead. UCLA smashed every team from the Pac-8 in their way, winning their first five games with the closest margin of victory a 15-point win over Washington State on the road. On January 22, the Bruins had a chance to redeem their only loss of the season. No. 3 UCLA and No. 7 Notre Dame squared off again, this time in front of 11,345 people at the Athletic and Convocation Center in South Bend.

Whereas the early-season matchup was a thrilling contest, the rematch was even better. Though significant chatter occurred after the game about the poor quality of the officiating, the players determined the outcome in the final seconds, and UCLA had a chance to come away victorious. With Notre Dame leading, 74–73, Wilkes stepped to the free-throw line for the Bruins for the front end of a one-and-one. After Notre Dame head coach Digger Phelps called timeout to ice the shooter, Wilkes again stepped up to the line as the wild crowd cheered as loud as they could. The ball left his hand well short, barely glancing the front of the rim. Bruce Flowers grabbed the rebound for Notre Dame. He was then fouled, made one of two free throws, and the Bruins were forced to throw up a long desperation shot that wasn't close. Notre Dame did it again. UCLA was 13–2, but both their losses came at the hands of the Irish.

UCLA dismantled the rest of the teams on its remaining schedule, with only Washington State able to keep within single digits of the Bruins. UCLA entered the NCAA Tournament with a 24–2 record, finishing 14–0 in Pac-8 play for its 12th straight conference championship. The team sensed another matchup with Notre Dame looming, but first they had to get there.

The Bruins took on Kansas, a team that finished with a strong 24–4 record in the regular season, in the first game of the tournament. Though the Bruins controlled the game much of the way, the Jayhawks hung around. UCLA won, but only by a seven-point margin, 83–76. Roy Hamilton led the way for the Bruins with 23 points and Raymond Townsend added 22.

The next task for the Bruins was even tougher. With an Elite Eight appearance on the line, UCLA took on the Arkansas Razorbacks. Under head coach Eddie Sutton, Arkansas played a much different style than the Bruins. The Razorbacks finished just 118th in the country in scoring but played lock-down defense, giving up just 61.6 PPG. The Razorbacks were the champions of the Southwest Conference. Ron Brewer, Sidney Moncrief, and Marvin Delph led the way for Arkansas, and on March 16, they shocked the basketball world.

UCLA students camping out before a game in 1978 (Southern Branch Collection).

In the first half, UCLA got off to a terrible start, falling behind, 42–29, at the break. Though the team inched its way back into the game, it couldn't quite climb the mountain. Arkansas won the game, 74–70. Delph was the leading scorer for the Razorbacks, scoring 23 points on 11-for-14 shooting. Though Greenwood, Hamilton, and Darrell Allums played well for UCLA, they didn't receive much help from the others. It was a brutal loss for the Bruins and their fan base, many of which believed they were the best team in the country despite their two losses to Notre Dame. For Coach Cunningham, his first season was a success in many ways, but at UCLA, things were different than at most schools. The Bruins did not win the title for the third consecutive year, and the unfortunate reality that the dynasty built by Coach Wooden was no more finally began to set in for most fans.

University of Kentucky won the NCAA basketball national championship in 1978.

1978–79

In 1978–79, the Pac-8 Conference became the Pac-10 Conference, with the addition of the University of Arizona Wildcats and the Arizona State Sun Devils. The Bruins had more competition within the conference, and though the addition of the two Arizona schools was primarily a football-driven decision, winning the Pac-10 in basketball became more difficult. Entering the season, UCLA had won 12 consecutive conference championships. Coach Gary Cunningham was in his second season in Westwood, and though his first year saw the Bruins improve over the two prior seasons under Gene Bartow, the Bruins only got as far as the Sweet 16 in the NCAA Tournament. The Bruins were in tight games in the 1979 season more than in any season in recent history. Though the Bruins took a step back from the '78 season in terms of wins and losses, they were once again a contender for the national title when March rolled around.

The Bruins of '79 were entertaining; though the team had long been one of the top scoring teams in the nation, it now relied more heavily on outscoring opponents. UCLA scored 85.6 points per game, but gave up 73.4, up from 67.4 the season before. Leading the way for the Bruins were four high scorers. Senior David Greenwood finished his Bruins career with a brilliant final season. The 6'9" forward averaged nearly 20 points and more than 10 rebounds per game. Fellow seniors Brad Holland and Roy Hamilton, the two starters in the backcourt, averaged 17.5 and 16.8 PPG, respectively. Kiki Vandweghe was a strong contributor, as well, pouring in 14.2 PPG from the small-forward position.

The Bruins began the season ranked as the No. 2 team in the country in the Associated Press poll and had expectations of greatness. The first three games of the season were quite simply warm-ups for the Bruins. In wins over Boise State, DePaul, and Santa Clara, all played at home in front of large crowds, UCLA looked outstanding, but its toughest non-conference rival was waiting. On December 9, No. 2 UCLA took on No. 3 Notre Dame at Pauley Pavilion.

David Greenwood, 1979 (Southern Branch Collection).

A crowd of 12,721 fans packed the arena and saw another Bruins–Fighting Irish classic. For much of the game, UCLA struggled to stop the potent Notre Dame offense. ND sophomore forward Kelly Tripucka exploited the weak UCLA defense, scoring 21 points. Matching Tripucka at the top of the scoring list was guard Rich Branning. Though Branning was from nearby Huntington Beach and grew up a UCLA fan, he was swayed to South Bend by Notre Dame head coach Digger Phelps. In front of 25 friends and relatives, Branning played one of the finest games of his career. Though UCLA climbed back in to tie the score at 62 with 6:30 remaining—after falling behind by 13—the Irish was the better team in the final minutes and won, 81–78. It was a heartbreaking loss for the Bruins, as they were looking to crush all rumors that the Irish had UCLA's number. For the third consecutive year, Notre Dame had gone into Pauley Pavilion and walked away with a victory, all the more impressive considering UCLA only had seven losses at home since Pauley Pavilion opened in 1965–66. Since 1974, the Bruins now had a 134–20 record, but seven of the losses came against the men from South Bend.

The Bruins won their next three games by a nearly 24 PPG margin before beginning Pac-10 action. When UCLA took on Stanford in front of a crowd of 7,946 at Maples Pavilion, few thought the game would be of much interest. UCLA was much better and was expected to blow out its rivals from up north. UCLA fell, however, losing again by three points and beginning conference play on a sour note. While the Bruins struggled in close games in December, January saw UCLA in many close affairs, and the results were much better.

On January 4, UCLA took on Oregon State at home. The Bruins didn't play their best, but still escaped with a two-point win. After thrashing Rutgers two days later, UCLA took on Oregon on January 7 and was in for another close affair. David Greenwood led the way for UCLA, and though they were not convincingly beating opponents, were still winning at a high clip. The Bruins narrowly beat Oregon, holding on to win by just three points. UCLA won by just three points again against USC five days later, before taking on the Arizona Wildcats in the first ever meeting between the two teams as conference foes. Though the teams had played in the past, the Wildcats hadn't beaten the Bruins since 1923. As was becoming all too familiar in 1979, the Bruins played down to the level of their opponent. Just five days prior, the Wildcats lost to Oregon State by 36 points. Against the Bruins, however, they played their finest game of the season and it came down to the wire. With six seconds remaining, the score was tied at 69 and Arizona reserve guard John Smith stood at the free-throw line. After knocking in one free throw, the Wildcats won, pulling off the stunning upset. Fans carried Smith off the court in their arms, the nets were ripped down, and Arizona had its biggest win in school history. Two days after the game, local restaurant Spaghetti Company offered all fans in attendance a free spaghetti dinner. The Wildcats were eating well and playing well, but they would meet the Bruins once again.

When January turned to February, the Bruins played better basketball. After losing to Arizona, UCLA won their next nine games, including a thrilling win over USC. The game went to overtime, the first ever OT game in Pauley Pavilion history, before UCLA pulled away for a 102–94 win. Though UCLA was inconsistent, it remained in the top six in the AP rankings all season. When they squared off against Notre Dame on February 11, the Bruins came in at No. 4, and the home team Fighting Irish were No. 2. This time UCLA got its revenge: UCLA 56, Notre Dame 52.

In the return to conference play, the Bruins were continually in high-anxiety, close games. With UCLA down, 83–79, against the Arizona State Sun Devils, Coach Cunningham and the Bruins pulled off some magic, scoring six points in the final nine seconds to come out on top. UCLA then smashed the University of Arizona, 110–86, to earn its 20th win of the season. Following the victory, UCLA vaulted to No. 1 in the national rankings. UCLA's hold on the top spot only lasted one week, however. On February 22, UCLA traveled to Seattle to play the Washington Huskies, falling by one point. Whereas the loss to the Huskies was frustrating, the game against the Washington State Cougars was exhausting. At halftime, the score was 42–42. At the end of regulation, it was still tied, now 82–82. The first overtime didn't solve the deadlock; neither did the second. Finally, Vandeweghe hit a clutch 20-foot jumper, and UCLA knocked down four late free throws to seal the victory in three overtimes.

Though the season had been frustrating, and UCLA's four losses seemed entirely too many, important goals were still attainable for the Bruins. After dropping to No. 3 in the polls, UCLA returned home and beat the California Golden Bears, 79–68, for the 1000th win in school history. Two nights later, UCLA destroyed Stanford, clinching the Pac-10 Conference title in the process, the 13th in a row for the Bruins.

Entering the NCAA Tournament, the Bruins were the No. 2 team according to the AP, and the No. 1 seed in the West Region. For the first and only time, the NCAA Tournament now comprised 40 teams. Two play-in games were in each region, and the winners then joined the 32-team bracket. After Pepperdine beat Utah, the Bruins had their opponent. On March 11, the top-seeded Bruins took on No. 8 Pepperdine at the Marriott Center in Provo, Utah. The game was surprisingly close, but the Bruins came out on top. Greenwood led the way again for UCLA, scoring 18 points and grabbing 10 rebounds.

Teams in the Sweet 16 were more competitive, but the Bruins increased their quality of play. The University of San Francisco was the No. 4 seed in the region and the overall No. 12 team in the country. The Bruins blew them out. The 99–81 victory not only moved the Bruins into the Elite Eight but eased the minds of some of the Bruins faithful. Two days later, it all came crashing down.

On March 17, 1979, UCLA played in another close game, and once again, they were on the wrong end of a classic. Perimeter play ultimately hurt the Bruins against DePaul University, a team the Bruins crushed in their second game of the season. David Greenwood was dominant on the inside, scoring a career-high 37 points. His big performance moved him into third place on the all-time Bruins scoring list, behind only Lew Alcindor and Bill Walton. It wasn't enough, however, as the massive early deficit was too much for the Bruins to overcome. UCLA trailed by 17, and though it cut the deficit to just four with several minutes to play, bad passing and poor shooting down the stretch cost UCLA the game. With the win, DePaul advanced to its first Final Four since 1943, and UCLA went home dejected. The Bruins had five losses on the season but had beaten every team played at least once.

At the end of the season, Coach Cunningham resigned and was soon replaced by an up-and-coming coach named Larry Brown. Things would get tougher before they got better.

Michigan State University won the NCAA basketball national championship in 1979.

CHAPTER 7
Larry Brown (1979–1981)

Larry Brown was born on September 14, 1940, in Brooklyn, New York. His childhood was difficult, and basketball became his outlet. The Brown family never had much money, and when Larry was just six years old, his father died, and desperation soon set in. Ann Brown was left to take care of the family, and though the United States had won World War II and the Great Depression was over, the Brown family still struggled. Larry's father, Milton, was just 43 years old when he died, and the first challenge for Ann was breaking the news to Larry and his brother Herb. Ann decided it best not to tell Larry right away. Instead, she sent her youngest son away to live with relatives for several weeks while she built a plan to keep the family afloat. Larry was told that his father was on the road working. Eventually he learned the truth, something that he suspected all along. Ann would now be forced to spend long hours working in the family bakery in Long Island, and though this was more difficult for the entire family without Milton, it gave Larry time to develop a passion, something that would define his life.

With their mother away for long hours, Larry and Herb took to the basketball courts in New York. While his game developed outside, his reputation was building inside when he reached high school. Larry attended Long Beach High School in Long Island and was a standout basketball star. He was one of the top prep players in America and had a choice of many of the top college programs in the country. At the urging of his high school coach, Brown chose to attend a military academy for one year before enrolling at the University of North Carolina in 1960. While at UNC, Brown learned the importance of hammering home fundamentals so they would become second nature to the team. Coach Dean Smith preached teamwork, unselfishness, and defense. These traits followed Larry Brown throughout his many stops in basketball.

In 1961, Brown represented the United States basketball team in the Maccabiah Games, held in Tel Aviv, Israel, where the Americans brought home the gold medal. As a Tar Heel, Brown was undersized but still productive. Standing at less than six feet tall, he had to use his brain to find spots on the floor where he could be successful. He was able to do that for the entirety of his career. As a junior, he averaged over 16 points per game, and as a senior he was named All-ACC.

Following his college career, Brown already had an eye for coaching, but he hoped to extend his playing career. Though he was drafted to the NBA, he chose instead to play for an AAU team based out of Akron, Ohio, called the Akron Wingfoots. Though he was one of the top players in the league, his greatest accomplishment came not with the Wingfoots, but back with the United States basketball team. He was a member of the 1964 national team and won a gold medal in the Tokyo Olympics.

Brown returned to North Carolina in 1965 as an assistant coach, a position he held for two seasons, but his time as a player was not yet over. In 1967, Brown began playing for the newly formed American Basketball Association (ABA), where he was one of the top point guards in the league. Though he played on five different teams over five seasons, he produced everywhere he went. He was three times an All-Star, won the All-Star Game MVP award in 1968, once had an ABA record 23 assists in a game, and won the ABA title with the Oakland Oaks in 1969.

In 1971, Brown finally put away his sneakers for good. His playing career was over, but his coaching career still had a long journey ahead. Brown coached in the ABA for four seasons, winning two titles. In his first year, he led the Carolina Cougars to a title, and in his fourth ABA season, he won his second title, this one with the Denver Nuggets. Brown continued to coach the Nuggets when they moved to the NBA, and though the Nuggets weren't able to bring home an NBA title, they continued to win at a high mark.

Brown's coaching career, like his playing career, involved many stops. Gary Smith of *Sports Illustrated* described Brown as the coach who would "come, conquer, and leave." Indeed it would be one of the things Coach Brown is now known for. Oftentimes as an NBA coach, he inherited teams that were struggling, quickly turned them into winners, and then left:

- In 1982, he took over the New Jersey Nets. The Nets won only 24 games in 1981 prior to his arrival. They won 44 and then 49 in his two seasons.
- In 1989, the Spurs won 21 games in Coach Brown's first year. It won 56 games the following season.
- In 1992, he took over the Los Angeles Clippers at midseason and led the team to the playoffs. He only stayed one more year, again leading the team to the playoffs.
- In 1994, he inherited a .500 Indiana Pacers team and led them to three playoff berths in four seasons, including trips to the Eastern Conference Finals in his first two seasons.
- In 1998, Brown took over the Philadelphia 76ers, which won just 22 games prior to his arrival. The team reached the playoffs in five of his six seasons, including a trip to the NBA Finals in 2001.
- Brown's greatest triumph came with the Detroit Pistons. After inheriting a strong team, he took the Pistons to the Finals in each of his two seasons, including an upset win over the Los Angeles Lakers in 2004.
- Brown coached the New York Knicks for just one year, but was unable to turn the team around.
- After inheriting a 32-win Charlotte Bobcats team, Brown won 44 games in his second year and reached the playoffs.

Brown was not just an NBA coach, however, and he was not successful everywhere he went. Brown was one in a string of successive coaches to try to carry the mantle at UCLA, and though he came close to doing what only one other coach has done at UCLA since John Wooden, he wasn't able to finish the job. His 1980 team was not one of the best in UCLA history, though it made a run deep in the NCAA Tournament that made most Bruins fans proud. The team was not without controversy, however, and Brown was not without fault. The NCAA had eyes on Coach Brown, and he was not long for Westwood, leaving for the NBA after just two seasons.

At Kansas, it was a different story for Brown. He coached the Jayhawks for five seasons, leading the team to the NCAA Tournament each year, winning the Big Eight Conference once, finishing second three times, reaching two Final Fours, and winning the 1988 national championship. Like the 1980 UCLA team, his 1988 championship-winning Jayhawks were not the best team of his tenure. They finished with the most losses for any Larry Brown-coached team at Kansas and finished in third place in the conference, but they got hot at the right time and brought home the title.

Brown returned to college one last time a quarter century after departing Kansas. For four seasons, he coached at Southern Methodist University, and though he again ran afoul of the NCAA, he again won games, finishing with a 94–39 record in four seasons and an American Athletic Conference championship in 2015. In 2018, Brown agreed to coach Fiat Torino of the Lega Basket Serie A (LBA) in Italy.

Though Brown has often been criticized for bouncing from job to job and not building on the success he usually achieves quickly, he is also considered one of the top coaches of the past 50 years at any level. Larry Brown was only in Westwood for two seasons, and despite the postseason success of the 1980 squad, his two seasons are rather forgettable. He found success in many places and is remembered by far more people for his time in Lawrence, Kansas, and

Detroit, Michigan, than for his time in Los Angeles, California. One could only guess what might have been for UCLA had Coach Brown stayed longer, but that was never his style. When he took over the Bruins, few knew what to expect, but now when Larry Brown signs on to coach a team, everyone typically has an idea of what is next. If only UCLA, or any other team for that matter, could just keep him a bit longer, more banners may fly overhead.

1979–80

The first goal for new UCLA head coach Larry Brown upon his arrival for the 1979–80 season was to revitalize school spirit. Over the previous four years, UCLA continued to draw large crowds at Pauley Pavilion to see the basketball team play, but gone was the sense of invincibility. No longer was Pauley Pavilion the site of a party each time the Bruins took the floor. UCLA's pregame festivities changed, with more organized chants, sleepovers inside of Pauley Pavilion, pom-poms for students, seats moved closer to the court, and earlier game times. Coach Brown's plans were viewed favorably, and the student body soon embraced him, but it wouldn't last long. The 1980 UCLA team struggled in ways that hadn't been seen in Westwood since most of the students were in diapers. UCLA lost more games in Coach Brown's first season than any UCLA team since 1962. Though Coach Gene Bartow and Coach Gary Cunningham were both seen as disappointments, Coach Larry Brown's first team lost more games in one season than either Bartow's or Cunningham's teams lost in two.

Though the 1980 season was borderline disastrous for UCLA, it almost become one of the most memorable in UCLA history. The Bruins were young, but when they finally hit their stride, they were in a position few thought was possible. The Bruins had three players average double-digit scoring in 1980. Sophomore guard Mike Sanders and freshman guard Rod Foster each averaged over 11 points per game. The top scorer for UCLA was senior Kiki Vandeweghe. Coming off a strong junior campaign, Vandeweghe backed it up with a stellar senior season, scoring 19.5 PPG. Beyond the three top scorers, UCLA was light on offense and was plagued by inconsistency among the supporting cast. Heading into the season, more questions arose about the quality of the 1980 UCLA team than in most years, and the only way to answer the questions was to toss the ball up and get the season under way.

The Bruins began the season in all-too-familiar fashion, beating several subpar opponents by large margins before falling to Notre Dame. Again, the game against the Irish was close, but UCLA lost by three points on the road. After falling to the Irish, UCLA lost by five points four days later to No. 11 DePaul. Though UCLA would get back on track, winning five of its next six games, the season was not what most fans expected. On January 12, the unthinkable happened.

After losing to USC, 82–74, and falling to 8–4 on the season, for the first time in 13 seasons, the Bruins were unranked by the Associated Press. The 221 straight appearances in the AP rankings is still the longest streak in college basketball history. Unfortunately, the fall from the rankings was not a wakeup call for the Bruins; they simply were overmatched in many games. Following the loss to USC, the Bruins lost two more games consecutively and three of their next five. Though UCLA had moments of great triumph, including a 26-point win over No. 2 Oregon State, the 1980 season was a continuous struggle. The streak of 13 consecutive conference championships came to a close, and if not for the expanded field, UCLA would not have made the NCAA Tournament. The Bruins finished with a 17–9 regular-season record, winning just 12 of the 18 conference games, and finishing in fourth place in the Pac-10. Though the results of the season were shocking, the results of the NCAA Tournament were even more shocking for UCLA, and this time, that was a good thing.

The Bruins were considered by many to have been the beneficiaries of their brilliant reputation. Skeptics of the Bruins believed they stood no chance in the NCAA Tournament. As the eight seed in the 12-team West Region, UCLA was a considerable underdog, but anything can happen in March on the hardwood. UCLA's opening-round opponent was the Old Dominion Monarchs. On March 7, Kiki Vandeweghe led the way for the Bruins, and after a slow start, the team started to click. Vandeweghe scored a game-high 34 points, and the Bruins pulled off the upset.

In the second round, the Bruins took on the top

UCLA vs. USC, 1980 (Southern Branch Collection).

overall seed and a team they had become familiar with over the previous 15 months. The DePaul Blue Demons were the No. 1 overall seed, winners in 26 out of their 27 games, and led by Mark Aguirre, one of the best players in America. Aguirre averaged nearly 27 PPG, and though slowing him down would be a challenge, UCLA could not simply let him beat them single-handedly. The first half was slow, with neither team making much of a run, which bode well for UCLA. At the break, the Bruins led, 34–32. The second half was much like the first, and though each team picked up the scoring pace, the Bruins outplayed the heavily favored Blue Demons. As time ran out, UCLA completed one of the few major upsets in its history so far. On March 9, 1980, UCLA, in its unusual position as an underdog, knocked off the top team: UCLA 77, DePaul 71. Aguirre scored 19 points and Terry Cummings scored 23, but the team play of the Bruins was more important.

Against Ohio State in the Sweet 16, the Bruins were again underdogs and they again shocked the nation. James Wilkes played a brilliant defensive game, and the offense did enough to win. UCLA was in the Elite Eight. When UCLA took on Clemson, the teams had two clear differences. The Tigers were much bigger, but the Bruins were faster. Rocket Rod Foster and Mike Sanders played well, and the Bruins clinched their spot in the Final Four, something few people thought was possible. Against Purdue, it was much of the same. The Boilermakers were led by a dominant center, Joe Barry Carroll, a seven-footer who averaged 22.3 PPG for the season. UCLA frustrated the big man, however, and forced the ball out of his hands for much of the game. Vandeweghe led the way for UCLA on the offensive end, scoring 24 points on just 12 shots. UCLA won the game 67–62 and was off to the national championship game!

On March 24, 1980, UCLA faced off against the Louisville Cardinals in front of 16,637 fans in Market Square Arena in Indianapolis. Former UCLA player and assistant coach Denny Crum coached the Cardinals, and his squad came into the game with a 32–3 overall record and the No. 2 overall seed. Senior guard Darrell Griffith starred for the Cardinals, averaging nearly 23 PPG for the season. Unlike the previous two games, UCLA and Louisville played similar styles. Neither team was big, but both were fast, athletic, and fundamentally sound. UCLA entered the game with a 10–0 record in national championship games but hadn't won a title in five years. With 4:32 to play in the game, UCLA appeared destined to raise banner number 11. The Bruins led, 54–50, but suddenly the offense went cold. The game was close the entire way, as neither team ever led by more than five points, and any offensive spurt would likely decide the outcome. The offensive spurt finally came, and the Cardinals prevailed. UCLA was held scoreless for the remainder, as Louisville scored the final nine points to win the national championship. Following the game, Coach Brown said, "I know a week from now I'll be a better man for this experience, but right now losing hurts. It hurts a lot." The loss was not the only thing that hurt. UCLA was in trouble with the NCAA.

After a one-year investigation, UCLA was forced to vacate all five NCAA Tournament victories following a report stating that the team broke NCAA rules. According to the *New York Times*, the violations dealt with compensation by the program, such as procuring discounted apartments for players, cosigning a car-purchase agreement for a player, giving money to a recruit, assisting a player in selling complimentary tickets for more than face value, facilitating car usage at reduced cost, and giving meals and entertainment to recruits and their families. According to the *Times*, "The university also failed to reduce the amount of financial aid to three players on another grant, and an assistant coach gave a recruit a school T-shirt." UCLA was also prohibited from competing in the 1982 NCAA Tournament. By that time, Coach Brown was already gone, and a new coach was left to clean up the mess he left. In '81, however, UCLA was simply looking to build on its tournament run and climb back to the top of the college basketball world.

1980–81

Coming off a national championship game appearance, a lot was expected of the Bruins basketball team in 1981. UCLA began the season ranked No. 6 in the country, and despite the up-and-down season of 1980, most pollsters thought UCLA would be improved. UCLA was, indeed, better in 1981 than in 1980 for the majority of the year, but second-year Head Coach Larry Brown was not without worries. UCLA was very young, without a single senior on the roster. The starting lineup consisted of a freshman, three sophomores, and a junior. Prior to the start of the season, Coach Brown said, "I am excited about our team and our attitude, but I'm very concerned about not having a senior class and the fact that we are limited in terms of experience. . . . We have some outstanding athletes, and I'm sure there will be times when we beat a team we shouldn't and that we will have some games where we are inconsistent because of our youth. I do feel we have great depth and that there is no reason that we cannot improve and again be a factor late in the season."

Junior guard Mike Sanders, who scored more than 15 points per game, led UCLA. Sophomores Darren Daye and Rod Foster were steady throughout the year, averaging just over 12.0 PPG each. Freshman Kenny Fields had a strong first year, scoring double digits per game, and the rest of the Bruins contributed in their own ways. Though UCLA did not have the star power that many previous teams had, it could brag about its depth. Coach Brown had proven in one year to be a top recruiter, and now he was tasked with proving himself as a coach.

The Bruins jumped out of the gates early, winning their first six games, including a blowout win over No. 10 Notre Dame at Pauley Pavilion. The 6–0 start was the best for a UCLA team since the 1975 Bruins began the year 12–0. In the fifth game of the season, UCLA beat the Temple Owls in Yoyogi National Gymnasium in Tokyo, Japan. The trip was the longest in UCLA's history, and the game was the first for the Bruins in a foreign country. Though UCLA was winning, Coach Brown had concerns. He said, "I don't think we're that physically impressive. I worry about us against a physical team, and I worry about us because of our inexperience."

Head coach Larry Brown, 1981 (Southern Branch Collection).

Against the top-ranked DePaul Blue Demons, it all came crashing down for the Bruins. UCLA was ranked No. 3, but they were clearly the inferior team. NBC's Al McGuire dubbed the matchup the "Game of the Year" prior to tip, but it was a dud. After UCLA knocked out DePaul in the NCAA Tournament the year prior, the Blue Demons got revenge. Mark Aguirre, Terry Cummings, Bernard Randolph, and Teddy Grubbs pounded the Bruins all game long. At the end, UCLA was on the wrong end of a 93–77 beatdown.

Though UCLA had moments that made fans proud, it never appeared to be a serious national contender the rest of the season. The Bruins were ranked as high as No. 6 later in the season, but with every good stretch came a disappointing loss. The Bruins played five ranked opponents the rest of the season and went 2–3. They lost in triple overtime on the road to No. 12 Arizona State and were crushed by No. 1 Oregon State in Corvallis. Late in the season, they played OSU again, still ranked No. 1; though the game was closer at Pauley, UCLA still fell short. The team knocked off top-ten Notre Dame and Arizona State, and the Bruins were still strong, but the setbacks were hard to get over. Not only did UCLA play poor basketball at seemingly the worst times, but also internal problems plagued the team. Midway through the season, Coach Brown kicked freshman Kenny Fields off the team, reportedly for disagreements with Fields's parents. Brown later changed his mind, however, and Fields was allowed to return.

Despite the up-and-down season, UCLA still finished in third place in the Pac-10 Conference and earned a berth in the NCAA Tournament. The Bruins held a 20–6 overall record, were No. 10 in the Associated Press poll, and were a No. 3 seed in the East Region. With a 48-team tournament format, 16 teams received a bye in the first round, including UCLA. After No. 6 BYU beat Princeton, that team took on the Bruins on March 14, 1981.

The game against BYU is one of the low points in UCLA basketball history. Over the previous six seasons, UCLA was believed to be close to pulling itself back atop the college basketball world. With the loss to BYU on March 14, the mystique of UCLA took a hit. No longer could fans count on UCLA playing for a national championship. It was just another program. BYU crushed UCLA. Danny Ainge, who played baseball in the summer and basketball in the winter and spring, scored 21 first-half points, 37 in total, as the Cougars beat the Bruins, 91–72. The loss was embarrassing, and it was the last game Coach Larry Brown ever coached for the Bruins. He was on the move, and UCLA was tasked with starting fresh once again in 1982.

Indiana University won the NCAA basketball national championship in 1981.

Michael Holton vs. Arizona State, 1981 (Southern Branch Collection).

CHAPTER 8
Larry Farmer (1981–1984)

Larry Farmer is a UCLA man through and through. After gaining fame as a Bruins player, he later became an assistant and then the UCLA head coach for three seasons. Since then, he has continued to stay involved in the game, but despite all his work with many teams, his legacy remains as that of a UCLA man.

Larry Farmer's life in basketball began on January 31, 1951. Originally from Denver, Colorado, basketball was difficult for Farmer in high school. As a sophomore, he struggled and nearly quit the Manual High School team. He decided to tough it out, and as he improved, so did his team. As a senior, the Manual High School team lost only one game, the state championship. Though Farmer was always the underdog, he had a confidence common in those who excel in sports. Though he was not recruited by schools nationwide like many of the UCLA players to come before and after him, Farmer knew he was good enough to play at the highest level. When he had to pick a college, the choice was easy. "I knew in my heart that I wanted to go to UCLA," Farmer later said. The choice worked out for everybody.

In Farmer's three seasons on the UCLA varsity basketball team, the Bruins finished with an 89–1 record. He was the only player to participate in every single game during the three years, and thus he is alone in holding the record for the highest winning percentage as a player over any three-year stretch in college basketball history. Though Farmer was a solid forward for the Bruins, averaging double-digit scoring in back-to-back undefeated seasons as a junior and senior, he chose not to pursue a professional career as a player. Farmer was drafted in both the NBA and the ABA, but he had his eyes set on coaching, and he was at exactly the place he wanted to be.

From 1973 to 1981, the UCLA basketball program experienced incredible staff turnover, but Larry Farmer was always the constant. Coach John Wooden hired Farmer right away upon graduation, and he served under his former coach for two seasons. As the UCLA head coaches continued to cycle in and out of Westwood, Farmer remained. In eight seasons as an assistant coach, he worked under four head coaches. He won a national title, lost in another title game, and felt the disappointment of seeing the UCLA immortality fade. At just 30 years old, Larry

Head coach Larry Farmer, 1982 (Southern Branch Collection).

Farmer was named the eighth head coach in UCLA basketball history.

Coach Farmer's brief stint as the UCLA head coach began in a tough situation and ended in mystery. The 1982 team was solid, but was ineligible for postseason competition due to NCAA violations that occurred prior to Coach Farmer's promotion. Two years later, after his worst season in Westwood, a strange offseason brought more change to UCLA. Former head coach Larry Brown would say of the UCLA job in 1984, "UCLA can be as good a job as there is in the country, but they need to let athletic people make athletic decisions and give the coach, whoever it is, the support he needs to run the program and do the job he's been hired to do." For Coach Farmer, winning games was not the only important thing that mattered. Defining expectations had been difficult for UCLA coaches and administrators following Coach Wooden's retirement, and new Athletic Director Peter Dalis had plans to personally help UCLA reach the pinnacle once again.

Along with Dalis, Vice Chancellor Elwin Svenson was key in the new strategy. They wanted to make the governance of the basketball program a group operation. All three had to play a role in the decision-making processes of the basketball team. The arrangement created confusion. Dalis said after the 1984 season, "Larry Farmer was the coach. We asked him what he needed to make this season successful. We wanted to be supportive of him. We had a meeting at the end of the season, and he told us what he wanted. We were prepared to give him those things." Everything wasn't so clear for Coach Farmer. Along with the pressure that comes with being the most scrutinized head coach by outsiders in college basketball, Coach Farmer believed he didn't have the support of the athletic administration. Dalis interviewed coaches personally to fill two assistant jobs, without the consent of Farmer, and wouldn't publicly speak well of his head coach. The pressure was building, and it finally got to him.

Following the 1984 season, the rumors swirling all season seemed to be put to rest. Though many thought UCLA was going to fire Coach Farmer, UCLA instead extended a two-year contract extension, which Farmer accepted. Three days later, however, Coach Farmer resigned. He could no longer work alongside Dalis. After notifying him at 12:30 p.m., Dalis announced that Walt Hazzard, the man he wanted to coach the Bruins all along, was now the head coach. Everyone was stunned, including Coach John Wooden. He said, "The only one who should have felt that kind of pressure was my immediate successor. He left because he had a chance to start a new program, become an athletic director, and make a lot more money. But why Larry Farmer left, I don't know. I never had any inkling that he wanted to leave. The only thing I can say is that sometimes people put undue pressure on themselves. Maybe he agonized over things you don't need to agonize over." Farmer has never publicly demeaned UCLA or Dalis and rarely speaks of his exit from the program. He simply moved on with his life.

Farmer, like Coach Larry Brown, was a lifelong teacher who made a lot of stops and helped a lot of young men. He continued to teach basketball from the sideline following his departure. From 1986 to 1988, he was the head coach at Weber State, but found minimal success, finishing with just a .386 winning percentage. He coached for two different teams in Kuwait, with a brief stint with the Golden State Warriors as an assistant sandwiched in between. In 1997, he returned to the college game as an assistant for Rhode Island, and one year later, he became a head coach again, this time at Loyola University of Chicago. In his six seasons, the Ramblers finished with a 71–102 overall record. After two years off, he became an assistant coach, a role he continued to fill until retiring in 2018.

Larry Farmer was not a great head coach. His overall record is 13 games below .500. He was, however, an excellent player for the Bruins during the most successful three-year period in college basketball history. He has proven to be a valuable assistant, a classy man, and a prideful Bruin. In the few times he has been back in Pauley Pavilion as an assistant coach, he looks up at the banners he helped raise, and smiles. Farmer is now nearly 70 years old, and the great Bruins teams that he was a member of played nearly 50 years ago. The memory of those teams flash into the minds of those that saw them play every time they look up and see the banners flying high. Farmer's legacy is set. He is a winner, and though he has spent far more time with a rolled-up program in his hand just like his mentor, he will always be most fondly remembered by those that saw him grace the floor with the four letters across his chest.

1981–82

The 1982 college basketball season was different for UCLA. Not only did they have a new coach, once again, but they were also banned from postseason participation. The ban was not only a blow to the Bruins, but to college basketball as a whole. UCLA was still the biggest name, generating the most intrigue come March. Without the ability to participate in the NCAA Tournament, Coach Farmer faced a unique challenge.

UCLA was expected to win around 20 games at the start of the season. It indeed reached the 20-win mark, totaling 21 at the end of the season—the 16th straight such season, setting an NCAA record. The last time UCLA won less than 20 games was in 1966, the year prior to Lew Alcindor's debut on the varsity squad and the last season the Bruins missed the NCAA Tournament. Even though the team couldn't compete in the tournament this season, fans hope for progress to begin competing for titles once again in '83.

The '82 Bruins were filled with familiar names in leadership roles but no clear star. Mike Sanders, Kenny Fields, and Rod Foster all averaged double-digit scoring, and Darren Daye, Ralph Jackson, and Michael Holton each contributed consistently. The Bruins were not a great offensive team, but they were solid defensively and improved greatly. The season didn't start great for Coach Farmer and the Bruins, however. UCLA began the season ranked No. 2 in the nation, but it immediately was given a wake-up call. The Associated Press voters overrated the team.

UCLA's first-game opponent, the BYU Cougars, entered the season unranked and left Pauley Pavilion with a stunning victory, 79–75. Though the Bruins would get their first win of the season the next night over Pepperdine, they fell to 1–2 when they lost to Rutgers on December 3. Though it seemed the Bruins recovered from their early-season slump when they beat rival Notre Dame and then won four more consecutive games, including an upset of No. 7 DePaul, they weren't quite there yet. The Bruins began conference play in miserable fashion. As 1981 turned to 1982, UCLA started the New Year with three straight losses to Pac-10 foes on the road. The Bruins were just 6–5, 0–3 in conference play, and Coach Farmer and staff were on the verge of losing the trust of the fan base.

Coach Farmer's philosophy on coaching was similar to that of his mentor, Coach John Wooden. He said his basketball philosophy was "comprised of three elements. The first is team play. . . . The second is that the team will be in great physical condition, and the third is that the team will be fundamentally sound." Though it took time for the team to see the dividends of the work players and their coaches put in, the season finally turned around, and it did so with a win over the Arizona Wildcats.

When UCLA beat UA, 65–56, at Pauley Pavilion on January 16, it was not only a streak-snapping win but also a streak-starting one. UCLA won 12 consecutive games to climb back into the Pac-10 Conference race. On January 29, UCLA took on No. 8 Oregon State at home and shocked the Beavers, handing them their first conference loss of the season. Against Oregon, "Rocket" Rod Foster scored 35 points, his best game of the season. Foster, like his team,

Darren Daye vs. ASU, 1982 (Southern Branch Collection).

started off the season slowly but played tremendous basketball as the year went on. He finished the season shooting 96 percent from the free-throw line, a new UCLA and NCAA single-season record. The UCLA record still stands today.

UCLA lost only one game following the dismal start to Pac-10 play, falling to Oregon State in the rematch in Corvallis. The Beavers won the Pac-10 Conference, and UCLA finished in second place. For Coach Farmer and the Bruins, the 1982 season was one of preparation. The players were playing primarily for individual and team pride, and the coaches were building a foundation for the coming years. The 1982 season was solid but unspectacular for the boys in Westwood, but 1983 would have to be even better. The tournament ban expired, and much was expected of UCLA going forward.

University of North Carolina won the NCAA basketball national championship in 1982.

1982–83

The 1983 UCLA basketball season was one of great success, at least when considering the still new, slightly lowered expectations of the program. After three straight years of failing to win the conference title, the '83 team had a flashback season. The Bruins sported their best conference and overall record in four years. Of course, UCLA would have to get the job done in March.

While UCLA's defense regressed in '83, its offense improved drastically. The Bruins scored over 80 points per game, an increase of 10 PPG from the last season. Kenny Fields, an extremely talented junior, showed in his first two seasons that he possessed the offensive ability to be one of the best scorers in the nation. Now as a junior, he scored with more consistency, leading the team with an 18.0 PPG scoring average. Senior Darren Daye had a breakout season, as well, finishing his career with his best season and averaging 15.7 PPG. Rod Foster was steady again as a senior, just one of the many backcourt pieces in UCLA's guard-loaded roster. The top performer in the frontcourt was Stuart Gray, a seven-footer with effective interior defense and rebounding.

UCLA began the season again with a matchup against the BYU Cougars. The Bruins started the season ranked No. 7 in the country; unlike the previous season, no upset happened this time around. UCLA went to Provo and snuck past BYU, 85–82, in front of a massive crowd of 23,023. The Bruins continued to play close games throughout the early portion of the season schedule. In just the second game of the year, DePaul pushed the Bruins to overtime. UCLA escaped with another three-point win. For the third time in three games, UCLA played a nail-biter on the road when it traveled to South Bend, Indiana, to take on the Fighting Irish. For the third time, the team defeated Notre Dame, 65–64. UCLA found its rhythm in the next three games, beating San Jose State, No. 7 Iowa, and LSU by an average margin of more than 15 points.

With a 6–0 record, the Bruins hit the road once again to take on unranked Maryland at Cole Field House in College Park. Approximately 14,500 fans saw one of the best games in the history of the venue. The game went to double overtime, and after the second OT period, the Terrapins topped the Bruins, 80–79. The loss was stunning, but it was soon relegated to the back pages, as Chaminade beat No. 1 Virginia in one of the biggest upsets in college sports history just hours after the Bruins fell.

Though sportswriters would write much more about the upset of Virginia, Coach Farmer had the

UCLA Spirit Squad, 1983 (Southern Branch Collection).

1983 UCLA team photo (Southern Branch Collection).

upset of UCLA on his mind. His team started the season well, but a loss to an unranked team was entirely unacceptable at UCLA. The memories of the January losing streak of last year were still on the minds of many. UCLA bounced back, however, and did so in a Bruins way. The team trounced its opponents, running up impressive scores over all teams, good and poor alike. After winning five straight games following the loss to Maryland, UCLA was in a familiar place: No. 1 in the country.

After beating California and Stanford to run its winning streak to seven, UCLA took a break from Pac-10 play to welcome an opponent from the SEC. When the Alabama Crimson Tide traveled west to take on the Bruins at Pauley Pavilion, few gave Alabama much chance at going back home with a win, but that's exactly what it did. Alabama players wore black patches on their shoulders in memory of legendary football coach Paul "Bear" Bryant, who died just days before the game against UCLA. Perhaps inspired by the legendary figure, or perhaps just more prepared from the jump, the Crimson Tide dominated much of the game. After building a 16-point lead, the Tide gave it back, as UCLA stormed all the way back to tie the game at 67 with under a minute to play. Alabama scored the final three points, however, and toppled the No. 1 team in the nation. UCLA had just two losses thus far during the season, but both were stunners.

After losing to Alabama, UCLA never quite looked the same. They played miraculous games but also mixed in subpar performances. The Bruins won a thrilling game over Washington State and clobbered No. 17 Washington but also lost to unranked Oregon State. They beat USC handily twice but lost to unranked Washington State. They beat Arizona by 53 points to clinch the Pac-10 title but then lost the final game of the regular season to unranked Arizona State. The Bruins finished the regular season with a 23–5 overall record, 15–3 in conference play, and won the Pac-10 title. The Bruins were certainly expected to be a national contender, earning the No. 2 seed in the West Region.

When UCLA took on the Utah Utes on March 19, it were expected to rout the future conference mates. Utah entered the 52-team tournament with the worst record of any team in the field at just 15–13. They snuck by Illinois in the first round before the

UCLA matchup. The Bruins shot 59 percent from the floor in the first half but couldn't put away Utah. Utah hung around and in the second half made its move. The game was slow, possessions were limited, and the Bruins began to falter. With 6:10 remaining on the clock, Angelo Robinson put the Utes up for good, 57–55. Utah played near flawless basketball the rest of the way and beat UCLA, 67–61. In a year of upsets, UCLA's season ended in one final shocker. All six of UCLA's losses came at the hands of teams unranked by the Associated Press.

North Carolina State University won the NCAA basketball national championship in 1983.

1983–84

The Bruins did not carry the momentum of 1983 into the 1984 season. Instead, the devastating and shocking loss to Utah in the NCAA Tournament led to a shocking collapse in '84. Coach Farmer's job was secure to be sure, but with the poor season in '84, combined with the often-overwhelming pressure of coaching the UCLA basketball team, enough was enough for Coach Farmer at the end of the season. His third season would be his last. Following the retirement of Coach Wooden, the name applied to the Ohio State football program in the 1940s could aptly be applied to the UCLA basketball program: it was the graveyard of coaches.

After averaging 10 more points in '83 than in '82, UCLA reverted in '84 back to '82 scoring numbers. Their defense was middle-of-the-road, as well. The situation led to predictably average results. Replacing Rod Foster, Darren Daye, and Michael Holton was difficult. Kenny Fields, now a senior, had another excellent season, averaging more than 17 points per game. Ralph Jackson and Stuart Gray had the finest seasons of their careers. Of the plethora of others to share the scoring load, most were inexperienced, and none could lift UCLA out of mediocrity. One freshman guard, however, eventually made his mark, but not during the '84 season. Reggie Miller, a skinny 6'7" shooting guard from Riverside, eventually became

Kenny Fields vs. BYU, 1984 (Southern Branch Collection).

one of the most recognized basketball players in the world. As a freshman, he averaged just 4.6 PPG.

The Bruins began the season ranked No. 9 and seemingly proved their worth early in the season, though the competition level was not particularly high. UCLA beat Notre Dame on the road in the third game of the season. After having lost five out of six to the Irish, the Bruins had now won the last seven matchups.

Though UCLA lost to an unranked New Mexico team on December 10, an unthinkably embarrassing loss, the team won its share of games the first six weeks of the season. After the New Mexico loss, UCLA dropped to No. 15 in the rankings but then reeled off seven straight wins, including three in conference, to climb back up to No. 6. The team was 10–1, and though they weren't flashy and high scoring, they were winning. Then the team fell apart.

On January 14, 1984, UCLA lost by double digits to the University of Oregon. It then traded wins and losses over the next six games, including a blowout loss at home against No. 2 DePaul. Following a triple overtime loss to Washington, UCLA fell out of the Associated Press rankings altogether and then lost two more and five out of six games to reach a new low point. The team that had been 10–1 was now 15–10. The Bruins played their most impressive game of the season on March 1, beating No. 13 Washington, 73–59. It was a nice win and ended a three-game losing streak, and the Bruins won two more games consecutively following, but they lost their final game of the season on the road to Oregon State. UCLA's record was just 17–11 and 10–8 in Pac-10 play. The team finished fourth in the conference it once owned, just the second time it finished that low in 42 years. The 17 total wins was the lowest for a UCLA team since 1960, and its 11 losses was the most since 1962.

The season was unquestionably one of the worst for the Bruins since Wilbur Johns was the coach. Everyone wondered where the program would go next. When Coach Farmer resigned, another coach got a shot. Walt Hazzard, a star on UCLA's first championship team in 1964, took control of the program he helped build.

Georgetown University won the NCAA basketball national championship in 1984.

Joe and Josephine Bruin, 1984 (Southern Branch Collection).

CHAPTER 9
Walt Hazzard (1984–1988)

Walt Hazzard is remembered differently by segments of the UCLA fan base. Many older fans remember Hazzard as one of UCLA's first great stars on the court, one of the top players to ever wear a UCLA uniform, a national champion, and a lifelong Bruin. Others who never saw him play or don't hear his name mentioned alongside Lew Alcindor or Bill Walton tend to think of him as a failed head coach. When UCLA basketball struggles, people remember Walt Hazzard's time as the head coach and understand that the college has had tough times before and prevailed.

Walter Raphael Hazzard Jr. was born on April 15, 1942, five years to the day before another Bruin, Jackie Robinson, made history with the Brooklyn Dodgers. Hazzard spent time as a youth in Delaware, Maryland, and then finally Pennsylvania, where he became a star at Overbrook High School in Philadelphia. The OHS varsity team finished with an 89–3 record in Walt's final three seasons, and as a senior, he was named city player of the year.

He then traveled to the West Coast and UCLA for college ball. After spending one season on the freshmen team, Hazzard joined the varsity squad and was a star during the best three-year stretch in UCLA basketball history to that point. As a sophomore, he averaged 13.2 points per game as a starting guard. The following year, he upped his scoring average to 16.3, and then finished his career with an 18.6 average as a senior, all while excelling as a rebounder, defender, and tremendous passer. Although Hazzard received numerous accolades for his playing, including twice being named All-AAWU, 1964 First Team All-American, and National Player of the Year, they would likely have been forgotten if not for the team's success during Hazzard's three years. In 1962, UCLA reached the first Final Four in school history. The next year, UCLA improved during the regular season, though it didn't fare as well in the NCAA Tournament. Finally in '64, it all came together for Hazzard, Coach Wooden, and the Bruins. UCLA finished with a perfect 30–0 record and won the national championship. Hazzard then added a gold medal at the 1964 Tokyo Olympics.

Walt Hazzard continued to play in Los Angeles, as so many Bruins would eventually; for three years, he was a member of the Los Angeles Lakers. As a rookie, he struggled, and was left to play mostly mop-up minutes. Hazzard improved, however, and as a second-year player in 1966, he averaged nearly 14 points and five assists per game. His third season saw a dip in production, and his flashy nature often led to frustration. During the expansion draft, the Seattle SuperSonics selected Hazzard. He had a new home, a new chance to play his style of basketball, and an opportunity to revamp his career.

Hazzard played just one year with the SuperSonics, but it was a memorable one. The 1968 season was the best of his NBA career. He averaged 24.0 PPG, and added 6.2 APG and 4.2 RPG, and earned a trip to the All-Star Game. Hazzard's career had seemingly turned around, and soon his name would change too. After three solid seasons with the Atlanta Hawks and after being introduced to Islam by Lew Alcindor, Hazzard converted to Islam in 1971 and changed his name to Mahdi Abdul-Rahman. He played three more seasons for four more teams before retiring from professional basketball as a player. Abdul-Rahman was never comfortable with how he believed the public perceived his name change and religious conversion, and though he didn't change his name back to Walt Hazzard, he would again use his birth name for the rest of his life out of "professional courtesy."

His future was uncertain following retirement. Coaching was not an immediate priority, but it did come calling, and Hazzard couldn't say no. Hazzard spent two seasons coaching at Compton College and two more at Chapman College. He was successful in his early coaching ventures, taking Compton to the Junior College state championship game. When he was hired by UCLA prior to the start of the 1985–1986 season, UCLA was searching for someone to bring stability. It hoped by hiring a Bruins legend, the coach would be there for the long haul and meet the lofty expectations of the fan base. Hazzard coached the Bruins for four seasons, winning one Pac-10 title and finishing with a 77–47 overall record. Following the 1988 season, Hazzard was fired.

Walt Hazzard would never coach again, though he remained in basketball, working a number of different behind-the-scenes roles with the Los Angeles

UCLA head coach Walt Hazzard, 1987 (Southern Branch Collection).

Lakers. On March 22, 1996, Hazzard suffered a serious stroke, and though he regained much of his strength and physical ability in the recovery, he never fully recovered and was less publicly active the rest of his life. On November 18, 2011, Walt Hazzard died following complications from heart surgery. He was 69 years old.

Hazzard was as a coach what he was not as a player. His teams were never great, nor were they ever poor. He was an average coach at UCLA.

His number 42 is retired by the UCLA program, though Hazzard graciously allowed Kevin Love to wear the number for one season in 2008. When Hazzard died, a new generation of fans was told his story, and this time, it wasn't about four disappointing seasons on the sideline. It was about a kid from Philadelphia who became a legend in Westwood.

1984–85

The 1985 season was, for UCLA standards, a disaster. In the tenth season since Coach John Wooden retired, Walt Hazzard was the fifth new coach. The Bruins were inexperienced, both on the court and on the sidelines. A new star emerged, and UCLA made a postseason run. But the team was generally a one-man show, and the run was in the wrong postseason tournament. UCLA won less regular-season games and lost more in '85 than in any season in a quarter century. Many fans thought it couldn't get any worse, but they were just beginning the most tumultuous four-year stretch since the 1940s.

As a sophomore, Reggie Miller had a breakout season and made a name for himself on the West Coast. The 6'7" sharpshooter became UCLA's primary scoring weapon, and though the three-point line would not be adopted in college basketball until his senior season, Miller was one of the best outside shooters in the sport. Miller eventually became one of the best-known basketball players in the world. He would develop a well-deserved reputation, as a trash talker and a clutch performer. In 1985, however, he was just trying to prove himself.

Though the sophomore from Riverside had a breakthrough season, UCLA's offense was not in the same class as those of teams Coach Hazzard had been a part of when he was a player. UCLA played slowly and had long periods of ineffectiveness on the offensive end. The Bruins averaged just 69.2 points per game, which ranked 141st in the country. Players like the senior trifecta of Nigel Miguel, Brad Wright, and Gary Maloncon all had moments of fine play, but to compete in the Pac-10 and on the national level, the Bruins needed more.

Expectations for the 1985 season actually were even lower than the final outcome. After repeated failed attempts in the NCAA Tournament, a declining win total, a depleted roster, and an uninspiring head coaching hire, fans thought 1985 would look more like the pre-Wooden teams than the post-Wooden ones. The UCLA yearbook said as much: "Not since 1939 when UCLA lost to 20th Century Fox and Bank of America was there so little expected from the Bruin basketball squad." Less than seven thousand fans showed up to see the Bruins in the first game of the year. Never before had many of the fans and students seen a UCLA team that was expected to be less of a factor on the national level. Seeing them unranked to begin the season was a reality that once seemed unthinkable. Despite the general negativity surrounding the program, UCLA began the season with a win, downing Idaho, 87–58. But one night later, UCLA lost to Santa Clara, an embarrassing defeat. Then in the first road game of the season, UCLA traveled to Chicago to take on DePaul, the No. 2 team in the nation and a regular on UCLA's schedule in those years. The Bruins were demolished, 81–60, and one week later, Memphis State blew them out 86–70. Wins over U.S. International and Oral Roberts, with losses to BYU and St. John's sandwiched in between, did nothing to ease the concerns of UCLA fans. When 1984 turned to 1985 and the conference season began, UCLA was just 3–5 and looked like a West Coast doormat.

The Bruins were able to right the ship in Pac-10 play, but it didn't come in the conference opener. Not only did UCLA lose to Oregon State, but the game was also dull. During UCLA's finest years, it was always known for offense. Against OSU, the team scored just 49 points and was handily beaten. Positive results came as the season wore on. Against Oregon on January 5, UCLA won in dramatic fashion. The game was again low scoring and ugly, but for all the poor offensive play throughout stretches of the season, UCLA played solid defense. Against the Ducks, the defense that kept the Bruins close, and finally in double overtime, they pulled away for a 67–59 victory. At least the Bruins were now seemingly headed in the right direction, at least for the time being.

The win over Oregon was the first game in a stretch in which UCLA won six out of seven games, with its lone loss coming by a single point against second-year head coach Lute Olson and the Arizona Wildcats in Tucson. Against Stanford, UCLA scored 100 points for the only time all season. The game was one of just five all season that the Bruins scored at least 80, which they only did one more time the rest of the season.

Though the Bruins had climbed out of the gutter and had started to win again at a respectable clip, they were just 9–7. Few thought they were a serious contender to even earn an NCAA Tournament bid.

Reggie Miller vs. Washington State, 1985 (Southern Branch Collection).

The first four games in the month of February all but sealed their fate. UCLA lost four consecutive heartbreaking games. In front of a large crowd at the Sports Arena, UCLA fell by one point to USC. The team then lost by one to Notre Dame, fell to Washington State in overtime, and lost another close one to Washington. The Bruins were back under .500, and all hope for a trip to the NCAA Tournament was now gone. UCLA and Coach Hazzard could have finished off the season with a handful more losses and geared up again the following season, but they didn't. The season ended on a strong note, even if it was on a smaller stage.

The Bruins won seven of their final eight regular season games, with the lone loss coming in four overtimes to USC, when the offense failed again, scoring only 78 points in 60 minutes. March was different for the Bruins in '85, as the irrelevance of the NIT substituted for the madness of NCAA Tournament. At just 16–12, UCLA was selected for the NIT field and accepted the invitation. UCLA thus played for the first time in the NIT, a tournament once considered important, but mostly ignored since. The Bruins played five teams as they continued to advance through the bracket, beating their first three opponents by double digits. In the semifinal game at Madison Square Garden, UCLA beat Louisville, 75–66, to earn its 20th win of the season, and finally against Indiana on March 29, the Bruins won again, taking home its only NIT championship in history. Reggie Miller was named Tournament MVP, a fine cap to a strong individual season.

Going forward, UCLA needed to improve. The NIT championship has been virtually erased from the minds of the UCLA basketball family. No banner flies overhead at Pauley Pavilion celebrating that title.

Villanova University won the NCAA basketball national championship in 1985.

1985–86

Whereas the 1985 season was a poor one that ended with success on a small stage and a glimmer of hope, the 1986 season was a disaster from beginning to end. No longer was UCLA a low-scoring team. It jumped from 141st in the country in scoring to 55th, adding 5.8 points per game. In '86, opponents scored 74.4 PPG, which ranked 240th in the country out of 279 Division I teams.

The '86 Bruins were led by three players. Reggie Miller was now a junior, and his third season would go down as one of the best in the history of the storied UCLA program. Miller averaged 25.9 PPG. Only Lew Alcindor in 1967 and 1968 ever averaged more points per game in a season than Reggie Miller in 1986. He wasn't alone. Montel Hatcher, a 6'1" guard, averaged over 13 PPG, and he was joined in the backcourt by a freshman that caught everyone's eye. Jerome "Pooh" Richardson, just beginning his stellar career, was an instant sensation. He was short but strong and was a good passer, good shooter, and excellent defender. His nickname was given to him by his grandmother, who believed he resembled Winnie the Pooh. As a freshman, his most important task was to get the ball to Reggie, and he did, leading the team in assists and earning Pac-10 Freshman of the Year honors.

While the story of the 1986 season is one of great personalities and interesting games, it is not a success story. The Bruins lost their first game of the year, a matchup with the University of North Carolina Tar Heels. UNC was coached by Dean Smith, led by Brad Daugherty and Kenny Smith, and ranked No. 2 in the country to begin the season. UCLA was unranked, something that would have been unbelievable just a couple of years prior. After UNC beat UCLA, 107–70, the gap between national contender and nonfactor was massive, and UCLA was part of the latter. The Bruins were never in the Associated Press rankings in 1986, the second consecutive complete season they were left out.

The Bruins finished with just a 15–14 record. Their winning percentage (.517) was the lowest for a UCLA team since 1948 (.480), the final season before Coach Wooden arrived. The most memorable games were not ones where the outcome was of any national importance. Against Oregon State University, Reggie Miller scored 41 points. He was just the fourth Bruin at the time to ever break the 40-point barrier, joining Alcindor, Walton, and Goodrich. Against Washington State, he scored 39. On January 25, 1986, UCLA lost to Cal for the first time in 25 years. The Bruins had won 52 consecutive games over their brothers from the north, the longest winning streak against a single opponent in NCAA history.

UCLA's season did not give hope heading into

the following year. UCLA lost to UC Irvine in the first round of the NIT. The Bruins have not played in the NIT since. Despite the horrendous results of the 1986 basketball season, UCLA made a run in '87. When all pundits counted out Coach Hazzard and the Bruins, they did what few expected. The '87 season would be a strong one for UCLA, but first they had to struggle through a long offseason. The Bruins just weren't winning enough and no one was happy. Coach Hazzard was on the hot seat already.

University of Louisville won the NCAA basketball national championship in 1986.

1986–87

The 1986–87 Bruins were the best team Walt Hazzard ever coached. The year before, junior guard Reggie Miller had one of the best individual seasons in UCLA history, but the team struggled, winning just 15 games. One year later, Miller was again brilliant, averaging 22.3 points per game, but now UCLA was again a contender. The Pac-10 Conference title had eluded the Bruins for the previous three seasons, but in '87, UCLA had a chance to bring back the title once again. Sophomore Pooh Richardson followed up his strong freshman season with solid sophomore season, and Montel Hatcher, Dave Immel, Jack Haley, and Charles Rochelin were also key contributors. While Miller was not alone, he certainly was the man who got the most attention, and in 1987, he had a new weapon at his disposal. Eight years before, the NBA adopted what was once see as a fluky new rule, and now it was time for the NCAA to get on board. In 1986–87, college basketball adopted the three-point line, and UCLA's best player just happened to be one of the best outside shooters in basketball history. The man who later became the NBA's all-time leader in made three-point field goals first started shooting behind the line for Coach Hazzard and the Bruins.

The greatly improved Bruins beat Santa Clara in the season opener, and then UCLA took on the University of North Carolina at Pauley Pavilion. The year before, the Tar Heels demolished the Bruins in Chapel Hill by 37 points. UNC entered the game ranked No. 1 in the country and finished the season with five starters that averaged double-figure scoring, led by senior Kenny Smith's nearly 17 PPG. The Tar Heels finished undefeated in ACC play and made a deep run in the NCAA Tournament, but on this day, the Bruins were the better team. Though the unranked Bruins topped the No. 1 team in the land by the score of 89–84, the players didn't see it as a shocker, and they said so. "This wasn't no upset," said Reggie Miller. It wasn't a shocker for UNC coach Dean Smith either. He said after the loss, "I've said all along we're overrated. Maybe now somebody will believe me."

After the big win over the Tar Heels, UCLA jumped into the rankings at No. 11, but the season soon took a turn for the worse. After trouncing Pepperdine, UCLA lost four consecutive games, including two in Pac-10 play. The struggling Bruins finally ended their losing streak against Long Beach State, but again the game was difficult. The Bruins of 1987 were not a dominant team, but they fared well in close games. Against LBSU, UCLA escaped with a two-point win at home, and two nights later, beat Cal State Fullerton by a single point. The two wins themselves weren't particularly impressive, but it was the beginning of a winning streak that turned around the UCLA season. On January 2, UCLA returned to conference play and beat Stanford by 20. They then beat Cal and Arizona State before taking on the University of Arizona in front of 13,024 fans at McKale Center in Tucson. With the Bruins trailing, 83–81, in the final seconds, everyone in the arena expected Reggie Miller to take the final shot, but another man, Craig Jackson, was the hero on this day. Pooh Richardson found Jackson for a long three-pointer that went right through the net as the buzzer sounded. UCLA won, 84–83, quieting the home crowd and extending UCLA's winning streak to six games.

A similar script was written three games later, but with a more predictable lead character. After beating Oregon and Oregon State, UCLA took on Notre Dame at home. Trailing 59–58, Miller hit a 24-foot three-pointer with 10 seconds left to lift the Bruins over the Irish. In a memorable season for Miller, the game against Notre Dame was not even his greatest individual performance. UCLA continued to win at a high rate, taking eight of their final 10 games to win the Pac-10 conference. In one final regular season game, however, Miller pulled off his greatest college performance. On February 28,

1987, UCLA took on defending national champion Louisville, and Miller put on a show. After starting slowly, Miller and UCLA trounced Denny Crum and the Cardinals. In the second half alone, Miller scored a school-record 33 points, which still stands today. He finished with a total of 42 on just 19 field goal attempts, 15 of which he converted. After the game, Miller was asked if this was how he would play during the postseason. He replied, "I'm not a gypsy. I'm not a fortune teller."

UCLA indeed participated in the NCAA Tournament for the first time since Coach Hazzard took over, but it would have to wait. In 1987, the Pac-10 conference played its own tournament for the first time. The No. 18 Bruins continued to do what they had done throughout the course of the conference season. They defeated the men in the different color uniforms. After knocking off Arizona State, California, and Washington, the Bruins were the first ever Pac-10 Tournament champions.

The 1987 NCAA Tournament consisted of 64 teams. It was the first time UCLA participated in the tournament since it expanded in 1985. In order to bring home another national championship, they would have to win six games. Though UCLA wasn't considered one of the favorites to win it all, many pundits considered the team a sleeper that could shock the nation. The Bruins were named the No. 4 seed in the West Region and began tournament play by taking on No. 13 Central Michigan in Salt Lake City. The Bruins had no problem with the Chippewas, beating them, 92–73. Miller led the way again, scoring 32 points and grabbing 13 rebounds.

UCLA vs. Arizona State, 1987 (Southern Branch Collection).

In the round of 32, things were different. While UCLA had clicked for most of the season, and the team was finding new ways to win each night, nothing went well for the Bruins against Wyoming. At halftime, UCLA led by six, but in the second half, they were held to just 24 total points, and the team fell in embarrassing fashion, 78–68 in favor of the Cowboys. Fennis Denbo torched the Bruins for 41 points, including seven three-pointers and 16 free throws. Miller scored 24 points, but he received little help. Miller's career was over.

The 1987 season saw stretches of team greatness, and many moments of individual greatness. The Bruins were Pac-10 champs, Pac-10 Tournament champs, and nationally relevant once again, but they didn't perform in March.

Miller was one of the best players in UCLA history, and he went on to become one of the best players in NBA history. But he never won a national championship at UCLA, and thus he is mostly remembered for his individual success there.

Moving forward, UCLA and Coach Hazzard had a tremendous hole to fill. For the previous three seasons, Miller was the unquestioned leader of the team, and still the Bruins did not win enough games. In 1988, Coach Hazzard would have to see another uptick in production. His seat cooled for one season, but soon the heat would be back.

Indiana University won the NCAA basketball national championship in 1987.

Reggie Miller

Reggie Miller is awkward. He was born with deformed hips and severely splayed feet and wore braces on his legs as a child. His stride on the court was strange. His shooting style, elbows flared wide, was unconventional, and he shot the ball with what some called too much arc. Reggie was rail thin. His ears are big, and sometimes his eyes are buggy. For much of his childhood, he was the awkward younger brother of a basketball phenom.

His older sister, Cheryl, is one of the best women's basketball players in history. Once coming from a game and scoring 39 points for Riverside Poly High School, Reggie burst into his home and bragged about his exploits. Cheryl just smirked. She had played a game too. Reggie asked, "How many did you get today, Cheryl?"

Her response was "A lot, Reggie."

"How many? Forty? Fifty?" he shot back.

"A hundred and five." Such was the life for Reggie growing up. He lived in the shadow of his legendary older sister.

Despite what Reggie looked like on the outside, and despite Cheryl's greater high school fame, Reggie was an excellent player from an excellent family. He grew up in Riverside, and his parents' story is just as interesting as the stories of the rest of his family. Saul and Carrie, his parents, met in Memphis, Tennessee, where Saul was a saxophonist, a cool man. Carrie later said, "All the girls had their eyes on Saul." Reggie's father may have had options in his younger days, but Carrie stole his heart, and the two later became the proud parents of one of America's greatest athletic families. Along with Cheryl and her many accomplishments, Reggie's brother Darrell played Major League Baseball and later became an MLB executive and his son, Darrell Jr., later played baseball at UCLA. Tammy Miller, two years younger than Reggie, attended Cal State Fullerton on a volleyball scholarship. While Darrell, Cheryl, and Tammy all have their own athletic accomplishments to be proud of, Reggie became the household name.

In 1983, Reggie stepped away from the shadow of his sister and decided to do things his own way. Whereas Cheryl had starred at crosstown USC, Reggie went to UCLA. As a freshman in 1984, he scored under five points per game. As a sophomore, he made a huge leap, scoring 15.2 points per game. In his final two seasons, was one of the greatest players in America, averaging 25.9 and then 22.3 PPG in a Pac-10-winning senior season. When the three-point line was instituted prior to his senior season, Miller had a new weapon, which ultimately build his legacy around. With the shot that once seemed fluky, Miller's college exploits were impressive. To this day, he is just one of six UCLA players to ever score 40 points in a

Reggie Miller vs. Oregon, 1987 (Southern Branch Collection).

game, doing so twice. His 33 points against Louisville in the second half in 1987 is still the school record. At the time of his departure, Miller was the second-leading scorer in UCLA history, behind only Lew Alcindor. While his scoring numbers were impressive, Reggie's legacy is about so much more. Against Notre Dame in 1987, he hit a game-winning three-pointer to lift the Bruins over their rival. Clutch shots would eventually become a part of Reggie's highlight reel on a regular basis.

In the 1987 NBA Draft, the Indiana Pacers selected Reggie Miller as the 11th overall pick by the Indiana Pacers. Indiana fans were not happy. While Reggie certainly had the qualifications to be picked that high in the draft, local fans clamored for Indiana University star Steve Alford. Time provee the team was right, as Reggie went on to become the greatest Pacer of all time.

In 18 seasons, all with the Pacers, Reggie scored a total of 25,279 points, good for 12th place on the all-time NBA scoring list at the time of his retirement. He made 2,560 career three-point field goals, most ever in NBA history at the time. As a rookie, he broke Larry Bird's rookie three-point field goal record, making 61 three-pointers. In Miller's third season, he scored 24.6 PPG, becoming the first Pacer to reach an All-Star game in 13 seasons. Over the course of his career, he scored at least 20 points per game during six seasons (three more if you round up). Miller averaged 18.2 PPG for the entirety of his career.

On November 28, 1992, Reggie set the Indiana Pacers single game scoring record that still stands today, pouring in 57 points against the Charlotte Hornets.

In the 1994 Eastern Conference finals against the New York Knicks, Reggie and filmmaker Spike Lee engaged in one of the most famous spats in sports history. Lee is a noted Knicks fan, an outspoken, brash, and confident trash talker, and the perfect figure to rile up Reggie's emotions, a legendary trash talker himself. Miller scored 39 points total, 25 in the fourth quarter alone, as the Pacers beat Lee's beloved Knicks in Game Five. Reggie put two hands around his own throat, gesturing in the direction of Lee that his team choked is one of the most iconic moments in NBA history.

That spat with Spike Lee and the Knicks is one of the two most memorable instances of Miller's career. The second is the 8.9-second game against the Knicks in 1995. On May 7, 1995, the Pacers trailed the New York Knicks, 105–99, when Reggie cut the lead in half with a catch-and-shoot three-pointer from an inbounds pass. On the ensuing inbounds play, the Knicks turned the ball over, throwing it directly to Reggie, after he nudged Greg Anthony, who flopped to the floor. Reggie quickly retreated to the three-point line and fired, knocking in the three and stunning the crowd. The score was tied, but then Pacer Sam Mitchell inexplicably fouled Knicks guard John Starks. Starks missed both free throws, and though Patrick Ewing grabbed an offensive rebound, he too missed, and Reggie then hauled down the defensive rebound and was fouled on the wild play. He knocked down both free throws, the Pacers held on to win, and his finest individual moment was cemented in NBA lore.

Reggie continued to thrill fans on the court through the 2005 season, and did so in his own always fascinating way. His career included countless clutch moments and game-winning shots. His late-game heroics quickly became known as "Miller Time," and eventually he even earned respect from New York Knicks fans at Madison Square Garden. In his final game in New York, fans chanted "Reg-gie! Reg-gie!" Miller was a member of the 1996 USA Basketball National Team that won a gold medal. He reached the NBA Finals in 2000, losing to the Los Angeles Lakers. He got in physical fights with Michael Jordan and Kobe Bryant and was seen by many as a dirty player. Eventually, he received respect. Although young players like Miller are often seen as brash, cocky, and unlikeable, many, like Miller, are later seen as devoted, competitive, and warrior-like when they get older.

Reggie remained active after retirement. He has worked for TNT, covering both the NBA all season and NCAA basketball in March, for the past 14 years. Miller resides in Malibu, California, where he has taken up the hobby, and developed a passion for, mountain biking. In 2007, he considered an NBA comeback, but chose to remain retired. His number 31 jersey has been retired by both the Indiana Pacers and UCLA basketball. In 2012, he was inducted into the Naismith Memorial Basketball Hall of Fame. Reggie can still be seen around the UCLA campus from time to time. He supports the Bruins of all sports, attending both baseball and basketball games, regularly tweeting support for all UCLA student-athletes, and donning his old school UCLA hat, sitting awkwardly on his small head.

Reggie Miller was not a natural athlete, and though he came from a talented sports family, he was always an underdog. Reggie's tenacity, focus, and the hours he spent shooting at the hoop at his Riverside home as a child helped him become a Bruin. His time in Westwood, playing under Walt Hazzard, helped him become an icon, and his continuous desire to beat the Knicks, to take down Michael Jordan and Kobe Bryant, took him to basketball immortality. Reggie Miller did not play on championship teams like many of the other great Bruins legends, but he did represent UCLA well and built a legacy uniquely his own.

1987–88

The 1987–88 Bruins, coached by Walt Hazzard, suffered through one of the most disappointing seasons in UCLA history. Under Hazzard, the Bruins struggled mightily for two seasons, but in 1987, they had a resurgence, winning the Pac-10 Conference. By 1988, Hazzard had lasted longer than any coach after John Wooden.. Each of the next three UCLA coaches after Wooden lasted only two years. Larry Farmer finally made it to a third year. The 1988 season was Coach Hazzard's fourth.

Reggie Miller was no longer around to lead the way on the court, and wins were hard to come by in 1988. Coach Hazzard needed to keep the momentum going from the previous season. He was coaching for his job.

But UCLA slipped back into mediocrity in 1988. Others stepped up to fill the scoring hole left by Miller's departure, but it was not enough. Sophomore forward Trevor Wilson was UCLA's leading scorer and rebounder, averaging 15.4 points per game and over nine rebounds per game. Senior Dave Immel had his best individual season, scoring 13.3 PPG. Pooh Richardson was now a junior and the clear leader on the team. He was steady again, as he had been from the day he arrived in Westwood. He was one of the top passers in the nation and averaged seven assists per game. A host of other players had big games for UCLA, and many players contributed, but the Bruins lacked consistency.

The Bruins began play in the Preseason NIT,

Trevor Wilson, 1988 (Southern Branch Collection).

and though they trounced Oral Roberts, 119–79, in the season opener, things quickly turned sour. Three nights later, the Bruins fell to the New Mexico Lobos, 77–66, and were eliminated from the tournament. The Bruins then lost their second game in a row against No. 12 Temple. After taking an early lead, UCLA fell apart in the second half. The Bruins continued losing early in the season. BYU and St. John's each beat the Bruins, and the losing streak reached four. UCLA had two games remaining on the nonconference slate before Pac-10 play began, and both were against subpar teams. The Bruins doubled up Penn, 98–49, in front of a small crowd at Pauley Pavilion. Three nights later, they beat UC Irvine, 116–100.

When Pac-10 play began, the Bruins had just a 3–4 overall record, and with the upcoming competition only getting more difficult, it was hard to imagine the 1988 season turning out any other way but disastrous. Conference play only affirmed the worries many had. UCLA was blown out by Cal and then suffered a heartbreaking double-overtime loss to Stanford, 116–110. Even the UCLA yearbook staff couldn't help but point out the wayward direction of the program. "The once-great UCLA basketball empire appeared to be crumbling into mediocrity.

UCLA vs. Cal, 1988 (Southern Branch Collection).

Critics were quick to assault the squad's coaching and apparent lack of leadership on the court." The writing was on the wall for Coach Hazzard. This would be his final season.

Despite the disastrous start to the season, UCLA and Coach Hazzard regrouped and turned a 3–6 start into a mediocre finish. But UCLA had many moments that made fans cringe. After losing by just seven points to No. 4 North Carolina, UCLA lost by a single point to Gary Payton and the Oregon State Beavers. The Bruins then won three out of four before falling to No. 1 Arizona. They finished the regular season winning nine of their last 12 games. In the quarterfinals of the Pac-10 tournament, UCLA fell to Washington State, 73–71. Their season was over.

Though the Bruins turned their putrid early season into a solid conference season, the 1988 Bruins were one of the worst UCLA teams in four decades. They were the first UCLA team to lose six games at home. No other team had even lost five in one season. Only two teams in the last 40 years at UCLA had finished with fewer wins than the 16 that the 1988 team earned. By the end of his fourth season, Coach Hazzard was clearly not the one to bring UCLA back to the top. On March 30, UCLA fired Hazzard. Its next coach, Jim Harrick, was unlike any of the five coaches who came before him at UCLA. Although moments of doubt during the Harrick tenure existed, so did moments of brilliance. It would take time, but UCLA was headed in the right direction once again.

University of Kansas won the NCAA basketball national championship in 1988.

CHAPTER 10
Jim Harrick (1988–1996)

Jim Harrick is UCLA's forgotten man. Sure, he is remembered by most UCLA fans and considered a fine coach. He rarely is mentioned among the key figures in UCLA's glorious history, however. He rarely speaks publicly about his eight seasons leading the Bruins' basketball program. The media speaks of his success, but mentions the star players and leaves out the name of the coach. Jim Harrick has coached basketball for more than 55 years, and though he found success in other places, his time in Westwood, unlike that of Larry Brown, was his crowning career achievement. UCLA sunk to levels few thought possible under Coach Walt Hazzard. Jim Harrick took them to where only John Wooden had before.

James Richard Harrick was born on July 25, 1938, in Charleston, West Virginia. Growing up in West Virginia and later spending more than three decades in Los Angeles, Jim saw the world in two very different lights. This was nothing new to him, as his father and mother were polar opposites. His father was a self-described hustler. He never held a steady job, but he found ways to make money, though never a lot. His mother was steady, strong, organized, and dependable. Jim's parents never owned a home; the family lived in a two-bedroom apartment. It was certainly nothing luxurious, but it was always enough for the Harrick family.

While there was never a great surplus of money during Jim's youth, he grew up in a family filled with love, and Charleston was the perfect place for the young boy. Jim never fit in with what some might think about West Virginia. He never worked in a coal mine and was not a small-town hick. He loved spending time in downtown Charleston, with a population of over 100,000 at the time, and he was most comfortable hanging out in a poolroom. Jim later wrote about his vivid memories of life in Charleston during World War II. He remembered the rationing, the mandatory community curfew, and all the sacrifices everyone made during the war. It helped to keep him grounded.

When Jim was eight or nine years old, he became fixated on sports—not just basketball but also baseball, football, horseshoes, and more. One year, Hot Rod Hundley, the neighborhood playground supervisor, took him under his wing. Their relationship spanned decades. After attending Lincoln Elementary School, where he was the best athlete on campus, Jim moved on to Lincoln Junior High School, a seventh—through ninth-grade prep school. At Lincoln Junior High, Jim played for Coach Al Ball, a strict disciplinarian, and the first coach to have a major influence on his life. During eighth and ninth grades, Lincoln won the league title, and as a ninth grader, Jim was selected to the All-City team.

At Stonewall Jackson High School, Jim continued to excel. Though he was a good football player, playing safety and quarterback, the basketball court was where he was at his best. As a sophomore, Jim played on the B team, which finished with a 20–3 record. When the season ended, Jim was one of two players called up to the A team for the playoffs. One year later, now a permanent fixture on the A team, Jim was a starting guard. He was not a primary offensive weapon, averaging just 11 points per game, but he was the best defensive player on the squad. As a senior, the team was expected to be better, and Jim was now one of the leaders. Stonewall Jackson High School's greatest athletic rival was East Bank High School, and its star guard was Jim's greatest personal rival. Though East Bank had never beaten Jackson High during Jim's time there, one player had the ability to take over games by himself. Jim Harrick and Jerry West had played against each other many times growing up. They were in the same grade and lived near each other. They were cordial with each other, though they would not become friends until years later. Jim always did well against West. He was not the quality of player that West was, but he held his own. West's brilliance pushed him to become a better player, and Jim's strong defense always tested West more than most opponents. When they met during the playoffs as seniors, however, it was a different story. The Stonewall Jackson Generals were considered favorites, but East Bank had West, and that's all it needed. West scored 45 points, East Bank won the game, and eventually it won the title.

In 1956, the year Jim graduated from high school, he was named the cowinner of the Most Outstanding Athlete Award at Stonewall Jackson High School, but winning the award didn't mean he had many fine options going forward. He was determined to continue his basketball career, and schools wanted him. But there was no perfect fit. He finally decided to attend Marshall University, where he would be a walk-on on the basketball team. Jim badly wanted to play, but he soon realized he wasn't good enough. He was a popular man on campus, becoming a socialite and a fixture around the university. Something was missing, however, and Marshall couldn't fill the void. After two years, he left Marshall and transferred to Morris Harvey College. He moved back home and commuted to school. Right by his side was his sweetheart. Sally Marple was one year younger than Jim, and following high school, she attended West Virginia University for one year. The two were away for long enough, and when Jim went to Morris Harvey, so did Sally. In 1960, Jim graduated with undergraduate degrees in speech and physical education. His time in college was over.

After graduating in spring and working a temporary summer job, Jim married Sally on August 20, 1960, and on the same day as their marriage, they hopped in a 1960 Chevy BelAir and went toward the setting sun. Jim was never able to describe why the couple decided to go to California. They each had job opportunities in multiple places, including at home in West Virginia, but California seemed right. Jim had heard from his cousin Bob years earlier about the wonders of the West and how different Los Angeles was from his hometown. When Jim was offered a teaching job in California, he immediately jumped on it. He didn't know where Smith River, California, was, but he figured it had to be similar to what his cousin Bob described to him years earlier. When he got to California, he found out it wasn't quite the same. Smith River was about a 15-hour drive north of Los Angeles and sat near the Oregon border. Despite the disappointment, Jim and Sally had a new adventure they were just beginning together, and despite living in a tiny garage that often leaked badly when the 127 inches of average rainfall per year came down, they enjoyed their first post-college stop.

Despite living in Smith River, Jim and Sally spent a considerable amount of time in El Segundo. Jim had family there, and during the holidays, the couple went south to be with them. After nearly a year and a half teaching in Northern California, Jim and Sally decided they weren't going back after spending time in Southern California during the holidays. Eventually they went up to pick up their stuff and move south. They had no jobs, no income, and no home to call their own, but they had a plan. Jim quickly found a job teaching at Hawthorne Intermediate School. The couple spent the majority of the rest of their lives in Southern California.

At this time in his life, sports were strictly entertainment for Jim. He played basketball at nights and enjoyed watching the Lakers and UCLA teams under Coach Wooden, but coaching was not on his radar. After settling into L.A., however, things slowly began to change. He volunteered to coach youth leagues in multiple sports for two years. In 1964, he caught the coaching bug and wanted more. Jim knew of an opening as an assistant coach at Morningside High School and decided to apply. He met with the head coach, the principal, and assistant principal. He nailed the interviews and was hired to coach the JV basketball and baseball teams, as well as teach English and driver's training.

For six years, Harrick coached at Morningside High School on either the JV staff or as an assistant on the varsity staff. In 1969, he was promoted to varsity head coach, a position he held for four years and thought he keep for the duration of his career. Eventually Harrick began to dream bigger, however. Harrick sought out several college coaching positions but was turned down. A connection built through a player helped Harrick climb the career ladder when he least expected it. Stan Love, who later became the father of Kevin Love, played JV basketball under Harrick at Morningside High School. Love later became a coveted recruit, and Frank Arnold, an assistant coach at Oregon, recruited him aggressively. In the recruiting process, Arnold and Harrick got to know each other. Arnold knew Harrick could coach at the next level and wanted to be the one to have him by his side when he finally made the jump. Arnold said to Harrick, "Jim, I'm going to get a head coaching job sometime, and when I do, Bae and I would love it if you and Sally came with us. I'd want you as one of my assistants." Though it didn't work out as he planned, Arnold was still the key man in luring Harrick away from high school ball. Two years later, Arnold wanted the Utah State job and was one of the finalists for the position. The job was offered to Dutch Belnap instead. After hearing the news, Arnold called to congratulate Belnap. Within the course of the conversation, Belnap mentioned that he'd like to hire an assistant coach from Los Angeles to help in recruiting. Arnold said to him, "Well, I've got a guy for you. Name's Jim Harrick."

For four seasons, Jim Harrick was an assistant coach at Utah State University. The position had little notoriety, but it jumpstarted his career at the college level. After four years in Logan, Harrick returned home, serving as an assistant coach at UCLA for two seasons under Gary Cunningham. In 1980, Harrick got his first shot at being a college basketball head coach. For nine seasons, Harrick coached the Pepperdine basketball team. Four times, Pepperdine made the NCAA Tournament, and twice it competed in the NIT. The team won five West Coast Conference titles and won 167 games and lost 97.

Prior to the start of the 1988–89 season, UCLA was once again in search of a new head coach. Walt Hazzard, the legendary former Bruins player, was fired, and UCLA had another chance to bring in someone who could get UCLA back to the top. Jim Harrick was not initially considered a serious candidate. He was far down the list, and the names ahead of him were all well known. Jim Valvano was interviewed first. UCLA wanted Valvano and it was reported that Valvano wanted UCLA. He traveled to L.A., was wined and dined, and offered the job. He stunned everyone when he turned it down.

After Valvano turned down UCLA, the focus of the job search turned to Duke coach Mike Krzyzewski. He expressed interest in the job, but his team was still playing deep in the NCAA Tournament, and he wanted to wait until after the season ended to have any serious discussions. Larry Brown, the Kansas coach and former UCLA coach, had no such personal problem with negotiating during the season. His Jayhawks went on to win the national championship, and during the run, he was in talks with UCLA the entire way. UCLA had put off discussions with Coach K, but they couldn't wait on Brown. Three days after Kansas won the title, Coach Brown was on UCLA's private plane discussing details of the contract. Everything was worked out. Larry Brown agreed to return to UCLA and became the head coach once again. He shook hands and sat back in his seat. The contract would be signed, but first Brown needed it to be kept secret for a few more days. He planned to fly back to Kansas, tell his players, then fly back to L.A., sign the contract, and have the formal announcement. On the way, he changed his mind. He instead went back to the NBA to coach the San Antonio Spurs. UCLA lost Brown, and in the process, lost Coach K also.

While the job search appeared to be a disaster for UCLA administrators and fans, it was a miracle for Coach Harrick. He wanted the job, interviewed for it, believed he was a better fit than Coach Brown, and knew he could provide stability that Brown never would. He was passed over for it, however, and he was heartbroken. When Brown reneged on the deal, Harrick was the man who benefited most. When the phone rang at his house at 7:00 a.m. on April 12, 1988, he didn't know who was calling. On the other end was Pete Dalis, UCLA's athletic director. "Jim, are you ready to come over and take the toughest basketball coaching job in America?"

Harrick answered, "Pete, I've been waiting 28

years for this opportunity. Yes, I'll take the job, and I won't let you down."

Jim Harrick's UCLA tenure was at times challenging. The Bruins didn't win the Pac-10 Conference until his fourth season, though they were instantly much better than they had been prior to his arrival. There were devastating and embarrassing tournament losses. Harrick was sometimes combative with the media and didn't have the most outwardly friendly personality to outsiders. Despite this, he did what no other UCLA coach besides John Wooden has ever done. He won a national championship, and he did it his way. While other coaches failed to live up to the massive expectations of the UCLA fan base and the unending pressure they and the media put on UCLA coaches, Jim Harrick chose a different strategy in dealing with the demands of the job. He chose to embrace the legend. He knew he was not John Wooden and never would be. He was not going to satisfy all UCLA fans. He was not going to shy away from the pressure, however, and he chose to embrace the challenge of bringing UCLA back. He knew Coach Wooden well, and he respected and loved the UCLA legend. He would do things his own way when necessary, but his entire coaching philosophy was based off what he learned from Coach Wooden. He had a large ego, but not so large that he couldn't try his best to duplicate everything Coach Wooden taught decades earlier.

Coach Harrick spent eight years as the UCLA coach, and more than 20 years since his departure, no other coach has won a championship. Harrick's career at UCLA was not without controversy, however. In 1996, he paid for a meal for two players at a student-athlete event, and though this was minor, Harrick's later actions made it a bigger story than it needed to be. Rather than reporting that he paid for the meal of the two players at his table, he instead listed the names of his wife and the wife of an assistant coach on an expense report. Paying for the meal itself was a secondary violation, but the cover-up was seen as unforgivable. He was given the choice to resign or be fired. He was fired.

The decision to fire Coach Harrick was certainly influenced by basketball, as well. Many believe UCLA had peaked under Harrick—everything came together for one season, but it wasn't likely to last much longer. Whether they are right or wrong, fans can only speculate. After taking a year off, Harrick got right back into coaching, leading Rhode Island to a 45–22 record over two seasons and Georgia to a 67–53 record in four years. Following the 2003 season, Harrick retired, though only temporarily. He coached the Bakersfield Jam of the NBA D League for just 16 games before resigning for personal reasons in 2007, and 11 full years later, he returned to the sidelines as an assistant coach for Cal State Northridge. Harrick has also spent time as an NBA scout and college basketball analyst.

Jim Harrick is not one of the most beloved symbols of UCLA athletic greatness, but he should be. In 1995, UCLA reached the pinnacle of the college basketball world. Jim Harrick and John Wooden have two things in common: they were both English teachers for nine years and were both champions. While Harrick will never earn the acclaim from Bruins faithful that Coach Wooden earned over the course of his career, he was once the coach of the best college basketball team in the world.

1988–89

The 1989 UCLA basketball season was a time of something new. Besides Coach Jim Harrick in his first year, working as new assistant coaches under Harrick were Brad Holland, Mark Gottfried, and Paul Landreaux. (All three would later become head coaches themselves.) Don MacLean, a 6'10" power forward from Simi Valley, was one of the most important recruits for UCLA since Coach Wooden's retirement. When he arrived in Westwood, there was a sudden changing of the guard. Trevor Wilson and Pooh Richardson each played well in 1988, but neither quite filled the void since Reggie Miller left in 1987. MacLean filled it. Wilson, Richardson, and MacLean formed one of the top trios in college basketball in 1989. As a freshman, MacLean averaged 18.6 points per game to lead the team. Scoring came naturally to MacLean, whose silky smooth mid-range game, touch around the basket, and tall frame with wide shoulders made him impossible for college players to defend. At the conclusion of his career, he was not only one of the best players in UCLA history, but one of the best in Pac-10 history. He is, to this day, the all-time leading scorer in Pac-12 history. Though MacLean's scoring numbers were impressive, Wilson was just behind him for the year, averaging 18.4 PPG and leading the team with 8.7 rebounds per game. As a senior, Richardson had his finest season. The 6'1" point guard scored 15.2 PPG and dished out a tremendous 7.6 assists per game. Kevin Walker, Darrick Martin, and Charles Rochelin were all important contributors as well.

The Bruins began the season unranked, but they played four straight opponents to begin the year to beef up their resume before taking on North Carolina once again. Away games at Miami and BYU, sandwiched in between home games against Texas Tech and Boston University, were no problem. UCLA was 4–0, and though the competition was not yet top notch, it was a stark difference compared to the horrendous start of the 1988 season.

When UCLA traveled to the Dean Smith Center for a matchup with No. 8 North Carolina on December 17, they were in for a rude awakening. The Tar Heels were balanced. Six UNC players averaged between 11.4 and 14.6 PPG, including Rick Fox. While the Tar Heels didn't have more stars than the Bruins, they played team ball, led by a coach with a vision and a plan. Coach Harrick had his own vision and plan, but success against the top college teams would have to wait: UNC 104, UCLA 78.

Despite the beatdown UCLA suffered in Chapel Hill, pollsters took notice of UCLA's improved team. When UCLA began conference play against its two Northern California rivals, they were ranked No. 20 in the nation. The two conference games were played at Pauley Pavilion, and the Bruins won each, but things soon took a shocking turn. On December 28, UCLA took on the UC Irvine Anteaters at Bren Events Center. Five thousand fans attended, and they witnessed one of the biggest shockers in UCLA basketball history. The Anteaters finished the season with just a 12–17 record and were the eighth-place finisher in the Big West Conference. On this day, however, they won the battle of the UCs, 91–90.

The loss to UCI was shocking, but the Bruins' response to the loss was not. Following major upsets, the favored teams can suddenly fall apart. Though UCLA beat North Texas and then stomped Oregon by 31 points, an unfortunate trend cropped up. For six consecutive games, the team traded wins and losses. The Bruins got hot at the end of January and into February, however, and after winning five straight games, their record stood at 15–5 overall and 10–2 in conference play.

On February 12, 1989, UCLA played No. 4 Louisville. The Cardinals were led by "Never Nervous" Pervis Ellison and still coached by Denny Crum. The Bruins played their finest game of the year. It was close throughout, but at the end, the 12,547 fans wearing blue at Pauley Pavilion were overjoyed. UCLA won, 77–75. Coach Jim Harrick's first season as the UCLA coach was not defined by triumphant moments, however, but by the inconsistency of his team. UCLA somehow lost to UCI, but beat Louisville. The team won five straight conference games prior to beating the Cardinals, but lost two straight following. Against No. 2 Arizona, UCLA was embarrassed the way it used to embarrass opponents. The Bruins were outclassed in every way, and Arizona's star player, Sean Elliott, had a night to remember. His 35-point, 11-assist, seven-rebound game in a 38-point Arizona win was impressive, but a record he broke rubbed salt into the Bruins' wound. With 7:10 remaining in the second half, Elliott knocked down a free throw to give him 2,326 career points, passing Lew Alcindor for most in Pac-10 history. Alcindor's record stood for 19 years. Elliott's record was broken by another Bruin in three.

UCLA closed the regular season strongly, but was clearly not yet ready to compete with the top college basketball teams regularly. After winning three in a row, UCLA took on Arizona again, this time at home, and though they played better, they still lost by three points. In the Pac-10 Tournament, UCLA beat Washington but lost to No. 12 Stanford at the Forum in Inglewood. The Bruins made the NCAA Tournament, but, to make a deep run, a series of improbabilities would have to occur. The Bruins were the No. 7 seed in the Southeast Regional. They beat Iowa State, 84–74, in the first round, but the team waiting for them in the second round was the North Carolina Tar Heels. The game was much closer than the early-season matchup in Chapel Hill, but UNC was the stronger team and won, 88–81. The Bruins had a nice bounce-back season in Coach Harrick's first year, winning 21 and losing 10, but things had to get better still. The Bruins were on the right track. It was time to climb back to the top.

University of Michigan won the NCAA basketball national championship in 1989.

1989–90

The 1990 UCLA basketball team was much like the 1989 team. The UCLA yearbook dubbed the 1990 winning formula the "4+4+4." Along with MacLean, senior forward Trevor Wilson, sharpshooting senior Kevin Walker, and sophomore Darrick Martin were all returning starters from the year prior. Four key contributors helped the cause: juniors Keith Owens and Kevin Williams, along with sophomores Darrin Dafney and Gerald Madkins, each played an important role for the team. UCLA also brought in four talented freshmen. Leading the way for the first-year players was 6'8" Tracy Murray from Los Angeles. In high school, Murray set the California all-time scoring record, and at UCLA, he continued his prolific scoring, averaging 12.3 points per game as a freshman, good for third on the team behind MacLean and Wilson. Joining Murray in the freshmen class were Zan Mason, Mitchell Butler, and Rodney Odom.

UCLA began the season ranked No. 13 in the country, better than they had been in the recent past. The Bruins' early-season schedule was abnormal. After beating Santa Clara, 66–62, in the season opener, UCLA jumped right into conference play. When the Bruins traveled to Washington to take on the Huskies and then Cougars, there were conference implications already, and the season was still brand new. UCLA didn't play particularly well against their conference mates, but it came away with two wins. UCLA was 3–0, and the schedule went back to a more typical early-season format. They didn't play the next conference game for over a month.

Don MacLean, 1990 (Southern Branch Collection).

After beating the University of San Diego to run their record to 4–0, the Bruins traveled to South Bend, Indiana, to take on the Notre Dame Fighting Irish, still coached by Digger Phelps. Taking on Notre Dame was never an easy task, and neither was slowing down ND star senior Keith Robinson. The Irish forward went 9-for-9 from the field, the most made shots without a miss in Notre Dame history. Robinson's big night was enough to lift the Irish over the Bruins in a close one, 86–84.

Following the loss, UCLA quickly got back to its winning ways in nonconference action. The team beat American by 15, Cal State Fullerton by 12, Fresno State by nine, and East Tennessee State by 49 points. The Bruins were 8–1 and ranked No. 15 in the country when they resumed conference play on January 3. In UCLA's return to Pac-10 action, it stomped USC by 17 points behind MacLean's 35-point performance. UCLA had just two nonconference games remaining, and one was next on the schedule, against one of the best teams in America. Though UCLA was a good team and an outside contender for the national crown, the Louisville Cardinals were one of the best teams in the country. The two teams met at Freedom Hall in Louisville in front of 19,455 crazed fans on January 7. Ten years before, the two great basketball programs met in the biggest stage of all, the national championship game, and though this game wasn't on that stage, a win by UCLA would help elevate UCLA into the forefront of the championship discussion. Denny Crum, Felton Spencer, and the rest of the Cardinals crushed UCLA, 97–80. UCLA was helpless in trying to defend the Cardinals.

Though UCLA got back on track, the defeat against Louisville exposed its porous defense. UCLA won seven of their next nine games, including a home win over a ranked Arizona squad. When the two Pac-10 rivals met again, however, it was in Tucson, and the Wildcats got their revenge. After beating UCLA, 83–74, UA won five of its final seven regular season games, while UCLA suddenly went in the wrong direction. After losing to the Wildcats, UCLA then lost to Cal, Stanford, Oregon, and Oregon State consecutively. It was out of the race for the Pac-10 title. Though UCLA won its final two regular-season conference games and won their first two Pac-10 tournament games, more heartbreak was on the way. In the finals of the Pac-10 Tournament, UCLA and Arizona played again, the third meeting of the season. Just as had happened in the second game, UCLA was thoroughly outplayed. The red-hot Wildcats won, 94–78, again scoring at will against UCLA's subpar defense.

Despite the disappointing close to the season, UCLA earned a berth in the NCAA Tournament in 1990. The No. 7 seed was not where UCLA envisioned itself after a sterling 16–4 start, but after limping to 4–6 finish in the last 10, the team had no cause for complaint. In the first round of the tournament, UCLA took on the University of Alabama Birmingham, the No. 10 seed in the East, coached by former UCLA coach Gene Bartow. The Blazers had finished the season with a 22–8 record and were a popular upset pick among those filling out their brackets. UCLA played well enough, however, showing solid defense and enough offense. It wasn't the formula most were used to seeing from UCLA, but it worked. After winning, 68–56, UCLA had a bigger challenge ahead. In the second round, they faced the No. 2 seed, the Kansas Jayhawks.

The game between UCLA and Kansas on March 18, 1990, in Atlanta, Georgia, is one of the best early-tournament games in the history of either program. The game was close throughout. At halftime, the Jayhawks held the slimmest of leads, 36–35. Roy Williams, the Kansas head coach, was one of the best offensive coaches in America. His team was 30–4 on the season and averaged 92.1 points per game. Five Jayhawks averaged in double figures, led by Kevin Pritchard's 14.5. Pritchard was his usual self against UCLA, scoring 15 points on efficient shooting, but the rest of the team didn't play as well. UCLA held Kansas to just 70 points, 22 below its season average. UCLA's offense, though solid, didn't have an easy way with Kansas's defense, however. MacLean only scored 10 points, but his teammates played extremely well. Trevor Wilson and Darrick Martin led the way with 18 points each. Still, the game was extremely close. With UCLA trailing, 70–69, with nine seconds left, freshman Tracy Murray stepped to the free-throw line for two shots. After knocking in the first attempt, the score was tied. Murray took his second shot and calmly drained it. UCLA went up, 71–70, stopped the Jayhawks, and shocked all college basketball fans tuning in.

UCLA was off to the Sweet 16, but the magic was left in the round of 32. Against No. 3 Duke, UCLA's defense failed again. The Blue Devils scored 90 points, allowing 81 to the Bruins, and went on to finish as NCAA runner-up. UCLA's season was over. It was an improvement on the season before, which was also solid. The Bruins had several important pieces to replace in 1991, but Coach Harrick looked to be the man for the job. UCLA was on the rise.

University of Nevada Las Vegas won the NCAA basketball national championship in 1990.

1990–91

The 1990–91 UCLA basketball season began and ended with great disappointment. Ed O'Bannon was just a freshman. The team was stacked with returning players from the already successful team of the year before. UCLA averaged 92.1 points per game for the season, and though it gave up 81.4 PPG and struggled on defense for the entirety of the year, the defense was usually enough for the team to win. Don MacLean was now a junior and the clear star of the team. MacLean finished the year scoring 23.0 PPG, good for sixth all-time in UCLA history. The only players to score more points per game than MacLean during any individual seasons were Lew Alcindor in each of his three seasons from '67 to '69, Gail Goodrich in '65, and Reggie Miller in '86. MacLean was just one half of a dynamic scoring duo. Tracy Murray had an incredible season, averaging 21.2 PPG and hauling down nearly seven rebounds per game. Darrick Martin was the leader in the backcourt, showing blazing speed with the ball and great court vision. Gerald Madkins, Shon Tarver, the high-flying Mitchell Butler, and former walk-on Keith Owens were all key members of the team. Still, the team needed more.

Just over one month prior to the start of the season, highly touted UCLA freshman forward Ed O'Bannon suffered a catastrophic knee injury. Several UCLA players, including O'Bannon and MacLean, were playing pickup ball in the John Wooden Center when the injury happened. After dunking a ball, O'Bannon landed awkwardly on his left knee, completely tearing his anterior cruciate ligament and meniscus. While ACL recovery over the last three decades has since become fairly standard, there was uncertainty in the fall of 1990 if O'Bannon would ever fully recover. He was expected to start his freshman season, and though he had a long road to recovery ahead of him, he did eventually return. UCLA fans dreamed of glory in 1991, and O'Bannon was front and center in their dreams. The basketball season went on without the man who one day became a UCLA basketball legend. While the UCLA basketball staff returned from a retreat in Palm Springs when they heard the news of O'Bannon, all they could do was prepare with the players they had. The 1990 UCLA team was again very good, but an opportunity for greatness was torn away during a game of five-on-five at the Wooden Center.

The Bruins began their season with a bang, albeit in an unusual place. UCLA tipped off the season in Anchorage, Alaska, playing in the 13th annual Great Alaska Shootout, and the first game of the season definitely lived up to the shootout billing. UCLA took on UC Irvine and put on an offense show. Sullivan Arena held 7,947 fans, and every seat was taken. The game was nothing if not unique. UC Irvine, led by head coach Bill Mulligan, emulated the offensive system run by Loyola Marymount, a frantic up-and-down, three-point shooting explosion of offense. The pace was fast, and UCLA played right into it. Coach Jim Harrick called the style of play "a disease," but, the Bruins were built to play that way. Murray led the way for the Bruins with 24 points. MacLean scored 22, and Shon Tarver scored 20 off the bench. UCLA scored 134 points, setting a new single-game team record. UCI shot 42 three pointers, three more than the previous NCAA record, but two less than Cal State Northridge shot that same night. The final score was UCLA 134, UCI 101. It was the highest-scoring game in the history of the Great Alaska Shootout, which was played every season from 1978 through 2017.

UCLA's season definitely started in an entertaining fashion, but Coach Harrick didn't enjoy the game. He wanted his team to play fast—but smart. He didn't want the games to be frantic. UCLA won its next two games in the Great Alaska Shootout to take the tournament championship, including a 15-point win over No. 18 Virginia in the finals. When they went home to continue nonconference action, however, the team waiting for them was just the one that Coach Harrick didn't want to see. He thought the game against UCI was often too fast. He was about to take on the kings of speed, Loyola Marymount.

On December 2, 1990, UCLA set another school scoring record. When Loyola Marymount came to Westwood, it wasn't the same team they had been in the past, though its system was still the same. Paul Westhead was gone, and Jay Hillock was the new coach. After winning 26 games the year prior, they only won 16 in Hillock's first year. The Lions weren't as successful, but they were always as entertaining. If ever a coach could be upset about a dominating performance, it was so when the Bruins played LMU. UCLA won, 149–98. Coach Harrick could not be upset with his players. They played extremely well and won by more than 50 points. The game was a trap, though, just as the UCI game was to begin the season. Bad habits are often created in games like those, and Coach Harrick was determined to make sure his team avoided those mistakes.

UCLA continued its high scoring as it continued to rack up wins and climb in the Associated Press rankings. After beating LMU, the Bruins beat four more quality teams, including Notre Dame and Coach Harrick's former team, the Pepperdine Waves. Though UCLA was 8–0, they continued to struggle on the defensive end and relied far too much on their offense. In the previous four wins, the offense scored 106 PPG, but gave up nearly 88. Finally, the struggling defense caught up to the team. On December 22, the Bruins traveled to Carver-Hawkeye Arena in Iowa and were greeted by unwelcoming guests. Though unranked at the time, the Hawkeyes dismantled the Bruins. Again, UCLA's defense was the main problem, giving up 88 points. In this game, their offense couldn't save the team and struggled for much of the game. When UCLA fell, 88–71, it was a shocker. The Bruins had risen to No. 5 in the country and were thought to be a legitimate national title contender. Instead, they were humbled and sent packing.

The Bruins did get right back to winning, but their defense was never strong throughout the season. In some games, the Bruins played slower, allowed less points, and locked down the other team in key spots, but they were never consistent. UCLA won its next five games, including an impressive all-around showing against Arizona State on January 10. The opponent next on the schedule was the Arizona

Wildcats, who had been building something special in the desert. UCLA was 13–1 on the season and ranked No. 7 in the country. The Wildcats were 12–2 and ranked No. 6. In front of 13,864 fans at McKale Center, the home team came out on top. While the win was big for Arizona, it sent UCLA into a tailspin. The Bruins lost three of their next five and five of their next seven, and by mid-February, UCLA was under .500 in conference play. The Bruins did recover to win six of their final seven games and finish in second place in the Pac-10 Conference, but after starting with a 13–1 record, the season was certainly disappointing. After four seasons, the Pac-10 Tournament was dissolved, and the winner of the regular-season title received an automatic invitation to the NCAA Tournament. UCLA didn't have to worry about being invited. They were in regardless. Still, UCLA needed to answer many questions. Could they perform in the NCAA Tournament as they had in December and early January, or was the team just decent, with no real chance to bring home the trophy? The answer soon came, and it wasn't the answer many wanted to see.

UCLA entered its first-round matchup against the Penn State Nittany Lions as heavy favorites. Although UCLA was the No. 4 seed and Penn State was the No. 13 seed, UCLA did not cruise; actually, it didn't even win. PSU was the better team on the day, despite being outclassed in the talent department. UCLA had six future NBA players, but Penn State had Coach Bruce Parkhill. Though his recruiting abilities were always in question and his teams were always underdogs because they lacked elite talent, Parkhill knew how to teach basketball, and his players bought into his system. The game was played at the Carrier Dome in Syracuse, New York, and it was in this enormous arena that one of the most stunning losses in UCLA history took place. UCLA jumped out to a quick start. MacLean was on fire early, hitting his first six shots, but Penn State hung around. With 8:00 remaining in the first half, UCLA was playing well, but led only 27–21. From this point, the Nittany Lions went on a run, and Coach Harrick and the Bruins could do nothing to stop them. PSU burst ahead to a 36–28 lead and never looked back. The game was close the rest of the way, but the Nittany Lions held on to win in shocking fashion, 74–69. UCLA's once promising season was over. Coach Harrick had just finished his third straight season with a disappointing loss and became the first UCLA coach to ever lose three straight years in the tournament.

Duke University won the NCAA basketball national championship in 1991.

Darrick Martin vs. Cal, 1991 (Southern Branch Collection).

1991–92

The year 1992 was one of basketball. In the summer Olympic Games held in Barcelona, the United States basketball team, dubbed the "Dream Team," was a marvel to watch. For the first time, professional players were allowed to play, and the United States was determined to bring home the gold. Not only did the Olympic team go undefeated en route to winning the gold medal, they put on a show like never before seen.

Before they took to the court, of course, other games were to be played, in the NBA and college. There was UCLA and the season of Don MacLean. Over the previous three years, MacLean, Coach Jim Harrick, and the Bruins had been remarkably consistent. In 1989, they finished with a 21–10 record. One year later, they finished 22–11. In 1991, the Bruins went 23–9. All were solid teams, but none were able to bring home the Pac-10 title or make a deep run in the NCAA Tournament. In 1992, MacLean and the Bruins wanted more. The team was improved, and for parts of the year, it was the best in the country.

Unlike the Dream Team of months later, UCLA did not rout every opponent. Close games were mixed in with blowouts. There were great individual milestones and great team disappointments. The team won more games than any UCLA team in 16 years, but as all had come to learn, the regular season meant little in Westwood. The biggest stage in March had the meaning.

The Bruins of 1992 looked much like the Bruins of 1991 in the scoring department. Though Tracy Murray overtook MacLean as UCLA's top scorer, averaging 21.4 points per game to MacLean's 20.7, the duo still remained as potent as ever. Much of the same supporting cast of the year before remained in 1992. Two new players joined the team, however, and though they didn't make much of an impact as freshmen, they would soon build legacies that will last forever in UCLA lore. Ed O'Bannon, fresh off the injury that cost him the entire 1991 season, returned in 1992. Still hampered by his bum knee for most of the year, O'Bannon scored just 3.6 PPG in his redshirt freshman campaign. Tyus Edney was also a freshman in 1992, and although he showed flashes, his time to shine came later.

The 1992 season was one of streaks for UCLA. When the first game against Indiana tipped off, the Bruins were immediately in for a huge challenge. Pollsters ranked UCLA the No. 11 team in the country to begin the season, but Bobby Knight and the Indiana Hoosiers were No. 2. The game was played at Springfield Civic Center in Springfield, Massachusetts, and the crowd saw UCLA take apart one of the top teams in the nation. UCLA won, 87–72. The Bruins and the Hoosiers would meet again in a much more important game, but for now, the Bruins looked like a major contender. When UCLA finally played again 15 days later, they were all the way up to No. 4 in the national rankings.

Throughout nonconference play and early in the Pac-10 slate, no team could play with UCLA. The offense was dynamic, scoring points in bunches just as the team had done the previous year, but now the defense was considerably improved. UCLA easily dispatched Long Beach State, Pepperdine, San Diego State, and Loyola Marymount. Cal State Fullerton played the Bruins close, losing by just six, but No. 2 UCLA destroyed Oral Roberts by 51 points and then beat Georgia in the final game before conference play began. UCLA was 8–0 when it began Pac-10 play and the quest for the conference crown.

On January 9, UCLA traveled to Tempe, Arizona, play Arizona State, and though the Sun Devils weren't in the same class as UCLA, it was a potential trap game. With Arizona looming, it could have been easy for UCLA to overlook the underdog home team, but early in the season, UCLA could not be stopped. It smashed Arizona State by 21 points. The University of Arizona Wildcats were next. UA was 10–1 on the season, ranked No. 6, and led by two dynamic players, Sean Rooks and Chris Mills. Playing in McKale Center in Tucson is never easy, and when the Bruins come to town, the energy is turned up even more. The game was close, as was expected. MacLean led the way for UCLA, scoring a season-best 38 points. "I was feeling it today. I had a feeling that if I got the ball on the wing and any of their guys were sticking me, I'd be able to score," said MacLean after the game. While MacLean was brilliant for UCLA, the Wildcats hung around. With UCLA leading, 87–85, Arizona's Wayne Womack hit a wild turnaround jump shot to tie the game with under 20 seconds to play. Everyone in the arena then expected MacLean to get the ball for UCLA, but another man was the hero on this day. After driving past Arizona freshman Damon Stoudamire, Darrick Martin threw up an off-balance, running jump shot. The ball left his hands with three seconds to play, and though it wasn't the shot that Coach Harrick wanted, it was a shot that Martin routinely took, often to the chagrin of his coach. When the ball came down through the net and the buzzer sounded, UCLA players rushed to celebrate with their teammate. Arizona's 71-game home winning streak was dead. UCLA's perfect season was alive.

As conference play continued, UCLA continued to rack up wins. It beat both the schools from Oregon, as well as its Pac-10 foes from Northern California. UCLA was 14–0 when it took on USC for the first time. The Trojans were ranked No. 25 in the country, and though UCLA was the heavy favorite, the Trojans were solid. UCLA quickly learned that they had underestimated its less successful Los Angeles neighbor. USC shocked UCLA, 86–82, ruining UCLA's perfect record.

The Bruins bounced back with seven consecutive wins to run their record to 21–1 in late February. Against Oregon State on February 13, history was made. Don MacLean stood at the free-throw line with one foul shot to take. He had just tied Sean Elliot's all-time Pac-10 scoring record and was one point away from breaking it. After calmly knocking down the free throw to put him at the top, MacLean thought he had just broken the record, but there was no recognition of his achievement in the road gym. He wasn't even 100 percent sure of his accomplishment until after the game. Though downplayed in Corvallis, the record has stood ever since, even with the expansion of the conference with Utah and Colorado. He is seldom mentioned with the likes of UCLA's greatest players, but his career was nothing short of marvelous.

Though everything was going well for UCLA, a tough three-game stretch was still ahead. Shockingly, UCLA was beaten by Notre Dame, lost a rematch to USC, and then fell to No. 1 Duke at home on March 1. The Bruins dropped to No. 9 in the country but won their final four regular-season games and clinched the Pac-10 crown before the start of the NCAA Tournament.

They earned the No. 1 seed in the West Region. In the first two rounds of the tournament, UCLA breezed past its opposition. After beating Robert Morris and Louisville the first week in blowout fashion, the Bruins were in the Sweet 16 for the second time under Coach Harrick. Their matchup was favorable. New Mexico State was just a 12 seed and pulled off two upsets to reach the second week of tournament play. UCLA was a determined No. 1 seed, looking to reclaim their spot at the top. NMSU played well, hung around most of the game, and were the clear crowd favorite, but UCLA was too much. After winning, 85–78, the Bruins were in the Elite Eight.

The final game of the season, the biggest yet in Coach Jim Harrick's coaching career, was a disaster. Three-and-a-half months earlier, UCLA convincingly beat Bobby Knight and the Indiana Hoosiers in the season opener. Now, it was Indiana's turn to return the favor. The Bruins could do nothing right. Knight outcoached Harrick, and the Hoosiers outplayed the Bruins. UCLA's improved defense was again inept, and though the offense scored 79 points, it wasn't nearly enough. The final score was Indiana 106, UCLA 79. The 27-point loss was the worst loss for UCLA in the NCAA Tournament to that point. UCLA won 28 games on the season and lost only five, but the last game left a sting that would last for years. UCLA had championship-level talent, but with one bad performance, it was all over. MacLean was off to the NBA, and junior Tracy Murray decided it was time for him to go as well. The 1993 Bruins would look much different than the 1992 Bruins, and Coach Harrick had a lot to prove. The pressure that so many coaches felt at UCLA had not yet enveloped Coach Harrick. He felt his job was safe and secure. After losing to Indiana, things would change. The Bruins faithful were not happy.

Duke University won the NCAA basketball national championship in 1992.

1992–93

In 1993, casual fans of UCLA basketball had new names to remember. The departure of Don MacLean and Tracy Murray meant over 40 points of production per game had to be replaced. The Bruins were talented but inexperienced. After Coach Jim Harrick's best season to date in 1992, the Bruins of '93 looked very much like the teams of his first three seasons—good, though flawed. While UCLA won its share of games, many of the same issues plagued the Bruins throughout the year. Their offense was quite good again, but the defense was subpar. Out of 298 Division I teams in the country, UCLA ranked 209th in defense.

The offense, however, was respectable, even with a new cast of characters leading the way. Three players set themselves apart from the rest for UCLA, and though none were new to the program, all were new to carrying the load. Shon Tarver was UCLA's leading scorer, averaging 17.2 points per game. Ed O'Bannon, the man with immense talent, set back by a devastating knee injury, looked like he was back to 100 percent health. He broke through as a redshirt sophomore, scoring 16.7 PPG and going through stretches where he was simply unguardable. Then there was Tyus Edney, the ever-reliable 5'10" point guard with incredible ball-handling skills, passing ability, and a knack for hitting clutch shots. Richard Petruska and Mitchell Butler each had fine seasons, as well, but the Bruins lacked depth, and were often predicable on offense.

On one front, at least, UCLA had a breakthrough. Coach Harrick, in his fifth season, was the first UCLA coach to make it that far since Coach Wooden retired nearly two decades earlier.

UCLA began the season ranked No. 24 in the country and participated in the Preseason NIT as part of a stacked field. The first two games of the season were played at Pauley Pavilion, and though UCLA beat Saint Louis by 14 and the University of Texas at El Paso by one, the Bruins certainly weren't impressive early on. As the tournament went on and UCLA reached the semifinal game at Madison Square Garden, the competition heated up. Now ranked No. 21, the Bruins had their first real test of the season against No. 6 Seton Hall. The Bruins were balanced on offense, with four players scoring in double figures, but Seton Hall was led by Terry Dehere's 27 points. It was enough for the Pirates to win, 73–64, and hand UCLA its first loss of the season. UCLA then bounced back to beat No. 7 Florida State, 86–83, in the third-place game. Five Bruins scored between 13 and 18 points.

Tyus Edney vs. Notre Dame, 1993 (Southern Branch Collection).

Despite dropping one game during the Preseason NIT, UCLA climbed to No. 16 in the rankings by the time it took the court again on December 5. After beating Santa Clara and San Diego behind big performances from O'Bannon and then Tarver, UCLA played in a unique atmosphere. In the Kuppenheimer Classic, UCLA faced off against the Georgia Bulldogs in front of a massive crowd of 28,885 fans at the Georgia Dome. O'Bannon was brilliant once again. He scored 24 points, pulled down 13 rebounds, and dished out four assists as UCLA won. The Bruins then smashed Cal State Northridge three nights later to run its record to 7–1.

UCLA played well early in the season, and though they had climbed to No. 11 in the country, the team was sure to have down games with such an inexperienced core of players. One of those down games came against Pitt. The game was on the road, but the Bruins were heavy favorites over the unranked home team. Again, UCLA played well on offense, this time with Edney leading the way, but the defense struggled mightily: Pitt 91, UCLA 79.

Despite moments of beautiful team play, UCLA never really hit its stride in 1993. O'Bannon and Tarver each scored 20-plus points against Cal State Fullerton in a win. Petruska then led the way with 22 against Houston to run UCLA's record to 9–2 when conference play began. UCLA had pieces that looked promising, but the puzzle was incomplete, lacking a championship quality. UCLA dropped its Pac-10 opener against Arizona despite a monster 29-point performance from O'Bannon, and though the team won four of its first seven conference games, losses against Oregon State and Cal were extremely frustrating for the Bruins faithful.

Despite the poor team play, Ed O'Bannon was a man on a mission. Over the first four conference games, O'Bannon averaged 25 PPG, scoring at least 20 in each game. Though O'Bannon and the Bruins struggled with consistency the rest of the season, UCLA clearly had a player to build the next two years around. O'Bannon was a special talent, and the college basketball world soon took notice.

By Valentine's Day 1993, UCLA was just 15–7,

but improving. After a rough stretch, the team won four in a row, then lost two straight, including to No. 9 Duke on the road, then won three of the final four games of the regular season. The Bruins finished 21–10 in the regular season and finished in third place in the Pac-10 Conference. The year was a significant step back from the 1992 season, but the Bruins earned another NCAA Tournament berth.

The Bruins were the No. 9 seed in the West Region and began the tournament in a tough matchup with No. 8 Iowa State in Tucson, Arizona. The two men that led the way for UCLA soon made it a habit to perform at their peak in the postseason. O'Bannon finished with 20 points, 13 rebounds, and three blocked shots. Tyus Edney scored 19, dished out six assists, and had five rebounds. Mitchell Butler had a strong game as well, and UCLA pulled the slight upset, winning, 81–70, and advancing to the second round.

Waiting for UCLA was the No. 1 seed in the West, the Michigan Wolverines. The men from Ann Arbor were a great team, and their starters were known as the "Fab Five." One year before, Michigan brought in one of the greatest recruiting classes of all time. The five freshmen would eventually all start together and make a run to the national championship game. They wore baggy shorts, black shoes, and low-cut black socks. They dunked, talked trash, and had a flair for the game that was uncommon in college basketball. In 1993, they were again a great team. The legendary starting five consisted of Chris Webber, Jalen Rose, Juwan Howard, Ray Jackson, and Jimmy King. UCLA pushed them to the brink. The 13,534 fans in attendance thought they were going to see Michigan roll over the Bruins. Coach Harrick had other plans. At halftime, UCLA led, 52–39. The offense was on fire, scoring at will, making the extra pass, and playing with a crispness that caught Michigan off guard. UCLA made seven of eight three pointers in the first half and shot 70 percent from the field. Michigan tightened up its defense in the second half, however, and started to click on offense. Whereas UCLA outscored Michigan by 13 in the first half, Michigan returned the favor in the second half, outscoring UCLA by 13. The game was tied at 77 at the end of regulation. In the second half, UCLA shot only 30 percent from the field and missed all three-point attempts. In the overtime period, the Wolverines did enough to advance, though it wasn't easy. The final score was Michigan 86, UCLA 84. The loss was tough for UCLA, as they had a great team on the ropes and couldn't finish them off. Michigan's season continued and UCLA's season was over.

In five years, Coach Jim Harrick had brought continuity to the program, and UCLA was winning games. Although 1993 was expected to be a down year for UCLA, the team exceeded expectations. In 1994, the expectations were sky-high. There were now students at UCLA who were not even born the last time a championship banner was raised to the rafters at Pauley Pavilion. This was entirely unacceptable.

University of North Carolina won the NCAA basketball national championship in 1993.

1993–94

Going into the 1993–94 season, two things were clear that weren't the year before. UCLA had its leaders. Ed O'Bannon, Tyus Edney, and Shon Tarver led the way for UCLA all year, each scoring between 14.4 and 18.2 points per game throughout the season and having individual moments of brilliance. George Zidek had a strong season as well, and Kevin Dempsey was an important contributor. Two freshmen made names for themselves in 1994. Charles O'Bannon, the younger brother of Ed, was an instant playmaker. The 6'5" forward averaged 11.6 points and 6.8 rebounds per game and was a bundle of energy. Cameron Dollar was a strong defensive player in his first year in the backcourt. Both became key pieces to UCLA's future.

While the leadership hierarchy on the court was clear, also clear was that pressure was on UCLA's leader on the sidelines. Coach Jim Harrick claimed he hadn't really felt any pressure to that point, but he noticed the newspaper headlines. Patience was wearing thin. The Bruins were indeed greatly improved in 1994, and Coach Harrick's job may have been saved by UCLA's strong regular season, but the season would be defined by one game, and it was more than four months away.

The Bruins began ranked No. 14 in the country, and it proved to be a magic number. UCLA tipped off their season on November 27 against Loyola Marymount.They beat the Lions, 115–77, at home, just one of UCLA's 14 consecutive wins to start the season. In the opener, both O'Bannon brothers and Tarver all scored over 20 points, Edney dished out eight assists and had four steals, and UCLA cruised. In the second game of the season, Charles O'Bannon went over the 20-point mark again, and in the third game, Ed led the way with 24 points. UCLA had quite the brother combo. Early in the season, it really didn't matter much who the Bruins played. They were unstoppable.

The toughest early-season opponent for the Bruins was the No. 25 Louisiana State University Tigers. On December 18, LSU traveled to Pauley Pavilion, but that team, like every one before, stood no chance. Five Bruins scored in double figures, Edney collected a double-double, and UCLA cruised to its fifth victory in as many games. The Bruins were 5–0, averaging 101.2 PPG and showing no signs of slowing down. After beating Houston and NC State, UCLA began conference play with a 7–0 record.

The Bruins climbed all the way to No. 6 in the rankings when they took on the Oregon Ducks on January 6. A total of 10,116 fans were in attendance at Pauley, and they saw what they had become accustomed to seeing. The Bruins were extremely balanced offensively and improved defensively, and they took apart their opponent with great precision. Two nights later, they were even better. In beating Oregon State by 33 points, Ed O'Bannon and Edney each scored 22, Tarver scored 20, and the team shot 56 percent from the field. UCLA was just getting started. Against Washington State, every starter scored in double figures. Against Washington, Zidek went over the 20-point mark for the first time all season. Against Arizona, the Bruins faced their toughest opponent yet. The Wildcats were ranked No. 9 by the Associated Press, but the game was at home for UCLA, and the 12,389 fans in attendance went away with another victory. Edney led the way with 26 points, and UCLA ran its record to 12–0. After beating ASU two days later, the Bruins shot up to No. 1 in the national rankings. The team struggled with Stanford next but came out on top once again. UCLA was 14–0, ranked No. 1 in the country, and seemingly unstoppable.

On January 30, 1994, the Bruins faced its UC rival, the Cal Bears, and ran into a buzz saw. Few thought UCLA would lose the game, and the way they lost was even more surprising. Cal took apart the Bruins, beating them by 15 points in front of a huge crowd at Oakland Arena. UCLA's high-scoring offense shot just 37.8 percent from the field and made just one of 19 shots from behind the three-point line. Charles O'Bannon played well, but he was the only one who did that night. The perfect record was no more. UCLA was 14–1.

The Bruins certainly didn't crash in 1994, but they no longer had the aura of invincibility. They bounced back to crush USC by 29 points but then lost again to Notre Dame. Monty Williams scored 28 points for the Irish in the upset. After winning three consecutive conference games, the Bruins suffered another massive blow. No. 8 UCLA went to the University of Arizona for a rematch and was hit with the best that the Wildcats had to offer. In a humiliating 98–74 loss, the Bruins looked outcoached, and again the Harrick doubters began to make their voices heard. To make matters worse, UCLA lost the next game at home to No. 17 Cal and lost twice more in the regular season, both on the road. After starting 14–0, UCLA won just seven of its final 13 games before the NCAA Tournament.

In hindsight, the possibility of firing Jim Harrick after the 1994 season seems ridiculous. Harrick's reputation soon changed, and he was soon a popular figure in UCLA circles again. But after the NCAA Tournament in 1994, few Harrick defenders were left. In the first round of the NCAA Tournament, UCLA played one of the worst games in school history. The school was the No. 5 seed in the Midwest Region; its first-round opponent was the No. 12 Tulsa Golden Hurricanes. The game was nothing if not disgraceful for UCLA basketball. The program that was once the winner of 10 national championships in 12 seasons sunk so low that it was unrecognizable. Just two minutes into the game, UCLA trailed, 10–0. With 6:17 left in the first half, the team was behind, 46–17. The Bruins made a run toward the end of the half—if cutting the lead to 25 could be considered a run. UCLA played well in the second half, but the resurgence was much too late. The final score was Tulsa 112, UCLA 102. Gary Collier led the way for Tulsa with 34 points. Shea Seals and Alvin Williamson each scored 20. Lou Alcindor Dawkins scored 14.

Despite the devastating loss, an important thing happened in the second half. Ed O'Bannon was clearly the best player on the team already, but with UCLA embarrassing itself on the court, O'Bannon had enough. He lit into his teammates, trying his best to inspire them to continue believing. He was a force on the court himself, scoring 30 points, grabbing 18 rebounds, dishing out six assists, and blocking four shots. More than just producing on the court, O'Bannon asserted himself as the sole leader of the team. Edney had great influence with his teammates, but O'Bannon was the man everyone turned to when things got tough. Going into 1995, O'Bannon was determined to make something out of the loss against Tulsa. The Bruins would not think about their 14-0 start. It didn't matter that they were the last undefeated team in the nation or the top ranked team at one point. What mattered was Tulsa. UCLA entered the arena wearing shirts that read "Refuse to Lose." O'Bannon took that to heart that offseason entering his senior season. He could always be remembered as a good player who made UCLA proud, or he could be remembered as a UCLA legend. He made his choice, and he made sure his teammates followed.

University of Arkansas won the NCAA basketball national championship in 1994.

1994–95

Thirty years before the 1995 UCLA basketball team took the court, Gail Goodrich and the 1965 Bruins had a job. The Bruins had won the championship; for the first time, they tried to repeat. The '65 Bruins finished with a 28–2 record and won the title for the second year in a row. In the years following UCLA's first 10 national championships, the team repeated seven times. In 1975, 20 years before the 1995 Bruins made a run of their own, UCLA won it again—Coach Wooden's final championship in his final season.

Few thought UCLA would go 20 years without raising another banner. In the two decades since Coach Wooden's retirement, UCLA showed the basketball program to be durable, capable of success, but as of yet unable to win the whole thing. The season-ending loss to Tulsa in 1994 was a turning point. It awakened something in Ed O'Bannon, Tyus Edney, Jim Harrick, and the rest of the Bruins that few knew they had in them. No longer would UCLA run from its past and crumble under pressure. Now was time for UCLA basketball to rise again.

The 1995 roster was made up of a unique blend of talent and character. Leading the way for UCLA in both statistics and leadership was Ed O'Bannon. Now a fifth-year senior, O'Bannon inserted himself into the upper echelon of UCLA's all-time greatest players. In his final season, he averaged 20.4 points per game to lead the team. The road was long to get to where he was, and the journey is worth the story. In 1990, Ed was named the National High School Player of the Year, and when he signed with UCLA, he was expected to be the missing piece that went alongside Don MacLean and Tracy Murray on a national championship contender. That changed when he tore his ACL in a pickup game. His recovery

1995 UCLA team photo (Southern Branch Collection).

Ed O'Bannon vs. Oregon, 1995 (Southern Branch Collection).

was slow, and though he returned, time was needed before he reached the level that many hoped for. He was more than just a good player, however, he was the Bruins' inspiration. He was the leader, and he made himself into a legend.

O'Bannon is the first person many think of when remembering the 1995 Bruins, but the most memorable play was made not by O'Bannon, but by Tyus Edney. A senior in 1995, Edney was a playmaker, and though he was small, he was dynamic, dependable, and clutch. As a high school prospect, even Coach Harrick wasn't sure if he made the right choice in recruiting Edney. He ranked other players ahead of him on the recruiting board, but Edney wanted UCLA, and the ease of his recruitment was one of the reasons Coach Harrick brought him in. Still, when he arrived, Coach Harrick didn't think much of him until the first day of practice. Tyus's jump shot caught Coach Harrick by surprise. In the first practice, he was knocking in every open shot. Over time, he learned that Edney was a complete player. He would smile at you on campus, greet you warmly, and then take apart opponents in Pauley Pavilion. His unselfish attitude, team-first mentality, and incredible all-around basketball skill made him one of the best point guards in America.

Charles O'Bannon was next, and though he wasn't the star player like his older brother Ed, he was every bit as important to the team. He was incredibly athletic, but raw. As a sophomore, things began to jell. He learned to play more fundamentally sound, read defenses better, and be more reliable. He averaged 13.6 PPG and finished second on the team in rebounds with 6.1 per game.

Tyus Edney falls to the ground, but Ed O'Bannon is right there to help him up, 1995 (Southern Branch Collection).

Charles O'Bannon, 1995 (Southern Branch Collection).

Of all the important players on the 1995 Bruins team, George Zidek is most often overlooked, though literally, it's quite difficult to do. Zidek, originally from Czechoslovakia, is a mammoth man—7'0" and 250 pounds. His work ethic, however, made him a productive player. Coach Harrick said, "He's just about the most intelligent and hardest working fella I've ever been around." His hard work on the court made him an important piece. Once considered a marginal player at best, he turned himself into a very good player and was one of the main reasons for UCLA's success. He would challenge his teammates to work as he did. "Hey, you're not working harder than I am today. I'm going to work harder than you," he typically said to his teammates. Zidek developed solid post moves, including a sweeping hook shot that became his go-to move down low. He was a 3.8 GPA student, graduated with a degree in economics, and spoke at least four languages. George Zidek is a Bruin through and through.

Two freshmen and a sophomore rounded out UCLA's core group of contributors. Toby Bailey and J. R. Henderson both arrived at UCLA and immediately made major impacts on the team in 1995. Toby was a local recruit. At Loyola High School, he averaged 26 points, 14 rebounds, and six assists per game. He was an unbelievable athlete and one of the best dunkers in UCLA history. Getting Bailey became Coach Harrick's primary recruiting mission since the time he saw him play as an eighth grader. By the time he was a high school senior, Bailey was like Edney before him—an easy recruit. Henderson was not as easy to recruit. While many athletes are high maintenance, Henderson was so low maintenance that it was hard to gauge his interest. He was extremely shy. At East Bakersfield High School, he averaged 27 points, 14 rebounds, six assists, and five blocks per game. His high school stats were almost identical to Bailey's, but the two were different players. Henderson was longer, standing at 6'9", and though he was quiet, he was fierce on the court. Henderson and Bailey each started for major portions of their freshmen seasons.

George Zidek, 1995 (Southern Branch Collection).

No player could be any more different on and off the court than Cameron Dollar. When visiting UCLA while still in high school, he showed up in a three-piece suit, and before talking in depth with Coach Harrick, he asked to speak with Pete Dalis, UCLA's athletic director. Before committing to the Bruins, he wanted to be sure that Coach Harrick would be there to guide and coach him. Once assured that he would remain in Westwood, Dollar decided he wanted to play for UCLA. He was respectful, charming, and a joy to be around. On the court, he was, as described by Coach Harrick, "100 percent pure-bred bulldog. I mean, he'll just bite your nose off. Terrific defensive player. Son of a coach. Incredibly tenacious."

Along with the core group of players, there were six others. Ike Nwankwo and Bob Myers, future general manager of the Golden State Warriors, were sophomores. Kevin Dempsey and Marquis Burns were juniors. Kris Johnson, son of the great Marques Johnson, and omm'A Givens were freshmen. Mark Gottfried, Lorenzo Romar, and Steve Lavin were the three UCLA assistant coaches.

The Bruins began their season on November 26 against Cal State Northridge, but it was one week later that they had their first real challenge. After beating the Matadors 83–60, No. 2 UCLA took on No. 3 Kentucky at the John R. Wooden Classic in Anaheim, California. The two heavyweights competed in front of 18,307 fans and 60 million television viewers in 80 countries. Coach Harrick described the atmosphere as Final Four–like. UCLA

J. R. Henderson dribbles down court, as Tyus Edney and George Zidek trail, 1995 (Southern Branch Collection).

and Kentucky, the two top college basketball programs in history, met for the first time since the 1975 national championship game. As with many early-season games, both teams started slowly. Edney struggled to keep control of the ball, and the entire team struggled at the free-throw line. For the game, UCLA was just 9-for-18 at the charity stripe. The Bruins kept it close, however, and after Edney nailed a three just before half, UCLA trailed just 38–33. The second half was close throughout. With 11:11 remaining in the game, Charles O'Bannon fouled out. He was then replaced with Henderson, but it didn't matter much. UCLA was out of sync, and with just over 10 minutes remaining, the Bruins trailed by 10. But over the final 10 minutes, UCLA played brilliant basketball. Edney got to every spot on the court that he wanted, either driving and dumping the ball off to Zidek, or creating enough space to feed Zidek in the post. He was scoring against one-on-one defense over and over. After Zidek scored to cut the Kentucky lead to just one with 18 seconds remaining, UCLA's full-court press forced a turnover. After calling a timeout, Edney was instructed to drive to the basket and either look to score or dish the ball to Ed. Kentucky had it covered, but Edney quickly spun away from the play and found Henderson under the basket. He went up and was fouled with six-tenths of a second remaining. Though only played in December, the game was nevertheless big for UCLA, and the man at the free-throw line was in just his second career game. Henderson calmly sank both free throws, and the Bruins won, 82–81.

Charles O'Bannon led the way for the Bruins in their next game, a 34-point win over Cal State Fullerton. Against LSU in the fourth game of the year, Coach Harrick expected the Bruins to be tested. The game was on the road in Baton Rouge, but the Tigers stood no chance. The Bruins won by 20, and Ed O'Bannon scored 28. On December 22, UCLA took on George Mason, now coached by Paul Westhead. Years earlier, Coach Harrick had called Westhead's offense at Loyola Marymount a "disease." Sure, it was effective for Westhead's teams, but it infected the other team with bad habits, including selfishness. UCLA beat the Patriots, 137–100. Both O'Bannon brothers, as well as Edney and Bailey,

Charles O'Bannon dunks against Cal State Fullerton, 1995 (Southern Branch Collection).

went over the 20-point mark on the day. The disease infected the Bruins, however, at least according to Coach Harrick, and they played individually-oriented, instead of team-oriented, basketball for the next few games. Still, UCLA was winning. Zidek's father came to the United States and saw his son play for the first time against NC State. UCLA won, 88–80.

On January 5, UCLA began conference play still undefeated and remained No. 2 in the country. The first conference game was against the Oregon Ducks at McArthur Court in Eugene, always a tough environment for the road team. The game was a shocker. UCLA came out hot and controlled the tempo and style of the game most of the way, leading, 56–43, with less than 15 minutes to play. But then UCLA collapsed. Coach Harrick lost his cool, earning two technical fouls and an ejection, and Oregon completed the comeback, 82–72. Fans rushed the court, and UCLA was no longer unbeaten. The next morning on the front page of the sports section of the *Los Angeles Times*, the headline read, "Harrick: Always a Question."

Following the loss, UCLA dropped to No. 6 in the rankings, but unlike past seasons, no upset loss would derail the 1995 team. Against Oregon State, the Bruins again struggled for a portion of the game and trailed by six at halftime. Coach Harrick had inserted Henderson into the starting lineup for Dollar, and he would start for the next 13 games. It didn't seem to be the spark that the team needed in the first half. In the second half, it worked, however. UCLA outscored the Beavers by 15 and cruised to a win. Henderson scored 16 points in his first career start.

The Bruins collected wins against the two schools from Washington, though the first game wasn't pretty. UCLA was starting too many games slowly, and the team again did so against the Huskies. After falling behind, UCLA came back to win. Against the Cougars, Coach Harrick challenged his team to get out to a better start. They led by as many as 30, and won, 91–78. Edney, a senior, dunked for the first time in his career.

Though the Bruins were 9–1 and back up to No. 4 in the national rankings, they still had many tough games ahead of them, including their next one, against No. 11 Arizona at McKale Center. The Wildcats were led by Damon Stoudamire and were always tough to play in Tucson. The Bruins played well, and so did their point guard. Coach Harrick wanted to instill confidence in Edney, telling him that Stoudamire was no match for him. UCLA was up, 35–26, at halftime and went on to win, 71–61. Edney finished with 19 points, nine rebounds, and five assists. Stoudamire scored 15 on just 6-for-21 shooting from the field. Though the final margin was just 10 points, it was the worst home loss for Arizona under Lute Olson to that point. The Bruins then beat a ranked ASU team. Charles O'Bannon and Bailey each scored 19. Stanford was next. They were ranked No. 17, and though the game was closer than expected, UCLA came out on top. Ed O'Bannon scored 23 and Zidek added 17.

After beating three straight ranked teams, UCLA went up against unranked Cal, and the defense let the team down. In the first half, UCLA was powerless to slow down the Golden Bears. Tremaine Fowlkes came off the bench and lit UCLA up for 24 points. The Bruins trailed by 14 in the first half. Cutting into the deficit is difficult when the defense can't get stops, and that was UCLA's problem against the men from Berkeley. The Bruins did finally ratchet up the defensive intensity and take a brief second-half lead, but that wasn't enough. Cal got going again and won, 100–93. Ed O'Bannon had 23 points, Henderson 22, and Edney 21, but the numbers were deceiving. Offense was not UCLA's problem; it was defense.

Cal later forfeited all wins from 1995 and 1996 after NCAA violations were discovered. Unlike games today, the result of the matchup was reversed, not simply vacated. UCLA was awarded the victory, though it doesn't really mean much. UCLA lost.

Following the loss to Cal, UCLA went on a winning streak that will be remembered fondly in UCLA lore forever. Against USC, Edney was sick with the flu and could not play. Dollar was inserted into the starting lineup, and UCLA came away with the win. Against Notre Dame, UCLA resurrected its press defense. After not using it for weeks, they unleashed it on the Irish in the second half. At the break, UCLA only led by two points. In the second half, the Bruins outscored Notre Dame, 63–28. Next was a trip up north and a teaching moment for Coach Harrick. The Bruins beat Washington, but what Coach Harrick did after the game was most important. While in Seattle, the players loaded into the team bus and secretly drove to the Kingdome, the site of the 1995 Final Four. Players were shown the facilities on a tour, and while some were bored, others visualized the moment when they would step foot in the Kingdome again. As the tour guide explained the layout of the arena, which was hosting an RV convention at the time, players realized that this is where a champion would be crowned. Why not UCLA? In the second game of the trip against WSU, UCLA won again. Henderson scored 28 points, Edney finished with a double-double, and the Bruins handled business.

Coach Harrick kept his players focused on each game, but UCLA was clearly one of the best teams in the nation. Against No. 13 Arizona State University, the Bruins were pushed to overtime, but they won at home. In the game against Arizona, Edney struggled with knee tendinitis and played only 19 minutes. Toby Bailey stepped up, however, finishing with 19 points. UCLA beat Arizona for the second time; during that game, Coach Harrick made an important decision. Despite Henderson's great production, Bailey was going to take over as a starter in the next game. It proved to be the missing piece. Bailey was coming on strong, and Henderson was a great team player and an asset coming off the bench. The Bruins had incredible diversity: When they wanted to go small, Bailey and Henderson played together, along with Edney and the O'Bannon brothers. When they wanted to pound a team inside, they still had their seven-foot center that was a matchup nightmare.

In the next game, UCLA trailed Stanford, 47–44, at halftime but turned it on in the second half and won, 88–77. Bailey scored 12 points, with Henderson scoring 19 off the bench. In the next two games, it was more of the same. UCLA was playing its finest basketball as the NCAA Tournament approached. The team crushed Cal in a rematch, winning, 104–88, at Haas Pavilion. The Bruins shot a then school record 66.7 percent from the field. Their next opponent was a recent power that had fallen on hard times. Duke had won two national championships under Coach Mike Krzyzewski, but he was on a temporary leave of absence to deal with back problems. The Blue Devils finished just 13–18 on the season in ninth place in the ACC. They were no match for UCLA. The final score was UCLA 100, Duke 77. Following the win, the Bruins were named the No. 1 team in the nation. They finished the regular season by smashing Louisville, Oregon State, and Oregon. The final game against the Ducks was senior day at Pauley Pavilion, and the day was emotional for Ed O'Bannon and the rest of the seniors. The final score was 94–78, and the crowd of 13,037 fans was the largest in Pauley Pavilion history. O'Bannon finished the game with 24 points and 10 rebounds and fellow senior Tyus Edney scored 22 points, dished out eight assists, collected seven steals, and played smothering defense. With the game well in hand, Coach Harrick pulled Ed from the game. As he jogged off, he veered over to the center circle, dropped down and kissed the court, and the crowd went wild. UCLA loved Ed O'Bannon, and he loved UCLA right back.

When UCLA began NCAA Tournament play in 1995, there was no reliable way to predict what would happen next. UCLA was the No. 1 overall seed and had won 13 consecutive games, but only the first-round game seemed like a cinch. All others were extremely difficult.

The Bruins began with a first-round matchup against Florida International and won by a large margin. Charles O'Bannon and Henderson led the way with 16 points each. Ed O'Bannon grabbed eight rebounds, and Edney dished out eight assists. Whereas the first-round game was comfortable, the second-round game was anything but, and the outcome was in doubt until the final seconds.

On March 19, 1995, No. 1 UCLA took on No. 8 Missouri at BSU Pavilion in Boise, Idaho. A total of 11,886 fans attended for what is now one of the most famous games in college basketball history. While UCLA always played fast, Missouri loved to play slowly. In the first half, the Bruins were frustrated. The Tigers controlled the tempo, playing tough defense and hitting contested three pointers. For the game, Missouri hit 12-for-19 behind the arc. At halftime, Missouri led, 42–34. As the second half began, the results were the same. Just minutes into the second half, Coach Harrick noticed the players with a desperate look on their faces that he hadn't seen all year. They dropped their heads and shoulders and seemed unsure of themselves—all except Ed O'Bannon. Sure enough, after trailing by nine UCLA went on a 15–0 run, led by O'Bannon. But Missouri wasn't done, and the game went down to the wire. With just under one minute to play, Missouri led by one, and UCLA had the ball. Ed got the ball in the post and scored again from eight feet out. UCLA was back on top, 73–72. After a UCLA foul, Missouri inbounded the ball with 40 seconds to play and a fresh 35 seconds on the shot clock. After 34 seconds of solid defense, Julian Winfield broke free for the Tigers, collected a pass under the basket, and scored the go-ahead layup. The Bruins were down, 74–73. Coach Harrick decided to take a timeout. UCLA had to go the length of the court with 4.8 seconds left on the clock.

As the players walked to the bench, all eyes were on Coach Harrick. Ed began imploring his teammates, "We are not losing this game! We are not losing!" Coach Harrick remained calm. "This is what we are going to do," he said. "Edney, I want you to get the ball. Hopefully you can get it around the foul line and push it down the floor like you always do, and they're not going to foul you. Take it to the rim. Take it to the rim! Ed, you spot up on the left side. Toby, you spot up on the right. J. R, you and Charles get in there and tip it in." As the buzzer sounded and the players headed back to the court, Coach Harrick said in Edney's ear, "Tyus, you shoot the ball. Make sure you shoot it! It's your ball. Your rock. Your game. Just go on and make it happen."

When the ball was inbounded to Edney, he was still 84 feet from the basket, but picking up a head of steam quickly. With 0:03.1 on the clock, Edney reached midcourt, where he made one of the most impressive ball-handling moves imaginable. Looking ahead, he saw another defender closing in on him to cut off his angle. With his left hand, Edney smoothly dribbled behind his back. He had an angle to the hoop at full speed ahead. At 0:01.8, Edney reached the top of the three-point circle. Ed called for the ball on the left side, but the pass was too difficult. Edney kept the ball. After driving past the foul stripe, the game was on his shoulders. With 0:01.2 remaining, Edney jumped. Derek Grimm, at 6'8", challenged the shot, but put his hands straight up. Edney reached back to get the shot around the challenging defender, and with 0:0.8 left, the ball left his hand. With 0:0.2 left, the ball hit high off the glass backboard, and the buzzer sounded as ball fell through the bottom of the net! UCLA won! Everything went quiet for Coach Harrick. UCLA players jumped on Edney. Several lifted him up in the air in celebration. Coach Harrick's wife, Sally, cried in the stands. Cameron Dollar saw a Missouri player laying on the ground and ran over to him. Dollar lifted him up, gave him a hug, consoled him, and then joined his team in celebration. The Bruins advanced to the Sweet 16 in the most dramatic way imaginable. For Tyus Edney and the Bruins, 04.8 is a magic number.

Four days after the miracle against Missouri, the Bruins had another game to play and another tough opponent trying to knock them down. Mississippi State was the No. 5 seed in the region and had plans to finish the job Missouri started. UCLA was on a mission, however. The team didn't play its best in the last game, and MSU felt the wrath of a focused team. At halftime, UCLA led, 40–19. When the final horn sounded, UCLA won, 86–67.

Toby Bailey vs. UCONN, 1995 (Southern Branch Collection).

all 12 players, and though the game was tied at halftime, it was well in hand when the final seconds ticked off. UCLA won, 74–61, but Tyus Edney was hurt.

In the closing minutes of the first half, Edney went down hard while defending a three-on-one fastbreak. After clutching his wrist in agony, Edney got up and returned to the action. Though Coach Harrick was mindful of the injury, he knew Edney was tough, and he dominated the rest of the game. The injury was worse than Edney let on, however, and part of his success in the second half must be attributed to adrenaline. In the postgame press conference, the team had other things to think about. When asked if anyone in the country can guard him, Edney had a playful look on his face and wasn't sure what to say. Ed interrupted, shouting out, "No!" The teammates laughed together, but the wrist was still a problem.

On Sunday, April 2, the day before the national championship game, Edney woke up in excruciating pain. His wrist swelled up overnight and was now basically useless. Although his wrist wasn't broken, Edney couldn't dribble a ball or shoot. The next night, no one knew what to expect from him. Players knew he would give his best effort. What they didn't know is that on that night, they wouldn't need him. On April 3, 1995, UCLA won the national championship virtually without one of the best point guards in school history. Edney played only three minutes, collecting no points, assists, rebounds, or steals. But he inspired a team.

In the Elite Eight, UCLA played No. 2 seed UConn, and the two teams erupted for a combined 198 points. Ray Allen scored 36 for the Huskies, but it wasn't enough. Bailey scored 26 for the Bruins, Edney added 22 points and dished out 10 assists, and Henderson scored 18 off the bench. UCLA was off to the Final Four.

Looking back, one can clearly see the 1995 Bruins as a team of destiny. After beating Missouri, everything seemed to click. However, a bad game, hot opponent, injury, or unlucky call can end a season. UCLA knew that going into their Final Four matchup with No. 4 Oklahoma State, and though the outcome of the game wasn't close, UCLA's chances at a title took a major hit. A total of 38,540 fans saw the Bruins dominate the Cowboys, especially in the final 10 minutes. Seven-footer Bryant Reeves, a.k.a. Big Country, had a good game for OSU, scoring 25 points, but the story was UCLA's team play. The O'Bannon brothers scored a combined 34 points and Edney scored 21. UCLA played

At halftime, the Bruins led by only one, but like they had so many times that season, the Bruins dominated in the second half and won, 89–78, for the 11th national championship in school history. Ed scored 30 points and grabbed 17 rebounds. Toby Bailey scored 26, and Zidek added 14.

In attendance was John Wooden, but he didn't see the clock expire. Originally, he didn't even want to attend the game. For 37 straight years, John and Nell Wooden attended the Final Four and the coaches convention, but when Nell died in 1985, Coach Wooden decided he didn't want

Ed O'Bannon and Cameron Dollar celebrate after winning the 1995 national championship (Southern Branch Collection).

The UCLA coaches celebrate as the final seconds tick off the clock in the 1995 national championship game (Southern Branch Collection).

UCLA students took to the streets in Westwood to celebrate the 1995 national championship (Southern Branch Collection).

to go anymore. After UCLA beat Oklahoma State in the semifinal game, he changed his plans. He knew what it meant to Coach Harrick for him to be there, and he knew what it meant for the UCLA community. When the game was no longer in doubt, Coach Wooden quietly exited the arena. He didn't want any of the attention that belonged to the team to instead be given to him. The team was about Coach Harrick, the assistant coaches, Ed O'Bannon, Tyus Edney, George Zidek, Cameron Dollar, and the rest of the supporting cast. Without the title in 1995, the UCLA basketball story would have only been about the success under Coach Wooden. With the newest

The 1995 Bruins pose together after winning the national championship (Southern Branch Collection).

title, it was about a program and about those who watched as another banner was raised to the rafters at Pauley Pavilion. The 1995 team was special. Coach Wooden once said, "Teamwork is not a preference, it is a requirement." The Bruins passed the test—they were the national champions.

Ed O'Bannon

Ed O'Bannon was never supposed to be a Bruin, never going down as the man most responsible for banner number 11 in Pauley Pavilion, and he was never expected to be the leader of a movement to reform college athletic amateur status and participation. Some see O'Bannon as a rebel. He was dissatisfied with the rules and intent on changing the system entirely. Ed O'Bannon nearly was a rebel at one time—a Running Rebel from UNLV—but with a twist of fate, he instead became a Bruin, a legend, and a college basketball icon. With one decision to change his college commitment from UNLV to UCLA, UCLA reclaimed power status, O'Bannon became a national star, and a generation of Bruins fans were given a moment, and a season, to cherish.

Ed O'Bannon was born on August 14, 1972, in Los Angeles and was an L.A. kid. He played at Verbum Dei High School before transferring to Artesia High School, putting up monster numbers and leading his team to the Division II State Championship. O'Bannon wanted to play at UNLV for legendary coach Jerry Tarkanian. At the request of the UNLV coach, however, O'Bannon slow-played the process. He committed to the Rebels but never signed a national letter of intent. UNLV was about to be hit with NCAA sanctions, and everyone knew it. When it was announced that the team would be placed on probation, O'Bannon decided to choose another path. The L.A. kid decided to stay home. In the summer of 1990, he enrolled at UCLA.

For Ed O'Bannon, nothing has been easy, and even his greatest years on the hardwood began not with glory but with adversity. In 1990–91, O'Bannon was expected to be an immediate star on a championship-quality team, but one week before the start of the season, he tore his ACL and missed the entire year. While ACL reconstruction is a fairly standard procedure now, it wasn't so sure nearly 30 years ago. Doctors replaced his ACL with the ligament from a cadaver, and no one knew how well it would hold up. The recovery was long, but eventually Ed made his way back to the court.

Ed O'Bannon in the 1995 national championship game (Southern Branch Collection).

the physical talent, but he also had the special gift inside him to inspire his teammates. Whereas UCLA has had better players come through Westwood since O'Bannon's departure, none have left the legacy of the lanky left-hander that kissed the court the final time he played at Pauley Pavilion. In 1995, he embarked on a new journey.

As O'Bannon sat in the SkyDome in Toronto on June 28, 1995, during the NBA draft, he had hopes for how the night would turn out. O'Bannon desperately hoped to be picked by a team on the West Coast. Though he ideally wanted to stay in Los Angeles, O'Bannon was content with other options. "I wanted so bad to go to Portland, or Phoenix. It didn't have to be the Lakers. I wasn't greedy. Just give me Utah or Denver, somewhere in the west, where I could shoot home on an off day. People who don't get homesick won't understand what I'm saying, but that's how I felt, and because of that, I just never got comfortable."

After redshirting in 1991, O'Bannon took to the court in 1992 wearing a Bruins uniform for the first time. Though he missed time early in the season still recovering from his injury, and though his contribution to the team was minimal, he was nevertheless working his way back to normal. As a sophomore in 1993, he made a huge jump in scoring. After averaging just 3.6 points per game a freshman, he scored 16.7, and then 18.2 as a junior and 20.4 as a senior. In 1995, he was named Pac-10 Player of the Year, consensus First Team All-American, and National Player of the Year by several outlets. His greatest contribution to the Bruins came not in individual accolades, however, but what he did as a member of a team. The 1995 Bruins had Ed O'Bannon and Tyus Edney, the two most recognizable players to don the UCLA uniform at the time, but more than anything, they had teamwork. O'Bannon was a star, but the biggest star was the team itself. Although O'Bannon is a legend because of the national championship, his unselfishness, leadership, and attitude made him special. He had

Not only did O'Bannon end up away from home, but also a team just about as far away as possible picked him. With the ninth overall pick in the 1995 NBA Draft, the New Jersey Nets selected Ed. With his girlfriend at the time, now his wife, sitting next to him, O'Bannon tried to hide the disappointment, but he couldn't. "Right then and there, my stomach dropped, and I started to get homesick," O'Bannon said. Despite going to a team he didn't want to play for, O'Bannon was now an NBA player, a dream for many, and with it came a three-year, $3.9 million contract. He bought a new car and a condo in Manhattan Beach, but his new home was far away from where he would play in 1995–96, and even farther from where he would spend the majority of his playing career.

For two years, Ed O'Bannon looked for answers and couldn't find them. As a rookie, he played in 64 games with the Nets, and then in 45 more in his second season before he was traded to the Dallas Mavericks. After 19 games with the Mavericks, he was traded to the Orlando Magic in the offseason and then released. In two seasons, he played in 128 games, averaging 5.0 points and 2.5 rebounds per game. The problems were numerous. He was a power forward forced to play shooting guard. He was too skinny to play consistently down low but didn't have the foot speed to keep up with guards. He continued to struggle with homesickness, both his knees gave him problems, and he lacked confidence. O'Bannon had gone down as a bust in the minds of many NBA analysts, but perhaps they should have seen the writing on the wall. The magical season of 1995 was the pinnacle of O'Bannon's playing career, and though he didn't last long in the NBA, he continued to play—even further away from home.

From 1998 to 2004, O'Bannon played professional basketball overseas, with the brief exception a short stint with the Los Angeles Stars of the semipro American Basketball Association in 2001. He spent time in Italy, Spain, Greece, Argentina, and Poland. In 2004, with no team in Europe willing to give him a shot, O'Bannon participated in a weeklong tryout for a Chinese league when he suddenly decided he was done. He no longer had the passion to play anymore. He wanted to return home, but he didn't know what to do. He called his wife, Rosa, and told her the news. "Come on home. We miss you. We'll start our new life. We'll turn the page, and everything will be good," she assured him.

O'Bannon has since worked as a car salesman, a high school basketball coach, and now as a director of marketing for an auto dealership. He began working not because of a need for immediate income following retirement, but because he and his wife recognized that the man lying around the house was not what O'Bannon wanted to be. He went to work to find purpose and instead found a career. O'Bannon has another passion, as well, and it is one that has stirred debate for years.

In July 2009, Ed O'Bannon filed a lawsuit against the NCAA claiming violations of the Sherman Antitrust Act. In the lawsuit, O'Bannon argued that players should be compensated for the use of their likeness for commercial purposes. The lawsuit has been both a win and loss for O'Bannon and the athletes. The Ninth Circuit Court of Appeals ruled that "while antitrust law requires that schools be allowed to provide these athletes with scholarships that cover all of their costs of attending college, including travel and personal incidentals, 'it does not require more,' such as what is termed 'cash sums untethered to educational expenses.'" While O'Bannon's suit has brought some change to the NCAA, and players have received greater benefits, a long way remains to achieve the end goal. Players still do not receive payment for the use of their likeness; yet, players' likenesses are rarely used for fear of future litigation. This has led to backlash from many outsiders. Popular video games have ceased production, including EA Sports college video games, and schools have almost completely stopped selling uniforms with player names on the back. In 2016, the Supreme Court chose not to consider the Ed O'Bannon case. To this day, he continues to fight for what he believes players deserve.

In 1996, UCLA retired Ed O'Bannon's number 31 jersey. O'Bannon's time in Westwood is unlike so many others. While legendary players are often taken for granted until years later, O'Bannon was appreciated at the time. A certain undefinable character trait in him caught the eyes of others. He was not just a great player but also a great leader, winner, determined force on the court, and fan favorite. When Ed O'Bannon walks into Pauley Pavilion, the cheers are as loud now as they were nearly a quarter century ago. It is a flashback to when Ed O'Bannon was the best college basketball player in the world—a time when the greatest show in hoops was in Los Angeles. UCLA will again raise a championship banner someday, and new basketball heroes will make their mark, but UCLA fans will always remember Ed and the Bruins in the spring of 1995.

1995–96

For the first time in 20 years, the Bruins entered the 1995–96 season as defending national champion. Under Coach Wooden decades earlier, UCLA was able to win championships, come back as a completely new team, and win again. Under Coach Jim Harrick, that was the goal in 1996. With Ed O'Bannon, Tyus Edney, and George Zidek gone from the championship team, four players remained from the previous team out of the core of key contributors. Toby Bailey, who alternated between his natural shooting-guard role and point guard, led the team with a 14.8 points per game scoring average. Fellow sophomore J. R. Henderson was right behind him in scoring, averaging 14.4 for the season, and steady Charles O'Bannon averaged 14.3 PPG. Cameron Dollar was expected to take over at point guard and see a major jump in his offensive production, but for much of the year, he dealt with injuries to both hands. His dominant defense continued. Kris Johnson was one of the surprises on the 1996 team. After losing 30 pounds in the offseason, Johnson became a key contributor. Freshman Jelani McCoy had a strong season, as well, taking over for Zidek and providing a strong presence down low. The Bruins of 1996 were not as explosive on offense, but they were every bit as efficient. Heading into the NCAA Tournament, UCLA led the nation in field-goal percentage. Though repeating as champions seemed like a daunting task, Coach Harrick and the Bruins were ready to give it a shot.

UCLA began the season ranked No. 4 in the country. The celebratory banner-raising ceremony had to wait, as the Bruins began their season in Hawaii, competing in the Maui Classic. In the first game, UCLA took on Santa Clara, and any hope that the Bruins would be as good from start to finish as the previous team was crushed. The Broncos took the Bruins apart. Marlon Garnett and Steve Nash each played well, and though O'Bannon and Henderson were solid for the Bruins, their play wasn't enough. UCLA was stunned: Santa Clara 78, UCLA 69. The Bruins bounced back to beat Wisconsin the next night but then fell to Vanderbilt in the fifth-place game to finish the tournament with just a 1–2 record. UCLA came home, but its high ranking did not come along. The team dropped all the way to No. 23.

On November 28, 1995, prior to the home opener against Cal State Fullerton, the 11th national championship banner was unveiled at Pauley Pavilion. Unlike nearly all other schools, only national championship banners are hung at UCLA, and despite the incredibly high standards, the rafters at Pauley are filled. All three seniors from the 1995 team were in attendance, and all three addressed the crowd. George Zidek said, "I just want to tell you, all of our guys and everybody on the basketball staff, we are proud to bring the banner back where it belongs to Pauley Pavilion." The Bruins then started slowly against the Titans but eventually took over in the second half and pulled away for a 79–63 win.

Clearly the Bruins had a way to go if they hoped to contend for another title. Against No. 2 Kansas on the road, O'Bannon scored 22, but his play wasn't enough, as Jacque Vaughn and Paul Pierce led the Jayhawks to a 15-point win. Despite the 2–3 start, the Bruins improved; following the embarrassing loss to Kansas, a winning streak started. UCLA beat No. 20 Maryland in the Wooden Classic, then crushed Stephen F. Austin University with the help of 23 points from Bailey. UCLA next beat Notre Dame by 25 and handed UNLV a loss on December 23. Henderson led the way for the Bruins against the Rebels with 25 points. After three weeks out of the AP rankings, UCLA climbed back in at No. 23 and then beat University of San Francisco before the start of Pac-10 play.

At 7–3, UCLA had started to turn their season around, but much improvement was still needed. The Bruins began conference play January 4 on the road at Washington State. The Cougars were a solid team and pushed the Bruins to overtime, but UCLA came out on top to run its winning streak to six games. J. R. Henderson scored 29 points on 11-for-13 shooting from the field. McCoy pulled down 15 rebounds, including five on the offensive end. Though the following game against Washington was decided by single digits as well, UCLA finished its first Pac-10 road trip with a sweep after beating the Huskies, 78–70. Henderson followed up his monster game against WSU with 22 points against UW.

When UCLA returned home and continued conference play, the winning streak continued as well. The Bruins beat No. 24 Stanford, holding that team to just 56 total points and 34.4 percent from the field. Against California, UCLA won again, but it was not the end result that was so surprising. It was the individual performance of one player. Marques Johnson's career-high scoring performance came against Cal in 1977. He scored 37 points. In 1996, his son Kris nearly matched his total. On 12-of-17 shooting from the field and 12 of 13 from the line, Kris Johnson poured in a career-high 36 points, as UCLA defeated the Golden Bears to begin conference play 4–0. UCLA then went to Tempe and beat ASU to run the winning streak to 10.

On January 20, UCLA fell to No. 18 Arizona.

Four Bruins scored at least 16 points, but the defense struggled to stop the Wildcats. Miles Simon went off for 28 points, and UCLA's undefeated conference record was no more. The Bruins bounced back by crushing USC behind 27 points from O'Bannon but then lost another heartbreaker to Louisville at home. The Bruins beat Oregon and then Oregon State. Against the Beavers, Bob Myers scored a career-best 20 points in the win. The Bruins continued to play solid basketball for the majority of the rest of the regular season, though the occasional hiccup was mixed in. They beat Cal again but lost to Stanford by one point. They beat Arizona by one in the rematch at Pauley Pavilion in a balanced team effort. They crushed ASU but played poorly against USC. It took a final-second shot by O'Bannon to knock off the Trojans. With just 0.4 seconds left, O'Bannon's 12-foot jumper was good, and UCLA survived. The Bruins were then crushed by Duke, but won their final four games of the regular season to clinch the Pac-10 crown with a 16–2 conference record. Overall, UCLA was 23–7, a significant step back from the previous year. Heading into the NCAA Tournament, UCLA was a hot pick to make a deep run. The team was up and down, struggling with consistency all year, but when the team was at its best they were capable of playing with any opponent. The NCAA Tournament of 1996 was unlike the tournament of 1995 for the Bruins, but UCLA still played one of the most memorable games in school history.

The game was ugly, one of those classic games that has lived on in NCAA Tournament lore. UCLA was the No. 4 seed in the Southeast Regional, and its opponent was the No. 13-seed Princeton Tigers, a slow-it-down, backdoor-to-death offensive team that played tight defense, made games boring, and hoped to execute better than its opponent down the stretch. Against the Bruins, their game plan worked to perfection. At halftime, the score was just 19–18, UCLA, and in the second half, the scoring didn't pick up by much, but the drama did. In front of 31,569 fans, the Tigers hung with the Bruins all game. After stopping UCLA with under 30 seconds to go, Princeton grabbed the rebound with the score tied at 41 and called a timeout. The shot clock was turned off (because less than 35 seconds were left), and this was Princeton's chance to knock off the champ. After running the clock down to under 10 seconds, the Tigers ran a series of backdoor cuts, and finally when the passing lane opened up they connected. Gabe Lewullis started in the right corner, snuck behind the defense, received a bounce pass on the right block, and made the go-ahead layup with 3.4 seconds left. UCLA quickly inbounded the ball and moved it up court and called timeout with 2.2 remaining. On the inbounds play, Dollar found Bailey, who got a shot off in the left corner, but it was well defended and sailed long. Princeton beat UCLA, pulling off one of the most stunning upsets in college basketball history. The game-winning play has since been dubbed by the Princeton faithful "The Game That Never Goes Away." David beat Goliath, and UCLA's season was over. Before the start of the next season, so was Coach Jim Harrick's career as the UCLA basketball coach. He brought UCLA a title but also brought great heartache.

University of Kentucky won the NCAA basketball national championship in 1996.

CHAPTER 11
Steve Lavin (1996–2003)

Steve Lavin was lucky. He was in the right place at the right time. No one expected the UCLA basketball job to open up before the start of the 1996–97 season, but it did.

Fresh off a national championship in 1995, Coach Jim Harrick had mostly silenced his doubters. Although some thought the 1995 championship team just had a fluke season, when the banner was lifted to the Pauley Pavilion rafters, the storm around Coach Harrick suddenly lifted. Then he was fired on November 6, 1996, just 15 days before the start of the season and six days before the first exhibition game, following minor NCAA violations and a major cover-up. Steve Lavin was named the interim coach for the rest of the season. Though UCLA underwent a national search, and one of the top names in consideration was again Larry Brown, the answer to who would coach the team over the long term was there all along. Lavin coached the Bruins for seven seasons.

Steve Lavin, born September 4, 1964, grew up in a basketball family. When Steve needed a basketball lesson, he just turned to his dad. Cap Lavin is a member of the San Francisco Prep Basketball Hall of Fame and the University of San Francisco Hall of Fame. He was a fancy dribbler, expert passer, and all-around great player. Two great passions that Steve developed from his father have helped to define what many people know about him today. Like his father, Steve has a heart for giving back, and he has a love of basketball. Along with his excellent playing career, Cap spent 43 years as an English teacher and was the cofounder and director of the Bay Area Writing Project at the University of California. He helped create writing centers across Northern California and eventually across the country. While Cap helped young men and women in their academic affairs and in developing their writing skills, Steve has spent much of his time, when not coaching or analyzing basketball, helping others as well. His philanthropic work may not receive the same attention as does his basketball skill, but he has made a difference in the lives of countless others because of his big heart.

As a boy, Steve was a basketball junkie. In high school, he played at Sir Francis Drake High School in San Anselmo, California, and won two state titles. During the 1981 and 1982 seasons, the team finished with a 65–1 overall record and won 57 consecutive games. Following graduation, Steve enrolled at San Francisco State, but he wasn't there very long. After two years, he transferred to Chapman University. As a senior in 1987, Lavin was named team captain and earned the Leadership Award. Meanwhile, Lavin had an eye for teaching. In 1984, while still in college, he started the Lavin Basketball Camps, teaching basketball to boys and girls from fifth through twelfth grades. With the help of others, he taught five one-week basketball camps per year. He continued to run the Lavin Basketball Camps until 1999.

Following graduation, Lavin's rise to coaching prominence was rapid. In 1988, he was hired as a graduate assistant at Purdue, a position he held for two seasons before being promoted to assistant coach for the 1990–91 season. Following his stint at Purdue, Lavin joined the UCLA staff as an assistant coach. In five seasons, he learned from Coach

Athletic Director Peter Dalis at the press conference to announce that Jim Harrick was terminated and Steve Lavin was the new interim head coach, prior to the 1996–97 season (Southern Branch Collection).

Harrick and those around him. He was a member of the 1995 national championship staff, and when he was given his chance as an interim coach of UCLA in 1997, he took full advantage. On February 11, 1997, "interim" was removed from Coach Lavin's job title. He was now officially the 11th head coach in UCLA basketball history. Over the next seven years, Coach Lavin had a steady run at UCLA, but like many coaches before him, his success was never enough. He was a strong recruiter, coached an exciting brand of basketball, and was a regular in the NCAA Tournament. UCLA won one conference title in his tenure, made the Sweet 16 four different times, and made the Elite Eight once. Following the 2003 season, Lavin was fired.

Shortly after Lavin was let go by UCLA, he found a new job as a college basketball analyst and color commentator with ABC and ESPN. For six seasons, Lavin provided his own touch to broadcasts and studio shows, appearing not only in-game but also on popular shows such as ESPN's *College GameNight*. In 2010, however, Lavin was given another shot at coaching and couldn't turn it down. For five seasons, he was the head coach of the St. John's University Red Storm basketball team, and with him came excitement. In his first season, St. John's finished with a 21–12 record and made the NCAA Tournament for the first time in nine years. Lavin wasn't able to keep the momentum going, however. He had more important things to worry about. Lavin coached only four games in 2012 after being diagnosed with prostate cancer. He beat the disease, but he was never able to get the Red Storm back on track. St. John's had three more winning seasons and made one more trip to the NCAA Tournament, but Steve Lavin was fired anyway following the 2015 season. He quickly found a job in television, working for Fox Sports, CBS Sports, and the Pac-12 Network.

Coach Lavin's years as the head coach with UCLA were often frustrating. When he was let go, it had been clear that new leadership was needed. The story of UCLA basketball since the retirement of Coach Wooden is the story of Steve Lavin. There were triumphs and disappointments, great wins and heartbreaking losses. Coach Lavin was not a bad coach. He was quite successful and built exciting teams. While the pressure on coaches has lessened over the nearly four-and-a-half decades since Coach John Wooden retired, UCLA's athletic identity remains solidly as a basketball school, so coaches must win basketball titles.

1996–97

After a tumultuous offseason, UCLA basketball took to the court again on November 21 with high expectations. The major changes involved the coaching staff, as much of the talent on the court was familiar. Charles O'Bannon was now a senior and had his best season as a Bruin, leading the team with a scoring average of 17.7 points per game. J. R. Henderson and Toby Bailey, the key freshmen on the 1995 team, were now juniors and continued their strong play, each averaging 14.1 PPG on the season. Jelani McCoy and Kris Johnson followed up their strong 1996 seasons with good years in 1997, and Cameron Dollar, now a senior, was as dependable as ever. The Bruins began the season ranked No. 5 in the country but had some kinks to work out. They were a strong offensive team, but for much of the season, they struggled on the other end. UCLA gave up 73.8 PPG, which ranked 236th in the country in scoring defense.

After two exhibition victories, UCLA took on Tulsa in the opening game of the season. The Bruins showed they had a lot of work still to do. Jelani McCoy finished 8-for-9 from the field and scored 19 points. His high efficiency from the field was normal, as he led the nation in field-goal percentage, but finding ways to use him was at times challenging. McCoy got off to a strong start, but the team did not. It fell to the unranked Golden Hurricanes and were 0–1. The schedule still had many difficult games on the nonconference slate. After beating Cal State Northridge behind 23 points from O'Bannon and a double-double from Toby Bailey, UCLA took on the top-ranked team in the nation, the Kansas Jayhawks. The Bruins did well to slow down star Paul Pierce, but he had plenty of help. Raef LaFrentz lit up UCLA for 31 points, and Jerod Haase and Billy Thomas combined for 40. The Jayhawks demolished UCLA, 96–83, at Pauley Pavilion.

UCLA was just 1–2, and Coach Lavin, the fifth youngest coach in Division I basketball, was in a difficult spot. He was an interim coach, hoping to land the job permanently, working in the most pressure-packed position in college basketball. But Coach Lavin kept working, and the Bruins started to improve. Though UCLA dropped a disappointing game against Illinois on the road, it won four of the final five nonconference games after losing to Kansas.

UCLA hoped to defend its Pac-10 title when conference play rolled around, but had stiff competition. The conference was strong. In the conference opener against WSU, a balanced scoring attack helped the Bruins run away from their opponent by a large margin. They then backed up their opening-game win with another, beating UW, 79–70. On January 9, 1997, UCLA played one of its worst games in school history. Against Stanford, nothing worked. O'Bannon and Henderson each shot just 3 of 10 from the field, Bailey had four turnovers, the team made just 13 of 23 from the free-throw line, and it turned the ball over 17 times. The Cardinal, on the other hand, played near flawless basketball. In the first half, Stanford shot 52.9 percent from the field, and in the second half, it upped that percentage to 60.0 percent. When the final seconds ticked off, the scoreboard read Stanford 109, UCLA 61.

Against California, O'Bannon pulled down a career-high 16 rebounds in the win, and against ASU, three Bruins each scored 17 points in the win. On January 18, UCLA took on No. 6 Arizona at Pauley Pavilion, and the game was a nail-biter. O'Bannon and the Bruins had played in big games before, and against the highly-ranked Wildcats, they were able to bring their A game. O'Bannon scored 24 and collected 13 rebounds, Henderson scored 19, McCoy added 15, and though it took an extra five-minute overtime period, UCLA pulled off the upset. The Bruins then backed up their big win with another over USC five days later.

The story of 1997 is that of a team that never let fans get their hopes up. Just as the team seemed to gel, things suddenly turned the other way. Though they played well, UCLA lost to No. 6 Louisville on the road and then lost two of the next three when conference play resumed. At 7–3 in Pac-10 action, UCLA needed to be more consistent down the stretch if it were to successfully defend the conference crown.

Over the final nine games of the season, the Bruins looked like one of the best teams in America. In the passion-filled rematch with Stanford, UCLA turned the tables on its northern rival. O'Bannon led the way, and UCLA won by 19. After reentering the AP rankings at No. 24, UCLA traveled to McKale Center to take on the University of Arizona, and just as they had earlier in the season, UCLA beat the No. 11 Wildcats in a close one. At halftime, the Wildcats led 33–32, but in the second half, UCLA outscored UA by three and won, 66–64. Just as he had done all year, O'Bannon led the way for UCLA, scoring 26 points on 10-for-14 shooting. The Bruins then beat ASU and USC before taking on No. 6 Duke in a nonconference game played at home. Henderson's scoring and O'Bannon's defense propelled the Bruins over the Blue Devils, 73–69, for their fifth consecutive win. After climbing all the way into the top 10, UCLA kept it going. It beat Oregon State and then Oregon to clinch the Pac-10 Conference, its third straight title and fourth in the last six years. The team then finished off the season by beating Washington and Washington State in two thrillers. Against UW, O'Bannon scored 31 points in the 87–85 victory. Against WSU, in the final game of the regular season, Cameron Dollar hit a driving layup at the buzzer to beat the Cougars 87–86 and extend UCLA's winning streak to nine.

When the NCAA Tournament bracket was announced, UCLA was in a similar spot—in the field and expected to contend for the title. The Bruins had turned their season around, Coach Lavin had been promoted to permanent head coach going forward, and the team was playing better than they had all season. UCLA was the No. 2 seed in the Midwest Regional and played No. 15 Charleston Southern in the opening game at the Palace of Auburn Hills in Detroit, Michigan. Despite 32 points from Charleston Southern's Brett Larrick, UCLA was too much for the underdog Buccaneers. Henderson and McCoy each scored 21 points and five Bruins scored 14 or more. UCLA won in blowout fashion. It was much the same against Xavier in the second round. Though the competition was tougher, UCLA was playing championship-level basketball. O'Bannon and Henderson combined to score 50 points and Jelani McCoy blocked five shots. UCLA cruised, 96–83.

In Coach Lavin's first year, UCLA was in the Sweet 16, something he became known for. No. 6 seed Iowa State, coached by Tim Floyd, was next on the schedule. In front of nearly thirty thousand fans in the Alamodome in San Antonio, the two teams played a classic. With the Cyclones leading, 73–72, in the final seconds of overtime, UCLA had the ball and was in need of a miraculous finish. That's just what it got. Cameron Dollar, the last-second hero against Washington State in the regular-season finale, repeated his heroics against Iowa State. After driving hard to the basket, Dollar's finger roll went through the net with 1.9 seconds left. As Iowa State looked to inbound the ball, Klay Edwards was unable to find an open man and was called for a five-second violation. Tim Floyd threw his clipboard, fell to the ground, and pounded his fists on the ground. UCLA won, 74–73, and advanced to the Elite Eight.

After winning 12 straight games, the season came to an end against the top-seeded Minnesota Golden Gophers. O'Bannon and Bailey played well, but they didn't get much help. Minnesota was a balanced team, and with the win, it improved its stellar record to 31–3. UCLA was outplayed in every way by a better team, and the season ended one game short of the Final Four. Though the Gophers later vacated their season for an academic-fraud case, that didn't matter for UCLA. Two brilliant seniors played their last game in a UCLA uniform, and replacing them was Coach Lavin's biggest challenge in his first full offseason as the UCLA coach. The only major pieces to the 1995 national title team that would be back in 1998 were J. R. Henderson and Toby Bailey. They knew what it felt like to be champions, and in 1998, they wanted to spread the joy.

University of Arizona won the NCAA basketball national championship in 1997.

1997–98

The 1997–98 season began with drama. The Bruins were led by three seniors on the court, and they were steady as can be. J. R. Henderson led the Bruins in scoring, averaging 19.0 points per game. Kris Johnson scored 18.4, and Toby Bailey 17.9. The three-headed monster was dynamic on the court, but so much of the success would come down to the new players. Jelani McCoy was now a junior, but he was the only other contributing player with any experience. The freshmen class was loaded. Baron Davis was one of the top incoming recruits in the nation. He was joined by Earl Watson, Travis Reed, Billy Knight, Rico Hines, Todd Ramasar, and Kevin Daley. One name was missing, however, and his loss was devastating for the Bruins' chances of success. Schea Cotton was a prep-athletics icon who was LeBron James before LeBron was ever in the public scene. He was famous for his basketball skills before ever reaching high school. He was the top recruit in the nation by the time he was a senior. Though many speculated that Cotton would follow Kevin Garnett and Kobe Bryant and continue the wave of jumping from high school to the NBA, Cotton wanted to attend college. Though injuries derailed his final two seasons in high school, when he committed to UCLA in April 1997, expectations were sky high. Cotton's admission to UCLA came with a contingency, however. He had yet to meet the qualifying standard SAT score to compete for the Bruins and had to retake the SAT before joining the team. Cotton did take the test again, and he received the necessary score. But because of a learning disability, Cotton was administered the test with larger font sizes and given extra time. According to the Educational Testing Service, this was appropriate given his diagnosis. According to the NCAA, it was not. Cotton never enrolled at UCLA and later sued the NCAA. Eventually, he enrolled at Alabama, and went on to play 10 professional basketball season but never reached the NBA.

The Bruins were without the man they expected to be a star, and soon things would get worse. After playing two exhibition games, UCLA began its season in a powerhouse vs. powerhouse matchup. On November 27, No. 7 UCLA faced No. 4 North Carolina in the first round of the Great Alaska Shootout. Unfortunately for the Bruins, they were without two more key contributors. Johnson and McCoy were each suspended indefinitely, which ended up being about three weeks, to begin the season for undisclosed reasons. The void was definitely felt in the season opener. UNC, led by Vince Carter's 22 points, ran the Bruins out of the gym. Baron Davis had 13 points and dished out seven assists in his first career game, but he was the lone bright spot. The final score was UNC 108, UCLA 69. The Bruins bounced back to win their final two games of the Great Alaska Shootout, but they went home disappointed.

After dropping to No. 15 in the country, the Bruins had their next chance to make a splash in the national picture. In the John R. Wooden Classic in Anaheim, Coach Steve Lavin and the Bruins played No. 8 New Mexico. Clayton Shields finished with 20 points and 10 assists for the Lobos, but it wasn't enough. The Bruins played their best game yet. Though Davis struggled for the first time, the rest of the team picked up the slack. Henderson led the way with 24 points, and 14 big points from Travis Reed helped push the Bruins over the top. UCLA's 69–58 win handed the Lobos their first loss of the season. As nonconference play continued, the Bruins really hit their stride. Against Cal State Fullerton, they scored a season-high 120 points. They forced 23 turnovers, and six Bruins scored in double figures, led by 23 from Henderson and a double-double from Watson. UCLA kept winning as nonconference play continued and it slowly climbed back up the rankings. Against Northern Arizona, Henderson and Bailey each finished 11-for-18 from the field and combined to score 55 points. Back from suspension, Johnson was one of three Bruins to score 20-plus points against Boise State. The Bruins continued their winning ways against UNLV on the road in front of a large crowd, as all five starters scored in double figures, and in the final tune-up before conference

Head coach Steve Lavin, 1998 (Southern Branch Collection).

play, the Bruins snuck by Illinois at home in a game too close for comfort.

UCLA was 9–1 when conference play began, and its toughest game was first on the conference schedule. The Arizona Wildcats were the defending national champions, and the Pac-10 opener was played at McKale Center in front of 14,551 fans. UCLA had climbed back up to No. 9 in the country, but the Wildcats were No. 8. The Bruins played well in the first half, leading, 41–38, at the break, but the second half was all Arizona. Miles Simon scored 27 and had plenty of help. Michael Dickerson added 24, and Mike Bibby scored 20 points. UCLA, on the other hand, looked lost. Seniors Kris Johnson and Toby Bailey each played well, scoring 28 and 17, respectively. Jelani McCoy scored 16 and pulled down 13 rebounds. The freshmen struggled mightily, however. Davis finished with just five points and was one of four Bruins to foul out. Watson scored just six, and UCLA's shrunken rotation looked tired in the second half. Arizona won, 87–75.

As the season progressed, a pattern began. UCLA was beating the teams they were expected to beat but struggling to break through against top-rated teams. After losing to Arizona, the Bruins beat ASU behind 31 points from Henderson. UCLA then easily handled Oregon State at home. Earl Watson and Baron Davis brought the crowd to their feet. After a steal got the Bruins in transition, Watson lobbed the ball off the backboard to a trailing Davis, who threw down a monster dunk. Two days later, the freshmen shined again. With the score tied at 66, Oregon had control of the ball in the final 30 seconds. Watson pressured the ball, stole it, and found Davis for the game-winning layup. UCLA won its third game in a row.

The winning streak reached four after another close win, this time over Cal on the road, but the next test was a tough one. On January 17, the Bruins were blown out by Stanford. UCLA shot just 40.7 percent from the field, turned the ball over 16 times, and was powerless to stop the Cardinal offense. Four Stanford players scored in double figures, and the Cardinal won by 13 points. The Bruins won their next four games, relying heavily on their offense to lead the way. After beating USC, the No. 9 Bruins knocked off Louisville. Henderson scored 32 points in the win. Against Washington State, five Bruins scored at least 16 points, led by 22 points and 11 assists from Bailey.

Though the Bruins were 17–3 overall, their resumé lacked big wins, but they had avoided bad losses. That would soon change. On February 5, the Oregon Ducks smoked the Bruins, shooting 66.7 percent from the field in the second half and running away with a win. The Bruins beat Oregon State two nights later. All three seniors scored 20 or more in the win. Against Stanford, the same three played well but received no help. Henderson, Johnson, and Bailey scored 60 of UCLA's 81 points but the Bruins fell. Despite the rough stretch, UCLA dropped just three spots in the AP rankings. After two wins, UCLA played its final nonconference game of the regular season. On February 22, the Bruins traveled to Durham, North Carolina, to take on the No. 2 Duke Blue Devils at Cameron Indoor Stadium. With the game nationally televised on ABC, Coach Steve Lavin and the Bruins were dismantled by Coach K and the superior Blue Devils squad. Trajan Langdon was the top scorer for Duke, pouring in a career-best 34 points. Roshown McLeod added 24 and Elton Brand scored 14. The Blue Devils shot 53.2 percent from the field and knocked down 15 three pointers, including 10 in the first half. The game was one of the worst performances in program history, Duke winning, 120–84. The 120 points was the most UCLA had ever given up in a single game. Following the loss, Duke was elevated to No. 1 in the country, while UCLA fell to No. 18. The Bruins went 2–2 in their final four regular–season games, beating Washington State and Arizona State, and losing to Washington and No. 2 Arizona. UCLA finished the regular season with a 22–8 overall record, including 12–6 in Pac-10 play, good for third in the conference standings.

The 1998 NCAA Tournament was much like the rest of the season, much like Coach Lavin's career. UCLA had some success but wasn't elite. The Bruins were named the No. 6 seed in the South Regional and took on Miami in the opening round. The game was low scoring, something uncommon for UCLA, but it worked well enough. The Bruins held the Hurricanes to just 37.7 percent from the field. UCLA shot 46.6 percent and was led by the two players with the most prior tournament success. Henderson scored 26, and Bailey scored 21 points, grabbed 11 rebounds, dished out seven assists, and had four steals. UCLA was on to the second round. Awaiting the Bruins was the No. 3 seed in the region—the Michigan

Jelani McCoy, 1998 (Southern Branch Collection).

Wolverines. In front of 19,423 fans in the Georgia Dome, UCLA pulled off the upset. Coming into the game, the biggest question for the Bruins was how they would defend down low. Robert "Tractor" Traylor led Michigan. The 6'9" Traylor was one of the strongest players in the country and one of the hardest to defend in the post. Coach Lavin and the Bruins wanted to speed up the Wolverines, pressuring them the length of the court. When they were able to slow it down and get the ball into Traylor, UCLA's defense would swarm him on the block, double- and triple-teaming him on the catch. Though Michigan scored 82 points and Traylor played well, the team shot only 40.6 percent from the field. Johnson led the way for UCLA, scoring 25 points, including eight clutch free throws in the final minute. UCLA won, 85–82, and advanced to the Sweet 16. There was one problem, however. Baron Davis, the Pac-10 Freshman of the Year, tore his ACL. His season was over. His future was in jeopardy, and the Bruins were without one of their best players.

The Sweet 16 was a comfortable spot for UCLA under Coach Lavin. Though the Bruins advanced to the Elite Eight in 1997, winning a third NCAA Tournament game proved to be too much for the Bruins of 1998 or during the rest of Coach Lavin's tenure. UCLA took on the No. 2 seeded Kentucky Wildcats, coached by Tubby Smith, and were dismantled. The balanced scoring for the Wildcats and smothering defense was too much. The Bruins shot just 29.1 percent from the field and turned the ball over 19 times, including eight by Watson. UCLA's season came to an end with a 26-point loss. Through two seasons, Coach Lavin had a record of 48–17, but 1999 was to be much harder. The brilliant college careers of Henderson, Bailey, and Johnson were over. The three were national champions, great players, and leaders.

University of Kentucky won the NCAA basketball national championship in 1998.

1998–99

Coaching a major college basketball team with an interim tag is difficult. Blending a talented group of freshmen incomers with an experienced group of former national champion seniors is a tough task also. Coach Steve Lavin's first two years were challenging, and his results were solid, though unspectacular. Replacing his stars from the year prior and continuing to win at a high enough level to satisfy the UCLA fan base was his job entering year three. The team was extraordinary young but also very talented. The top 10 scorers were all freshmen or sophomores. The brilliant duo of Baron Davis, fully recovered from his knee injury by midseason, and Earl Watson took significant steps forward in 1999, with Davis leading the team in points and assists per game. Watson was right behind him in each category. Three freshmen were the next highest scorers. Forwards JaRon Rush and Jerome Moiso each averaged double-figure scoring, and center Dan Gadzuric had a solid season, as well. Travis Reed, Ryan Bailey, and Rico Hines each contributed off the bench during their sophomore seasons, as freshmen Ray Young and Matt Barnes played important minutes as well.

The uncertainty leading into the season was reflected in the opening Associated Press rankings. UCLA was extremely talented. With two straight loaded new classes, Coach Lavin had worked wonders on the recruiting trail, but the team was mostly unproven. The Bruins began the season ranked No. 11.

Guard Earl Watson vs. Stanford, 1999 (Southern Branch Collection).

The team was still without Baron Davis for the first handful of games and working him back into the rotation took time. In the season opener, UCLA knocked off Santa Clara at Pauley Pavilion. Rush and Moiso led the way, and Watson was his usual steady self. After beating the University of San Francisco in a low-scoring game, it was time to play the big boys. On consecutive nights, No. 10 UCLA played No. 5 Maryland and No. 4 Kentucky in the Puerto Rico Shootout. Against the Terrapins, nothing worked for the Bruins on offense. Terence Morris and Steve Francis of Maryland combined for 40 points, and UCLA lost its first game of the year. The next night, it was much of the same. Though Moiso had a huge game, scoring 25 points, UCLA only scored 62 against Kentucky and lost. The Bruins were 2–2, but their spark plug was soon to return.

On December 2, Baron Davis rejoined the Bruins. He played only 16 minutes against Delaware State and took only five shots, making one. He wore a large brace on his knee and was noticeably rusty. Still, UCLA won big, and Davis came away from the game healthy. Three nights later, UCLA won their biggest game yet. In the John R. Wooden Classic, played in Anaheim, UCLA beat No. 11 Oklahoma State. Davis played a limited role again, and it took a complete team effort to pull out the victory. After beating the Cowboys, the Bruins began to click. After beating UNLV, they trounced the Cal State Northridge Matadors, 114–97. Seven Bruins scored in double figures, led by 21 points from Travis Reed. The Bruins then ran their winning streak to six since Davis's return, beating American and Loyola Marymount.

The 1999 Pac-10 season began on January 2, and for the second consecutive year, UCLA and Arizona played in the opening game. The Bruins were ranked No. 10 in the country and Arizona came to Los Angeles at No. 6. Jason Terry was one of five Wildcats to score in double figures, but his play wasn't enough. Davis had his finest game since returning. UCLA had slowly brought him along, increasing his minutes played throughout the nonconference schedule. Against the Wildcats, he was all the way back. He played 34 minutes, scored 20 points, dished out six assists, and had two steals. The Bruins held the Wildcats to just 37.7 percent from the field and won, 82–75. UCLA then beat ASU in overtime two days later to begin the conference season with a home sweep.

After winning eight straight games since Davis's return, the Bruins hit their first speed bump on their first Pac-10 road trip. Against the Oregon State Beavers, the UCLA offense struggled again. During Coach Lavin's first two years, UCLA was an offensive team, scoring a lot of points and holding opponents down just enough to come away on top. After finishing in the top 20 in scoring nationally the previous two years, UCLA fell to number 35 in 1999. Games with scores in the 60s were rare in previous years, but the low-scoring games became more common in Coach Lavin's third year. Against Oregon State, UCLA fell, 65–63. The Bruins shot just 28.4 percent from the field.

The Bruins bounced back with two more wins, but were then trounced by No. 4 Stanford on January 16. Mark Madsen led the way with 16 points for the Cardinal, and the Bruins again struggled from the floor, shooting just 40.6 percent and making only one three-pointer. Against USC, the free-flowing offense was back, as if UCLA flipped a switch. Four Bruins scored at least 16 points, the team shot 53.6 percent, and UCLA routed USC again. The Bruins then won four of their next five, losing only to Washington on the road. Davis and Watson each went over 20 points against the Huskies, but that wasn't enough.

Despite a stellar 17–5 record and top-15 national ranking, the Bruins showed they were national contenders. Baron Davis played better than ever, showing explosiveness uncommon in college basketball, but with a nucleus made up entirely of freshmen and sophomores, the Bruins struggled to play consistently all year. In a rematch with Stanford in Palo Alto, the Bruins lost again, and two nights later, the California Golden Bears blew them out. The Bruins snapped the losing streak against USC, and Rush and Davis exploded for a combined 50 points in a nonconference win over No. 21 Syracuse. Against Washington State, five Bruins scored in double figures, as Davis finished with 17 points and 11 assists. The Bruins then beat Washington and Arizona State after Earl Watson had two consecutive big games. In the Pac-10 and regular-season finale, UCLA fell to Arizona to finish with a 12–6 record in conference play, good for third place in the Pac-10 behind Stanford and Arizona.

Making a deep enough run in the NCAA Tournament was always Coach Steve Lavin's biggest problem at UCLA. In 1999, the Bruins were one-and-done. After being named the No. 5 seed in the South Regional, UCLA lost to No. 12 Detroit. The offense let down the Bruins, as they shot just 38 percent from the floor and turned the ball over 17 times. Davis played well, but it was the last time he would put on the uniform for the Bruins.

After a brilliant second half of his sophomore season, he earned All-America acclaim and was a top NBA prospect. After the season, he was selected with the third overall pick in the NBA draft. He went on to play 13 seasons in the NBA for six teams. He was a three-time All-Star, and though his NBA career was hampered by injuries, he was one of the most exciting players in the league when healthy.

For UCLA, it was time to look to the future. Davis was gone, and it was time to put the disappointing season behind them. The twentieth century soon ended, and the Bruins hoped to ring in the twenty-first century with more elite basketball.

University of Connecticut won the NCAA basketball national championship in 1999.

1999–2000

Coming into the new millennium, UCLA's future looked bright. Sure, they had to replace Baron Davis, one of the most talented Bruin players in the last decade, but others were capable of doing the job. Earl Watson, steady as always, was back for his junior season and was clearly the team leader. Six sophomores, including JaRon Rush, Dan Gadzuric, and Jerome Moiso all played meaningful minutes and took on important roles. Rush missed 24 games in the middle of the season due to issues with the NCAA but returned late in the season after being cleared. A new offensive star came forward, and he was just a freshman. Jason Kapono, an Artesia High School product, was one of the top recruits in the country. At 6'8", Kapono had good size for a small forward, but his shooting ability made him special. Wearing his patented headband, Kapono found openings in the defenses he faced and fired away from long distance at will. He was one of the best shooters in UCLA history, productive from the first moment he stepped foot on the court. Kapono later played in the NBA for nine seasons and was the first player in NBA history to lead the league in three-point shooting percentage two seasons in a row. He won two consecutive Three-Point Shootout contests at NBA All-Star Weekend, and he won an NBA title with the Miami Heat. Before Kapono was in the NBA, however, he was a Bruin, and for four seasons, he was one of the best to ever don the UCLA uniform.

The Bruins tipped off their season against Fairfield University on November 23 as the No. 13-ranked team in the nation. Moiso led the way with 20 points and 10 rebounds, and the Bruins began the season with an expected win. The first three games of the year were at home against subpar opponents, but the fourth game was against a team building a reputation as a strong West Coast basketball program. The first real test of the year for the now No. 11 Bruins came against No. 24 Gonzaga. The Bulldogs, coached by Mark Few, slowed down the pace, took good shots, and played lockdown defense. Gonzaga shot just 40.4 percent from the field, but the Bruins were even worse. UCLA shot 28.1 percent in the first half and just 24.1 percent in the second. The Bruins were just 4-for-26 from behind the three-point line and attempted only eight free throws the entire game. UCLA turned the ball over 16 times and Kapono was the leading scorer with just 10 points. In an ugly game, Gonzaga beat UCLA, 59–43.

UCLA was inconsistent throughout the rest of the early season nonconference slate. Against No. 19 DePaul, the Bruins played well. Kapono led the way with 20 points, and Ray Young, Gadzuric, and Moiso each had 15 or more. UCLA won, 76–58. The Bruins then beat Maine in the first game of the Pearl Harbor Invitational but followed that up by losing, 55–54, to Colorado State. Against South Florida, UCLA was pushed to overtime, but 20 points each from Moiso and Watson helped the Bruins escape with a win. The games remained close throughout the rest of nonconference play. On December 28, UCLA beat Pepperdine by just two points, and two days later, beat Purdue by just two again. The Bruins were 8–2 when Pac-10 play began and ranked No. 24 in the nation. Though some wildly believed that the world would end, UCLA rang in the New Year, new decade, new century, and new millennium just as it had in previous years. It was strong, looking to improve, and hoping to make a splash in the Pac-10 conference.

On January 6, UCLA traveled to Key Arena in Seattle for the first conference game of the year, and just like previous games, the score was close at the end. The Bruins led for the majority of the game but were never able to separate from the Huskies. At halftime, UCLA led, 31–27. In the second half, the Bruins scored 31 again, but UW did just enough to escape with a win. The Bruins shot 50 percent from the floor in the second half but repeatedly turned the ball over. Despite another big performance from Kapono, the Bruins lost, 63–62. It was a disappointing defeat and just the beginning of a terrible conference season.

Following the loss to Washington, the Bruins began an unfortunate win-one-lose-one trend. They bounced back to beat Washington State but then fell to USC. Against the Trojans, the Bruins played well on offense, though they couldn't stop Jeff Trepagnier and lost, 91–79, at the Sports Arena. The Bruins then snuck by North Carolina in a battle of unranked former powers at the Dean Smith Center, but five days later they had a tougher challenge. Though the Bruins made their way back into the AP rankings, coming in at No. 25, the ranking didn't last long. No. 2 Arizona beat the Bruins by 15 at Pauley. UCLA then beat ASU and finally broke the win-lose-win-lose string by beating Oregon State. UCLA was just 12–5 overall, including 3–3 in conference play, and their tailspin was just beginning.

On January 29, the Oregon Ducks blew out the Bruins on McArthur Court in Eugene. Stanford and Cal then swept UCLA the following week. Suddenly, UCLA was on the verge of missing the NCAA Tournament. On February 9, the Bruins broke their three-game losing streak with a five-point win over USC. Kapono led the way with 27 points, and Watson finished with 22 points and seven assists. Moiso scored 17 and grabbed 15 rebounds. Despite the encouraging performance, the Bruins weren't able to build off their win. No. 4 Syracuse beat UCLA in front of 29,731 fans at the Carrier Dome, and then Eddie House and the Arizona State Sun Devils blew out UCLA. While Kapono put on a good shooting display for the Bruins, scoring 24 points, House stole the show. He led all scorers with 40 points, and the Sun Devils beat the Bruins, 104–75. No. 4 Arizona handled business two days later, beating UCLA, 99–84. UCLA was now just 13–11 overall and chances of making the NCAA Tournament were quickly fading away. Just six games were left in the regular season.

When the Bruins returned home on February 24 to take on the Oregon Ducks, little optimism was left in the fan base. After losing six of the previous seven games, UCLA seemed to have little chance to turn the season around, but that's just what it did. Watson scored 22 points and grabbed 10 rebounds against Oregon in a win. He led the way against OSU the next game in another win. The winning streak reached three when UCLA traveled to Berkeley and destroyed the Golden Bears. Kapono scored 20 points, making five three-pointers, and UCLA won, 83–62. Things had quickly turned around for UCLA, but the next opponent was its toughest yet.

On March 4, 2000, unranked UCLA took on No. 1 Stanford on the road at Maples Pavilion. CBS televised the game, which turned out to be one of the most thrilling of the college basketball season. The Bruins donned navy blue alternate uniforms and played their best game of the year. At halftime, the score was 43–41, Stanford. Both teams were balanced in their scoring, and the game was close throughout. David Moseley led the way for the Cardinal, scoring

22 points. Four others who scored at least 10 helped, including Casey Jacobsen and Mark Madsen. Six Bruins scored in double figures, led by 19 from JaRon Rush. In the second half, UCLA outscored Stanford, 39–37, sending the game to overtime. With less than 40 seconds left and Stanford leading by one, the Bruins held the ball. A six-second differential was between the shot and game clocks, and the Bruins were letting the clocks run down as far as they could. With 12 seconds on the game clock, Ray Young took a contested mid-range jump shot from the left elbow. It came up short, but hit the bottom of the rim and bounced straight down. There was a mad scramble for the loose ball. Finally, the ball ended up in the hands of JaRon Rush on the left baseline. Rush looked to the basket and quickly fired a shot. No one was around him, and he knocked it down with 0:03 remaining on the clock. Stanford inbounded but was unable to get anything other than a half-court heave that landed well short. UCLA's bench stormed the court, dogpiling on top of Rush. Coach Steve Lavin jumped up and down celebrating the win. UCLA knocked off the No. 1 team in the nation and kept its tournament hopes alive.

In the final week of the conference season, the Bruins avoided the all-too-common letdown performance following a big win. They beat Washington State and then Washington to finish the regular season with a record of 19–11. Their 10–8 conference record was good for fourth place in the Pac-10. Though some Bruins faithful were concerned about UCLA's tournament prospects, the win over Stanford placed UCLA solidly in the tournament field, and by winning its final six games, the team was trending up. UCLA was the No. 6 seed in the Midwest Regional and began with a first-round matchup against the Ball State Cardinals.

On March 16, UCLA beat Ball State, 65–57, in the first round of the NCAA Tournament. After a sloppy first half, the Bruins turned it on in the second to seal the win. UCLA won the rebounding advantage, 46–34, though it turned the ball over 18 times. In the second round, the Bruins had a much tougher test. The Maryland Terrapins were the No. 3 seed in the region, a stacked team, and the clear favorite. But they stood no chance against the red-hot Bruins. Five Bruins scored in double figures. Watson finished with 17 points and a miraculous 16 assists and zero turnovers. Everything worked for UCLA in the first half. UCLA shot 21-for-29 from the field in the first 20 minutes and led, 49–33, at the break. In the second half, the squad picked up right where it left off. UCLA outscored Maryland, 16–2, in the first three minutes and were sparked by four three pointers by Watson. Watson turned in a truly a magnificent performance, but he suffered a facial injury in the second half that required four stitches and a minor procedure. The Bruins won, 105–70.

Watson played in the Sweet 16 matchup the following week, but like so many times in Coach Lavin's career, the Bruins couldn't get past the second week of tournament play. The Bruins, now a trendy pick to win the region to compete for the title, were blown out by No. 2 seed Iowa State. With the exception of Jerome Moiso, no one on the Bruins played well, and the team lost, 80–56. The season was over.

Michigan State University won the NCAA basketball national championship in 2000.

2000–01

While Coach Lavin was not yet on the hot seat, patience was running out. After reaching the Elite Eight in 1997, the Bruins failed to make it past the Sweet 16 the next three years. They hadn't been to the Final Four since the championship season in 1995, and the team lost at least eight games in each season since. In 2001, the Bruins were expected to be good. Leading scorer Jason Kapono was back for his sophomore year. He again led the team in scoring, averaging 17.2 points per game. Earl Watson was now a senior and had his best season yet. Juniors Dan Gadzuric and Matt Barnes increased their production, helping to make up for the loss of Jerome Moiso, who left UCLA early for the NBA draft. The schedule was difficult early, as UCLA competed in the stacked field at the Coaches vs. Cancer Tournament. No. 17 UCLA began its season against No. 7 Kansas at Madison Square Garden.

The opening game of the season was essentially a three-on-three battle. Jayhawk stars Kenny Gregory, Drew Gooden, and Kirk Hinrich combined for 63 points, while Bruins Jason Kapono, Earl Watson, and T. J. Cummings scored 67. Defense was optional in the first half, or so it seemed, as both teams scored at will. At the break, Kansas led, 57–51. Though UCLA outscored the Jayhawks, 47–42, in the second half,

Kansas won, 99–98. The Bruins shot 50.8 percent from the field and made 13 three-pointers, including six by Kapono, but defense and rebounding let them down. Kansas shot 54.8 percent from the field and outrebounded the Bruins by 15. UCLA was 0–1.

The Bruins bounced back against another tough opponent in the second game of the tournament. In a 97–92 overtime win against Kentucky, Kapono, Watson, and Ray Young each went over the 20-point mark, holding off Keith Bogans, Tayshaun Prince, and the Wildcats.

After returning home with a 1–1 record, the Bruins began the supposedly easier portion of their schedule. At the Pauley Pavilion, they faced Cal State Northridge. But the Matadors stunned UCLA. Jeff Parris scored 27 for the visitors. Though the Bruins had five players score in double figures, they turned the ball over 24 times and blew a seven-point halftime lead. The final score was CSUN 78, UCLA 74.

The Bruins were never quite able to find their rhythm in nonconference action. After beating UC Santa Barbara, they fell to Georgia Tech in the John R. Wooden Classic in Anaheim. Turnovers and poor second-half performances continued to haunt the Bruins. The men in blue and gold won three of their final four nonconference games before the start of Pac–10 play, with the lone loss coming against No. 15 North Carolina in Pauley Pavilion. Against the Tar Heels, Watson scored 30. But Joseph Forte of North Carolina scored 29, and UNC outrebounded the Bruins by 11.

When Pac-10 play began, UCLA was just 5–4 and were statistically just an average team. Just as they had one year earlier, suddenly the Bruins looked like a different team when they really needed to excel. After an uninspiring, often embarrassing conference season in 2000, UCLA looked to start Pac-10 play with better results in 2001, and they did. On January 4, UCLA beat the University of Washington, 86–64. Though the end result was a blowout win, the final score was a bit deceiving. The Bruins played a brilliant first half, shooting nearly 60 percent from the field, holding the Huskies to under 20 percent, and building a 49–16 lead at the break. Many of the same problems remained, however. UCLA played poorly in the second half and were outscored by 11. They turned the ball over 23 times, including five players with at least three turnovers. It was a win, and a dominant one in many ways, but UCLA still had much to improve on.

The Bruins continued to win and improved as the season went on. UCLA beat Washington State, despite a poor game from Kapono, and then knocked off No. 19 USC at home despite giving up 31 points to Sam Clancy. After running their winning streak to four, the Bruins then crushed Villanova. Leading the way was Kapono with 28 points. In their first road conference game of the year, UCLA easily handled Arizona State. Four Bruins scored at least 16 points, and the Bruins extended their winning streak to six. When the streak ended, it did so in blowout fashion. No. 17 Arizona beat UCLA by 25 points at McKale Center in front of 14,562 fans. Gilbert Arenas led the Wildcats with 22 points, and though Ray Young and Ryan Bailey played well for the Bruins, they were the only two to score in double figures. The Bruins turned the ball over 21 times, were outrebounded by 10, and again were demolished in the second half. After leading by eight at the break, UCLA was outscored, 55–22, in the second half.

UCLA won two of the next three, but as had been all too common over the previous two seasons, when UCLA lost, they lost big. On February 1, the Bruins lost by 29 points to the California Golden Bears, and two days later, they had a much tougher test. One year earlier, UCLA knocked off the No. 1-ranked Stanford Cardinal on the road. This year, led by Casey Jacobsen and Jason and Jarron Collins under Coach Mike Montgomery, the Cardinal came into the game with a perfect 20–0 record. The team would likely not finish the season undefeated, but the Bruins were unlikely to knock Stanford off. Coach Lavin and the boys hoped to prove people wrong. Unlike the previous season, the game was not a classic, and there was no dramatic ending, but the result was still the same. UCLA played well in the first half, shooting 56.7 percent from the field compared to Stanford's 40 percent, knocking down four threes compared to Stanford's one, and leading 40–37. Stanford remained in the game at the free-throw line, however. The home team attempted 15 free throws, making 12, and UCLA only reached the stripe three times, making two. Though the Bruins had struggled mightily in the second half of games throughout the year, they didn't against Stanford. UCLA won the second half, 39–36, and the game,

79–73. The two teams were even in turnovers, and UCLA outrebounded Stanford by three. The problems that plagued the Bruins throughout the year were set aside for one day, and the Bruins played clean basketball. Billy Knight led the team with 22 points, and Watson scored 20 points and dished out six assists. It was an unlikely victory following the blowout loss to Cal just two days earlier, but the Bruins desperately needed it.

Following the big win over Stanford, UCLA began playing its best basketball. For the second time, unranked UCLA beat a ranked USC team, this time knocking off the No. 22 Trojans at home. UCLA then knocked off DePaul behind 28 points from Kapono. The team beat No. 8 Arizona, despite Gilbert Arenas scoring 30. Gadzuric led the way for UCLA with 22 points and 17 rebounds. UCLA kept the winning streak alive against ASU, as Billy Knight's 23 points lifted the Bruins over the Sun Devils. The winning streak eventually reached eight games after wins over Oregon, Oregon State, and Cal. On March 3, the Bruins played the Stanford Cardinal in the much-anticipated rematch at Pauley Pavilion, with 12,523 fans in attendance. UCLA was red hot, now up to No. 12 in the rankings, and Stanford was still the No. 1 team in the country, sporting a 26–1 record, with its only loss coming against the Bruins exactly one month earlier. The game was well played on both sides. UCLA shot 51.5 percent from the field in the first half, but Stanford shot 60.7 percent. In the second half, UCLA shot 50 percent and Stanford shot 42.9. The Bruins played their best game of the year in the turnover department, forcing 14 for the Cardinal and turning it over just seven times themselves. The difference came in the rebounding category. The Cardinal outrebounded UCLA, 40–27, and had 11 more shot attempts at the end of the game. Matt Barnes had a career day for UCLA, scoring 32 points, but Stanford's balanced attack was enough to hold off the Bruins. Jacobsen, the Collins twins, and Ryan Mendez all scored 16 points, and the Cardinal beat the Bruins, 85–79. The Bruins then split their final two conference games to finish the regular season with a 21–8 overall record, 14–4 in Pac-10 play.

The Bruins were seeded No. 4 in the East Regional, and though their path through the first week of the NCAA Tournament seemed clear of serious danger, they were on a second week collision course with another basketball power. UCLA easily took care of Hofstra in the first round, though it actually trailed by four at the half before cruising in the second half to a big win. The second round provided no real challenge either. Utah State shot just 28.3 percent from the field, 22.2 percent from three, and 66.7 percent from the free-throw line. The Bruins easily advanced, beating the Aggies, 75–50, and moving on again to the Sweet 16.

After advancing to their fourth Sweet 16 in the last five years, UCLA took on the top-seeded Duke Blue Devils. Coached by Mike Krzyzewski, the Blue Devils entered the game with a 31–4 record. They were the second-highest scoring team in the nation and had a roster loaded with stars. Jay Williams was their leading scorer, averaging 21.6 PPG. Shane Battier scored 19.9 PPG, and Mike Dunleavy, Nate James, Carlos Boozer, and Chris Duhon were all important contributors. For UCLA, nothing went right offensively. Though players were able to control the Duke offense and slow that team down, it wasn't enough because of the offense. Despite trailing by just seven at halftime, UCLA wasn't able to seriously threaten the Blue Devils in the second half. Twenty-three total turnovers and porous free-throw shooting ultimately cost UCLA the game. Williams and Battier were unstoppable for Duke, and Williams finished with a game-high 34 points. Battier scored 24, and Duke advanced after beating UCLA, 76–63.

Duke University won the NCAA basketball national championship in 2001.

2001–02

The 2001–02 UCLA basketball team had higher expectations going into the season than any other team coached by Steve Lavin. The Bruins began the season ranked No. 3 in the nation by the Associated Press, and the mix of veteran and incoming talent was expected to produce significant results on the court. Jason Kapono was back for his junior season, and he again led the Bruins in scoring. Though Earl Watson left for the NBA, UCLA was expected to make up for his production with the help of others. Billy Knight, Matt Barnes, and Dan Gadzuric had their best seasons as seniors, with each averaging double figures in scoring. As a sophomore, T. J. Cummings was improved, and two freshmen, Dijon Thompson and Cedric Bozeman, were top

30 recruits nationally. For Coach Lavin, the 2002 season was make or break. He had proven that he was a quality coach, but he had yet to prove he could lead an elite program with high expectations. By the end of the season, many of those sitting on the fence had their answer. While the 2002 season wasn't Coach Lavin's final season in Westwood, it was the beginning of the end for him.

The season began on November 19 with a win over Houston in the Maui Invitational Tournament, but one day later he season went off the rails. Against the Ball State Cardinals, the No. 3 Bruins were blown out. Kapono scored 26 and Cummings added 15, but turnovers were the story—UCLA turned it over 22 times and forced only three. The Bruins lost, 91–73. After the devastating loss, UCLA beat South Carolina but then lost again in the home opener against Pepperdine. When the Bruins found success in 2002, they did so with a balanced offensive attack. When they didn't, oftentimes they relied too heavily on Kapono. In the loss against the Waves, Kapono scored 28 and knocked down five three pointers. The Bruins got back on track in nonconference play, but the two early-season losses stuck with the team throughout the year. The Bruins beat UC Riverside and then won a big nonconference game against No. 16 Alabama in the John R. Wooden Classic. Four Bruins scored in double figures, and the Bruins limited their turnovers to just nine. They then escaped with a one-point win over UC Irvine before beginning Pac-10 play.

The Bruins began conference play early, with the first game coming on December 20 against the University of Washington. The game was played at Hec Edmundson Pavilion in Seattle and was the first of a stretch of games won by the Bruins by single digits. The Bruins beat the Huskies, 85–79. Gadzuric led the way with 23 points and 13 rebounds. He then followed up his strong performance against the Huskies with another good one against the Washington State Cougars, scoring 20 points and leading UCLA to a five-point win. The Bruins then took on two more nonconference foes, beating Columbia and No. 20 Georgetown at home. Five Bruins scored at least 16 points against the Hoyas in the win. After four close wins, the Bruins returned to Pac-10 action, taking on the two Washington schools again in a scheduling quirk, and beating each by a dozen points. Against Washington State, Billy Knight scored 32 points to lead the team.

The Bruins were 11–2 overall and 4–0 in Pac-10 play when they took on the USC Trojans at the Great Western Forum on January 10. UCLA had won nine in a row, but USC was a strong team as well. The Bruins outshot the Trojans but were killed on the boards. Gadzuric pulled down 16 rebounds, but the Trojans relentlessly attacked the glass. USC had 24 offensive rebounds, including eight by David Bluthenthal. USC's aggressiveness brought its players to the free-throw line all night. The Trojans attempted 22 more free throws than the Bruins, knocked in 13 more, and won the game by four points.

After losing to USC, the Bruins took on a much better opponent, the top-ranked Kansas Jayhawks. In front of 12,280 fans at Pauley Pavilion, UCLA played its finest game of the season. For the third season in a row, UCLA knocked off the top-ranked team in the nation. The Bruins played a complete game. They led, 46–35, at halftime and went on to win 87–77. The Bruins got it done despite just 10 points from Kapono. Matt Barnes scored 27 points on just 14 field-goal attempts, and Billy Knight added 20 points. The game was truly a shocker, and after finishing with just a 1–1 record during the week, UCLA climbed up to No. 9 in the rankings.

As it turned out, the win over Kansas was the last time the Bruins looked like a serious national contender during the 2002 regular season. UCLA lost three of the next five conference games, falling to No. 15 Arizona, No. 17 Stanford, and unranked Oregon. The Bruins bounced back to beat Oregon State and then USC, but fell again to the Villanova Wildcats in Philadelphia. Despite just a 16–7 record, the Bruins remained ranked by the Associated Press, coming in at No. 20, when they faced No. 9 Arizona at Pauley Pavilion. Against the Wildcats, UCLA played from behind most of the way. With 10 minutes remaining in the game, UCLA was behind by eight, but then went on a spurt. With 5:34 remaining, Knight tied the score for UCLA with a three-point play. UofA then went on a run itself to build the lead back up to five, but UCLA wasn't done yet. A three-pointer by Kapono and a free throw by Barnes brought UCLA to within one. After Arizona hit a free throw to extend the lead to two, Kapono knocked down another three to put the Bruins on top, 74–73, with a little over a minute remaining. Jason

Gardner, who scored 25 for the Wildcats, followed up Kapono's big shot with one of his own, knocking down a three on the next possession to give Arizona a two-point lead. Kapono wasn't done, however. With 19 seconds left and trailing by two, Kapono caught a pass from Barnes and drained another three, putting UCLA up, 77–76. Arizona couldn't answer, and the Bruins won the game. Kapono finished with a team-high 20 points in the win.

Unfortunately for Coach Lavin and the Bruins, they didn't build off the win over Arizona and finish the season strongly. After trailing ASU by 14 in the second half, UCLA stormed back to take the lead, but couldn't hold it and lost, 69–68. Cal blew out UCLA the following week, and though the Bruins beat No. 10 Stanford on the road, they finished with just a split against the two Oregon schools. Over the final 16 games of the regular season, UCLA had just an 8–8 record. To make things worse, the Pac-10 tournament returned in 2002, but the Bruins weren't around very long to experience it. They lost to No. 25 Cal, 67–61, in front of a large crowd at Staples Center. UCLA was just 19–10 in the regular season and sixth in the Pac-10 conference, and the team was eliminated in the first round of the conference tournament.

Despite the struggles, the Bruins were invited to the NCAA Tournament. After being named the No. 8 seed in the West Regional, UCLA took on Ole Miss in the first round. The Rebels never stood a chance. UCLA shot 50.9 percent from the field and held Ole Miss to 33.9 percent. The final score was UCLA 80, Ole Miss 58. Despite the rough regular season for the Bruins, the team could play well against the best opponents. In the second round, the team had to do so again. On March 17, the Bruins took on the top seed Cincinnati Bearcats in Mellon Arena in Pittsburgh. The Bruins played a poor first half but didn't quit. After falling behind by 13, they began the long march back into the game. By the time the two teams went back to their locker rooms at halftime, UCLA trailed, 47–37. In the second half, UCLA flipped the switch. Kapono scored 17 of his 19 points in the second half, and Barnes scored all 17 of his points in the half. Gadzuric had a career day, scoring 26 points and grabbing 13 rebounds. Still, the fine performances weren't enough. At the end of regulation, the score was tied. At the end of overtime, it remained tied. The game went to a second overtime period, and UCLA finally pulled away from the top seed and won the game, 105–101. Leonard Stokes scored a career-high 39 points for the Bearcats, but UCLA's defense on All-American Steve Logan and Cincinnati's balanced offensive attack was the difference. The win was the first double-overtime game for UCLA in the NCAA Tournament since 1974, when Bill Walton and the Bruins famously lost to North Carolina State, ending the stretch of seven consecutive Bruins titles.

Following the big win that sent UCLA to the Sweet 16 for the fifth time in the last six seasons, Matt Barnes confidently said, "When we come to play, we can beat anybody in the country." The belief in much of the college basketball world was the same. UCLA was as talented as anyone in the country, but inconsistent. If the team were to peak at the right time, it could make an impact the rest of the way. Unfortunately for UCLA, the squad was never able to put it all together for more than a brief spurt. After beating the top-seeded Cincinnati Bearcats, UCLA lost to No. 12-seed Missouri, coached by Quin Snyder. The game was a letdown for all Bruins, and in the minds of many, it was an unacceptable loss. UCLA was out of the tournament again, and once more, the players had to watch as another team raised the championship trophy overhead.

University of Maryland won the NCAA basketball national championship in 2002.

2002–03

The 2003 UCLA basketball team was like many of the recent Bruins teams entering the season. It was ranked No. 14 in the country and was expected to win a lot of games. For UCLA, this was the new normal. They would mix in years of serious competition for the national title, but more often than not, they were just good, not great. In 2003, this new normal was unacceptable, and the Bruins had to find a way to break through and rejoin college basketball's elite tier. Coach Steve Lavin was on the hot seat and making another Sweet 16 and losing was not likely going to help him keep his job. The team had an historic win-loss record. Unfortunately for Coach Lavin and the Bruins, that wasn't a good thing.

While Coach Lavin had always been a good recruiter, his charm no longer had the same effect. The Bruins brought in just one top-100 recruit, Michael Fey, a seven-footer from Washington, but his contribution was minimal. Ryan Hollins, another seven-foot center, also joined the program, but as a freshman, he was too raw to make much of a difference. Marcedes Lewis saw some playing time, as well, but the 6'6" forward was a football player first and a basketball player second. His contribution was minor. The Bruins relied not on new faces but on the ones they had counted on over the previous years. Jason Kapono, now a senior, finished his career with another splendid season, leading the Bruins in scoring for the fourth season in a row. When his career came to an end, his name littered the UCLA record book. Kapono is UCLA's all-time leader in made three-pointers, attempted three-pointers, most three-pointers made in a season (2002), and most three-pointers in a game January 4, 2003). He is second all-time in three-point field-goal percentage, sixth in free-throw percentage, seventh in made field goals, ninth in games played, ninth in career points per game, and tenth in free throws made. Kapono finished his career with 2,095 points, third all-time at UCLA, behind only Don MacLean and Lew Alcindor. While Coach Lavin could always count on Kapono, sophomore Dijon Thompson was new to his role as a premier player. After a solid freshman season, Thompson scored 14.0 PPG as a sophomore. Junior T. J. Cummings and senior Ray Young averaged double-digit scoring as well.

After a disastrous exhibition season that saw the Bruins lose twice, UCLA began the regular season against the University of San Diego at home. Dijon Thompson scored 21, but the Bruins were killed on the glass, as USD outrebounded UCLA, 49–31, including 21 offensive rebounds. The Toreros shot 36 free throws to the Bruins' 17 and pulled off the major upset. UCLA was 0–1, and things were going to get much worse. Four days after the season-opening loss, the Bruins took on No. 4 Duke and lost again. Though the game was relatively close, J. J. Redick and the Blue Devils prevailed. After starting 0–2, UCLA dropped out of the AP rankings and wouldn't rejoin for nearly three full years. The Bruins finally got their first win of the season against Long Beach State in the third game. Kapono scored 28 points, and then Dijon Thompson scored 23 against the Portland Pilots in the fourth game. Though UCLA had played better against two poor opponents, they quickly slid back down. The Northern Arizona Lumberjacks handed UCLA another loss in nonconference play, and then No. 19 Kansas blew out the Bruins in Lawrence. The Jayhawks were led by Kirk Hinrich, who scored 27 points. The Bruins returned home, but the losing streak continued when they faced the University of Michigan. UCLA shot just 41.7 percent from the field and lost, 81–76.

The Bruins were just 2–5 overall when Pac 10 play began but were lucky to begin against perennial Pac-10 bottom dwellers Washington and Washington State. Against the Huskies, the Bruins offense was a mess. The players made 29 turnovers but still hung on to win. The Bruins played a cleaner game against Washington State two nights later, and Jason Kapono's performance grabbed the headlines. In 37 minutes, Kapono put on a shooting show for the ages. He finished 14-for-19 from the field and 9-for-10 from beyond the three-point line, and he made all seven of his free-throw attempts. His nine made three-pointers is a school record that still stands today. He finished with 44 points, six assists, five rebounds, and just one turnover. UCLA won, 98–83.

The two wins over the Pac-10 schools from Washington were rare moments that the Bruins could celebrate in 2003. On January 8, they returned home and began one of the worst stretches in UCLA history. The Bruins lost their next nine games, including three to ranked teams, and twice to USC. On January 18, No. 2 Arizona beat the Bruins by 35 points at Pauley Pavilion on national TV. The Bruins finally won another game on February 8 against Georgetown, their first win in five weeks, but the celebration was short-lived. Their next game was against No. 1 Arizona, this time in Tucson, and the result was much like the first time they met. Andre Iguodala was one of five Wildcats to score in double figures, as Arizona blew out UCLA, 106–70. Following the loss, UCLA won four out of the final seven regular-season games, but the season had already been a complete disaster. Not only did the Bruins lose many games, but also they often looked like they quit on Coach Lavin. Against Oregon, the Bruins scored just 48 points in a 31-point loss.

The Bruins finished with just a 6–12 record in Pac-10 play before the Pac-10 tournament. Standing in UCLA's way in the first round was the No. 1 team in the country. Arizona had beaten UCLA twice already, with the average margin of victory an astounding 35.5 points. As UCLA had done so often under Lavin, they rose to the occasion when no one expected the team to do so. The Bruins got off to a terrible start, trailing by 15 early, but they clawed back. In the second half, Arizona made another run, stretching the lead back to 15 with under 15 minutes to play, but again UCLA responded. With 15 seconds remaining, UCLA trailed by just one and had the ball. They went to their best player. Kapono got a shot off, but missed from 15 feet out, and Arizona got the rebound. After Salim Stoudamire knocked down two free throws, UCLA's season was on the line. While everyone expected UCLA to go to its sharpshooting senior star, another senior took the shot. Ray Young knocked in a three-pointer with 4.9 seconds left to tie the game. UCLA got a stop in the final seconds, went to overtime, and outplayed the Wildcats in the extra session. For the fourth year in a row, the Bruins beat the top-ranked team in the country. With the win, UCLA passed Notre Dame for most wins over the No. 1-ranked team in the country with 10.

The big win for UCLA was simply just one moment of joy in an otherwise maddening season. The Bruins lost to Oregon the next night and their season was over. For Coach Lavin, this was the end. He couldn't survive a 10–19 season at UCLA. It was the team's first losing season since 1948, the year before Coach John Wooden arrived. Their 54 consecutive seasons with a winning record is the most in NCAA history. When the Bruins took the court again in the fall, things looked different. Many of the players remained, but Coach Lavin did not. He was replaced by Ben Howland. In Coach Lavin's seven seasons as the UCLA head coach, the Bruins finished with a 145–78 record but won only one Pac-10 title and never reached the Final Four.

Syracuse University won the NCAA basketball national championship in 2003.

CHAPTER 12
Ben Howland (2003–2013)

Ben Howland, born on May 28, 1957, is one of the best coaches in UCLA basketball history. Although Coach John Wooden was the best, there is significant debate about the order of the rest. Jim Harrick won a national championship in 1995, Larry Brown took the Bruins to the championship game in 1980, and Gene Bartow and Gary Cunningham each won conference titles in their two seasons. Some may rank Howland the second-best coach in UCLA basketball history. Others will place him further down the list. At the time Howland was hired in 2003, he was already an established coach, perhaps the most accomplished coach in UCLA history at the time he was hired. He was different in many ways than the men who came before him and similar in other ways. Coach Howland embraced what it meant to lead the Bruins. He didn't shy away from expectations, though there were seasons of disappointment. Coach Howland was different in another way, perhaps what he is most remembered for now. While UCLA has long been a program built on spectacular offensive play, Coach Howland was a defense master. His greatest teams at UCLA played incredible defense, harassing teams and making their guards pay. Coach Howland was unique. His big men hedged, his forwards were active, and his guards embraced the challenge of staying in front of their man. He called timeouts after scores to set up his defense, his voice booming throughout Pauley Pavilion shouting defensive instructions, and he stressed the little details that made teams great. By the time Coach Howland arrived at UCLA, he had a well-defined leadership and coaching philosophy, built around a life in basketball.

As a kid, Ben Howland was obsessed with basketball and obsessed with UCLA. Howland was born in Oregon but spent most of his youth in California, first attending Dos Pueblos High School in Goleta and then finishing his final three years of high school in Cerritos. By the time Howland was a star in high school, he knew what he wanted to do with his life. In eighth grade, he told friends that he was going to be a Division I basketball coach someday. His love of basketball began in the Boys and Girls Club in Santa Barbara County. In trying to channel his youthful energy, his mom sent him there, the beginning of a path that led toward him becoming one of the most well-known college basketball coaches of the last two decades. He went to school, to the courts, back home to eat, and then to play more basketball at night. During basketball season, he was either playing with his team, playing at the club, or watching UCLA basketball replays on his small black-and-white television at night. Just as many remember where they were in some of the most memorable moments in history, Ben Howland remembers just where he was when he saw UCLA lose to North Carolina State in the 1974 NCAA Tournament, ending its streak of seven consecutive titles. He watched the game at a local department store and went home crushed.

At Cerritos High School, Ben played just how he coached later. He was a hard-nosed, in-your-face defensive player. After playing zone during his sophomore season, Howland convinced his coach that man-to-man defense was the sure way to win games, the best and most effective way to shut down any offense. There were no gaps in great man-to-man defense, but a good offensive team could always beat the zone. His coach listened. Other coaches came calling for Ben as well. The Cerritos High School football coach told Ben that he should play football and that basketball players were wusses. The comment enraged Ben. He was not a wuss, and he spent every day trying to prove how tough he was. Still, after two years as an all-league and all-CIF (California Interscholastic Federation) performer in high school, he didn't have many options to continue his playing career.

In 1976, Ben Howland enrolled at Santa Barbara City College. He played two seasons for the Vaqueros before transferring to Weber State for his final two years. While in college, Howland was as fiery as ever. He knew he could play college ball, but he was constantly doubted. He played with rage and intensity unmatched by anyone else he faced. His jump shot was good, especially at the top of the key, but his defensive play made him stand out. In his two seasons at Weber State, the Wildcats made the NCAA Tournament each year. Howland, who knew that he wanted to coach, used his college playing career as a time to learn about coaching. During scrimmages, he yelled to his teammates on defense, "Get your hands up! Get your hands up!"

While at Weber State, Howland met his future wife, Kim, captain of the cheer squad. He also mapped out his future coaching plans. Though he played one year of professional basketball in Uruguay, he knew he wanted to coach, first at UC Santa Barbara and eventually UCLA. He just had to figure out how to get there. In 1981, Howland took his first coaching job, a graduate assistant position at Gonzaga. He helped coach the team while he also completed his master's degree in administration and physical education. One of his tasks as a coach was to work directly with future NBA superstar John Stockton.

The following year, Howland moved on to UC Santa Barbara, in a place he always wanted to be. While at Weber State, his teammates got tired of hearing about how much he liked living in Santa Barbara. Returning home was a dream come true. For 12 seasons, Howland was an assistant coach for the Gauchos. Beginning in 1992, he began to seek out head coaching jobs, but he wouldn't get his opportunity for a couple more years. In 1994, Ben Howland became the head coach of the Northern Arizona University Lumberjacks, where he had plans to do things his own way. He wanted tall, mobile athletes with long arms, quick feet, and tenacity, who played smothering defense and made life hell for opposing offenses. This wasn't easy at first at NAU. Recruiting the type of athletes he needed to Flagstaff was always going to be his biggest challenge, and he struggled in his first two seasons. The offense wasn't dynamic enough, and he didn't have the athletes he needed to play the defense he wanted. He had to change his strategy, and he did. Howland started bringing in more shooters, spreading the court, and taking a lot of threes. After finishing with just a 14–38 record in his first two years, the Lumberjacks won the Big Sky conference in 1997 and 1998, leading the nation in three-point percentage and scoring a school-record 80.2 points per game in 1998 and reaching the NCAA Tournament. After another strong season in 1999, the Pittsburgh Panthers came calling, and Ben Howland was off to the Big East. While at Pitt, Howland did what he had done at NAU. He was now able to play the style he preferred, and the results were positive. After just a 13–15 record in his first year, the Panthers won the Big East in his third and fourth seasons, reaching the Sweet 16 of the NCAA Tournament each year. Ben Howland was now a well-known college basketball coach and a hot commodity. He was already at a top job, but he wanted more and wanted to be somewhere else. Following the abysmal 2003 season for UCLA, Steve Lavin was fired, and Ben Howland was hired as the 12th basketball coach in UCLA history.

Coach Ben Howland's tenure at UCLA is best described in two distinct periods. His first five years were positive. It took time to turn around the Bruins, and his first season was difficult, but the Bruins were headed in the right direction. They continued to improve, and by 2006, they were one of the top teams in America. Following the 2008 season, however, the Bruins began to slide. They were still good for four of his final five years, but they often underperformed, and off-court problems piled up. Fans grew tired of his coaching style, as UCLA didn't score many points, was rarely flashy, and was no longer playing at an elite level. Prominent UCLA basketball alumni were vocal about their issues with Howland's style,

Ben Howland (Dick Hansen Collection, CC by 2.0, cropped).

including Bill Walton. The Bruins won the Pac-12 Conference in Howland's final season, but they failed to make a Sweet Sixteen appearance in his final five years. As top college programs continued to lose freshmen to the NBA, whether they were ready or not, Coach Howland had more difficulty building a winner at UCLA. Following 10 years, Ben Howland was fired in 2013. While coaching the Bruins, he won 233 games and lost 10. Howland made seven trips to the NCAA Tournament, three to the Final Four, and one to the national championship game. He won four Pac-10/12 titles in the process.

For two years after he was fired, Ben Howland was out of basketball. For the first time in his professional life, he wasn't on a sideline. Finally, on March 24, 2015, Mississippi State hired Howland as the 20th head coach in school history. Like each of his three previous stops, Coach Howland had a tough task on his hands early but was able to turn it around. In his first season, the Bulldogs won just 14 games, but by year three, they won 25. At Mississippi State, expectations are lower, players are more likely to stay longer, and Coach Howland has been given ample time to make his mark.

When discussing Ben Howland among UCLA fans now, the answers are different than they used to be. No other coach in recent UCLA football or basketball history has spurred debate like Ben Howland. He is a good coach; few deny that. His success for a short time was unquestionable. He also lost control of the program, was slow to adapt to the changing college basketball world, and was criticized for many other things. Like any coach, Ben Howland had faults. But for three years in the middle of his run, Ben Howland was one of the best coaches in America, and UCLA was one of the best teams. His tenacity that made him a star in high school, a defensive stopper in college, and a rising assistant coach helped carry him to UCLA. His success at NAU and Pitt was a precursor to the success he had at UCLA, and then later at Mississippi State.

2003–04

Following the Bruins' 10–19 season in 2003, Coach Ben Howland had a tough task on his hands in his first year. Not only did UCLA struggle the previous year, but also its best player, Jason Kapono, was off to the NBA. The Bruins played a different style of basketball under Coach Howland than under Coach Lavin, dedicating more time in practice to the defensive end and being more selective on the offensive side. The Bruins were in a complete rebuild, and time was needed to see the results of their work. But players were committed from day one to Coach Howland's style. The 2004 Bruins weren't among the most talented teams to ever play in Westwood. In fact, the team struggled mightily and was in desperate need of a talent infusion, but players did play hard. Dijon Thompson, now a junior, was UCLA's best player. He led the team in scoring with 14.4 points per game. Along with Thompson, senior T. J. Cummings, one of the most dependable Bruins of recent years, had another strong season, finishing second in scoring on the team. Junior Cedric Bozeman, once one of the top recruits in the country, and sophomores Ryan Hollins and Michael Fey all struggled for parts of the season, but all were important contributors to the team, as was the oft-injured Brian Morrison. Only one freshman played significant minutes for the Bruins, and he showed sky-high potential. Trevor Ariza, a 6'8" forward, averaged 11.6 points and 6.5 rebounds per game and was a solid defensive player.

Ben Howland began his UCLA career, and the 2003–04 Bruins began their season, on November 29 against the University of Vermont Catamounts at Pauley Pavilion. The game was uncomfortably close, and in the first half, a disaster seemed in the making. Vermont led, 34–23, at the break, UCLA shot just 31 percent from the field, and the Bruins looked too slow and unathletic to play the lockdown defense Coach Howland demanded of them. Forward Taylor Coppenrath scored 20 points in the first half to give the Catamounts the double-digit lead. In the second half, however, the Bruins turned it around. Coppenrath continued his scoring barrage, finishing with 38 points, but he was alone. UCLA climbed back in the game, and thanks to a career-high 20 points from Michael Fey and the go-ahead free throw by Ryan Hollins with 4.8 seconds left, the Bruins escaped with a one-point win.

In the second game of the year, UCLA won again, and this time it was junior guard Brian Morrison who was the star. Though his season was limited by injuries to his hamstring and ankle, Morrison was a talented player and had several big games for the Bruins early in the season. Against UC Riverside, he finished with a game-high 28 points in the win.

The Bruins were 2–0, but the competition would get much more difficult. In the John R. Wooden Classic in Anaheim, UCLA took on Kentucky, the No. 9 team in the country, in front of 17,816 fans at the Arrowhead Pond. Much like the opening game of the season, UCLA got off to a slow start, and in this game, its offense let the team down. UCLA did a fine job defending the Wildcats, holding them to just 29 percent shooting in the first half, but UCLA shot just 24 percent. At halftime, UCLA trailed, 27–17, which was much closer than it looked like it would be early in the game. They had fallen behind, 7–0, just minutes in, and Kentucky stretched its lead to 23–6 midway through the half. In the second half, the Bruins picked up their offense a bit and continued to hold the Wildcats offense down. Though UCLA was able to get close, Kentucky led the entire way. The final score was Kentucky 52, UCLA 50.

After UCLA's first loss, they traded wins and losses for the rest of nonconference play. Occasionally, UCLA looked like a solid team, but more frequently it seemed a long way from being a contender. UCLA beat Loyola Marymount, though an overtime period was needed to secure the win. Against UC Santa Barbara, the Bruins played poorly again at home and suffered an embarrassing loss, 61–60. The Bruins bounced back to upset Michigan State at home in an ugly game but then traveled to Ann Arbor and lost to the University of Michigan the next game. Dijon Thompson scored 21 points, but a balanced attack by the Wolverines was too much for the Bruins. When 2003 turned to 2004 and conference play began, UCLA was just 4–3, and the schedule was going to get a lot more difficult.

UCLA's 2004 season ended with a streak of poor play unmatched by any team since before John Wooden took over, and the team was not a contender on the national level or even in the Pac-10. But they could play solid basketball in spurts and had a short stretch of solid play that made college basketball fans take notice. UCLA's best spurt came at the beginning of Pac-10 action. On January 2, the Bruins faced the Oregon State Beavers in the Pac-10 season opener. It was, so far, the best game UCLA had played all season. Ariza led the Bruins in scoring, collecting 24 points on just 13 field-goal attempts with 11 makes, and he also collected nine rebounds. The Bruins were 1–0 in conference play and just getting started. Against Oregon, Cummings and Bozeman each scored 12, Thompson and Janou Rubin each scored 13, and the Bruins won again. Despite 17 turnovers, the Bruins were able to beat the Ducks by shooting 52.9 percent for the game and holding Oregon to just 40.3 percent.

After the opening-weekend sweep, the Bruins kept their good play going the following week. In a preview of what was to come in later years, UCLA put on a defensive clinic on the road against the Washington State Cougars. In front of a crowd of just 2,861 fans, the Bruins held WSU to just 29.6 percent shooting in the first half, 37.5 percent for the game, and 30.8 percent from from the three-point arc. UCLA limited possessions with slow, deliberate offense, and though they only scored 48 points, that was enough: UCLA 48, WSU 45. Neither team collected any fast-break points. Two days later, the Bruins won again, but the win wasn't satisfying for Coach Howland. UCLA's smothering defense was suddenly gone, and the Washington Huskies scored far too often for Coach Howland's liking. Will Conroy scored 29 points for the Huskies and led a second-half comeback that forced the game to overtime with the help of 24 UCLA turnovers. UCLA gave up 48 second-half points, more than it gave up all game against Washington State. At the end of regulation, the score was tied at 75. The Bruins outscored the Huskies, 11–9, in the extra five minutes and won their fourth in a row. The Bruins then beat Arizona State at home to run their record to 5–0 in Pac 10 play. Cummings and Thompson combined for 40 points in the win, and the Bruins defense was again suffocating. Though the early-season success in conference play was encouraging for those rooting for UCLA, the collapse that ensued over the final 16 games was heartbreaking. The 2004 season was an extremely rare one for UCLA in that the Bruins were not used to seasons with no real expectations for success. Fans understood that the team was not likely to compete for the conference title in Coach Howland's first year, and success on a national level was not even a consideration yet. Still, losses are painful, and losing streaks can be unbearable. The Bruins were about to begin one of the worst stretches in school history.

On January 17, the 9–3 UCLA Bruins took on the 10–3 Arizona Wildcats, ranked No. 7 in the country, but coming off a loss to USC two nights earlier. The game was televised nationally on ABC, and in front of 12,621 fans at Pauley Pavilion, the Bruins were blown out. Arizona finished the season with the number-one scoring offense in the country, and UCLA was powerless to stop the team. The final score was 97–72 in favor of Arizona, and it could have been worse. Channing Frye scored 26 for the Wildcats, Salim Stoudamire had 25, and Hassan Adams scored 23. Things only got more difficult the next week. UCLA played undefeated No. 2 Stanford and lost again. Cal, USC, St. John's, and Washington State all knocked off UCLA as well. Against St. John's, Ariza scored 19, but no other Bruin had more than six points. After losing six in a row, UCLA finally won another game, this time against the University of Washington. Though Brandon Roy scored 30 points for the Huskies, a balanced offensive attack for the Bruins and a dominant performance on the boards helped UCLA get back in the win column.

The joy of the win over UW didn't last long, and UCLA was soon back to losing games in bunches. On the Bruins' trip to Arizona, UCLA had two frustrating losses. Against ASU, the Bruins pushed the Sun Devils to overtime, but fell. Ike Diogu finished with 27 points and 13 rebounds for ASU. Arizona then blew out the Bruins, 107–83. Salim Stoudamire was unguardable, finishing with 34 points. The Bruins finally fell under .500, with their record now standing at 10–11.

Though the Bruins beat California, it was their last win of the season. No. 1 Stanford came south to Los Angeles and went home with another win. USC beat UCLA by a single point in overtime, and Notre Dame, Oregon State, and Oregon all did enough to beat the Bruins. With the regular season over, UCLA had just a 7–11 record in Pac-10 play. After starting 5–0, the Bruins finished in eighth place in the Pac 10, the worst finish for the Bruins since the conference expanded to 10 teams. In the first game of the Pac-10 tournament, it was much of the same. The Washington Huskies beat the Bruins, 91–83, and UCLA ended its season with a six-game losing streak. Coach Howland's first season, one that saw promise early in the Pac-10 season, was finally over. The Bruins won just two out of their final 16 games, finishing with back-to-back losing seasons for the first time since 1942.

University of Connecticut won the NCAA basketball national championship in 2004.

2004–05

The 2004–05 UCLA basketball season was different than all others under Coach Ben Howland. After struggling mightily during the second half of the previous season, the Bruins improved greatly in Coach Howland's second year. The offense jumped from 234th in the nation in scoring to 60th. The defense, however, Ben Howland's calling card, was worse. UCLA fell to number 245 in the nation in scoring defense. The Bruins certainly weren't where Coach Howland wanted them to be, but more positive signs were in year two than in year one.

Dijon Thompson, now a senior, was UCLA's clear leader. He led the team in points and rebounds, averaging 18.4 points and 7.9 rebounds per game in his final season in Westwood. Junior Michael Fey was a steady presence at center, and Brian Morrison and Ryan Hollins were key figures again. New additions arrived, as well, and Coach Howland's 2004 recruiting class was one of the best in recent UCLA history, one that helped turn the tide of the program. Jordan Farmar and Arron Afflalo were two local recruits that made big impacts for the Bruins as freshmen. Farmar, a 6'2" guard, had a smooth style, a knack for getting where he wanted to be on the court, good vision, and a solid jump shot. Farmar averaged 13.2 PPG and led the team with 5.3 assists per game. At 6'5" 215 pounds, Afflalo, also a guard, was like a bulldog—strong, physical, and relentless. He moved well without the ball and put himself in spots to score. He was a very good shooter, a great on-ball defender, and one of the most competitive players to ever put on the blue and gold uniform. Josh Shipp, a streaky scorer at small forward, and Lorenzo Mata, a defensive force at center, were important players, as well, and their roles would continue to increase as their careers went on.

The Bruins began their season with four straight wins over lower-level opponents. A far cry from the season prior, UCLA took care of the teams it was supposed to beat and looked good doing it. Four Bruins scored in double figures in the season opener against Chicago State, and UCLA outrebounded the Cougars 41–21. The Bruins then beat Western Illinois, UC Irvine, and Long Beach State. Against LBSU, Thompson finished with a game-high 25 points, and Afflalo added 21 points and six assists. Coming off two straight terrible seasons, few thought that UCLA would have a smooth ride from beginning to end in 2005, and bumps in the road were expected. Against Boston College in the John R. Wooden Classic, the Bruins hit one of those bumps. The Eagles beat the Bruins, 74–64, behind 20 points from Craig Smith. UCLA won two of its final three before conference play began, beating Pepperdine with the help of 25 points from Farmar, escaping with a two-point win over Michigan, behind 29 points from Thompson, and then falling to Michigan State. The Bruins were 6–2 when conference play began.

UCLA tipped off in the Pac-10 opener on New Year's Eve and felt the sting of defeat. The Bruins outrebounded the Beavers, 43–27, shot a better percentage from the field, scored 10 more points in the paint, and had more than double the Beavers' second-chance points. UCLA turned it over 19 times, however, and the Beavers had only 10. OSU hit two more three pointers as well, and though UCLA led by five at the break, OSU came out on top, 85–80.

The Bruins bounced back to win their next four conference games. Five Bruins scored at least a dozen points in a win over Oregon. Against Washington State, the Bruins played a horrendous first half, falling behind by 15 at the break, but came all the way back in the second half to force overtime. One OT period wasn't enough, and the game went to a second OT. UCLA finally prevailed, 80–77. Two nights later, the Bruins played one of their finest games of the Ben Howland era thus far. In front of a large crowd at Pauley Pavilion, UCLA knocked off No. 12 Washington, 95–86. Thompson again starred for UCLA, leading the way with 29 points and nine rebounds. Brian Morris scored 19 and Jordan Farmar had 13 points and seven assists. The Bruins won the turnover battle, won the rebounding battle, had more second chance points, and scored more fast-break points. The Bruins then snuck by ASU the following week to keep their winning streak alive.

Though the 2005 Bruins were greatly improved over 2004, great concern arose during stretches. After winning four in a row, UCLA lost three straight, although, unlike 2004, UCLA righted the ship to win games at a high clip. The Bruins played a close game against a ranked Arizona team on the road but then looked lackluster and struggled against Stanford and Cal at home. On January 29, UCLA beat USC at the Sports Arena, 72–69. Dijon Thompson scored 24, outdueling Nick Young, who scored 22 for the Trojans. Against Washington State, the game again came down to the wire, just as their first meeting at Pauley Pavilion had one month earlier. Thompson scored 24 again, and the Bruins beat the Cougars in overtime. The Bruins weren't able to keep their momentum going, however, and lost three of their next five. With a 14–9 record, UCLA was headed toward missing an NCAA berth. The team needed to make a late-season run, and that's just what it did.

On February 24, UCLA beat USC again, in the first of what turned out to be a four-game winning streak to close the regular season. Against the Trojans, Afflalo led the way with 22 points and the Bruins were once again dominant on the boards, outrebounding USC, 42–26. The Bruins then beat Notre Dame, holding that team to under 40 percent shooting, and finished the season with a home sweep over Oregon and Oregon State. The Bruins finished the regular season 18–9 overall and 11–7 in Pac-10 play. After finishing in eighth place in 2004, the Bruins climbed all the way up to third place in 2005. Despite losing to Oregon State in the first round of the Pac-10 tournament, UCLA had done enough to earn a trip to the NCAA Tournament for the first time under Coach Howland.

The Bruins were named the No. 11 seed in the Albuquerque Regional and took on Texas Tech, coached by Bobby Knight, at Tucson, Arizona, in the first round. The Bruins weren't yet ready to be a serious contender in March, as the Red Raiders beat the Bruins, 78–66. The Bruins shot 50 percent from the field in the first half, but the Red Raiders shot 57.1 percent. In the second half, UCLA slowed down on offense, but Texas Tech continued shooting the lights out. The Red Raiders ended up shooting 61.5 percent from the field for the entire game and ended UCLA's season in dominant fashion. Dijon Thompson's career came to an end, and though UCLA had many pieces that excited fans going forward, the Bruins still appeared a ways away. But the success came faster than anyone imagined. The 2006 Bruins were going to make a statement.

University of North Carolina won the NCAA basketball national championship in 2005.

2005–06

In 2006, the Bruins did what no one expected. The Bruins ascended back into the realm of the college basketball elite, the contenders that compete for the title year in and year out, which most thought was at least another year away. Coach Howland had needed time to make his mark, to shape a team in his image. By 2006, the Bruins were very close to what he envisioned. After finishing 245th in scoring defense in 2005, the Bruins finished 10th in the country in 2006. They were long, athletic, and motivated on the defensive end. They lacked firepower on offense, but they took good shots, played smart basketball, and rarely beat themselves. Dijon Thompson was gone, but the Bruins had others to fill the void left by their former top scorer. Arron Afflalo and Jordan Farmar followed up their solid freshmen seasons with even better sophomore years. Afflalo led the team in scoring with 15.8 points per game, and Farmar led the team in assists per game for the second season in a row. As seniors, Cedric Bozeman and Ryan Hollins had their best seasons, mostly contributing on the defensive end with their length, timing, anticipation, and athleticism. Josh Shipp suffered through injuries throughout his sophomore season and was limited to just four games. Joining the returning players was a freshmen class that helped turn around UCLA's program. Luc Richard Mbah a Moute, a 6'8" forward from Yaoundé, Cameroon, was the team's top rebounder, an elite defensive player, and, in a quiet way, a leader, exemplifying everything Coach Howland looked for in a player. Joining Mbah a Moute was another freshman that built his Bruins legacy through hard work, determination, and clutch play. In 2006, Darren Collison was primarily a backup point guard, though in time his role increased, and he, like Mbah a Moute, became a crowd favorite. Three other freshmen, Alfred Aboya, also from Cameroon; Michael Roll, a knockdown shooter; and Ryan Wright, a 6'9" power forward from Canada, played smaller roles but were still important to the overall team success.

After falling out of the Associated Press rankings toward the end of the 2002 season and remaining on the outside looking in, UCLA finally had a number next to its name again at the beginning of the 2005–06 season. The Bruins began the season ranked No. 18 in the country when they took on the New Mexico State Aggies in the NIT Season Tip-Off at Pauley Pavilion. The Bruins were sharp to begin the season. Afflalo led the way with 23 points, and Farmar finished with 18 points and eight assists. The Bruins outrebounded the Aggies, finished with less turnovers, and shot 55 percent from the field in the win. The season was off to a fine start, and more winning was to come. The Bruins held Temple to just 47 points and Delaware State to 37 in the remaining two games of the NIT Season Tip-Off at Pauley Pavilion. The Bruins continued the nonconference showcase event at Madison Square Garden, but now the competition was much more difficult. Against the No. 11 Memphis Tigers, coached by John Calipari, the game was a contrast in styles. Memphis was one of the top offensive teams in the country, and UCLA was one of the top defensive teams. Something had to give. Unfortunately for UCLA, offense won this matchup. Shawne Williams led the way with 26 points for the Tigers, and Farmar's contribution of 28 points, seven assists, and five rebounds wasn't enough. The Tigers shot over 60 percent from the field in the first half and 53.4 percent for the game and scored 88 points. The Bruins played well offensively themselves, but fell by eight.

Over the remainder of the nonconference slate, UCLA looked more like the defensive powerhouse that fans saw in the first three games. Though it wasn't pretty, UCLA finished the NIT Season Tip-Off with a 57–56 win over Drexel at Madison Square Garden. The team then beat Albany and Coppin State at home before knocking off No. 17 Nevada at the Wooden

Classic in Anaheim. Farmar finished with 24 points on 10 of 13 from the field against the Wolfpack. The Bruins then beat Michigan in Ann Arbor and Wagner College and Sacramento State at home before the beginning of Pac-10 action.

The Bruins were 10–1 when conference play began, and the team was now ranked No. 11 in the country and looked like a serious conference contender. The next few games were against familiar opponents. The Bruins beat Stanford, 71–54, to run their winning streak to eight, but disappointment was right around the corner. Although UCLA held Stanford to just 29.2 percent from the field, the California Golden Bears shredded the UCLA defense to shoot 52.2 percent two days later. Against the Cardinal, Afflalo played well in the win, but against Cal, he couldn't win the game alone. UCLA fell to the Golden Bears, 68–61. Though the 2006 UCLA basketball team is remembered for how the season ended, such a game showed it wasn't always an elite team.

After losing to Cal, UCLA bounced back with three straight wins, and fans regained confidence. The team traveled to Tucson, Arizona, and beat a ranked Wildcats team before sneaking by ASU and Washington in two close games. UCLA then lost two of their next three against tough competition, in what was a low point. No. 13 Washington traveled to Los Angeles and beat No. 11 UCLA on January 14, and one week later, No. 12 West Virginia did the same. The games were low scoring, as were many others the rest of the season. Even when UCLA won, the team never made games easy. In the final 17 games of the regular season, the Bruins scored 80 or more points only two times.

After falling to West Virginia, the Bruins began to click. Against Oregon, Mbah a Moute finished with 15 points and 10 rebounds, and the Bruins held the Ducks to just 32.2 percent from the field and won, 56–49. The results were much the same the rest of the way. The defense was elite, the offense did enough, and the team was tough. Players took smart shots, limited possessions, and relied on offensive execution, fanatical hustle, and mental sharpness to outlast their opponents. Mbah a Moute was again key in a win over Oregon State, Farmar and Afflalo shined against Arizona State, and Afflalo outdueled Arizona's Hassan Adams in another win. Against Washington State, the Bruins put on a defensive show. The game was played at Beasley Coliseum in Pullman, Washington, and the fans saw their home team Cougars suffocated by UCLA's defense. In the first half, the Cougars shot just 26.1 percent from the field. In the second, they shot 28.6 percent. For the game, they were just 14-for-51 from the field, or 27.5 percent, and didn't make a single three pointer all game. They attempted just five throws and made only two. Aron Baynes was the leading scorer for WSU, and he scored only 10 points. No other Cougar scored more than four. UCLA won, 50–30, to collect its 20th win of the season.

Just as the Bruins looked to be playing their best basketball, they suddenly lost two straight, and all momentum was gone. They were in a tight race with the Washington Huskies for the Pac-10 title; when No. 21 Washington beat No. 13 UCLA on February 11, the race became much more difficult. The Bruins then lost to USC eight days later and fell to 10–4 in conference play. Over the final two weeks, however, the Bruins got back on track. They blew out both Oregon and Oregon State, winning by an average margin of 17.5 points. Against Cal, the game wasn't as easy. Afflalo started slowly and Farmar struggled for much of the game. At halftime, UCLA trailed, 31–20. In the second half, Afflalo took over. He scored 21 of his 25 points after halftime, leading UCLA all the way back and forcing overtime. Midway through the OT period, Afflalo knocked in a big three-pointer to put UCLA ahead for good. The final score was UCLA 67, Cal 58. With the win, the Bruins and the Bears split their regular season series for the eighth year in a row, and more important, UCLA clinched at least a share of the Pac-10 title for the first time in nine years. That wasn't enough, and that wasn't the goal. After the game, Afflalo said, "Right now, we're co-Pac-10 champs. We're definitely not satisfied with that. We'll enjoy this bus ride and enjoy tonight, but after that, it's business as usual. Being cochamps was not one of our goals. It was being Pac-10 champs." Two days later, the Bruins did indeed take care of business and rout the Stanford Cardinal to win the Pac-10 title. The Bruins played one of their cleanest games of the year, shooting 50 percent from the field while turning the ball over only seven times, outrebounding the Cardinal by nine, and winning on the scoreboard, 75–54.

The Bruins weren't done collecting trophies when the regular season ended. The surging Bruins had the Pac-10 tournament to play, and by now, they were a force. In front of large crowds at Staples Center, the Bruins demolished Oregon State, Arizona, and Cal on three consecutive nights. Against the Beavers, Ryan Hollins finished with 17 points and eight rebounds to lead the way. Darren Collison was the Bruins' leading scorer against the Wildcats in the semifinals with 15 points off the bench, and Afflalo led the way for the Bruins in the championship game against Cal. The Pac-10 tournament championship was the first for UCLA since Reggie Miller and the Bruins won in 1987 (no tournament existed from 1991 to 2001).

When the NCAA Tournament bracket was announced, much of the discussion was about UCLA. The team was surging, clearly presenting itself to the selection committee as one of the top teams in the country. When the brackets were unveiled, UCLA was where most thought they would be: the No. 2 seed in the Oakland Regional. The top seed was the Memphis Tigers, a team UCLA lost to early in the season.

But the Bruins couldn't focus on what potentially lay ahead; first, they had to beat their opponent in the opening round. In a battle of the Bruins, No. 15 Belmont took on No. 2 UCLA at the Cox Arena in San Diego. The game was no challenge for UCLA. Mbah a Moute led the Bruins in both points and rebounds and was one of three UCLA Bruins to collect three steals. The Bruins of Belmont shot just 28.8 percent from the field, as UCLA cruised to a 78–44 win. The second round saw a tougher opponent and a tougher than expected game. The Alabama Crimson Tide, coached by former UCLA assistant Mark Gottfried, was the No. 10 seed in the region and put up a tough fight. The game was tied at halftime, and when time expired, UCLA barely came away with a win, 62–59. Competition was about to get even more difficult.

For football, many UCLA fans' most vivid memories of the last 30 years are the games that meant the most to them. Maybe they think of the 1992 game against USC, or the 2006 and 2012 games against USC. Maybe they think of 1998 against Miami or the 1994 Rose Bowl. For basketball, the season of 1995 and the three-year stretch from 2006 to 2008 under Coach Howland spring to mind. So to do the games

UCLA point guard Jordan Farmar (Erkki Corpuz Collection).

in the Final Four and the disappointments. There is also Gonzaga, in the Sweet 16, in 2006.

The Gonzaga Bulldogs were the talk of the college basketball world for much of the 2006 season. The perennial underdog, Cinderella team in March, was no longer a long shot. It was a top team, led by one of the best players in America. Adam Morrison was First Team All-West Coast Conference, WCC Player of the Year, a consensus All-American, and the National Player of the Year in 2006. He led the nation in scoring, averaging an astonishing 28.1 PPG for the season. While Gonzaga was the No. 3 seed in the region and UCLA was No. 2 in the tournament, the Bulldogs were actually ranked higher than the Bruins in the Associated Press poll. The game was truly a toss-up, and it turned out to be a classic.

The game was not UCLA's best, and for the majority of the game, it looked like the promising season was going to come to a close in the most disappointing of ways. The Bruins were getting blown out early. In the first half, they trailed by as many as 17 points. The usually dominant defense struggled, and the offense couldn't get anything going. At halftime, UCLA trailed, 42–29. While the Bruins were only able to shoot 25.9 percent from the field, the Bulldogs had no such problem. They carved up the UCLA defense, shooting 57.7 percent.

In the second half, the Bruins turned up their aggression, playing tougher defense and slowing down Gonzaga. Still, they were unable to climb all the way back. Whenever they made a run, Morrison and J. P. Batista answered right back. With 3:26 to go, Morrison knocked down two free throws to extend the Gonzaga lead to nine, 71–62. Then, one of the most incredible finishes in UCLA history unfolded. Mbah a Moute began the late run by hitting two free throws. The Bruins went to their full-court press, a decision that ultimately turned the tide of the game. After forcing a turnover, Farmar missed a three-pointer, Morrison missed a jumper, and then Mbah a Moute cut the deficit to five with a putback layup. After getting another stop, Darren Collison forced a foul, but missed the front end of a one-and-one. Smothering defense by Bozeman then forced Morrison into a contested shot, and UCLA got the ball back with 1:01 on the clock and still trailing by five. On the ensuing possession, Farmar took control. After beating his defender to the right, he took a floater, which he knocked down to bring the score to 71–68. Tough defense forced Adam Morrison into another long, contested shot, and on the rebound attempt, Hollins was fouled by Batista and sent to the free-throw line for another one-and-one with 19.6 seconds remaining. At just 60.9 percent from the line for the season, Hollins approached the stripe and knocked down two free throws, certainly the most clutch shots of his career. The score was now 71–70. UCLA had scored eight straight, but still trailed by one. Following the second make, Coach Howland substituted Hollins out of the game for Mbah a Moute. The following sequence is one of the most memorable in UCLA basketball history. Legendary announcer Gus Johnson, with one of his classic calls, said it best: "They throw it to Morrison. He holds on . . . and a steal. Farmar, inside . . . the freshman, up and in—oh, and they go in front!" After inbounding the ball to Morrison in the corner, UCLA trapped him. After he threw a crosscourt pass to Batista, Bozeman and Farmar converged, forcing a turnover. Farmar collected the ball and instantly turned and found Mbah a Moute under the basket for the go-ahead layup. Gonzaga, with no timeouts left, inbounded the ball. Johnson continued, "Raivio, last chance to dance . . . fumbled on the play . . . what a game! What a game! U-C-L-A! Unbelievable! After being down by 17 . . . heartbreak city!"After inbounding the ball, Gonzaga guard Derek Raivio rushed up court, but lost the ball. Bodies dove to the court, Mbah a Moute got his hands on the ball, and a jump ball was called. The possession arrow pointed UCLA's way. It was a turnover to UCLA, which was up by one, with 2.6 seconds remaining. The bench went wild, the players on the court jumped up and down in celebration. The fans were ecstatic. Gus Johnson had one of his all-time greatest calls.

Afflalo knocked in one free throw, and though the Bulldogs got a shot off, Batista missed it, and the Bruins won. After jumping up and down in celebration on the court, Arron Afflalo left the scrum and walked over to Adam Morrison, sitting on the court in shock and in tears. Afflalo lifted up Morrison, helping him to his feet and hugging him. One by one, his teammates followed. It was a poignant moment following one of the best moments in Afflalo's life and one of the worst in Morrison's young life. The show of sportsmanship touched Morrison. After the game, he said, "It's just a sign of obviously a great program and great people. They had enough guts as [men] to come over, and in their moment of victory, to pick somebody off the floor. If I could thank them, I would. It's more than basketball."

The Bruins survived, but the season wasn't over. In the Elite Eight, they had a rematch with Memphis, a team they had lost to in the fourth game of the year. This time, defense prevailed. UCLA put the clamps on Memphis and beat them, 50–45. The Bruins were off to the Final Four once again.

On April 1, the Bruins took on the LSU Tigers at RCA Dome in Indianapolis, with a chance to reach another national championship game. The Bruins were playing better basketball than any time since the 1995 title and not only were playing the brand of basketball Howland preferred but also were arguably the best defensive UCLA team in history. Against LSU, they proved those statements true again. At halftime, the Bruins led big, outscoring the Tigers, 39–24, over the first 20 minutes, holding the Tigers to 30 percent from the field, and controlling the tempo. In the second half, the Bruins didn't let up defensively. They held the Tigers to just 20 points, never allowing them to seriously threaten the Bruins. Glen Davis scored 14 points but was just 5-for-17 from the field. Tyrus Thomas was held to just five points. Mbah a Moute led the Bruins in scoring with

17, rebounds with nine, and steals with two. UCLA won, 59–45.

On April 3, 2006, the Bruins played in the national championship game for the 13th time in school history, in search of their 12th national championship. Their opponent was the Florida Gators, the No. 3 seed out of the Minneapolis Regional. The Gators were led by Coach Billy Donovan and were a balanced team. No real stars were on the roster, though many of the players would make a name for themselves over the ensuing years. Joakim Noah, Taurean Green, Corey Brewer, Al Horford, and Lee Humphrey all averaged in double figures. The Gators were good offensively and defensively, though not elite on either end. Like the Bruins, they entered the game with a 32–6 record. They were winners of their last 10 games, while UCLA entered with a 12-game winning streak. Most betting services had Florida as a one- or two-point favorite, though certain others had more belief in the Bruins. The game turned out to be one few, if any, expected. Florida beat UCLA handily, sending them back to Westwood without the title they coveted. At halftime, the Gators led by 11. When time expired, they won by 16. The Bruins played a fine defensive game, but their offense was not dynamic or consistent enough to come away with the championship. Four Gators scored in double figures, they only turned the ball over six times, and outshot the Bruins from the field, the three-point line, and the free-throw line. The national championship was Florida's first in basketball, and in 2007 all major contributors returned. The two teams were to meet again.

2006–07

Coming off a trip to the national championship game and a school-record 32 wins in 2006, the Bruins of 2007 had sky-high expectations, but they also had a hole to fill. Jordan Farmar went to the NBA, staying home and playing for the Los Angeles Lakers. In two years, Farmar had been one of the top players in the Pac-10 Conference, so replacing his production was a challenge. Luckily for Coach Howland, Arron Afflalo, an Honorable Mention All-American in 2006, returned for his junior season in 2007. He had the finest season of his career and helped make UCLA a contender once again. Afflalo led the team in scoring and was dominant on the defensive end. For his incredible season, Afflalo was named Pac-10 Player of the Year and was a consensus All-American. Joining Afflalo was Josh Shipp. After playing in only four games and being granted a redshirt season, Shipp returned as a third-year sophomore in 2007. He finished second on the team in scoring with 13.3 points per game. Darren Collison, now the starting point guard, had a strong season as well, and Luc Richard Mbah a Moute and Lorenzo Mata were dependable all season.

While his contribution was minimal as a freshman in 2007, one new player who joined the program has left a lasting legacy in both college and the NBA. Russell Westbrook, a 6'3" guard from Hawthorne, was born to play basketball. His competitiveness, hustle, energy, and skill have made him one of the best players in the world. When he arrived at UCLA, he was raw, in need of fine-tuning. His athleticism was off the charts. Over time, he developed not just into a better version of himself but also into a legend. In the NBA in 2017, he led the league in scoring and averaged a triple-double for the season, the first and only player to do that since Oscar Robertson in 1962. He was named MVP of the league. One year later, he averaged a triple-double again. As a freshman at UCLA ten years earlier, Westbrook was tasked with the same job that Collison had the year before. He was a backup guard; his time to shine would come later.

The Bruins began the season ranked No. 6 in the country and began with a win. At home in front of a large crowd, the Bruins beat the BYU Cougars, 82–69. Mbah a Moute led the way with 24 points and 11 rebounds. Collison finished with a double-double, 16 points and 10 assists. The game against BYU was just one in a series of early-season UCLA blowouts. The Bruins were ready when the season began and looking to finish the job this time around. The Bruins crushed the field at the Maui Invitational, beating Chaminade by 13, No. 20 Kentucky by 25, and Georgia Tech by 15. When the Bruins returned home, they were now No. 2 in the country, one spot too low. The Bruins crushed Long Beach State by 30 and then UC Riverside by 23. They were blowing out everyone that dared step on the court with them early in the season. They played efficient offensively and elite defensively. The 2007 Bruins, like the 2006 team, finished the year ranked No. 10 in the country in scoring defense, and the 2007 team allowed just 57.8 PPG, down 0.9 from the year before. After starting the season 6–0, winning by nearly 20 points per game, the Bruins were named the No. 1 team in the country.

Seeing the number one next to UCLA was not a distraction, nor did it add any pressure to the Bruins. They just kept winning. The Bruins routed Oakland, 78–54. Afflalo led the way with 20 points. Four days later, the Bruins played their toughest team yet. The No. 6 Texas A&M Aggies were led by Acie Law IV, one of the most clutch players in America. Like UCLA, Texas A&M relied on its defense, teamed with opportunistic offense. The game was close. The Bruins didn't play particularly well but got enough stops down the stretch to hold on and win, 65–62. The Bruins then blew out Oakland by 21, Sam Houston State by 14, and Michigan by 37 points to close out the early season nonconference slate. The Bruins were a perfect 11–0.

While the nonconference season went as well as anyone could have hoped, things would be tougher in conference play. The Pac-10 was strong, and UCLA had to play well each night to come out on top. The first opponent was the Washington State Cougars, an elite defensive team with just enough offensive firepower to challenge any of the top teams in the country. Though the Cougars were unranked at the time of the meeting, WSU finished in the top 15 in the national polls at the end of the year. The game was slow and defined by two distinct halves. In the first, UCLA was terrible, as was Darren Collison. He finished the first 20 minutes with zero points, three turnovers, and three fouls. UCLA trailed by 10. In the second half, he turned it on and carried UCLA over the finish line. Collison finished the second half with 13 points and the game-winning three-pointer. UCLA won, 55–52.

Beating the Washington Huskies proved to be much easier three nights later. Afflalo finished with 27 points, including five three-pointers, and UCLA cruised to its 13th straight victory. Against Oregon State, the Bruins weren't flashy, but they were effective, winning once again. While UCLA was able to get away with a poor first half against Washington State and come back to win, they weren't able to do the same against the University of Oregon. After allowing the Ducks to shoot 70 percent from the field in the first half to build a 10-point halftime lead, the Bruins almost did enough to come away with a win. Trailing, 66–63, Collison brought the ball up the court, and, seeing that the defense was playing off him, he calmly pulled up and drilled a three to tie the game. Oregon guard Aaron Brooks came right back, however, and knocked down a short jump shot on the right baseline to give the Ducks the lead. The Bruins had time for another shot, but Josh Shipp's forced, closely defended jump shot was well off, and the game was over. Oregon fans rushed the court. UCLA was no longer undefeated.

The Bruins turned in another lackluster performance one week later when they traveled across town to take on the USC Trojans. The Bruins again were trailing late, but this time, they wouldn't be denied. They went to their leader, their All-American, and he delivered. With USC leading, 64–63, Collison crossed halfcourt with 18.5 seconds remaining and then quickly passed the ball to Afflalo on the right wing and cleared out. After the ball swung around the perimeter, it was back in the hands of Afflalo in the same spot. Just 10 seconds remained on the clock when he went to work. After two dribbles to his left, Afflalo pulled up from 15 feet out and knocked down the game-winning shot. UCLA survived.

Though the games were closer, UCLA was winning at a high clip. It beat Arizona State and Arizona at home, Afflalo again leading the way. The Bruins then beat Cal, but fell on the road for the second time, this time going down in Palo Alto to Stanford. In a rematch against Oregon, UCLA came out on top at Pauley Pavilion on February 1. The Ducks were ranked No. 9, UCLA was ranked No. 5, and the game was played in front of 12,113 fans. The Bruins held the Ducks to just 36.8 percent from the field and won, 69–57. UCLA then smoked Oregon State by 42 points and knocked off No. 21 USC for the second time.

The Bruins won five of their final seven regular-season games to finish 26–4. For the second season in a row, they won the Pac-10 Conference, but unlike 2006, they weren't playing their best basketball at the end of the year. Though the Bruins beat ranked Arizona and Washington State teams in the final month, they also lost to unranked West Virginia and then unranked Washington in the season finale. UCLA followed up their loss to Washington with an overtime loss to Cal in the first round of the Pac-10 tournament.

With their late-season struggles, the Bruins gave up what once seemed like a lock as a No. 1 seed in the NCAA Tournament. Instead, they were named the No. 2 seed in the West Regional. The opening round opponent for the Bruins was a familiar team for Coach Ben Howland: Weber State, Howland's alma mater. The game was played at ARCO Arena in Sacramento, and the Bruins easily took care of the Wildcats, 70–42. Afflalo finished with 22 points and eight rebounds in the win. The second round saw UCLA face a tougher team, the No. 7 seed Indiana Hoosiers, and though the game wasn't pretty, UCLA won. Indiana shot just 32.7 percent from the field and made only five three pointers. UCLA shot poorly as well, but the difference was made at the free-throw line. UCLA knocked down 18 of its 24 attempts, while Indiana only made 10 out of 21 from the stripe. UCLA won, 54–49, and advanced to the Sweet 16. Waiting for the Bruins was another opponent Coach Howland had gotten to know in the past. The Pitt Panthers, now coached by Jamie Dixon, were 29–7 entering the game and the No. 3 seed in the region. The Bruins, as they did so often, smothered the Panthers, holding them to just 36.4 percent from the field. Afflalo led UCLA with 17 points and seven rebounds. Shipp scored 16, and the Bruins got a boost with eight points and nine rebounds for Lorenzo Mata.

In the Elite Eight matchup, UCLA made a statement: the ranking committee was wrong in giving the top seed in the West Region to the Kansas Jayhawks. UCLA, the second seed, took apart Kansas, 68–55, to win its 30th game of the year. Afflalo finished with 24 points and was named the West Regional's Most Outstanding Player. The Bruins forced 21 turnovers, outrebounded the Jayhawks, and scored more fast-break points. UCLA advanced to the Final Four again, and waiting for them was a familiar opponent—the Florida Gators.

Though the two memorable players on the Florida Gators in 2006 and 2007 played mostly inside, Joakim Noah and Al Horford, the team was stacked in the backcourt as well. They were extraordinary balanced. Taurean Green led the team in scoring with a 13.3 PPG average, just ahead of Al Horford and Corey Brewer, each averaging 13.2 for the season. Noah and Lee Humphrey rounded out the starting lineup, the same five that beat the Bruins one year earlier. The rematch was not much different than the first game. Florida jumped out to a halftime lead, 29–23, and slowly extended it in the second half. The Bruins lost, 76–66. The Bruins shot under 40 percent from the field, while the Gators were well over 50. UCLA's season came to an end in heartbreak. For many fans, the season was championship or bust. When UCLA was forced to go home, it was a bust. Afflalo, like Farmar one year earlier, would leave school early. His career as a Bruin was exemplary, and replacing him would be an incredible challenge in 2008.

University of Florida won the NCAA basketball national championship in 2007.

2007–08

The 2008 UCLA basketball team was one of the most talented in school history. While Arron Afflalo left, more than enough talent remained, with new talent coming in. The Bruins signed just two players in the 2007 recruiting class, but one was one of the best players in the country, a five-star recruit from Lake Oswego, Oregon, who was named the number one recruit in the country by Scout recruiting service. His name was Kevin Love, and for one year at UCLA, he was brilliant. At 6'10" 260 pounds, Love could play down low. He used his big body to get position, clear space, and score at the basket. He also had the ability to stretch defenses, utilizing his outside game more as the season progressed. More important, Love was an elite rebounder at the college level and became one of the top rebounders in the NBA also. In his one season in Westwood, he pulled down 10.6 rebounds per game. His most unique skill, and perhaps his most impressive, was not his scoring or rebounding, however. When basketball historians talk about outlet passing, two names immediately come up—Wes Unseld and Bill Walton. Love's middle name is Wesley, named in honor of Unseld, who played professionally with Love's father, Stan. Bill Walton, of course, was a Bruin, and like Unseld, Stan Love fell in love with Walton's outlet-passing ability. Now when outlet passing is discussed, Kevin Love's name must be brought up with Unseld and Walton. After grabbing a rebound, he turned and fired passes to streaking teammates with incredible accuracy. He quickly fired length of the court passes for layups after made baskets. Love's outlet passing was a thing of beauty, and so was his overall game.

The Bruins of 2008 were stacked from top to bottom. Along with Pac 10 Player of the Year and All-American Kevin Love, Darren Collison was now a junior, and he finished second on the team in scoring, averaging 15.5 points per game. As a sophomore, Russell Westbrook moved into the starting lineup, playing primarily as a shooting guard alongside Collison. Westbrook saw a huge jump in his year-two production. He averaged nearly 13 points per game, led the team in assists, and was named Pac-10 Defensive Player of the Year. Josh Shipp and Luc Richard Mbah a Moute were back, as well, and were as reliable as ever.

While the talent level on the Bruins roster was off the charts, so was much of the Pac-10 conference. The Pac-10 was the best conference in America, led by freshmen. O. J. Mayo (USC), James Harden (Arizona State), and Jerryd Bayless (Arizona) were just a few of the top freshmen in the Pac-10 in 2008. The Pac-10 was hardly unique, however. As UCLA would see throughout the season, talent was everywhere, and the Bruins had to play their best if they were to win it all in one of the best college basketball seasons of all time.

The Bruins began the season ranked No. 2 in the country, and though there was more talent than ever in Westwood under Coach Ben Howland, the formula stayed the same. The Bruins played superb defense, finishing No. 10 in the country in scoring defense for the third consecutive year. The season tipped off at home against Portland State, and the Bruins put on a show. Love finished with 22 points

Kevin Love shoots against Youngstown State, while teammate Russell Westbrook crashes the boards, 2008 (Erkki Corpuz Collection).

and 13 rebounds in his debut, Shipp scored 18, and the Bruins cruised to victory. For much of the early part of the season, Love and the Bruins lived up to all the hype. Against Youngstown State and Cal State San Bernardino, UCLA won by an average of 33 points, and Love averaged 20 PPG. On November 19, UCLA beat Maryland by double digits in the College Basketball Experience Classic, and then the next night, the team beat No. 10 Michigan State. Against the Terrapins, Love finished with 18 points and 16 rebounds; then against the Spartans, he finished with 21 points and 11 rebounds. There was nothing Love didn't do well early in the season, and UCLA looked like a complete team.

After beating Yale by 34 points, the Bruins were named the No. 1 team in the country. UCLA then dismantled George Washington before taking on the No. 8 University of Texas Longhorns in the Big 12/ Pac-10 Hardwood Series. For the first time all season, the Bruins struggled. The Longhorns outshot the Bruins from the floor, outrebounded them, and showed much more depth, trouncing them in bench scoring, 63–6. Still, the Bruins hung in. They made more three-pointers, made more free throws, and won the battle in the paint. The performance wasn't enough, however. After clawing back from 16 down, UCLA ran out of gas, and the Longhorns closed out the victory.

Following the loss, UCLA fell from the top spot all the way to No. 8 in the rankings—a disappointment to be sure, but much basketball remained. The Bruins won their final five nonconference games to take a 12–1 record into Pac-10 play. Against Davidson, UCLA held All-America guard Steph Curry to 15 points on 6-for-19 from the field. The Bruins showed their depth throughout nonconference play, with a different star seemingly every night. Against Davidson, Mbah a Moute scored 21 points. Against Idaho State, Collison led the way with 20. Love had a monster 17-point, 16-rebound game against Michigan in Ann Arbor. Meanwhile, Westbrook was steady the whole way, contributing on offense and dominating on defense. The Bruins were ranked No. 5 in the country.

The Bruins were the clear Pac-10 Conference favorite, but the competition was fierce. They began at No. 20 Stanford in a battle of the big men. Love and the Lopez twins, Brook and Robin, from Stanford, grabbed the headlines before the game, but Josh Shipp stole the show. He finished with a game high 21 points, and UCLA handed Stanford just its second loss of the season. Two nights later, Love starred with 21 points and 14 rebounds in a win over Cal. But the lasting memory of that game was not any play by Love, but one by Westbrook. After driving down the middle of the court in a semi-fast-break, Westbrook raced past two defenders, took off from one full step inside the free-throw line, and hammered a dunk over Cal's Jamal Boykin. The crowd in Berkeley, with just as many UCLA fans in attendance as Cal fans, was stunned. Later that night, it was the number one play on SportsCenter's top 10. The Bruins then knocked off Washington and Washington State to run their conference record to 4–0. Against the Huskies, Russell Westbrook led the way with 18 points. Love dominated the physical Washington State Cougars, finishing with 27 points and 14 rebounds.

When UCLA faced USC on January 19, the pregame talk was all about O. J. Mayo and Kevin Love. Both were named the top overall recruit in the country by various recruiting outlets, they shared magazine covers, and now they shared the court for the first time in college. While Mayo and Love were stars as freshmen, Davon Jefferson of USC starred in this game. Jefferson finished with a game-high 25 point,s and USC carved up UCLA's usually brilliant defense. The Trojans shot 60.9 percent from the field. Though Love played well, Westbrook and Mbah a Moute struggled. In their worst game of the regular season so far, UCLA lost, 72–63.

Following the loss, UCLA dropped to No. 7 in the national rankings, but quickly climbed back up. The Bruins beat Oregon, 85–62, at McArthur Court. The game was personal for Oregon fans and Kevin Love. The hometown fans once believed that Love, an Oregon native, was theirs to lose on the recruiting trail. Ultimately, Love chose UCLA, and Oregon fans chose anger. Love won the battle, making Oregon fans look silly. He finished with 26 points and 18 rebounds, including eight offensive rebounds. Every time the Ducks crept close, UCLA went to Love, and he delivered. Two nights later, he had 16 points and 21 rebounds against the Oregon State Beavers. The Bruins then returned home to face the two Arizona schools and beat them both. Against Arizona State,

UCLA held James Harden to just nine points, and Love and Shipp each went over 20. After beating ASU by 33, UCLA beat UA by 22. Love scored 26, and Westbrook added 21 in the win.

When UCLA traveled to Pullman, Washington, to play the WSU Cougars, both teams were going in the right direction. WSU was ranked No. 17 in the country, the Bruins were ranked No. 4, and both teams were vying for the conference title. The two teams both shot the ball well, but the pace was incredibly slow, and scoring was still limited. The Bruins shot 55.1 percent from the floor, topping the Cougars at 52.3 percent. The Bruins lost the turnover battle by one, but outrebounded WSU by nine. After entering the second half tied at 26, UCLA outplayed WSU in the final 20 minutes and won, 67–59. Collison led UCLA with 18 points. Just as the Bruins looked like they were going to cruise to another Pac-10 title, they were upset. Two nights after beating WSU, the University of Washington shocked UCLA. Love shot just 3-for-8 from the field, Westbrook was just 5 of 16, and Collison was 1-for-8. Nothing worked for UCLA offensively, and though the team played a fine defensive game, Justin Dentmon and the Huskies came away with the win.

The Bruins were 21–3 when they returned to Los Angeles to take on the USC Trojans at the Sports Arena. After losing to USC earlier in the year, this game was a chance for the Bruins to get payback. This time the show really was the two freshmen. Love finished with another double-double, while the defensive combination of Collison and Westbrook shut down Mayo. By the end of the game, he had clearly quit on his team. He finished with just four points and turned the ball over 10 times. UCLA won, 56–46.

Mayo later was found to have taken extra benefits while in high school that lured him to USC. The Trojans vacated the entire 2008 season. Mayo's problems were not over. He had a rocky NBA career, filled with underperformance, steroid use, and off-the-court problems. In 2016, his NBA career came to a close. On July 1, Mayo was banned from the NBA for repeated drug violations.

The rest of the regular season for the Bruins was filled with wins and Russell Westbrook highlights. The Bruins beat Oregon State by 35 and then Oregon by 10. Against the Ducks, Westbrook stole a pass on the left side of the court, dribbled all the way down himself, and threw down a vicious dunk over LeKendric Longmire. Westbrook finished with 16 points on the day.

For the second time of the year, UCLA destroyed Arizona State on February 28, holding Harden to 11 points and winning, 70–49. The Bruins then went into hostile McKale Center in Tucson and came away with another win. UA fans, as they typically do, were quick to blame officiating for their loss. The Bruins, however, were the more aggressive team. Still, Arizona shot 25 more free throws than UCLA, more fouls were called on UCLA, and the Bruins played more inside, outscoring Arizona in the paint. The biggest difference, however, was UCLA had Kevin Love, and Arizona did not. Love finished with 24 points and 15 rebounds. Chase Budinger and Jordan Hill each had big nights for the Wildcats, but UCLA did enough to win, 68–66.

The Bruins then returned home to take on the Stanford Cardinal with the Pac-10 title on the line. Two games separated the two teams, and two games were left to play. With a win, UCLA would win the conference again. The game was difficult for UCLA. The Cardinal led UCLA, 30–18, at halftime, but the Bruins came right back. Trailing by two with 7.5 seconds remaining, the ball was inbounded to Darren Collison, who raced down the court. He was fouled with 2.5 seconds remaining. Collison stepped to the line and calmly knocked down both free throws. The game went to overtime, where Westbrook, Love, Mbah a Moute, Collison, and Shipp all played flawlessly. UCLA won, 77–67. The win gave the Bruins their third straight Pac-10 title, with Coach Ben Howland the first UCLA coach to do that since John Wooden. The win also pushed UCLA's record to 27–3. The 27 regular-season wins set a new school record. The Bruins then finished off the regular season by winning their 28th game, beating Cal, 81–80, on a wild buzzer-beating shot by Josh Shipp.

The Bruins then cruised through the Pac-10 tournament, beating Cal, Stanford, and USC. After being selected as a No. 2 seed in the NCAA Tournament for two consecutive seasons, UCLA was named a No. 1 seed in 2008. The Bruins were in the West Regional, close to home, and had a clear path to the Final Four. In the opening game, played at the Honda Center in Anaheim, the Bruins put on a show. Against helpless Mississippi Valley State, they dominated. Love finished with 20 points and nine rebounds, but played only 21 minutes. He wasn't needed any longer. UCLA won, 70–29, holding the Delta Devils to just 19.7 percent from the field. The games would get harder, everyone knew, but a big challenge came a little earlier than expected. In the second round, UCLA took on the extremely athletic Texas A&M Aggies. The game was ugly. UCLA shot just 43.2 percent from the field, 0.1 percent better than TAMU. Love finished with 19 points and 11 rebounds and Collison finished with 21 points, but no other Bruin scored more than five. The Bruins were better from beyond the arc, however, and that ultimately was the difference: UCLA 51, TAMU 49. The Bruins survived the first weekend.

In the Sweet 16, the Bruins took on the No. 12 seed Western Kentucky Hilltoppers and won comfortably. Tyrone Brazelton had a brilliant game for WKU, but UCLA had a star of its own. Brazelton finished with 31 points. Kevin Love finished with 29 points, 14 rebounds, and four assists. The difference was the rest of the team. UCLA was deep and talented, and beyond the usual stars, others waited to emerge. Against WKU, James Keefe had his finest day. He finished with 18 points and 12 rebounds. UCLA won, 88–78, and advanced to the Elite Eight. The Bruins faced off against No. 3 seed Xavier, searching for its third straight trip to the Final Four. Like WKU, Xavier couldn't hang with the better Bruins. At halftime, UCLA led, 33–24, and by the end of the game, the score was 76–57, in favor of UCLA. Love and Collison each scored 19, and Westbrook had 17 points and played his usual dominant defense, including three steals. The Bruins held Xavier to just 36.2 percent from the field. UCLA won the region, and their season continued.

For much of the season, Memphis and UCLA were considered by pundits the two favorites to win the NCAA title. Now they squared off on April 5, 2008, for a chance to play in the championship game. Like much of the country, Memphis had a freshman on its squad with special talent, but he was not alone. Derrick Rose was eventually drafted No. 1 overall in the 2008 NBA Draft, but Chris Douglas-Roberts was Memphis's best player, an All-American and the leader of a brilliant team. John Calipari coached the Tigers, and the team had a 37–1 record entering the game. The first half was close, and the style of play favored UCLA,. Still, with both teams shooting below 50 percent, Memphis led, 38–35. In the second half, things began to open up on the offensive end for the Tigers, and UCLA went cold. Douglas-Roberts finished with 28 points, and Rose scored 25. The gap in team athleticism was very apparent, and for many of the Bruins, the game was too much to handle. Westbrook played well, scoring 22 points for the Bruins and keeping the score close for most of the second half, but his play wasn't enough. Memphis collected another win, proving many doubters wrong and advancing to the NCAA title game, 78–63.

Like USC, Memphis later was forced to vacate all wins from the 2008 season due to NCAA infractions. Of course, that didn't matter for UCLA because its season was over. Westbrook and Love both left early for the NBA, and both are in the middle of incredible careers that will eventually land them in the Basketball Hall of Fame. The future for UCLA following the season was uncertain. There was great confidence in Coach Howland, and many elite prospects would continue to go west and join the Bruins. Still, the loss stung, and the 2008 Bruins were UCLA's last great team for at least the next decade.

University of Kansas won the NCAA basketball national championship in 2008.

2008–09

Reinforcements were on their way to replace the departing Love and Westbrook. UCLA signed the No. 1 recruiting class in the country in 2009 according to Scout, Rivals, and ESPN recruiting services. Five new scholarship players joined the team, and though replacing the unique skills of Love and Westbrook was hard, the Bruins were still the preseason Pac-10 favorite. Along with four-star recruits Jerime Anderson, Drew Gordon, and Malcolm Lee, UCLA added five-star recruits Jrue Holiday and J'mison Morgan. Along with the newcomers were the reliable, familiar faces:

- Josh Shipp led the team in scoring, averaging 14.5 points per game in his final season.
- Darren Collison, the best overall player on the Bruins, scored 14.4 PPG and led the team with 4.7 assists per game.

- Alfred Aboya, once just a defensive player with a very limited offensive game, had his finest season of his career. As a senior, he averaged 9.9 PPG.
- Nikola Dragovic, now a junior, was an outside shooting threat, though his streaky play and often poor shot selection frustrated many fans.
- Junior Michael Roll was also a solid shooter.

Of the highly-touted freshmen to join the squad, only Jrue Holiday played a prominent role in 2009. He averaged 8.5 PPG, 3.8 RPG, and 3.7 APG. It was certainly a solid debut season, but as a consensus top-three recruit in the nation, his only season in Westwood was disappointing for some.

Though no one quite knew it yet, the 2009 season was the beginning of the UCLA slide under Coach Ben Howland. Despite coming up just short in the NCAA Tournament, Coach Howland and the Bruins were brilliant over his first five years, but the next five wouldn't be so easy. The 2008 recruiting class not only was disappointing on the court but also had off-the-court problems. When UCLA's play on the court began to slip, much of the talk eventually shifted to off-the-court problems. The first cracks came in 2009.

UCLA's defense, usually elite under Coach Howland, took a major step back in 2009. The Bruins were still solid, giving up just 64 PPG—but a full five points per game more than the year prior. The team was flawed, but voters for the rankings couldn't see that at the beginning of the year.

After two straight exhibition wins, No. 4 UCLA began the season against Prairie View A&M on November 12 in the 2K Sports Classic. In the season opener, Collison led the Bruins with 19 points, and Holiday and Lee scored in double figures in their collegiate debuts. One night later, UCLA beat Miami (Ohio) behind strong performances from Collison and Shipp. As the tournament shifted from various sites across the country to Madison Square Garden, the competition increased as well. Though unranked, the Michigan Wolverines were tougher than the previous two opponents, and much tougher than UCLA could handle. The Bruins struggled on offense, turning the ball over 17 times and shooting only 42 percent from the field. They were just 5-for-11 from the free-throw line, scored only two points in the paint, and had zero fast-break points. Michigan won, 55–52.

The Bruins bounced back to have a strong nonconference season, but the shocking loss to Michigan reset expectations. Alfred Aboya scored 22 points in a win over Southern Illinois, and Holiday led the way with 20 points on a perfect 8-for-8 from the field against Florida International. The Bruins were No. 11 after the two wins but then fell to the University of Texas for the second year in a row in the Big 12/Pac-10 Hardwood Series. Collison scored 22 points but made 22 attempts to get those points. A. J. Abrams, on the other hand, scored 31 points and hit five three-pointers for Texas. The Bruins again shot poorly from the field and from the free-throw line in the 68–64 loss.

Fortunately for UCLA, the rest of the nonconference schedule was loaded with subpar teams. Balanced offensive efforts helped the Bruins knock off Cal State Northridge and DePaul. UCLA's defense shut down a bad Loyola Marymount team, holding it to just 25 percent shooting and 1-for-17 from behind the three-point line. Michael Roll hit four three-pointers against Mercer and provided a big boost with 16 points, and then he followed that up with 25 points in a win over Wyoming. Against the Cowboys, the Bruins scored a season-best 113 points and shot 60.3 percent from the field. Drew Gordon finished with 14 points and 11 rebounds. The Bruins then trounced Louisiana Tech in their final tune-up game before Pac-10 play.

Going into the conference season, the Bruins had a stellar record—10–2, ranked No. 9 in the country—but they had yet to beat a quality opponent. The season got much tougher, but for the time being UCLA continued winning. The Bruins began conference play with a dominant win, and they did it in the way Ben Howland loved—with their defense. The Bruins smothered Oregon State, holding them to just 46 points and 43.6 percent from the field, outrebounding the Beavers, and forcing 20 turnovers. Roll and Collison each scored 16 in the Bruins' 69–46 win. Two nights later, the Bruins made it an opening-week sweep with an 83–74 win over Oregon. Collison scored 22 points and dished out nine assists in the win.

Though USC was still a solid team in 2009, much

of the luster around the rivalry was gone after 2008. Love and Mayo were off to the NBA, and the two freshmen, Holiday and DeMar DeRozan, didn't draw the attention like Love and Mayo, despite being held in high regard. The Bruins struggled for much of the night, but so did USC. UCLA outshot USC from beyond the three-point line and won. Four Bruins scored in double figures, including 13 from Holiday. The following week, UCLA blew out Arizona before taking on a strong ASU team at Pauley Pavilion. The Bruins came into the game ranked No. 7 in the country and riding a 10-game winning streak, but ASU, led by star sophomore James Harden, was no slouch. It was ranked No. 15 in the country. The Bruins played ahead for much of the game, but when ASU went to a matchup zone down the stretch, the Bruins fell apart. Over the final eight minutes of regulation and five minutes in the overtime period, UCLA scored only one basket. Harden finished with 24 points, and ASU shocked UCLA, 61–58.

With the loss to ASU, the Bruins were no longer undefeated in Pac-10 play, and soon they lost more games than they should have. The Bruins hung on to beat Washington State, 61–59. Dragovic scored a career-high 20 points for UCLA's 16th-straight win in

Jrue Holiday vs. Washington State, 2009 (Erkki Corpuz Collection).

Pullman. The Bruins then lost a game that ultimately cost them the Pac-10 title. The unranked University of Washington upset No. 11 UCLA, 86–75, despite 25 points from Josh Shipp. Isaiah Thomas scored 24, and the Huskies outscored UCLA, 36–10, at the free-throw line.

The Bruins got back to their winning ways but couldn't sustain their run. After knocking off four unranked teams, Cal, Stanford, USC, and Notre Dame, the Bruins traveled to the state of Arizona for a tough Pac-10 road trip. On February 12, ASU knocked off UCLA for the second time that season. Five Sun Devils scored in double figures, led by 15 points, 11 assists, and seven rebounds from James Harden. Darren Collison played well for UCLA but didn't receive much help. Holiday finished with zero points and just one assist in 33 minutes. Two nights later, Nic Wise, Jordan Hill, and Chase Budinger proved too big, athletic, skilled, and good for the Bruins. Arizona knocked off UCLA, 84–72. Following the two straight losses, the Bruins fell from No. 6 in the national rankings to No. 15.

For the rest of the regular season, the Bruins were trying to make up for lost opportunities. The Pac-10 race was tight, but they gave away too many games. Though the Bruins beat Washington in a rematch, they fell to Washington State, 82–81. The loss was heartbreaking in itself, but devastating for UCLA's conference chances. Taylor Rochestie scored a career-best 33 points for the Cougars, outdueling Nikola Dragovic, who scored a career-high 23 for the Bruins. Klay Thompson added 15 for WSU, and Collison scored 20 for the Bruins, but WSU's duo was better, and the final score was 82–81 in favor of WSU. The win was the first for the Cougars over the Bruins at Pauley Pavilion since 2005, and though the Bruins still led the all-time series, 94–14, the 2009 loss hurt.

The Bruins finished the season with four consecutive wins, including a February 28 victory over Cal on a day in which ESPN's popular show *College GameDay* was at UCLA. Over the final four regular-season games, Josh Shipp played his finest basketball for the Bruins, averaging over 23 PPG. In the end, his play wasn't enough for the Bruins to take home another Pac-10 title. They finished one game behind the Huskies and had to settle for second place. Though the Bruins beat Washington State in the quarterfinals of the Pac-10 tournament in a defensive battle, they weren't able to beat USC for the third time and fell in the semifinals, 65–55. With the loss, UCLA entered the NCAA Tournament with a solid yet unspectacular 25–8 record. The eight losses were already the most for UCLA in four years.

When the tournament field was announced, UCLA was the No. 6 seed in the East Regional. Their opening-round opponent was the Virginia Commonwealth University Rams, led by star senior point guard Eric Maynor. The game was anything but pretty for the Bruins. UCLA shot just 40.4 percent from the field and struggled all game to pull away from the pesky underdogs. VCU, which struggled from the field as well, hung close throughout and finally had a shot at the end to knock off Goliath. After cutting the UCLA lead to 63–62, the Rams got the ball back after Larry Sanders blocked a Darren Collison shot. They had time for one shot, and everyone in the arena knew who was taking it. So did Collison. In the final seconds, Collison stuck to Maynor like glue and forced him into a contested 17-foot jump shot at the buzzer. Maynor missed, and the game was over. UCLA survived, but the game wasn't easy.

Finally, UCLA had no more thrilling wins left. After three consecutive Final Fours and a 26-win season in 2009, the season came to an end. In the second round, Villanova trounced the Bruins. Collison finished with 15 points in his final career game, and Shipp scored 18 in his last game as a Bruin. Though it wasn't known at the time, Jrue Holiday played his last as a Bruin as well. He finished with just four points on 1-for-6 shooting. The final score was Villanova 89, UCLA 69.

Understandably, the 2009 Bruins took a step back. The talent lost to the NBA was too much to overcome, but UCLA did have a strong team. In 2010, things drastically changed at UCLA and for Coach Howland. The Bruins soon began a slide from which Coach Howland never quite recovered.

University of North Carolina won the NCAA basketball national championship in 2009.

2009–10

Going into the 2009–10 season, a fresh new group of Bruins joined the squad. While Coach Ben Howland didn't sign the No. 1-ranked recruiting class in the country, he did bring in what was considered by most recruiting pundits to be one of the finest classes in America. Nearly everyone believed UCLA would stay near the top of the college basketball rankings despite its youth. The new crop of freshmen was different, however. The class was tall, talented, and troublesome. Tyler Honeycutt was the star of the class, a five-star recruit from Sylmar, California. Brendan Lane, Mike Moser, and Anthony Stover were all four-star recruits, and Reeves Nelson, a 6'7" three-star recruit from Modesto, rounded out the class. The signing class brought in to Westwood in 2009 was supposed to keep the Bruins relevant. Instead, the players were Coach Howland's worst nightmare. Reeves Nelson and Anthony Stover were eventually both kicked off the team. Tyler Honeycutt was a good player for UCLA, but stayed only two years, and later had his own very serious off-the-court problems. In 2018, Honeycutt committed suicide following a reported shootout with police. Brendan Lane stayed three years at UCLA, but his contribution was minimal, and he eventually transferred to Pepperdine. Mike Moser was the best player in the class, but not at UCLA. After one season, he transferred to UNLV, where he earned Honorable Mention All-America acclaim. He then transferred again and played his final season at Oregon.

Despite all the negative press resulting from the 2010 season, there were also bright spots. As a senior, Michael Roll had his finest season, averaging 14.1 points per game to lead the team. Malcolm Lee, now a sophomore and part of the highly-touted recruiting class of the prior year, also had a major breakthrough season, scoring 12.1 PPG and having a strong defensive season. Nikola Dragovic continued to frustrate fans as a senior, but he sometimes shot the ball well. Though he dealt with injuries, sophomore Drew Gordon showed many flashes of great talent. Of the freshmen, Reeves Nelson and Tyler Honeycutt were the most effective. Nelson averaged 11.1 PPG on the season. He had a scrappy, tough-guy mentality that drew him to fans. Honeycutt, too, was a major contributor. He led the Bruins in rebounding and showed flashes of solid shooting and playmaking ability.

Despite the many talented pieces, Coach Howland had difficulty making the 2009–10 roster into a team. Clashing personalities, underachievers, and cancerous members held the squad back. From the very beginning, trouble was clearly brewing in Westwood. In the first exhibition game played before the official start of the season, UCLA beat NAIA (National Association of Intercollegiate Athletics) opponent Concordia University Irvine by just 62–61. A lot of work was still to be done.

The Bruins began the regular season in the most shocking of ways. Entering the season opener against Cal State Fullerton, the Bruins had beaten the Titans in nine straight meetings, but this season was different. The game went to overtime, and then another. At the end of double overtime, the Titans prevailed, 68–65. The Titans played zone defense and forced the Bruins to shoot from the perimeter. Shot after shot, UCLA missed. The Bruins shot just 31 percent from the field, 17.2 perfect from three, and 47.1 percent from the free-throw line. The season-opening loss was the first for UCLA since Steve Lavin's final season.

The loss was one of many for the Bruins in 2010. Though they were able to pick up a victory over Cal State Bakersfield and then add another win over Pepperdine, the season soon fell apart. On November 26, the University of Portland blew out UCLA in the 76 Classic, 74–47. The loss was one of the most embarrassing for UCLA in its rich history. The Bruins played better the next night, hanging close with No. 12 Butler until the end. With 0.6 seconds remaining on the clock, however, Bulldog forward Gordon Hayward stepped to the line and knocked down two free throws to win the game. The Bruins then lost by 11 to Long Beach State, 12 to No. 1 Kansas, and 18 to Mississippi State in the John R. Wooden Classic. The Bruins were 2–6.

Over the final four nonconference games, UCLA won three, and though the three wins all came against low-level competition, Coach Howland and the Bruins would take any wins in 2010. Five Bruins scored in double figures against New Mexico State, led by 20 points from Lee. UCLA won, 100–68, over the Aggies. Following a loss to Notre Dame, spoiling a brilliant 29-point performance from Lee, the Bruins used a balanced attack to beat Colorado State and then were led by 21 points from Reeves Nelson

UCLA Spirit Squad, 2010 (Erkki Corpuz Collection).

in a win over Delaware State. When conference play began, the Bruins were an astonishing 5–7, despite playing only two ranked teams.

UCLA began Pac-10 play with a New Year's Eve win over Arizona State, 72–70. Dragovic led the way with 23 points, knocking down six three pointers. The Bruins shot 83.3 percent from the field in the first half but barely hung on in the second half for the close win. One final victory in 2009 didn't foreshadow good things to come in 2010. The Pac-10 season would be one of the toughest for UCLA in history. The Bruins were blown out by Arizona, and though they snuck past Cal to get the second conference win, the season was going in the wrong direction. UCLA lost to Stanford and then USC. They beat both Washington schools, including another one-point win over UW, but then lost to Oregon.

Throughout the entirety of the Pac-10 season, UCLA never put together a string of wins to give anyone confidence. Against Oregon State, the Bruins dominated statistically. They shot 65.7 percent from the field and held the Beavers to 37.3 percent. Nelson finished with a double-double, 14 points and 12 rebounds. The Bruins backed up their win over OSU with a win over Stanford. They played a clean offensive game, turning the ball over only five times. Nelson again led the way with 18 points. Whenever they put together a couple wins, however, crushing losses were sure to come next. After finally getting back to .500 with an 11–11 record, UCLA lost to Cal and then USC. Against the Golden Bears, Michael Roll scored 22 points, but no other Bruin had more than nine. Against USC, Roll was again the star for UCLA, scoring 21 points, but UCLA missed nine free throws in the five-point loss.

No matter what Coach Howland tried, nothing seemed to work for more than one or two games. Against the Washington State Cougars, UCLA won by 20, but two nights later, they lost to the University of Washington by 29. On February 25, UCLA beat Oregon State, but two nights later, threw away a game against Oregon. A total of 14,407 fans at McKale Center in Tucson, Arizona, saw the home team Wildcats hand UCLA its 16th loss of the season, guaranteeing the Bruins would finish with a losing record.

After losing to ASU in the Pac-10 regular-season finale, the Bruins finished with an 8–10 record in Pac-10 play. Only twice in the previous 50 seasons had UCLA finished with less than eight conference wins. Somehow, the Bruins pulled themselves together for one final strong performance. In the opening round of the Pac-10 tournament, the Bruins took on the same Arizona team that beat them seven days earlier, and this time, they came out on top. The game was played at Staples Center, and though neither team was particularly good, a large crowd still showed up to see the traditional western powers. Nelson finished with 19 points and 10 rebounds, and Dragovic and Roll each scored 18 for the Bruins. UCLA shot 53.2 percent from the field, outrebounded Arizona, and scored more at the free-throw line. The final score was UCLA 75, Arizona 69, and the win was UCLA's last for the season. One night later, Cal easily defeated the Bruins. Roll scored 27 points in his final game in a Bruins uniform, but Cal's dominant offense, shooting 60 percent for the entire game, was too much.

The tumultuous season, finally over, was a disaster for the Bruins. Nothing was left to do but put the season in the rearview mirror, focus on the future, and strive to be better. The year 2011 would be a bounce-back season.

Duke University won the NCAA basketball national championship in 2010.

2010–11

Following the disastrous and surprising 2010 season, Coach Ben Howland and the Bruins recovered in 2011, increasing their win total substantially and challenging for the Pac-10 title. The Bruins improved statistically in both scoring offense and scoring defense, and though they still lacked star power that could take them to the next level, the five Bruins starters were all solid in 2011. Sophomore Reeves Nelson, coming off a strong freshman season, improved greatly. He led the team in both scoring (13.9 points per game) and rebounding (9.1 rebounds per game). Malcolm Lee, the dependable 6'5" shooting guard, finished second on the team in scoring, with a 13.1 PPG average. Tyler Honeycutt improved from his freshman to sophomore year as well, and he finished third on the team in scoring. Two newcomers also played important roles for the Bruins in 2011. Josh Smith, a five-star recruit, had the highest expectations of any of the incoming freshman, and he played the biggest role in his first season. Though Smith was notably overweight (with the weight being an issue during his entire career), coming it at a listed 350 pounds, he had the ability to score on the inside that was rare in college hoops. Joining him was a JC transfer from Chicago named Lazeric "Zeke" Jones. As a junior, and in his first season in Westwood, Jones contributed solidly, leading the Bruins in assists with 3.6 per game.

After two straight exhibition wins at Pauley Pavilion, the Bruins tipped off the 2010–11 season in impressive fashion. The opponent was Cal State Northridge, a struggling team from the Big West, and the Bruins did as much as they could to provide fans some optimism. The Bruins held CSUN to just 29 percent shooting, forced 27 turnovers, outrebounded the Matadors, scored more in the paint, chipped in more second-chance points, and scored more in transition. After winning, 83–50, the Bruins were 1–0.

In the second game of the year, the Bruins didn't play as well but still beat Pepperdine. They followed up their win over the Waves with a win over the University of the Pacific Tigers before taking on tougher competition in the NIT Season Tip-Off. Against the No. 7 Villanova Wildcats at Madison Square Garden, the Bruins proved that, though improved, they were behind other top programs in the country. Corey Fisher scored 26 for the Wildcats to lead the way, and though the game was close statistically, Villanova won at the free-throw line. The game was a foul fest, and when it came to a close, the Wildcats made 10 more free throws and won by eight points. The Bruins were 3–1. In the tournament third-place game the next night, UCLA lost again, this time to VCU. After a strong start against inferior competition, the Bruins fell in their first two against tougher opponents, and the path going forward was still very difficult.

On December 2, the Bruins traveled to Lawrence, Kansas, to take on the fourth-ranked Kansas Jayhawks. Going into the game, Kansas had a school-record and national-best home winning streak stretching back 63 games. The game was physical throughout, but both teams played extremely well. Two players led UCLA, Josh Smith, who recorded his first career double-double, and Tyler Honeycutt, the best player on the floor for either team. At halftime, Kansas led by just three. In the second half, UCLA hung in the entire way. Trailing, 75–71, Smith scored to bring the Bruins within two with 37 seconds to play. The Bruins fouled, and then Kansas guard Tyshawn Taylor made one of two free throws to give the Jayhawks a three-point lead. The Bruins were then unable to score, and the game seemed over. But drama was to ensue. With 19.6 seconds remaining, Kansas's Marcus Morris missed the front end of a one-and-one. Players fought for the rebound, and the ball got tied up; the possession arrow pointed in Kansas's favor. The Bruins set up their press defense, and after Tyrel Reed received a pass, he quickly turned it over while trying to find a teammate. Honeycutt collected the errant pass at the top of the key, and after circling under the basket and back out to the perimeter, he passed the ball to Lee, who quickly returned it to Honeycutt. Beginning on the left wing outside the three-point line, Honeycutt took two dribbles to his right and launched a long three pointer. With 4.0 seconds remaining on the clock, he buried the shot to tie the game. Kansas had no timeouts and quickly inbounded. UCLA guard Malcolm Lee and Kansas guard Mario Little raced for a loose ball. With just over one second remaining, Little picked up the ball and fired at the basket. He missed, but a whistle sounded. A foul was called on Lee. The two players touched as they reached for the ball, and unfortunately for UCLA, the foul was called on Lee. When the whistle blew, Coach Howland grabbed his water bottle and threw it to the floor. He was furious, and he had a right to be. The contact was incidental, minor, and not worthy of a foul call. Honeycutt finished with 33 points, including five made three-pointers, but because of the late foul, Kansas won the game. Little knocked down one free throw and the final score was 77–76. The Bruins then returned home three days later and lost their fourth in a row, this time to the University of Montana. Suddenly, the Bruins were again looking very similar to the 2010 team.

UCLA fortunately snapped out of its early season funk, and it did so in a big way. After beating Cal Poly and UC Davis, the Bruins took on the 18th-ranked BYU Cougars in the John R. Wooden Classic in Anaheim. BYU played well offensively, but the Bruins were the more disciplined team. Jimmer Fredette led BYU, and he finished with 25 points. Brandon Davies and Jackson Emery also played well for the Cougars, combining for 33 points, but no other BYU player scored more than six. Reeves Nelson scored a team-leading 23. The difference on the scoreboard came in the turnover department. UCLA turned it over only 10 times, while BYU turned it over 19. Though the Cougars shot a higher percentage from the floor, UCLA had ten more attempts and won, 86–79. The Bruins then won their final two nonconference games before the start of Pac-10 play.

UCLA began conference play on December 29 against Washington State at home and came away with a win. Klay Thompson led the way with 26 points for WSU, knocking down all 12 of his free throw attempts, but 21 points each from Lee and Nelson helped UCLA. The opening-game win was quickly followed by two frustrating losses. Against Washington and USC, the Bruins never got on track offensively. Against the Huskies, the Bruins shot just 35.3 percent from the field, and against USC, they shot just 39.6 percent. The offense struggled, though the defense played well. Following the two straight losses, the Bruins did enough against Oregon State and Oregon, though the offense was still ineffective for long stretches during each game. The Bruins beat the Beavers with their defense, forcing 21 turnovers, and then they knocked off the Ducks two nights later with another strong defensive showing. Against Cal, it was a different story. UCLA's usually strong defense was poor, but its offense came alive. Lazeric Jones and Reeves Nelson each tallied 24 points, and despite giving up more points than in any of their previous 12 games, the Bruins won, 86–84. The game came down to the wire. After blowing a big lead late, Nelson tapped in a missed shot at the buzzer for the win. The Bruins then beat Stanford two nights later to run their winning streak to four. Lee led all scorers with 23 points.

The Bruins lost to the University of Arizona, the eventual Pac-10 champion, on January 27, but the team was dramatically improved over the prior year, and it would not fall apart as conference play progressed. Rather, the team made a run. The Bruins beat ASU by one in overtime in Tempe to begin a stretch of six consecutive wins. Against USC, defense and rebounding propelled the Bruins over the Trojans. The same could be said in a win over Steve Lavin-coached St. John's, though the Bruins had to overcome 22 turnovers and a monster 32-point performance from Red Storm guard Dwight Hardy. In back-to-back wins over the two Pac-10 schools from Oregon, Lee averaged 22 points, and a balanced performance pushed the Bruins over the Stanford Cardinal on February 17.

The winning streak ended at six when Jorge Gutierrez torched the Bruins for 34 points and the Cal Bears beat the Bruins in Berkeley, but more positive moments were on the horizon for UCLA. The Bruins collected their 20th win of the season against the ASU Sun Devils at Pauley Pavilion, but the game two nights later has gone down in as one of the finest moments in UCLA basketball history.

On February 26, 2011, UCLA took on No. 10 Arizona in the home finale at Pauley Pavilion. The majority of the game itself was not particularly noteworthy, though the Bruins enjoyed a blowout win over a favored opponent. A basket by a walk-on in the final seconds garnered the attention. The 2011 season marked the end of an era. Pauley Pavilion first opened in 1965, and the 1966 UCLA basketball season was the first at Pauley Pavilion. In the first-ever game, Lew Alcindor and the freshmen Bruins beat the two-time defending national champion varsity squad, 75–60, in an exhibition. Alcindor finished with 31 points and 21 rebounds. John Wooden, of course, coached the varsity. For the next 46 seasons, the Bruins played their home games at Pauley Pavilion, but 2012 would be different. Though major renovations began in 2010, the team still played throughout the 2011 season in the storied arena. UCLA was set to take its show on the road, as the Pauley Pavilion renovation construction continued. The game against Arizona was the last game at "Old Pauley." With the Bruins leading by 21 points with under one minute to play, Coach Howland pulled out his starters and emptied the bench. The walk-ons were coming in. With 25.8 seconds remaining, the final basket at old Pauley Pavilion was scored, and the player who laid in the ball after catching an air ball was Tyler Trapani, the great-grandson of John Wooden. In the house that Wooden built, there could be no better player to score the final basket. UCLA fans and players jumped for joy. The moment was not lost on them. It was an incredible moment for not only Tyler Trapani and his family but for the UCLA family as well. Another 20 months elapsed until UCLA played in Pauley Pavilion again, but all were left with another moment to cherish.

Trapani scores the final basket in "Old Pauley" (Erkki Corpuz Collection).

the Sweet 16, they would first have to beat the Florida Gators, the No. 2 seed in the region. Like they had done to the Bruins before, Florida played great team ball, jumped out to a lead, and slowly extended it until the game was out of reach. UCLA didn't play poorly, but the better team won: Florida 73, UCLA 65. The 2011 season was over.

UCLA, improved greatly from the year before; 2012 would be a different story, unlike any season in recent UCLA history. The 2012 team had no home court and had diminished fan support. The Bruins lost talent from the roster, and Ben Howland lost control of the team.

University of Connecticut won the NCAA basketball national championship in 2011.

2011–12

The 2011–12 season brought moderate expectations and also extreme challenges. Tyler Honeycutt went to the NBA, and Malcolm Lee decided to skip his senior season and go to the league as well. Reeves Nelson was the Bruins' leading returning scorer, but by the time his junior season rolled around, his attitude problems began to wear thin on everyone, and he was kicked off the team early in the season. Josh Smith, now a sophomore, had the same problems in his second year as he did in his first. Despite rumors all offseason that he was losing weight, the rumblings proved to be false. He was still much too heavy to be a consistent, dominant force inside that the Bruins hoped he would be. The Bruins instead relied on players to step into roles that they were perhaps not capable of filling. Lazeric Jones was a good player, but in 2012, he was forced to carry the team. He did an admirable job, showing talent, heart, and tenacity from beginning to end. Jones led the team in both scoring and assists. Two new players joined, and both were starters. David and Travis Wear are identical twins who played with nearly identical styles. They transferred from the University of North Carolina, and, after sitting out one year due to transfer rules, they were both eligible

In the final week of the conference season, the Bruins split a pair of games with the Washington schools and finished in second place in the Pac-10 conference, an incredible turnaround from the year before. The Bruins went into the NCAA Tournament on a sour note, however, losing to Oregon in blowout fashion in the Pac-10 Conference Tournament quarterfinals.

UCLA entered the NCAA Tournament as the No. 7 seed in the Southeast Regional and took on the No. 10 seed Michigan State Spartans in the opening round. The Bruins jumped out to a huge lead at halftime, dominating the Spartans in every facet of the game. At the break, the score was 42–24, Bruins, but MSU wouldn't quit. In the second half, things flipped upside down. The Spartans played brilliantly, and the Bruins went cold. Over the final 20 minutes, MSU was unstoppable offensively, but UCLA held them off just long enough to secure the win. Four Bruins scored in double figures, and despite 24 points, 11 rebounds, and 10 assists for Draymond Green, the Bruins survived. Their second-round opponent was a familiar one. If the Bruins hoped to advance to as redshirt sophomores. Tyler Lamb improved as a sophomore, Jerime Anderson had his finest season as a senior, and Norman Powell showed flashes as a freshman, though all certainly had their share of struggles as well.

Ultimately, the 2011–12 Bruins were grinders. Following the dismissal of Reeves Nelson in December, the shunning of Anthony Stover (who was kicked off the team after the season), and the improved team chemistry, UCLA turned what could have been one of the most embarrassing seasons in school history into a somewhat understandable year of ups and downs. The Bruins, to be clear, were not great, but they played hard. On the defensive end, the 2012 Bruins were the best team since 2008, and all their work was done without any home-court advantage. The 2011–12 season was the UCLA road show. While Pauley Pavilion was closed for renovations, UCLA played its "home" games on the road. Of the 18 UCLA home games, 14 were played at the Sports Arena, the old, raggedy arena just south of campus at USC, within walking distance of the Los Angeles Memorial Coliseum and Galen Center. The other four games, including the John R. Wooden Classic, were played at the Honda Center in Anaheim.

The Bruins began the season with a home game against Loyola Marymount at the Sports Arena. UCLA was ranked No. 17 in the country, but it was not yet capable of playing high-quality basketball. With many new pieces, poor team chemistry early in the season, and an adjustment period for traveling for every game, the Bruins needed time to jell. They lost their season opener to LMU, 69–58, fell out of the AP rankings, and wouldn't rejoin the top 25 until the following year. Things went from bad to worse in the opening game of the Maui Invitational against Middle Tennessee State University. Josh Smith led the Bruins with 15 points, but he didn't receive much help. The Bruins shot just 37.3 percent from the field, while the Blue Raiders shot an incredible 71.4 percent from the floor and knocked down 10 out of 11 three-pointers. UCLA fell, 86–66.

The Bruins finally got in the win column in their third game, beating Chaminade, 92–60. Jerime Anderson scored 20 points, and Lazeric Jones played a complete game, totaling 19 points, seven assists, and six rebounds. Despite the blowout win, things were going to get more difficult for the Bruins before they got better. In the Maui Invitational semifinal, No. 14 Kansas blew out the Bruins, and then one night later, No. 15 Michigan took apart UCLA and handed the team its fourth loss in the first five games.

When UCLA returned to the Sports Arena, not many fans greeted them. Attendance for the season dipped dramatically playing away from the Westwood campus. Against the Pepperdine Waves, only 3,885 fans made the trek through traffic to see the Bruins play. UCLA played its best defensive game thus far, holding Pepperdine to just 39 points. The Bruins struggled from the field as well, but took good care of the ball and outlasted the Waves to win, 62–39. Five days later, the Bruins had their final chance to collect a marquee out-of-conference win. They played the University of Texas, and though they grabbed a six-point lead at halftime, they couldn't hold it over the final 20 minutes. Jones scored 21 for UCLA, but it wasn't enough: Texas 69, UCLA 59.

In the remaining nonconference games, the Bruins padded their win-loss record, but against subpar opponents. The Bruins beat Penn at the Honda Center and then Eastern Washington at the Sports Arena. By now, Jones had taken full control of the reins as UCLA's leader, averaging 20 PPG in the two wins. Against fellow University of California schools, Davis and Irvine, the Bruins won by an average of 36 points. UCLA held UC Davis to just 23.6 percent from the floor and then used a balanced, efficient offensive attack to take care of UC Irvine. Against the Richmond Spiders, the Bruins struggled on the offensive end but dominated on the boards to escape with another win, their fifth in a row before the start of conference play.

The conference was different than in previous years—the Pac-10 expanded, adding Colorado and Utah to become the Pac-12 Conference. Though the main reason for conference expansion in the west, and throughout the country, was for football, it affected basketball as well. The double round-robin schedule was no more. Eighteen conference games would still be played each season, and UCLA would always play USC both home and away. In 2012, the Bruins only played the new conference members once, in Los Angeles. Future trips to Boulder and Salt Lake City would be challenging, but that was for another time. With the added competition, winning the Pac-12 was a major challenge.

The Bruins began Pac-12 play on December 29 against Stanford in Palo Alto. Entering the game, the Bruins had a 7–5 record and were winners of their previous five, but in order to make the NCAA Tournament in March, they would need to make a serious run in conference play. Against the Cardinal, the game was a one-man show for the Bruins. Jones led UCLA with 26 points. Though the Bruins hit just 9 of 27 shots in the first half, they only trailed by one. UCLA's defense was strong throughout the game, holding the Cardinal to just 34.5 percent from the floor, but the offense let UCLA down. The final score was Stanford 60, UCLA 59. Following the heartbreaking one-point loss, the Bruins felt the sting of a blowout loss. Cal took apart UCLA's usually sharp defense. Allen Crabbe led the way with 20 points, and the Bears beat the Bruins, 85–69.

On January 5, the Bruins took on the Arizona Wildcats at the Honda Center. The John R. Wooden Classic, usually reserved for a nonconference game, was played as a conference game in 2012, against the Wildcats. The Bruins played well. Travis Wear finished with 20 points, and the Bruins came away with a win. They were then able to make it a perfect weekend with a commanding win over ASU two days later.

The 2012 season didn't have many high points, but one of them came on January 15 against USC. The game was played at the Galen Center, a home game for the Trojans, with the new arena sitting right near the old Sports Arena. The Bruins played a complete game against the rival Trojans. They shot 51 percent from the floor, held the Trojans to 36 percent, outrebounded them, 44–19, scored more in the paint, had more second-chance points, and scored more in transition. Travis Wear finished with 19 points and eight rebounds. Jones scored 15 points and dished out five assists. UCLA walked out with a 66–47 win.

Following the win over USC, the Bruins proved they were scrappy enough to play hard and win their share of games with effort, determination, and fundamental play, but they also lacked talent like few teams in UCLA history. The Bruins lost two close games in Oregon to the Beavers and the Ducks, but blew out their new conference mates, University of Utah and Colorado, in their first meeting as Pac-12 opponents. Against the Utah Utes, the Bruins played efficiently on offense, but their defense again led them to victory. Against Colorado, the story was the same. Jones finished with 17 points and nine assists, and the defense played extremely well.

Against the Washington Huskies, the Bruins lost in heartbreaking fashion. After leading for most of the game, UCLA squandered a lead late, and Terrence Ross and the Huskies stole a win. The Bruins then won three of their next four, losing only to Cal, but beating USC once again. This time the game was at home, played at the Sports Arena, where USC students could walk to the game from their dorms. Over the final five games, the Bruins reinforced what many had already come to know: they were a solid team, certainly not bad, but also not tournament quality. On February 18, Steve Lavin and St. John's beat UCLA, 66–63. The game was surely one of Coach Lavin's finest in an otherwise poor season for the Red Storm. UCLA then won three of their final four games, losing only one close game to the University of Arizona on the road. The Bruins finished with an 11–7 record in Pac-12 play, placing them in fifth place at the end of the regular season.

While some prognosticators considered the Bruins to be a bubble team going into the Pac-12 Tournament, they were in reality just off the bubble and likely needed to win the Pac-12 Tournament to make the big dance. The Bruins beat the USC Trojans in the first round, holding them to just 40 points, their third win over USC in the third different venue in Los Angeles, none of which was Pauley Pavilion. But UCLA lost the next night to Arizona, and the season was over. UCLA finished with an overall 19–14 record.

For the Bruins, the 2012 season was frustrating. They began the season ranked, lost their first game, never rejoined the AP rankings, and missed the NCAA Tournament. There was trouble within the program, and a *Sports Illustrated* article damning Ben Howland, Reeves Nelson, and more was soon on the way. The team played hard, reaching near its maximum potential, but was missing pieces. Coach Howland cleared out many of the bad apples within the program, but questions remained. Coach Howland was on the hot seat. After nine seasons, many, including vocal critic Bill Walton, had seen enough. The No. 1 recruiting class in the country was on its way. The Bruins were greatly improved for 2013. Would that be enough to save Coach Howland's job? With Pauley Pavilion reopening, and elite talent coming to Westwood, Coach Howland needed to put up or shut up. UCLA fans demanded a return to greatness. Coach Howland was coaching for his job.

University of Kentucky won the NCAA basketball national championship in 2012.

2012–13

Entering his 10th season, Coach Ben Howland had just signed the No. 1 recruiting class in the country, but many believed he wouldn't know what to do with his talented roster. Coach Howland's style was built on developing players, fine-tuning their athletic gifts, teaching them to play tough defense, and winning with disciplined offense. In an era filled with players who left early for the NBA, this was getting harder to accomplish, especially at a high-profile program like UCLA. In order to save his job, Coach Howland had to turn back the clock and make UCLA nationally relevant again.

According to the Scout recruiting service, the Bruins signed three five-star recruits and one four-star recruit, and along with several key returning players, the expectations were higher for the 2013 Bruins than in any season since 2008. Shabazz Muhammad was the crown jewel of the 2012 recruiting class, a consensus five-star recruit, and seen by some as the No. 1 overall player in the class. Though Muhammad missed the first three games of the season following an appeal with the NCAA regarding his eligibility, he was eventually ruled eligible and allowed to compete for the Bruins. Muhammad was a strong left-handed guard. At 6'6" 225 pounds, the star from Las Vegas used his body to attack defenders, relentlessly driving to the hoop. He was a good enough outside shooter and a strong-willed competitor. In his lone season for the Bruins, he led the team in scoring, averaging 17.9 points per game.

Along with Muhammad, Kyle Anderson, Tony Parker, and Jordan Adams were part of the top-ranked recruiting class. Anderson, like Muhammad, was a consensus five-star recruit. At 6'9", Anderson presented unbelievable matchup problems. Nicknamed "Slow Mo" because of his often-deliberate pace when controlling the ball, Anderson is one of the most unique players to ever pass through Westwood. Much debate concerned what Anderson's position of the future would be. His passing ability was his greatest strength, and while playing at the legendary St. Anthony's program in New Jersey, he was a point guard. At UCLA, he too would play point guard, but not until his sophomore season. As a freshman, he

Former UCLA guard/forward Kyle Anderson (Erkki Corpuz Collection).

was a small forward, and his biggest contribution was his rebounding. In 2013, he led the team with 8.6 rebounds per game. Tony Parker, a 6'9" center from Georgia, was raw. As a freshman, his minutes were limited, and his contribution was minor. Of the four-man recruiting class, Jordan Adams was the least regarded of the four players, but as a freshman, he was the most complete player. Adams, like Anderson, was slow of foot but loaded with skill. He was UCLA's best shooter and most natural scorer, and he was an instinctual defender and clutch performer. He finished second on the team in scoring and third in assists; often, he was the go-to man down the stretch.

Of course, players returned from the prior year. Travis Wear was solid as a junior, scoring 10.9 PPG, while twin David was a steady contributor. Larry Drew II, like the Wear twins, was a transfer from North Carolina, and in his one season with UCLA, he was the starting point guard. Drew had his finest college season in 2013, earning All-Pac-12 First Team honors, averaging 7.3 assists per game and breaking Pooh Richardson's single-season assists record with 256 total.

On November 9, 2012, the Bruins returned to a place of comfort, and fans joined them for a celebration. Pauley Pavilion was once again open, celebrities flocked to see the Bruins play at home again, and the arena was better than ever. UCLA was ranked No. 13 in the country, and a record crowd of 13,513 filled new Pauley Pavilion to see the Bruins take on Indiana State University. Coach Howland promised his team would play a new brand of exciting, offensive basketball, and in the season opener, the Bruins didn't disappoint. Adams led the team with 21 points in his career debut, Anderson collected a double-double with 10 points and 10 rebounds, and the Wear twins combined for 30 points and 17 rebounds. The Bruins won, 86–59, and were 1–0 on the season.

The Bruins followed up their impressive season-opening performance with a clunker. Against UC Irvine, the Bruins were pushed to overtime. After falling behind, 79–78, in the OT period, Larry Drew II drove to the basket and made the game-winning layup with 17 seconds left. The Bruins escaped. Despite winning the game, UCLA was in need of a boost. Prior to the game, freshmen Kyle Anderson, Jordan Adams, and Tony Parker all donned shirts that read, "Free Shabazz." Following UCLA's 100–70 win over James Madison, the NCAA cleared Muhammad. The Bruins traveled across the country to Brooklyn, New York, to take part in the Legends Classic tournament, and despite the excitement of Muhammad's debut, the Bruins fell flat. Muhammad scored 15 points off the bench, and Adams led the way with 22. But the Bruins shot just 40.9 percent from the floor, and the Georgetown Hoyas took them down, 78–70.

The next night, Muhammad was inserted into the starting lineup and led UCLA with 21 points in a win over Georgia, but the Bruins needed time to click as a team. On November 25, UCLA lost to Cal Poly at home. It was an embarrassing defeat, and the following week the team dropped completely out of the AP rankings. Norman Powell led the way for UCLA against Cal State Northridge with 17 points off the bench, but UCLA then fell to No. 23 San Diego State in the John R. Wooden Classic. Those who held out hope that Coach Howland was still the man for the job were hard-pressed to defend their stance. The Bruins would make a run, however, and it began with a win over Texas.

Against the Longhorns, UCLA's defense rose to the occasion. The Bruins held UT to just 37.1 percent from the floor and 20 percent from beyond the three-point line. Muhammad, Adams, and Anderson all scored in double figures for the Bruins, and though UCLA struggled from the field too, they did enough to come away with the win. A late spurt by Adams put the Bruins over the top. After trailing most of the game, UCLA scored 12 of the final 14 points and won, 65–63. The surprising win helped catapult UCLA into a winning streak. UCLA beat Prairie View A&M by 42 points, Muhammad leading the way with 25. The Bruins beat Long Beach State, getting a combined 45 points from Muhammad and Adams, and then blew out Fresno State. Against the Bulldogs, the freshmen again played brilliantly. Muhammad scored 27 points, Adams finished with 25 points and five assists, and Anderson scored 20 points, pulled down 17 rebounds, and dished out seven assists. After winning four straight, the Bruins had their toughest test yet. Against No. 7 Missouri, 11,854 fans at Pauley Pavilion saw the surging Bruins take on the Tigers. The game was a shootout. At halftime, the game was tied at 47. At the end of regulation, it was tied at 88. In the OT period, both teams struggled from the floor, but UCLA hit the big shots. A three-pointer from Muhammad and a short jumper from Travis Wear put the game away for UCLA, which sealed the deal with a defensive stop in the final seconds. Muhammad tied his career high with 27 points, and Wear set his career high with 22. It was UCLA's fifth consecutive win.

On January 3, the Bruins began Pac-12 play against the California Golden Bears and continued their winning streak. Anderson played well again, leading the Bruins with 19 points and 12 rebounds. Drew dished out five assists, and the Bruins played lockdown defense. Two nights later, the Bruins won again. Muhammad scored 23 points, including 10 from the free-throw line, and UCLA beat Stanford, 68–60. When the Bruins made their first trips to Salt Lake City and Boulder as conference mates with the Utah Utes and Colorado Buffaloes, they were riding a seven-game winning streak. The two games each came down to the wire, but in each game, the Bruins came out on top. Muhammad finally struggled against the Utes, as did much of the team, but the defense was stifling. UCLA escaped with a 57–53 win. Against Colorado, Travis Wear scored a new career-high 23 points, and despite Spencer Dinwiddie matching him shot for shot, the Bruins came away with another win.

Following their ninth consecutive win, UCLA finally reentered the AP rankings at No. 24 and then promptly extended its winning streak to 10 against Oregon State. UCLA had a short stay in the rankings, however; after losing to No. 21 Oregon at home on January 19, the Bruins were again on the outside looking in. Over the next four weeks, the Bruins were very inconsistent. On January 24, they had their finest performance of the year to date, knocking off No. 6 Arizona in Tucson. Muhammad scored 23 points, David Wear and Jordan Adams each added 15, and the Bruins defense was solid as usual. They couldn't build off the big win, however; against ASU, the team shot just 34.7 percent from the floor in a loss. The Bruins then inexplicably lost to a poor USC team the following week despite another big performance from Muhammad.

While UCLA had their share of ups and downs in 2013, so did the rest of the conference. Despite giving away games they should have won, the Bruins were in the thick of the Pac-12 race. They beat both Washington—on a last-second buzzer beater from Drew—and Washington State but lost to Cal. The Bruins then outlasted Stanford, relying again on the trio of freshmen to carry the load. Muhammad, Adams, and Anderson scored 63 for the Bruins. The Bruins were 20–7 overall with three weeks remaining in the regular season.

Over the final five games, the Bruins made a push for the Pac-12 crown. They demolished USC, holding the Trojans to just 35.3 percent from the floor, and then survived against ASU in overtime. Against the Sun Devils, Adams led the team in scoring with 22, and Muhammad and Anderson each scored 21. Drew dished out 14 assists. Then on March 2, in front of 13,727 fans at Pauley Pavilion, the Bruins played in their most important game of the season, against No. 11 Arizona. The winner would be in the driver's seat for the conference crown. The game was evenly played throughout. UCLA shot slightly better than Arizona from the floor, but Arizona shot better from three. Arizona outrebounded UCLA but also turned it over more. UCLA scored more in the paint, but Arizona got more from its bench. At halftime, UCLA led by just four, and in the second half, it was tight throughout. With every big play from Arizona came an answer from UCLA. The Bruins finally closed out the game with sharp play in the final minutes and won, 74–69. Muhammad and Anderson combined for 35, but the steady hand of Drew was the difference. He finished with 14 points and nine assists.

With the victory, UCLA needed just one more win in the following week to take home the Pac-12 title, though the team made that difficult. The Bruins lost to Washington State but clinched the title with a win over Washington in the final game of the regular season. The conference title was UCLA's first in five years.

Back in the AP rankings, No. 21 UCLA knocked off ASU in the opening round of the Pac-12 Tournament behind a game-high 20 points from Drew, setting up a third meeting between the Bruins and the Arizona Wildcats. On March 15, UCLA faced No. 18 Arizona at MGM Grand Garden Arena in Las Vegas, and a crowd of over thirteen thousand fans saw a brilliant game. Like they had done so many times in the past, the Bruins and Wildcats played in a thriller that came down to the wire. With one minute remaining, UCLA led 64–61, but the Wildcats controlled the ball. After catching a pass at the top of the key, Grant Jerrett knocked in a game-tying three with 54.6 seconds remaining. UCLA inbounded the ball and ran down the clock. With 26.5 seconds remaining, Adams took a three-point shot on the right wing but came up short. The rebound bounced to Kyle Anderson, and with 22.1 seconds left, he scored the go-ahead layup. After Arizona took a timeout, UCLA set up on defense for the final possession. The Bruins got a stop and won the game, but all was not right. Jordan Adams, closing out on Solomon Hill, leaped to defend the shot, came down awkwardly on his right leg, and broke his foot. His season was over, and the dreams of the Bruins were dead.

In the Pac-12 Tournament championship the following night, five Bruins scored in double figures, but UCLA missed the firepower needed to win. The Oregon Ducks handed UCLA its ninth loss of the season, and six days later, the Minnesota Golden Gophers handed the Bruins their 10th. Despite being the favored seed in the first round of the NCAA Tournament, No. 6–seeded UCLA was a shell of what it was just a week earlier. Without Adams, UCLA's season was essentially over, and Coach Howland's time as the Bruins' leader was over with it. UCLA finished the season 25–10, won the Pac-12 regular-season title, and was exciting, playing with a more free-flowing offense. Still, that wasn't enough to save Coach Howland. He had coached admirably in his time in Westwood, proving he was a quality coach, but the time was right to move on. Shabazz Muhammad left for the NBA, and Larry Drew II left as well. Still, the Bruins returned a great deal of talent to the team in 2014, and the future looked bright. There would be a new coach, one that brought brief excitement and prolonged anger.

University of Louisville won the NCAA basketball national championship in 2013.

CHAPTER 13
Steve Alford (2013–2019)

Steve Alford is not a UCLA man. He didn't play for the Bruins like Wilbur Johns, Gary Cunningham, Larry Farmer, and Walt Hazzard. He didn't work as an assistant for the Bruins like Steve Lavin or spend time as an athletic administrator like Wilbur Johns. He was never fully embraced like Ben Howland once was, he never experienced the success of Jim Harrick, and no one will ever have an impact like Coach John Wooden. Steve Alford will never leave a positive impression now that he is gone from the team. Steve Alford is a basketball man, never to be confused with a Bruins man. He has had notable success as a player and a coach. At UCLA, however, Alford was always an outsider. His personality never meshed with the Hollywood glamour of UCLA, and more important, his teams consistently underperformed. Coach Alford frustrated many fans. Following Ben Howland was a tough task. Coach Howland saw success, but even his accomplishments weren't able to save his job. Coach Alford was not tasked with repeating what Howland did, but improving upon it. Prior to his arrival at UCLA, Steve Alford had already been a college basketball head coach for 22 years. He had seen every possible scenario on a basketball court, but nothing could prepare him for UCLA.

Steve Alford has won a lot of basketball games as a coach, and as long as a university employs him, he'll continue to win a lot of games going forward. He has had notable success at multiple stops during his coaching career, and he has seen many of his players go on to great success in the NBA. His longest-lasting legacy, however, will be the great success he had as a player. Steve's father, Sam, was a high school basketball coach in Indiana, and Steve played for his dad. While others were out enjoying their teenage years, Steve often stayed home and practiced shooting. He had a passion for basketball and an incredible skill. He became one of the greatest outside shooters in Indiana state high school history as well as one of the top shooters in college basketball history. As a sophomore at New Castle Chrysler High School, Alford was one of the top players in the area. As a junior, he was even better, making a huge jump and earning statewide acclaim. As a senior, Alford accomplished every personal accolade imaginable for a high school boy from Indiana. He went over the 2,000-point career mark, averaged 37.7 points per game, scored 57 points in the state semifinals, was named Indiana Mr. Basketball, and was named All-State for the second consecutive year.

In college, it was much of the same for Steve. He went to local Indiana University, playing for Bobby Knight and the Hoosiers, and continued to shred nets with his incredible shooting. As a freshman, Alford started 27 games, scoring 15.5 PPG, and shooting over 91 percent from the free-throw line. Following the season, Alford continued to play for Bobby Knight, but in the summer of 1984, he took off the Indiana University jersey and put on the USA basketball uniform. Playing alongside other amateurs, Michael Jordan and Patrick Ewing among them, Alford helped team USA take home the gold medal. He averaged 10.3 PPG during the tournament, and his excellent showing during the Olympic Games helped propel him into stardom back at Indiana. As a sophomore, Alford earned a spot on the First Team All-Big Ten team, and the Hoosiers made it to the final of the NIT Tournament, losing to UCLA in the championship game. Alford continued to improve in his final two seasons, though now he was fully recognized as the star he was. After increasing his scoring to 18.1 PPG as a sophomore, Alford averaged 22.5 as a junior and 22.0 as a senior. In his final season, 1987, Indiana finished with a 30–4 record and won the national championship. That year was when NCAA adopted the three-point line, and Alford took advantage of it, knocking down 53 percent of his attempts, including seven in the National Championship Game. When Alford's college career ended, his accomplishments were incredible. Three times he was named First Team All-Big Ten, and twice he was named a consensus First Team All-American. He had won a national championship, was named Big Ten MVP, and graduated as Indiana's all-time leading scorer with 2,438 career points. He is considered by many one of the 10 greatest players of the 1980s and one of the top 50 college basketball players of all time.

Despite Alford's incredible college career, many doubts about his ability to score against tougher competition in the NBA existed. He was a shooting guard in a point guard's body. He stood at just 6'2" and wasn't particularly quick, fast, or much of a leaper. What he did, however, he did extremely well. His shooting ability was unquestioned, his conditioning was exemplary, and his dedication was never doubted. Leading up to the 1987 draft, the hometown Indiana Pacers wanted Alford. The Pacers drafted 11th, and many expected to hear Alford's name called. When it was time to make a pick, however, Alford's name was not called, but that of Reggie Miller. Alford instead slid all the way to number 26 in the draft. He was selected by the Dallas Mavericks, where he played for one full season and part of another before he was released. Alford then signed with the Warriors, finishing off the 1988–89 season. At the end of the season, he was released by the Warriors and re-signed with the Mavericks. He played for two more seasons in Dallas, averaging just 4.4 PPG for his career. He signed with the Kings, but was cut shortly thereafter.

Following his unplanned early retirement from playing, Alford and his wife Tanya found themselves in the next phase of their life. Steve Alford the player became Steve Alford the coach. Following a 0–7 start to its season, tiny Division III Manchester University needed a new coach. The previous coach resigned, dealing with health issues that forced him to step away, and the new man to take over was the 27-year-old Indiana legend. Manchester was just a small farming town in Indiana. The basketball program was a perennial loser, with just two winning seasons in the previous 30 years, but now there was hope. Alford was beloved, and there was a belief in Alford not based in anything other than dreams. If he was able to lead the Hoosiers to a national title, and he was able to inspire a state that loved basketball, maybe he would be able to turn around Manchester. After inheriting a 0–7 team, the Spartans finished 4–16 in his first season. Over the next three years, Alford did what everyone hoped he would. In his first full season, the Spartans reached the Division III NCAA Tournament. The next two years, Manchester won the Heartland Collegiate Athletic Conference. In 1995, it had a 30–0 record before falling in the Division III national championship game. Though Alford left Manchester nearly a quarter century ago, he is not forgotten. In 1999, he was inducted into the Manchester University Athletics Hall of Fame.

Following the 1995 season, Coach Alford was on to bigger and better things. For four seasons, he was the head coach at Southwest Missouri State, where he finished with a 78–48 record. His finest season came in 1999. The Bears made a run in the Division I NCAA Tournament, winning two games to reach the Sweet 16 before losing to Duke. Coach Alford made two more stops along the way before landing at UCLA, and he found success in both places. For eight seasons, he led the Iowa Hawkeyes, making the NCAA Tournament three times and the NIT another three. His time in Iowa City was not without controversy, however. In 2002, Iowa's leading scorer, Pierre Pierce, was charged with rape. Coach Alford was his loudest defender. He was adamant that Pierce was not guilty. Eventually Pierce agreed to plead guilty to a lesser charge. Pierce was not kicked off the team, however, but his problems were not behind him. In 2005, Pierce pled guilty to assault with intent to commit sexual abuse, burglary, and criminal mischief. He served 11 months in prison after he was kicked off the team. Despite Alford's success, the events surrounding Pierce and Coach Alford's handling of the situation lost him the support of much of the

Iowa fan base. Following the 2007 season, Alford decided to move on, accepting a job with the New Mexico Lobos, taking a seeming step down from the Big Ten to the Mountain West Conference. In six seasons with New Mexico, Alford proved himself a capable coach, winning four conference titles and twice advancing to the second round of the NCAA Tournament, but never making it further. He finished with 155 wins in six seasons, never winning less than 22 games in a season.

When Ben Howland was fired following the Pac-12 championship season of 2013, UCLA fans were eager to see the Bruins replace a quality coach with an even better one. On March 30, 2013, Steve Alford was announced as UCLA's next basketball coach, signing a seven-year contract worth over $18 million. The announcement came just three days after Alford had agreed to a 10-year extension at New Mexico. Two segments of the fan base took extreme positions—some fans were excited, and others thought he was a terrible choice. Many fans were in the middle, believing UCLA could have made a better choice and also could have done much worse. Alford would have to answer questions about his handling of the Pierre Pierce situation at Iowa, and he faced many more tough questions during his time at UCLA. In his first season with the Bruins, Coach Alford inherited a talented roster. The cupboard was not bare and the pressure to win was on him from the very beginning. Over the next five and a half years, the Bruins won many games, but being a consistent winner is the expectation at UCLA.

Steve Alford (Dick Hansen Collection, CC by 2.0, cropped).

Coach Alford never won a national championship at UCLA or even reached the Final Four or Elite Eight. He never even won the Pac-12 Conference, the only UCLA coach to fall short of a conference crown since Larry Brown. Entering the 2019 season, finding Alford defenders became difficult. In UCLA's 100th season, many fans simply wanted a new coach. Few believed that Coach Alford would ever turn UCLA into a national championship contender again. Finally, the UCLA athletic department could wait no longer. On December 31, 2018, midway through his sixth season, Steve Alford was fired, becoming the first UCLA basketball coach in history to be fired during the middle of a season.

2013–14

The 2013–14 Bruins were loaded with talent. Jordan Adams led the Bruins in scoring, averaging more than 17 points per game as a sophomore. The big star, however, was Kyle Anderson. After a strong freshman season, Anderson considered jumping to the NBA, but decided instead to return to UCLA. As a sophomore, now playing his more natural position of point guard, Anderson was one of the best players in America. His mid-range jump shot improved, and with his tremendous height advantage over all other point guards, he was able to get into the middle of the paint and elevate over smaller defenders. Anderson was multitalented, however, and in his sophomore season, he showed off all his skills. After averaging 14.6 points, 8.8 rebounds, and 6.5 assists per game, Anderson was named to the All-Pac-12 First Team, and All-America Third Team. He became the first player in Pac-12 history to record 200-plus rebounds and 200-plus assists in a single season and the first player in Division I history with 500-plus points, 300-plus rebounds, and 200-plus assists in a season. Joining Adams and Anderson were Norman Powell, Zach LaVine, Bryce Alford, Tony Parker, and the Wear twins, Travis and David. The Bruins were undoubtedly one of the top offensive teams in the nation, scoring 81.2 p.p.g., but just as they did over the next five seasons, they struggled mightily on the defensive end.

UCLA began the season ranked No. 22 by the Associated Press, and after two exhibition wins, the team began its season on November 22 against the Drexel Dragons. After a strong first half, the Bruins struggled in the second but held on to win, 72–67. Anderson finished with 12 points, 12 rebounds, and seven assists. Adams led the Bruins in scoring with 16. David Wear played well, and so did Zach LaVine, a high-flying freshman playing in his first career game.

Over the next six games, the Bruins took care of business against lower-tier opponents. They beat Oakland by 31 points, with Tony Parker collecting a double-double with 21 points and 12 rebounds. They beat Sacramento State by 36, and snuck past Morehead State, thanks to 30 points from Jordan Adams and a triple-double from Kyle Anderson, the first for a Bruin since Toby Bailey in 1995. The Bruins then blew out Chattanooga by 41. After winning their first five games, the Bruins climbed to No. 19 in the rankings and then easily defeated Nevada and Northwestern in back-to-back games in the Las Vegas Invitational. Against the Wolfpack, Adams and LaVine each scored 21 points, and against the Wildcats, Adams, LaVine, and Bryce Alford each scored 18. Kyle Anderson finished with 16 points, nine assists, and nine rebounds in UCLA's 95–79 win. The Bruins then ran their record to 8–0 after knocking off UC Santa Barbara in another high scoring game.

On December 7, the Bruins took on the Missouri Tigers in Columbia, Missouri, and lost their first game during the Steve Alford era. They shot poorly from the field, gave up 10 three-pointers, and couldn't keep the Tigers off the free-throw line. Jabari Brown, Jordan Clarkson, and Earnest Ross each went over the 20-point mark for Mizzou, and UCLA fell, 80–71. Following the loss, UCLA dropped out of the AP rankings, and though the team easily beat Prairie View A&M in its next game, the Bruins had a tough opponent upcoming. On December 19, the Bruins took on the Duke University Blue Devils, ranked No. 8 in the country, at Madison Square Garden. The two blue-blood programs squared off before 15,410 fans who saw that UCLA was not in the same class as Duke. Jabari Parker led the Blue Devils with 23 points, and despite the score being tied at halftime, Duke went on to win big, 80–63. UCLA then won its final two nonconference games against Weber State and Alabama before beginning Pac-12 play.

The Bruins began the conference season against USC with something to prove. New USC coach Andy Enfield, in a pitch to potential recruits, publicly stated, "If you want to play slow, go to UCLA." His comments were made in an open USC practice, surely planned for the media to spread. It appeared to be a shot at Coach Alford and UCLA. Enfield, recently hired by USC from Florida Gulf Coast, hoped to build off his reputation as the architect of "Dunk Coast" and bring style and flair to USC basketball. UCLA had something to say about that. The Bruins ran USC out of the gym. The game was played at Pauley Pavilion, and UCLA showed who runs L.A. and who always will. The Bruins shot 57.7 percent from the floor, knocked down 11 three pointers, outrebounded USC, and scored more in the paint, off turnovers, and from fast-breaks. Anderson finished with 23 points, Adams scored 21 and collected six steals, and Bryce Alford scored 20 off the bench. UCLA's walk-ons were on the court before time expired, with UCLA winning, 107–73.

Despite the thrill of crushing USC, the Bruins could not relax. The next opponent was Arizona, the No. 1-ranked team in the country. On January 9, 13,283 fans packed Pauley Pavilion to see the Bruins and the Wildcats square off. At 15–0, the Wildcats were off to a tremendous start, thanks in part to Nick Johnson, Aaron Gordon, Kaleb Tarczewski, Rondae Hollis-Jefferson, and the rest of their stacked roster. The game was close throughout. Both teams struggled from the floor in the first half. Arizona picked up in the final 20 minutes, but UCLA's edge in the turnover department kept the game close. After trailing by four at the break, UCLA was unable to cut into the Arizona lead, and the two teams played the second half even. Four Bruins scored in double figures, but the cold shooting of Adams and Anderson doomed the Bruins: Arizona 79, UCLA 75.

The Bruins were a strong team in 2014, and despite the early conference loss, they legitimately contended throughout Pac-12 play. LaVine scored 19 against ASU in a win, and Powell scored 19 against Colorado the following week. The Bruins held the Buffaloes to just 40 percent from the floor, and despite cold shooting themselves, they came out with a win. Against Utah, the poor Bruins shooting continued, but this time, they weren't able to get away with it. Despite 28 points, seven rebounds, and seven assists from Anderson, the Bruins dropped to 14–4 after losing in Salt Lake City.

UCLA won seven of their next eight games, dropping only a close contest to Oregon State in Corvallis. Against Stanford, the Bruins collected 15 steals in a win. In the rematch against USC, this time played at the Galen Center, the score wasn't as decisive as the first meeting, but the Bruins still came out on top. Anderson finished with 15 points, 10 rebounds, and eight assists, and the Bruins won by 10. Anderson continued his fine play throughout the rest of the conference season. Against Colorado in the second meeting, he scored 22 points, dished out 11 assists, and pulled down seven rebounds. This was becoming standard for Anderson, and while he was the man who grabbed most of the headlines, Jordan Adams continued to pour in points from all over the court. Against Utah, he scored 24 points, including a perfect 3-for-3 from three-point land, to lead UCLA to another win. Against Cal, he scored 28 and continued to show great anticipation and quick hands on the defensive end, collecting five more steals.

At 21–5, the Bruins were playing their best basketball, but everyone expected more bumps in the road. On February 22, UCLA lost to Stanford, and five days later, they played in the most frustrating game of the season. In need of a bounce-back win, the Bruins played without their two best players. Anderson and Adams were each suspended for one game for a violation of team rules. UCLA was shorthanded, but the game was not short on drama. With 1:01 remaining on the clock, the Bruins trailed by seven. Bryce Alford hit two free clutch three pointers to bring the score to 69-68 in favor of the Ducks, then Joseph Young knocked down two free throws before David Wear hit a miraculous shot. With the Bruins trailing by three with 1.2 seconds remaining, Travis Wear threw a long pass to David Wear on the left wing, well beyond the three-point line, and Wear swished a three-pointer at the buzzer to send the game to overtime. UCLA couldn't finish it off in the extra period, but neither could the Ducks. Both teams went ice-cold in the OT period, scoring only two points apiece, and the game went to a second OT, where Oregon outscored UCLA, 14–10, and won, 87–83. The performance by a shorthanded Bruins team was valiant but still a loss. Alford scored a career-high 31 points, and LaVine finished with 18.

The Bruins won two of their final three Pac-12 games to finish with a 12–6 record in conference play. Despite showing moments of greatness, the Bruins finished in second place, a full three games behind the University of Arizona. In the Pac-12 tournament, the Bruins caught fire. They shot 56.6 percent from the floor in their opening game, easily beating the Oregon Ducks. The following night, they blew out Stanford. Powell scored 22 points, Anderson played a complete game, and the defense held the Cardinal to under 40 percent from the field. Finally, in the championship game, the Bruins faced Arizona again. They had yet to play the Wildcats since facing them over two months earlier. Arizona entered the game ranked No. 4 in the country, but on this day, the Bruins were the better team. At halftime, UCLA led, 43–40, and the game came down to the wire. With under one minute to play, the score was tied at 68, and the Bruins had the ball. After bringing the ball upcourt, Anderson found Adams, who quickly fired a contested three-pointer at the top of the key. Adams knocked down the difficult shot to put the Bruins ahead. They never relinquished the lead, getting multiple stops in the final minute to close out the game. The Bruins were the Pac-12 Tournament champions.

Entering the NCAA Tournament, the Bruins were commonly mentioned as a sleeper national title contender. The road would be tough, but they were talented and, coming off the big conference tournament win, they were confident. As a No. 4 seed, they were the heavy favorite in their opening-round matchup. The Bruins took on the Tulsa Golden Hurricanes and easily came out on top. After missing the NCAA Tournament in 2013 as a freshman because of a broken foot, Adams scored 21 points and led the Bruins with eight rebounds in his tournament debut. Tulsa shot just 36.8 percent from the floor and turned the ball over 16 times. UCLA won, 76–59, and advanced to the second round.

The Bruins' second-round game was very much like the first. They beat Stephen F. Austin, 77-60, with Adams, Anderson, and Powell leading the way. The Bruins played solid defense, were efficient on the offensive end, and collected their second consecutive minimum-stress NCAA Tournament win. The Bruins advanced to the Sweet 16, and a familiar team was there to meet them. On March 27, UCLA took on the Florida Gators, the No. 1 seed in the South Region, and winners in 34 of their 36 games on the season. Just as the Gators had done to the Bruins in years past, they beat UCLA with a balanced offensive attack, solid defense, and smart, tough basketball. The Bruins never got it going on the offensive end. Adams scored 17 points, but took 15 shots to get them. Anderson finished just 4 of 11 from the field, Powell finished 3-for-8, and LaVine and Alford combined for just seven points on 12 shots. The final score was 79–68 in favor of Florida. UCLA's season was over.

University of Connecticut won the NCAA basketball national championship in 2014.

2014–15

Coming off a solid first season under Coach Steve Alford, the Bruins looked to build off year one and make a deeper run in year two. But UCLA's top two players, Kyle Anderson and Jordan Adams, each left early for the NBA. Norman Powell, now a senior, was called upon to do more, and he delivered. The 6'4", 215-pound athletic wing from San Diego had his finest season. He averaged 16.4 points per game and provided countless highlight-reel plays for the Bruins. Bryce Alford, son of Coach Steve Alford, now a sophomore, also had to carry a heavier load in 2015. As a freshman one year prior, Alford and fellow freshman Zach LaVine were key contributors off the bench, but LaVine was now gone, as well, jumping early to the NBA, and Alford remained to take on much of the scoring burden for the Bruins. While Alford was a strong shooter, he struggled in other areas. Far too often, he overpenetrated, finding himself in trouble under the basket. He was a shooting guard forced to play point guard, a solid contributor forced to take on the load of a star player. Despite his faults and the constant criticism that came with being the son of the head coach, Alford had moments of excellent play. As a sophomore, he finished second on the team in scoring, averaging 15.4 PPG, and leading the team in assists with 4.9 per game. Three other Bruins averaged in double figures on the season. Kevon Looney, a long-armed 6'9" freshman from Milwaukee, was an excellent rebounder and solid scorer in his lone season in Westwood. Tony Parker, now a junior, saw an increase in playing time, and like Alford, he was both a frustrating and important piece of the Bruins puzzle. Isaac Hamilton, a sophomore forced to sit out the previous season after a transfer appeal was denied, lacked elite athletic ability, and left UCLA fans scratching their heads at times, but he was a solid contributor as a sophomore, averaging 10.6 PPG Thomas Welsh, a McDonald's All-American from Redondo Beach and soon to become a fan favorite, was a freshman, as well; over the next four years, his role increased dramatically.

With the losses of key personnel came a drop in outside expectations for the Bruins. They began the season unranked by the Associated Press pollsters.

On November 14, the Bruins put on an offensive show during the first game of the season against Montana State. The team shot 57.4 percent from the field. Powell led the Bruins with 25 points, and Looney finished with 20 points and nine rebounds in his collegiate debut. Two nights later, the Bruins collected their second win of the season. Coastal Carolina didn't stand a chance. Five Bruins scored in double figures, led by 17 points and 14 rebounds from Looney. Against Nicholls State in the third game of the year, three Bruins scored over 20 points. Bryce Alford led the team with 28, knocking down six three-pointers. Powell added 23, and Parker scored 20. Finally in the last tune-up game against lower-tier competition, the Bruins easily beat Long Beach State, 77–63. Though the Bruins struggled from the field as a team, they took care of the ball, turning it over only five times in the win.

With a 4–0 record, the Bruins climbed into the AP rankings at No. 22 when they traveled to the Bahamas to take part in the Battle 4 Atlantis tournament. In the opening game, the Bruins took on Oklahoma and struggled mightily. Both teams failed to make open shots, and the game was ugly throughout. Alford led the Bruins in scoring with 19 points, but with 18 attempts. Looney finished with 16 points, but with 15 shots. Buddy Hield led the Sooners in scoring with 24, and Oklahoma knocked off UCLA, 75–65. The next night, UCLA took on North Carolina and were blown out. The Tar Heels entered the game ranked No. 5 in the country and proved they were the better team. The final score was UNC 78, UCLA 56.

After the two losses, the Bruins won four straight, beating University of Alabama at Birmingham, Cal State Fullerton, University of San Diego, and UC Riverside, but winning was going to get much tougher going forward. Three of the next five opponents were ranked in the top 10. On December 13, No. 9

Gonzaga blew out UCLA, 87–74, and one week later, the result was even worse. No. 1 Kentucky put on a first-half clinic against the Bruins. The first meeting between the two top programs in college basketball history in eight years quickly became a rout, and the Bruins were on the wrong side. Kentucky scored the first 24 points of the game and led, 41–7, at halftime. UCLA shot just 8.1 percent from the field in the first half, knocking down only three shots, none from beyond the three-point line, and one free throw. While the Bruins picked up their play in the second half, that wasn't saying much. Kentucky won, 83–44. The 39-point loss was just nine shy of the worst loss in program history.

Coming off back-to-back humiliating losses to top-10 opponents, the Bruins continued their poor play, even against lesser competition. Unranked Alabama beat UCLA, 56–50, and then the Bruins lost their first conference game as well. Unranked Colorado beat UCLA, 62–56, in Boulder, and UCLA began Pac-12 play on the wrong foot. The humiliation continued for Coach Alford and the Bruins when they took on Utah in Salt Lake City. The Bruins scored just 39 points against the No. 10 Utes and were blown out of the gym by 32 points.

The Bruins finally ended their five-game losing streak on January 8, winning their first game in nearly a month. They beat the Stanford Cardinal, but only after two overtime periods. After falling behind by 13 with under eight minutes to play, the Bruins went on a 15–1 run over the next four minutes to take the lead. In the final four minutes, however, both teams went cold. UCLA couldn't score a single point, Stanford knocked down just one free throw, and the game was tied at 66 at the end of regulation. In the OT period, UCLA trailed, 75–73, but with 6.3 seconds remaining, Bryce Alford took an inbounds pass from underneath the basket and hit a fade away go-ahead three-point jump shot from the right corner to put the Bruins ahead. Stanford came back, however, and after a questionable call on the other end, Chasson Randle knocked down one free throw to tie the score and force a second OT period. The Bruins did enough to come away with the victory, 86–81, in the first double-overtime victory for the Bruins since 2011. Kevon Looney finished with 27 points and 19 rebounds in the win.

Though the Bruins had moments of great disappointment in 2015, they salvaged the season to avoid more embarrassment. Following the win over Stanford, they picked up more wins. The Bruins beat Cal and USC in dominant fashion, but then traveled to Oregon and lost to both the Beavers and the Ducks. On January 29, the Bruins got their biggest win of the year to date. In a rematch against the Utah Utes, Norman Powell scored 23 to lead the Bruins, and they knocked off No. 11 Utah, 69–59. Two nights later, UCLA avenged its earlier loss against Colorado, as well, beating the Buffaloes by 13 at home.

In the second half of the conference season, the Bruins began to round into shape, though there were a few hiccups. They beat Stanford again but lost a close game to Cal. With the Bruins leading by one, Dwight Tarwater hit a three for the Bears to give them the lead and ultimately the win, 64–62. The Bruins responded with two straight convincing home wins, beating Oregon State and Oregon to move to 16–10 on the season. Just as they did all throughout the season, the Bruins raised the hopes of many but then quickly brought them back down. After leading ASU at halftime, UCLA blew the lead and lost in Tempe. No. 7 Arizona then shut down the Bruins with elite defense, holding UCLA to 47 points in a Wildcats win.

At 16–12, UCLA was on the bubble and needed a strong finish just to get into the NCAA Tournament conversation. That's exactly what it got. The Bruins finished with three straight wins, beating Washington and Washington State at home. Norman Powell averaged 26 PPG in the two games. In the season finale, UCLA beat USC behind a strong performance from Bryce Alford in front of a big crowd at Pauley Pavilion. Eight days later, the Bruins took on USC again, this time in the quarterfinals of the Pac-12 Tournament, and a different man took charge. Isaac Hamilton was seldom in the spotlight for the Bruins as a sophomore, but against USC on March 12, he was. Hamilton scored 36 points, making 13 of his 17 shots from the field, including seven three-pointers. The Bruins shot 60.3 percent from the floor and crushed the Trojans, 96–70. Though UCLA lost to Arizona the next night, the strong close to the season was enough to get the Bruins in the NCAA Tournament, though the choice was not without controversy.

The Bruins were named the No. 11 seed in the South Regional and took on No. 6 SMU in the first round. The game was low scoring throughout, and in the final seconds, UCLA trailed, 59–57. With 10.9 seconds remaining on the clock, Bryce Alford heaved up a contested three point shot over two defenders. The ball was clearly short and off to the right, but SMU center Yanick Moreira jumped to grab the rebound, misjudging the flight of the ball and interfering while the shot was above the cylinder. Though the shot was off the mark, he still goaltended. Looney was under the basket and ready to clean up the deflection for an easy two, but the Bruins were instead awarded three, putting UCLA up, 60–59. SMU got two shots off, including an attempt at the buzzer, but both fell short, and the Bruins won in miraculous and controversial fashion. The Bruins then crushed No. 14 seed UAB in the second round. Tony Parker led the Bruins with 28 points and 12 rebounds. Despite a frustrating season, the Bruins were off to the Sweet 16 once again.

On March 27, UCLA took on No. 2 Gonzaga in NRG Stadium in Houston. A crowd of 21,168 attended, and though the Bruins were seemingly lucky to be in the position they were, they also hoped for more. Gonzaga was a better team, however, and they outplayed the Bruins. The final score was 74–62, and UCLA's season was over. Norman Powell led the Bruins in scoring with 16 points, but his last game as a Bruin came in another tournament loss. Powell left for the NBA, and UCLA continued to search for the right answers. The 2015 season was a step back for UCLA, and there were many questions going into the following year. While many fans were still on the fence about Coach Steve Alford after his second year, few remained in his corner after year three. That year, 2016, would be a disaster.

Duke University won the NCAA basketball national championship in 2015.

2015–16

The 2016 Bruins were one of the worst teams in the post-Wooden era at UCLA. The Bruins' greatest problems continued to be on defense. Out of the 351 Division I college basketball teams, UCLA ranked 285th in scoring defense, giving up 76.7 points per game. The Bruins lacked athleticism; talent was on the team but not enough to make the Bruins a winner. In the scoring department, a pair of juniors led the way for UCLA. Isaac Hamilton and Bryce Alford were forced to carry a load much too big for UCLA to have any success. Each scored more than 16 PPG on the season, but every high point was accompanied by many low points. Tony Parker finished third on the team in scoring. Parker, the lone player remaining from Ben Howland's final recruiting class, was a load under the basket who often put up big games statistically against inferior opponents. Taller players gave Parker fits, however, and like the rest of the team, he struggled with consistency for much of the year. The remaining two starters were both new to the Bruins lineup. Thomas Welsh was a sophomore, and after spending much of his freshman season sitting next to Coach Alford on the bench, he saw his role increase as a sophomore. The 7'0" center was unique in what he brought to the table. He was a good rebounder, solid interior one-on-one defender, and a calming presence, but his greatest asset was his jump shot. Welsh was one of the best short to mid-range shooters in UCLA history. His jump shot from 10 to 15 feet, especially on the baselines, was a thing of beauty. As his career progressed, his range increased, but when UCLA really needed a bucket, Welsh's bread and butter, his silky smooth shot from mid-range, was often the answer. Lastly, Aaron Holiday, brother of former Bruin Jrue Holiday, was a bulldog, a 6'1" guard constantly in attack mode. As a freshman, he averaged 10.3 PPG.

The Bruins began their season on November 15 at home against the Monmouth University Hawks. Each year, the Bruins play a handful of teams often mocked, called "cupcakes," to rack up wins while the team tries to get better. Monmouth was one of these teams, but in Coach Steve Alford's third year, nothing came easy. At halftime, UCLA led just 34–30. The Bruins struggled in every facet, shooting just 36.7 percent from the floor and missing seven free throws. Monmouth picked up its game in the second half, and UCLA could do nothing to stop it. The Hawks shot 51.6 percent in the second half, forced the game to overtime, and won it in the extra period. UCLA began the season with an unfathomable loss.

Two days later, the Bruins played the Cal Poly Mustangs, and though they again struggled, they came away with a win. The game was high scoring, with both offenses finding great success, UCLA doing much of its scoring inside, while Cal Poly was prolific from the perimeter, knocking down 13 three-pointers. Thomas Welsh led the Bruins with 22 points, Bryce Alford scored 18 and dished out eight assists, and Parker finished with 16 points and 14 rebounds. After beating Pepperdine four days later, the Bruins had a winning streak, just in time for tougher competition. On November 23, UCLA beat UNLV in the Maui Invitational at the Lahaina Civic Center. Alford and Welsh each scored 20, Holiday finished with 18, and the Bruins escaped with a narrow two-point win.

After the opening-game loss, UCLA had won three in a row, but in the Maui Invitational semifinals, it faced the Kansas Jayhawks, the fifth-ranked team in the country. The game was a rout. Kansas was unstoppable offensively. The UCLA defense was nonexistent early, and by halftime, the game was essentially over. At the break, the Jayhawks led, 59–33. When the game ended, the final score was Kansas 92, UCLA 73. Perry Ellis led the Jayhawks with 24 points in only 27 minutes. The next night, UCLA lost to Wake Forest in the third-place game to drop to 3–3 on the season.

Though the Bruins beat Cal State Northridge on November 29, the following game was against the No. 1 team in the country, the same program that humiliated the Bruins the year before. Kentucky was 7–0 when it traveled to Pauley Pavilion to take on the Bruins, and nearly everyone believed they were sure to run their record to 8–0. The Bruins, however, dominated the game from start to finish. They shot 50 percent in the first half and 56 percent in the second. They outscored Kentucky in the paint, scored more off turnovers, outrebounded the Wildcats, and got to the free-throw line at a higher clip. At halftime, they led by eight. At the end of the game, they were on top, 87–77. UCLA beat a No. 1-ranked team for the first time since beating Arizona in March 2003, and the victory was a team effort. All five Bruins starters scored in double figures, led by 21 points and 11 rebounds from Welsh. Hamilton and Alford each scored 15, Parker added 11, and Holiday finished with 10 points and seven assists. Off the bench, Prince Ali finished with eight points, including a tremendous dunk over Alex Poythress in the second half. For a brief time, the Bruins looked like they turned the corner. The season had a long way to go, however, and conference season hadn't even started yet.

The Bruins built off their big win over the Wildcats, and though all three games were settled by just single digits, the Bruins beat Long Beach State, No. 20 Gonzaga, and Louisiana-Lafayette to run their winning streak to five. Two games were left for UCLA before conference play, including one against a traditional basketball powerhouse program. On December 19, No. 22 UCLA took on No. 11 North Carolina in the CBS Sports Classic in Brooklyn, New York. Unlike the earlier game against Kentucky, the Bruins had no magic in them, and there would be no upset. Isaac Hamilton scored 23 for the Bruins, but UCLA was unable to slow down the Tar Heels. Brice Johnson had a monster game for UNC, leading all scorers with 27 and leading the Tar Heels over the Bruins, 89–76. UCLA dropped out of the rankings, and though it beat McNeese State in the final game before conference play began, the team had just a mediocre 9–4 record.

On New Year's Day 2016, the Bruins began Pac-12 action with a game against the Washington Huskies in Seattle. The game ended with two dueling headlines. First, it was a foul fest. Referees called 64 fouls, and the two teams combined to attempt 90 free throws. The night was another embarrassing one for Pac-12 referees, as the game had no flow, rhythm, or resemblance to a beautiful basketball game. For much of the way, players marched from end to end to shoot free throws. Late in the game, another story emerged, about Bryce Alford. His clutch shooting carried the Bruins, turning the game into a thriller. After starting 0-for-11 from the floor, Alford found his shot when the Bruins needed it most. Trailing, 71–68, Alford hit a three-pointer with seven seconds remaining to send the game to overtime. Trailing, 83–80, in overtime, he did it again. In the second overtime, the Huskies learned their lesson. Again trailing by three in the final seconds, Alford brought the ball upcourt, but this time, UW fouled him with 1.8 seconds remaining. He knocked down both free throws, though on the second attempt, he was trying to intentionally miss. The Washington lead was cut to one, but Andrew Andrews, who finished with 35 points, knocked down two more free throws, and the final margin was three points. Despite the heroics of Alford late in the game, UCLA lost a heartbreaker and began Pac-12 play in the basement. For much of the season, the Bruins had the same problems. They were a strong offensive team that couldn't stop anyone. They played well in spurts, and even played well enough to collect wins over good teams, but they also played down to competition and lost games they should have won.

Following the defeat at Washington, UCLA dropped another game two nights later at Washington State. In the conference home opener, UCLA celebrated the return of one of its greatest recent players. The evening was Russell Westbrook Night at Pauley Pavilion, and the Bruins did what Westbrook has done so many times—they won with style. Taking on No. 7 Arizona, UCLA played its finest game in over a month. After falling behind big, however, Arizona stormed back in the game. In the final seconds, the game was tied at 84, and UCLA had the ball. After running the clock down, Alford was the man the Bruins called on again. After dribbling to the right and pulling up on the wing for a deep three-pointer, he let it fly. With 1.8 seconds left, Alford swished the shot, putting the Bruins up three. Arizona couldn't get a shot off, and the Bruins pulled off the upset. Westbrook stood and cheered from his courtside seat.

The win over Arizona was the last positive moment for the Bruins all season. Their record stood at 10–6, and soon it took a dive. Many individual good games ensued, but UCLA was never able to put everything together and play as a team. Hamilton scored 26 against ASU, Parker had 27 against USC, Alford had 28 against Washington, Holiday had 19 against Oregon, and Jonah Bolden, Prince Ali, and Thomas Welsh all had moments of fine play as well. None of it mattered, however, as UCLA struggled mightily. It won just five more games all season and lost 11. The Bruins lost to USC in all three meetings and lost to Arizona in a rematch. They finished the season with five consecutive losses and missed the NCAA Tournament for just the eighth time in the last 50 years. The Bruins' 10th-place finish in the conference standings is the worst in school history. Despite the dismal 2016 season, hope was alive going into the 2017 season. Reinforcements were on their way.

Villanova University won the NCAA basketball national championship in 2016.

2016–17

The 2017 Bruins were the best team of the Steve Alford era. After a terrible 2016 season, the Bruins improved dramatically. Bryce Alford and Isaac Hamilton, now seniors, had their best seasons yet, both having many moments of superb play, but they also took a backseat to their new teammates. Aaron Holiday and Thomas Welsh each continued to play well for the Bruins. After starting every game the previous season, Holiday came off the bench in 2017, often providing a much-needed spark. Welsh continued to be a rock-solid contributor for the Bruins. The greatest improvement came with the addition of new players. The Bruins signed only three freshmen, but they were all contributors, and two of them immediate stars. Ike Anigbogu, an athletic big man from Corono, was an important player for the Bruins, but Lonzo Ball and T. J. Leaf temporarily elevated UCLA back into elite status.

When Lonzo Ball arrived in Westwood, things changed. While his father LaVar made a name for himself with outrageous declarations, Lonzo just played. He was not flashy, though he was fascinating. At 6'6", he was taller than nearly every other point guard who tried to defend him. He was a good leaper, a solid outside shooter—though his shot was extremely unorthodox—and he was a good defender. His greatest strength, however, was his passing. As a five-star recruit, much was expected of him coming into the season, and he delivered. In his lone season in Westwood, he averaged 14.6 points, 7.6 assists, and 6.0 rebounds per game. He shot 55.1 percent from the floor and 41.2 percent from three, and was the best perimeter defender for the Bruins. More important, however, Ball changed the way the Bruins played. Passing became contagious, as good shots were passed up for great shots. The basketball rarely stuck in the hands of the guards, as it did in previous years. Bryce Alford was able to move to his more natural shooting-guard position, Isaac Hamilton received passes where he was best able to operate, and the UCLA big men received the ball on time and on target in their sweet spots. On the other end of many of Ball's assists was T. J. Leaf. Another five-star freshman, the 6'10" forward from San Diego could do it all. Leaf led the team in scoring and finished second on the team in rebounding. On the offensive end, Leaf was unguardable. Though he was thin, he could play down low, as his tremendous skill was displayed on the block against bigger and slower opponents. He could shoot from mid-range and from three, drive, and dunk. Leaf was a good ball handler, a good passer, and unselfish.

He was the perfect complement to Lonzo Ball. With the addition of the fantastic freshmen class to the remaining players, the Bruins were again a national contender. While much could be said about UCLA's brilliant offense, as they finished second in the nation in scoring, much more can be said about its team defense. When the Bruins won games, they simply outscored opponents. Defense was a problem all year, despite having a talented roster. The Bruins gave up 75.5 PPG, which placed them 259th in the country in scoring defense.

The Bruins, ranked No. 16 nationally, began their season on November 11 against the University of Pacific Tigers. In the opener, the Bruins put on an offensive show. In the first half, they shot 58.3 percent from the floor and knocked down 10 three-pointers. They were just getting started. In the second half, they shot 63.6 percent from the floor and made eight more threes. Alford led the team with 30 points, Holiday scored 18, Hamilton added 17, and the two new freshmen starters starred as well. In his first game, Leaf scored 22 points and pulled down 15 rebounds. Ball finished with a near triple-double—19 points, 11 assists, and eight rebounds. UCLA won, 119–80. The 119 points is the 17th-highest scoring performance in UCLA history.

Two nights later, the Bruins again showed what they could do against lower-tier competition. UCLA beat Cal State Northridge convincingly, again with incredible offensive production. Seven Bruins finished in double figures, and UCLA beat CSUN, 102–87. The Bruins continued to impress over their next six games, winning all of them and scoring a lot of points. Against San Diego State, Leaf led the way with 26 points and 10 rebounds. The Bruins then trounced Long Beach State, 114–77, shooting 64.8 percent from the field and knocking down 12 three-pointers. In the Wooden Legacy tournament, the Bruins took care of business as well. The Bruins' balanced scoring attack helped them easily defeat Portland and Nebraska to reach the tournament final. Though their offense was held in check for the first time against Texas A&M in the tournament final, they escaped with a 74–67 win to remain undefeated. UCLA then returned home on November 30 and crushed UC Riverside. Hamilton led the Bruins with 27 points, and Leaf and Welsh each collected double-doubles.

Though the Bruins were 8–0, they had yet to be tested like they would on December 3. UCLA was now up to No. 11 in the rankings but was a clear underdog when they traveled to Rupp Arena in Lexington, Kentucky, to take on the No. 1-ranked Kentucky Wildcats in front of 23,976 fans. Though UCLA beat No. 1 Kentucky at home the year before, this game was a much tougher task. Kentucky, like UCLA, was led by freshmen. De'Aaron Fox, Malik Monk, and Bam Adebayo were all tremendous players, and all played well against UCLA. The difference in the game, however, was UCLA's depth. The game was a shootout. Both teams were relentless in their offensive attack, and though UCLA was the underdog, it was the better team. At halftime, UCLA led, 49–45, and the second half had no let up. Though Adebayo got to the free-throw line and knocked down 10 attempts, and though Fox and Monk were aggressive in their attack, scoring a combined 44 points, the Bruins met every Kentucky run with a run of their own. The game was a true offensive show. Six Bruins scored at least 13 points. Hamilton led the Bruins with 19 points; Leaf finished with 17 points, 13 rebounds, and five assists; Welsh, Ball, and Alford each scored 14; and Holiday added 13 off the bench. UCLA knocked down 10 three-pointers, made 17 of their 21 free throws, and were clutch down the stretch. For the second season in a row, UCLA knocked off No. 1 Kentucky, this time by the score of 97–92. UCLA outshot Kentucky from the field, from three, and from the free-throw line, and the team outrebounded the Wildcats. Kentucky forced twice as many turnovers as the Bruins, scored more in the paint, had more second-chance points, and scored more in transition. The game was wonderfully played on both sides and a tremendous win for the Bruins. Kentucky would not go away, however.

After UCLA's big win on the road, they shot all the way up to No. 2 in the country, and the feeling on campus was unlike any other season since 2008. The Bruins were real contenders, and fans knew it. On December 10, the Bruins returned to Pauley Pavilion, and 13,571 Bruins fans were there to greet them. The Bruins took on the Michigan Wolverines and tore them to pieces. Leaf and Ball combined for 40 points and UCLA won, 102–84. The Bruins finished nonconference play with three more wins, all coming in convincing fashion. Against UC Santa

Barbara, Leaf finished with a near triple-double, tallying 25 points, 10 rebounds, and eight assists. Against Ohio State, Holiday and Alford each scored 20 in a win, and against Western Michigan, the team again shot 50 percent from the floor in a convincing win. UCLA was 13–0 and averaging nearly 97 PPG on the season when Pac-12 play began.

UCLA began the conference season against one of the top teams on the West Coast, the No. 21 Oregon Ducks. From the very beginning, the Ducks clearly were not going to roll over and succumb to UCLA's offensive attack. They had the talent to combat UCLA's skill with precision basketball of their own. The Ducks led for much of the way, stretching their lead to 12 with three minutes left in the first half. The Oregon offense was on fire. The team shot 53.3 percent from the floor, knocked down seven threes, and racked up 52 points at the break. A late run by the Bruins cut the Oregon lead to five, however, heading into halftime. In the second half, both teams slowed down on offense, trading baskets for much of the half, but the Bruins eventually took the lead and built a cushion. With under seven minutes to go, UCLA led by eight, but the Ducks weren't done. Slowly, Oregon cut into the Bruins' lead, and with 12 seconds remaining, Payton Pritchard hit a long three to bring the Ducks within one. Oregon sent Alford to the line, but he missed the front end of the one-and-one, and Oregon grabbed the rebound. After dribbling down court, Pritchard found Oregon star Dillon Brooks at the top of the key, and after two dribbles to his right, Brooks let a long three-pointer go, and he knocked down in at the buzzer. UCLA fell, 89–87, dropping its first game of the year.

A seeming fluke was needed for the Ducks to beat the Bruins. Oregon played well, UCLA struggled down the stretch, with one of its usual clutch performers missing a key free throw, and Oregon needed a long three-pointer at the buzzer to win. The loss hurt, and Oregon was a top contender for the conference crown, but the Bruins were still elite. They quickly bounced back to win six consecutive games following that loss. Ball finished with 23 points against Oregon State, Leaf added 21, and the Bruins won their first conference game. The Bruins then returned home, and in front of consecutive sellout crowds, easily beat both Cal and Stanford. UCLA was 16–1 when it traveled to Boulder to take on the Colorado Buffaloes. Though games in Colorado are never easy, Bryce Alford made sure no upset happened this time. Alford finished with 37 points, knocking down nine three-pointers in the Bruins' win. The Bruins then won a nail-biter against Utah, hanging on to beat Kyle Kuzma and the Utes, 83–82, in Salt Lake City. Five days later, the Bruins trounced Arizona State at home to collect their 19th win of the season. Hamilton finished with a game-high 33 points, matching Alford's nine threes from one week earlier with nine of his own against the Sun Devils.

Following the Bruins' six-game winning streak, they faced major adversity for the first time. UCLA lost convincingly in back-to-back games to the University of Arizona and then to USC. The 14th-ranked Wildcats beat the Bruins, 96–85, as UCLA's defense was again shown to be its great weakness in 2017. Ball had 24 points, eight assists, and six rebounds in the loss. UCLA was still in a fine position in the conference standings, but after losing four days later to USC, it fell behind. The unexpected loss ultimately cost UCLA a shot at the Pac-12 crown. Following the defeat, UCLA dropped to No. 11 in the AP rankings.

Though UCLA's season hit a major speed bump, it showed itself to be a tremendous team. UCLA won out in the regular season, finishing with nine consecutive conference wins. Against Washington State, T. J. Leaf dominated. The freshman star scored 32 points and grabbed 14 rebounds. Against the University of Washington, much of the pregame discussion was about Lonzo Ball vs. Markelle Fultz, the eventual top two picks in the NBA Draft. Fultz finished with 25 points, but he was alone for the Huskies. Meanwhile, four Bruins, including Ball, finished with at least 20, and UCLA demolished Washington, 107–66.

The biggest game for UCLA in the second half of the conference season was the rematch against the Oregon Ducks. Despite the anticipation for the rematch at Pauley Pavilion, UCLA came out slowly. Oregon jumped all over the Bruins early, building a 19-point lead in the first half. As quickly as Oregon built its lead early, UCLA came back late. Five Bruins scored in double figures as UCLA climbed the mountain and overtook Oregon. The final score was UCLA 82, Oregon 79.

UCLA fans looked forward to two particular games the most. They were both revenge games, and UCLA came ready to play in each. After beating Oregon State, UCLA was back up to No. 6 in the rankings when it faced USC on February 18 at Pauley Pavilion in front of 13,659 fans. The Bruins shot 53.8 percent from the floor, 50 percent from three, and knocked in all of their free-throw attempts. They played their finest defensive game of the season, holding the Trojans to just 33.8 percent shooting. Alford led the Bruins with 26 points, and he had plenty of help from his friends. Welsh scored 16 points and grabbed 16 rebounds; Leaf finished with 19 points, eight rebounds, and three blocks; and Ball had another near triple-double. UCLA routed USC, 102–70. Revenge was sweet.

The Bruins then played a superb game against ASU before taking on UA on February 25. The game was played in Tucson at McKale Center, always one of the toughest road venues for any team in the Pac-12. The Bruins started slowly and trailed at halftime, but in the second half, they got it going, eventually taking the lead and never looking back. UCLA beat Arizona, 77–72, avenging all three of their early Pac-12 losses with wins in the second half of the Pac-12 season. The Bruins then finished with consecutive wins over Washington and Washington State to close the regular season with an overall record of 28–3. Despite the brilliant season, the Bruins finished in third place in the Pac-12, one game behind both the Ducks and the Wildcats. UCLA's loss to USC earlier in the season cost them the conference crown.

In the Pac-12 Tournament quarterfinals, the Bruins took on USC for the third time. The game came down to the wire. UCLA led, 38–35, at halftime, but in the second half, the Trojans hung around. UCLA led by as many as 14 before USC made a late charge. After knocking down a three with 4.1 seconds remaining, USC attempted to foul the Bruins, but UCLA beat the press, avoiding the Trojans and running out the clock. The game was close, but UCLA survived, 76–74. One night later, UCLA wasn't as fortunate. For the second time during the season, Arizona beat UCLA. Lauri Markkanen dominated for the Wildcats, scoring 29 points. Meanwhile, the Bruins struggled mightily from the floor and lost, 86–75.

Despite being ranked No. 3 in the country by the Associated Press the previous week, UCLA was named just a No. 3 seed in the NCAA Tournament by the selection committee. The Bruins were in what was considered to be the most difficult region, the South Regional, and had a tough task ahead of them if they hoped to reach the Final Four. Still, the Bruins had a chance. In the first round, the Bruins took on No. 14 seed Kent State and easily won. Leaf finished with a game-high 23 points and was one of five Bruins to score in double figures. Holiday finished with 15 points and 11 assists off the bench for the Bruins. UCLA's 30th win of the season came in style, with the Bruins shooting 62.7 percent from the field. In the second round, though the game wasn't as pretty, the result was the same. Playing the uberathletic Cincinnati Bearcats, the Bruins offense was slowed in the first half. At halftime, UCLA trailed, 33–30, but in the final 20 minutes, UCLA exploded for 49 points and cruised to a 79–67 win. UCLA turned the ball over just three times and again used a balanced attack to overcome an opponent.

For the third time in Coach Alford's first four years, the Bruins advanced to the Sweet 16, but this season, UCLA was no longer the underdog. Though the Kentucky Wildcats were seeded higher than UCLA, the Bruins had beaten Kentucky already and knew they could play with anybody. The game on March 24 was different than the one on December 3, however. Kentucky outplayed and thoroughly outcoached UCLA from start to finish. The Bruins played well offensively, shooting an efficient 52.7 percent from the floor, but Kentucky was better. UCLA turned the ball over 13 times and forced just six. The Wildcats outrebounded UCLA, made more threes, made more free throws, and were more clutch down the stretch. Kentucky also had one player UCLA couldn't stop. The Wildcats repeatedly called for screen and rolls at the top of the key with De'Aaron Fox handling the ball, and UCLA was powerless to stop him. Ball was screened off, UCLA's big men sagged in the paint, and Fox hit short jump shots over and over. UCLA made no adjustments and never forced Kentucky coach John Calipari to stray from his game plan. Fox took over the game, torching the Bruins for 39 points. Kentucky won, 86–75. UCLA's season was over.

Despite winning 31 games, the fourth most for a Bruins team ever, the season ended far too early. They beat every team on their schedule, but a win in December is easily forgotten when you are eliminated with a loss in March. Ball, Leaf, and Anigbogu all left UCLA for the NBA draft. Alford and Hamilton graduated and moved on as well. The Bruins looked much different in 2018 than they did in 2017. One of the most talented teams in UCLA history had its chance and couldn't take advantage.

University of North Carolina won the NCAA basketball national championship in 2017.

2017–18

In his fifth season, Coach Steve Alford lost the majority of UCLA fans still holding out hope that he was the right man for the job. While many had long given up on the idea that Coach Alford could get UCLA back to the top, the 2017 season changed the minds of some. The Bruins disappointed in the tournament, but throughout the season, they were one of the best teams in America. Despite the talent losses to the NBA and graduation, UCLA needed to build off its success. Ultimately, the team failed to do that, though the season couldn't quite be called a disaster. By March, Bruins fans were again flying flags over campus, begging UCLA administrators to find a new coach.

After spending the entire 2017 season as the Bruins' sixth man, Aaron Holiday returned to the starting lineup as a junior and took over as UCLA's top scorer. Holiday was relentless in his offensive attack, driving to the basket, firing deep three-pointers, and pouring in points at a higher clip than any Bruin since Ed O'Bannon in 1995. Holiday was consistent throughout the season, shining in both nonconference and conference games. He became the first Bruin to lead the conference in scoring since Reggie Miller in 1986. Holiday found the proper balance between aggressiveness and control, at least for the most part. In his previous two seasons, Holiday's decision making was questioned, as he far too often took bad shots, forced bad passes, and played outside the normal rhythm of the offense. Though he still had moments where he struggled with his decision-making, most notably in UCLA's final game, he cut back on his mistakes, and he and the team were better for it. Along with leading the team in scoring with 20.3 points per game, he led the team in assists with 5.8 per game and steals with 1.3 per game.

Sharing leadership duties with Holiday was a senior, one of the most popular players in recent UCLA history, Thomas Welsh. For three seasons, Welsh was a dependable, important piece and a key team player. The 7'0" center was loved by his teammates and coaches. Every day in practice, he shook Coach Alford's hand, thanked him for helping him personally grow as a player, and went about finding ways to improve individually. By his senior year, Welsh was a trusted, beloved member of not just the UCLA basketball team but also the UCLA campus. While fans came to trust Welsh in all his sweet spots, he was asked to extend his range as a senior, and he did just that. Prior to the 2017–18 season, Welsh had only attempted one career three-pointer, knocking it down one year earlier. In his final season in Westwood, Welsh attempted 112 three-pointers, hitting 40 percent for the year. In his senior season, he played his finest basketball. He finished with career highs in scoring and rebounding, averaging 12.6 PPG and 10.8 RPG for the season.

While Holiday and Welsh grabbed many of the headlines, others contributed as well. Kris Wilkes and Jaylen Hands were each five-star recruits, and though both struggled with consistency during their freshmen seasons, they each showed great potential and were important pieces to the team puzzle. Prince Ali, after missing the entire 2017 season with an injury, was back for his redshirt sophomore campaign in 2018, and he, like the two new freshmen, struggled with consistency. Ali was a streaky scorer and at times looked like a star in the making, but he also went through long stretches of poor play. G. G. Goloman, Alex Olesinski, and Chris Smith all played important roles for the team too.

Prior to the season, three Bruins created a controversy that grabbed national headlines. Freshmen Cody Riley, Jalen Hill, and LiAngelo Ball were arrested while the Bruins were in China for the season opener. The trio was caught shoplifting, and the saga dragged on far longer than anyone hoped. The charges were eventually dropped and the players were allowed to return home. It was an institutional embarrassment, however, and could not go unpunished. Riley, Hill, and Ball were each suspended indefinitely, and on December 22, UCLA announced that the suspensions would last the entirety of the year. Riley and Hill were contrite and apologetic, and they did everything necessary to get back in the good graces of the Bruins faithful. LiAngelo Ball, younger brother of Lonzo, chose a different path. He dropped out of school and began his professional career in Lithuania.

After beginning the season ranked No. 21 in the country, the Bruins narrowly escaped against the Georgia Tech Yellow Jackets in Shanghai, China. Kris Wilkes led UCLA in his first career game with 18 points, and though the game was ugly on both sides, UCLA won, 63–60. Back home five days later, the Bruins began the Hall of Fame Classic, taking on Central Arkansas at Pauley Pavilion. The game was closer than all expected. Jordan Howard scored 35 points for the Bears, and none were bigger than his three in the closing seconds of the second half. Trailing by two, Howard knocked down a three-pointer with three seconds remaining to take the lead. In UCLA's last dash to the hoop, however, Jaylen Hands was fouled; after missing the first free throw, he knocked down his second attempt to force the game to overtime. Central Arkansas scored the first four points of the OT session, but UCLA came right back and took control, winning, 106–101. Holiday led the Bruins with 24 points.

As the Hall of Fame Classic continued, predicting what the Bruins would bring from night to night was hard. After the close call against Central Arkansas, the Bruins crushed a poor South Carolina State team, 96–68. Hands led the Bruins with 22 points, and fellow freshman Chris Smith added 15 off the bench. Despite the solid win, things were going to get worse for the Bruins. Against Creighton, the old problems crept up and bit the Bruins again. UCLA's defense was atrocious. Despite strong offensive performances from Holiday, Welsh, and Ali, the Bruins fell, 100–89. Finally, the Bruins closed out the Hall of Fame Classic with a tight win over Wisconsin in the third-place game. With the score tied at 70, Holiday drove to the basket and scored with 0.8 seconds remaining to give UCLA the win.

The rest of the nonconference season was frustrating. The Bruins showed they could play high-level basketball, but they also struggled in ways that the team hadn't the year before. After a perfect nonconference season in 2017, the 2018 Bruins lost three times, equaling the total for the entire 2017 regular season. Along with the loss to Creighton, the Bruins lost in overtime to Michigan in Ann Arbor, handing the Wolverines a game the Bruins should have won. One week later, they were blown out by Cincinnati at home. The Bruins collected five more wins, however, four of which came against low-level competition. Ali led the Bruins with 21 points against UC Irvine, Welsh collected another double-double against Cal State Bakersfield, Hands finished with 23 points off the bench against Detroit, and five Bruins scored in double figures against South Dakota. UCLA's biggest nonconference win came against a familiar foe. For the third consecutive year, UCLA beat Kentucky in the regular season. This time, the Wildcats were ranked No. 7 in the country, and the game was played at Smoothie King Center in New Orleans. After falling behind early and trailing for most of the first half, the Bruins made a late charge, and at halftime, the game was tied at 39. In the second half, it was all Bruins. They quickly jumped out to a 12-point lead, and though the Wildcats made runs of their own, UCLA countered each time and held on to win, 83–75. Holiday and Wilkes each scored 20, Welsh finished with 13 points and 11 rebounds, and UCLA outshot Kentucky. When Pac-12 play began, the Bruins held a 9–3 overall record.

UCLA began the conference season with a two-game home stand against their Pac-12 foes from Washington. First, against Washington State, Aaron Holiday scored a game high 33 points and had a career-high 11 rebounds in a 13-point win. Two nights later, the Bruins won convincingly again, beating the University of Washington, 74–53. UCLA's much-maligned defense held the Huskies to just 27.9 percent from the floor. Despite the good start, things soon fell apart. The following week, Stanford beat UCLA in Palo Alto, though two overtime periods were needed. After leading by five at halftime, the Bruins were unable to slow down Stanford in the second half, as the Cardinal shot 60 percent from the floor to tie the game. At the end of regulation, the score was 85–85, and in the OT period, it was much of the same. The two teams played evenly, forcing another OT period, and Stanford ultimately came out on top, 107–99. Holiday again played well for the Bruins, scoring 31 points. The loss to Stanford was just one of many for the Bruins during Pac-12 play. After beating Cal and Utah, the Bruins then dropped three consecutive games. Against Colorado and Oregon State, the Bruins defense was not the main issue; it was the offense. UCLA averaged just 61 PPG in the two games and lost both. Finally, against

Oregon, the offense was proficient, but the defense was nonexistent: Oregon 94, UCLA 91.

For parts of the 2018 season, UCLA seemed ready to turn the corner and become a real contender in the poor Pac-12 conference. After losing three straight, the Bruins won six out of their next seven, including a win over No. 13 Arizona in McKale Center. By the back half of the conference season, the roles of every player on the UCLA team were clearly set, and at the top was Aaron Holiday, who led the team in scoring in each of the final 10 games of the regular season. During the team's four-game winning streak, Holiday scored over 20 points in three out of the four games. Against Arizona, he scored a team-high 17 points, but he had plenty of help. Five Bruins scored in double figures, including G. G. Goloman , who scored 16 points. After dropping a game to Arizona State, the Bruins won two more, beating both Oregon State and Oregon at home. Against the Ducks, Holiday scored 29 points and knocked in five three-pointers in the win.

Despite UCLA's 19–8 record, many college basketball pundits did not think the Bruins were definite to make the tournament. The Pac-12 was down, and though the Bruins had one quality win over Kentucky in nonconference play, that was their only one. When the Bruins dropped their next two games to Utah and Colorado, their chances at receiving an NCAA Tournament berth seemingly took a major hit. Just one game was left in the regular season, against USC at the Galen Center, so the Bruins needed to make a splash in the Pac-12 Tournament. After beating USC, 83–72, behind a career-high 34 points from Holiday, the Bruins finished the regular season with a 20–10 record and were third in the Pac-12 Conference standings.

UCLA added one final win before the NCAA selection committee met and announced the tournament field. In the quarterfinals of the Pac-12 Tournament, Holiday scored 34 points for the second consecutive game, and the Bruins toppled Stanford, 88–77. The next night, they hoped for a similar result, but the team they faced was much tougher. The semifinal game against Arizona went to overtime, but the Wildcats pulled it out in the end. UCLA lost, 78–67. Welsh finished with 17 points and 17 rebounds, but Holiday struggled, going 5-for-20 from the field.

The Bruins were 21–11, and though they were seen by many as controversial, they were selected to be part of the NCAA Tournament—kind of. On March 13, UCLA played in one of the play-in games, officially called the First Four. The winner of the game between UCLA and St. Bonaventure would slot in as the No. 11 seed in the East Regional. The Bruins were atrocious from start to finish. Though they shot better than the Bonnies from the floor and from three, outrebounded them by 10, and scored more second-chance points, turnovers killed the Bruins. Holiday finished the game with 20 points, but was just 7 of 17 from the field and turned the ball over an astonishing 10 times. Welsh grabbed a game-high 15 rebounds but scored only two points. At halftime, UCLA trailed by five and then lost, 65–58. Though the Bruins officially were a part of the NCAA Tournament field, it is hard for anyone to see it that way. UCLA was not part of the frantic action of the two days of first-round play. The loss to St. Bonaventure was the last straw for many. Fans wanted Coach Alford gone, and it was nearly unanimous. Despite the wishes of the fan base, he was not fired, and he returned for the 2018–19 season with what many called his deepest roster yet. It was time for him to win or pack his bags. Coach Alford's seat was burning up.

Villanova University won the NCAA basketball national championship in 2018.

2018–19

The 2018–19 UCLA basketball season was the 100th in school history, and it was a mess. The Bruins entered the season with relatively high expectations. Coming off a 21-win season the year before, many pundits expected UCLA to make a leap in 2019, despite losing both Aaron Holiday and Thomas Welsh to the NBA. Though the fans had almost unanimously given up on the prospects of major success under head coach Steve Alford, there were reasons to be optimistic going into Alford's sixth season in Westwood. According to 247Sports, the Bruins signed the No. 6 overall recruiting class in the country in 2018. The Rivals recruiting service ranked the Bruins' class as the fifth best, and ESPN claimed UCLA's recruiting class was No. 3 in the country. The star of the class was Moses Brown, a 7'2" center from New York City. While Brown brought considerable physical talent and dominated inside, his game remained raw and he had struggles in his debut season. Brown's greatest strength as a player was his ability to run, jump, and finish above the basket. He struggled with offensive moves and was inconsistent, but throughout the season, he proved to be a valuable piece of the puzzle. Joining Brown were five other players, only two of which were able to contribute as freshmen. David Singleton and Jules Bernard, a pair of local recruits, showed promise throughout the season. Singleton was UCLA's best outside shooter and best perimeter defender, though he spent much of his freshman season looking for ways to fit in. Bernard, on the other hand, stood out from the very beginning. He is an aggressive, left-handed guard who seeks to attack the basket nearly every time he touches the ball. Like Brown and Singleton, Bernard had an up-and-down freshman season. Kenneth Nwuba was part of the class, as well, though his time on the court was extremely limited. A pair of players that were expected to contribute significantly never saw the court. Before the season even started, point guard Tyger Campbell tore his ACL and was forced to have a redshirt season. Shareef O'Neal, son of legendary basketball player Shaquille O'Neal, was found to have a rare and serious heart abnormality. O'Neal underwent open-heart surgery, forcing him to miss the season as well. Both Campbell and O'Neal were expected to make full recoveries and join the Bruins in time for the 2019–20 season.

Some players from the prior season returned. Sophomores Kris Wilkes and Jaylen Hands, once high-profile recruits, took on a larger role. Wilkes led the team in scoring, averaging 17.3 points per game. Hands finished second in the scoring department at 14.2 per game, while leading the Bruins with 6.1 assists per game. Junior Prince Ali had a solid season, though like many Bruins, he was inconsistent, and he missed much of the season with an injury. Sophomore Chris Smith showed improvement, and redshirt freshmen Cody Riley and Jalen Hill contributed too.

Despite the deep team, the Bruins struggled to jell, and coaching remained a problem. Murry Bartow, son of former UCLA coach Gene Bartow, was brought in as an assistant coach, and he was expected to revamp the Bruins' defense. UCLA had a long, athletic lineup that showed defensive potential at times. Despite this, UCLA continued to struggle on that end. Out of 353 Division I teams, UCLA ranked 321st in points allowed. It was not a recipe for winning, and it was not a recipe for keeping a job in coaching, as coach Steve Alford later finally found out.

The Bruins began their season on November 6, ranked No. 21 in the country, against Purdue Fort Wayne. UCLA was led by Kris Wilkes and Moses Brown. Wilkes scored 27 points and hauled down 10 rebounds, while Brown finished with 19 points and 17 boards. Hands and Smith each scored in double figures too. Three nights later, the Bruins took on Long Beach State and again showed great balance in their offensive attack. Six Bruins scored in double figures. The Bruins shot 50 percent from the floor, and despite missing 11 free throws, they came away with a win, 91–80.

On November 16, the Bruins collected their third win of the season. The Moses Brown hype train reached new levels. Against Saint Francis, Brown scored 23 points, pulled down 14 rebounds, and had eight blocks. By now, many in the media were comparing Brown to former Bruin Kareem Abdul-Jabbar. The lofty standards were a compliment, but a bar much too high for anyone to meet. Brown's solid, unspectacular play the rest of the season was sure to disappoint those who believed the comparison was worthwhile. Against Presbyterian in the fourth game of the season, Brown scored just 10 points, but help came from many others. Hands led all Bruins scorers with 19 points, and Jalen Hill grabbed a career-high 20 rebounds. UCLA was 4–0, but the competition was going to get much tougher.

On November 22, No. 17 UCLA took on No. 11 Michigan State in the Las Vegas Invitational semifinals. The Spartans took the Bruins apart. MSU shot 60 percent from the floor in the first half, 51.6 percent for the game, and led big nearly the entire way. At halftime, MSU nearly doubled up the Bruins, leading 51–26. When the game finally ended, UCLA's perfect record was no more. The team fell, 87–67. The competition didn't get any easier. In the third-place game the next night, UCLA fell again, blown out for the second night in a row. The University of North Carolina beat UCLA, 94–78. The meltdown was just beginning.

After the disastrous trip to Las Vegas, UCLA returned home for a four-game home stand, hoping to get back on track. Against Hawaii, they did just that. Prince Ali led the way with 23 points, and UCLA held the Rainbow Warriors to just 35.9 percent from the field. The Bruins then beat Loyola Marymount before welcoming an old rival back to Pauley Pavilion. On December 8, UCLA played Notre Dame in front of 12,985 fans at Pauley Pavilion. The game was low-scoring throughout and sloppy on both sides. In the first half, UCLA shot just 32.4 percent, but the Irish shot a measly 22.9 percent. At the break, UCLA led, 31–20. In the second half, Notre Dame picked it up, and the Bruins did not. With the score knotted at 62, Notre Dame had the ball and was looking to get away with a win, no matter how ugly. With 8.0 seconds remaining, ND guard Prentiss Hubb attempted a wild, spinning shot. It was blocked by Jalen Hill off the backboard and picked up by Ali off the bounce. Ali then raced up the court and hit a trailing Wilkes. He rose for three with 2.5 seconds remaining and drained the game-winning shot with 0.1 seconds remaining. Wilkes, dealing with cramps late in the game, fell to the floor, and his teammates celebrated with him on the court. UCLA won in dramatic fashion. It was the last win for Steve Alford as the coach of the UCLA men's basketball team.

Despite the thrill of the exciting win for UCLA, things weren't going well. One week later, UCLA lost to Belmont at home in an embarrassing collapse. The Bruins missed an astonishing 16 free throws in 28 attempts. For the season, UCLA shot just 63.3 percent from the charity stripe, 342nd in the country in free-throw percentage and last in the nation for any team from a power conference. After the loss to Belmont, things continued to spiral in the wrong direction. Against Mick Cronin and the Cincinnati Bearcats, the Bruins were blown out at home. Cincinnati shot a higher percentage from the two-point area, three-point area, and free-throw line. It outrebounded UCLA, forced more than twice as many turnovers, scored more in the paint, scored more off turnovers, made more second-chance points, and got more scoring from its bench. The Bruins were embarrassed again: Cincinnati 93, UCLA 64.

Four days later, the Bruins lost their third in a row to Ohio State, and then on December 29, they were blown out at home by Liberty University. That was the final straw. Two days later, on December 31, 2018, Steve Alford was fired as the UCLA head coach. He is the only UCLA basketball coach to ever be fired midseason. Murry Bartow finished the remainder of the season as the interim head coach for the Bruins. The long, frustrating Steve Alford era was finally over.

Bartow is a proven solid coach, but he isn't a miracle worker. The 2018–19 Bruins were flawed, and though less head-scratching, in-game coaching blunders were made the rest of the way, the team was Alford's and there wasn't much Bartow could do to make the team an immediate winner. The first game for Bartow came on January 3 and was the Pac-12 opener for the Bruins. Against the Stanford Cardinal, the Bruins played well, winning, 92–70, and two days later, they crushed Cal, 98–83. The opening week of conference play was a good one for the Bruins, but the competition was weak, as Stanford and Cal were subpar teams. Competition got tougher, though the Pac-12 was in the midst of one of the worst seasons in conference history.

On January 10, UCLA traveled to Eugene, Oregon, and pulled off a thrilling come-from-behind victory. After trailing nearly the entire game, UCLA made its move in the final minute. The Bruins had already cut the Oregon lead from 17 to eight with 44 seconds remaining, and though prospects looked bleak, UCLA did the impossible. Hands knocked down a three with 38 seconds left and then Prince Ali got a quick steal and found Hands, who was fouled on a three-point attempt. Hands hit all three free throws to cut the Oregon lead to two, 76–74. With 20 seconds remaining, Victor Bailey Jr. knocked down a pair of free throws for the Ducks to extend the lead back to four. The game appeared over when Hands missed a jumper shortly after, but an offensive rebound and a three by Ali kept the Bruins alive. The score was 78–77 and the Bruins were forced to foul with three seconds remaining. Payton Pritchard went to the line and knocked down a pair for the Ducks to give them a three-point lead. Oregon coach Dana Altman chose to foul rather than give the Bruins a chance at the game-tying three. With two seconds left, Hands went to the line. He made the first, and then missed the second intentionally. Brown got his fingertips on the ball and Chris Smith raced in to grab the offensive rebound. He grabbed it, made a layup, and drew a foul! Smith then missed the free-throw attempt, and the game went to overtime. In

OT, UCLA outscored Oregon, 7–4, and came away with the most improbable win of the season. UCLA was 3–0 in Pac-12 play.

For the rest of the season, there was little to celebrate for the Bruins. Following the big road win over the Ducks, UCLA lost three in a row, including a blowout defeat against USC. The Bruins beat Arizona in the lone meeting of the year. In front of a big crowd at Pauley Pavilion, Wilkes scored 34 points to break the Bruins' losing streak. The rest of the season was up and down, however, made even more frustrating by the weakness of the conference and the opponents UCLA played. When conference play ended, the Bruins were just 9–9 against Pac-12 foes. In a year that the Bruins needed to improve, they finished in seventh place in the worst power conference in America. To make the NCAA Tournament, UCLA needed to win the Pac-12 Conference tournament, and though it beat Stanford in the first round, it fell to Arizona State in the quarterfinals and the season ended. UCLA finished the year with just a 17–16 record.

All eyes turned to the coaching search. Though the job had been open since New Year's Eve, nothing was likely to happen during the season. The season's end marked the time for action. UCLA swung big, and rumors swirled about the highest-profile names in college basketball heading to Westwood. On April 9, UCLA hired Mick Cronin as the 14th head coach in UCLA history. Cronin, formerly of the University of Cincinnati, has a stellar resume, and though the reviews of his hiring were mixed, he has proven to be a capable coach. In 2019–20, he will be at the helm of the greatest college basketball program in history. In one hundred years, the Bruins have an all-time record of 1,890–856, 37 conference championships, 18 Final Four appearances, and 11 national championships. The first Bruins century was defined by greatness. Here's to the next hundred.

University of Virginia won the NCAA basketball national championship in 2019.

The UCLA Spirit Squad on their way to the 1965 national championship rally (Southern Branch Collection).

UCLA student section, 1978 (Southern Branch Collection).

Joe and Josephine Bruin, 1984 (Southern Branch Collection).

Joe Bruin with a child, 1985 (Southern Branch Collection).

Balloons fall as UCLA wins their 11th national championship in school history, 1995 (Southern Branch Collection).

The Bruin Bear on campus (Erkki Corpuz Collection).

UCLA legend Bill Walton stands near the statue of John Wooden outside Pauley Pavilion (Erkki Corpuz Collection).

UCLA Spirit Squad, 2008 (Erkki Corpuz Collection).

UCLA Yell Crew, 2009 (Erkki Corpuz Collection).

UCLA Spirit Squad, 2014 (Danielle Alvari Collection).

UCLA Cheerleaders backflip after every made free throw (Danielle Alvari Collection).

CHAPTER 14
Assistant Coaches

A- Don Ashen (1939–1959), Frank Arnold (1971–1975)

B- Al Barnes (1923), Ken Barone 1989–1991), Duane Broussard (2013–2018), Murry Bartow (2018), Kory Barnett (2019)

C- Richard Callahan (1927–1928), Denny Crum (1959–1960, 1968–1971), Gary Cunningham (1966–1975), Ernie Carr (1987–1988)

D- Phil Davis (1925–1928), Albert Dowden (1921–1924), Charlton Dukes (1925–1926), Donny Daniels (2003–2010), Scott Duncan (2007–2011)

E- Carl Eardley (1924–1926), John Ecker (1974–1975), Chuck Evans (1980–1981), Tyus Edney (2017–2019)

F- Larry Farmer (1975–1981), Tony Fuller (1982–1992)

G- Joe Guion (1921–1925), Si Gibbs (1924–1939), Keith Glass (1979–1981), Mark Gottfried (1988–1995), Scott Garson (2006–2013), David Grace (2013–2018)

H- Leroy Hill (1942–1943). Jim Halsten (1958–1959), Lee Hunt (1975–1977), Jim Harrick (1977–1979), Jack Hirsch (1984–1988), Brad Holland (1988–1992), Michael Holton (1996–2001)

I- Craig Impelman (1977–1979, 1981–1984)

J- Wilbur Johns (1926–1939), Kris Jason (1984–1987)

K- Carl Kraushaar (1950–1951), Kerry Keating (2003–2007)

L- Art Lane (1925–1926) Milford Layman (1925–1926), Marvin Lee (1947–1948), Dick Linthicum (1932–1939), Mel Lippman (1920–1921), Fred Little (1921–1922), Chris Lippert (1981–1983), Paul Landreaux (1988–1989), Steve Lavin (1991–1996)

M- Jack Montgomery (1942–1945), Andre McCarter (1984–1988), Gerald Madkins (2001–2003), Phil Mathews (2010–2013), Korey McCray (2011–2013)

N- Melvin Nielson (1924–1926), Jerry Norman (1956–1968)

O- George Owen (1925–1926), Kevin O'Connor (1979–1984)

P- Isador Prinzmetal (1925–1926), Bill Putnam (1945–1951, 1954–1962), Ed Powell (1948–1952), Barry Porter (1956–1957)

Q-

R- Robert Robinson (1925–1927), Deane Richardson (1955–1957), Frank Ryan (1986–1987), Lorenzo Romar (1992–1996)

S- Doug Sale (1949–1952), Alan Sawyer (1952), Jim

Saia (1996–2003), Steve Spencer (1997–2001), Patrick Sandle (2001–2003), Ed Schilling (2013–2017)

T-

U-

V-

W- Caddy Works (1919–1921), Bugs Woodard (1925–1926), Eddie White (1955–1956), Sidney Wicks (1984–1988), Greg White (1995–1996)

X-

Y-

Z- Ernie Zeigler (2003–2006)

CHAPTER 15
Players by Jersey Number

0. Jerome Moiso, Russell Westbrook, Drew Gordon, Anthony Stover, Nick Kazemi, Alex Olesinski

1. Marvin Lee, Jason Flowers, Dijon Thompson, Jordan Farmar, Malcolm Lee, Mike Moser, Tyler Lamb, Wanaah Bail, Wonder Smith, Moses Brown

2. Janou Rubin, Darren Collison, Spencer Soo, Kenny Jones, Kory Alford, Noah Allen, Lonzo Ball, Cody Riley

3. Ted Forbes, Dick Birnie, Tom Brown, Bill Rankin, Ralph Jackson, Richard Petruska, Billy Knight, Brian Morrison, Josh Shipp, Malcolm Lee, Nick Kazemi, Jordan Adams, Aaron Holiday, Jules Bernard

4. Orv Appleby, Lloyd Anderson, Richard Perry, Grant Clothier, Owen Stewart, Corey Gaines, Trevor Wilson, Marquis Burns, Kevin Daley, JaRon Rush, Spencer Gloger, Marcedes Lewis, Trevor Ariza, Arron Afflalo, Tyler Trapani, Norman Powell, Isaac Wulff, Jaylen Hands

5. Clem Clements, Bob Alshuler, Ralph Witt, George Stanich, Cameron Dollar, Baron Davis, DeAndre Patterson, Joe Crispin, Jerime Anderson, Kyle Anderson, Kevon Looney, Prince Ali, Armani Dodson, Chris Smith

6. Ernie Handlesman, Johnny Stanich, Frank Freriks, Mel Stoner

7. Larry Gittler, John Fryer, Jack Heald, Chuck Clustka, Bob Waterfield

8. Marvin Lee, Chuck Stewart, Ron Pearson, Dick Bernie

9. Bob Null, Jack Dooling, Jeff Asher

10. John Moore, Fred Ferroggiaro, Tom Grant, Dave Minor, Ray Alba, Rod Foster, Ryan Walcott, Janou Rubin, Mustafa Abdul-Hammid, Alex Schrempf, Larry Drew II, Isaac Hamilton, Isaac Wulff, Tyger Campbell

11. John Fryer, Ben Lewis, Don Barksdale, Mike Sanders, Curtis Knight, Corey Gaines, Kevin Williams, Tyus Edney, Todd Ramasar, Jordan Farmar, Ryan Wright, Spencer Soo, Reeves Nelson, Lazeric Jones

12. Dick West, Glen Grant, Don Miller, Montel Hatcher, Gerald Madkins, David Boyle, Toby Bailey, Josh Shipp, Alfred Aboya, Anthony Stover, David Wear

13. Sandy Cameron, Bill Ward, Roger Terry, Bruce Sieck, Dick Hough, Gene Williams, Doug Sale, Charles O'Bannon, Travis Reed, Gene Barnes, James Keefe, Matt Demarcus, David Brown, Ike Anigbogu, Kris Wilkes

14. Mickey Panovich, Alan Sawyer, Glen Grant, Brad Holland, Michael Holton, Stu Meinert, Rodney Zimmerman, Lorenzo Mata-Real, Alex Schrempf, Jack Haley, Nick Kazemi, Zach LaVine, G. G. Goloman, Kenneth Nwuba

15. Clark George, Jack Baddeley, Don Borden, Dick Blurton, Bill O'Neill, Jack Haley, Darrick Martin, Ryan Hollins, Blake Arnet, Shabazz Muhammad, Jerrold Smith, Armani Dodson

16. Ainsley Bell, Dave Brown, Guy Buccolo

17. Orv Appleby, Audre Richardson, Frank Bowman, Bob Arnold

18. Don Ashen, John Ball, Alex Rafolovich, Jackie Robinson, Bob Jones, Marvin Lee, Chuck Stewart

19. Mickey Panovich

20. Clem Melancon, Roger Hillis, Bill Putnam, Jim Harrison, Sonny Skjervheim, Mike Huggins, John Lyons, Tyren Naulls, Darryl Morris, Jeff Bronner, Brandon Loyd, Michael Roll, David Wear, Brendan Lane, Bryce Alford, Isaac Wulff

21. Ken Lucke, Alex Farolovich, Noah Curti, Richard Perry, Gordy Matteson, George Englund, Rod Palmer, Darrin Dafney, Shon Tarver, Ryan Bailey, Cedric Bozeman, David McGrat, Jrue Holiday, Brendan Lane, Khalid McCaskill, Alec Wulff

22. John Ball, Wilburn Monkers, Don Seidel, Morris Taft, Walt Torrence, Bob Berry, Larry Gower, John Galbraith, Henny Heitz, Tommy Curtis, Raymond Townsend, Jerald Jones, Chris Kenny, Steve Elkind, Rico Hines, Ike Williams, Kelvin Kim, Chace Stanbach, J'Mison Morgan, Reeves Nelson, Josh Thomas, Noah Allen, Gabriel Bell-Williams, T. J. Leaf, Armani Dodson, Shareef O'Neal

23. Horace Haight, Chet Lappen, Harley Humes, Bill O'Brien, Hal Michaels, Lindy Kell, Gary Baker, Cliff Brandon, Kenny Washington, Lee Walzcuk, Kenny Booker, Bill Leonard, Mitchell Butler, Matt Barnes, Andre Patterson, Luc Richard Mbah a Moute, Matt Demarcus, Tyler Honeycutt, David Brown, Tony Parker, Prince Ali

24. Chet Freeze, Lloyd Anderson, Courtney Borio, Art Hutchins, Bill Hicks, Gail Goodrich, Chuck Darrow, Larry McCollister, Gene Sutherland, Rick Betchley, Dave Cumberland, Roy Hamilton, Randy Arrillaga, Jermone Richardson, Bob Myers, Jason Kapono, Joey Ellis, Matt DeMarcus, Travis Wear, Justis Bell-Williams, Jalen Hill

25. Bill Reitz, Gerald Sieck, Noah Curti, Ron Livingston, Dave Hall, Rafer Johnson, Stan Anderson, Ron Lawson, Rich Gugat, Chuck Darrow, Gail Goodrich, Don Saffer, Andy Hill, Pete Trgovich, Nigel Miguel, Keith Owens, George Zidek, Earl Watson, Matt McKinney

26.

27. Ralph McFadden, Bob Calkins

28. Paul Peek, Stanley Price, Roger Terry

29. Don Piper, William Robinson, Jack Seiter

30. Luther Hiltner, Denny Crum, Duane Barnes, Jim Rosvall, Steve Lock, Kent Graham, Neville Saner, Curtis Rowe, Vince Carson, Chris Lippert, Darren Daye, Dave Immel, Tracy Murray, Kevin Dempsey, Sean Farnham, Kevin Schmidt, Khalid McCaskill, Aubrey Williams, Joseph Wallace

31. Harry Holt, Swen Nater, Rich Washington, Gig Sims, Reggie Miller, Ed O'Bannon

32. John Wells, Orv Appleby, Don Brown, Grover Luchsinger, Gene Williams, Carl Kraushaar, John Moore, Ben Rogers, Kent Miller, Dave Waxman, Doug McIntosh, Steve Patterson, Bill Walton, Brett Vroman, Darrell Allums, Brad Wright, Greg Foster

33. Paul Slaughter, Willie Naulls, Nolan Johnson, Warnell Jones, Lew Alcindor

34. Crossan Hays, Dick Irmis, Bob Ballard, Nolan Johnson, Dick Skaer, Bill Wagoner, Bill Hicks, Kim Stewart, Vaughn Hoffman, Jim Nielson, John Chapman, Dave Meyers, David Greenwood, Cliff Pruitt, Sean Lamb, Jonah Naulls, Jelani McCoy, Ray Young, Josh Smith, Ikenna Okwarabizie, David Singleton

35. Jack Cooper, Ray Alba, Ed Feenstra, Mike Hibler, Conrad Burke, Ron Wallace, John Berberich,

Fred Slaughter, Mike Lynn, Sidney Wicks, Ralph Drollinger, James Wilkes, Mark Eaton, Ike Nwanko

36.

37. Jack Montgomery

38. Jack Bradley, Karl Kroshoor, Ralph Joeckel

39. Robert Null, Paul Klein, Johnny Fryer, Grover Luchsinger

40. Ray Weldie, Larry Gittler, Bob Bell, Bob Miller, Rich Levin, Freddie Goss, Terry Schofield, John Vallely, Marvin Vitatoe, Casey Corlis, Thomas Welsh

41. Nikola Dragovic

42. Bob Alshuler, Ron Bane, Dick Banton, Bob Fisher, Bill Ellis, Walt Hazzard, Mike Serrafin, Lucius Allen, Terry Schofield, Bob Webb, Darrell Allums, Kelvin Butler, Don MacLean, Kevin Love

43. Roger Hillis, Eddie White, Jack Arnold, Fred Crabtree, Bill French, Kent Graham, Steve Brucker, Brice Chambers, John Chapman, Terry Schofield, Greg Lee, Rennie Kelly, Chris Lippert, Tony Wang, Stephen Brumback, Rodney Odom, T. J. Cummings, Jonah Bolden, Russell Stong

44. Mark Costello, Jim Halsten, Bill Kilmer, Jim Milhorn, Kenny Washington, Mike Warren, Lee Walczuk, Jim Spillance, Dean Sears, Jeff Dunlap, Zan Mason, James Diefenbach, Tyler Trapani, Sooren Derboghosian

45. Denny Miller, John Green, Fred Goss, Mike Serafin, Bill Sweek, Henry Bibby, Andre McCarter, Tony Anderson, Charles Rochelin, Michael Fey

46. Ernie Handlesman

47. Cordner Gibson, Kenneth Lueke

48.

49.

50. Ted Bell, Jack Hirsch, Bill Ureda, Kent Taylor, Fred Gray, Gary Franklin, Marvin Thomas, Kevin Walker, omm'A Givens, Dan Gadzuric, Adria Gasol

51. Dick Killgore

52. Jerry Norman, Mark Costello, Don Bragg, Allen Harring, Bob Archer, Pete Blackman, Rich Levin, Randy Judd, Dick Lynn, John Ecker, Keith Wilkes, Mike Sanders, Craig Jackson, J. R. Henderson, John Hoffart

53. Wayne Boulding, Tom Williams, Al Herring, Nate Brewer, Roger Nichols, Keith Erickson, Lynn Shackelford, Larry Hollyfield, Wilbert Olinde, Gary Malancon

54. Dick Irmos, Alan Sawyer, Dick Ridgway, Bill Eblen, Brain Kniff, Jim McFerson, Kim Stewart, Edgar Lacey, Larry Farmer, Marques Johnson, Kenny Fields, Kris Johnson, Josiah Johnson

55. Eldon Bennett, Barry Parlovich, Hank Steinmann, Henry Steinman, Carroll Adams, Roland Underhill, Gary Cunningham, Keith Erickson, Bill Winkelholz, Joe Chrisman, Bill Seibart, Rick Betchley, Gavin Smith, Kiki Vandeweghe, Stuart Gray, Mike Lanier, Jon Crispin, Quinn Hawking, Nican Robinson, Matt Lee

56. Guy Buccolo, Don Bragg

57. Chuck Clustko, John Matulich, Ron Bane

58. Ralph Joeckel, Paul Saunders

59. Alan Sawyer, Jerry Evans

60.

61.

62.

63.

64.

65.

66.

67.

68.

69.

70. Gene Logan

71. Barry Porter

72. Art Apler, Jack Davidson

73. George Stanich, Don Johnson, Bill Johnston

74. Don Seidel, Ernie Bond, Gene Logan

75. Eddie Sheldrake, Ron Livingstone

76. Ernie Johnson, Rolf Engen, Ed White

77. Fred Holzer, Courtney Borio

78. Ron Pearson, Mark Costello, Bob Ballard

79. Andy Thomas

80.

81.

82.

83.

84. Dick Ridgway

No Regular Number or Unknown Number *(alphabetical):*-James Armstrong, Bill Athey, Jim Baker, Robert Baker, Sam Balter, Ray Bartlett, Buck Beeson, Gary Benccolo, Joe Berry, Carson Binkley, Julius Blum, David Brees, Horace Bresee, Lloyd Bridges, George Brotemarkle, Carl Brown, Ralph Bunche, Lamar Butler, Morris Caldwell, Chuck Church, John Colla, Cyril Eaton, Louis Eilers, Les Ewing, Silas Gibbs, Bill Gilbert, Bill Goertz, David Graham, Harley Humes, Shelby Johns, Wilbur Johns, Jack Ketchum, Carl Knowles, Ted Lemeke, James Leyh, Dick Linthicum, Frank Lubin, Bill Maxwell, Raymond McBurney, Ernest McRitchie, Vic Millar, David Milne, Will Munkers, Mickey Panovich, Franklyn Pierce, Erwin Piper, Edward Prigge, Bill Reitz, Howard Roberts, Max Rogers, Lou Rose, Eddie Rossell, Howard Rossell, Doug Sale, Tom Scott, Al Sheppard, Carl Shy, Hal Smith, Harold Smith, James Soest, Kenneth Springer, Chuck Stewart, Al Sunseri, Warren Thornberg, Sterling Tipton, Dudley Tower, Duke Trotter, Dick von Hagen, Len Wellendorf, Carlton West, George Westphal, Lewis Whitney, Alex Widlicska, Charles Wilbur, Larry Wilds, Arthur Williams, Dave Williams, Spencer Williams, Freddie Winter, Larry Wilde, Ralph Witt, "Bugs" Woodard, William Woodruff, Norris Woodward, Milo Young

CHAPTER 16
This Day in UCLA Basketball History

JANUARY 1
In 1928, former UCLA basketball player Alan Sawyer was born.

JANUARY 2
In 1896, former UCLA basketball coach Pierce "Caddy" Works was born.

JANUARY 3
In 2012, former UCLA basketball head coach Gene Bartow died at the age of 81.

JANUARY 4
In 2003, Jason Kapono scored a career-high 44 points in a 98–83 win over Washington State.

JANUARY 5
In 2013, UCLA beat Stanford, 68–60. Shabazz Muhammad led the Bruins with 23 points, 17 of which came in the second half.

JANUARY 6
In 1978, David Greenwood tied his career high with 23 rebounds against Washington.

JANUARY 7
In 1910, UCLA Athletics Hall of Fame basketball player Frank Lubin was born. He won a gold medal with Team USA in the 1936 Summer Olympics.

JANUARY 8
In 2014, Lonzo Ball committed to UCLA.

JANUARY 9
In 1997, UCLA lost to No. 21 Stanford, 109–61. The 48-point margin is the largest in school history.

JANUARY 10
In 1964, the Bruins played their first game as the No. 1-ranked team in the nation, beating USC, 79–59.

JANUARY 11
In 2018, UCLA beat Utah, 83–64, behind 20 points from Aaron Holiday.

JANUARY 12
In 1924, the Southern Branch of the University of California (UCLA) beat Caltech, 51–20. The win made head coach Caddy Works SBUC's all-time leader in wins. Works retired with 173 career wins, a record that stood until 1957.

JANUARY 13
In 1996, Kris Johnson scored a career-high 36 points for the Bruins in a 93–73 win over Cal.

JANUARY 14
In 1920, the Southern Branch of the University of California (UCLA) lost to Redlands, 34–21, marking the first loss in school history.

JANUARY 15
In 1994, No. 5 UCLA beat Washington, 82–62, to run its record to 11–0 on the season.

JANUARY 16

In 1970, the Pac-12's all-time leading scorer, Don MacLean, was born.

JANUARY 17

In 1974, No. 1 UCLA won its 88th consecutive game, beating Iowa, 68–44.

JANUARY 18

In 1925, former UCLA basketball All-American John Stanich was born.

JANUARY 19

In 1974, Notre Dame beat No. 1-ranked UCLA, 71–70, ending UCLA's NCAA record 88-game winning streak.

JANUARY 20

In 1967, UCLA's 48-game winning streak was snapped by the No. 2 University of Houston Cougars. The game was played in front of 52,693 fans in the Astrodome and was dubbed the "Game of the Century." The Bruins avenge their lone loss on the season by beating Houston, 101–69, in the Final Four.

JANUARY 21

In 1967, Lucius Allen scored a career-high 37 points in a 119–75 Bruins win over UC Santa Barbara.

JANUARY 22

In 2018, Moses Brown committed to UCLA.

JANUARY 23

In 1971, No. 1 UCLA lost, 89–82, to No. 9 Notre Dame. The Bruins did not lose another game for nearly three years.

JANUARY 24

In 1996, UCLA beat USC, 99–72, shooting a school-record 72.1 percent from the floor.

JANUARY 25

In 1973, Bill Walton set a career high with 27 rebounds against Loyola-Chicago.

JANUARY 26

In 1974, No. 3 UCLA beat No. 1 Notre Dame, 94–75. one week after the Fighting Irish snapped UCLA's 88-game winning streak.

JANUARY 27

In 1973, No. 1 UCLA beat Notre Dame, 82–63, for its 61st consecutive win, setting a new college basketball record.

JANUARY 28

In 1956, Willie Naulls set a UCLA record with 28 rebounds against Arizona State.

JANUARY 29

In 1967, Lew Alcindor scored 45 points in a win over Illinois.

JANUARY 30

In 1971, No. 2 UCLA beat UC Santa Barbara, 74–61. It was the first win in what became an NCAA-record 88-game winning streak.

JANUARY 31

In 1919, UCLA four-sport star Jackie Robinson was born.

FEBRUARY 1

In 1969, No. 1 UCLA beat Stanford, 98-61, to run its record to 16–0 on the season.

FEBRUARY 2

In 1962, UCLA beat No. 5 USC, 73–59.

FEBRUARY 3

In 2001, UCLA beat No. 1 Stanford, 79–73, at Maples Pavilion.

FEBRUARY 4

In 1981, former four-time All-Pac-12 forward Jason Kapono was born.

FEBRUARY 5

In 1949, UCLA beat Pittsburgh, 51–48, at the Men's Gym.

FEBRUARY 6

In 1996, former All-Pac-12 forward Kevon Looney was born.

FEBRUARY 7

In 1959, Walt Torrence scored a career-high 38 points for the Bruins against Idaho.

FEBRUARY 8

In 1956, UCLA Athletics Hall of Fame member Marques Johnson was born.

FEBRUARY 9

In 1962, former All-American Kenny Fields was born.

FEBRUARY 10

In 2005, Dijon Thompson scored a career high 39 points for the Bruins as they defeated Arizona State, 95–76.

FEBRUARY 11

In 1979, No. 4 UCLA beat No. 1 Notre Dame, 56–52, at the Athletic & Convocation Center in South Bend.

FEBRUARY 12

In 1921, the Southern Branch (UCLA) beat Whittier College, 26–24, to sweep the season series.

FEBRUARY 13

In 2003, UCLA lost to No. 1 Arizona, 106–70. UCLA's record dropped to 5–15 on the season. With the loss, UCLA was guaranteed a losing record for the season, ending its NCAA record streak of 54 consecutive winning seasons.

FEBRUARY 14

In 1973, UCLA Athletics Hall of Fame member Tyus Endey was born.

FEBRUARY 15

In 2007, No. 7 UCLA beat ASU, 67-61, in Tempe.

FEBRUARY 16

In 1929, UCLA lost, 47–31, to California, dropping to 6–9 on the season and guaranteeing its first losing season in school history.

FEBRUARY 17

In 1951, Ed Sheldrake scored a career-high 38 points for the Bruins as they defeated the Stanford Indians, 90–67.

FEBRUARY 18

In 1922, the Southern Branch of the University of California (UCLA) beat Pomona College to finish the season with a 9–1 record. The Bruins won their second consecutive Southern California Intercollegiate Athletic Conference title.

FEBRUARY 19

In 1920, the Southern Branch of the University of California (UCLA) beat Redlands, 23–17, finishing the first season in school history with a record of 12–2.

FEBRUARY 20

In 1992, Tracy Murray scored a career-high 36 points for the Bruins in a 96–70 win over Stanford.

FEBRUARY 21

In 1976, No. 5 UCLA lost to Oregon, 65–45, ending their 98-game home winning streak.

FEBRUARY 22

In 1928 at Olympic Stadium, UCLA beat USC for the first time, 34–27.

FEBRUARY 23

In 1922, former UCLA basketball player Davage "Wheelhorse of Steel City" Minor was born.

FEBRUARY 24

In 1923, the Southern Branch of the University of California (UCLA) beat Occidental College, 61–12. The 61 points scored was the most in school history to that point.

FEBRUARY 25

In 1967, Lew Alcindor scored a UCLA-record 61 points against Washington State. Alcindor set the school record for most made field goals in one half with 13—he did it in each half. He finished with a career-high 24 rebounds as well.

FEBRUARY 26

In 1977, Marques Johnson scored a career-high 37 points in a 91–69 win over California. Eighteen years later, in 1995, Ed O'Bannon scored a career-high 37 points in a 100–77 Bruins win over Duke.

FEBRUARY 27

In 1960, John Green scored a career-high 38 points for the Bruins against the University of Washington.

FEBRUARY 28

In 1987, Reggie Miller set a UCLA record with 33 points scored in the second half against Louisville, finishing with 42 for the game. The Bruins won, 99–86.

FEBRUARY 29

In 1996, No. 17 UCLA beat Oregon State, 68–66, to collect its 20th win of the season.

MARCH 1

In 1971, No. 1 UCLA beat Washington, 71–69. Curtis Rowe hit the game-winning jump shot with under 30 seconds to play.

MARCH 2

In 1956, Willie Naulls scored a career-high 39 points for the Bruins as they defeated California, 85–80.

MARCH 3

In 2014, Aaron Holiday committed to UCLA.

MARCH 4

In 2000, UCLA beat No. 1 Stanford, 94–93, in overtime.

MARCH 5

In 1971, Sidney Wicks set a career high with 22 rebounds against California.

MARCH 6

In 1986, Reggie Miller scored 41 points as UCLA beat Oregon State, 74–63, in Corvallis.

MARCH 7

In 1970, No. 1 UCLA beat USC, 91–78. It was the first win in what became a Pac-12 record 50-game conference winning streak.

MARCH 8

In 1975, David Meyers scored a career-high 39 points as the Bruins defeated Oregon, 107–103.

MARCH 9

In 1980, UCLA beat No. 1 overall seed DePaul in the second round of the NCAA Tournament.

MARCH 10

In 1956, No. 10 UCLA set a school record for most made and attempted free throws in a game, knocking down 47 of 61 attempts.

MARCH 11

In 1950, No. 7 UCLA beat Washington State, 52–49, to win the Pacific Coast Conference championship. It was UCLA's first conference championship since joining the PCC.

MARCH 12

In 1965, Gail Goodrich became the first UCLA Bruin to score 40 points in a game. He scored 40 for the Bruins in a 100–76 NCAA first-round win over BYU.

MARCH 13

In 2003, UCLA beat No. 1 Arizona, 96–89, in the first round of the Pac-10 Tournament. It was the last win of Coach Steve Lavin's tenure at UCLA.

MARCH 14

In 1949, UCLA lost to Oregon State in the Pacific Coast Conference playoffs, 46–39. Despite the loss, UCLA finished with a record of 22–7 in Coach John Wooden's first season. It was the most wins in school history in a single season to that point.

MARCH 15

In 1979, Roy Hamilton scored a career-high 36 points for the Bruins in a 99–81 win over USF.

MARCH 16

In 2015, former UCLA basketball player Jack Haley died at the age of 51.

MARCH 17

In 1979, David Greenwood scored a career-high 37 points for the Bruins against DePaul.

MARCH 18

In 1967, UCLA beat Pacific, 80–64, to advance to the Final Four.

MARCH 19

In 1995, UCLA beat Missouri, 75–74, to advance to the Sweet Sixteen of the NCAA Tournament. The Bruins won on a game-winning layup at the buzzer by Tyus Edney.

MARCH 20

In 1965, UCLA won its second consecutive NCAA title, beating top overall seed Michigan, 91–80, in the national championship game. Gail Goodrich finished with 42 points.

MARCH 21

In 1964, UCLA beat Duke University to win its first national championship in school history. The Bruins finished the season with a perfect 30–0 record.

MARCH 22

In 1969, UCLA beat Purdue, 92–72, to win its fifth national championship and third in a row. The Bruins finished with a 29–1 record on the season.

MARCH 23

In 1968, UCLA beat the University of North Carolina, 78-55, to win its fourth national championship in school history. The Bruins finished with a 29–1 record on the season.

MARCH 24

In 1950, UCLA played in its first ever NCAA Tournament game, losing to top-seeded Bradley University, 73–59. Thirty years later, UCLA lost the national championship game to Louisville, 59–54.

MARCH 25

In 1967, UCLA won its third national championship, beating the University of Dayton, 79–64, in the national championship game. UCLA finished with a perfect 30–0 record. Five years later, UCLA beat Louisville to cap another perfect 30–0 record with another national championship.

MARCH 26

In 1973, UCLA won its seventh consecutive national championship, beating Memphis State, 87–66. Bill Walton led the way with 44 points on 21 of 22 from the field.

MARCH 27

In 1971, UCLA beat Villanova, 68–62, to win its seventh national championship.

MARCH 28

In 1992, UCLA lost to Indiana University, 106–79, in the Elite Eight. The 27-point loss is the largest margin of defeat for UCLA in an NCAA tournament game.

MARCH 29

In 2008, UCLA beat Xavier, 76–57, to advance to its third consecutive Final Four.

MARCH 30

In 2013, Steve Alford was named the 13th head coach in UCLA basketball history.

MARCH 31

In 1975, UCLA beat Kentucky, 92–85, to win its 10th national championship. It was Coach John Wooden's final game as the UCLA head coach.

APRIL 1

In 1995, UCLA beat Oklahoma State, 74–61, to advance to the national championship game. Twenty-one years later, UCLA beat LSU to advance to the national championship game once again.

APRIL 2

In 2008, Kevin Love was named a finalist for the John R. Wooden Award.

APRIL 3

In 1995, UCLA beat Arkansas, 89–78, to win its 11th national championship.

APRIL 4

In 2018, UCLA forward Kris Wilkes announced he was going to test the NBA draft waters.

APRIL 5

In 2008, UCLA lost, 75–63, to Memphis in the Final Four.

APRIL 6

In 2006, UCLA coach Ben Howland was named National Coach of the Year by CollegeInsider.com.

APRIL 7
In 1969, the Milwaukee Bucks selected Lew Alcindor with the first overall pick in the NBA draft.

APRIL 8
In 1963, former All-Pac-10 basketball player Nigel Miguel was born.

APRIL 9
In 2016, it was announced that the contracts signed by former Bruins multisport star Jackie Robinson and the Brooklyn Dodgers would be displayed at Collectors Café in New York City.

APRIL 10
In 1972, the New York Knicks selected Henry Bibby in the fourth round of the NBA draft.

APRIL 11
In 2012, Shabazz Muhammad committed to UCLA.

APRIL 12
In 1987, All-Pac-10 guard Michael Roll was born.

APRIL 13
In 1979, former All-American point guard Baron Davis was born.

APRIL 14
In 2008, Kevin Love was named team MVP at UCLA's annual basketball banquet.

APRIL 15
In 1942, former UCLA All-American player and coach Walt Hazzard was born.

APRIL 16
In 1947, Kareem Abdul-Jabbar was born.

APRIL 17
In 2008, Kevin Love and Russell Westbrook each announced their intentions to leave UCLA and enter the NBA draft.

APRIL 18
In 2004, Russell Westbrook verbally committed to UCLA.

APRIL 19
In 1944, former UCLA basketball All-American Keith Erickson was born. Erickson also played on the 1964 Team USA men's volleyball team.

APRIL 20
In 1954, two-time national champion Ralph Drollinger was born.

APRIL 21
In 1953, two-time national champion Dave Meyers was born.

APRIL 22
In 1977, former Bruin Kareem Abdul-Jabbar set a career playoff high with nine blocks against the Golden State Warriors.

APRIL 23
In 1943, UCLA Athletics Hall of Fame Member Gale Goodrich was born.

APRIL 24
In 1954, the Syracuse Nationals selected Jack Davidson in the 10th round of the NBA draft.

APRIL 25
In 1950, the Rochester Royals selected George Stanich 22nd overall in the NBA draft.

APRIL 26
In 2010, Phil Matthews was hired as a UCLA basketball assistant coach.

APRIL 27
In 2008, Darren Collison announced he was returning to UCLA for his senior season.

APRIL 28
In 1971, former Bruin Kareem Abdul-Jabbar had 23 points and 21 rebounds for the Milwaukee Bucks against the Baltimore Bullets in Game Three of the NBA Finals.

APRIL 29
In 1999, former Bruin Reggie Miller tied a career high with 12 rebounds against the Charlotte Hornets.

APRIL 30
In 1997, former All-Pac-12 forward T. J. Leaf was born.

MAY 1
In 2008, Chase Stanback announced his intention to transfer from UCLA.

MAY 2
In 1953, UCLA Athletics Hall of Fame member Jamaal Wilkes, formerly known as Keith Wilkes, was born.

MAY 3
In 1967, the San Francisco Warriors selected Mike Lynn in the fifth round of the NBA draft.

MAY 4
In 1964, the Los Angeles Lakers selected Walt Hazzard with the second overall pick in the NBA draft.

MAY 5
In 1985, former Bruin Kareem Abdul-Jabbar set a career high with six steals and another career high with nine offensive rebounds against the Portland Trail Blazers.

MAY 6
In 1965, the Los Angeles Lakers selected Gail Goodrich with the third overall pick in the NBA draft.

MAY 7
In 1960, former UCLA guard Mike Sanders was born.

MAY 8
In 1983, former Bruin Jamaal Wilkes finished with a career high seven assists against the San Antonio Spurs.

MAY 9
In 2014, Russell Westbrook had 23 points, 13 assists, and eight rebounds against the Los Angeles Clippers in Game Three of the Western Conference semifinals.

MAY 10
In 1993, Bill Walton was inducted into the Naismith Memorial Basketball Hall of Fame.

MAY 11
In 1966, the San Francisco Warriors selected Ken Washington in the eighth round of the NBA draft.

MAY 12
In 2010, UCLA held a groundbreaking ceremony, officially beginning the Pauley Pavilion renovation.

MAY 13
In 2010, former Bruin Kareem Abdul-Jabbar suggested to the Associated Press that the NBA should raise the minimum age limit to 21.

MAY 14
In 1966, former UCLA point guard Jerome "Pooh" Richardson was born.

MAY 15
In 2018, former Bruin Kevin Love had 22 points and 15 rebounds against the Boston Celtics in Game Two of the Eastern Conference finals.

MAY 16
In 1980, former Bruin Jamaal Wilkes finished with a career-high 37 points against the Philadelphia 76ers.

MAY 17
In 2006, it was announced that former Bruin Andre McCarter would be inducted into the Philadelphia Overbrook High School Hall of Fame.

MAY 18
In 2015, former UCLA guard Zach LaVine was named Second Team All-Rookie.

MAY 19
In 1984, former UCLA football and basketball player Marcedes Lewis was born.

MAY 20
In 2005, former Bruin Reggie Miller played in his final NBA game.

MAY 21
In 1999, Jason Kapono signed a national letter of intent with UCLA.

MAY 22
In 1990, former UCLA guard Malcolm Lee was born.

MAY 23
In 2006, it was announced that UCLA would take on Texas A&M University in the 2006 John R. Wooden Classic.

MAY 24
In 1998, UCLA guard Isaac Wulff was born.

MAY 25
In 1993, former All-Pac-12 guard Norman Powell was born.

MAY 26
In 2010, it was announced that David and Travis Wear were transferring from North Carolina to UCLA.

MAY 27
In 1957, former UCLA basketball star David Greenwood was born.

MAY 28
In 1974, the Portland Trail Blazers selected Bill Walton first overall in the NBA draft.

MAY 29
In 1975, the Los Angeles Lakers selected Dave Meyers with the second overall pick in the NBA draft.

MAY 30
In 1985, former Bruin Kareem Abdul-Jabbar finished with 30 points, 17 rebounds, and eight assists in Game Two of the NBA Finals against the Boston Celtics.

MAY 31
In 1969, former UCLA captain Keith Owens was born.

JUNE 1
In 1965, former UCLA guard Corey Gaines was born.

JUNE 2
In 1987, former Bruin Kareem Abdul-Jabbar had 14 points, 10 rebounds, and four blocked shots in Game One of the NBA Finals against the Boston Celtics.

JUNE 3
In 1982, former Bruin Kareem Abdul-Jabbar had 22 points, 11 rebounds, six assists, and three blocks in Game Four of the NBA Finals against the Philadelphia 76ers.

JUNE 4
In 2010, John Wooden died at the age of 99.

JUNE 5
In 1977, the Portland Trail Blazers beat the Philadelphia 76ers to win the NBA Finals. Former Bruin Bill Walton was named Finals MVP.

JUNE 6
In 2008, five-star recruit center J'Mison Morgan signed with UCLA.

JUNE 7
In 2017, former Bruin Kevin Love collected a career high six steals against the Golden State Warriors in the NBA Finals.

JUNE 8
In 1976, the Kansas City Kings selected Richard Washington with the third overall pick in the NBA draft.

JUNE 9
In 1978, the Golden State Warriors drafted Raymond Townsend with the 22nd overall pick in the NBA draft.

JUNE 10
In 1977, the Milwaukee Bucks drafted Marques Johnson with the third overall pick in the NBA draft.

JUNE 11
In 2008, Josh Shipp announced he was returning to UCLA for his senior season.

JUNE 12
In 1979, former All-Pac-10 guard Earl Watson was born.

JUNE 13
In 2004, Darren Collison orally committed to UCLA.

JUNE 14
In 1987, former Bruin Kareem Abdul-Jabbar won the NBA Finals as a member of the Los Angeles Lakers.

JUNE 15
In 1978, former UCLA center Jerome Moiso was born.

JUNE 16
In 1948, three-time national champion Terry Schofield was born.

JUNE 17
In 2006, Arron Afflalo announced that we would return to UCLA for his junior season.

JUNE 18
In 2006, former Bruin Drew Gordon was named a finalist for the USA Basketball Men's U18 National Team.

JUNE 19
In 1984, the Milwaukee Bucks drafted Kenny Fields with the 21st overall pick in the NBA draft.

JUNE 20
In 2011, Jordan Adams committed to UCLA.

JUNE 21
In 2018, the Indiana Pacers drafted Aaron Holiday with the 23rd overall pick in the NBA draft.

JUNE 22
In 1987, the Indiana Pacers drafted Reggie Miller with the 11th overall pick in the NBA draft.

JUNE 23
In 2017, former Bruin guard Lonzo Ball threw out the first pitch at Dodger Stadium.

JUNE 24
In 1948, three-time national champion Steve Patterson was born.

JUNE 25
In 1979, the Chicago Bulls drafted David Greenwood with the second overall pick in the NBA draft.

JUNE 26
In 2017, former UCLA guard Russell Westbrook was named NBA MVP.

JUNE 27
In 1989, the Minnesota Timberwolves drafted Pooh Richardson with the 10th overall pick in the NBA draft.

JUNE 28
In 1995, the New Jersey Nets drafted Ed O'Bannon with the ninth overall pick in the NBA draft.

JUNE 29
In 2016, UCLA shooting guard Kobe Paras withdrew from school.

JUNE 30
In 1985, former UCLA forward Trevor Ariza was born.

JULY 1
In 2018, former Bruin Thomas Welsh and the Denver Nuggets began mini-camp.

JULY 2
In 1949, UCLA Athletic Hall of Fame member Curtis Rowe was born.

JULY 3
In 2007, Jrue Holiday orally committed to UCLA.

JULY 4
In 2017, rappers Kanye West and 2 Chainz visited the UCLA basketball team at practice.

JULY 5
In 1947, former UCLA four-sport star Jackie Robinson finished 2-for-4 with one run scored for the Brooklyn Dodgers, raising his season batting average to .313.

JULY 6

In 1944, former UCLA four-sport star Jackie Robinson refused to move to the back of the bus while stationed at Camp Hood in Belton, Texas. He was court-martialed but later acquitted.

JULY 7

In 2018, former Bruin All-Pac-10 forward Tyler Honeycutt died.

JULY 8

In 1994, former All-Pac-12 guard Jordan Adams was born.

JULY 9

In 2012, former UCLA three-time national champion Kenny Heitz was born.

JULY 10

In 2018, it was announced that former Bruin Billy Knight had died two days earlier of suicide.

JULY 11

In 1990, former Bruin guard Kenny Jones was born.

JULY 12

In 1990, former UCLA forward Drew Gordon was born.

JULY 13

In 2010, UCLA Athletics Hall of Fame member Ernie Johnson died at the age of 84. Johnson played football under Red Sanders and basketball under John Wooden. He also played on the club rugby team.

JULY 14

In 1967, former UCLA basketball player, head basketball coach, and athletic director Wilbur Johns died at the age of 63.

JULY 15

In 1955, former UCLA national champion and All-American Richard Washington was born.

JULY 16

In 2013, UCLA forward Wanaah Bail had surgery on his left knee.

JULY 17

In 1942, John Wooden enlisted in the United States Navy.

JULY 18

In 1975, former UCLA national champion Kris Johnson was born.

JULY 19

In 2018, the UCLA basketball youth summer camp began.

JULY 20

In 1957, former UCLA All-American Roy Hamilton was born.

JULY 21

In 1972, former Bruins four-sport star Jackie Robinson sent a letter to Clyde Sukeforth, who scouted him and briefly served as his first major-league manager, stating in part, "I have always considered you to be one of the true giants in this initial endeavor in baseball, for which I truly appreciate."

JULY 22

In 2009, former UCLA All-American Ed O'Bannon was named as the lead plaintiff in a lawsuit against the NCAA over the use of player images.

JULY 23

In 2003, John Wooden received the Presidential Medal of Freedom, the nation's highest civilian honor.

JULY 24

In 2018, former Bruin Kevin Love signed a four-year, $120 million extension with the Cleveland Cavaliers.

JULY 25

In 1971, former All-Pac-10 forward Tracy Murray was born.

JULY 26

In 1975, former Bruin All-American Keith Wilkes began the process to change his name to Jamaal Abdul-Lateef.

JULY 27

In 2011, it was announced that Jerime Anderson was

suspended from the UCLA basketball team following an offseason arrest.

JULY 28
In 2004, three-time national champion Steve Patterson passed away.

JULY 29
In 2012, Kevin Love scored 14 points for Team USA in the opening game of the Summer Olympics.

JULY 30
In 1996, Reggie Miller and Team USA beat Brazil, 98–75, in the quarterfinals of the Summer Olympics.

JULY 31
In 2014, UCLA announced that it needed to replace the Pauley Pavilion floor following a flood after a pipe burst on Sunset Boulevard two days earlier, flooding much of the campus.

AUGUST 1
In 1958, former All-Pac-10 forward Kiki Vandeweghe was born.

AUGUST 2
In 1973, former UCLA national champion George Zidek was born.

AUGUST 3
In 2016, Latrell Spreewell told the *New York Post* that he hated Reggie Miller as a player but respected him.

AUGUST 4
In 1961, Michael Holton was born.

AUGUST 5
In 2016, former UCLA All-American Kareem Abdul-Jabbar endorsed Hillary Clinton for president.

AUGUST 6
In 2018, Shareef O'Neal signed a scholarship with UCLA.

AUGUST 7
In 1904, former UCLA basketball player and valedictorian Ralph Bunche was born. Bunche later won the Nobel Peace Prize and the Presidential Medal of Freedom, among many other honors.

AUGUST 8
In 1954, UCLA four-sport star Jackie Robinson collected three RBIs in the Brooklyn Dodgers' 20–7 win over the Cincinnati Redlegs.

AUGUST 9
In 2005, UCLA sophomore Jordan Farmar was named a preseason Top-50 candidate for the John R. Wooden Award.

AUGUST 10
In 1979, former UCLA guard Jason Flowers was born.

AUGUST 11
In 1990, former UCLA guard Lazeric "Zeke" Jones was born.

AUGUST 12
In 1936, the Team USA basketball team, including five UCLA Bruins, beat the Philippines, 56–23, in the quarterfinals game. Two days later, it won the gold medal.

AUGUST 13
In 1948, former Bruin Don Barksdale won a gold medal as a member of the USA Basketball Olympic team.

AUGUST 14
In 1972, UCLA Athletics Hall of Fame member Ed O'Bannon was born.

AUGUST 15
In 1925, Krekor Ohanian, professionally known as Mike Connors, was born. Ohanian played basketball at UCLA and later earned fame as an actor.

AUGUST 16
In 2017, rapper Drake played pickup basketball at UCLA wearing a Kentucky jersey.

AUGUST 17
In 2013, former UCLA basketball coach Ben

Howland hosted a 70th-anniversary party for the United Boys and Girls Club of Santa Barbara County.

AUGUST 18

In 1935, UCLA Athletics Hall of Fame member Rafer Johnson was born. Johnson was a member of the UCLA basketball team and track and field team. He won a gold medal and set the world record in the 1960 Summer Olympics in the decathlon.

AUGUST 19

In 2010, ESPN reported that John Wooden once hit a hole in one and a double eagle on a par 5 in the same round of golf in 1939.

AUGUST 20

In 2008, UCLA announced the inaugural Dribble for a Cure event would take place on November 2.

AUGUST 21

In 2016, the UCLA basketball team arrived in Australia for a three-game exhibition series.

AUGUST 22

In 2012, the UCLA basketball team arrived in China to begin the China Goodwill Tour.

AUGUST 23

In 1987, All-American guard Darren Collison was born.

AUGUST 24

In 1965, UCLA Athletics Hall of Fame member Reggie Miller was born.

AUGUST 25

In 1953, former UCLA champion Andre McCarter was born.

AUGUST 26

In 2017, Bill Walton appeared at the San Diego Festival of Books, where his book *Back From the Dead* was featured.

AUGUST 27

In 1947, three-time national champion Lynn Shackelford was born.

AUGUST 28

In 2012, the Bruins took on the Shanghai Sharks in their third game in the China Goodwill Tour. The Bruins won the exhibition game, 92–63, with Kyle Anderson scoring 21 points and collecting 11 rebounds.

AUGUST 29

In 2015, former UCLA basketball star Russell Westbrook and Nina Earl, a former UCLA women's basketball player, got married.

AUGUST 30

In 2007, *Lindy's College Basketball* tabbed UCLA as the number-one team in the country in its preseason poll.

AUGUST 31

In 1981, former UCLA forward T. J. Cummings was born.

SEPTEMBER 1

In 2003, Coach John Wooden's book *Inch and Miles: The Journey to Success* was released.

SEPTEMBER 2

In 2013, Trevon Bluiett committed to UCLA. He later decommitted and enrolled at Xavier University.

SEPTEMBER 3

In 2005, former UCLA two-sport star Marcedes Lewis and the UCLA football team beat San Diego State, 44–21, in the football season opener.

SEPTEMBER 4

In 1981, former UCLA basketball player Carl Knowles died at the age of 71. He won a gold medal as a member of Team USA in the 1936 Summer Olympics.

SEPTEMBER 5

In 1979, former Bruin Ann Meyers signed a contract with the Indiana Pacers, becoming the first woman to ever sign a contract with a major professional sports team in America.

SEPTEMBER 6

In 1960, UCLA two-sport star Rafer Johnson won

the gold medal in the decathlon in the 1960 Summer Olympics.

SEPTEMBER 7

In 1988, former All-American Kevin Love was born.

SEPTEMBER 8

In 2018, Ray Allen called former Bruin Reggie Miller "the greatest shooter I've ever seen."

SEPTEMBER 9

In 1986, UCLA forward Luc Richard Mbah a Moute was born.

SEPTEMBER 10

In 2011, the ninth-annual Ralph J. Bunche Classic high school football game took place in honor of former UCLA basketball player and American icon Ralph J. Bunche.

SEPTEMBER 11

In 1980, former UCLA forward Spencer Gloger was born.

SEPTEMBER 12

In 1947, Jackie Robinson was named National League Rookie of the Year, though 13 games were still left to be played in the regular season.

SEPTEMBER 13

In 1908, former UCLA basketball player Carl Shy was born. He won a gold medal with Team USA in the 1936 Summer Olympics.

SEPTEMBER 14

In 1940, former UCLA basketball coach Larry Brown was born.

SEPTEMBER 15

In 1980, a sculpture was dedicated in honor of former UCLA basketball player and American icon Ralph J. Bunche at Ralph Bunche Park in New York City.

SEPTEMBER 16

In 1977, former UCLA forward Sean Farnham was born.

SEPTEMBER 17

In 2015, it was announced that former UCLA head coach Steve Lavin was joining Pac-12 Networks as an announcer.

SEPTEMBER 18

In 2009, UCLA coach Ben Howland underwent an appendectomy.

SEPTEMBER 19

In 1949, UCLA Athletics Hall of Fame member Sidney Wicks was born.

SEPTEMBER 20

In 1993, former UCLA All-American Kyle Anderson was born.

SEPTEMBER 21

In 1990, former Bruins forwards Travis and David Wear were born.

SEPTEMBER 22

In 1950, former UCLA basketball player and American icon Ralph J. Bunche became the first African American to earn the Nobel Peace Prize.

SEPTEMBER 23

In 2018, Russell Westbrook arrived at the Oklahoma City Thunder media day wearing a UCLA football jersey.

SEPTEMBER 24

In 2016, a statue of John Wooden was dedicated at Purdue University, his alma mater.

SEPTEMBER 25

In 2018, former UCLA All-American Kevin Love represented the Cleveland Cavaliers at media day.

SEPTEMBER 26

In 1947, Lucius Allen was born.

SEPTEMBER 27

In 1949, former UCLA four-sport star Jackie Robinson was featured in an article in *Look Magazine*, which called Robinson its "Athlete of the Year."

SEPTEMBER 28

In 2018, it was announced that UCLA freshman

Shareef O'Neal was going to undergo open-heart surgery and miss the entire 2018–19 season.

SEPTEMBER 29
In 2016, UCLA legend Bill Walton was the keynote speaker at the third annual Navigate Conference.

SEPTEMBER 30
In 1996, former All-American Aaron Holiday was born.

OCTOBER 1
In 2018, UCLA Athletics announced the itinerary for the UCLA Athletics Induction Ceremony five days later.

OCTOBER 2
In 1951, former Bruins four-sport star Jackie Robinson finished 3-for-5 with one HR, one run scored, and three RBIs against the New York Giants.

OCTOBER 3
In 1948, two-time national champion John Vallely was born.

OCTOBER 4
In 2007, Ben Howland signed a seven-year extension with UCLA.

OCTOBER 5
In 2018, former UCLA player, assistant coach, and head coach Larry Farmer was inducted into the UCLA Athletics Hall of Fame.

OCTOBER 6
In 2016, UCLA Athletics Hall of Fame member Fred Slaughter died at the age of 74.

OCTOBER 7
In 1934, UCLA Athletics Hall of Fame member Willie Naulls was born.

OCTOBER 8
In 2012, CBS Sports named Shabazz Muhammad the No. 1 impact freshman in the upcoming season and No. 3 overall player in the country.

OCTOBER 9
In 2018, UCLA announced that freshman Tyger Campbell would miss the 2018–19 season with a torn ACL.

OCTOBER 10
In 1960, Rod Foster was born.

OCTOBER 11
In 2018, Steve Alford, Kris Wilkes, and Jaylen Hands participated in the annual Pac-12 media day, representing UCLA.

OCTOBER 12
In 1948, three-time national champion John Ecker was born.

OCTOBER 13
In 1999, UCLA center Moses Brown was born.

OCTOBER 14
In 1910, John Wooden was born.

OCTOBER 15
In 1909, UCLA Athletics Hall of Fame basketball player Sam Balter was born. Balter was an All-American at UCLA and won a gold medal with Team USA in the 1936 Summer Olympics. He later became the "voice of UCLA football and basketball" as a radio announcer.

OCTOBER 16
In 2008, UCLA freshman guard Jrue Holiday publicly predicted UCLA would win the national championship.

OCTOBER 17
In 1981, former UCLA guard Ryan Mollins was born.

OCTOBER 18
In 2018, former Bruin Lonzo Ball and the Los Angeles Lakers began their season with a 128–119 loss to the Portland Trail Blazers.

OCTOBER 19
In 2018, UCLA announced that the latest Dribble for the Cure event, held five days earlier, raised a record $130,000.

OCTOBER 20

In 2005, Coach Ben Howland and the UCLA coaching staff conducted their annual UCLA coaching clinic.

OCTOBER 21

In 2011, The 100 Black Men of Los Angeles, Inc., awarded former Bruin player and coach Walt Hazzard their Lifetime Achievement Award.

OCTOBER 22

In 2018, UCLA was ranked No. 21 in the Associated Press preseason poll.

OCTOBER 23

In 1972, former UCLA four-sport star Jackie Robinson died of a heart attack.

OCTOBER 24

In 2017, former Bruin Kevin Love had 20 points and 12 rebounds against the Chicago Bulls.

OCTOBER 25

In 2017, former Bruins guard Russell Westbrook had 28 points, 16 assists, and 10 rebounds against the Indiana Pacers.

OCTOBER 26

In 2012, a bronze statue of John Wooden was unveiled outside of Pauley Pavilion.

OCTOBER 27

In 1997, former All-American guard Lonzo Ball was born.

OCTOBER 28

In 2011, the media voted UCLA as the favorite to win the Pac-12 Conference.

OCTOBER 29

In 2007, UCLA was named No. 2 in the nation in the preseason Associated Press poll.

OCTOBER 30

In 1976, former UCLA national champion J. R. Henderson was born.

OCTOBER 31

In 2013, Kevon Looney committed to UCLA.

NOVEMBER 1

In 2017, UCLA beat Cal State Los Angeles, 111—80, in an exhibition game.

NOVEMBER 2

In 2007, UCLA beat Azusa Pacific, 111–81, in an exhibition game.

NOVEMBER 3

In 2008, UCLA beat Cal Baptist, 76-42, in an exhibition game.

NOVEMBER 4

In 1928, former UCLA All-American basketball player George Stanich was born. Stanich was the first All-American to play for Coach John Wooden. He also won a bronze medal in the high jump in the 1948 Summer Olympics and played professional baseball following graduation.

NOVEMBER 5

In 1952, Bill Walton was born.

NOVEMBER 6

In 2018, No. 21 UCLA beat Purdue Fort Wayne, 96–71. Kris Wilkes led the Bruins with 27 points.

NOVEMBER 7

In 2008, No. 4 UCLA beat Biola University, 76–42, in an exhibition game.

NOVEMBER 8

In 2013, UCLA beat Drexel, 72–67, in Steve Alford's first game as the UCLA head coach.

NOVEMBER 9

In 2012, Pauley Pavilion reopened after major renovations forced the Bruins to play their home games away from Westwood the previous year. UCLA beat Indiana State, 86-59, in front of 13,513 fans.

NOVEMBER 10

In 2010, Norman Powell orally committed to UCLA.

NOVEMBER 11

In 2016, No. 16 UCLA beat Pacific, 119–80. Bryce Alford led the Bruins with 30 points.

NOVEMBER 12

In 1988, former UCLA guard Russell Westbrook was born.

NOVEMBER 13

In 1992, former All-American Shabazz Muhammad was born.

NOVEMBER 14

In 2015, UCLA basketball began its season with a 113–78 win over Montana State. Norman Powell, who scored 25 points, led the Bruins.

NOVEMBER 15

In 2012, No. 13 UCLA beat James Madison, 100–70, in the first round of the Legends Classic.

NOVEMBER 16

In 2018, No. 20 UCLA beat Saint Francis, 95–68. Moses Brown led UCLA with 23 points and 14 rebounds.

NOVEMBER 17

In 1890, Fred Cozens, the first basketball and football coach at the Southern Branch (UCLA), was born.

NOVEMBER 18

In 1992, No. 24 UCLA began its season with a 68–54 win over Saint Louis in the Preseason NIT.

NOVEMBER 19

In 1975, former national champion Toby Bailey was born.

NOVEMBER 20

In 2004, the Bruins began their season with a 64–53 win over Chicago State.

NOVEMBER 21

In 1996, No. 5 UCLA lost to Tulsa, 77–76, in overtime in Steve Lavin's first game as the UCLA head coach.

NOVEMBER 22

In 2013, Kyle Anderson finished with the fourth triple-double in school history. In a win over Morehead State, Anderson finished with 13 points, 12 rebounds, and 11 assists.

NOVEMBER 23

In 1984, UCLA beat Idaho, 87–58, in Coach Walt Hazzard's first game as the UCLA head coach.

NOVEMBER 24

In 1949, three-time national champion Henry Bibby was born.

NOVEMBER 25

In 1972, UCLA beat Wisconsin, 94–53, in the first game of Coach John Wooden's 25th season in Westwood. Bill Walton led UCLA with 26 points and 20 rebounds in only 25 minutes. It was UCLA's 46th consecutive win.

NOVEMBER 26

In 1977, No. 6 UCLA beat BYU, 75–73, in Coach Gary Cunningham's first game as the UCLA head coach.

NOVEMBER 27

In 1965, the UCLA freshman team, led by Lew Alcindor, beat the No. 1-ranked UCLA varsity team, 75–60, in the first game played in Pauley Pavilion. Alcindor had 31 points and 21 rebounds in the exhibition game.

NOVEMBER 28

In 1981, Larry Farmer collected his first win as head coach of the Bruins, beating Pepperdine, 76–69.

NOVEMBER 29

In 1975, No. 2 UCLA lost to No. 1 Indiana, 84–64, in Coach Gene Bartow's first game as the UCLA head coach.

NOVEMBER 30

In 1979, UCLA beat Idaho State, 82–40, in Coach Larry Brown's first career game as the UCLA head coach.

DECEMBER 1

In 1973, Bill Walton set a Pauley Pavilion record with 27 rebounds against Maryland.

DECEMBER 2

In 1990, UCLA beat Loyola Marymount, 149–98. The 149-point total is the most for the Bruins in school history.

DECEMBER 3

In 1966, Lew Alcindor set the UCLA record for most points in the first half with 32 against USC. In his first career varsity game, Alcindor had 56 points and 21 rebounds.

DECEMBER 4

In 1971, No. 1 UCLA beat Iowa, 106–72. Henry Bibby led the way for the Bruins with 32 points.

DECEMBER 5

In 1925, the Southern Branch of the University of California (UCLA) began its season with a 33–19 win over the Los Angeles Athletic Club. SBUC finished with a 14–2 overall record and won its fifth conference title over seven years.

DECEMBER 6

In 1963, UCLA beat BYU, 113–71. UCLA's point total was the most in a single game in UCLA history to that point. The Bruins closed out the season with a 30–0 record and won their first national championship.

DECEMBER 7

In 1927, UCLA played the first basketball game since changing its name from the Southern Branch of the University of California. UCLA beat Caltech, 52–16.

DECEMBER 8

In 1973, Bill Walton recorded the first triple-double in UCLA history. In a win over SMU, Walton had 25 points, 16 rebounds, and 11 assists.

DECEMBER 9

In 1995, Jelani McCoy recorded the second triple-double in UCLA history. In a win over Maryland, McCoy finished with 15 points, 10 rebounds, and 11 blocks.

DECEMBER 10

In 1921, UCLA beat Caltech, 30–12, winning the first game of Pierce "Caddy" Works's college coaching career.

DECEMBER 11

In 1971, No. 1 UCLA beat Texas A&M, 114–56. The 64-point margin was the largest for UCLA during its 88-game winning streak. Walton finished with 23 points, 18 rebounds, and eight blocks.

DECEMBER 12

In 1919, the Southern Branch of the University of California (UCLA) played its first ever basketball game, beating Manual Arts High School, 46–38.

DECEMBER 13

In 1969, No. 2 UCLA beat LSU, 133–84, at Pauley Pavilion. The 133 points was the most for the Bruins in school history to that point.

DECEMBER 14

In 1963, UCLA beat Kansas, 75–54, to run its record to 4–0.

DECEMBER 15

In 1970, former UCLA guard Mitchell Butler was born. By the end of his college career, Butler had played in more games than any Bruin in history to that point.

DECEMBER 16

In 1972, John Wooden missed the game for UCLA after being hospitalized with a mild heart condition. UCLA beat UC Santa Barbara, 98–67, with Bill Walton scoring 30 points and grabbing 22 rebounds.

DECEMBER 17

In 1994, No. 2 UCLA beat LSU, 92–72, in the Pete Maravich Assembly Center.

DECEMBER 18

In 1995, Toby Bailey collected the third triple-double in UCLA history. In a win over Stephen F. Austin, Bailey had 23 points, 10 rebounds, and 10 assists.

DECEMBER 19

In 1964, No. 5 UCLA beat Boston College, 61–52, in the Milwaukee Classic.

DECEMBER 20

In 1946, UCLA beat the Los Angeles Police Club team, 83–18. The 65-point margin set a UCLA record, which was tied in 1954 and 1967.

DECEMBER 21

In 1973, No. 1 UCLA beat Ohio, 110–63. Bill Walton finished 11-for-11 from the field, with 25 points, 15 rebounds, and nine assists. The win was UCLA's 80th in a row.

DECEMBER 22

In 1954, No. 17 UCLA beat New Mexico, 106-41, topping the 100-point mark for the first time in school history.

DECEMBER 23

In 1969, Pete Maravich set thc record for most field goal attempts in a game at Pauley Pavilion with 42. Maravich was 14-for-42 from the field, and No. 1 UCLA beat LSU, 133–84.

DECEMBER 24

In 1979, an article by Larry Keith appeared in *Sports Illustrated* with the headline "The Bruins are in Ruins." UCLA appeared in the national championship game exactly three months later.

DECEMBER 25

In 1955, former national champion Brett Vroman was born.

DECEMBER 26

In 1925, the Southern Branch (UCLA) beat Montana State, 36–21, to move to 5–0 on the season.

DECEMBER 27

In 1969, No. 2 UCLA beat Georgia Tech, 121–90, in the first round of the Bruin Classic.

DECEMBER 28

In 1968, Lew Alcindor scored 40 for the Bruins in a win over Princeton.

DECEMBER 29

In 1971, No. 1 UCLA beat the University of Texas, 115–65. The Bruins collected a program-record 84 rebounds in the game. The game was UCLA's seventh straight with 100 or more points scored, also a program record.

DECEMBER 30

In 1988, Don MacLean finished with a career-high 41 points against North Texas.

DECEMBER 31

In 1954, No. 15 UCLA beat No. 4 Dayton, 104–92, in the ECAC Holiday Festival at Madison Square Garden.

Sources

Abdul-Jabbar, Kareem. *Becomng Kareem: Growing Up on and off the Court.* New York: Little, Brown and Company, 2017.

———. *Coach Wooden and Me: Our 50-Year Friendship on and off the Court.* New York: Grand Central Publishing, 2017.

Alcindor, Lew. "UCLA Was a Mistake." *Sports Illustrated*, November 3, 1969. http:// https://www.si.com/vault/1969/11/03/611046/ucla-was-a-mistake.

Baker, Chris. "Marques Johnson Told: Surgery and 3-Month Layoff—or Retire." *Los Angeles Times*, November 25, 1986.

Beigel, Bill. "The World War II Dead of University of California at Los Angeles (UCLA)." *WWII Researcher* (blog), February 4, 2014. https://www.ww2research.com/world-war-2-dead-ucla/.

Berkowitz, Steve. "Supreme Court Will Not Consider the Ed O'Bannon Antitrust Case against NCAA." *USA Today*, October 3, 2016.

Bisheff, Steve. "Cunningham Doesn't Regret Leaving UCLA." *Seattle Times*, January, 10 1993.

Bonk, Thomas. "Miller Has 42, Is Too Much for Louisville." *Los Angeles Times*, March 1, 1987.

———. "O'Bannon of UCLA Suffers Knee Injury: Basketball: Freshman from Artesia High Injured in Pickup Game. He Will Have Surgery, Miss the Season." *Los Angeles Times,* October 11, 1990.

———. "UCLA's 89–84 Victory Stuns North Carolina." *Los Angeles Times*, December 2, 1986.

Boswell, Thomas. "Irish, Crowd Defeat UCLA." *Washington Post*, January 23, 1978.

Bourret, Tim. "Retrospective: Jan. 19, 1974—Notre Dame Ends Longest Streak in College Basketball History." University of Notre Dame Athletics, January 17, 2014. https://und.com/news/2014/1/17/Retrospective_Jan_19_1974_Notre_Dame_Ends_Longest_Streak_in_College_Basketball_History.aspx.

Cave, Ray. "Cincinnati Is No. 1, No. 1, No. 1!" *Sports Illustrated,* April 2, 1962. https://www.si.com/vault/1962/04/02/593540/cincinnati-is-no-1-no-1-no-1.

Celtics Life. "What the Hell Happened To . . . Sidney Wicks?" October 23, 2011. http://www.celticslife.com/2011/10/what-hell-happened-tosidney-wicks.html.

"Coaches Bio: Steve Lavin: Men's Basketball." *UCLA*, April 17, 2013. https://uclabruins.com/news/2013/4/17/208184915.aspx

Cook, Kevin. "Team Miller: Plenty of Discipline, a Basketball Hoop in the Driveway and Oatmeal Every Morning—That's the Millers' Recipe for Success." *Los Angeles Times*, October 6, 1991.

Crowe, Jerry. "A Grand Opening: Pauley Pavilion and UCLA's Best Freshman Team Made Their Debuts Together 25 Years Ago." *Los Angeles Times,* November 27, 1990.

———. "Arizona Streak Gets Martinized: UCLA: Senior Guard Hits the Winning Shot as Wildcats' Home String Ends at 71 Games. MacLean Scores 38." *Los Angeles Times*, Jaunuary 12, 1992.

———. "NCAA Basketball Tournament: UCLA, Murray Put Kansas on Ice: East Regional: Freshman's Free Throws Give Bruins a 71–70 Victory over Jayhawks in the Second Round." *Los Angeles Times*, March 19, 1990.

———. "Playing for Bruins Was Only Option." *Los Angeles Times*, March 13, 2006.

"Don Barksdale." College of Marin. http://athletics.marin.edu/alumni/Don_Barksdale?view=bio.
"Don Barksdale, 69, One of First Blacks To Play in N.B.A." *New York Times*, March 11, 1993.
Doyel, Gregg. "Duke 120, UCLA 84." *Chicago Tribune*, February 23, 1998. https://www.chicagotribune.com/news/ct-xpm-1998-02-23-9802230011-story.html.
Eggers, Kerry. "Wicks Keeps NBA Life in Past." *Portland Tribune*, February 16, 2006. https://pamplinmedia.com/component/content/article?id=97367.
Ejercito, Emmanuelle. "UCLA's Royal Backcourt." *Daily Bruin*, February 19, 1998.
ESPN. "AP All-Time Top 100 College Basketball Programs." March 29, 2017. http://www.espn.com/espn/wire/_/section/ncb/id/19032638.
———. "Collison, No. 2 UCLA Thwart No. 7 Stanford in OT for Pac-10 Title." March 7, 2008. http://www.espn.com/mens-college-basketball/recap?gameId=280660026.
———. "Free Throw in Final Seconds Lets Kansas Extend Home Winning Streak to 64." December 3, 2010. http://www.espn.com/mens-college-basketball/recap?gameId=303362305
———. "Gadzuric's Career Game Gets UCLA Back to Sweet 16." March 17, 2002. http://www.espn.com.au/mens-college-basketball/recap?gameId=224000003.
———. "Huskies Overcome Bruins, Bryce Alford's 3s to Force Both OT Periods." January 2, 2016. http://tv5.espn.com/mens-college-basketball/recap/_/gameId/400841288.
———. "James' Dunk Seals No. 8 Texas' Upset of Top-Ranked UCLA." December 2, 2007. http://www.espn.co.uk/mens-college-basketball/recap?gameId=273360026.
———"Loss Ends Arizona's 10-Game Winning Streak." March 14, 2003. http://www.espn.com.au/mens-college-basketball/recap?gameId=230720012.
———."Maynor Misses Would-Be Game Winner as UCLA Prevails." March 20, 2009. http://www.espn.com.au/mens-college-basketball/recap?gameId=294000023.
———."Michigan State's Big Comeback Falls Short as UCLA Moves On." March 18, 2011. http://www.espn.co.uk/mens-college-basketball/recap?gameId=310760026.
———."Nelson's Buzzer-Beater Tip-In Lifts UCLA over Cal." January 21, 2011. http://www.espn.com/mens-college-basketball/recap?gameId=310200026.
———."No. 1 UCLA Hands No. 6 Aggies Second Loss in Five Days." December 11, 2006. http://www.espn.com/mens-college-basketball/recap?gameId=263430026
———."No. 13 UCLA Barely Avoids Upset by UC Irvine in OT." November 14, 2012. http://www.espn.in/mens-college-basketball/recap?gameId=323180026.
———."No. 23 UCLA Escapes with 106–101 Win over Central Arkansas." November 16, 2017. http://www.espn.com/espn/wire/_/section/ncb/id/21430233.
———."Rochestie's Career-Best 33 Carry Wazzu Past No. 15 UCLA." February 22, 2009. http://www.espn.in/mens-college-basketball/recap?gameId=290520026.
———."Second-Half Surge Helps No. 13 UCLA Survive at Cal." March 3, 2006. http://www.espn.in/mens-college-basketball/recap?gameId=260610025.
———."Shabazz Muhammad, UCLA Down No. 7 Missouri in Overtime." December 29, 2012. http://www.espn.co.uk/mens-college-basketball/recap?gameId=323630026.
———."Sun Devils Snap Bruins' 10-Game Streak with OT Triumph." January 18, 2009. http://www.espn.com.au/mens-college-basketball/recap?gameId=290170026.
———."Top-Ranked Bruins Rally, Squelch Wash. St.'s Upset Bid." December 29, 2006. http://www.espn.co.uk/mens-college-basketball/recap?gameId=263620026.
———."UCLA Ends with 12–2 Run to Close Texas." December 9, 2012. http://www.espn.com.au/mens-college-basketball/recap?gameId=323430251.
———."UCLA Scores Final 11 Points in Stunning Comeback over Gonzaga." March 24, 2006. http://www.espn.com/mens-college-basketball/recap?gameId=264000014.
———."UCLA Slips by Washington St. behind Dragovic's Career-High 20." January 23, 2009. http://www.espn.com.au/mens-college-basketball/recap?gameId=290220265.
———."UK Starts with 24–0 Run, Holds UCLA to Lowest Points Total (7) in Half." December 22, 2014. https://abc7chicago.com/sports/uk-starts-with-24-0-run-holds-ucla-to-lowest-points-total-(7)-in-half/445077/.
———."Year After Embarrassing Loss, UCLA Dominates No. 1 Kentucky in a Rematch." January 2, 2016.

http://www.espn.com/espn3/event/_/id/2691334/ncaam-basketball/kentucky-vs-ucla-m-basketball.

Feinstein, John. "Griffith, Louisville Rule NCAA, 59–54." *Washington Post*, March 25, 1980.

———. "Questions Still Punctuate the Sentences at UCLA." *Washington Post*, April 7, 1984.

Foster, Chris. "Walt Hazzard Dies at 69; Former Bruins Basketball Star and Coach." *Los Angeles Times*, November 19, 2011.

"Games Jan. 20, 1968." *Los Angeles Times*, February 10, 1991.

Goodrich, Gail, and Rich Levin. *Gail Goodrich's Winning Basketball*. Washington: Regnery, 1976.

Griffin, Cal. "Where Are They Now: The O'Bannon Brothers." *All Things Hoops*, February 9, 2018.

Gustkey, Earl. "Taking Her Shot: A Funny Thing Happened to Cheryl Miller, Who Went From Booth to the Bench at USC." *Los Angeles Times*, December 1, 1993.

Hansen, Greg. "1. Arizona 102, UCLA 64, February 18, 1989." *Arizona Daily Star*, June 24, 2017.

———. "Arizona Wildcats' Spirit of '79 Lives on with USC, UCLA Arriving." *Arizona Daily Star*, February 23, 2017.

Harrick, Jim, John McGill, and Tom Wallace. *Embracing the Legend: Jim Harrick Revives the UCLA Mystique*. Los Angeles: Bonus Books, 1995.

Healey, Carrie. "How March Madness Started: History of the NCAA Basketball Tournament." AOL.com, March 10, 2017. https://www.aol.com/article/news/2017/03/10/how-march-madness-started-history-ncaa-basketball-tournament/21878668/

History.com "'March Madness' Crowns Its First Men's NCAA Champion." https://www.history.com/this-day-in-history/march-madness-is-born.

Hoffarth, Tom. "Game by Game: The UCLA Winning Streak, from 1 to 88." *Daily News*, August 28, 2017.

"Houston Wins, 60–50, in N.C.A.A.; Utah Upsets U.C.L.A. by 6." *New York Times*, March 20, 1983.

Howard-Cooper, Scott. "Pioneer Barksdale Spent His Life Opening Doors for Others." NBA.com, February 14, 2013.

Hudson, Maryann. "UCLA Was Big, But the 'E' Proved Bigger: College Basketball: Hayes Helped Houston End Bruins' Winning Streak at 47 Games Jan. 20, 1968." *Los Angeles Times*, February 10, 1991.

Hughes, Rich. *Netting Out Basketball, 1936: The Remarkable Story of the McPherson Refiners, the First Team to Dunk, Zone Press, and Win the Olympic Gold Medal*. Victoria, BC: FriesenPress, 2011.

IMDB. "Marques Johnson." https://www.imdb.com/name/nm0425759/?ref_=nv_sr_1?ref_=nv_sr_1.

Impelman, Craig. "How Coach Wooden Created the Pyramid of Success." *Success*, March 15, 2017.

Indiana Basketball Hall of Fame. https://www.hoopshall.com.

Jares, Joe. "Out West, DePaul Had a Ball." *Sports Illustrated*, March 26, 1979. https://www.si.com/vault/1979/03/26/823480/out-west-depaul-had-a-ball.

Jones, David. "Penn State's 1991 NCAA Upset of UCLA Was Triumph of Guile and Teamwork over Raw Talent." PennLive.com, May 19, 2011.

"The Journey." CoachWooden.com. http://www.coachwooden.com/the-journey.

Kamenetzky, Brian. "Walt Hazzard, 1942–2011." Los Angeles Lakers (blog). ESPN, November 18, 2011.

Just All-Star. "Players Who Played the NBA All-Star Game in Their Rookie Season." https://www.justallstar.com/nba-all-star-game/player-lists/rookies-all-star-game/.

Keith, Larry "Another Irish Roast out on the Coast." *Sports Illustrated*, December 18, 1978. https://www.si.com/vault/1978/12/18/823252/another-irish-roast-out-on-the-coast-with-rich-branning-a-southern-california-emigre-and-kelly-tripucka-leading-the-way-notre-dame-won-its-third-game-in-a-row-at-ucla.

Kulik, Hannah. "Gail Goodrich: A Native Legend." Fansided (blog). Lake Show Life, September 24, 2015. https://lakeshowlife.com/2015/09/24/gail-goodrich-a-native-legend/.

Kwartler, Zach. "Princeton 43, UCLA 41: The Game That Never Goes Away." *Princeton Alumni Weekly*, March 2, 2011. https://paw.princeton.edu/article/princeton-43-ucla-41-game-never-goes-away.

"Larry Brown Biography." *Encyclopedia of World Biography*. https://www.notablebiographies.com/news/A-Ca/Brown-Larry.html

Lewis, Jason. "Black History Month: Don Barksdale Achieved Many Firsts on and off the Basketball Court." *Los Angeles Sentinel*, April 8, 2017.

Litsky, Frank. "Gene Bartow, U.C.L.A. Basketball Coach after Wooden, Dies at 81." *New York Times*, January 4, 2012.

Lowell, Craig. "A Look Back at the NCAA Dunk Ban and Forward to Basketball's

Future." Gizmodo, January 30, 2014. https://studioatgizmodo.kinja.com/a-look-back-at-the-ncaa-dunk-ban-and-forward-to-basketb-1505786580.
Mapleston, Peter. "Pipe Dreams Coming True." *Plastics Engineering* 65, no. 3 (2009): 10–15.
Marquette, Ray. "1976 Indiana Hoosiers: No Doubt—Indiana's the Top Banana." *Indianapolis Star*, November 29, 2015. https://www.indystar.com/story/sports/college/indiana/2015/11/29/retroindy-1976-indiana-hoosiers-no-doubt----indianas-top-banana/76302080/.
McCormick, Lisa Wade. *UCLA Basketball.* New York: Rosen Central, 2014.
Middleton, Yale, and Parker Davis. "100 Unforgettable John Wooden Quotes." *Addicted 2 Success*, June 10, 2017.
Miller, Bryce. "Bill Walton Scorches Memphis State in Record Setting Title Game." *San Diego Union Tribune,* September 16, 2016.
Moss, Irv. "Farmer Recalls H.S. Loss Harder to Bear." *Denver Post*, May 7, 2016.
Myslenski, Skip. "Overconfident UCLA Caught in Tulsa Hurricane, Gets Blown Away." *Chicago Tribune*, March 19, 1994. https://www.chicagotribune.com/news/ct-xpm-1994-03-19-9403190131-story.html.
National Association of Collegiate Directors of Athletics. "Gary Cunningham Bio." No longer available online.
Newhouse, Steve. "Great Moments in Allstate Arena History." 247Sports, March 1, 2017. https://247sports.com/Article/Great-Moments-in-Allstate-Arena-History-74922197/.
The Nobel Prize. "Ralph Bunche—Biographical." NobelPrize.org, February 14, 2017. https://www.nobelprize.org/prizes/peace/1950/bunche/biographical/.
Norwood, Robyn. "Bruins Run to Record: College Basketball: UCLA Beats UC Irvine, 134–101, Setting a School Scoring Mark." *Los Angeles Times*, November 24, 1990.
———. "Game of the Century." *Los Angeles Times*, January 19, 2008.
Not in Hall of Fame. "Marques Johnson." http://www.notinhalloffame.com/home/news/basketball/1702-16-marques-johnson.
"Notre Dame Upsets UCLA 89–82." *New York Times*, January 24, 1971.
Novak, Thad. "UCLA Basketball: The Top 50 Players in School History." Bleacher Report, April 12, 2017. https://bleacherreport.com/articles/930386-ucla-basketball-the-top-50-players-in-school-history.
Olson, Lisa. "Morrison's Bitter End Becomes Uplifting Finish." *New York Daily News*, March 24 2006.
Maves Jr., Norm. "McArthur Court Memories: Best Games—Oregon-UCLA 1974 and What Else?" *Oregon Ducks Beat* (blog). *Oregonian,* March 4, 2010. http://blog.oregonlive.com/behindducksbeat/2010/03/mcarthur_court_memories_best_g.html.
Pac-12. "1970 NCAA Championship Team to Be Honored at Oregon Game." February 23, 2010. https://pac-12.com/article/2010/02/23/1970-ncaa-championship-team-be-honored-oregon-game.
———. "Stanford Basketball And The Original 'Miracle at Maples.'" January 26, 2010. https://pac-12.com/article/2010/01/26/stanford-basketball-and-original-miracle-maples.
Pallette, Philip. *The Game Changer: How Hank Luisetti Revolutionized America's Great Indoor Game*. Bloomington, IN: AuthorHouse, 2005.
Papanek, John. "At the Top of His Profession." *Sports Illustrated*, November 10, 1980. https://www.si.com/vault/1980/11/10/825131/at-the-top-of-his-profession-marques-johnson-who-may-well-be-the-best-forward-in-the-nba-performs-high-above-the-opposition-stopping-time-defying-gravity.
Pucin, Diane. "The Day the Bruins Finally Got Floored." *Los Angeles Times*, December 15, 2007.
———. "Howland Was a Real Wild Cat While Playing at Weber State." *Los Angeles Times*, March 15, 2007.
Rosenthal, Phil. "50 Years Later, TV Hoops Legacy of Eddie Einhorn and UCLA-Houston Looms Large." *Chicago Tribune*, January 19, 2018. https://www.chicagotribune.com/sports/college/ct-spt-basketball-game-of-century-1968-ucla-houston-kareem-astrodome-sports-media-20180118-story.html.
Schwartz, Jerry. "1998 N.C.A.A. Tournament: Second Round—South; U.C.L.A.'s Foul Shots Undercut Michigan." *New York Times*, March 16, 1998.
Sheinin, Dave. "Ed O'Bannon Has Gone From the Hardwood to the Sales Floor." *Washington Post*, June 14, 2009.
"The Sidelines: UCLA Set to Retire Numbers of Jabbar, Walton, Meyers, Curry." *Los Angeles Times*. January 23, 1990.
Smukler, Eli. "A History of Wooden's Early Years in Westwood." *Daily Bruin*, June 6, 2010.
Sondheimer, Eric. "Gail Goodrich Returns to Where It All Started—Madison Middle School." *Los Angeles Times*, November 6, 2015.

Spears, Marc. "What's in a Name? Walt Hazzard's Struggle with Islam & Identity in the NBA." The Undefeated, December 15, 2016. https://theundefeated.com/features/whats-in-a-name-walt-hazzards-struggle-with-islam-identity-in-the-nba/.
"The Sports Archives—1971 USC, 24-2, Misses NCAA Basketball Tournament!" The Sports Archives (blog), April 2, 2011. https://thesportsarchivesblog.com/2011/04/02/the-sports-archives-—1971-usc-24-2-misses-ncaa-basketball-tournament/.
Sports Reference LLC. "Basketball Stats and History." SportsReference.com. https://www.basketball-reference.com. The site contains historical information for the NBA, ABA, WNBA, and top European competition.
———. "College Basketball Stats and History." SportsReference.com. https://www.sports-reference.com/cbb/. The site contains historical information for UCLA and other basketball programs, in addition to conference and tournament summaries.
Stueve, Spencer. *UCLA Football Encyclopedia: From Tears to Touchdowns.* New York: Sports Publishing, 2016.
Truman State University. "Truman Hall Of Famer Gene Bartow Passes Away." January 4, 2012. https://trumanbulldogs.com/news/2012/1/4/GEN_0104120910.aspx.
UCLA. "Tributes: John Wooden Spotlight." http://www.spotlight.ucla.edu/john-wooden/life-and-times/. No longer available online.
UCLA "Aaron Holiday." https://uclabruins.com/roster.aspx?rp_id=5556.
UCLA. "Athletic Department Mission Statement." https://uclabruins.com/sports/2013/4/17/208274085.aspx.
UCLA Basketball—College Basketball. Des Moines, IA: Sports Illustrated Kids, 2006.
"U.C.L.A. ON PROBATION IN BASKETBALL." *New York Times*, December 9, 1981.
UCLA "UCLA Men's Basketball Roster." https://uclabruins.com/roster.aspx?path=mbball.
"U.C.L.A. Upset by Alabama, 70–67." *New York Times*, January 29, 1983.
"UCLA Yearbook Collection." Internet Archive, https://archive.org/details/uclayearbooks.
University of Notre Dame Athletics. "Notre Dame —UCLA Renew Basketball Rivalry." December 16, 2009. https://und.com/news/2009/12/16/Notre_Dame_UCLA_Renew_Basketball_Rivalry.aspx.
"Walt Hazzard, Former Star and Coach for UCLA, dies at 69." *New York Times,* November 18, 2011. https://www.nytimes.com/2011/11/19/sports/basketball/walt-hazzard-former-star-and-coach-for-ucla-dies-at-69.html.
Walton, Bill. *Back from the Dead.* New York: Simon & Schuster, 2017.
Wang, Jack. "David Wear's Miracle Shot Forces Overtime, but UCLA Loses to Oregon." *Daily News*, August 28, 2017.
White, Gordon S. "B.Y.U. Gains in East, as Does Notre Dame." *New York Times*, March 15, 1981.
"Wilbur Johns Dies at Home." *Eugene-Register Guard.* Google News Archive, July 16, 1967. https://news.google.com/newspapers?nid=1310&dat=19670716&id=hthVAAAAIBAJ&sjid=ReEDAAAAIBAJ&pg=2272,2852793.
'Wilbur Johns Will Retire from UCLA." *Pittsburgh Post-Gazette.* Google News Archive, February 9, 1963. https://news.google.com/newspapers?id=9shRAAAAIBAJ&sjid=XmwDAAAAIBAJ&pg=4144,1142431&dq=wilbur-johns+player&hl=en.
Wojciechowski, Gene. "Back Home in Indiana: After His NBA Career Fizzles, Former Hoosier Steve Alford Returns to Become Coach at Manchester College." *Los Angeles Times*, January 12, 1992.
Wooden, John, and Steve Jamison. *Wooden.* New York: Contemporary Books, 1997.
Wooden, John, and Jack Tobin. *They Call Me Coach.* New York: Contemporary Books, 2004.
World History Project. Adolf Hitler Timeline. http//:worldhistoryproject.org/topics/adolf-hitler.
Yamaguchi, Scott. "Bruins Hoist 11th Championship Banner." *Daily Bruin*, April 5, 1995.
Zabar, Kai EL'. "Jamaal Wilkes Tells the Story of an NBA Champion in His Memoir, Smooth As Silk." *Chicago Defender*, March 30, 2015. http://chicagodefender.com/jamaal-wilkes-tells-the-story-of-an-nba-champion-in-his-memoir-smooth-as-silk/.